DIXIE HERETIC

Religion and American Culture

SERIES EDITORS

John M. Giggie
Charles A. Israel

EDITORIAL ADVISORY BOARD

Catherine A. Brekus
Paul Harvey
Sylvester A. Johnson
Joel W. Martin
Ronald L. Numbers
Beth Schweiger
Grant Wacker
Judith Weisenfeld

DIXIE HERETIC

The Civil Rights Odyssey of Renwick C. Kennedy

Tennant McWilliams

The University of Alabama Press | *Tuscaloosa*

The University of Alabama Press
Tuscaloosa, Alabama 35487-0380
uapress.ua.edu

Copyright © 2023 by the University of Alabama Press
All rights reserved.

Inquiries about reproducing material from this work should be addressed to the University of Alabama Press.

Typeface: Janson

Cover image: Black-robed Renwick Kennedy on the steps of Camden Associate Reformed Presbyterian Church, Camden, Alabama, c. 1956; photo by Hugh C. Dale Jr.
Cover design: Lori Lynch

Cataloging-in-Publication data is available from the Library of Congress.
ISBN: 978-0-8173-2161-1 (cloth)
ISBN: 978-0-8173-6088-7 (paper)
E-ISBN: 978-0-8173-9455-4

To Susan Lee Johnson McWilliams,
soulmate, indeed kidney mate,
and
to Betty Gaines Kennedy,
la raconteuse of reality and *la grande dame* of the Gaines Ridge Dinner Club

Let's dedicate ourselves to what the Greeks wrote so many years ago: to tame the savageness of man and make gentle the life of this world. Let us dedicate ourselves to that and say a prayer for our country and for our people.
—ROBERT F. KENNEDY, INDIANAPOLIS, APRIL 4, 1968

Contents

Preface xi

Overture: They Were Two 1

Part I. Mandated Idealist, 1900–1945 9
1. Origins 11
2. Evolution 24
3. The Wilcox Move 40
4. Dual Mandates 61
5. At Bay 94
6. Attack 121
7. More Attack 166
8. All-Out War 192

Part II. Tormented Pragmatist, 1945–1985 237
9. "Home, Again" 239
10. Somewhere to Go 265
11. The Limits of Ascent 298
12. Wallace's Troy 325
13. Breakfast at Ren's 356
Coda: What He Was 371

Appendix: The Writings of Renwick C. Kennedy 381
List of Abbreviations 387
Notes 389
Bibliography 461
Index 489

Maps follow page xii.
Illustrations follow page 225.

Preface

In Wilcox County, Alabama, deep in America's Black Belt, history stares you in the face. From that stare some Wilcoxons, old and even new, take romantic hubris. Others advance their own political and financial interests by manipulating historical tragedies so apparent in the stare. But there also are the "in between" Wilcoxons. They engage the stare's profound burden: out of the past, compassionate and honest navigation forward. Many of these multihued community builders have aesthetic interests—architecture, pottery, painting, writing, photography, quilting. Rallied around the cooperative artistic venue in Camden, Black Belt Treasures, they find not just comradeship and ideas but a shared spiritual desire for quietly happy interracial life. That spirit can find reinforcement from more individual hearts: members of the Camden city government; members of the Wilcox County Historical Society reaching out beyond the tourism afforded by a unique range of antebellum homes to include Black history sites; a white businessman tirelessly working to develop an interracial Little League baseball program; a veteran Black civil rights advocate advancing BAMA Kids, aiming for fewer high school dropouts and better parenting skills. Although a few white families long have sent their children to "Black public schools," today a few Black families now have enrolled their children in the "white private schools." All of which prompts a plea.

Ahead is the story of a white Wilcoxon confronting Black Belt life of the nineteenth and twentieth centuries—to him, a saga of abject racial sorrow. And that makes it all the more important for a person reading his story not to forget this brief editorial about the complex terrains of modern-day Wilcox. Many sources of this man's sorrow remain. Polarization across America only makes them more difficult. Still, were he still with us, this World War II veteran who waded ashore at Normandy undoubtedly would rush to salute the growing heroics of community and character gaining a beachhead on land long and perversely dominated by complexion.

In the 1970s, when I first thought about writing this story, I could not have imagined such a personal editorial. But the succeeding half-century yielded up a range of new perspectives. They came out of the unfolding Wilcox experience. They also came from within me personally and often owing to different individuals challenging my thoughts. For these influences at this moment I thank foremost my wife, Susan Lee Johnson McWilliams, the late Renwick C. Kennedy, the late Richebourg Gaillard McWilliams, the late William J. Jones, the late Mary Moore Kennedy, the late Mary Conway Kennedy Dickinson, Margaret Kennedy Ausley, the late Viola Jefferson Goode Liddell, Veronica Woods, Betty Gaines Kennedy, Sheryl Threadgill-Matthews, Will and Ruth Liddell, Tammi Sharpe, Betty Anderson, and Marian P. Furman. Colleagues from both sides of the Atlantic also rendered major assistance: Samuel L. Webb, Edwin C. Bridges, John Milton Cooper Jr., Matthew Tinker, Dan T. Carter, Yvonne Crumpler, Howell Raines, Thomas Winton Davis, Harvey H. Jackson III, Fred Fey, Robert Bullock, Jonathan Bass, James Baggett, Martin Olliff, James Hogg, Lowry Ware, Walter B. Edgar, Scotty Kirkland, Erskine Clarke, Martin Lanaux, and the late Clarence Mohr. As for actual publication, I thank the good family of the University of Alabama Press as well as those essential to visuals in this book, photographer Cynthia McCrory and graphics specialists Craig Remington, Joe Comer, Edith Brawley, Sara Morrison, the late Chares Carlisle, and the late Lowry Ware.

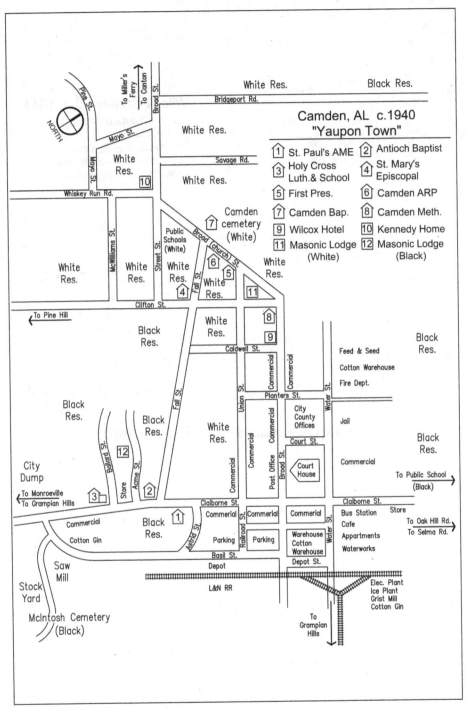

Camden, Alabama, "Yaupon Town," c. 1940.

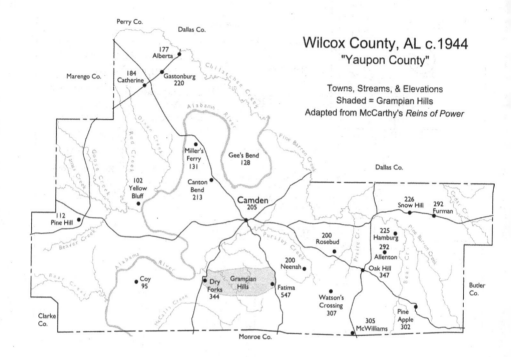

Wilcox County, Alabama, "Yaupon County," c. 1944.

The "Black Belt" counties within the state of Alabama.

Overture

They Were Two

In the late1940s, amid America's continuing celebration of victory over Japan and Germany, a Scotch-Irish preacher in Alabama's Black Belt agonized over his nation's embrace of the very behaviors it had just helped defeat: racial fascism. By the 1980s, muted if still resolute, his worries stood as sorrowful prophecy for some of today's America. That preacher's name was Renwick Carlisle Kennedy. This book tells the odyssey of his life.

Kennedy's concerns parallel, if not presage, warnings by Robert Penn Warren and some of the preacher's other intellectual contemporaries who saw alarming comparisons between American life—especially in the South—and the fascism of Nazi Germany. Kennedy's concerns also resonate with more recent thoughts of historian Robert Paxton, who describes fascism as "political behavior marked by obsessive preoccupation with community decline . . . working . . . in collaboration with traditional elites . . . without ethical or legal restraints . . . for a goal of internal cleansing and expansion." Kennedy's disturbing insights also deepen the story behind Isabel Wilkerson's recent assertion that certain groups even will "sacrifice themselves and their ideals for the survival of the group from which they draw their self-esteem"—a "malignant narcissism which gives rise to fanatical fascist politics." And his prognostications about myth and lying anticipate recent descriptions of a nation woefully hindered by "post-truth in electoral politics," including strong components of what others have termed the "creeping fascism" accompanying "white displacement" fear.[1]

Still, unlike these critics and perversely even contrary to what Adolf Hitler ever planned, Kennedy focused on connections between racial-fascist politics and a particular strain of Christianity, not just within Alabama but well beyond. Through a prism of modern social science and neo-orthodox Christian theology, he saw a growing white racial paranoia and refusal to accept truth feeding off the aggressive, "blasphemous" behaviors of "Half Christianity." He urged this long before some accused today's religious right of fostering "Christian fascism." He also did it almost a century before the

2020 US Census further documented the steadily growing minority status of white Americans, raising strong argument for a national "conscious minority" aggressiveness all too reminiscent of the ethnonationalism behind the Confederate States of America and the bloody US Civil War.

Kennedy also had passionate political views. An adamant member of the Democratic Party, he likely was unmatched as a white southerner critical of twentieth-century Republicans. Yet even during his early-adult embrace of Christian Socialism, he never advocated political action similar to the Christian Democratic movement of post–World War II Europe and Latin America. He revered separation of church and state.[2]

In fairness to the reader, here at the start I want to be clear about who is telling this story. As echoed through his diaries, letters, and writings, Kennedy largely has center stage. But off to the side, occasionally front and center, I am the narrator and interpreter. To play that role with as much scholarly objectivity as possible I draw on extensive interviews with Kennedy, as well as with his family, friends, and critics. I also employ insights of historians, journalists, philosophers, physicians, novelists, soldiers, theologians, geographers, and psychologists. Know this, too: though Kennedy's story is that of a passionate Christian, that I am not. And while his also is the compelling saga of a Scotch-Irish man—a much debated "type" in American life—depending on definition and despite my name, I probably am not that either. Finally, fearful of empowering liars and laggards, I avoid the modern opioid of tribal voting: I am not one to follow a party line. Yet this story could not have emerged were it not for my family's shared experiences with Kennedy and the place of his adult life, Wilcox County. Indeed, given that no true story has a definable beginning, this personal nexus offers a useful way to begin.

It was a Saturday afternoon in late August 1934. On my family's front porch in Wilcox County the humidity and the heat stifled all but one human endeavor: talking, slowly. This also meant it was prime time for a preacher to get you cornered, especially in a place as small as Oak Hill, population 130. Yet the thirty-four-year-old preacher who visited that afternoon had no such plan. As Renwick C. Kennedy drove up the red clay drive, the furthest thing from his mind was evangelizing.

After the Civil War, the house hosted families of broad intergenerational mix. By 1934, title to the place had long since passed to my great-aunt, Matt ("Nannie") McWilliams Boykin. There, she and her husband, physician Samuel Swift Boykin, were living out their final days, he still practicing out of the office attached to the house. But looking after them were my aunt and uncle, Joyce Clopton Carothers Jones and William Junius ("Bill") Jones. Every weekend they came from Camden—fourteen miles to the northwest—to oversee the home place Joyce had known from growing up there.

These people were well favored by the preacher coming up the drive that afternoon. Ever since Kennedy's move to Wilcox in the spring of 1927, he often dropped by just to philosophize. During the work week Bill saw him regularly in Camden. Kennedy's Associate Reformed Presbyterian (ARP) Church of Camden was a ten-minute walk down Broad Street from Bill's office as Wilcox County school superintendent, across from the courthouse. But Kennedy's bond with the superintendent and his family quickly eclipsed church and small-town affairs. They looked at the whole world the same way.

Directly descended from Lowland Scots forced to move to Ulster Plantation in northern Ireland, Kennedy came from a noted Old South family of upcountry South Carolina. After Erskine College, in Due West, South Carolina, he went on to Princeton Theological Seminary (PTS). He loved Franklin D. Roosevelt. He loved conversation. And he loved a cocktail or two. For Nannie and Dr. Sam and Joyce and Bill, here was their kind of person. They called him neither "Mr. Kennedy" nor "Reverend Kennedy." They called him what family and close friends called him: "Ren." Nannie even named one of the green rockers on the front porch for him: "Ren's rocker," a two-seater.

Kennedy shared their deep concerns about the rising currents of racial totalitarianism in Europe and Japan—especially the fascism of Germany, the weighty topic on the agenda for that afternoon. He who became my father, Richebourg Gaillard McWilliams, age thirty-three, was home at Oak Hill for a few days. With Joyce, he had grown up there in the house and would inherit it from Nannie. He had a few days left before returning to Harvard where he was a doctoral student in literature and creative writing. In the summer of 1932, while Bill was a Rosenwald fellow at Columbia Teachers College in New York City, Richebourg was at the University of Munich studying the German language, a requirement of his doctoral program. Recently, he had been working on a short story drawing on that experience. Back in Wilcox Richebourg's personal "Hitler Report" was quite the talk. Ren and Richebourg vaguely knew each other from happenstance introductions back in the summer of 1927 in the dining room of Camden's Wilcox Hotel. But as Ren quickly accepted the Oak Hill invitation for a special retelling of "Richebourg's Hitler Report," a more substantive friendship was about to form.[3]

In Germany, my father got more than he anticipated. At the theater one early afternoon in mid-August 1932, he sat directly behind the man himself: "I could have touched him." Hitler was on the verge of becoming chancellor. Large, burly, black-booted guards ushered him in. "Once he took his seat the curtain finally went up—over twenty minutes late." From three feet away my father "felt [Hitler's] fascism": the hubris, the power, the lies, the evil. "Frightful," he recalled years later.

Ren Kennedy wanted a Hitler report. He got one. He and Richebourg promised to stay in touch.[4]

Shortly, my father found the noted transatlantic short-fiction magazine, *Story*, eager for his piece, "They Were Seven"—an antiwar short story based on a German family devastated by World War I. So, in early June 1935, he departed Harvard. Minus the doctorate—his major professor, Robert Hillyer, advising it was "unnecessary" for a fiction writer—he moved home to Oak Hill to become "a writer." He took with him three short stories about Wilcox life drafted in Hillyer's writing workshop. Most every day he drove to Camden to write in a small office just off the courthouse square. There, the recent trip to Germany still much on his mind, he began expansion of those stories into a novel about daily life in Wilcox. It would be a "Black Belt novel."[5]

Geologically speaking, of course, Wilcox barely touches the true Black Belt—that arc of profoundly nutritious prairie running from Georgia to Mississippi. But a blue-black marl underlies much of northern Wilcox. And over the eons an equally rich alluvial soil came to rest along the banks of the Alabama River as it carved its serpentine diagonal across the county. My father had a rough idea of all this. From his earliest mapping of Wilcox, noted Alabama state geologist, Eugene Allen Smith, was a friend of his father and grandfather. On our Oak Hill porch many a time did that scientist hold forth on the surrounding landscape. But my father also understood that what happened on this rich one-third of Wilcox's earth dominated human life in the rest of the county. Not that white columns and vast cotton fields had ever filled the Wilcox landscape, he knew. But there indeed were sufficient big-cotton enterprises for Wilcox's people—white and Black, and vestiges of red—to live as one convoluted Black Belt county.[6]

As the summer unfolded, Ren and Richebourg met for lunch several times a week at the Wilcox Hotel. They found they shared a lot more than growing up in raised Carolina cottages and shooting quail from horseback— including concerns about the Depression, fascism, and war. Kennedy, too, wrote portraits of Wilcox. They became close. They chided each other over who had the "better" typewriter: Ren's 1928 portable Underwood versus my father's 1928 portable Remington. With apparently no fear of one scooping the other, they also shared research notes.[7]

They mulled over Richebourg's work. A Black barber formed the core of his tale: a narrator springing from the real life of one Martin Van Buren Jones, of Oak Hill. His parents, John and Lucinda Jones, had been slaves owned by my father's great-grandmother, Martha Harriss Jones. For some twenty years the people of Oak Hill—Black and white, male and female, old and young—went to his shop for haircuts. But Black people also went there for private counsel on navigating segregated life. On July 13, 1934, despite

Sam Boykin's best efforts, Van (as he was known) succumbed after a month-long bout with "laryngeal pneumonia." He was fifty-six. He "lived bravely," my father wrote in early drafts, "truly a great man." Still, despite New York publishers' surging interest in books revealing "the real South" and repeated queries about "your Black Belt novel"—Scribner's, Simon and Schuster, Harper, and especially Knopf—plus subsequent successes as a writer and a professor, he did not finish Van's story. "I quit," he told me in 1979, "never could make it work right . . . being the voice of Van." Fair enough. In a society where one group has total control over another, and this power is reinforced by ancient ethnic myths, regardless of the strength of long-term friendship it is indeed a challenge for a person of the controlling group to think in an accurate and nuanced way like one of the controlled group.[8]

Kennedy was different. He had a less complicated way of writing about south Alabama. He also felt mandated to stay on it. In contrast to my father—vaguely an ARP through youth but by early adulthood an intellectual for whom Sunday was "just another day"—Kennedy was not only an intellectual but also a devout Social Gospel/Christian Socialist preacher who believed that God had a mandate for him to make a goodly number of white Alabamians "true Christians." To him, the "Half Christianity" of only Bible reading and pietism fell far short of the "Full Christianity" of Jesus' teachings acted upon in contemporaneous life: helping fellow humans regardless of their color and gender, regardless of their sexual and religious preferences, regardless of their general station in life. So Kennedy's plans included writing and a whole lot more.[9]

For a long time, "quitting" on his typewriter never occurred to Kennedy. Through chiefly *Christian Century* and *New Republic*, he had considerable success with fictional vignettes of white people drawn from his daily life set in a place he called "Yaupon." Overwhelmingly, here were people of his same transatlantic and indeed Carolina background, Scotch-Irish Christians. Instinctively, he knew them to the core—none of the "voice" problems his friend Richebourg had. Kennedy's vignettes could include riveting characterizations, from "kind" and "loyal" to "strange," "hypocritical," "violent," and "fascist," and indeed "blasphemous." Ultimately, still, his lack of success with growing white hearts, coupled with inability to expand his publishing beyond a few journals, gnawed down his creative energies for writing. Visceral feelings of defeat turned this idealist into a shrewdly pragmatic politician. At times, he quietly returned to concrete reform endeavors. But these did little to ease his private lingering torment about God's Mandate for far larger change within white Christians all around him every day and beyond.

In 1943, despite years as a confirmed Christian Socialist pacifist and by this time too old to be called up by the World War II Selective Service,

Kennedy volunteered for military service. He went to Europe as a chaplain with the famed 102nd Evacuation Hospital. At home he had confronted racial control and violence and abject poverty. Overseas he found the same—just in far greater extreme. With Normandy, the Battle of the Bulge, and on to Buchenwald and Dachau, he came face to face with humanity's most grotesque horrors. Yet, far different from Alabama and all of America for that matter, in Europe he also experienced frontal assault on institutionalized racial fascism and, more to the point, its defeat.

In late November 1945, on return from the war, he told Camden ARPs he had no notion of what the war "did" to him. His forty years of postwar life, however, gradually made it clear. Up to a point, he recovered from the overseas blood and horror. He also resumed life as a high-profile minister while developing a second career as a professor and administrator—essentially a lobbyist—at nearby Troy State Teacher's College. Too, he published five high-profile articles on Cold War America. Still, privately, he felt increasing anguish over the many Americans, especially Alabamians, professing national pride in the "Victory" over Germany and Japan—fascist racial orders—yet lacking the morality, courage, and Full Christianity to work for the same at home. Consider that but a clue as to what the war "did" to him.

A crucial element in Kennedy's story is his private diary. It survives chiefly as some thirty-five notebooks. His entries could be hurriedly jotted phrases, well-crafted paragraphs of thirty to fifty words, or indeed essays of five hundred to a thousand words. In the diary-writing he scrupulously sought to protect the confidential personal details revealed to him in pastoral counseling sessions. Occasionally, he also used secretly coded notes employing a combination of letters and numbers. But when it came to politics, race, and economics, not to mention his personal ruminations about God, he was vivid and meticulous. He wrote in the diary up until two months before his death.

For his times, Ren Kennedy was an overt racial liberal. Many Black people talked openly with him. A few white people did, too. Because of his regularly going against the Old South orthodoxy, one of these liberal whites baptized him "Dixie heretic"—a loaded label. So you might think the mass of white conservatives around him saw him as "a meddling outsider" or, more severe, "a serious threat to our way of life." Yet even the reactionary land-owning elite, while politely rejecting his politics, enjoyed his company socially, and many rarely missed his sermons—another tantalizing part of his story.

Beginning in the early 1970s, and for the decade to come, my father sought to guide our regular conversations into Wilcox stories centered either on Van or Ren or both. Increasingly, he became downright insistent. "You *must* write about Ren Kennedy. Get to know him. A fine southern writer.

See if he will talk with you. . . . One summer in the 1930s we regularly met for lunch at the Wilcox Hotel. I was writing. So was he. You will find him interesting."[10]

In fact, I cannot remember a time when my father and my uncle Bill did not talk about their dear friend. As for me, in September 1961—only a few weeks after starting college—I met Kennedy for the first time on our front porch at Oak Hill. He was chatting with Bill. Yes, the same green rockers. After we shook hands, I went on back to the kitchen and sat at the table with Joyce until their conversation ended. Later, in 1980, I was in the Bethel ARP Church at Oak Hill when Kennedy gave the eulogy at Joyce's funeral. He had written remarks to include two lines from Edmund Spenser's *Faerie Queene*. But he got on a roll. Three or four minutes later—major portions, verbatim, with people squirming—we finally got back to burying Joyce.[11]

So, as my father repeatedly urged me to get to know Ren, up to a point my mind could grasp him. I remembered his accent: at core, antebellum South Carolina upcountry, yet also regular hints of Ivy League. I knew the softly syncopated pauses in his sentences. I knew, too, the way he looked—pushing a straight six feet, white shirt sleeves rolled to just above the elbows, dark tie profiling a perfect Windsor knot, full head of gray hair, neatly cut. And I knew at least something about his eyes, a penetrating deep brown, if over time I also sensed a deceptiveness in their serenity. Finally, a decade into my career as a professional historian, I telephoned him asking if we could talk.[12]

On my arrival in Camden in 1983, there he was in the house where he and his wife, Mary, had raised their two daughters and hosted a lot of grandchildren. We sat in his study. Though physically aged and sick, his mind was sharp and his memory precise and subtle. He asked how my father was doing. I reported he was old but doing all right. He said it was the same for him. Then he asked about the Remington portable typewriter. "He still has it . . . and uses it." I asked if he would help me in writing about him. Brown eyes twinkling, he replied, "Well, you know, yes . . . [pause] *if* you like." Had I been "had" by two aging comrades of the 1930s? I never found out for sure. And for a while that worried me.

Introductory interview complete, he asked Mary to take me upstairs to a bedroom. She pointed to a trunk under one of the beds. "He wants you to see this." It was his World War II army trunk. Manuscripts. Battle ribbons from the European theater. Bundles and bundles of string-tied letters. The diaries—notebooks. Then, again on his instruction, she took me to the garage. Covered partially by rotting canvas were molding boxes; Mary volunteered that the canvas came from his once-upon-a-time World War II–surplus Jeep. I had heard a lot of stories about that Jeep and did not focus when she added something like, "Those old boxes are Red Cross stuff. He won't throw away anything." Little did I know. . . . After that interview there were three others, plus lengthy long-distance phone calls.[13]

In December 1985 Kennedy died. I could not attend the funeral. At the time my father was going through his own final countdown, succumbing two months later. Still, Kennedy had said he would leave me his papers. In March 1986 I returned to Camden. The family presented the paper contents of the trunk. Then they pointed to piles of paper in his private study: some on desktops, some in file cabinets. I was stunned. Altogether here were around five thousand letters, the intimate diary-notebooks, manuscripts—published and unpublished, handwritten and typed—and notes written upon everything from old calendars to the backs of blank checks. All this would reveal his experience as a prolific writer, which so tantalized my father. But that was just for starters, it turned out.

As I discovered over the succeeding years—being "had" ultimately irrelevant—there was so much more. Inside this heretic's odyssey was a prophet's tale. With considerable sadness, and without a clue of the way futuristic social media would both intensify and expand the "rationality inequality" and myth addiction behind so much of American prejudice, Kennedy came to predict some of today's most trying times. Interwoven within his own tortuous twentieth-century story is the narrative of steadily growing fascist ways, surely dominant among many white people of the twenty-first century South but of America as well. Here at last is the story Ren and Richebourg lived and that Ren managed to tell. They were two. And if still alive, undoubtedly these white Black Belters would want you to know not just the way it was but, should history be allowed to repeat itself, what that portends for now.[14]

Part I

Mandated Idealist, 1900–1945

Ren Kennedy came from a part of South Carolina rife with Scotch-Irish Associate Reformed Presbyterians. They lived by biblical infallibility and a strain of individual piety and salvation focused on the hereafter. In the early 1920s, Kennedy's ministerial studies took him to Princeton Theological Seminary. There, he encountered the deep chasms over science and fundamentalism and the Social Gospel. This changed him forever, leaving him open to rapid embrace of new thought. Like some neo-orthodox, young Kennedy stayed true to the literalist Bible, salvation, and piety allegiances of his youth. He continued daily prayer—usually at nightly bedtime. Yet he also embraced not just the Social Gospel's mandate to solve earthly problems of poverty and prejudice, but many cardinal perspectives of modern science.

In 1927, Kennedy moved to Wilcox County. Shortly he married—always far from a "perfect" relationship—and started a family. Meanwhile, his ministry for social change dominated his Wilcox pastorates, filled with the very people from whom he derived, the Scotch-Irish. Quietly, he came to believe that God had a Mandate for him: to confront and change some of the behaviors of these people, notably their attitudes about race and poverty. And to do this, he soon found, he had to attack what he considered the traditionalist Christian hypocrisy facilitating those attitudes, their "Half Christianity," which he came to associate with a "blasphemous" proto-fascism, if not fascism itself. Soon he grasped that changes in law and policy were fruitless without deeper changes in daily human behavior. In turn, he became a confrontational writer and an advocate for US intervention in World War II with hopes that defeating racial fascism abroad might somehow grow white hearts at home. This was not a life for the equivocating. And in most ways his own life was anything but that.

1

Origins

Cross the Atlantic to one of the most difficult chapters in the long story of the British Isles. In the late 1600s, as England and Scotland struggled on toward their 1707 "union," most Scottish Presbyterians wound up with considerable freedom to worship when the English crown ultimately approved creation of the Presbyterian Church of Scotland.

But a strong-willed minority of these Presbyterians refused to go along, a people to whom history has devoted considerable debate. Many of them came from the physically remote, culturally isolated pockets of southern Scotland—the Lowlands—where their chiefly Celtic ancestors, according to would-be Roman conquerors, had a "savage ignorance of the virtues of peace," some even "delight[ing] in the taste of human flesh." Indeed, it was not until the sixteenth century Protestant Reformation that Western civilization finally pierced their primal "leave me alone" mentality. And even then, explains geographer Barry Vann, the Calvinistic sense of purity and "chosenness" only reinforced their endemic determination to be isolated. They rejected whatever human authority—the king, the Church of England, even the Church of Scotland—might intrude on their individual covenant with the Holy Ghost. Ultimately, the crown managed to relocate some of these "recalcitrants" to Ulster Plantation in northern Ireland. Here, some of the Scottish Covenanters intermarried with earlier settlers in northern Ireland—English, German, French—as well as Irish. And the whole bunch, whether pure Lowlander Scot or the new mix, soon became known as "Ulster Scots" to distinguish them from pure-blooded Irish.[1]

But not all Covenanters moved from southern Scotland to Ulster. In the 1680s, armed with Bibles and pistols, red scarves flagrantly flying from their necks, many rose against the English crown in repeated and violent guerrilla warfare. In response, during 1688 and 1689 alone, the king's soldiers killed some fifteen hundred of the fierce Covenanters. None of these was more noted than Ren Kennedy's probable ancestor, James Renwick, originally from

Moniaive, in Dumfriesshire County, Scotland. On Wednesday, February 17, 1688, in a cold and gray morning mist, soldiers of King James II hanged twenty-six-year-old James Renwick from the gallows at Edinburgh's market square, pitching his decapitated torso into the pit of other Redneck remains at Greyfriars burial grounds.

Within a year of James' death, the Glorious Revolution ushered in the reign of William and Mary. Attacks on Covenanters ceased, and the British Isles moved on down their agonizing journey toward religious peace. But the deed was done. Non-Anglican Protestants became a dramatic part of British migration around the globe. At best they took along bad memories of being uprooted by England, at worst deeply seared stories of those bloody "stains on the heather" and what shortly was called "the Killing Time." Actually, despite the drama of the Covenanter narrative, more Borderlander/Ulsterites—people of southern Scotland, northern England, and northern Ireland—ultimately embraced Baptist and Methodist denominations than radical Presbyterianism. But for all who made it to America, at least, the word *redneck* followed them, regardless of denominational affiliation, and after their arrival yet another term came their way.[2]

Between 1713 and 1773 some 300,000 Borderlanders—many Ulsterites—came to America. By the time of the American Revolution, their "cross breeding" had extended beyond Aryan types to include a modicum of Africans and Native Americans, though a Celtic/Borderlands appearance clearly remained dominant. These people thought of themselves as "Americans." Yet the popular culture of the Anglo-American colonies decided that was not specific enough. It proclaimed them the "Scotch-Irish," a term that stuck in everyday talk if not in many US government records.

One of the first broadly read books about these people—read amid a surging Aryanism on both sides of the Atlantic—Charles Knowles Bolton's *Scotch-Irish Pioneers* (1910), celebrated the Scotch-Irish as a "courageous" and adventuresome force in the Anglo conquest of North America. On into the mid-to-late twentieth century the Bolton profile received continued ballyhoo.

Still, the different research strategies and social values of more recent times produced a vastly different Scotch-Irish profile. They were obstinate and overtly "individualistic," indeed, "wild and impulsive" as they searched for "natural liberty." And while "[loyal] to friends," they were filled with "hatred for enemies": at the slightest challenge to their honor they gouged eyes and slashed throats. Over time they provided a uniquely violent component in the Anglo genocide of Native American peoples. Andrew Jackson, George Patton, and George Wallace were downstream products of this "pool."

More recently still, a substantial body of historians has advanced the wrongheadedness of this negative stereotype. From Ulster to America, they urge, the Scotch-Irish reflected far more diverse ethnic origins and cultural characteristics than heretofore granted. For all the hyper-individualistic Scotch-Irish eye gougers there also were sophisticated Scotch-Irish community builders. Meanwhile, granting ample exceptions, others counter with yet more assertion of the rough Scotch-Irish "backwoods homogeneity." And still others see those places as seedbeds for a persisting Scotch-Irish influence supportive of white privilege, "guns," evangelical religion, and opposition to government. All of which is to say that, out of this complicated Scotch-Irish experience evolved Ren Kennedy's heritage. The Ulster-to-America narrative, as he came to understand it, played a cardinal role in his sense of self as well as his eventual notion of Half Christianity.[3]

In the decade following the American Revolution, some eleven thousand Scotch-Irish Americans identified with radical Scottish Presbyterianism—some of Covenanter roots, others from another wave known as "Seceders." In 1782 many of these came together in Philadelphia to establish the Associate Reformed Presbyterian (ARP) Synod of North America. Here, after years of fomentation, began Ren Kennedy's church.

ARPs grounded themselves in the Westminster Standards. They focused on individual piety and salvation, and the implied infallibility of the Bible as interpreted through strict Calvinistic doctrine. For their strong emphasis on predestination, some have considered them "Providentialists." Others have seen them as "religious fatalists." They sang no hymns, only psalms; and their ministers wore no Anglican-style black robes. The congregation "called"—elected—a minister. An ordained minister had to be at least twenty-four years old and well educated. Yet, regardless of a minister's education or stature, his role never exceeded that of "moderator." Power resided with the people of individual congregations. They elected a board of elders, which, with the minister, constituted the chief congregational administrative body—the session. In turn, a group of congregations formed a presbytery, and a group of presbyteries a synod.[4]

While Philadelphia—and its immediate western frontier—provided their originating site, most ARPs were not comfortable there. Quakers were in control, with strict laws and high-priced property. Some ARPs headed to Maryland and Virginia and on into the Ohio Valley, where other white people welcomed them for their violent guerrilla-style Indian fighting. Others, perhaps as many as six thousand, journeyed south to the Appalachian Mountains, and substantial numbers of these wound up in South Carolina, notably Fairfield, Lancaster, Chester, and Abbeville counties. Here they merged with other, more recently arrived Borderlanders who crossed over to Charleston, then to the upcountry.

By the mid-1700s ARP congregations—rarely larger than thirty members—punctuated the frontier of South Carolina. Occasional counterattacks from Cherokees, regular assault from mosquitoes, copperheads, water moccasins, and poison ivy, plus some bad crops and going hungry—all this happened. Even so, compared to the rugged Scottish Lowlands, this likely was the most nurturing place of their family histories. For here also were abundant creeks, a few rivers with rich alluvial soil, and red-dirt hills filled with pines, hardwood, and game. Most seemed to love the place—the isolation, cheap land, and freedom from authority.[5]

Few were more steeped in these southern Scotch-Irish/Ulster-Scot/ARP experiences than the ancestors of Renwick Carlisle Kennedy. Consider his first name: Renwick. Long before its association with James Renwick the Martyr, the word seems to have been used in what became Dumfriesshire for one who lived among isolated creeks and hills where there were abundant crows, or ravens. For a short period, indeed, *renwick* referenced a specific hilly area with creeks near Dumfriesshire.[6]

At any rate, in 1767 Covenanter preacher John Renwick, from the village of Ahoghill (Dervock, County Antrim) in Ulster Ireland, shipped out directly to Charleston. With his wife, Elizabeth, he moved to the interior—to Newberry County. He built a cabin near Gilder's Creek, raised pigs, and grew corn. Over time the family apparently acquired four or five slaves.

Reverend Renwick had an aura. Locals on both sides of the Atlantic considered him a direct descendant of martyr James Renwick. More likely they were of the same extended family, with John possibly being the nephew of James. Regardless, Rev. John Renwick entered South Carolina with an esteemed pedigree. He also delivered on it. In Newberry County he developed Cannon's Creek ARP Church, founded a few years before he arrived. Nearby he founded King's Creek ARP Church. And from those two he led creation of Head Spring and Prosperity churches. ARPs thrived as homesteaders next to isolated springs and creeks. So their churches often popped up there. If they did not put a biblical name on a church—Bethel, Prosperity, Enterprise—they put a creek or spring name on it.

On his death in 1775 Reverend Renwick's son, John Jr., stepped up. He pastored at Gilder's Creek and Warrior Creek ARP churches. The other son, James William Renwick, built on the family's farm life. In time he was joined by his son, John Simpson Renwick. They developed a comfortable life based on cotton and slaves. In 1837 John married Mary Toland, of another Gilder's Creek family. Hers hailed from County Tyrone, in Ulster Ireland. They built a cabin on Gilder's Creek and began having children—over time, eight.[7]

With this union the Renwick family also moved to planter status. Under John's careful development they ultimately owned some two thousand acres on which they grew chiefly cotton but corn and wheat, too. Contrary to Renwick and Kennedy family lore, they were not among the largest slaveowners in the county. In 1860 about a dozen Newberry County planters owned more than 110 slaves, Chancellor Johnstone with the most at 183. The Renwicks were just below this tier with 107 slaves.

In 1853 John and Mary Renwick built a white-columned and raised "Carolina cottage" at Beth Eden, about three miles from Gilder's Creek. In the "Dutch Fork" formed by the Broad and Saluda rivers, Beth Eden had emerged from a 1740s arrival of German and Swiss settlers, Lutherans all. When the Renwicks began construction, the area was no longer rough frontier. Just down the road was Patrick Calhoun's estate—where John C. Calhoun grew up. The Calhoun home was far grander. But for that setting at that time the Renwicks' home was still an estate of note, with a private schoolhouse, peacocks strutting on the lawn, and some thirty slave cabins. It was destined for an iconic role among Renwick descendants.

All this took money and social clout. Though too old for Confederate military service, John Renwick stood out in Newberry County's pro-secession ranks. Cotton cultivation through slave labor was the family's core business. Yet he also had a large cotton gin in the town of Newberry, the county seat eight miles from Beth Eden. There, too, he was president of the Bank of Newberry and served on the board of the other bank. More subtly, he personified that strain of Scotch-Irish pig farmers who eclipsed the angry mentality of "leave me alone" and other debilitating tribal ways of their more or less Redneck origins. Even before the Civil War, assisted mightily by slavery, he ascended not just to the moneyed, white-columned life and status of a community builder but, indeed, to the informal rank of "Colonel."

Among John and Mary's eight children was Emma Elizabeth Renwick, born in 1851. Private tutors educated her in the family's tiny brick school. By 1866 she was a precocious fifteen-year-old when she enrolled at Due West (South Carolina) Female Institute; since the 1830s, Due West was also home to the ARP's Erskine College for men. This was a big day for Colonel John Renwick. In the late 1850s, he had been one of the ARP leaders to urge that Due West Female Institute be developed into a full *college* for women. And Emma now became the first of his children to go there. Still, as she headed off to college that fall of 1866, higher education was not the only thing on Emma's mind. An "older man"—a decorated Confederate veteran and a doctor—had her attention, too.[8]

His name was Thomas Coleman Carlisle. A native of Goshen Hill, in Union County just north of Newberry County, Coleman descended from the very Carlisle family from which Carlisle, England, gets its name. Located in northwest England, in Cumberland County, and technically in the

Borderlands, Carlisle was anything but a hotbed of radicalized Presbyterians. Indeed, it provided the crown a base for launching raids far deeper into the Borderlands to kill the likes of James Renwick. Still, a significant number of risk-takers moved from that area of England to northern Ireland about the same time the Scots settled there, and at least one was a Carlisle. He wound up in County Tyrone, Ulster, the same county from which Mary Toland Renwick's grandfather came. In the 1760s his Methodist minister son, Robert, migrated to Edgecombe County, North Carolina. Several generations later this devoutly Methodist family had a small farm in Union County, South Carolina.

Then came the rising prices of cotton. Thomas A. Carlisle and his wife, Catherine ("Kittie") Peacock Teal Carlisle, expanded the farm into a substantial plantation with at least twenty slaves. So much money came from this endeavor that a son, Coleman Carlisle, born in 1836, went to The Citadel for college and then on to the spanking new medical college of New York University. With South Carolina's secession, the newly minted MD hurried south to join his five brothers in fighting for the Confederacy. He doctored all over the Virginia theater, ending the war with General Joseph F. Johnston's surrender at Greensboro, North Carolina.[9]

In August 1866 Dr. Carlisle arrived in the town of Newberry—the county seat—looking for a place to open a private practice. He chanced upon Colonel Renwick. Undoubtedly a man in transition, Renwick had invested heavily in Confederate bonds for the good of that cause. Now, of course, this money was gone. Yet, he still owned vast stretches of land, and was one of the first in the county to make the transition that historian Gavin Wright describes as "land-lord to labor-lord"—that is, a transition to agricultural wealth based on recently freed slaves used as tenant farmers.[10] The fact that many of his former slaves (perhaps twenty-five) stayed on with him under the new system may help explain his quick recovery.

At any rate, whether it was business thoughts or family life, or a mix, when he encountered this young doctor from a family he knew, the Colonel moved like lightning. There were too many doctors in Abbeville and Newberry, he advised. Carlisle had a better chance at building a practice in the Beth Eden area. Colonel Renwick proposed renting him a room upstairs in his home as well as office space in the schoolhouse. He could take meals with the family.

Coleman moved in at Beth Eden just two days before Emma headed off to Due West. Despite the age difference between Emma, fifteen, and Coleman, twenty-eight, things happened fast. For three years she tried to keep her mind in Due West while her heart pulsed thirty-five horse-and-buggy miles eastward in Beth Eden. John and Mary Renwick provided astute

Victorian oversight of the in-house courtship ensuing on holidays and occasional weekends. Along the way the good doctor left the Methodist Church for the ARP.

In late May 1869, with Coleman's religion improved and Emma's degree in literature and music completed, full attention moved to wedding plans. On September 16, 1869, they married at King's Creek Church, founded by the bride's great-grandfather. A dinner followed at the Beth Eden big house. After guests departed, Emma moved upstairs into Coleman's room. As was so common among plantation families of that era, the two began married life right there with her parents.

Out of this elite ARP union of Coleman and Emma came one Mary Emma Carlisle—Ren Kennedy's mother. The Renwick money never returned to the levels of prewar years, but for the late nineteenth-century South, Mary Emma still grew up in relative luxury. When Colonel Renwick died in March 1889, Coleman Carlisle continued the shrewd management of the various Renwick family enterprises—farming to banking to cotton ginning, with new investments in cotton textiles. And he did this while still practicing medicine. By the time daughter Mary Emma in turn headed to Due West Female Institute, in 1895, her father had a larger public profile than even her grandfather. He was the biggest landowner in the county. The ARP newspaper, the *Associate Reformed Presbyterian (ARP)*, beamed: "Dr. Carlisle can write as large a check as any man in Newberry County."[11]

At Due West, Mary Emma instantly became infatuated with a young man of similar past, though certainly not future. He would be Ren Kennedy's father. Isaac ("Ike") Newton Kennedy was his name. He was a second-year student at Erskine Theological Seminary.

His father, William Patton Kennedy—with family roots deep into Ulster-Scot life—also had the Scotch-Irish background of being born on a small farm in 1837 and reaching young adulthood on a Newberry County plantation with slaves, near the village of Wideman's. He was as compulsive about plantation management as he was about the ARP church. After the Civil War, in which he lost an arm, he also worked as part of the original management team of Calhoun Mills. The same story applied to Isaac's mother. Margaret Elizabeth McFarlan McLane Kennedy descended from Ulsterites who rode cotton and slavery to plantation life near Long Cane Creek, in McCormick County. From childhood Margaret was known as "Muddie"; her eyes were a "soft, clear, penetrating muddie brown." Most of Muddie and William's nine children got these eyes. Their grandson Ren Kennedy did, too.[12]

By 1880 William and Muddie could afford to keep the plantation and still buy a large home several miles to the west in Due West. Here, they believed, the children could get better education, and continue to eclipse the

Redneck ways of so many of their distant relatives. Yet why they chose Due West is a bigger story than just seeking town life or even "college-town life" for their children. This requires a pause in the Renwick and Kennedy stories. It requires a brief foray into religion, education, race, and social change—and more on Ren Kennedy's cultural inheritance.[13]

As with other types of Presbyterians, ARPs had a unique connection with education. Back across the Atlantic, Presbyterians always had valued literacy among their general church members. But this emphasis rarely extended beyond basic biblical reading and elementary computational skills. Nor—as numerous scholars have shown—did the historic Presbyterian emphasis on mass education include more "humanistic" or "aesthetic" uses of literacy. So, on the American frontier Presbyterian mass education rarely intruded on the "savage" slaughter of Native Americans, or the harsh treatment of Black slaves. Profoundly different stood the historic education of Presbyterian clergy. Advanced studies not just in Christian theology but also in history and philosophy (including science)—essentially, Western culture—formed the required standard. This had dramatic impact on denominational growth in America. Without such restrictive clergy requirements, Methodist and Baptist churches grew far faster than Presbyterian groups, including ARPs.

Still, like other Presbyterians, southern ARPs had their growth spurts. By 1822, unhappy with northern comrades' lack of diligence with regard to evangelism, psalm-singing, Sabbatarianism, and communion, southern ARPs seceded from the ARP Synod of North America to become the Associate Reformed Presbyterian Synod of the South. The new synod benefited from the Great Awakening, counting at least four thousand members by 1835. And by 1839—intensely focused on gaining more ARP ministers—they had built at Due West, South Carolina, their own Erskine College and Seminary, named for recently deceased Ebenezer Erskine, a noted Scottish Covenanter. As antebellum life developed, southern ARPs grew even more. America's rapidly expanding population, Second Great Awakening passions, Indian removal, pursuit of the "white gold" of cotton especially in Alabama and Mississippi—by 1860, all this had pushed ARP growth to more churches and indeed presbyteries all across the South.

Embedded in this growth, of course, was the issue of slavery. About 60 percent of all antebellum southern ARPs had at least two to five slaves. A few had ten to twenty, and a tiny number—like Ren Kennedy's grandfather, Colonel Renwick—around a hundred. Still, some slaveowning southern ARPs flaunted state slave codes prohibiting a master from teaching a slave basic reading and writing, Colonel Renwick being one. And a portion of these, in turn, joined some nonslaveowning southern ARPs, not to mention those of the Midwest and Pennsylvania, in openly criticizing inhumane treatment of slaves, Colonel Renwick *not* being one. Finally, in 1858, with sectionalism at high tide, midwestern ARPs joined with Pennsylvania brethren to form the generally antislavery United Presbyterian Church. Already well distanced from these people on theological issues, and now on slavery, southern ARPs—then numbering around five thousand—immediately jumped at the resultant naming opportunity. They dropped "of the South" from their name. The ARPs of Dixie became *The* Associate Reformed Presbyterian Synod. And Erskine College and Seminary, of Due West, South Carolina, became the ARPs' iconic southern place.[14]

As a bastion of conservative, though rigorous, Christian education set in rural isolation, Erskine never grew as did some other denominational colleges. Still, in the 1880s Due West was a vibrant Victorian community of around twenty-four hundred—modest cottages, white picket fences—where farmers of the area traded and socialized amid Erskine's staff, students, and faculty. Well into the 1890s, as legalized segregation descended on the South, at least one Black person held membership with the white Due West ARP Church. Town leaders, often including Erskine faculty, remained vigilant in blocking Ku Klux Klan activities. Given the exceptions of racial segregation, a rigid ban on alcohol, and a few self-righteous ARPs, here nevertheless was a Deep South place of relative tolerance.

It is hard to think of Due West as a "Holy City," what a few ARPs have called Due West and what many people have called Charleston, South Carolina, with all its churches—especially Episcopal. But "Holy Hamlet"? Due West indeed was that for ARPs. And so, in 1880, William and Margaret Kennedy did not just move to a town or to a "college town." They moved to the Holy Hamlet. The transition went smoothly: a large white-columned home just down Church Street from the college, William an elder at the church and a member of the town council, their children with access to every level of education—spiritual as well as conservative-secular.[15]

The second of their children, Ike (born in 1874) had no interest in William Kennedy's businesses. In 1891, he entered Erskine College dead-set on emulating his brother, Ebenezer. He, too, would be an ARP minister. By September 1895, when Mary Emma came to town, he was in his second year of seminary. As she completed her first year, and Ike his final year in seminary, Mary Emma's romance with the "brown-eyed pure Christian" had moved to a six-month whirlwind. Muddie had to oversee all this alone. William died of pneumonia in March 1892, after Ike's first year in college.

With his master's in theology from Erskine, Ike became the youngest ARP minister ever licensed, four months shy of twenty-one, though he still had to wait until his twenty-fourth birthday to be ordained. His first call took him to Prosperity ARP Church, eleven miles south of Fayetteville, Tennessee. "Prosperity" is a popular name among ARPs. It made the voyage from Ulster. Four ARP churches subsequently carried that name. It evolved from numerous biblical references to a vibrant group of Christians being "prosperous" as well as the notion that such vibrancy God will reward with material prosperity.

Never, however, has "prosperity" found reflection in the way ARPs pay preachers. Well before the wedding, Ike explained all this to Mary Emma, whom Ren Kennedy remembered as naïve but "fine and uncomplaining." Ike's salary of about fifty dollars a month permitted at most two trips home per year. Fayetteville, Tennessee, is 350 miles from Beth Eden, South Carolina, roughly the same from Due West. The train—Chattanooga to Atlanta to Anderson or Abbeville—cost twenty dollars per round trip. For a man making what he made and trying to save for marriage, that was tough. Raised in luxury at Beth Eden, Mary Emma, while mildly concerned over how her love of dancing weighed on Ike, seemed unfazed as she pondered her humble material future. She graduated in May 1899. Dr. and Mrs. Carlisle caucused with Muddie Kennedy. And a wedding of great note, indeed of "prosperity," unfolded on November 22, 1899, at the Beth Eden plantation.

For that night, Ike moved into Mary Emma's room. The next day Dr. and Mrs. Carlisle took the bride and groom to Newberry to catch the train. Just a few of the wedding presents went along. Their honeymoon was the twelve-hour train ride to Fayetteville, economy coach. Shortly the Elk Valley ARP manse underwent some changes. Dr. and Mrs. Carlisle sent the couple furniture as well as a Black maid (with her salary covered for two years). Though recollections of the maid attending Ike's Elk Valley ARP Church survived in Kennedy family memories, her name did not.[16]

Well equipped, Ike and Mary Emma wasted no time in starting a family. On October 1, 1900, their first child arrived. They returned to Beth Eden for Dr. Carlisle to oversee the actual delivery. After an arduous process, one Renwick Carlisle Kennedy finally popped out, opening those Muddie eyes. They called him Ren. And in the following years a plethora followed: William McLane, Gladyce Mildred, and Richard Newton (who soon died). So, in late 1904 another Richard Newton arrived. Then came Leon Toland, Emma, and Elizabeth. Dr. Carlisle's decline, then death in 1904, required delivery of the last five in Newberry.

By the time he was eight, because of his mother's periodic absence, Ren helped his father run the house and manage the ever growing stream of infant Kennedys. If Ren was not born responsible, he got that way fast. By age nine he even chaperoned the trek to school. All ages were educated at Harms, a mile-and-a-half walk that crossed the majestic stone edifice, the Elk River

Bridge. In rough weather Ike took them in the family buggy pulled by Jim, the family's black horse. Ren also had the assignment of protecting the family's two cats, Reek and Joe. The other children, he reminisced, "chased them in a fully un-Christian manner."[17]

After twelve years in Fayetteville, Ike Kennedy accepted a call to Bethel ARP Church in Ora, South Carolina, in Laurens County. In 1790, Mary Emma's great-grandfather, Rev. John Renwick, had founded this church. Even more, the call located the family closer to both grandmothers. Ora was some fifty miles from Beth Eden and about the same from Due West.

There, Grandma Emma helped them buy a used Ford, a black Model T. This permitted long weekends, holidays, and summer vacations at Beth Eden. Two more little Kennedys appeared in Ora as well, Margaret McLane and Mary. Upon telegram-notice Ike easily took the Ford to Beth Eden to witness both big events, topping off their child production. With such a large family, Ike's pay of one thousand dollars a year provided a spartan life. But as the years unfolded, the "Tribe of Isaac" (what the children later called the family) had only happy memories. No one starved. Everybody got educated. Everybody got loved.

So close to Ora, Beth Eden provided a large part of this happiness. Both grandmothers were attentive to the kids. Though fifteen years Emma's senior, Muddie outlived Emma. Those eyes finally closed for good on July 13, 1933, age ninety-three plus three months and two days. But Emma, the *grande dame* of Beth Eden, had the greater social impact on the grandchildren.[18]

Emma's home was in the countryside, Muddie's "in town"—a subtle if potent hierarchy for traditionalist southerners. The walls in Emma's main hall held stories from the 1850s, those of the "kitchen" back to the 1830s. It was not just the historical depth of Beth Eden that resonated with the kids. With sharecroppers substituted for slaves, Emma continued the "old way" up to around 1920. So while Emma died in 1930, three years before Muddie, it was Emma who had the energy, personality, and iconic family setting to get Ike and Mary's children, and some ten other grandchildren, well blended into the family's dramatic journey—from the isolated, rugged, often violent hills of southern Scotland to Ulster, and from the rough-hewn cabin and pig farm to the Carolina big house.

This was complex. Ren Kennedy recalled those years as "charmed" and "aristocratic—by blood, by wealth, certainly behavior." Though he came from the purest strain of Scotch-Irish, it also was one that evolved with money, social clout, indeed community building. He remembered crisp fall weekends hunting quail from horseback. He remembered summer holidays clerking at the Beth Eden store "making forty cents an hour selling soda pop to Negroes." Unlike his ARP preacher home, the Beth Eden place let him be a privileged white kid living in the seemingly endless Old South cotton-culture, less a myth than a time warp.

Yet he seems to have received even more than elevated material ways and social expectations. For at least five generations back, his family had included educated preachers—highly literate people. And at least back to his great-grandparents, this family seems to have had wide-ranging readers with sophisticated tastes and manners. If not sufficiently humane and aesthetic to forsake slavery, their sophistication still led them to advocate *college*—not finishing school—for women. For sure, his grandparents felt a stake not just in God, family, home, and land, but critically in the life of their own minds. That, in turn, permitted at least some of them to begin to penetrate the New South myths of moonlight and magnolias. When you think about Emma Renwick Carlisle's Old South upbringing, not to mention adulthood, what she did with books is especially striking.

She read to her grandchildren about what lay around the corner. She did this with the ferocity of a person certain time was running out not just for herself but also for her way of life. But she was anything but angry. "She read us *The Long Roll* and *Cease Firing* by Mary Johnston." Here was one of the first white southerners to challenge the carefully orchestrated myths of the Lost Cause. "She read them to us," Kennedy recalled, "and then we had to be part of discussing them . . . what they said about the past and future. And she told me never to use the word *nigger* . . . never use *that* word. . . . My parents already drilled this into me, but she was strong on it also."

When the doctor died, Emma's younger brother, Hubert, moved in at Beth Eden. He also read. "Uncle Hubert had a huge library. My father had a lot of books, too. But Uncle Hubert read to us and got us to read modern fiction he had just finished. He got me to read *Ishmael*, by Mary Southworth. I remember discussing her with him." Here was conversation about a friend of Harriet Beecher Stowe, author of *Uncle Tom's Cabin* and a leading social reformer of Washington, DC.[19]

If this seems to have been as potent a part of Ren Kennedy's "inheritance" as his British Borderlands background, it is hard to be precise about how it all worked. There is a good chance Beth Eden hinted at a forked road. Was it more than books read by Emma and Hubert? Was Christianity the reason they raised the need for new thought? That is hard to argue; they were surrounded by people of equal Christian fervor who fought change relentlessly. Did their thought broaching reconciliation between past and future signal some "social mutation" in a long story of evolving social thought? Was it, after all, their reading that extended the "mutation"?

At the least, if they felt deep connection to an emotional road to the past, far in the haze they likely sensed an intellectual road embracing a changed future. At the split, undoubtedly leaning to the past, but accepting the probability that change happens and straight-thinking people channel it in order not to live defeated; and, even more, full Christians channel it so as not to be angry, which is contrary to what Jesus preached and therefore un-Christian: is that where Emma and Hubert stood?

The full impact of these family origins remains unclear. Yet two elements of it shine through. First, family upbringing counts, with Ren Kennedy's reflecting an abundance of sophisticated reading atypical among the mass of Scotch-Irish. Second, Beth Eden never left him.

2

Evolution

As much as Ike and Mary Emma liked Ora, they found its high school weak and undisciplined, an insufficient place for a young man wanting college. For his final year they sent Ren to the stronger Laurens High School. Every morning at 8:15 he caught the train at Ora. For twenty cents it delivered him the seven miles south to Laurens. The 2:40 p.m. train took him home. It was a stiff curriculum: geometry, English, history, and second-year Latin—Caesar's *Gallic Wars*, first Latin to English, then the far more difficult English to Latin.[1]

In September 1917, a month shy of seventeen, Kennedy moved on to well-known turf. He became one of 110 students at the Holy Hamlet's Erskine College. He took along his new, blue-vested Sunday suit. On the right side, at the bottom, the vest sported a watch pocket. Here, rested a gold, seven-jeweled Elgin timepiece Grandma Emma gave him for his high school graduation. As he proudly noted in his little black book—calendar and important addresses—his Elgin had case number 627771, works number 19543236. On special occasions he could spread across his front the accompanying slender, understated gold chain. Virtually all gentlemen of that era obsessed about "time." It unlocked the door to "efficiency," which led to the door to "success" and on to the ultimate door, "status." But this obsession—memorializing the Elgin's numbers in his little black book—undoubtedly reached an even greater fervor inside Ren Kennedy. It exuded a quiet personal "statement." Redneck origins be damned. Ren Kennedy arrived on campus a Scotch-Irish Victorian gentleman, efficient, mannered, deliberate, focused, responsible, and indeed punctual.[2]

Because he was a year short of draft age for World War I, which the United States had entered the previous April, and Armistice arrived midway through his junior year, that pocket watch ticked off four uninterrupted years. As a preministerial student he received financial aid from Erskine. His father and two grandmothers helped from time to time as well. Managed meticulously, his check stubs reflect a frugal if comfortable life. He first rented a room from

Mrs. Maude Pressly, later from Mrs. Tom McDill—going rate about $5.50 a month. He had his Sunday suit pressed once every other month, thirty cents each time. Two or three times a year he rented a typewriter. Fifteen years earlier the US government had moved virtually all of its communications to typewriters. Increasingly, now, they were a part of college life as well. For his term papers typed on a rented Royal—a few wealthy students had them—one dollar got him five hours. Each year he made donations of a dollar each to the Armenian Relief and the YMCA. But checks also went to merchants and others whose extended families helped create the Holy Hamlet and would prove dramatic parts of his later life—Bonners, Presslys, Millers, Carothers, Dunns, Dales, Brices, Joneses, Griers, and Hoods.[3]

As for academics, Kennedy had fleeting moments when biology enticed him toward becoming a physician. Still, he was generally focused on the ministry. His father deeply wanted this. Too, Ike's brother, Ebenezer—whom Ren idolized—was by this time an esteemed Yale- and Sorbonne-educated professor of Latin and French at Erskine. Ren decided on English as a major and pursued the liberal arts curriculum Erskine by that time required of all students: from history to foreign languages, from physics to literature to classics. Above all was the emphasis on advanced writing. He recalled "the war" all English faculties waged against comma splices. His March 10, 1919, in-class physics examination reflects numeric precision delivered through equally precise grammar and syntax required of science students, at least in that era. Likewise, no comma splices appear in his essays on elasticity in metals and temperature-pressure correlations in gases, nor in his December 21, 1920, in-class examination in geology, explaining diastrophism, volcanism, and gradation. As for his preministerial essays treating the Bible, ethics, and history of the Christian church—the same written rigor.[4]

At Erskine, young Kennedy's father had been the stereotypical future preacher, forever preoccupied with the Bible. Ren was not. Physically, he was well suited for athletics at 5 foot 10 inches, 155 pounds, with a 31 inch waist. His athletic attainment, however, seems to have been more in the area of intensity than actual accomplishment. For the Erskine Seceders, he played guard on the basketball team, center fielder on the baseball team, and halfback (offense *and* defense) on the football team, just begun in 1915. During Kennedy's time, at least, these generally were winning years for the Seceders—later known as The Flying Fleet. Still, his most "remembered football game" was *not* the 1917 defeat of South Carolina. The memorable one happened in his senior year. Erskine lost to Clemson, 53–0. But his younger brother, William, finally started as quarterback, and Ren caught one of his down-and-out passes. He did not score. He just caught it. Teammates nicknamed him "Venerable."

When it came to leadership, however, he soared. He liked being "in charge," no doubt an extension of sibling-raising duties at an uncommonly young age. By his junior year he served as assistant coach in baseball and football, arranging transportation and host families for away games and providing statistical analysis of player performance. He showed similar talents as advertising manager for *The Erskiana*, the college's yearbook, and general campus social life as well. In his junior year the already suave Mr. Kennedy took up the pipe—off-campus only, for Erskine students "did not smoke." An active dater, doubtlessly assisted by those Muddie eyes, in his senior year he earned the accolade of "quiet" but "foremost" by editors of *The Erskiana*. What a distance from eye-gouging.[5]

Kennedy also ran around with people of long-term ARP families decidedly undestined for the ARP ministry. While remaining an ARP, his best friend, Ralph Blakley, became a teacher and meteorologist. His roommate, Andrew Hood—son of revered ARP minister, James Boyce Hood—focused on history before heading to law school at Georgetown University and ultimately a career as a professor and noted Washington, DC, judge. Andrew's brother, William—who later married Ren's sister, Gladyce—moved through Erskine College and Seminary only to leave the ARP for less conservative Presbyterian churches.

He also spent a lot of time with his distant cousin and the future writer, Erskine Caldwell, William's roommate and fellow member of the football team. Ren remembered him as "a quiet young man but cynical." Erskine Caldwell's father, too, was an ARP preacher. But Sylvester Caldwell was dramatically different from Ike Kennedy. Wherever he landed in Georgia, South Carolina, and Tennessee, he acted upon a fervent Social Gospel Protestantism. Unhappy in conservative Due West, after two years Erskine Caldwell departed for the University of Virginia. His subsequent fiction writing about the American South followed much of his father's liberal reform views, if not his vocabulary. "We talked about many things, particularly literature," Kennedy recalled. "I enjoyed him." Much later, after Caldwell's *Tobacco Road* (1937) hit print, he regularly defended his cousin's writing style, even to his pious father. "What Erskine wrote is rather tame and mild compared to the complete frankness of many present-day novelists."[6]

In his senior year, 1920–21, Kennedy seemed drawn more to the debate club than to classes. The club had a yearlong program on America's role in world affairs. Participants had to demonstrate the relevance of noted Greek philosophers—Euripides, Sophocles, Aeschylus—in assessing ethical dimensions of contemporary international affairs. In that context, Kennedy argued for the legitimacy of the League of Nations and the greatness of Woodrow Wilson.

Raised in a pro-Wilson family, Kennedy here for the first time publicly articulated an enduring resentment of Republicans. He was not focused on Civil War and Reconstruction as a "tragedy" rendered on white southerners by Republicans. Instead, he resented Republicans' blocking US membership in the League of Nations. In fact, as he explained in several debates, Republican action was downright "sinful." The defeat of the League in the US Senate, he was sure, "meant more war." And "since war meant more killing, and Jesus said killing was a sin, Republicans were sinners."

Likewise, he saw the Republican position as "unethical" within the context of more secular universals. Aeschylus had urged "that the Greek god, Zeus, commanded humans do good deeds for the improvement of civilization, here and now. What could be more civilized than order and peace?" In essence, Kennedy used Aeschylus to argue that Republicans, in violating a central ethic of classical Greek thought, transgressed upon foundational values of Western and American culture.[7]

In May 1921 Kennedy completed his baccalaureate degree. His grade-point average ranked third out of twenty-one; the English faculty named him their best senior English major. He spent the following summer in Bartow, Florida, a locale about to explode with Roaring Twenties real estate development. One of his father's old ARP friends, Edward C. Stuart, was a wealthy businessman in Bartow. He had known Ike's oldest from early childhood, when the family visited Bartow where Ike's brother, Ebenezer, then pastored the ARP church. Word that "a pipe has been noticed in a photo" required Ren to promise Stuart he would not smoke. But with that promise, he undertook office work in Stuart's Florida Ice and Light Company and helped in whatever ways needed at the Bartow ARP church.[8]

With a little cash to apply to school costs and considerable financial scholarship provided by ARP donors, Kennedy spent the next two years in Erskine Seminary. It had three faculty members. He studied Greek and Old Testament with sixty-seven-year-old Francis Young Pressly. Born in Due West, son of an august ARP family, he was an Erskine graduate (BA, MTh) and had an honorary doctorate from Westminster College in Pennsylvania. Kennedy studied New Testament and Hebrew with another South Carolinian, sixty-year-old Robert Milton Stevenson. He, too, was an Erskine graduate (BA, MTh) and had an honorary doctorate from Erskine. A temperance man and one of the leading Prohibitionists of the South, Stevenson served as editor of the *Associate Reformed Presbyterian*. Finally, Kennedy studied church history, homiletics, and pastoral theology with Gilbert Gordon Parkinson. An east Tennessee native, Parkinson was an Erskine graduate (BA, MTh) with an honorary doctorate from Erskine. Parkinson also did graduate study at Princeton Theological Seminary and McCormick Theological Seminary in Chicago.

For this faculty Ren Kennedy was a star student both in the classroom and in the pulpit. By Christmas break of his first year, he was in a pulpit. Undoubtedly through his father's invitation, he preached the afternoon service on Christmas Eve back home at Bethel, in Ora. He wrote out his sermon on sixteen pages of 5 x 8 inch notepaper. With perfect syntax, grammar, and economy of words, he stiffly recounted the birth of Jesus. Then he wound up with straightforward Calvinism, surely pleasing for his father: "It is useless to fight against [God]. For He will triumph. Let skeptics and wicked men and devils go to whatever extreme.... It will all avail nothing but their own ruin."[9]

The following summer he returned to Bartow for work again with E. C. Stuart, undoubtedly without pipe. He also got in some preaching. Sunday, August 22, he delivered the main sermon at the Bartow ARPC. From Daniel 3:16–18 he preached on the faith of the Hebrew children, urging that such commitment provided courage undefeatable in the face of earthly adversity—a message right out of traditional ARPism and his father. Still, his language was less stiff than back in Ora. People in front of him he called "friends"—not "you."

Erskine Seminary faculty were so impressed with Ren they proposed him for preaching in October 1922 for the presbytery meeting at Due West. He got turned down. Still, he returned to the pulpit on Sunday, November 12, 1922, at Clinton, South Carolina—Ralph Blakley's hometown. This was a practice run for a required sermon before the seminary faculty. Not happy with Clinton results, Kennedy worked until near midnight on November 15, then delivered the sermon at 11:00 a.m. the next day. From 2 Peter:11–12, he preached on the need for Christians to be steadfast in their purity even when under the pressure of being among sinners. For at the end of the day God would hold you accountable no matter what. Again, this was the type of judgmental message he had been studying—conventional ARPism. The eleven handwritten, legal-size pages must have taken him at least forty minutes to deliver. In spring 1923 he gave similar sermons at Vidette, Georgia, and Bethlehem and King's Creek, South Carolina. In later life the length would be different, even more the message.[10]

In May 1923 Ren Kennedy departed Erskine Seminary with the Bachelor of Divinity degree. Shortly, the Second Presbytery of the ARP Synod meeting at Unity Church, in Lancaster County, South Carolina, licensed him to preach. The summer of 1923 he took "supply" pastorates at Mount Zion ARPC and Elsberry ARPC, both in Elsberry, Missouri—sixty miles northwest of St. Louis. Each congregation had around fifteen members.

As Isaac's son, he was well prepared for most of the nonpulpit elements of the Elsberry ministries. He lived in a rented room at the back of a congregation member's house. He enjoyed dinner in congregational homes. Still, with far less money than ARPs of Due West, most of his church members lived scattered across the countryside, which posed a problem. They all wanted to be visited, regularly. Yet he had no car, and no money to buy one. For short runs he borrowed a horse and buggy. Otherwise, he had to rent a Ford from one of three wealthy congregation members. Ten miles took him two hours in a buggy, thirty minutes in a Ford.

Happily, in those three months he grew the tiny Elsberry ARPC congregation by four, "Stanley Miller, wife and two children, by letter." Unhappily, he buried the former elder at the Mount Zion church, seventy-eight-year-old James Thomas Finley. As he wrote his father, "[His] dying was an awful sight ... glassy eyes and gasps of breath. ... I saw the death sweat on his brow and heard the death rattle in his throat, things of which I had heard but never seen. ... Got along alright."

In July 1923, the Elsberry postman brought a letter from Princeton Theological Seminary (PTS). Just before commencement back at Erskine, Professor Parkinson—who attended Princeton during 1900–1901—had asked Kennedy if he were interested in further study at PTS, as Erskine could nominate from among their top students. He was. If admitted, PTS covered all tuition and books for his pursuing the Master's in Theology. Kennedy got in.

E. C. Stuart still made big money in various ventures around Bartow and Lakeland, Florida. When he received Kennedy's inquiry about a loan for living expenses at Princeton, he sent a check for $300 to help with 1923–24. Grandma Emma also would help from time to time in smaller amounts. Kennedy seemed on his way.[11]

On Friday, September 14, nine days before he left Elsberry, however, something almost derailed him. The diary shows he did whatever it was by his own choice. It gave him great pain and a sense of crisis. He compared it to "St. Francis of Assisi receiving the *stigmata*," that is, painful attacks to feet, hands, and head such as Jesus had received at his crucifixion. Worried about self-importance, he then backed off: no, St. Francis had it worse: "What proved to be my torture [however] in no way compared to his?" In that Kennedy had no scars on his hands, the consequences must have been psychological. Gluttony or sloth? Unlikely. Envy, pride, anger? Maybe. Lust? Possibly, for an attractive young woman in the Elsberry congregation had been coming to see him "too frequently," making him ponder—wisely—the liabilities of his dating a member of his church.[12]

Whatever it was, by Sunday, September 23, he undoubtedly was ready to leave it behind. After church he and his two large suitcases caught a ride to the St. Louis train station. Some twenty-four hours later—Chicago, Washington, New York City—he disembarked at Princeton station, New Jersey.

Both before and after the Civil War, Ivy League colleges and universities received many white southerners who had benefited from slavery and plantation life. For a lot of them, the Ivy League had little impact on their world view. Instead, with enhanced connections to East Coast money and politics, they became even more powerful—and glib—in keeping the South a captive of its historic feudal oligarchies. A few southerners, however, headed to the Ivy League and were changed forever. Ren Kennedy was one of these.[13]

On September 24, 1923, the freely pipe-smoking gentleman from South Carolina, Elgin watch poised in vest pocket, moved into Room 313 of Hodge Hall at Princeton Theological Seminary. At registration the next morning he declared intentions to major in New Testament. Beneath the suave exterior lurked the fear. It was one thing to puff pensively on a pipe before declaring a major. It was another to have a realistic idea of what lay ahead. This was his first venture beyond small-town life.

He was to be one of a ninety-seven-student class. His Erskine Seminary class had had twelve. True, some of his future colleagues also hailed from small, denominational colleges—Calvin, LaFayette, and Maryville. At least half, however, had graduated from bigger, more imposing places: Princeton, Brown, Chicago, London, Pennsylvania, Virginia, and Trinity College in Dublin. Regardless of their backgrounds, "All had read everything," Kennedy later recalled. "I could tell just by their level of conversation." "Complicated ideas" were just part of their normal talk. "They all knew what was on the editorial page of the *New York Times* that morning."

He also found out with whom he would be studying. For that term it would be Geerhardus Voss, J. Gresham Machen, J. Ritchie Smith, Charles R. Erdman, and William B. Greene. Back at Erskine, Professor Parkinson had mentioned a few of their names. But they turned out to be the foremost Protestant theologians of that era, and young Kennedy now was in the same building with them—in the same classroom. "I was scared."[14]

With Erskine Seminary's intended isolation, no Erskine faculty member, much less Kennedy himself, could have anticipated precisely what he walked into at PTS. Granted, issues had been bubbling up for some seventy-five years. But now a volcano erupted. It was far more than a Presbyterian conflict. It was a Protestant Christianity psychic crisis.

In the United States, immediately after World War I, surging nativism and a general cultural inwardness warred with a strident liberal Christianity spawned by Charles Darwin's *Origin of Species* (1858) and urging non-literal interpretations of the Bible. Out of this conflict many traditionalist Christians became fearful of anything "different," a fear devouring Princeton Theological Seminary. Would it stick with the old-line "Princeton theology," the long-held orthodoxy based on "infallibility" of the Bible? Would it embrace a "new Princeton theology" open to science?

At the 1923 General Assembly of the Presbyterian Church USA (PCUSA), which sponsored Princeton Theological Seminary, a majority sided with the practical, flexibly toned Auburn Affirmation, which let individual presbyteries decide where they stood on the two approaches. From his pulpit at the First Presbyterian Church of Princeton, PTS professor J. Gresham Machen counterattacked that the Bible was infallible. Adhere to the Five Fundamentals: "the Deity of Christ, the Virgin birth, the blood atonement, the Resurrection, the inerrancy of the Bible," shortly crystallized in his classic, *Christianity and Liberalism* (1923). At its next annual meeting, the PCUSA defrocked Machen and shortly made adherence to the Five Fundamentals an optional matter, expecting PTS faculty to comply. Subsequently, Machen and four other conservative PTS faculty departed for Philadelphia, where in 1929 they formed the fundamentalist Westminster Seminary and later the Orthodox Presbyterian Church.

In short, by the late 1920s most Presbyterians and many other "mainline" Protestants increasingly accepted this *new* and flexible Princeton theology. Yet fundamentalists—including most southern Presbyterians, some Baptists (who joined the Southern Baptist Convention), and certainly ARPs—did not. In this way American Protestants moved to a traumatic parting of ways, enduring as a visceral conflict well into the twenty-first century.

More to the point, right in the middle of this theological war stood Ren Kennedy's PTS professors, the combat generals. Under a recent, hotly debated curriculum reform pushed through the faculty by PTS president J. Ross Stevenson, Kennedy had required courses but also a few electives. A fifty-eight-year-old moderate in this great debate, Stevenson urged electives as a way to help students sample different viewpoints. So, as the year unfolded, Kennedy had opportunity to consider the two main oppositional views and many others in between—if he wanted. He did. As a young ARP minister, not to mention Ike's son, he had reached the age of twenty-two with no encouragement to consider any theological position other than the old orthodoxy, indeed, a conservative ARP version of that orthodoxy. But the tentatively experimenting mind so apparent back in Due West clearly wanted more.[15]

For sure, he received a full dose of the conservative approach. In 1923–24 Gerhardus Voss taught him in three classes—"Biblical Theology of the New Testament," "The Teachings of Paul," and "Pauline Eschatology," which is essentially the Bible's take on human destiny. Kennedy received his adamant imploring of the literal truth of the Bible, the Five Fundamentals. With a more politicized edge, the thirty-two-year-old Machen—youngest on the faculty but four-star general for the conservatives—also taught Ren the literal-truth message in his class, "The Birth of Jesus."

That year Ren also sampled more moderate views. He studied "The Prophecies of Daniel" with John D. Davis, who did not have the tone of moral certainty Voss and Machen did. Though theologically conservative, Davis accepted the usefulness of the debate. The same went for the conservative William Benton Greene Jr., who taught Kennedy "The Metaphysics of Christian Apologetics."

Even more open to debate, and indeed one moving rapidly to a pragmatic, optional approach to the Five Fundamentals, stood fifty-seven-year-old Charles R. Erdman. Relative to others on the faculty, Erdman was "liberal." But that label distorts his belief. Personally, he also was a theological conservative. Still, in his courses "The Gospel of John" and "General Epistles," both of which Kennedy took, Erdman came across as a man not interested in having Protestantism stand in front of a train. Already a potent force, scientific thought only grew stronger each day. Rather than Protestants losing out by requiring an orthodoxy denying this, he urged, they should pragmatically open their theology to options.

Erdman and Machen regularly attacked each other. Though the personal conflict deepened as Erdman replaced Machen at Princeton's First Presbyterian Church, their differences also stemmed from their pasts. Machen came from a prominent Baltimore family with strong Confederate ties. He held enduring sympathies for the Southern Presbyterian Church. Many in Princeton saw him as a "southern aristocrat" with little interest in domestic or foreign missionary work beyond "spirituality." They identified him with classic southern beliefs on race: no Presbyterian missionary should advocate social action leading to a government solving social problems if such action challenged the traditional racial order. Erdman felt differently. He came from a Philadelphia family that fought against the Confederacy. He wanted Protestant Christianity engaged in secular life. Jesus urged helping the poor. Enough reading, urged Erdman; go do it. Over these issues the two had many personal conflicts. And PTS president Stevenson—from upstate New York—normally sided with Erdman.

In 1923–24 this was Ren Kennedy's world, one of the greatest cultural wars in American history. His two surviving classroom essays reflect agreement with the old orthodoxy's biblical infallibility. His lengthy piece on evolution, submitted to Machen, concludes it to be an unproven theory and hence in no way contradicting the Genesis version of the origin of man. His essay "The Evolutionary View of the Origin of Sin," written for William Brenton Greene, reveals the same approach. "The Biblical doctrine of sin is truthfully set forth in Calvinistic theology" as emphasized in "the Westminster Shorter Catechism.... The Covenant being made with Adam not only for himself but for his posterity.... Man's present estate consists of 'the guilt of Adam's first sin." In other words, while evolution from ape to man did not occur, evolution of sin within man indeed did. None of his written work for the less orthodox Erdman survives. Through classes with Erdman, still, Kennedy likely encountered his first formal theological instruction on a Christian's overt mandate from God to help those less fortunate, the core of Social Gospelism.[16]

Kennedy's strong performance boosted his self-confidence and encouraged embrace of other things "Princetonian." He became an ardent fan of Ivy League football. His appearance changed. From a Trenton optometrist he bought a pair of stylish, Ivy League–looking, horn-rimmed glasses. A Princeton tailor shortened his pants to a top-of-the-shoe look. He bought calf-length argyle socks and the garters to hold them up. He embraced the bow tie. The only anachronism in his East Coast 1920s "new look" was the timepiece. Despite wristwatch popularity for men since World War I, the Elgin stayed.

More important, his mind could not get enough. In April 1924 he wrote his father on how his new knowledge affected his view of theological education back in the Holy Hamlet. In the middle of moving to his last call, at Mooresville, North Carolina, just north of Charlotte, Ike Kennedy must have been caught off guard. It was not just what his son said. It was how he said it. "When I got . . . here [at Princeton] I knew . . . nothing of the Bible. I knew nothing of dealing with men. . . . [The Erskine faculty] . . . turned me out ignorant. I am still ignorant, but now I know it, which is much gain. . . . I want to come back next year and study the Bible. I want to take everything John Davis teaches. . . . He teaches you more about it than any man I know. There are some other courses I would take, also. . . . It may mean going further in debt."

The father was not happy; even for an ARP minister, scholarly inquiry had its limits. But he did not try to block his son's plan. After having his appendix removed in Trenton, young Kennedy moved forward. He arranged for another loan from his father's friend, E. C. Stuart. He lined up another summer job in Elsberry. He confirmed his plan to be back in Princeton the following year. And then in May 1924 he graduated with the Master's in Theology. Out of that PTS class of ninety-seven, he finished number three. Close to brilliant, if not that, he outworked most of the students from Penn, Virginia, Princeton, and Chicago.[17]

The second summer in Elsberry was different from the first. Though it included the same churches, the same congregation members, indeed the same rented room, whatever the great crisis of the previous September had been, it did not recur. Even more, Kennedy became deeply engaged in the Red Path Chautauqua.

From the early 1900s forward, the Red Path orchestrated summer-long programs as a "big tent" alternative to the infighting Protestants increasingly engaged in over science and the Bible. Based in Chicago, these liberals erected tents where guests could listen to preachers who at least were supposed to sound the ecumenical message. Before and after the rallies, audiences partook of wide-ranging music—secular as well as religious—plus literacy instruction and drama profiling religious tolerance, woman suffrage, consumer protection, civil service reform, and other midwestern liberal ideas. By the early 1920s some of these "meetings" were dubious—secretly, profit-making schemes. But the one that Chicago's Harry P. Harrison established near Elsberry had much of the older purity.

Fellow PTS students out of Chicago got Kennedy excited about this effort to "apply Christianity to the real world." It had to be concrete, direct action. His papers from that summer even include detailed drawings of how to erect the tents, down to the number of pegs needed per yard for a certain size canvas. Although extensive hours he spent "out at the tents" drew criticism from Elsberry elders, Kennedy persisted. Indeed, within two weeks of hammering pegs and pulling rope, he found himself a part-time employee. The one hundred dollars that Red Path paid him he then used to rent an automobile for regular pastoral visits to congregation members living in the countryside. Criticism of his time "out at the tents" eased up.

In this particular Chautauqua the spirit behind "the tents," if ecumenical, still had formal religious focus. Fellow PTS students who guided Kennedy to Red Path had him reading the *Christian Century*, published in Chicago—especially articles by its editor and noted Christian Socialist, Charles Clayton Morrison. Just like his acclaimed mentor, Reinhold Niebuhr, at Manhattan's Union Theological Seminary, Morrison advocated the neo-orthodox "compromise" between old and new.[18]

Neo-orthodoxy was a reaction. Profoundly influenced by new waves in science and industry, many nineteenth-century Protestant liberals rejected biblical miracles as scientifically untenable and essentially symbolic. Rational and at core optimistic about human nature, they also called on Christians to become more engaged in solving problems of the new urban and industrial society. Even so, in the eyes of Niebuhr, Morrison, and their theological brethren on both sides of the Atlantic, Christian liberalism only further eroded society and therefore worsened, rather than eased, industrial and urban problems. Some of these neo-orthodox theologians called for reassertion of biblical inerrancy, and virtually all urged a renewed emphasis on individual piety and salvation. In contrast to the traditionalist orthodox, however, the neo-orthodox agreed with liberals on Christians helping to solve earthly problems of unfortunates—poverty, greed, prejudice, and the wars they created.

"We [students] talked about Morrison," Kennedy recalled in 1983. "Not so really in the PTS classes"—PTS did not have a focused neo-orthodox faculty member until the 1930s—"but among ourselves . . . the big ideas of it and some of its variations." Still, through their teaching, Erdman and Stevenson's theological flexibility, not to mention open criticism of Old South slavery, undoubtedly reinforced the emphasis on solving earthly secular problems, and probably paved the way for Kennedy's growing interest in neo-orthodoxy and, it turns out, Christian Socialism.[19]

The 1910s had witnessed the final decline of violent labor-management confrontations in America, those involving radical socialists like Eugene V. Debs. But on through the 1920s and 1930s Christian Socialism still focused on education and preaching about the inequities of capitalism as contrary to the teachings of Jesus. Many Christian Socialists, viewing capitalism as a cause for war, were pacifists. Niebuhr showed no particular interest in racial divisions caused by capitalism. Yet a good many Christian Socialists did, and especially in the American South. Kennedy was to be one of them.[20]

Organized through any number of groups, but notably the Fellowship of Christian Socialists, these direct-action reformers always had a small following. Yet through the *Christian Century* they spoke with powerful voices, not just Niebuhr and Morrison but also writers such as William Dean Howells and theologians like Karl Barth. Kennedy recalled he joined the fellowship that summer in Missouri and remained "a member for a while." More to the point, with neo-orthodoxy he found a comfortable meeting between his past and future: it provided theological grounding for overtly helping others, while posing no conflict with the Calvinist orthodoxy of his ARP background. The endurance of such comfort would be another matter.

For that summer he managed to follow his father's advice regarding pulpit performance. "Son, stay in touch with the people in front of you." His sermons for that time were conventional ARP; with a "careful harness on my new enthusiasms," he was "neither intellectual, nor liberal, nor Princetonian." Still, much like the private comfort, the "harness," too, would prove but an evolutionary step.

On his way back to Princeton, in August, Kennedy took a fateful detour through Charlotte, North Carolina. This stretched him financially, but three things made him ultimately decide to do it. A cousin had marriage plans; he would attend the ceremony. He also would check on his parents, plus pursue a romantic interest first kindled at Erskine. The young woman was Louise Elliott Guerard. Her noted ARP family descended from the original French Huguenots who fled the revocation of the Edict of Nantes. By this time, she was teaching at Long Creek School, near Charlotte, and also had plans to attend the wedding. Kennedy's first two endeavors went as planned. The third turned into serendipity of life-altering consequences.[21]

At a party the night before the wedding it was clear to Kennedy that the old flame was moving on; she had wanted marriage soon, he did not. So, as the weekend proceeded, he pragmatically found himself deep in conversation with the fellow Long Creek School teacher Louise was staying with in Charlotte—one Mary Elizabeth Fitzhugh Moore. A good year and a half older than Ren, Mary had a degree from Davenport College, in Lenoir, North Carolina, noted for its Christian fundamentalism. She also had completed one summer of postgraduate work in literature at Teacher's College of Columbia University. Her mother was a polished product of a northern Virginia plantation called River View, near Scottsburg. Her father was an executive with the International Harvester Credit Corporation in Charlotte. Her conservative Methodism was devout.[22]

When Kennedy first saw her "on the front porch . . . five-foot five, dark hair surrounding a Celtic-dark oval face . . . wearing [something] dark in color and a string of ribbon across [her] throat," he was smitten. Decorum he managed for the wedding ceremony and festivities following. But the following Sunday evening he came knocking at the Moore residence. Mary was reticent. Still, his idealism, Christianity, intelligence, wit, and Muddie's eyes framed by Ivy League horn-rims and indeed the pipe (as she later would tell): beneath the reticence Mary just "quivered." Repeatedly, Kennedy palmed the Elgin as he apologized for staying so long. After a few puffs on the pipe, he then plunged into another conversation. At 2:00 a.m. her father finally ushered him from the drawing room. Twelve hours later he was back. With a cousin's car he took her riding. Finally, at dark, he walked her to the door. When he kissed her, she wrote him within the year, she indeed "received it." Despite the "quiver," however, she confessed she "hated kissing people." Still, Kennedy seemed undeterred—for a while.[23]

After two more days with his parents, Kennedy returned to Princeton as a "special graduate student," not officially pursuing any degree. He plunged into "Introduction to Prophetical Books" with his hero, John Davis, and "Christian Ethics" with William Brenton Greene. But he also enrolled in classes taught by noted scholars new to him: Robert Dick Wilson, Frederick W. Loetscher, and Casper W. Hodge. The second term of 1924–25 he ranged further. Over in the university he took two courses in philosophy and two in classics. Student records for those university programs in the mid-1920s do not survive. But Kennedy recalled he studied with some "greats"— including noted Greek history specialist, Shirley Howard Weber—which "dwarfed" his earlier Erskine study of Aeschylus and Euripides.

Kennedy's vague plan to earn the MA in philosophy, counting some of his PTS and classics courses toward the degree, did not work out. Still, he achieved his goal. He wanted to know more, and he did. Again, nothing suggests that the personality conflicts and turmoil of ideas and faith surrounding him every day had anything other than a scintillating effect on him. For Ren Kennedy the Protestant conflict proved only fertile ground for learning.

Even so, to peg him intellectually and theologically during 1924–25—to compare him to these internationally acclaimed PTS figures and other noted theologians of the era—he reflected a lot of Charles Erdman's pragmatism, which then opened him up to embrace of Niebuhr and Morrison's new brand of neo-orthodox Social Gospelism. He was increasingly enthusiastic about "using Christianity to help the world," as he later wrote—"a social-gospel approach, not just a spiritualist one. . . . Christian Socialism held this together for me, plus it was clear that society needed something even more liberal than what [President] Wilson tried to do." Yet this view did not lead him to reject the Bible's literal infallibility. Nor did it steer him away from individual salvation and piety, which he embraced as an ARP and learned so much more about with John W. Davis. Contradictory? Not to some who embraced neo-orthodox Christianity. And he remained that way the rest of his life, even if over time prioritizing the two strains of Protestantism became a profound part of his life, leading him to critiques of Half versus Full Christianity.[24]

The same complexity increasingly characterized this Princetonian's love life. By the first week of October, Mary Moore—despite self-avowed displeasure at kissing—advised that she had received a marriage proposal in North Carolina from one Louie Thunderburk, a young attorney. Indeed, she now wore an engagement ring. On October 16, Kennedy countered with lengthy quotes from Shakespeare, then sarcasm, then noted phrases of Greek philosophers, and finally . . . football—rambling and virtually endless. He was not just "through with Louise [Guerard]" but indeed "through with all women." His thoughts were with learning at Princeton and enjoying grid life of the Ivy League.

Seven days later, however, he wrote Mary: "I am now a free-lancer as far as love goes, and I am conducting several new investigations. . . . Using deductive thought . . . true to Baconian science . . . you [Mary] are the most interesting of my investigations." Now, to return to football. "Saw Princeton beat Amherst 40 to 6, and last Sat saw Princeton and Lehigh tie 0 to 0. . . . Gee, but it was a good . . . bloody game. . . . I will look for a letter from you by Oct. 25—the day before the Notre Dame game. Two things to look forward to on that day." This epistle went on so long that Kennedy's two one-cent stamps failed to get the job done. When Mary received the letter, she found the postmaster in Huntersville had written in red on the back, "Miss Moore, you are due [to pay] 2 cents on this letter."[25]

The epistle bore fruit. On November 1, Kennedy received another letter from Mary, what he called in his November 2 return letter "a delightful surprise" written with "true literary style." Even if she was engaged, he much wanted to get to know her beyond letters. She wrote back. By the end of the month he turned up the heat, comparing his correspondence relationship with her to the fate of Woodrow Wilson as president of Princeton. "Wilson was practically kicked out of Princeton by . . . aristocratic snobs," he started off. Here were people "with whose prejudices Wilson's democratic ideas did not jibe. But . . . he soon became governor of New Jersey and then president of the United States. The *New York Times*, when [Wilson] died last February, said that Princeton kicked him out but he fell upstairs." Now, succinctly, he homed in. "I got kicked out by Louise, but I fell upstairs . . . to you, Mary."

This intellectualized "flattery will get you everything" strategy continued on November 26. He lectured her extensively on different approaches to loving. Next, he asked if she was starting to love him "for the chase" or for something more serious. Clearly, "Venerable" applied to more than Erskine athletics.

They made plans to see each other at Christmas. Mary would be with her parents in Charlotte, Ren with his in Mooresville. He had guest-preaching assignments lined up in Abbeville and Mooresville to help pay for the trip, at about five dollars a service. When he called on Mary the night of December 26, he found her status "clarified." Three days before Christmas she had returned the engagement ring to Louie Thunderburk. After two days of gusto dating, Mary had Ren's photo and his Erskine pin, a tentative step toward "going steady."[26]

On December 29 Kennedy returned to Princeton, Mary to the teacherage at the Long Creek School. The Christmas gusto had her nervous. On January 3, 1925, she wrote Ren she "felt like a divorced woman" and needed time to sort out her life. For the upcoming summer, she had decided to enroll in a correspondence course in American literature through the University of North Carolina Extension Service and planned to take two courses, either at Columbia or Chicago. She was happy for their relationship to grow gradually, if it happened to. Still, she would be taking her time and remained comfortable with the chances that their relationship might not work out.

In reply, he insisted he had a dream about her being his wife. She wrote back: "Young men dream dreams and old men see visions. . . . So you dreamed a dream [where] you saw me as your wife. . . . I've seen that picture myself in days past, though I know I'm not that perfect fit for you. . . . I'm going to take some time off [from grading papers] to dance and to play bridge. . . . I adore dancing. . . . Imagine a preacher's wife talking so!"

That tone lasted about four days. Whatever he wrote back, by January 8 she felt like "a ship which has recently come into port after being tossed about stormy waters. . . . Ren, I didn't have any idea I'd ever love you. You made me do it!" Letters soon moved to possibilities of an engagement ring, with

Kennedy's caveat that, *if* he gave her one, she would not wear it—after all, they might not actually marry.[27]

Meanwhile, Kennedy started looking for a job. Relieved that his son's ARPism survived Princeton, Ike Kennedy worked hard behind the scenes. In late April 1925 young Kennedy accepted an invitation to "supply" at the Russellville, Arkansas, ARP Church. A serious interview followed. No sooner had he returned to Princeton than, on May 5, the church sent him their synod-approved call.[28]

Though he was yet to focus on the Scotch-Irish of the American South, Princeton's complex environment ultimately offered pivotal modern sources for that focus. His new level of analytical thought, urbanity, awareness of Midwest and East Coast reformism, not to mention embrace of neo-orthodox, Social Gospel Protestantism and, indeed, Christian Socialism: all this left him a committed Christian attuned to changing human behaviors, soon to be applied to those of his own transatlantic origins.

Other things, still, seemed not to have changed. Again, with neo-orthodoxy he did not leave the literalist Bible, individual salvation Calvinism of the ARP Synod. Likewise, he arrived at Princeton a southern gentleman—and he left as one, too, just more sophisticated. On departing, he even thought that his old-fashioned gentleman's quintessential search for the "perfect woman" was about to deliver results. Well educated, assertive, easily Kennedy's match in the Victorian art of courtship through contorted correspondence, Mary Moore still was a deeply conservative Protestant. Her brand of Methodism just allowed card-playing (*not* gambling) and dancing. And, it turned out, these were more than negotiable, as she navigated terrains of heart and mind with a man swept up in convoluted changes perhaps best described by historian Daniel Joseph Singal as "Victorian to Modernist."[29]

3

The Wilcox Move

Kennedy's temporary move to Russellville, Arkansas, as a supply minister played a key role in his subsequent decision to seek a life in the deepest South. Seat of Pope County, the town of Russellville is some seventy-five miles northwest of Little Rock. In 1925 its population was around sixty-five hundred, and it was mainly a farming community with a little coal mining. Ethnically, it was a rounded blend of African American, English, Germans, Scots, Irish, Scotch-Irish, and a dabble of French. Arkansas's Scotch-Irish ARPs hardly had the numbers or the history of their brethren in the Carolinas, Georgia, Tennessee, and Alabama. It was not until April 1893, with a major national depression hanging over their heads, that seventeen dynamic souls had launched the Russellville ARPC. Even so, when Kennedy arrived in early June 1925, the congregation numbered around seventy-five, with some sixty attending regularly—a vibrant church by ARP standards.

Like so many Americans who quickly forgot the economic hardships of the early 1890s, Russellville ARPs saw only a booming economy ahead in the 1920s. With borrowed money they started construction on a new, three-story modern facility at a cost of $30,000. The ARP Synod would pay half, the congregation would pay the rest. Hit hard even by earliest downturns leading to the financial crash of 1929, however, the congregation ultimately splintered over financing their half of the deal. Kennedy arrived well before this—just as the building reached completion. Yet congregation members were already fighting over the specifics of paying off the debt. Only the Robert M. Oates family, and several others that were well off, had steadfast optimism that church finances would work out.[1]

The Oates family also opened doors for Kennedy. Through them he rented the back portion of a modest home at 801 Walnut Street. He easily walked to work, thankfully. No car was forthcoming on his salary of $1,500 a year, a goodly portion of which he had to use for immediate repayment of loans to E. C. Stuart. He accomplished this, only to have Stuart make him a gift of what he had repaid out of appreciation for his becoming an ARP minister. With several hundred dollars in the bank, the social entrée of the Oates family, and the Arkansas Presbytery ordaining him at a called session in neighboring New Edinburgh, Arkansas, his Russellville life looked promising.

Indeed, regardless of where they stood on the church funding fight, Russellville congregants liked Kennedy. In this generally unlettered, rural setting he again wisely refrained from being "Princetonian," though not without consequences to himself. Too, as in Elsberry, nothing indicates he used his pulpit to advocate Christian Socialism. He delivered the straightforward orthodox ARP message. According to the *Associate Reformed Presbyterian*, people saw him as "scholarly and intensely spiritual . . . with a quiet enthusiasm which went direct to the hearts of his hearers." They appreciated his role as center fielder on the ARP baseball team. They extolled the personal interest he took in their family histories, as on one occasion when he helped a widow sort out her father's accounts of the Civil War. Even more, they beamed with community pride over his sermons before Russellville's "union" services—July Fourth, Thanksgiving, and Christmas Eve services—in which Presbyterians of all stripes joined Baptists and Methodists in calling a temporary truce on the pulpit and baseball fronts and all worshipped together.

Yet his general sophistication indeed had uses. He navigated among the different cliques of the congregation. When budget stresses over the new building bled into current operating monies, and nobody would meet even to discuss an effective insurance policy for the church, Kennedy personally worked out a deal with a local insurance agent that ultimately satisfied the factions . . . and saved them a thousand dollars a year. Likewise, the fiscal fight had church social life tensely divided. But he stayed covered over with dinner invitations from congregation members of the different cliques. Mainly as a walker, but occasionally catching a ride, he spent at least every Wednesday, Saturday, and Sunday afternoon making pastoral calls to congregation members in their homes and in the hospital. These were not ten-minute visits; they were hour-long conversations, or more. With two elderly families, however, he found himself listening more than counseling. Their vivid recollections of Civil War "Bushwhackers and Jayhawkers" he found captivating.[2]

Although his congregation and the people of Russellville generally thought highly of him—and were interested in his being more than their supply minister—the job not only entailed the vexing congregation fight but had him far removed from the South of his youth. Granted, the deep South's cotton-and-slavery past continued to stymie many modern changes. But—as he knew from synod and his father—the Dixie of old plantations also included a few ARP congregations of considerable education and sophistication, people not automatically threatened by a Princeton intellect. Some, his father advised, might even be intrigued by sermons with modern Social Gospel thoughts and quotations from Shakespeare. Indeed, young Kennedy had barely landed in Russellville and sampled the local population when he asked his father to quietly put out the word that he did not want to stay in Russellville, even if they wanted to hire him beyond supply status. He wanted to get back farther south. Here was a pivotal thought of his life. It also would not pan out as planned.[3]

Meanwhile, a quick Christmas trip to Charlotte revealed full turmoil in his personal life. Over three days he and Mary saw each other twice. Much like Louise before, Mary now sought not just wearing a ring but making concrete marriage plans. Ren saw marriage as a possibility—just not soon. On his return to Russellville the unabating letters from Mary only showed their further chaos. From Huntersville, North Carolina, where she taught high school French, she reported that his reluctance had led her to a decision to date others. In reply, Kennedy complimented her on the literary quality of her letter; he was keeping all of them (which he did), while having occasional dates himself. In turn, she told him to burn her letters and "forget all they stand for." He told her she was "too distant, reserved, unanimated, and not naturally expressive of her feelings." She retorted, "Women in our family [are] distant and reserved. . . . I'm glad I found out before too late that you wouldn't be satisfied with a love that I could give." As a couple they were "unfitted," she said. Ren replied with questions on how she felt about marrying and having children despite their lack of full compatibility. She thought that doing so would violate "God's concept of marriage." On through 1926 things continued this way: they were not dating—each other—but marrying was not off the table.[4]

Such discomfort in both personal and professional life plagued him. Writing to his Bartow, Florida, benefactor, E. C. Stuart, he asked for intimate advice. The June letter explained his uncertainties about Mary and, more generally, his problems not just in finding a future wife suitable to him personally but also one who would be a good fit for pastor-wife duties. That letter does not survive. Yet Stuart's extensive reply does, giving much of what Kennedy wrote as well as Stuart's own advice. Clearly a man untouched by the feminism of the 1920s, he advised no more Mary: "Drop back to the generation just coming of marriageable age . . . they have all the advantages of the older ones plus the energy and adaptability of early years. . . . Don't get a stale old hag."[5]

On the preaching front, Kennedy received something more civilized from long-time friend and fellow ARP pastor, A. B. (Coot) Love, who had recently moved to the Covington, Tennessee, ARPC. Again, Kennedy's plea for help does not survive. But Love's letter suggests his friend wanted a more educated congregation than he found in Arkansas. He saw his church's paralysis over money as a forecast of his own inability to "get big things done." Likewise, the young minister naïvely interpreted the congregation's financial infighting as symptomatic of an unsophisticated population, people who had not even "read Shakespeare." Love replied that "God is putting you through the mill. He means for you to learn from what you are passing through.... Bury Princeton. Let the sands of time shift even over old Erskine ... and make a study of the Holy Spirit." In other words, pray and look to the Bible for guidance. But Coot Love, a combat veteran of World War I, also was a pragmatic man. Do this soul-searching for six more months, he said. After that, "if you have not had your head above water for a good breath, then it will be time for you to leave there."[6]

Weighted by such conflicts of heart and mind, Kennedy may well have prayed, but he also sought relief through something he would do for much of his subsequent life. He turned to writing. He threw himself into drafting an essay about the significance of Woodrow Wilson. In 1922, Cleveland Dodge, Bernard Baruch, Franklin D. Roosevelt, and Raymond Fosdick had created a fund to encourage appreciation of their hero. The new Wilson Foundation offered a cash prize of $25,000 for the winning submission. In 1924 the first award went to Sir Robert Cecil, English barrister and diplomat and an early architect of the League of Nations. Despite this level of competition, Kennedy felt confident. And, *if* he won, he wrote Mary, they could use the money to help pay for the wedding and set up household operations—*if* they married. Just before Thanksgiving 1926 he completed an initial, 2,345-word version. It was a long-term project. Meanwhile, something else yanked him out of the doldrums.[7]

Early Friday morning, December 3, well shy of Coot Love's deadline, Kennedy boarded the train at Little Rock. Late that afternoon, attorney John Miller and his wife, Clyde Purifoy Miller, met him at the Montgomery, Alabama, depot. Miller was a leading member of the Camden, Alabama, ARPC. Before the Civil War, his grandfather had been a seminal force in building ARP congregations in Wilcox County. From Montgomery, the Millers drove Kennedy fifty miles west to Camden, seat of Wilcox County. Here, the deep South lived—and its ARP church needed a preacher. Kennedy went there to be interviewed.[8]

Camden's ARPs had been without a regular pastor since the revered Boyce Hemphill Grier became ill and then died in June 1925. They had strong interest in Kennedy as a replacement: he was of the fold and reverberated with continuity. When his father, Ike, took the Ora, South Carolina, pastorate in 1912, it was to fill the position opened when Reverend Grier moved to Camden. To their Wilcox cousins, the Holy Hamlet network—Joneses,

Dales, Brices, Hoods, Youngs, Griers—had sent glowing endorsements of "Ike's son." Now he was in town.[9]

Kennedy stayed with the Millers. Up early Saturday morning, they took him on an extended automobile tour, lecturing as they went on the history of the place they wanted him to embrace. After showing him stately antebellum homes inside Camden, he recalled in the early 1980s, they drove north to several large plantations still functioning at Canton Bend and Miller's Ferry. Surely, Kennedy thought of Beth Eden. But the Millers urged caution. Most of the county, Clyde explained, was not like this. If she elaborated—and she likely did—the narrative would have explained that the bottom two-thirds of Wilcox consisted of modest farms, at best, created by Scotch-Irish who departed South Carolina for the Red Hills of Wilcox. In central and southern Wilcox, land generally was not "good"—not highly fertile. They did not care. Early on, as Daniel Fate Brooks has demonstrated, cotton was not much on their minds. That came later, when Eli Whitney's cotton gin made it so valuable. The modest ground of the Red Hills, with winding creeks rippling down through private hollows, reminded them of home. Ideal for corn, pigs, a garden, the land also was cheaper than land in the Carolinas.

At this point a significant intrusion into the Millers' tour seems appropriate. Between 1815 and 1850, historians believe, at least five thousand of these Scotch-Irish came to Wilcox alone—no Alabama county got more. With property, freedom, an even greater chance to be left alone, they branded the landscape just as their immigrant ancestors did the upcountry of South Carolina: with Scotch-Irish directness. For the waters of Wilcox, Native American names survive in only two cases: Alabama River and Chilahatchee Creek. Otherwise, they named the endlessly flowing streams with Scotch-Irish family names (Wardlaw, McCall, Jones) or descriptive words direct from the Scotch-Irish lexicon (Prairie, Shoal, Cedar, Gravel, Little Gravel, Pine Barren, Big Flat). Names of places were the same. Granted, there is Neenah (Creek Indian for "source of water") and two German-named places, early Hamburg and more recent Vredenburgh. And there are also the Grampian Hills. With elevations running to 547 feet, the highest in Wilcox, the Grampians got that name from one of the storied mountain ranges of the Scottish Highlands, most likely compliments of one Swene McIntosh. Native of Inverness-shire, in the Scottish Highlands, McIntosh made money in North and South Carolina before coming to Wilcox in the early 1820s to homestead at Neenah, in the Grampian foothills. But other than these exceptions, and two more experiments with English names—one a failure, Barbourville, the other, Camden, enduring—place-names overwhelmingly were and remain Scotch-Irish direct: Yellow Bluff, Peach Tree, Lower Peach Tree, Oak Hill. For sure, unlike Virginia, Wilcox geography carries no names out of high English royalty—no Prince George, no King William.[10]

At any rate, John Miller continued, given the predominance of the poor Scotch-Irish, what made for the exquisite white-columned homes in Camden and northward, with names such as Youpon, White Columns, and Liberty Hall? It was mostly about the ground of northern Wilcox and the alluvial flatlands close to the Alabama River. There, in contrast to the Red Hills, the richest of black soil—the Black Belt—offered dramatic fortunes for agriculturalists using slave labor to grow cotton.

And that is what happened. In the early 1820s two Virginia-based families were first to see possibilities for great cotton wealth in Wilcox: those of Joseph Gee and even more Charles Tait. By the late 1820s and early 1830s others followed. With one notable exception, their ancestry was predominantly Highlander Scot, Irish, and English. Virtually all were well moneyed and, for the times, well educated. Unlike the first settlers, they already had made it—in many cases inherited it—in Virginia, the Carolinas, Georgia, and one in Haiti. Historians would add that they also understood world trade patterns, technological change, scientific management of land, and the textile revolution unfolding in England. And they had few, if any, qualms about the morality of slavery. They quickly grasped what rich soil and large-scale slave labor portended: big cotton production, which meant big money . . . and big homes. Not that all small-scale farmers to their south remained without slaves, nor that they stayed clear of cotton despite less fertile land. But most of Wilcox's major cotton plantations emerged to the county's far north and down toward the county's center along the Alabama River.

The Millers seem not to have pursued the question of the numbers of slaves involved in this enterprise. But an interjection of such data, from the Federal Census, further demonstrates their point. By 1860 a few of the Wilcox Red Hillers had ten to twenty slaves, but some 70 percent had between three and none. The same year, however, of the 17,797 slaves in Wilcox, just 139 of the county's 7,000 white farmers owned 9,581 of them. And 134 of those 139 white farmers functioned from Camden northward, while the other five worked the alluvial soil to the west and near southwest of Camden.[11]

Next, John and Clyde apparently launched into a long digression on the biggest of these early planters: Charles Tait. A Virginian by birth, but long a Georgian, in 1819 Tait moved to Alabama. A childhood horse accident had him hobbling on a wooden leg, but—Clyde emphasized—"he arrived anything but a cripple." Historians know that back in Georgia he had been an influential tobacco planter, educator, attorney, jurist, and statesman. As a US senator from Georgia, he sponsored the bill bringing Alabama into the union in 1819. Not that he did this without personal stake. Since 1817 he and his son, James Asbury Tait—a Creek War veteran—had been buying up land and slaves for future cotton plantations in Monroe and Wilcox counties. Their investments hinged on Alabama statehood. When that happened, their wealth soared—especially in Wilcox. There, just by 1820 the family had moved from an initial squatter farm to some 800 acres and held some twenty slaves. By 1835 their Wilcox ventures included 135 slaves. And at the start of the Civil War, John Miller emphasized, "that had turned into something probably unmatched in Alabama": 20,000 acres, 400 slaves, and "a grand home, Dry Forks"—on the high, relatively cool western end of the Grampians.

An astute observer of politics, and destined to be a revered Circuit Court judge, John Miller explained that "Charles Tait did not live to see his empire's zenith." But even by 1835, when he died, Tait had established his family as one of the most influential in the state and unquestionably a determining force in Wilcox. Indeed, Kennedy later recalled John Miller saying (in Kennedy's words), "[Tait] had the air of an aristocrat, like in Old Virginia, and a lot of people thought of him like that. After all his son [James Asbury Tait] married a woman kin to Thomas Jefferson's sister." And this could go against him, history tells. His early expectation to be one of Alabama's new US senators did not work out; the man who got the job, Selma planter William Rufus King, had not voted to give himself a pay raise as a US senator from Georgia and was not associated with rich planters from Georgia and Virginia—the Broad River group—trying to rule Alabama politics. But Tait still had the connections for President James Monroe to name him Alabama's first federal district judge.

Yet, apparently unbeknownst to the Millers and to Kennedy himself even some sixty years later, Charles Tait's origins were different from those of most of his rich Washington, DC, colleagues—and, actually, different from his own public sense of self. He did not descend from Old Virginia elite, much less from wealthy English, Irish, or Scots. He descended from the rough Tait clan, the same uncivilized British Borderlanders producing Ren Kennedy's Scotch-Irish line and John Miller's, too. As a down-and-out Covenanter, one James Tait—possibly indentured—made the migration to Philadelphia, ultimately joining other Scotch-Irish in prerevolutionary Baltimore where he eked out a living as a tailor. Still, from these humble origins, James Tait and family rapidly grasped the "American dream," initially growing tobacco in Hanover County, Virginia. Indeed, two generations later—aided mightily by slavery— his grandson, Charles Tait, was a US senator from Georgia, a regular in White House social life, then a US District Court judge, and a dominant planter in Alabama, as well as a noted amateur botanist and paleontologist elected to the American Philosophical Society. Indeed, Tait was so secure at the top that he politely declined President Monroe's offer of the biggest plum in American diplomacy—the London-based post of Minister Plenipotentiary and Envoy Extraordinaire at the Court of St. James. So, behind the potent antebellum family of Wilcox lived one convoluted tale. Granted, that December day in 1925 Kennedy apparently got few of these finer points. But he remained fascinated by the Millers' general portrait of the judge and his family, and throughout his subsequent Wilcox ministry he had to deal with that tale's seemingly endless reverberations.

The tour continued. John Miller drove up near the bank of the Alabama River at Canton Bend and parked the car. The three got out. When Alabama came into the union in 1819, Clyde started off, local commissioners chose "Wilcox" for their county's name. They selected that name to honor the US Army's Lt. John Wilcox, who died in 1814 from Creek War fighting. He finally succumbed where the Pursley Creek flows into the Alabama River—some ten miles down the winding river from where the three stood. Nothing suggests the Millers got to Joseph Wilcox's equally interesting family background: in Connecticut, the family moved from indentured-servant weavers to entrepreneurs; in England they were weavers, too, but before that for some three hundred years the Wilcoxon family of the southern reaches of the British Borderlands were so renowned for stubbornness and fighting, they also lived as an adjective—*wilcoxon*, meaning "excessively obstinate."

At any rate, for a county seat, the same commissioners designated a settlement on the south side of the river, less than a half-mile back from where the three stood. For reasons unknown to the Millers, "Canton" had been placed on that sweeping bend in the river. Canton Bend (or Canton) became Wilcox's first county seat. Then John Miller pointed far across to the northern side of the river. There, many years back, had stood another town, Prairie Bluff.

In fact, even before explosion of the cotton economy in the 1830s, Prairie Bluff (later Prairieville) soon dwarfed the county seat of Canton. "Adjacent to the most productive cotton lands in far north Wilcox," they told, "Prairie Bluff—unlike Canton Bend—was too high above the river to flood." Massive slides took cotton bales to the paddle wheel boats below, which then headed downriver to Mobile where the cotton was sold and exported. Prairie Bluff grew like magic: three hotels, lawyer and doctor offices, a paved and lighted street, and postal roads to other key cotton centers, Selma and Greensboro. Prairie Bluff was so prosperous, indeed, that when the state legislature debated movement of the Alabama capital from Cahaba, in 1825, it lost out to Tuscaloosa by only two votes.

For a significant political and civic future with Wilcox, still, Prairie Bluff had flaws. It was in the northern part of the county, John Miller went on, and "the State legislature wanted county seats near the center of a county" to equalize access for all with county business. The Alabama River cut it off from the bulk of the county. Aided substantially by nearby Miller's Ferry—owned by Canton physician and planter, Abijah Miller (no kin to John Miller and wife)—Canton Bend therefore remained as the county seat.

Ultimately, however, the regular flooding of Canton's low-lying ground, plus the occurrence of yellow fever, led to talk of moving the county seat some five miles back southeasterly from the river. Here, closer to the center of the county, there was higher ground accented by a clear and bubbling spring. To encourage this move, one of the earliest of Wilcox settlers, Thomas Dunn, gave "twelve acres [to be sold to build the new Courthouse] . . . that did it." By late 1832 the new town was emerging. Undecided on what to call it, or just not caring, people accepted what the US Post Office was forced to use: "Courthouse, Wilcox, Alabama."[12]

But the matter was far from settled. Given something to react *against*, a small degree of civic interest emerged. Some began to call the place "Shavertown." Lore told that certain Canton Benders felt cheated, the Millers explained: friends and cousins six miles inland from the river unfairly shaved off their county-seat status. Others thought *shaver* sprang from an old British Isles word connoting "young," as indeed the new county seat was. Then there was the simple fact that one could get a barber-bought shave there.

So, John related, sometime in late 1833 the heretofore "Camden discussion" of no major concern over the town's name suddenly shifted to a focused call for "Courthouse/Shavertown" to be changed to something more substantial—like "Barbourville." Kennedy asked why "Barbourville"—a question staying with him for years to come. In retrospect, it is worth noting that, in 1833, the Wilcox County Commission consisted of planters Littleberry Mason, Robert Henry Gregg, Abijah Miller, and Franklin King Beck (who married Charles Tait's granddaughter, Martha Jefferson Tait). But the commission apparently left no records to elucidate the name change, nor even lore, which might have provided something for the Millers to pass along to Kennedy. At the time Barbourville had a newspaper, but its only surviving issue offers nothing on the town's name.[13]

Still, the curious might wonder if Charles Tait played a role. Not only was he the baron of Wilcox, but from US Senate years he and the Virginia senator, James Barbour, remained close friends. When Congress was in session, the two even rented rooms on the same floor at Dawson's Boarding House near the White House. On numerous occasions they were trusted colleagues in advancing federal protections for slavery and keeping the tariff low. In the late 1820s and early 1830s they still were close, exchanging long letters about scientific agriculture, family life, and growing stresses of the nation. Yet this history only suggests strong possibilities for a Tait role in renaming the county seat after his friend—nothing more. As far as documentable developments go, only one thing is clear. In late 1833 "Courthouse" and/or "Shavertown" indeed became "Barbourville."[14]

The Millers continued the story. "Many" of Wilcox's South Carolina–descended white people "were not happy with Barbour's name on their town . . . a fancy Virginian's name." Yet they deferred. As the national depression of 1837 came on, no doubt they focused on more pressing matters. Still, as the depression deepened, in 1838, a fellow Scotch-Irish man moved to town. Less daunted by hard times and more inclined to open civic endeavor, his name was John Daniel Caldwell. "He was a young physician from South Carolina," explained John Miller. "He carefully stirred the pot for a few years, talking about another town name—Camden."

As one who proudly shared Caldwell's South Carolina background, John Miller held forth on how Caldwell spent his early years in Camden, South Carolina. It is doubtful that this etymological exploration continued on to connect "Camden" to the great English barrister, Charles Pratt, 1st Earl Camden, PC.

Granted, a group of Deep South Scotch-Irishmen naming anything after an English earl seems dubious. But as English nobility went, Pratt was atypical. Hating all government bureaucracy, especially taxation, he urged the English crown and its greedy aristocracy not to increase taxes on American colonials. This earned him iconic status in the American colonies—and as many as five American towns were named for him. Of course, his message about the colonies proved futile. Yet it still resounded with freedom for those of future Camden, South Carolina. And if Dr. Caldwell had happened to have told the earl's story to fellow Wilcoxons, those many who were Scotch-Irish must have found it balm for their anti-English, anti-authority, often obstinate souls so attuned to what recent president Andrew Jackson had preached as democracy for the "common man." At any rate, John Miller related, in late 1841 the (new?) County Commission announced that the county seat had become an "incorporated" community and that at the first of the new year its name would be changing. In this way, on January 1, 1842, "Barbourville" became the legal, incorporated entity of "Camden"—with its new "intendent" (mayor) being that Scotch-Irishman from South Carolina, John Daniel Caldwell.[15]

The three drove on—northward across the river, then some fifty miles more to Marion Junction, in Dallas County. Here Reverend Grier's other ARP church, Prosperity, also needed a pastor. Then, back in Camden, they headed for "dinner"—that is, lunch—at Emma Newberry's white-brick Wilcox Hotel, a block north of the courthouse on Broad Street. While they waited for a table, Mrs. Newberry, recently widowed, "talked [Kennedy's] head off about all the Newberry people back in South Carolina." Ultimately, they plunged into a meal of "fried meat and greasy vegetables," Kennedy recalled, and much talk about the Civil War in Wilcox.[16]

Wilcox, of course, felt the Civil War's enduring cultural concussion. Yet it was spared the gore and extreme destruction so devastating in other areas of the South. While the Cooks of Possum Bend sent thirteen to war of whom only five came home, that was not typical. Of the 1,650 Wilcox white people who fought for the Confederacy, only 42 died. The lack of war's physical impact also revealed itself in what the Millers had shown Kennedy all morning: those majestic homes, none of them burned. Why? Because, the Millers emphasized, Yankees did not get to Wilcox until after the war. How that happened requires still another sidebar to the Millers' account.[17]

On Thursday afternoon, April 20, 1865, Union soldiers seem to have made their first recorded appearance in Wilcox. It happened some fourteen miles southeast of Camden, at Oak Hill. At the top of that hill stood a fulsome grove of ancient white oaks, where—lore had it—early in the Creek War a beautiful copper-colored bride had slashed her wrists and died over her husband's death. But since 1844 that hill had also hosted a raised Carolina cottage—a large white house with dark green shutters and cypress-shake roof. A half-century later, on its broad covered porch, Richebourg McWilliams would give his "Hitler Report." But that day in 1865—eighteen days after Selma fell, eleven after Robert E. Lee surrendered at Appomattox Courthouse, and eight after Montgomery and Mobile capitulated—on the porch stood a sole, diminutive lady. She had just returned from visiting her mother in nearby Allenton. As her buggy had entered the drive, she saw beyond the trees her eighteen-year-old daughter, Joyce, and two young cousins sitting astride the roof, accessible by a side porch covered with wisteria vines. They yelled out, "The Yankees are coming! The Yankees are coming!" Immediately she marshalled them down from their perch and issued the firm instructions, "Go hide the horses." Only minutes later, from the top of the front porch stairs, she stared down on the red clay drive as ninety blue-clad soldiers slowly trotted up among the milk cows and guineas.

Her name was Elizabeth Martha Harriss Jones, born in Rockford County, Virginia, and brought to Wilcox by her parents in the 1820s. At forty, she stood there, a woman enduring big change. Eight years earlier, her South Carolina/Hamburg–rooted husband, physician James Harvey Jones, had died of pneumonia. Three years earlier her son, Harriss, age seventeen and a Confederate private, had died of pneumonia after capture at Island No. 10. Two years earlier she had called her twenty-two slaves to the house and told them they were free. Most remained at Oak Hill, among them the future parents of one Martin Van Buren Jones.

On that Thursday, April 20, no one seems to have known, for sure, if the war was over. The Union cavalry was part of a regiment recently formed in Louisiana; it consisted mainly of foreigners looking for a meal, plus New Orleans citizens of strong Union sentiment. According to Jones family lore, it also included one private from Ohio. He told Mrs. Jones that all he wanted to do was go home to Ohio to finish college at Oberlin. She allowed as how that was a grand idea. But the commanding officer, Major Raymond H. Perry, native of Bristol, Rhode Island, had more immediate business at hand.

His assignment was to round up—if necessary, destroy—certain roving remains of Lt. Gen. Nathan Bedford Forrest's Confederate cavalry. After barely escaping the Selma battle, Forrest and his men spent some three weeks as essentially Black Belt guerrilla rovers. Most of the unit stayed with Forrest, ultimately escorting him to an odd dinner at Cahaba with the man who had just whipped him at Selma—Brig. Gen. James H. Wilson. Then Forrest headed west to Marengo County, where he finally called it quits. But, according to Union intelligence, as this unfolded, several groups of Forrest's men still roamed separately. Cunning and vicious, they were suspected of not caring if the war was over—just living off the countryside while slashing at anybody even appearing to be a Union soldier or sympathizer. There was rumor of such a group—perhaps twenty men—operating in the Camden area. If this was so, Major Perry's company, along with other Union forces to follow, were to eliminate it. To Mrs. Jones, however, Perry seems only to have said that he had come up from the Blakeley battle on Mobile Bay's eastern shore, on through Monroeville, and needed a place to bivouac for the night. They wanted to use the house.

Major Perry's commanding officer, Maj. Gen. Thomas J. Lucas, often had cautioned him about his "hot-headed" personality. And, initially, there at Oak Hill, when Mrs. Jones indicated his plans did not coincide with hers, he seems to have been true to form. Yet he soon calmed down. One glance at the Martha Harriss Jones portrait still hanging in the hall tells why Major Perry showed great wisdom in changing his approach. Some of her more outspoken female descendants, of which she had many, called the face in that portrait "hard-mean and ugly." From an early twenty-first-century male perspective, "sorrowful" seems more appropriate. Regardless, that painting reveals a person with whom one had best not tangle. Ultimately, they negotiated a deal. Only Major Perry and three other officers slept at the house—in the hall on the floor. Others either bivouacked on the ground in the yard or down the road in Bethel ARP Church.[18]

Early the next morning, Friday, April 21, Perry's unit departed. Other than leaving behind stray canteens, tin cups, and at least two belt buckles, those who had bivouacked at the Jones place and the church exited Oak Hill just as they had found it. They headed to the outskirts of Camden, winding up southwest of town at the confluence of Pursley Creek and the Alabama River. At this stage there is a big blank in the story. Still, on Saturday afternoon, April 22, 1865, Perry's horse soldiers merged with some 500 Union troops offloaded from a flotilla at Black's Bluff. On their way up the Alabama River to help ensure order at well-surrendered Montgomery, they would assist as needed in the search for Forrest's raiders. Light skirmishes followed the next day, leaving two Wilcoxons dead and the head of the state militia in Wilcox, Sheriff Robert Larkin Goode, in Yankee custody. Finally, on Sunday morning, April 23, at 9:00 a.m., Union troops marched down Clifton Road to "take Camden"—no battle, no surrender.

They found not a trace of Confederate raiders; by this time, it turns out, Forrest had corralled virtually all of them westward in Marengo County. But Union soldiers commandeered hams, chickens, mules, horses, and harnesses, and burned a few outbuildings. They also burned a portion of the courthouse out of frustration over the many essential land-title records that were missing—being well hidden in the woods north of town. And they killed two Wilcox deputies trying to escape town with a couple of prisoners. Late in the afternoon, officers then checked into the Wilcox Hotel, built by Jeremiah Fail in 1848 for Judge Tait's son, James Asbury Tait—right where Kennedy and the Millers were eating lunch. Already thinking about postwar business ventures with northerners—angering many Camdenites for years to come— Tait tried to make them comfortable. The bulk of the Union forces, however, spent the night in Jeremiah Fails's peach orchard just off Broad Street. A safe choice. To protect his fruit from prying hands, Fail had surrounded the orchard with an 8 foot high brick wall, then "dressed" the top with shards of broken glass.

But that was about it for what Yankees officially dubbed "the Camden Expedition." On Monday, April 24, they marched to Bridgeport Landing northeast of town on the Alabama River. There, the big boats waited to take them on upriver to Montgomery. The war was more than over. And in Wilcox it had resulted in no major battle, no rape, no extensive pillage, no burning of homes—and no discovery of any of Forrest's noted cavalry.[19]

From the hotel Kennedy and his tour guides next headed southeast to Oak Hill—not so much for Civil War history as for something even closer to home. There, Hugh McMaster Henry long had pastored the Bethel ARP Church, the church founded by Judge Miller's grandfather and the church where the Yankee horse-boys spent the night and did no damage. An "institution" unto himself, sixty-four-year-old Henry wanted to meet Ike's son. Even more, he had History Lecture No. 2 for the job candidate.

Many details of Dr. Henry's lecture remain unrecorded. Still, this local historian of not just "scholarly knowledge" but "addiction to talking history" undoubtedly spoke of significant ARP life in Wilcox, starting with a tightly knit group of pure Ulster Scot descendants. In 1818, a year before Alabama became a state, James Bonner and his wife, Mary Laird Bonner, departed Abbeville County, South Carolina. They journeyed well down the Federal Road to Burnt Corn, some thirty miles shy of Fort Claiborne on the Alabama River. According to Wilcox historian Bonnie Mitchell, not far from Burnt Corn alongside Flat Creek they started a farm. All their family went along except for two daughters, who had just married two Abbeville County brothers: Martha Bonner married Joseph Jones; Peggy Bonner married Robert Jones.

Those two young Jones couples tried farming in Missouri, not far from St. Louis. But the weather was cold, and it was not like Abbeville. When Peggy suddenly died and her Burnt Corn parents were needed to help raise her ten children, widower Robert plus Joseph and Martha sold their Missouri land and headed for south Alabama. They stopped some thirty-five miles short of Burnt Corn at a creekside campground in west-central Wilcox. Two years earlier they had overnighted here in route for a family visit to the Flat Creek farm. This time overnighting was not their plan. The campground was a stone's throw from the banks of Pine Barren Creek, all too remindful of Abbeville County, South Carolina.

As Dr. Henry the ARP scholar surely explained, by no means were the Joneses the first from South Carolina to settle in this part of Alabama. By 1822, a few others had built a log cabin church—the first ARP church in Alabama—some fifteen miles west of Selma in Dallas County at a crossroads ultimately named Marion Junction. Still, by 1823 the Jones brothers had a patent on 320 acres along Pine Barren Creek and were hard at work building log homes and barns. Pigs, corn, a patch of cotton, a gristmill, and a godly ARP life—and at first no slaves: that was their vision for the place they soon discovered had been dubbed "Hamburg" by a German frontiersman who beat them there by about a year, only to make a quick exit, likely after hearing that, some sixty miles to the north in Perry County, the new cotton mecca of Marion offered better prospects for fruit growing. For sure, the Jones brothers planned otherwise.[20]

In 1825, James and Mary Bonner decided that thirty-five miles away on the Flat Creek farm was not close enough. They decided to move to Hamburg and patented land. But just as they were loading and about to depart, James suddenly died. The grieving widow yet frontier ARP stoic pressed on. James's "barely cold body" tied across the top of the wagon holding all her worldly goods, Mary moved on alone for the next day and a half over the muddy trail northeast to Hamburg. On arrival, there must have been at least some comfort for her to find ample South Carolina attendees for James's burial. Wide-ranging cousins and friends from back in Abbeville County already were there building an ARP colony, not just at Hamburg but seven miles west at Darlington. And an ARP Scotch-Irish family from Rockford County, Virginia—Francis and Anne Diguid Harriss with three children— had wound up at Hamburg, too. Unlike the South Carolinians, the Virginians came with slaves—perhaps five. Shortly, William, Samuel, John, James, and the other Flat Creek Bonners came along as well.[21]

With "great reverence," Kennedy recalled years later, "Dr. Henry proclaimed, in an uncharacteristically low tone, that these resolute souls named their Hamburg ARP church 'Lebanon.'" Each year for a month Lebanon received a supply preacher out of South Carolina, one very church-filled month. Even so, no amount of prayer could combat the extraordinary aggression of water moccasins and mosquitoes along Pine Barren Creek. For these Scotch-Irish Hamburgians—undoubtedly the same for "the German"—snakebites and yellow fever were nonstop. In short, when ARP prayer and the rugged Scotch-Irish persona cannot handle the situation, your village planning screams out for renewed thought.

Accordingly, in 1846 the Joneses (including the young James Harvey) and the Harrisses (including daughter, Elizabeth Martha), along with the Bonners, Dales, McReynolds, Millers, Lairds, Newberrys, Purifoys, Bonhams, and Presslys, relocated to hills several miles to the south. They bought the land from several other white families, notably "the Armstrong brothers," who had acquired it via military service with Gen. Andrew Jackson in the War of 1812 and "Indian removal" incursions. On these hills they created Allenton as well as Oak Hill, originally called "the Ridge" and at 410 feet the third highest point in the county. Likewise, the Harriss family's approach to labor may well have guided the South Carolinians to gradually buy slaves and expand their vision to modest cotton production. Even so, these pursuits quickly were dwarfed by the rapidly emerging Allenton plantation (ultimately fifty slaves) of Joshua B. Grace, descendant of an Irish Delaware family that seemingly prospered in Georgia's Broad River cotton enterprises and chief manager of the Taits' vast Wilcox cotton endeavors. Finally, in 1856, following a major yellow fever epidemic in Hamburg, the ARP churches of Hamburg and Darlington merged to form Bethel ARP Church at Oak Hill. With that they could afford a minister—Judge Miller's grandfather, John Miller.[22]

This native of York County, South Carolina, already had supplied the Lebanon church when he got Bethel's call. He arrived at Oak Hill in time to saw and hammer as the church structure went up. Shortly Miller married a Wilcox woman, Sarah Pressly, of course a native of Abbeville County. They had six sons and four daughters. Over time Dr. Miller became a noted church scholar and was offered the presidency of Erskine College. He elected to stay at Bethel and to run the Female Institute in Camden. In 1878 he died of typhoid fever.

Within the year the Chester County, South Carolina, native, Hugh M. Henry—Kennedy's vociferous instructor—succeeded him. After gaining his Bachelor of Arts degree at Erskine College, Henry became one of the two 1876 graduates of Erskine Seminary. He had been doing home mission work across Alabama when Miller died. So he jumped at the chance to come to Oak Hill: an ARP congregation pulsing with life, even possessing a manse. For someone of his youthful age, it was a plum call. Six years into his new life he went to the ARP well, the Holy Hamlet, and returned with a wife, Mary Evelyn Young, daughter of his mathematics professor back at Erskine. They had eight children.

Why did Dr. Henry want Kennedy to know all this? It explained the roots of the Camden ARP Church. From Miller and Henry's leadership, and with history at that point being all too right for ARPs, Bethel prospered beyond all expectations. In 1888 it had a countywide membership of 101, a robust number for a rural ARP church. By 1890 it seemed so strong that a few Bethel members living in Camden had sufficient following and money to gather in the Broad Street home of William Joel Bonner—the first home in Camden (built by Thomas Dunn)—and establish a Board of Trustees for a new ARP church. Bonner served, as did William Clarence Jones and two sons of Dr. Miller, Joseph N. Miller and Benjamin Meek Miller. The board then struck a deal with remaining trustees of the defunct Cumberland Presbyterian Church, on Broad Street. For $400 they got the building and the half-acre lot it sat on. They then spent some $2,000 refurbishing it.

Camden ARPC had an initial membership of twenty-eight. They got by—even grew—with supply preachers. Finally, in 1900 they accumulated the money to call Dr. Grier. By 1926, when he died, the church had ninety members. They were up and running. Yet Bethel's place stayed firm. As the saying went, before getting to Heaven an ARP had to pass through Due West. But the soul of a Camden ARP had a crucial detour to take before Due West: Oak Hill's Bethel.

Camden's growth resulted in no immediate losses for Bethel. On the eve of the 1890 spinoff expansion, Bethel had 101 members. A decade later it had grown to 125, only to fall off to 89 in 1927. As Reverend Henry underscored, "Any experienced church person knows that numbers never tell the whole story." Even so, Henry pronounced in his booming voice, as far as an ARP ministry went in Wilcox, or indeed any in Alabama, the churches at Oak Hill and Camden were just one notch down from the Due West ARPC. "Young man, do you understand me?" the booming continued. "This is very, very important."

So went Dr. Henry's narrative of the evolution of the church Reverend Kennedy was considering for his future. Camden ARPC emerged out of the heyday of ARP success. It also echoed Scotch-Irish ARP growth stories dating back to the 1790s. It sounded so much like Newberry and Abbeville counties. Not just the story line, but even down to the names of families.

Yet there was one nuanced difference. Possibly from his father and assuredly from synod meetings, Kennedy later noted, he visited Wilcox already thinking that the county's ARPs had considerable financial, educational, and professional attainments—more than those in Arkansas, indeed, even more than those of the Carolinas. Recently, the Camden church had been struggling financially, granted. But he saw this less as a comment on limited growth and more as an indication that the church had gone too long without a regular, dynamic minister.[23]

On Sunday, December 5, Kennedy preached the morning service at Camden ARPC. From the text of Matthew 20 he focused on "Inequality of Life" and the relativity of God's rewards. At 2:00 p.m. he preached again, this time on Proverbs 10–12 and "Righteousness" and the practical advantages of love over hatred. Both abstract and spiritual: safe. Marion Junction folks attended. So did many from Oak Hill, including Joyce and Bill Jones (Bill had just been named superintendent of the Wilcox schools). The train schedule permitted no time for dinner afterward, much less for more socializing; the Millers returned him to the Montgomery train station.[24]

On Saturday morning, December 18, the Russellville postman brought the call. Camden and Marion Junction wanted him. While negotiations unfolded, all done in constant consultation with congregation members, Kennedy went to Charlotte for Christmas. He gave Mary the full report on Camden, minus a few key facts. From Mary's standpoint his coming to Charlotte went well. "I am surely glad you came home," she wrote on January 6, 1927. "I think we had some pleasant visits together. I am sure things will work out the way we want them."[25]

But that tone did not last. As January gave way to February, they both expressed major doubts about ever finding genuine compatibility; Mary even told their mutual close friends they had broken up. At the same time, she kept writing him for details about the Camden manse, just in case they decided they *were* compatible. And in that case, indeed, she thought it would be "a good idea to marry late in the summer [of 1927]. . . . If you should go to Camden before June 1 [1926], perhaps you could 'sound out' the situation for us. . . . [Through a teaching job] I could help get things for the parsonage. Is it pretty decent looking? Don't you think it will be furnished? . . . I want it to look pretty." In reply, he kept telling her how well his Wilson essay was progressing, never mentioning what John Miller had told him about the manse. The church badly needed the income from renting it. Even if it did not, however, the current renter—"stubborn and seemingly immovable"—was plantation-overseer-turned-mail-carrier-turned-Wilcox-sheriff, Fleetwood ("Fleet") Foster Tait—great-grandson of Charles Tait.[26]

Meanwhile, he continued negotiations with the ARP Synod on better financial support for his "new church," should he accept the offer. Camden congregates became nervous; Clyde Purifoy Miller got the assignment to turn up the heat. Kennedy never forgot his lengthy conversations with Clyde during the two nights of his interview visit, plus the touring. One smart, sophisticated lady. On January 16 she reiterated to Kennedy: "We believe you are just the right person for us and will suffer the keenest disappointment if you turn down the call. . . . In time we can pay more through church assessment as we grow."

Camden postmaster Hugh Dale, whose ancestors had helped create the Cedar Springs ARP Church back in Abbeville County, also wrote. "We sincerely hope all obstacles may be surmounted and you will come." Named for Rev. Hugh Henry at Oak Hill's ARPC, Dale felt a deep stake in the Camden church. "We have a boy fifteen years old," he went on. "You might say he has had a pastor only three or four years. Should you not come we feel our church here is of the past." Since Hugh Dale served as the perennial treasurer for the church, Ren explained the holdup. Money. Housing.[27]

Final negotiations went this way. For serving the Camden and Marion Junction congregations, it looked like the salary would be $1,000 a year. But several Camden ARPs thought $1,000 a year was too much to pay a preacher, even a Princeton-educated one. They regularly made significant gifts to the church; their voices were strong. Hugh Dale had to compromise.

These discussions finally ended with the offer of $83.33 per month—or $999.96 a year. (In early 2021 values, that $999.96 was equivalent to $14,996, or $5,164 below entry-level annual pay for McDonald's employees.) If no congregation member were available to drive him twice a month back and forth to Marion Junction, 107 miles per round trip, or to the many pastoral visits required out in the county, he was to rent a car out of this salary. Several congregation members said they would be happy to rent him one. The deal reverberated with the stereotypical "truth" about most Scotch-Irish and money. More Scotch than Irish. Ren vented to Mary: "Some people!" Still, he wanted the job. On February 6 he accepted it.[28]

The synod asked Kennedy to stay in Russellville until May. They needed time to find a replacement. He agreed. Things got awkward when Camden people proudly placed an announcement of the change in the *Associate*

Reformed Presbyterian a week before Kennedy planned to break the news to his congregation. Still, Russellville continued to appreciate him. When a dogfight broke out in the sanctuary while he was preaching, and a deacon felt it best to pull the fire alarm, Kennedy did not skip a beat—though at his conclusion the crowd had moved from thirty to just three. This became the adoring talk of the town. Likewise, one of his more scholarly sermons, "Barabbas," drawing on Matthew 27, appeared in the *Associate Reformed Presbyterian*. He brought three more members into the church—people not from local ARP families. He took the congregation through another selection of elder and deacons, not easy with the money fight.

Rev. W. W. Orr, writing for the synod, asked him to pressure the Oates family to come up with more money to entice a new pastor. To get a good person in that difficult a situation, Orr said, would require a salary of $2,000, plus a manse, assuming they were married. Ren, who was making $1,500 and paying for an apartment, did it. The synod and Russellville folks finally settled on John L. Boyd, who was twenty years Kennedy's senior and came from Brighton ARPC, in Tennessee. They heard him preach but were not willing to offer a "call" until another visit. When the Mississippi River flooded out all transportation to Russellville, that visit fell apart. The two financial sides of the church argued over how to proceed. Finally, the synod and Boyd asked Kennedy to convince the church it should bury its hatchets for the moment. Skip the visit and just make the call. He prevailed. His summary of all this for Mary—the flood, the negotiations—reflected a pride that made Mary ask, "Do you regret leaving?" Despite the salary cut, the answer was no. His final day in Russellville would be Sunday, May 8.[29]

If Kennedy was excited about this move back South, the situation with Mary constantly weighed on him. Most recently, she had asked, *if* they got married, would he help plan the wedding. He replied he would be well engaged in the planning of the ceremony, *"if"* they got married. Next, they mutually decided they should keep dating others so nobody would think they were getting married—because they might not. Still, if they did, she wanted "nice furniture . . . for the manse." Never addressing the Sheriff Tait problem, he said "a few chairs and plenty of bookshelves" were all they needed. His head hurt, he told her. She said that was because he needed new glasses. Also, he was too preoccupied with his Wilson essay. He should do something other than read and write. Her eyes did not hurt because she had good diversions thanks to dating: going to dances, playing bridge, going to the polo matches on Sunday afternoon at nearby Southern Pines. "Don't you like the Virginia reel?" None of that strained your eyes. *If* they got married, he replied, her dancing and polo matches on Sunday could not continue in Camden. No, he had not done the Virginia reel. No, he did not dance. To that she replied: "You are a grumpy boy! I am almost afraid to marry you due to the fact that if anything goes wrong, you'll say I told you to do it." Honest? Shrewd?

But she still wanted an engagement ring. Since her father, a Charlotte financial advisor and accountant, was on temporary assignment in Havana, there could be no formal proposal. On the grounds they might marry, however, Ren mailed her a ring. Immediately she wrote about her happy quandary. Should she actually wear it? What if people thought . . . she was engaged? What if she were not? She was still dating. She could wear it on her right hand? Remember, Ren said, we decided on an engagement ring that could pass for a nonengagement ring, if necessary. But to be sure, do not say anything. "Let people wonder." That way, if they did not get married, "there is no embarrassment." She agreed. That was the prudent course. Now, back to the parsonage. Since "they have used some paint on the church," she queried, "I hope it won't be too long before they put some on the parsonage."[30]

Thus, Kennedy's Russellville life had roads both straight and forked. The preaching part seemed clear. On May 8, he left Russellville for a presbytery meeting in Little Rock, then the synod meeting in Fayetteville, Tennessee. At the synod he roomed with his father. They reminisced about Ike's early years preaching there. By invitation from the Board of the Synod, Ren preached at the main synod service—an honor for someone his age. After the service Robert Grier, president of Erskine, asked if he could come to Due West in late May to give the commencement address. He said he easily could deliver a talk on Woodrow Wilson, but the schedule could be tough—so soon after arriving in Camden. They agreed to pursue the matter.

Clearly, Ike's son was off and running: a natural in the pulpit, an effective negotiator and leader, a genuinely kind and attentive pastor, a rising scholarly star within the ARP Synod. On modern Protestantism he was complicated, but at ease. Though he had not shown it in Arkansas, he was on a steady path toward the Social Gospel, in fact, Christian Socialism. He also stuck with the literal Bible. For him these roads were anything but forked. They ran parallel; with neo-orthodoxy, indeed, they fed off each other. It was in his personal life where the roads forked more profoundly and decisions appeared tougher.[31]

After the May 12 synod meeting Coot Love drove Ren to Huntsville, Alabama, where he caught the train to Birmingham. Across from the Birmingham Terminal Station he enjoyed a fried snapper lunch at Sarris's Café, and then walked several blocks to the YMCA to get a room for the night. He had time to burn. He did not enjoy the stroll around town—"the filthy air and clanging sounds of the adjacent iron-making plant." It made him reflect on a *New York Times* article of October 1925, "The New South Throbs with Industrial Life." He had clipped it . . . actually had it with him in one of the big trunks with books checked back at the station.

On reboarding the next day, he wrote Mary his Birmingham impressions. He mailed the letter when the train picked up passengers twenty-five miles south at Columbiana. He was all too ready to get beyond not just "the Arkansas South" but "the Birmingham South." The Deep South of his youth called him; the History Lectures by the Millers and Dr. Henry enticed him.

As to how the East Coast, urban, Social Gospel Christian in him would react to that call, or how it would react to what he later labeled, "Wilcox—a Scotch-Irish colony," he left no record of prognostication. Nor is there record of how his conscious decision to move to the deepest South comported with the message of another clipping he had in his trunk. It was from the *Christian Century* of February 3, 1927. News of a Chicago choir—happening to be a Negro choir—singing in French and Russian prompted the editorial: "The color-line has little distinction in the field of art." He was just happy. No doubt in Wilcox County his personal life would get the momentum his professional life had. After all he was engaged to be married—sort of.[32]

4

Dual Mandates

On Tuesday afternoon, May 17, 1927, Hugh Dale picked up Kennedy and his bags at the Montgomery train station and headed for Camden. There, the historic Wilcox Hotel awaited the new preacher. At 6:00 p.m. Emma Newberry checked him into Room 20 on the second floor. For the foreseeable future this would be home.

Years later Kennedy reminded the diary what Room 20 was like. The walls "were green kalsomined [lime-based paint] with white border . . . [and] above [there were] picture moldings and a white ceiling." From those moldings hung an eclectic collection of framed prints: a portrait of Ferdinand Foch, famed French general of World War I; then "two cows in a stream" and "one of geese." He had "a washstand, clothes horse, bookshelves, table, bureau, water pitcher, bowl and [slop] jar." A screened door fronted the room's wooden door. The floor was bare. There was a small, coal-burning fireplace. All guests hauled their own coal from a pile at the back of the hotel, or paid someone to do it for them. Adjacent to his room was the floor's communal bathroom providing "constant music of [the] flushing commode." A chinaberry tree stood just outside his window. It hosted "a box of purple martins."[1]

That first evening he was unpacking and sorting books when Mrs. Newberry knocked on the door. Before he could get out his request for two more bookshelves, she advised that he had mail down at the front desk. He straightened his tie, put his coat back on, and descended. There in the lobby he read the letter. Mary had not skipped a beat: "I hope you get a nice place to stay until I come and we have a home of our own." She wrapped up by urging him to do the Erskine commencement speech; this way he "could also come home" to see her.

With Mrs. Newberry's promise of at least one more bookshelf, he returned to getting organized. Late that night he wrote Mary, "I am not sure how long I will be here [at the hotel]. It could be a while." Two days later

Mary pled again: "I'm crazy to know if you are coming home to make the Erskine address."

It turns out that back at the synod meeting, when Kennedy equivocated on the Erskine speech—the institution could only cover partial travel expenses—President Grier lined up someone else. This suited Kennedy fine; he just had neglected to tell Mary until a letter dated May 23. Anyhow, other commencement duties would have blocked the Erskine trip. Wilcox ARPs already had him committed in Camden.[2]

On the afternoon of Sunday, May 22, his baccalaureate message to graduates of Wilcox High School seems to have been a slightly refocused version of what he offered his own ARP flock at that Sunday's 9:00 a.m. service. But it was a double-barreled message for Camden in more ways than that. Unlike in Arkansas, he thought he faced an educated audience who wanted to know where he stood—on just about everything.

With the vaguely optimistic title, "You and Your World: Be Ready in the Morning," he began with passages from Exodus 34. This describes the "spectacular pageant of Israel coming out of Egypt." Just as Israelites needed to be "ready" for what lay ahead, so did, now, the Wilcox class of 1927. Modern society had more "wealth," more "science" and more "material accomplishment" than any in the history of civilization—"radios . . . cars . . . even aero planes." These on their own could be good things. Still, outside of "scientific and physical accomplishment," modern society had "moral corruption" from the most local to international arenas. Leaders at all levels were "weak." Western man's "control over the forces of nature" had "moved far beyond his moral power to exercise it. Witness the World War." As these discouraging circumstances increasingly merged with "the yellow peril" and "Nordics," we were arriving "at an uneasy and restless time." "One year from now . . . this decaying center of the universe may again belch out with a Hell of war." As for confronting such difficulties, he urged "lofty ideals . . . reading . . . study, especially the fine arts . . . a personal religion [of] old-style faith—don't be ashamed of it." With these tools one could confront the depravity of modern civilization. "Be ready in the morning."

Just beneath the surface, here was a full dose of Christian Socialism. Recently, he had been reading the fiction of socialist Sinclair Lewis and the modern history written by socialist-turned-communist, Scott Nearing. These plus his steady diet of anything on the tragedy of Woodrow Wilson had him down on Western culture, especially in America. After all, if one as powerful as Wilson proved unable to eclipse the forces of greed and narrow nationalism both at home and abroad, things were not good.

That afternoon it is doubtful that Kennedy's "lofty" thoughts had much effect on the graduating seniors before him; their minds likely surged with visions of postcommencement revelry at somebody's camp house over on the river. But the adults—whether at church that morning or in the school audience—likely heard him loud and clear. Surely, most suspected the new preacher of being "a liberal nut." And those who heard neither set of remarks shortly could read them. On June 1, 1927, the *Wilcox Progressive Era* published major portions of his sermon and speech. At the least, Camdenites realized a new preacher was in town. And, as the years unfolded, most came to the firm realization that he was indeed liberal—yet far from a nut.[3]

Kennedy's life quickly took on a schedule. With little choice, it was a walking life. By 10:00 a.m. he had done the ten-minute walk up Broad Street to where it becomes Church Street and to his office at the back of the ARP Church. Monday through Friday he worked on sermons, met with congregation leaders and committees, maintained the church grounds, and counseled those in need. Carefully he crafted notices to place in the *Progressive Era* announcing ARPC services: "Sabbath school every Sunday morning at 10:00 a.m., preaching every Sabbath morning except the second Sabbath of the month, preaching services on the first and third Sabbath evenings of each month, prayer meetings on the first and third Wednesdays at 7:00 p.m. Public cordially invited."

Most afternoons he walked from the church to homes of various congregation members. He listened to what they had to say about anything. He talked about books he had just read. Thursday afternoons he went to baseball practice. He was a fielder on the Camden baseball team. This was the heyday of small-town baseball in America; in Wilcox, virtually all games took place on Saturday and Sunday afternoons. "In game against Forest Home I lucked a spectacular catch in left field and made a perfect throw home to cut off another runner and retire the sides." As for football, his interests spawned at Erskine had become almost an obsession while he was at Princeton. That focus now began to make him—his words—"the greatest University of Alabama football fan ever to come out of South Carolina." During football season he listened to games on the radio propped in an open window at the courthouse. He also served as a linesman-referee for high school games.

Unless there was a home-supper invitation, Kennedy took his meals in the hotel dining room. Overnight guests and Camden residents eating out sat at small tables for four. They surrounded a large round table seating twelve— the "communal table" where Ren and other boarders ate family-style. Elegant hotel eating, he had learned from the interview lunch, this was not. "A carpenter [who is] working at the Wilcox Hotel cutting large rooms into smaller ones . . . sits down at dinner table. I ask him to pass me the peas. He did so, ramming his rustic, dirty thumb far down into the peas as he gripped the dish." "The player piano [in the dining room] of the hotel . . . music lovers ... play a roll of paper with holes in it ... subliminal expressions feeding the soul. Hideous." While Mrs. Newberry provided cloth napkins, she washed them only once a week. "You never knew whose napkin you had." And there was the much-celebrated large pitcher of syrup anchoring the table. It was for cornbread. Black ants often floated at the top.

After supper he might walk the block up to the courthouse to "loaf" with whatever "local color" was still hanging around. He found such "color" to be "useful" but also "intoxicating" ... fascinating. He puffed on the pipe and nodded, more than he talked. Then he headed up to his room. He read and wrote until between 2:00 and 3:00 a.m. Thursday nights he reserved for writing his next sermon. "Always have your sermon ready two or three days in advance," his father had preached, "for you never know when someone will die and you are needed for a funeral." Other nights there were as many as four letters a night to Mary, relatives, and fellow ARP ministers, and for a while to come the Wilson essay. But always his nocturnal writing—later he would note, "My mind works better at night"—wrapped up with detailed, carefully crafted entries in his diary before prayer and bed.[4]

Kennedy's diary was no majestic, leather-bound volume with creamy bond paper. From the mid-1920s to the late 1940s, his entries went into inexpensive black-and-white student notebooks (the size of "bluebooks" still used by college students). In later years he used large calendar/daybooks. During 1926 and 1927, he moved from writing only about pulpit experiences to social life around a "meeting"—what ARPs call a "revival"—and then to recently read books and conversations in front of the courthouse or at the barbershop. If it was a personal matter related to a member of his church and it underscored something about the ministry, he covered it but rarely mentioned the name. Occasionally, he even added to the top of an entry coded messages to himself—an X with numbers 1, 2, or 3 inserted in the small V of the X, or the letter A or C sometimes accompanied by 1, 2, or 3. On the other hand, when he met people who interested him and saw no reason for confidentiality, he wrote all he knew about how they came to be the way they were.

These entries could be glowing. They also could depict some of the rawest life in and around Wilcox. Despite his initial enthusiasm about moving from Russellville to Camden, in fact no more than three months after his move the diary shows a recurring note of sarcasm: "Life in the *Great* State of Alabama!" Increasingly, he was conflicted over his decision. Indeed, this conflict about his initiation to Wilcox ultimately took him to psychic crisis.[5]

As spring 1927 unfolded, Kennedy had other conflicts on his plate as well. No sooner had he written Mary about the change of plans on the Erskine speech than he started back-pedaling again on the romance. Just two days after his high school commencement address he queried Mary, who was at home in Charlotte for much of the summer, on whether she was wearing the ring he gave her. If she did, he worried that her friends would think they had definite marriage plans. "I don't exactly understand what I'll do about the ring," she replied. "You said you wanted me to wear it, but you didn't want people to know what it meant. . . . I don't have to tell when we are planning to marry, if that's what you mean. I didn't exactly understand what you did mean." But she probably did. "I hope you find some good friends there in Camden," she continued. "Are there many girls there? I am not so anxious for you to meet them."

Within ten days things had further deteriorated. Kennedy's letter does not survive. Even so, according to Mary's correspondence, he wrote her "in an outburst" not to wear the ring on her left hand. Though he professed love for her, he wasn't sure they should marry. She replied: "I scarcely know what to say. . . . This is something you'll have to decide in a measure for yourself. . . . No one is going to force you to marry me. . . . You said you haven't had a date since Christmas, but it may be some girl that caused the outburst against me. . . . I am not saying you ought to have dates [in Camden]. But please be careful. You get so far along before you take stock." She moved the ring to her right hand. And waited.

In fact he had not been dating. Yet, while he continued to write Mary at least three times a week, and she him, his letters to her were increasingly distant. It was not until mid-June that he even mentioned to her his full job description—that he had an additional church, Prosperity ARP Church up at Marion Junction where he preached the second Sunday of the month. Marriage talk moved to definite postponement. Maybe in another year.[6]

Another problem emerged, too. As in Arkansas, young single women in his church found his intellect and those "Muddie" eyes all too appealing. Some flirted aggressively, as happened on the night of June 29, 1927. That evening he married Marlowe Bonner to Blake Field in an 8:00 pm service at his church. Their courtship had high drama. Blake came from a well-pedigreed Boston family. He was a distant relative of Marshall Field, multimillionaire department store executive of Chicago. At Harvard, Blake and Hunter Farish, a Wilcox (Black's Bluff) native, took a few graduate history courses together. "They sat next to each other," Kennedy heard, "Field and Farish both being 'F' names." On a March spring break visit with the Farish family, Hunter introduced Blake to Marlowe, daughter of Alabama state senator J. Miller Bonner, and perennial elder in Camden ARPC. Two intense nights later Blake and Marlowe were talking marriage.

Normally, Kennedy would have waxed eloquent in the diary about such a tantalizing nexus of Black Belt and Boston. But a far higher drama dominated his diary that night. After the wedding, on the sidewalk in front of the church, "a young female"—one of Marlowe's close friends who was "singularly vapid and altogether void of thought—publicly horses me to kiss her. Where upon a combat of wits ensued in which I feel that I came off the victor. I left her without satisfying her inordinate desire."[7]

Another, more subtle young woman received a different response. She was Jane Elizabeth Bonner. Locals called her Elise. She was the daughter of noted Camden physician Ernest Bonner—like Senator Bonner, descended from the Bonner brothers who helped bring ARPism from Due West to Hamburg and Oak Hill. Indeed, born in Oak Hill, Elise was a petite, twenty-six-year-old graduate of Alabama College for Women, at Montevallo. A specialist in phonetics, she now taught at the Camden elementary school. Because of the Bonners' leadership in his church, Kennedy was in and out of Dr. Bonner's home on a regular basis. They lived only two blocks up from the Wilcox Hotel, across the street in the historic Dunn home. Ren and Elise's first date did not go unnoticed.

On Sunday morning, July 3, Kennedy completed his transition steps as the new preacher. At that service he was "installed" by orders of the Tennessee-Alabama Presbytery. Dr. Henry of Oak Hill's Bethel Church executed the "charge to the pastor." One of the most prominent ARPs in the county and a heralded Confederate cavalryman under Gen. Joe Wheeler, eighty-five-year-old John Taylor Dale, also of Bethel Church, executed the "charge to the congregation." That night Ren wrote to Mary of this milestone. She wrote back that she was visiting her aunt in northern Virginia—and dating. He also wrote of his "installment" to his old college friend and now brother-in-law, Cy Hood, in business in Mooresville, North Carolina. For Cy, however, church news was not his main purpose for writing. He wrote about his romantic quandary: he was not sure about marrying Mary, plus he wanted to ask Elise out. Cy's July 12 advice straddled the issue: "Hell Fire, don't I know you will use your own judgment.... T'aint nobody's business. Don't let any mere man (and, by all means, no woman) influence you, pro or con," on marrying Mary.[8]

It turns out that Kennedy did not wait for Cy Hood's reply. On Wednesday, July 13, he did his standard 8:00 p.m. prayer meeting. As people departed, he asked Elise to walk back up Broad Street with him. She invited him in. This was no pastoral visit. This was a date. And it created a stir. He savored the diary entry. "The whole town knew [of the date] before the next morning." And the following day "one elderly female with a marriageable daughter—a bleary-eyed girl with an underslung and heavy jaw—facetiously demanded when I planned to marry ... wanted to know which of the Camden girls I had elected.... 'Young man, we have got our eyes on you.' She said it jokingly. [But] there was almost a vicious note of warning in her voice. Wouldn't these old girls croak with glee should I slip a bit some day?" Still, "the scene" must have given him pause. Although he forever remained "sweet on Elise," as his daughters would recall years later, right away his letters to Mary warmed up.[9]

Kennedy's momentum as a new and forceful preacher in the county continued to build. Camden's most prominent citizens praised his pulpit performances. Their children joined his church. His momentum was so strong that, despite his having arrived only two months earlier, his congregation leaders were fine with his accepting Rev. Joseph Lowry Pressly's invitation to do a revival "meeting" down toward the Florida border in Covington County. He spent the last ten days of July in Covington. Here, Pressly pastored Deen's Memorial ARP Church at Red Level. Through horse and buggy, he also provided home-mission assistance to three ARP congregations of the surrounding countryside—Salem (at Loango), Mt. Horeb, and Mt. Sinai.

The first ARPs in Covington were South Carolinians and Georgians who fought with Jackson. They liked the area's remoteness and came back to settle. Yet theirs was not the 1920s ARP life of Pine Apple, Oak Hill, Camden, and Canton, nor of the Grampian Hills. Because of Covington's soil, these settlers had gotten little out of the cotton culture. After 1900, Red Level and Andalusia came along with the railroads. But in the late 1920s most of the county lived much the way most frontier people of the 1820s lived in Wilcox—rough, subsistence farming. Many indeed had descended to hit-and-miss tenant-farming life, well beneath subsistence level. In short, as much as anything else, since 1906 Reverend Pressly had been running a social-uplift enterprise—even providing instruction in basic reading, writing, and numerical skills.[10]

Despite Pressly's warning, the abject poverty, levels of illiteracy, and decrepit state of people's homes that Kennedy found among these Covington County ARPs left him stunned. Those who read only read the Bible. Few knew anything about the news of the world. In an ARP family with sons drafted in 1918, most of the family thought Wilson had *started* World War I. A Mormon turned up at one of his sermons. Reverend Pressly explained that this was the local bootlegger. Outside of the ARP families, many of the local children did not know who their fathers were. Itinerant Holiness preachers worked this area: according to Pressly, they "measured their success not just by the number of converts or the size of the offering but by the number of children they could create in a week's time."

When the "meeting" ended—after ten days and fourteen sermons—Kennedy departed, admiring the participants' faith. He ate their humble vittles: grits, cornbread, beans. And he graciously accepted the offering of eight dollars raised among the sixty who heard him preach. After all, out of the bunch he had eight converts.

He also took meticulous notes. He could not get over how extreme cultural isolation and poverty influenced people's daily lives, down to what they named their children. Kennedy had the natural eye and nose for their stories. Their "curious poetry" made him want to write about them. On return to Camden he did not get back to work on the Wilson piece. Instead, into his diary went an essay on Covington County, Alabama. It remains as thirty-five pages of well-crafted prose—his first attempt to write not as a preacher or a scholar, but as a journalist. He was not sure what he would do with it.

He wrote Mary about it. After all, she was taking a course on the sociology of the South. But her reaction was anything but enthusiastic. She worried that *if* they married, she might have to be around such "primitive" people, "careless in speech and dress," "ignorant and superstitious." This she did not want. She preferred "more cultured people . . . cars and civilization." Plus, all that effort and virtually no money. "$8.00?!"[11]

A lot of time passed before Kennedy sought a publisher for the Covington County story. But it was not Mary's lack of enthusiasm that brought the project to a long-term halt. It was more pressing matters of race.

In the mid to late 1920s, as Black veterans of World War I increasingly challenged segregation, racial violence spread across the South. Often delivered by the Ku Klux Klan, lynchings by rope, gun, knife, whipping, drowning, burning, or dragging behind a horse or car were rampant. In Arkansas, an especially violent state in these years, Kennedy experienced the results of one such killing. "In 1925," he recalled, "a Negro was hanged some miles from Russellville." The day afterward, when news of the event reached him, he rented a car and drove "to the family's place and that afternoon buried the man." For the interment to be completed, he had to "lift [the] wailing widow from the casket." This was his sole personal experience with racial violence before coming to Wilcox.

Actually, in the years leading up to Kennedy's arrival, Wilcox had fewer lynchings than some other areas of Alabama. White control over Black residents was so severe in the county that Black people usually avoided anything that might precipitate retaliation. Likewise, in Wilcox the Klan had far less support among whites compared to what it had in other counties; most white planters considered the Klan an intrusion on their own control over the county.[12]

Nonetheless, lynchings certainly occurred in Wilcox. In 1927, Kennedy's conversations with several Negroes and one with "a leading white lawyer," probably Miller Bonner, revealed specific memories of a Negro being hanged on the courthouse square in the late 1880s. The lynched man had killed another Negro at a church revival. With no trial, "he was hanged twice and finally had to be choked to death." This never made it into a newspaper. In the 1890s, as historians now know, Wilcox had two lynching cases that can be documented: those of William Lewis, at Lamison, on April 14, 1894, and

Riley Gulley, at Pine Apple, on September 9, 1895. In the early 1900s—again, as historians now know—there were others that can be documented: Arthur Stewart, at Pine Apple, on December 27, 1903; Ephreium Pope, at Pine Apple, on June 22, 1904; brothers Edward and William Plowley, at Pine Apple, on March 4, 1905; and also in 1905 one of "unknown" name at Midway (a hamlet near Prairie Bluff no longer existing). Then, between 1907 and 1925—based on Kennedy's conversations with "a local lawyer" (probably Miller Bonner) and a local physician active in the KKK (likely Ernest Bonner)—lynchings without newspaper or legal record in Wilcox numbered between seven and ten, at least two of them in or near Pine Apple according to another white resident. While the *Wilcox Progressive Era* covered nonviolent activities of the Klan—gifts to schools and churches, theft of KKK stationery, children's poetry extolling the Klan—it remained silent on Klan-associated violence.

Although Camden's new Christian Socialist preacher could not have had this picture of lynching, he clearly knew plenty and each day learned more. Like Kennedy, the Georgia writer, Lillian Smith, kept a diary; the racial horrors she wrote about were so far beyond the pale that "'some things she [did not fully accept as true] until she saw them staring back on the page' of the diary." Whether Kennedy's reactions were similar to Smith's is not clear. Certainly, however, his diary writings about racial violence affected him profoundly. In the summer of 1927, writing to Mary, he described lynching as "dire un-Christian behavior" and felt called upon "to do something" about it. For a while, Kennedy confronted this "behavior" privately. Still, over time he became compelled to find more public methods of "doing something." And in this evolution, his usage of the word *behavior* also changed from what was accepted and customary to something far more sophisticated—a concept in which changes of behavior became the essential precursor to meaningful changes in law and policy.[13]

On the morning of July 27, 1927, an itinerant Baptist minister Ira W. Stout knocked on the door of Kennedy's church office. He asked if he could use the extensive grounds of the ARP Church for a tent revival. The visiting minister said he expected a big crowd; the local Klan had promised support. Kennedy sent him packing. But to his astonishment the next day he saw posters all over town announcing: "Big Tent at Camden . . . Why the Ku Klux Klan?" The event was scheduled for the coming week, every evening at 7:30 p.m., with a grand finale on Sunday at 2:30 p.m. Camden Baptist Church, across the street from the ARP Church, would let it occur out in front of its white columns. Kennedy asked John G. Dobbins, the Camden Baptist's preacher and a known Klan opponent, how this could happen. Dobbins said his deacons, some of whom were Klan members, wanted it to happen.

The Sunday before the Camden Klan rally, Kennedy gave a strong anti-Klan sermon at his own Camden church. Actually, it was less a sermon than a lecture to the community on using moral courage to do what Jesus would do. Never employing the word *behavior*, he described those who engaged in racial violence, and indeed those who even tolerated such actions, as "not following Jesus" and as "a disgrace to the community." The KKK rally still occurred. After four days and a rapidly declining turnout, however, the "revival" moved on.[14]

Even if Klan visitors got a lackluster reception in Camden, to Kennedy they still reached some people in a bad way. They presented Wilcox County High School with two new water coolers. Under pressure from Superintendent Jones, the principal, Curtis Matthews, was reluctant to give them credit. For months the coolers remained boxed near the principal's office. But local Klansmen on the county school board—the board to whom Jones reported—applied pressure. Ultimately, they were installed in the hall outside administrative offices, beneath them a poster: "Sign here to say thank you to the KKK for this present." Some twenty students signed. Matthews also sent a thank-you letter to the Klan, published in the *Wilcox Progressive Era*.[15]

But of far greater concern was what happened on Monday morning, August 8, in front of the courthouse on Broad Street. There, three Camden white men grabbed a young Negro man, threw him in a car, and whisked him to the city limits for a brutal flogging. Both Elise Bonner and banker Joe McReynolds (Mac) Moore witnessed the capture and immediately told Kennedy what had happened. At noon, Kennedy found Wilcox sheriff Fleet Tait at home for dinner at the ARP manse, which he still rented. He told Tait he had heard "certain facts"; if they were true, he wanted to know "what actions will be taken" against the white men. "The sheriff explained that the three already had been arrested. They admitted guilt. They were fined $500 each and released."

While Kennedy found this deeply troubling, what happened next both floored and enlightened him. There, in the sheriff's living room, according to the diary, he found himself under repeated verbal assault by an "antebellum relic" living down the street from the sheriff—one Bess Cochran. Here was the spinster daughter of Samuel G. Cochran: New Yorker by birth, Wilcox planter, friend of James Asbury Tait, Confederate soldier, law partner of Franklin King Beck. Born only three months after the 1863 Emancipation Proclamation, Miss Cochran was too young to remember her father's fifty-seven slaves gradually departing the family's plantation northeast of Camden. But she knew the end of slavery had rendered her life dramatically different from that of her parents. Instead of white columns down the Clifton Road and fancy shopping in Manhattan, she and her sister, Sara Louisa (Lou), had a modest home on Broad and were advertising small pieces of old furniture for sale in newspapers—if not "working." She deeply resented the abolition of slavery.

Miss Cochran attacked Kennedy for his concerns about flogging. She seemed an educated person. He had heard that she and her sister were two of the few remaining members of St. Mary's Episcopal Church. So, falling back on Woodrow Wilson, he tried to guide her harangue into a discussion about the rights of all people to "self-determination" within the common-sense limits of civilized society. She countered: "I believe in putting my foot on [the Negroes'] neck and keeping it there.... Do you know there are nine Negroes for every white person in this county? What about your self-determination?"

That night Ren wrote Mary about this striking day—the range of white responses to the horrible incident. Mac Moore was horrified, not just from the capture but from sounds on the community outskirts afterward. "He told me he had never heard a human being scream so piteously and with such terror." Dr. Bonner's daughter, Elise, was horrified, too. "She told me she heard the Negro's mother wailing . . . and she heard the bell the Negro's ring when this sort of thing happens . . . she told me he is in the Selma hospital now." The sheriff said the Negro man had "a bad name," meaning he would challenge white people. Apparently, Kennedy continued, after the Klan rally out front of Camden Baptist, "these Southern Gentlemen . . . had been waiting for some specific indiscretion on his part to purge their Eminent Community of his presence. . . . Public sentiment condones it." As for Miss Cochran, she believed floggings were necessary. The key to successful democracy, in her mind, was "Rousseau's social-compact theory." But there could be no such compact between white and Black people. So force was required to keep order. "She is a fossil . . . a pathetic piece of broken-down aristocracy clinging like grim death to a handful of blasted illusions."[16]

In short, the entire event brought to the surface the daunting range of white behaviors toward Black people and racial violence—from the act of flogging to an intellectual rationale for it. Along this spectrum, Kennedy seemed especially concerned about the role of the self-perceived white aristocracy. Granted, with the dramatic increase in lynchings following World War I, Frank Tannenbaum, H. L. Mencken, and a few other East Coast writers attacked the image of an "aristocratic" (old-monied, responsible, wise) New South leadership. In August 1927, however, the closest Kennedy might have come to such broadsides against the mythologized South would have been an occasional article in Grover Hall's *Montgomery Advertiser*—Hall being a Mencken devotee and correspondent—or references to Mencken and Tannenbaum in the *New York Times*. And nothing documents that he read any of that. His New South aristocracy critique appears to have resulted from his own unique and isolated setting: a Christian Socialist reacting to white

Wilcox behaviors. What role would such self-identified "aristocrats" now play in shaping a new, more Christian racial order? The Social Gospeler was not encouraged.

Still, his 1920s discouragement over southern "aristocracy" held seeds of other thoughts possibly offering him a modicum of hope. Kennedy's use of the term "broken-down aristocrat" implied a belief that southern history also included "*non*-broken," that is, true aristocrats. This perception found reinforcement—possibly even its original source—in memories of his early Beth Eden experiences. He remembered his Renwick-Carlisle grandparents as "aristocrats"—powerful, educated, wealthy—guided by an abiding *noblesse oblige* both in plantation affairs and in those of neighboring communities. That Grandmother Emma and Uncle Hubert overtly sought to shoulder the burden of what they perceived to be a new understanding of the Negroes' role in society, and did this as *Scotch-Irish* aristocrats, made this family reference all the more meaningful for him. In retrospect, of course, such filial identity was at the least suspect. The Renwick-Carlisle lineage included no multigenerational experience with great wealth; quite the opposite, it was a pig-farm-to-big-house story unfolding over a mere century. Likewise, as with the eighteenth-century tobacco elite of Tidewater Virginia, the Renwick-Carlisle people worked hard and claimed no hereditary high-society credentials—not what real aristocrats did. The succeeding decade of Depression and war would see him thinking quite differently about "aristocracy." But for the time being his Beth Eden barometer for "aristocracy"—"broken" (not embracing abolition) versus "unbroken" (embracing abolition)—seemed to prevail.[17]

At the end of August 1927, Kennedy took the train to Charlotte for a two-day visit with Mary and an opportunity to check on his parents in nearby Mooresville. The second night he borrowed the car of his brother-in-law, Cy Hood. He and Mary took in a movie. It was a good weekend. The romance appeared to be ongoing, although both would continue dating others—something not all that uncommon before "going steady" came along after World War II.

With his love life more settled, Kennedy now pressed even harder on nonromantic fronts. On Friday, September 16, he finally mailed his essay to the Woodrow Wilson Foundation. Elise Bonner had typed it for him. It was twenty pages on Woodrow Wilson's wisdom. Granting his flaws associated with critical moments of inflexibility (Kennedy seems not to have had knowledge that historians later would have on Wilson's debilitating stroke), he urged that modern society lost profoundly when Wilson was unable to eclipse the forces of greed and ignorance overtaking Western culture. Now he faced the agonizing wait for results. He sent Mary a copy; she wrote congratulations: Wilson was a far better topic than the "uncivilized" folk of

Covington County, Alabama. Shortly, Kennedy received notification of the Woodrow Wilson Foundation's decision: Charles Lindbergh won the contest. Later, when it became known that the decision revolved around Lindbergh's notoriety with airplanes, rather than any profound thoughts on Wilson, the contest devolved to termination. Kennedy regretted the way the thing turned out; he was sorry to see the contest go. But when Lindberg's anti-Semitism, America First isolationism, and possible fascism emerged in the mid-1930s—which Kennedy considered a direct affront to Woodrow Wilson—and the Wilson Foundation did not retract Lindberg's honor, Kennedy turned on the foundation and resented its 1927 decision all the way into his grave.[18]

Meanwhile, white Wilcoxons remained front and center in Kennedy's awareness. Propelled by events of July, he launched into extensive "investigations" of local race relations, especially Klan endeavors. Grover Hall's *Montgomery Advertiser* provided state and national reports of Klan activities; these became context for what Kennedy discovered on the Wilcox KKK through talking with locals. As with the Covington County investigations, his results then went into the diary. Later, they too would be used as starting points for writings. For now, however, here are samples of Klan notes he wrote in the early hours of the morning in the late summer and fall of 1927.

"Most folks say 'ignore it' and 'it will die'; 'it must go, it cannot live.' A few more years and most people will forget about it . . . keep mouth shut and do nothing." "Klan has secret order within called 'Black Robes' . . . a group . . . of knaves. . . . [Klan] officials make them do the dirty work out of their fear of exposure, example a man guilty of rape might be made to flog his own father in preference to exposure"; "Rev. N. H. Nall, a former Baptist preacher in Camden, got in debt and in trouble with woman and had to leave . . . when he left, congregation paid him one month raised salary and paid off bank note. Nall [now] wanted in Georgiana [Crenshaw County, Alabama] for Klan flogging of a woman—but just left for Texas"; "Miller Bonner opposes Klan but still says, 'Lord means for white people to enjoy the country and Negroes to work it . . . need to give Negro less education than now—give more and bring on a race war.'"[19]

At this point, what struck Kennedy most was not just the rank racial views of some white persons but, as he wrote Mary, "the lack of action to deal with those views among the over-whelming majority of educated white Christians." He did not probe the cause for this "lack of action." But while he continued with his investigations, he determined he had to do something about the behavior the investigations so blatantly revealed. Mary feared such a step. "Please don't attempt to do anything like that. I don't believe it will do any good. . . . These men have done some horrible things, and I'd never have a peaceful moment if I thought you had mixed it up with them. Promise me you won't do it, will you?" But Ren had not given Mary many peaceful moments. And she was not about to get one now.[20]

His sermon of Sunday, October 2, reflected a strategic plan: use a concrete problem—and a problem caused by Klan influence on public policy—to demonstrate un-Christian behavior among even those who were not in the Klan. He called the sermon, "Sin at the Door." Though never identifying himself as Christian Socialist, he explained how capitalism fostered greed, which in turn created not just war but grotesque disparities of wealth and un-Christian concepts of labor. He read passages from Scott Nearing's *Where Is Civilization Going?* He then went to the Old Testament's Book of Lamentations, 1:22: "Is it nothing to all ye that pass by? Behold and see if there be any sorrow like unto my sorrow?"

In that context, he next urged that the Negro's life in Wilcox was a natural by-product of this un-Christian capitalistic malaise. Whites viewed Negroes simply as cheap labor to be exploited, just like cheap land or cheap minerals or cheap horses. Strategically, he admitted that ownership of slaves was very much a part of his own family's history. Culpability he did not deny. Thus, he emphasized that "we" have given the Negro only "meat and bread and shelter we wouldn't eat and . . . wouldn't use. We have shown him scant more consideration than our animals." Then, homing in on recent Klan activity, and lack of public condemnation of it, "We . . . curse him and beat him. . . . Some Eminent Southern Gentlemen even feel their week is not complete unless they experience the refined pleasure of applying the lash to a Negro's back."

Now to education policy, his strategic hook—indeed, a hook all too reflective of the complex family ties in Black Belt life. Several days earlier Kennedy had asked Superintendent Jones for a breakdown on race and education funding in Wilcox. And despite Jones's being Miller Bonner's nephew—Jones's mother, Jessie Taylor Bonner Jones (1869–1926) was Bonner's sister—Jones provided Kennedy the unvarnished truth. Hence, according to Kennedy, openly quoting Jones, Wilcox included sixteen white elementary schools and two white high schools, one in Camden, another in Pine Apple. Black elementary schools numbered about thirty single-room structures and six high schools, two with dormitories, one with a hospital. Black high schools had had northern Presbyterian financial assistance dating back to Reconstruction. However, some of the Black elementary schools also offered reading and mathematics instruction through the high school level, thanks to Missouri Lutheran support orchestrated by the local Black education activist, Rosa Young, and several white ARP leaders of Oak Hill and Rose Bud: Jacob C. Harper, John T. Dale, J. Lee Bonner, and Bethel ARP pastor, Robert M. Henry. Jones also provided extensive data on how public schools in Alabama were funded and how that money was divided in Wilcox.

Hook well placed, Kennedy next launched his broadside again using Jones's data. After summarizing types and numbers of schools, regardless of the noted white support for some Black schools, he bore down on student competencies and money. In 1926, he told his congregation, of the 2,000 white students of all levels in Wilcox, 1,700 had basic competency in reading and writing. That was good. Yet only 3,200 of the county's 8,000 Black students had the same learning skills. Why the difference? He laid out Bill Jones's data.

> [From the State] the county gets $4.59 per child. The county gets around $33,000 for schools on the basis of its Negro children and $13,000 on the basis of its white children.... Of this $33,000 the Negro children bring in, $4500 of it is spent on them and the rest on the whites. The county has a 3-mill tax amounting to $20,000 and $1000 [from] poll taxes for its schools. All of this goes to the white schools. In other words, the county spends annually $62,500 on its 2000 white children and $4500 on its 8000 Negro children. The fifty Negro schools of the county have an average run of four months and their teachers receive $22.50 per month. Out of every $4.59 each Negro child brings to the county he receives 62 cents in schooling and $3.97 goes to the white children in addition to their own $4.59.

Finally, back to where he began. "Is it right, fair, Christian ... to treat [the Negro] so? ... I hear the voice of the Negro crying. Remember the Book of Lamentations: 'Is it nothing to you, all ye that pass by? Behold and see if there be any sorrow like unto my sorrow'.... The Church and the Christian people can't ignore them." He left them with Matthew 25:40: "In as much as ye have done it unto one of the least of these my brethren you have done it unto me."

On facts alone here was a riveting message. It also reflected complex thought on Kennedy's part. To borrow the words of literary historian Fred Hobson, his message reflected two religious strains of the southern white racial experience. He sought action on behalf of Blacks with an emergent twentieth-century appeal to white "racial guilt and repentance." Yet, he appeared to make this less threatening to his flock by wrapping the message in a nineteenth-century white proclivity to "honor and shame." Some white southern liberals of the 1930s believed such efforts at changing others provided mighty assistance in changing their own hearts as well. Indeed, for a few their own racial conversion may have been their subconscious priority. And this may have been working inside Kennedy, too, further explaining the duality of "racial guilt and repentance" alongside "honor and shame," though it is difficult to document. At any rate, as fascinating as this may be to historians and theologians, Kennedy's own feelings about the sermon were anything but fascination.

That night he turned to his diary woefully discouraged. Some of the reactions he received after church he had anticipated. Joyce and Bill Jones offered congratulations. Miller Bonner did not speak. B. M. Miller spoke but with ignorant insensitivity: "I walked home with Judge Miller . . . [who] said, 'You can find plenty of Negroes willing to teach for $20 a month.' He believes in justice, but he is blind to the system here." But it was the others—the overwhelming majority—who distressed him the most. They extended "pleasant greetings and talked about the weather, no comment of any kind on the pressing matter at hand."[21]

These reactions tell a lot. Compared to post-Reconstruction conservative Protestant orthodoxy in the South, Kennedy's message was heretical. Although it had little to no impact on local racial views, equally important, it had little if any effect on his flock's admiration for him. By Monday morning even Senator/Elder Bonner was on good speaking terms with Kennedy. Core perceptions of Black inferiority persisting from the Old Order apparently remained so dominant that Kennedy's message did not penetrate even enough to threaten.

Later, at a local barbecue, he was one of ten men standing around the open pit listening to Miller Bonner recall how a Black teenager, enrolled at Snow Hill Institute, recently took to the woods to escape a white man seeking to use him for target practice. Bonner elicited a range of comments, as Kennedy later noted: "Many would have approved had he killed the Negro. But some would have not. Miller Bonner said he would not have approved. A twenty-seven-year-old part-time town constable, Monette Curtis—son of a former Wilcox sheriff—said he would have approved just because 'these nigger schools don't do nuthin' but ruin niggers. Makes 'em so they ain't fit for nuth'n.'" Shortly, Kennedy distilled his discouragement for Ernest N. Orr, at First ARPC of Gastonia, North Carolina; Orr's reply, indicating he faced similar problems, undoubtedly summed up where Kennedy was: "God is holding us responsible for the way the Negro is treated."

Lengthy conversations over the next two days only furthered this "low" feeling. On October 2, John Miller briefed him on why local legal action on behalf of improved Negro education could be useless. Kennedy's summation: "The Governor [Bibb Graves] is a Klansman"; in Wilcox all "three jury commissioners" (those who oversee jury selections) "are KKK appointed by Governor. They [are authorized by the Governor] to throw out any name [in the pool] known to oppose the Klan." Kennedy found little encouragement in Miller's caveat: compared to other Alabama counties, however, "there are so few KKK" who might get into a jury pool that Graves's strategy was not always effective.[22]

The following morning in came more KKK news. Quickly recovered from the sermon, B. M. Miller casually mentioned: "By the way, a women's KKK [is] in Camden." Actually, such WKKK groups were relatively common across the South of the 1920s and even more in the Midwest, particularly Indiana. In most ways, they espoused the essential views of their male counterparts: anti-Catholic, anti-immigrant, anti-Negro, anti-Jew. Though usually nonviolent, they provided local "intelligence" about local Blacks whom male KKK members could then address with whips or other weapons. The women's "eyes and ears," to borrow Glenn Feldman's words, even extended to a curious confluence with the era's surging "social feminism." They reported white men known for violating traditional Victorian standards by engaging in drunkenness, adultery (with nonprostitutes), or spousal abuse. On occasion this extended to Klan members punishing a fellow Klan member. Female "Kluxing" was so pervasive in some areas that middle- to upper-class women's clubs—some associated with the American Federation of Women's Clubs (founded in Birmingham)—could reflect leadership chosen from WKKK chapters. And at meetings of clubs supposedly focused on music, books, or art, the discussions were known to evolve into pressing Klan matters.[23]

To B. M. Miller, Wilcox's female KKK endeavors represented nothing new—"everyone knew," regular life since right after World War I. But years later Kennedy recalled he was "stunned" by what B. M. Miller reported. Even though "Klan women" were strong in Arkansas, especially Little Rock, his reaction suggests he likely had not encountered this before Wilcox.

He pressed Miller for more. Casually, "hands in pockets out front of Courthouse," the judge continued with Kennedy: "Mrs. Arnold Cook is president or Kleagle . . . of the Camden chapter. . . . One night she went to a party instead of KKK meeting. Mrs. Felix Tait [the Sheriff's wife], a pillar of the organization, wrote her a personal note upbraiding her for [the absence]. Mrs. Cook replied that she had done more for Mrs. Tait than Mrs. Tait had ever done for her. . . . She even had defended Mrs. Tait when all the other women wanted her thrown out because she rarely came to meetings. . . . Both women are high-stepping and fire-eating." Miller and Kennedy seem not to have addressed Klan memberships in the best known of Camden women's groups, the Culture Club.[24]

Kennedy was beside himself. The Klan, the "broken aristocracy," the status of the Negro, and, just as compelling, virtually all educated white Wilcoxons—including in his own churches—remaining passive in the face of horrors and injustice all around them: he could not fathom it. As Lowry

Ware has written about ARPs of this time, "a few . . . vigorously resisted any change in the church's position toward Blacks. Fewer still agitated for change. Most . . . sat back, uncomfortably," and did "nothing." Depressed, Ren unloaded on Mary. Though he had been in Wilcox just over a year, based on what he had experienced, he saw no future in making "these self-professed white Christians" act more like Christians. He had no illusion about getting all white persons to think Black people deserved better treatment. He just wanted enough whites to change so that grotesque violence toward Blacks would cease and education for Blacks could get significant improvement. He wondered who were the "better Christians": the poor and ignorant white people of Covington County or the well-off and educated—yet passive—whites of Wilcox? If this continued for years and years, he told Mary, he could see himself "leaving Wilcox defeated and ashamed of himself by the time he was in his early fifties. . . . He would leave town, the county, and whatever family [he] had and the ministry, too, a disgrace in the eyes of God." Mary showed little sympathy, even echoing the very passivity so upsetting for Kennedy. "Don't be such a Gloomy Gus. . . . Thank the Lord for the smallest pleasures. Do what you can for Him and let the rest go."[25]

On Friday, October 7, Kennedy went to Carlowville, some twenty miles northwest of Camden in Dallas County. There, local ARPs were interested in restarting a home mission congregation. After carefully canvassing other clergy in the area to determine what type of ARP life might work, he was not encouraged. The tiny place—a quarter the size of Camden—already hosted four Protestant churches. Still, in surveying the situation, he made an important new friend—Justice Smith Jones, Episcopal priest at St. Paul's. Native of Flat Rock, in western North Carolina, Jones had attended the University of the South (Sewanee) theology school before coming to Carlowville in 1927, two months before Kennedy's arrival in Alabama.

Unrelated to ARP prospects, Justice Jones told Kennedy something he did not want to hear. Charleston Episcopalians had helped create Carlowville; the Episcopal Diocese of Alabama sent Jones there thinking that his distant family connections to South Carolina's noted Pinckney and Middleton families could assist him in breathing new life into St. Paul's. But Jones had found these once-rich plantation families little interested in growing a church or much of anything else. "They just look out for themselves . . . an attitude that must be in their blood." On racial views, Jones reported that his parishioners were nonresponsive to his outspoken opposition to the Ku Klux Klan and lynching. They also questioned why he taught part-time at Calhoun Colored School, in neighboring Hayneville, and why he befriended the school's director, the Connecticut socialite-turned-racial-reformer, Charlotte R. Thorn. Although Kennedy returned to Camden thankful for this new friend, some ten years his senior, he also took the conversation with Justice Jones as further reason to doubt his possibilities for ministerial success in Wilcox.[26]

Other aspects of church life, however, temporarily eased this troubled mentality. In mid-October, the Tennessee-Alabama Presbytery convened at Oak Hill. Here was a major undertaking: housing and feeding delegates from ARP churches of both states. Camden ARPs plus a few from Marion Junction and Red Level pitched in. The two days he found "immensely successful," climaxed by his being elected moderator of the Tennessee-Alabama Presbytery—a position he would hold for some fifty years to come. After presbytery, he caught a ride with Red Level attendees to another ten-day meeting in Covington County. By ARP standards it was a productive stint. Twelve services at Mt. Horeb—511 total attendance, five teenagers baptized and brought into the church—plus adult literacy lessons, his Chautauqua passions still strong.

Against the poverty and humility of the Covington people, the letters he received from Mary were especially difficult. When he returned to Camden, she wrote, he would find a gift from her: a box of ten-cent cigars. He chided her on waste; there was no need for anyone to smoke a ten-cent cigar. She shot back: "I'll give you ten-cent ones if I want to. Next time I'll put them in a five-cent box." She also cranked up on the parsonage, which was still occupied by Sheriff Tait. "Do you know whether the parsonage has an open fireplace? We must have an open fireplace in our living room. I simply couldn't get along without that." He did not respond. In late October, he hitched a ride back to Camden. The transition was not easy.[27]

On Monday, October 31, Alabama's Fourth Circuit Court convened in the Camden Courthouse, Judge Thomas E. Knight, of Greensboro, presiding. Kennedy observed and wrote. He was struck by the crudity of the scene: "Heavy course-weave carpet in the aisles . . . serves as an absorbent—a spittoon—for those sitting on the ends of the benches. . . . The bar, for the lawyers, [is] a place enclosed by railing [with] spittoons on the floor. . . . The [Judge has] . . . private judiciary spittoon. . . . Tobacco spray flying through the air. Floor mucky with spit." When it came to the cases, however, the stakes were far greater than atmosphere. Doubts about his future in Wilcox came rushing back to the surface.

Jesse Kennedy, a Negro, had a case involving moonshine whiskey. His wife testified that, at the time of Jesse's arrest, he was at work on the farm where he normally worked, the Phillips place, and that "the still [was] hers and she runs the whiskey. . . . The prosecution said she did so because it would go easier with a woman and that the court hardly knows what to do with a woman. [The jury] gave Jesse a year and a day. . . . I suppose, [because] one of them was guilty. Might as well take it out on Jesse." But that turned out wrong. Even at the level of moonshine, Wilcox law for Black tenant farmers took a more disconcerting approach. "Discussed case with Frank Dale. He told me, 'Juries don't try the nigger. They try the landowner and whose place the nigger lives. If [landowner] stands well, they protect him [so he will not lose the labor]. Otherwise, it would have been ten years for Jesse.'"

The "accepted corollary" to this approach to law also appeared in the succeeding case. "Three white men were held for grand jury on charge of flogging a Negro. Grand jury did not indict." When the announcement came out, "a Negro with the last name of Walton" sitting next to Kennedy stated the obvious: "These people always stick together in a matter like that. I knowed they wouldn't do nuthin to them fellows."[28]

So, he entered November 1927 again heading "down"—down but writing furiously. It was not just race. "Loafing" at Clark Jones's Drug Store— Clark being the brother of school superintendent, W. J. (Bill) Jones—he overheard five men from old plantation families discussing B. M. Miller's political career. Because of his anti-Klan position, Miller recently had lost reelection to the Alabama Supreme Court. But he was far from through with politics. Banker William Joel Bonner asked the group what they thought of Miller's recent Montgomery speech against the Klan. Responses pragmatically focused on Miller's unlikely political future if he kept attacking the Klan. None praised Miller or condemned the Klan.

The only deviation came from John Albert Winters, originally from Mobile and a devout Catholic. He was in a difficult situation. In these years the Winterses were one of only five or six practicing Catholic families in Wilcox. Built in 1860, Camden's wood-frame Catholic church shut down in 1914; in the 1920s priests occasionally came from Selma for services in Wilcox homes. But Catholics were not just few in number, they also suffered from Klan aggressions. Wilcox's only "Catholic doctor," Oak Hill's Dr. Samuel Swift Boykin, saw his patient list dwindle as Klansmen flogged Black people and boycotted businesses of white people who went to him for treatment. Indeed, one spring Sunday in 1926, hooded Klansmen invaded Boykin's yard to verbally harass his family and the Winters's while a Jesuit priest, William A. Wilkinson, from Selma, tried to offer Mass on the front porch.

More to the point, in November 1927, as the barbershop group mulled over B. M. Miller and the Klan, Kennedy had reason to wonder what tack Albert Winters would take. Years later, he could not recall specifically what Winters had said. He only remembered: "The others waited to see what [the Catholic] would say . . . and [what he said] was diplomatic—diplomatic but sad." Still, Kennedy's diary for November 1927 had Winters's exact words: "It's a terrible thing . . . friend against friend."[29]

Such unhappiness only further stoked Kennedy's cynicism about other elements of Black Belt life. Increasingly, he appeared preoccupied with behaviors of social irresponsibility among well-off (or once well-off) whites. Could there be any significant changes in law without accompanying changes in behavior? What he first observed in antidemocracy and "broken aristocrat" comments of Bess Cochran morphed into broader critique of white people, eclipsing—if never excluding—race. On Wednesday night, November 23, for example, he accompanied Benjamin Meek Miller to a PTA dinner at the Coy school house. Miller appeared "large and pompous, very heavy gold watch chain and pendant . . . white stiff collar, black suit, large paunch . . . symbol of his position as an aristocrat, his wealth, and superiority. What all does that charm and pendant represent!" Miller's remarks were "same old inane, banal hokum: Columbus and his ships . . . freedom . . . America . . . the Brooklyn Bridge! More beyond! The people gulped it whole." And who were these people, Miller's audience—the citizens who were not well off? "The simple rustics trying so hard to have a good time, all dressed up and stilted in manner . . . one little girl with poetry in her eyes, another a little older, already married, with dull rebellion in hers—the poetry long since crushed out." And what of these children's school? "Dingy green and brown painted pine walls . . . dirty scabrous desks. Thus does civilization advance."[30]

Two nights later, back in Camden, the disparity between Miller's gold-chained hokum and the country girl with no more poetry in her eyes returned him to a novel he had read several months earlier, Sinclair Lewis's 1920 blockbuster, *Main Street*. Here was a riveting profile of the unthinking, insensitive, and haughty nature of a well-off modern American consuming society in the Roaring Twenties. But as the Lewis profiles melded with images of the Coy dinner, then with conversation among young adults Kennedy encountered at a large Thanksgiving dinner hosted by a Camden family, a new idea was born: "Black Belt Mainstreetism." Kennedy encountered "Main Street" attitudes within many of Camden's plantation-descended elites—people with "little interest" in changing Wilcox ways "to help a few more country girls have poetry in their eyes." "You can't evacuate Mainstreetism from their raising." Materialism and greed of the 1920s only magnified values long inculcated by the planter-class sense of self. Searing, depressing stuff, and by one definition original, too.

As James Cobb probes in *Away Down South: A History of Southern Identity* (2005), by 1927 a few other critics of southern "aristocracy," notably Broadus Mitchell at Johns Hopkins University, had made the connection between Old South planter-class greed and 1920s New South materialism. And, if we extrapolate on Cobb's connecting the 1890s New South Cavalier myths to the Northeast's parallel Gilded Age myths, and the Roaring Twenties being more or less the Gilded Age gone wild with new technologies, then

Kennedy's "Black Belt Mainstreetism" makes all the more sense. At any rate, in 1927 Kennedy had read nothing by Broadus Mitchell. And one who was to become a noted critic of rampant consumerism among the New South's middle- and upper-class white population, Tulane's Herman Clarence Nixon, was still a good three years away from publishing "Whither Southern Economy" in *I'll Take My Stand* (1930). To this day Kennedy's coinage of "Black Belt Mainstreetism"—something he never published—remains, at the least, unique.[31]

Such extreme, unhappy social criticism also appeared that November in Kennedy's reflections about animals and death, an area where he believed Black Belters of all colors and strata were in regular conflict with God. In retrospect, here were thoughts of a proto-Christian-animal-rights advocate. To him, however—normally one prone to slicing analysis of the most everyday happening—they were but another source of sadness about Black Belt life. Though a hunter in youth, by now his absorption of Christian Socialism had made him a consistent pacifist. This extended to the killing of animals. On November 21, it was "opening of hunting season for quail. Scores of hunters out. Much murder done today . . . murders satisfying their lust to kill." On November 23, at the Coy dinner with Miller, the advertised "turkey dinner" tuned out to be "1 turkey, 100 squirrels, 70 quail, 2 possums, 10 chickens. Men hunted all day . . . killing for the supper. Thus, the little wild creatures died . . . were murdered . . . for us to consume. . . . Wrong to kill God's little wild creatures, [but] Judge [Miller] enjoying his carnivorous debauch."

Kennedy appears not to have shared his broader "killing thoughts" with anyone. Though he and Bill Jones and a few others talked regularly about human killings, notably Klan lynchings, his sadness over the small animals and songbirds stayed inside him for another twenty years. Undoubtedly, he correctly understood how others of those times, and later, would react, calling a person crazy and a critic of hallowed tradition—with cruel harassment to follow. But such "proto-animal-rights" sensitivities made the privacy of Room 20 of the Wilcox Hotel all the more his inner sanctum. It was not only a place for the most intimate of diary writing. It was a place secure from public view where he—unto himself—could practice his reverence for one of the least noticed elements of "God's world," and more.

Here, safe from attack by the plethora of mousetraps spread throughout the hotel, one particular mouse was his "friend." "Feeding my mouse a piece of chocolate candy from a box the Coopers sent me. Put candy in hole in the wall and mouse dragged it off . . . they cannot help being mice . . . that is their only offense." But he was not exclusive. "[When] I drop a crumb [for the mice, and they do not come,] the ants do and devour it. [But] how do they know about it?" Birds outside his window, appreciated since his first moving into the hotel, got even greater appreciation: "Martens, roosting in trees . . . people don't like them . . . got shotguns and slaughtered them . . . incensed me . . . made effort to stop them but failed. Boll weevils [killing cotton] now multiply." And to animals drawn to where the hotel fed hogs out back: "The stray dog out back. . . . Mrs. Newberry got Joe Wallace to shoot it at noon. I used to hear it whimpering at night. . . . Ben Miller is a sadist . . . burns cats alive and buries them alive." Later, living in other settings, it was the same. "The cattlemen here do not provide feed in winter, counting on losing a percentage of cows every winter. Seems cruel to me." "Bennett Slade is another killer of quail. . . . I am for the birds and against the murderers." "God will deal with men for their sinful cruelty to little dumb animals." Here, Kennedy went beyond traditional explanations for southerners and hunting—"sport" in a generally isolated environment, perverse expression of male insecurities through attachment to weapons, and celebration of the mythological Cavalier ways of the Old South. He saw hunting the way he viewed killing in general: a key thread in the broader tapestry of addicted "blood-thirstiness" and violence.[32]

On Saturday, November 26—sometime between 12:30 a.m. and 2:00 a.m.—amid all these private and prescient ruminations in the room, his "darkness" pled for relief. He had come to Wilcox excited about assisting "God's world"—all of it. Now, his initiation to Wilcox behavior had him deeply discouraged. He approached the precipice of quitting—not two decades later, as he had recently mentioned to Mary, but immediately. As a last resort, still, he did what his father had always advised about overpowering decisions: overpowering prayer. Since early youth he had prayed before going to sleep at night. But his father's advice went to something far greater, turning to John Calvin's *Institutes for the Christian Religion* (1536). Here, Calvin urges an overwhelmed Christian to pray for guidance while fasting. And this is what Kennedy did, if not quite as planned.

The diary gives his plan. From 6:00 p.m., Saturday, November 26, to 8:00 am, Monday, November 28, he would fast and pray, leaving Room 20 only to use the bathroom down the hall. And this he did. "There was a constricted feeling in my stomach Sabbath night. I slept 1 and one-half hours Sab. afternoon. I had a slight headache Sab. night. I had no food for 38 hours. Nothing but water entered my system."

Yet he also permitted variations from the plan. And considering their ironic nature, they hinted at the outcome ahead.

Late Saturday morning, before the seclusion commenced, Kennedy was finishing up breakfast in the hotel dining room when Bill Jones dropped by. They moved to the front porch, where Bill gave him news of suddenly developing Klan plans—rallies set for the next few nights. Bill said he planned to attend—"to let them know I came to observe"—and asked if Ren would go with him. How their discussion went from there remains unrecorded. But clearly Kennedy joined him.[33]

Sunday night he told the diary: "Klan rally Camden [tonight] . . . burn cross . . . speeches . . . parade through town in robes. Jesse McLeod [Wilcox County judge of probate and Coy planter] easily recognized by his height . . . Dr. Ernest Bonner by his thinness . . . others by [a] shaking arm or improper use of unaccustomed robes which displayed their faces at times." The following night, November 28, he and Bill observed another rally at a "rough baseball field" just southwest of Oak Hill, and the following night another one ten miles west of Oak Hill at Watson's Crossing and Burl. There, Superintendent Jones found organizers planning to use grounds of the Watson Crossing [white elementary] school; he made them relocate to a spot several hundred yards away from the school. That night Kennedy noted, "KKK in Watson Crossing and [in] Burl . . . two towns together and separated by railroad . . . people in Watson Crossing all KKK . . . people in Burl are all non-KKK . . . rough necks in Watson, better people in Burl."

It is hard to imagine what John Calvin would have advised about taking time out from a cloistered conversation with God to observe a KKK rally, much less three. But whether serendipitous cacophony or predestination, the whole thing seems to have worked for Ren Kennedy. "It did me good," he noted in the diary. Granted, "good" remains vague: what precisely took place between him and God is unclear. But much else is indeed clear. "Good" was something solemn and profound . . . and resolution.[34]

For the rest of his life, if in varying levels of intensity, he would feel this God Mandate to seek conversion of white people to a full Christian embrace of Black people This embrace needed to be an appreciation of Blacks as American citizens deserving of equal treatment under the law. But it also went beyond law. He wanted white hearts open to a full Christian acceptance of Blacks as equal children of God. Within the ARP Synod, theological efforts inched in this direction for whites, with "Social Regeneration" and "Whole Gospel." But neither the social goals, nor the theology behind them, broached Kennedy's idea of full Social Gospel Christianity. At this stage, granted, his vision seems to have lacked clarity on change within the context of segregation versus change eclipsing segregation. That clarity would come later. Still, if regular defeat ultimately would see him consistently on the ropes, even down on the canvas, he never stayed down for the count. As for the essential predicate of his own racial conversion, it seems not to have derived from a notable deciding moment as chronicled by his fellow South Carolina Presbyterian, professor-writer Charles McBride Dabbs and a few other southern white liberals of that era. Kennedy's own racial conversion narrative gradually evolved with influences of parents and grandparents. Then, despite extreme Calvinistic salvation-and-piety influences of his ARP education, from the Princeton and Red Path Chautauqua environments, it developed further with a neo-orthodox Protestantism that prepared him theologically and socially for attacking mistreatment of others, notably people of color.

Little is known of his encounter with the Missouri lynching. But, for sure, when he encountered such blatant behaviors in Alabama, it took less than one year for him to get clear thought about race reform. He would start at the top of the heap—the ruling whites. From there, time and energy permitting, he would work down through the myriad not in control. And over time he even took them on, in public, about killing "God's little creatures." Regardless of its major challenges, such mandated clarity brought relief and an end to the "darkness," at least for a while. Indeed, there were immediate signs. On the night of Friday, December 2, he ate dinner at Oak Hill. "Bill Jones and his wife and [her brothers] Fritz Carothers and Ed Sadler Carothers, with their Catholic uncle, Dr. [Sam] Boykin, all [are] violently hostile to the Klan." He felt buoyed.[35]

For months Mary had been urging him to "come home for Christmas." "Don't let anything happen to keep you from coming!" On December 10, he wrote her he would not be coming. This made her "sick"; she urged they make marriage plans for June 1928 instead of waiting until August. He acknowledged her idea . . . but focused elsewhere.

Despite "the ring," they had agreed they would each have casual dates with others, and his interest in Elise Bonner clearly had grown. While Kennedy politely tolerated Elise's father, Dr. Bonner—Klan member, functional alcoholic, and rumored morphine source for anyone with the money—he was entranced by Elise's warm vivacity. In mid-November, he had rented Joe Dunn's Chevrolet at fifteen cents a mile and taken her on two "car dates"— the liberating craze of the 1920s. Elise seemed "vague" when he mentioned "Browning and Tennyson . . . [and said she had] read one page of [Sinclair Lewis's] *Main Street* [and] stopped." But "riding in the rain just after dark with her: . . . she says she likes to ride in the rain . . . so do I, especially with her." He sent Mary "a handsome piece of luggage" for Christmas. She sent him a belt buckle and a watch chain. All bases covered.[36]

Ten days before Christmas, Kennedy's Camden congregation gave him fifty dollars—by ARP standards one huge gift. It also was a strong vote of confidence, buoying him further. Perhaps he was reaching some—or at least they were not rejecting his message. "God's hand?" he wondered. At any rate, with that and another fifty dollars he had saved by not going to Charlotte, he caught a ride to the Selma Stationery Shop and bought a portable Underwood typewriter. "A typewriter," he wrote Mary, "can be a wonderful thing."

Still hurt from the cancelled Christmas plans, she responded: "You can't even type. Are you going to do this with two fingers? . . . Enough speed, I suppose, for your purposes."

Unfazed by her sharp tone—maybe even relieved?—and excited about the Underwood, Kennedy embraced the holidays in Camden. Each night he typed long passages from his favorite classics. He knew these words were not his. But it still excited him. Christmas day he had dinner with John and Clyde Miller. That night he was yet again typing in his room when John Miller dropped by to tell him that he would be getting a twenty-dollar-a-month raise. This moved him up to around $1,228 for the next year.[37]

In that upbeat mood—somehow sensing his mandate from God actually achievable?—Kennedy finished off 1927 by meeting a person destined to become one of his closest comrades, and one of the most difficult. The evening of December 30, he went to a dinner party at Frank and Helen Dexter's home on Bridgeport Road. The small gathering included the Dexters' across-the-road neighbor, Camden native Emmett Kilpatrick. He was on Christmas break from teaching in the foreign language department at the University of South Carolina, in Columbia. Before that gathering, all Kennedy knew about this man, some ten years his senior, was that he owned "fine pine woods" across from the Dexter house and "he won't have it cut." Over cocktails Kennedy told Kilpatrick of recently walking through his grove—"tall and slender and straight pines, with a carpet of pine needles." The owner of the trees "purred."

At dinner, where he was seated to Kilpatrick's left, "electric talk" revealed much about the purring tree owner, a man of "slight stature with sandy red hair." He came from an old Camden family. After earning a bachelor's degree in French from Maryville College, he headed for Johns Hopkins University. There, under the direction of noted John Holiday Latané, he earned a master's in political science and international relations. But his plans to go on for a doctorate took one convoluted detour compliments of World War I. After a year with the 117th Battalion of the American Expeditionary Force, Kilpatrick's language skills landed him a post as a lieutenant assigned to Woodrow Wilson's staff during the Versailles peace negotiations. From there, he joined the American Red Cross as an international aid worker. He was assigned to Russia, then still in revolution. This, Kilpatrick explained, led the Bolsheviks to arrest him on suspicion of being a spy for Wilson. Captured and jailed, he finally was freed by the US State Department after substantial lobbying by his old friend, Marie Bankhead Owen, daughter of US senator John H. Bankhead. Back in Paris, he enrolled at the Sorbonne, emerging three years later with the doctorate of letters, his dissertation—written in French, of course—on the coming of the Civil War in Alabama. As Kilpatrick proudly explained, he was "the first U.S. citizen ever to earn a doctorate from the Sorbonne." Back in the States, at Mrs. Owen's suggestion, he spent one term in the Alabama Statehouse, elected out of Perry County where he had relatives, before taking the job at the University of South Carolina.

Though he soon would recognize Kilpatrick's propensity for exaggeration, that night Kennedy focused on his intellect, sophistication, devotion to Woodrow Wilson, and "photographic memory for the greatest lines of best literature." Kilpatrick "is not a Xtian," Kennedy noted late that night, but "he . . . admires Xtianity . . . [as] the finest thing the world has known . . . and [he] says Lewis' *Elmer Gantry* [1927] is the funniest book he has ever read." As if that were not enough, the next week Kennedy told Bill Jones: "And he is a socialist, too!"[38]

The year 1927 closed with Ren Kennedy having gone through tortuous initiation, culminating in crisis and then resolution through mandate—something for which he seemed ready. It also ended with his wondering what else in Wilcox he might have been missing. Emmett Kilpatrick, he correctly surmised, was beyond match. But perhaps it offered more than the Klan and killing. Maybe some of the "home" he had thought he would find in Wilcox and chances for a successful pastorate, after all, were there. Indeed, perhaps beyond the "broken aristocrats" there might even be some true aristocrats.

But it turns out his early Wilcox agonies still had a way to go. In January and February 1928 Mary continued her three-a-week correspondence campaign. She congratulated Ren on the pay raise; they would need it to set up housekeeping in the manse. He replied like any committed Christian Socialist not wanting marriage, at least to a specified person. He "would rather live in two rented rooms that belong to someone else than . . . have a house of my own. You can travel through life lightly laden . . . and that's the way I like to take it."[39]

Still, a blend of secular ethics and Calvinist theology now moved Kennedy to acceptance of what had been a long and shrewdly developed Mary Mandate. On March 13, in the diary, he probed the "insanity" and "irresponsibility" of being totally honest with Mary—and probably Elise—about his marriage confusion. "The arbitrary device outside of me" is "indecision and the shifting of responsibility to Fate." This is "a character weakness in me." In that he identified Fate with the Will of God, the devout Calvinist felt deep guilt with the downside to predestination: "What happens will happen for the best." While one waits for Fate to "work out" things, there is ample opportunity for conflict. He thought he could live with the conflict and resultant guilt so long as he wrote about it and prayed—a type of therapy. But what about people influenced by his waiting for God's action—for Fate's resolution? They suffered mightily. And he was responsible for their suffering. He felt "dishonorable" and "guilty" in not taking responsibility for the consequences of his actions. So, he felt he had no alternative but to step outside his traditionalist religious ethics and turn to Free Will.

For several days this "discovery" caused him consternation. But over the next month his thoughts evolved, heading him to a new reality. Much as he had done with literalist Bible Christianity alongside Social Gospel Christianity, finding compromise in neo-orthodoxy, he accepted himself as contradictory by some standards but "modern" by others: one foot in secular ethics, the other in Christian ethics. And though he debated marriage with Mary for several more months, by May it appeared they had a firm plan.[40]

On May 2, 1928, Kennedy headed to Fayetteville, Tennessee, for presbytery. From there, as promised, he went on to Charlotte for synod and to see Mary, who was home from teaching. They talked wedding plans. Either August 16 or 17, 1928, was the magic date. For financial reasons it would be a small affair at Mary's Charlotte home. Mary felt good: "the minutes passed so fast," she wrote. "They were gone before I knew it . . . [but] August is not that far off."[41]

Meanwhile, Elise Bonner took a big step. While she had dated Ren, she also dated Walter Hickey, a Birmingham native who had recently moved to Camden to manage its Standard Oil distributorship. When Ren returned from Charlotte, he told Elise of his marriage plans. Swiftly, she decided on a future with Walter. Dr. Bonner pled with her to hold up; Ren easily could change his mind. She would not agree, even asking Ren to do the honors in his church. On the night of June 12, he did it; Walter paid him a twenty-dollar gold piece, and shortly the newlyweds joined Kennedy's church. After the ceremony, back in Room 20, he wrote Mary that a church conflict prohibited his marrying her on August 16. But he indeed would marry her on August 17 despite his "imperfect" love. If she would convey "the marriage question" from him to her father, that would move things on along. A day later he distilled his feelings for the diary: "A woman in North Carolina is going to marry me. I see no way out. She is a good woman. I do not want to hurt her. . . . Oh, she's got me now." The Mary Mandate prevailed.[42]

With the big day still a way off, Kennedy seemed cooperative. Mary told him what suit to wear. He agreed. She told him they would walk down her stairs together and then into the foyer for the ceremony. He agreed. As mid-August got closer, however, it was the opposite. On July 3, he wrote Mary he "would rather die than marry." Yet by July 10 he had explained that he had come to his senses, even though, as he said that, he confided to the diary: "At least, I will find relief when I get to Heaven." Her mandate prevailed. On August 15 he caught Southern Railway No. 30 out of Montgomery to Charlotte. And at 6:00 p.m., August 17, 1928, they married.[43]

The honeymoon was five days of train rambling—Atlanta, Chattanooga, Birmingham, Selma. Along the way they took excursions to Missionary Ridge, Chickamauga, and other Civil War sites. On August 27, Clyde Purifoy Miller drove them from Selma to Camden. At the hotel's front desk gifts awaited: a $200 check from Camden ARPs, a $25 check from Marion Junction ARPs, a $25 check from the groom's parents, and another set of $25 checks from his grandmothers. With Mary's trunks wedged in between the piles of Ren's books, Room 20 must have offered an intriguing scene. Fate helped as the mouse decided not to greet the bride.[44]

Fate failed to help the next day when physician Huestis Jones hosted a party for them. It was bannered as a "fish fry and goat-watching" event: all were to mill around eating fried fish while carefully speculating on which goat would be first to scale a crude hog-wire fence, ten feet high. Here was Mary's introduction to life in Wilcox. Ren's diary, Tuesday, August 28: "Heustis . . . curiously scheduled it for 6:00 a.m. . . . so people could get back to town by 8:00 a.m. We went out with John Miller. Got up at 4:15 a.m., left at 5:00 a.m. and got there at 6:00 a.m. . . . [But] no fish had been caught. [Huestis got] chickens and had them dressed and we ate breakfast at 11:00 a.m. We were all weak and faint and bored to death [watching goats climb] and conversation was very heavy and difficult. 30 or 40 people there. All suffered intensely . . . one of the most painful experiences of my life."[45]

Three weeks later things improved dramatically. The newlyweds checked out of the Wilcox Hotel and into a four-room furnished apartment on the west side of Mrs. Lottie Beck's home, at 312 Clifton Road—known locally as "the Beck apartments." It was to be a short-term arrangement. As Kennedy left for the marriage in Charlotte, B. M. Miller had a direct talk with Sheriff Tait—who was Lottie Beck's nephew—about vacating the manse. Shortly, he moved out. The church then hired a carpenter to deal with extensive damages resulting from the sheriff's stay. While Kennedy deeply regretted leaving Room 20 ("it had been my home since the latter part of 1927"), the apartment obviously had more room, plus Mrs. Beck would let him grow a vegetable garden out back. Even more, another Lottie Beck apartment hosted none other than Kennedy's closest friend. Bill and Joyce stayed there during the week, then weekended at the family place up at Oak Hill. All this had Mary ecstatic—a spacious apartment in an antebellum home and, at last, concrete plans for moving into the manse. Plus, Kennedy now had just a twenty-foot walk to join Bill for increasingly frequent evening cocktails. To the public the Kennedy couple seemed off to a good start.[46]

But not in all respects. The more the Kennedys got to know Lottie Beck, the more they found her a problem. She was born in 1877 as Charlotte Vass Tait—great-granddaughter of US senator and federal judge Charles Tait. In

1898 she married her first cousin, James Tait Beck, Wilcox's probate judge and son of noted planter and Confederate officer Franklin King Beck and Martha Jefferson Tait Beck. Judge Beck died in 1906. "Miss Lottie," as she was called locally, stayed on in the Beck home.

In essence, Lottie Beck came from the biggest money and influence of antebellum Wilcox. And she had never recovered from it. Much the fan of Charles Dickens, in characterizing such people Kennedy borrowed a term seemingly coined from *Oliver Twist* (1839): "High Cockolorum," a person of high pretension. For years "Miss Lottie the High Cockolorum" had been short on money, Kennedy found, yet refused to work—take a job. She had gotten by through renting out space in her home. Assuredly, some in Wilcox had a more positive opinion of her. But to Kennedy, in this self-determined downward mobility, she struggled to maintain a semblance of social profile through endless gossip, intermittent activity in the Women's Klan Club, leadership in the United Daughters of the Confederacy, and service on every possible committee at St. Mary's Episcopal Church.

Back came his intergenerational aristocracy concerns. He compared her to Senator/Judge Tait; to his son, James Asbury Tait; and to the baron's grandson, Felix Tait—"sophisticated, educated people of great influence." If, here, he omitted editorial comment on their levels of "brokenness" on race, he still thought Miss Lottie was "not very graceful" compared to her antecedents, and was "very angry." His thoughts turned to her noted nephew, the sheriff, Fleet Tait: "sour gutted and conceited . . . cheap at heart . . . stubborn, a Kluxer. . . . I wonder if he is crooked . . . though his children are fine. Taits used to be aristocrats here. What happened?" Granted, if Kennedy had lived into the early twenty-first century, he could have found Tait descendants of substantial self-made and professional accomplishment. But that was his reading on the family in the late 1920s and for a long time afterward, and it seemingly presaged by several years thoughts about social degeneration in the South soon to surface in writings of William Faulkner, Thomas Wolfe, and others of the "Southern Renaissance."[47]

The brutally cold winter of 1928–29 deepened his understanding of Miss Lottie and shed some light on other Wilcoxons like her. Miss Lottie's roof was so "corroded" that water leaked in everywhere . . . into their apartment, into Bill and Joyce's apartment, even into Miss Lottie's own quarters. At night "the water would freeze on the floor and on tops of tables." The Kennedys' lease had her providing coal for the grates in their apartment. They asked her for some. "Haughty and incensed," she said there was "no money for repairing the roof, much less buying coal." So, Kennedy bought coal for their apartment, and bought some for her, too.

In payment for the coal, Miss Lottie turned to one fancy artifact owned by her late husband. As nephew of US senator and US vice president William Rufus King, of Selma, Judge Beck had inherited King's famous walking cane. It sported a jeweled stiletto hidden in the handle. Down and out, Miss Lottie handed over King's walking cane. Kennedy had asked for no payment. But he accepted it "mainly out of curiosity." Shortly, however, the coal and the cane appear to have tightened his focus on "broken aristocracy." She paid for coal, he concluded, "with the only currency she had—the past." But, likely comparing her to Grandma Emma and Uncle Hubert of Beth Eden, he granted her no sympathy. "These people who once were high and mighty . . . and spoiled off another man's labor [slavery] . . . wait stubbornly, angry and in vain, for history to reverse itself so *they* will not have to change. Broken aristocrats."[48]

With the manse in need of more rebuilding than anticipated, and the church's renovation funds dependent on donations that came in sporadically at best, the Kennedys wound up living at Lottie Beck's place much longer than anticipated. So, it was there, alongside Miss Lottie—and much to the Kennedys' worry—that they did their best to settle into Wilcox life as a couple. His work continued unabated. Much the rising minister in the ARP, he had constant invitations for revivals as well as increasing obligations to synod committees, not to mention his service as moderator for the entire Tennessee-Alabama Presbytery. When he traveled, Mary's severe anxiety about "the woman on the other side of the wall" required her staying with others: the John Millers, George Alfords, Stanley Godbolds, the Walter Hickeys (with Elise and Walter living in an apartment in the home of her parents, the Ernest Bonners). Indeed, they "clamored" to host her, each family having her for two or three nights at a time until her husband returned.[49]

In late November 1928 Mary found she was pregnant. Combine Victorianism, first pregnancy, and small-town life, plus Miss Lottie Beck and the low salary of an ARP preacher, and the result was an explosion in the Kennedy household. By standards of the day, Mary believed she was not to "show"—that is, to appear pregnant—much less talk publicly about her status until several months before delivery. They had no money to buy another wardrobe, not even money to hire a seamstress. For regular augmentation of Mary's dresses they had to count on help from a trusted friend, Frances Allenby Jones, Clark Jones's wife. As in any small town, however, privacy was hard to come by.[50]

It all came to a head in May 1929. With Mary six months pregnant, Ren had to attend a synod meeting in Tennessee. In a long missive, Mary used her well-honed skills as letter writer to unload on Camden life. First, she set the scene. "Mrs. Beck is telling 'people' in Camden how 'big' I am getting . . . over the phone!" (Remember, in a small town in 1929, "over the phone" meant the town operator knew virtually everything said "on the line.") Mary continued. "[Lottie Beck] called Mrs. Howard Turner, who didn't know I was pregnant . . . and I don't know who else. Mrs. Clem Jones says she heard it from Mrs. Marguerite Jones, and she told Mrs. Tom Moore." Then, her Christianity temporarily on the ropes, Mary bore down. "It's none of Mrs. Beck's dam [sic] business . . . The miserable coward wouldn't dare do much while you are here. . . . It makes me so angry I could kill her. . . . Mrs. [Clark] Jones told me not to tell you this, but I have to tell you . . . to get it out of my system. I can't leave all this poison in my heart to saturate my baby's nature. . . . I did well to hide my figure six months, didn't I?"[51]

Finally, they gave in. On June 28, 1929, a good two months before delivery, Mary went home to Charlotte—well removed from Camden gossips. There she also had access to a female gynecologist, Maude Pressly, product of the Due West/ARP network and one of Kennedy's old friends. Frightened over costs of having a baby, from Camden Kennedy regularly wrote Dr. Pressly about projected expenditures. On August 21 she sent him a letter designed to calm him: "Delivery room use at Presbyterian Hospital, $10.00; anesthesia, $5.00; room per day, $4.00; baby care per day, $1.00—grand total depending on length of stay." She said she would waive her fee: that thrilled Ren, but Mary nixed it: "Surely we will pay her."[52]

After a difficult delivery, the baby finally came at 8:15 a.m., Wednesday, August 28. Kennedy was still asleep in the apartment. Marriage and the move to Lottie Beck's only had intensified his nocturnal reading and writing; he often worked until daylight, then slept until late morning. Such was the case that day. First light arrived in Camden at 5:00 a.m. He finally shut down his writing and headed to bed. Then "about 9:30 a.m. I heard the phone ring" through the wall. "Mrs. Beck called me saying there was a telegram for me. . . . The Western Union operator read me the telegram: 'Fine girl seven pounds eleven ounces born 8 today. Mary and baby doing well. Maude.' I was elated . . . proud . . . thrilled . . . happy. . . . I wanted to see Mary and my little girl. I wonder what she looks like. What color eyes and hair. I need to see her. I love her."[53]

They named her Mary Conway after Mary's grandmother of Riverview plantation in Halifax County, Virginia. Happiness abounded. On October 16, mother and daughter headed to Wilcox. In trips to watch Selma baseball, Kennedy made a good friend in Camden deputy sheriff Sam McNeill. He admired the deputy's kindness toward Black people, despite reporting to Sheriff Tait, and he liked riding in McNeill's Ford Roadster. Over time, here was to be one of Kennedy's most heartfelt friendships. But that October morning he focused on Sam's car. He borrowed the Roadster and, top down, headed southeasterly the fifty-three miles to the Greenville train depot. To protect his newborn from the sun, he raised the top just before the Pullman arrived.

"At 12:07 pm. . . . I . . . had the first sight of my first (and for the present only) child . . . a little Kewpie [doll] in the bright sunlight. . . . I held her . . . She slept as we rode . . . and cried as we went through Camden . . . a pretty baby, bright and interesting."[54]

No less pleasing was the final bill. Maude Pressly ran roughshod over Mary's prideful exhortations. Half of the doctor's relatives were ARP preachers—she knew full well what the Kennedys tried to live on—and she waived her own fifty-dollar fee. The total bill came to $108. Three days later John Miller appeared at the Kennedys' door with a "congregation gift" for $100. Mary Conway "cost" the Kennedys eight dollars—what her father brought in from ten days at a Covington County revival.[55]

In retrospect, their first-born's "cost" was anything but an indication of her significance. Instantly, she—and another to follow—made "more than workable" what Mary Conway called seventy years later "an ill-suited relationship." Granted, for a long time to come a few of Camden's more addicted cloistered cacklers would salivate over rumors of "Elise and Ren"—the only documentation for which remains enduring friendship. But Ren and Mary persisted. They moved beyond the agony of the romance and the relief of the vows to a family life with spontaneous love. If the love revolved more around offspring than parents, it still was binding and nurturing for the whole family and "more than workable" for two adults who, it turned out, had little problem living apart for extended periods of time. Writing long letters—they never stopped. In short, the Mary Mandate proved doable. As for the God Mandate, that was another matter.[56]

5

At Bay

In the late morning of Thursday, September 27, 1928, a "run" began on the Bank of Camden. The bank did not open the following day. By Saturday afternoon, key stockholders had agreed to sacrifice some two-thirds of their stock as well as the president, William Joel Bonner—Miller Bonner's brother. That, plus a large infusion of new funds by the Vredenburgh lumber mill family and reorganization under their leadership, permitted the bank to reopen at 9:00 a.m. on Monday, October 1. Depositors lost not a dime.

As fortunate as that was, the magical reopening also had a downside. It sent a signal of security to Wilcox's well-off when that was the last thing they actually needed. In the summer of 1928, the stock market crash may have been thirteen months away, but the economic slowdown delivering the Depression already was well under way. Cotton prices had declined throughout the 1920s: 1922, $215 a bale; 1928, $100 a bale. Birmingham's heavy industry had experienced declining orders since 1926. In this sense, despite the boosterism of the decade, the Crash of 1929 was but a *coup de grace* to some five years of declining economy. Still, with the Bank of Camden's continuing stability, most Wilcox white people echoed so many others in America: they stuck with the carefully orchestrated boosterism of the decade: "Perhaps a dip or two but everything will turn out as always—good."[1]

If still at Miss Lottie's in the final months before the Crash, the Kennedy family seemed part of this tenuous Camden security. Others of the family were less fortunate. Back in Charlotte, Mary's father, John T. Moore, already had been terminated from his executive position with the International Harvester Corporation and was trying to keep his head above water with temporary work as an accountant specializing in foreclosures—and selling encyclopedias door to door. Compared to this, the career of Rev. Renwick C. Kennedy seemed steadily ascendant.[2]

In some ways he was "one of the guys." Beyond playing town-league baseball and refereeing high school football, Kennedy not only continued his baseball trips with Sam McNeill but became another Wilcox convert to University of Alabama football. For some games he went to Tuscaloosa, compliments of congregation members; for others he was in the crowd outside the Wilcox courthouse for the play-by-play blasting out the window from the large Philco radio.

As a new member of the Wilcox County Ministers Association, he stepped out front to organize occasional "union services" in different towns. Methodists, Presbyterians, and ARPs normally participated, occasionally Baptists. One of the more educated families in the county, the Purifoys of Snow Hill—Clyde Purifoy Miller's family—was so appreciative of these efforts they gave him a six-month subscription to *New Republic*.

Kennedy also guest-preached. Camden's historic Black church, Antioch Baptist, invited him twice a year. Here he became friends with lay leader Joe Allen, whose father had helped found the church during Reconstruction. That friendship led to Kennedy's regularly offering prayer sessions at Camden Academy, the Black school on the hill south of town where Allen was principal. Foremost, however, his ministerial life stayed focused on growing the Camden and Marion Junction ARP congregations. His nonministerial attention to congregation members was just as consistent. "August 30, 1929: Went to Mrs. W. J. Bonner's where I helped her twins [his baseball companions] fill out application blanks for admission to Columbia University though I felt they [Jo and James] would never go." Between 1928 and 1935 Prosperity Church at Marion Junction grew from 40 to 52 members, Camden's ARPC from 90 to 131: "growth" by ARP standards. Even his diehard Methodist wife, Mary, took time away from dodging Miss Lottie and, on June 16, 1929, finally agreed to join her husband's church—nearly a year after they married. "Not easy," her husband noted, "but necessary."

When word spread to the synod that ARP life in Wilcox was looking up, Erskine College increased the "goal" Kennedy was to raise for its endowment campaign. He delivered, but more through the substantial help of three or four Wilcox families and his own personal loans from the Bank of Camden than from broad-based giving. In early July 1929, following considerable advance notice in the *Associate Reformed Presbyterian*, he offered a five-day meeting in Due West: eleven sermons, total attendance 1,700, pay to him of $54.71. In late July he did another meeting down in Covington County, for Red Level, Salem, and Mt. Sinai: fifteen sermons, total attendance 755, pay to him of $9.00. While Mary noted Covington's increase over the previous year, his father wrote: "I suppose you are back in Camden now rejoicing in a finished campaign."[3]

All this further legitimated Kennedy in the eyes of those looking at him every day; they talked with him ever more openly. Indeed, when the economy finally went into full crash in late October 1929, and Wilcoxons who had had money finally saw the harsh prospects ahead, their Depression fears resulted in even more talk with him, about their fears, strategies for survival, and priorities. He was stunned by what he heard: more selfishness than concern for others and even greater hostility toward Blacks, beyond what he encountered in the year of "initiation." In short, despite his own relatively happy personal life, and significant professional accomplishment, his worries about un-Christian behavior only intensified. He did not return to fasting and an extended cloistered session with God. Yet his concerns reached such intensity that he ultimately felt encircled like a wild creature surrounded by dogs, "at bay."

Even before Mary Conway's birth, in August 1928, it was apparent that Kennedy's ministerial mobility opened him more to Wilcox, including many who were not of his congregations. That fall came the presidential election of 1928. The contest pitted California Republican Herbert Hoover against New York Democrat Alfred E. Smith. Most ex-Confederate states went for Hoover, and some 48 percent of Alabama did, too—perhaps the first indicator that the white South might someday be predominantly Republican. Many Hooverites apparently believed the "Roaring Twenties" prosperity Republicans had brought on showed careful economic policy, not what it turned out to be. Ever the loyal Democrat—and ever the critic of "sinful" Republicans—Kennedy supported Al Smith. Most around him in Wilcox, it turned out, did too, but not primarily out of concern for what happened to the League of Nations.[4]

It was a brutal election season in Wilcox. The fact that Smith was both Catholic and "wet"—opposed to prohibition—placed many of the normally passionate Democrats of Wilcox in one difficult bind. And if they turned to Hoover, they found themselves in even more of one: voting for something just as "evil"—the party they held responsible for "freeing the slaves," conquering the white South, and ramrodding Reconstruction. A product of primal feelings about race and outside interference, plus more recent historical experiences with the Civil War, religion, and booze, their historic fighting moved to a new level. Virtually every segment of the voting population divided: pro-Klan whites and anti-Klan whites; businesspeople whose forebears had cooperated with Reconstruction Republicans, or not; civic groups, church congregations, indeed families and marriages.[5]

One of the most fascinating white-on-white divides involved the sons of Charles E. Tait, great-grandsons of Charles Tait. One of the sons, Felix, married a great Catholic-hater from Georgia. Her name was Carlotta—ironically, the name of one of the Catholic world's most noted personalities, Luisa Carlotta, early-nineteenth-century Duchess of Cadiz. In 1928, according to Kennedy's diary, Wilcox's Carlotta could not fathom a Catholic, Al

Smith, becoming president. She made her husband, Felix, promise to vote for Hoover. When Felix's brother, Fleet—the sheriff—discovered what his brother was about to do, and indeed did, he hit the ceiling.

During the 1920s the current Tait generation had continued its efforts to clear its family name after earlier Tait "collaboration" in business deals with Yankee Republicans of Union forces and Reconstruction. To their great consternation, in 1923, one of Fleet and Felix's cousins, Sara Tait Ervin, even continued such "collaboration" by marrying Fred Henderson, descendant of the "biggest carpetbagger of all," Judge William Henderson. Fleet agonized over having Tait blood coursing through Yankee veins. And now his brother, Felix, was "soiling" (Kennedy's word) the family name yet again by actually voting for a Republican to be president of the United States. For over a year following the 1928 election Felix would not speak to the Republican sympathizer, Fleet. Nor would Fleet speak to Felix, the Catholic supporter. Yet, Kennedy concluded: "They didn't shoot each other, and they well might have."[6]

Church congregations of Wilcox also fought viscerally. Some four months before the election, on Sunday, July 28, 1928, Camden Baptist's Reverend Dobbins openly preached against the Catholic, Al Smith. This "created quite a furor in the village," Kennedy noted in his diary. Perhaps most of Dobbins's congregation liked the message. Yet some Baptists definitely did not. Among them was recently retired Wilcox tax collector, Will McWilliams, grandson of south Alabama's frontier builder of Baptist churches, Miles Levi McWilliams. After the "sermon," he encountered Kennedy on Broad Street. "'If a nigger runs for president under the Democrats,'" he urged, "'and a white under the Republicans, I vote for the nigger . . . no pro-nigger Republican for me.'"[7]

Other Baptists felt even more strongly. "Monday [July 23] afternoon I went to Dr. Heustis Jones' office. He . . . condemned Dobbins' sermon violently. Said he was going to get his letter [written documentation of church membership] and throw it in the Pine Barren Creek"—which he never did—"and told his wife to get hers and put it in the ARP Church," which she in fact did on December 28, 1930. "And said if I ever preached such a sermon [in the ARP church] he would take hers and throw it in the Pine Barren Creek, too."

Later that day, unaware of Heustis Jones's reaction, Dobbins went to the doctor's home. Jones was treasurer of Camden Baptist, and Dobbins asked for his salary check plus a special one-time augmentation of the church's operating budget. The doctor responded: "Alright, I'll give it to you because I promised it, but . . . I want my letter. Going to throw it in the river. Wherever it lands, even if it's a nigger church, they can pick it up and put it in their church. . . . This is a white man's country and I'll vote the Democratic ticket even if the nominee is the blackest nigger out of Africa."

Dobbins took his money and left. He was an odd duck. His normally anti-Klan position had cost him his earlier pulpit in Luverne, Alabama. But Dobbins also was a big "dry" and strongly anti-Catholic. In October, two months before the election, he started up again by hosting Rev. Robert Reynolds (Bob) Jones, "evangelist and Catholic hater" of Montgomery and on his way to major national impact. Bob Jones worked for the Hoover campaign and, according to Kennedy's notes, pled with Camden Baptists to reject Smith as a "Catholic who drinks whiskey and thinks the Pope is actually God."[8]

Some Klansmen now became fearful that the powerful Rev. Bob Jones actually would swing Wilcox for Hoover. Their true concerns eclipsed the specter of a Republican president further freeing Blacks. Privately, they detested Prohibition and feared a strong anti-Smith vote would bring on even more stringent liquor bans. Kennedy fully understood that angle.

For "years," Miller Bonner advised Kennedy, John Newberry, Joe Wallace, Sheriff Tait, and other *publicly* "dry" Klansmen had been quiet conduits between Camden's rich and the bootlegging and prostitution shack called Rachel's Place, below Vredenburgh—barely inside the Monroe County line. In October 1928, the core of Bonner's "advice" on Rachel's Place actually came to Kennedy inside her establishment when the two men stopped there for "a bottled drink." "She is a protected . . . bootlegger and whore . . . never raided . . . blond, blue eyes, small, pretty in a way, face a bit coarse . . . voice a bit coarse, culture not present . . . 35 yrs old . . . interesting lady." Not wanting to lose Rachel's bootlegging business, a few other Kluxers eased around the county threatening a Klan boycott of businessmen who supported Hoover. Yet, Wilcox reflected anything but a unified Klan sentiment. For wide-ranging reasons of self-interest, "morality," and prejudice, it was about equally split between Hoover and Smith.

And "the Klan *would know*," as Clark Jones—one of the businessmen so threatened—told Kennedy. At that time, voting in Wilcox was anything but "secret ballot." Governor Bibb Graves had placed KKK personnel in control not only of county jury pools but of county voting processes. Fearful for his drugstore business, Clark Jones told Kennedy: "I hated to vote for Smith but did after Sam Lee Jones told [me] they were watching me and would ruin my business." Clark's brother, Bill, the school superintendent, openly supported Smith.[9]

Though a devout Democrat, Kennedy assiduously kept the hateful election out of his pulpits in Camden and Marion Junction. His senior counterpart at Bethel ARPC in Oak Hill did not. "Dr. Henry shook the woods . . . three different times with sermons against Al Smith. Made many mad but none quit the church." John T. Dale—again, a revered Confederate veteran and key leader at Bethel—saw Dr. Henry's words as "wrong, very wrong." A long-time Democrat, Dale ultimately voted for Hoover. But he saw Henry's remarks as contrary to the ARPs' historic commitment to separation of church and state. "No politics in the pulpit. The people vote on their own."

Ultimately, the executive committee of the Wilcox County Democratic Party resolved to support Al Smith. They placed their recommendation in the *Progressive Era*. "The issue is Democracy or Republicanism, and there are no anti-Smith Democrats." When the *Montgomery Advertiser* reported that the Republican national convention nominating Hoover had over a hundred voting Negro delegates, their rhetoric intensified. Kennedy noted what B. M. Miller said all over Wilcox: "There was not a seat for [even one] nigger at Houston," where Democrats convened. "No nigger helped nominate Al Smith." Bonner, Miller, and other Wilcox Democrats, of course, got the local results they wanted. Futilely, Wilcox voted 266 for Hoover, 979 for Smith.[10]

Not long after Hoover's victory, Kennedy's analysis of Wilcox election sentiment led him to certain predictions. First, though they could not vote, all of Wilcox's "educated Negroes"—people such as "[Legon] Wilson, [Curtis] Simpson and old N. B. Cotton," who were heads of the United Presbyterian schools in the county—"took much interest in the election." "In another generation," he told the diary, "the Negroes in the South will be voting." Yet, he believed that only a few Black Belt white persons "comprehended the depth of Negro interest in voting." He predicted they would blame other whites, particularly northeastern Republicans, for "inciting Negroes to demand their rights at the polls." And to Kennedy, here was "[white] Black Belt reasoning—plain as day." Finally, because "the [prohibitionist] Anti-Saloon League supported Hoover and fought Smith," he predicted whites of the Black Belt would be "through with the Anti-Saloon League for the present." His first predictions proved essentially correct, the last one not.[11]

While local talk of the presidential election provided Kennedy the highest profile of topics for digesting white behavior, he was no less engaged—and disturbed—by what he found in conversations about lower profile and occasionally secretive developments. From his first months in Wilcox, he had been concerned about poor whites to his south in Covington County. With Wilcox's ground more suitable for cotton, and long prospering off slave labor, Kennedy's county had fewer poor whites. But it still had whites living off "sweet potatoes, squirrels and fish from the creeks." Shawnee, just east of Camden, and the lumber mill and railroad town of Vredenburgh, on the Monroe County line, had a goodly share of this white poverty. As the Depression came on, his attention turned even more to them.[12]

Poor whites rented rundown houses on the edge of Camden. From those families, pretty women occasionally landed low-level clerical jobs downtown. Here, they were vulnerable to abuse by white businessmen—"not all that uncommon," John Miller told Kennedy, as he confided details of two recent cases. One occurred in December 1928, the other in January 1929.

Both women wound up pregnant by their rich bosses. One of the men was from a well-known plantation family from nearby Possum Bend and a leading Methodist, the other from similar background in Lower Peach Tree and active at Camden Presbyterian Church. One of the women was married to a skilled sawmill worker who had been permanently injured in a job accident and was unable to work; the other was single. When the women told their bosses of their pregnancies, the men solved their potential problems—marital stress, public ridicule, loss of face, perhaps even Klan reprisal—with insidious manipulations. To ensure that the women and their families left town, the men first terminated them for some "office reason." Then they not only made sure nobody in Camden would hire them, but secretly "arranged" cancellation of their rental agreements and a ban on their getting others. "As long as they were producers," the Christian Socialist editorialized, "Camden kept them and was glad to have them. But when stricken, the bourgeoisie shipped them away."

Actually, the two pregnant women John Miller described still were living on the outskirts of Camden with friends, trying to determine where to go next. Kennedy acted. Through the Episcopal minister in Carlowville, Justice Jones, he helped one of them find a job and a place to live in Selma. Then he approached "the Liddell family," pillars of the Camden Presbyterian Church, about funds to help the woman abused by "the Presbyterian." The Liddells opted for a special gift to the Wilcox County Red Cross, where their close friend, Bill Jones, was director. Jones saw to it that the Liddells' gift covered six months' rent for the woman and her family in a new rental arrangement in Monroeville. For Kennedy, here was just one more element in a pattern: the "Cockerlorum planter crowd . . . the type with no ethics . . . in the old, once fine houses."[13]

As for relatively well-off whites not of the "Cockerlorum" class—businesspeople and farmers—some were Klan devotees, some nominally of the Klan but essentially inactive, and some closeted Klan opponents. For them, it was much ado about going to church. But most had little in their lives related to "art and culture." They could be "drab and dull and colorless." They were faithful readers of the *Wilcox Progressive Era*, which "didn't even have an editorial page . . . just town gossip . . . [and] syndicated bilge and advertisements." Their "cultural deadness" Kennedy sampled in a conversation at Clark Jones's drugstore. "A: Not many good dogs now. B: Shore ain't. A: More poor dogs than is good run around here, ain't they? B: Shore is."

"Cultural deadness," however, did not always include "drab and dull." Business-class whites included a set who sought to help "aging singles find someone to date or marry." Behind closed doors and drawn shades, they sponsored "kid parties . . . [where] these aging adults . . . moronia [state of acting like a moron] all . . . dressed as children . . . [and] played games like children at a birthday party. Quite odd . . . a fifty-year-old woman dressed in the clothes of a six-year-old, stumbling drunk. . . . Some sat around laughing, aggressively ridiculing her. Others saw the whole thing as *avant garde*." Much like Heustis Jones's goat-watching party, here was a perplexing blend of impetuosity, comedy, numbness, and the extreme macabre.[14]

Still, white life included some individuals with cultured ways. They read sophisticated literature. They traveled—and not just to Tuscaloosa for football games or to distant hunting clubs. The majority of them had college degrees, some from institutions outside Alabama. If Kennedy bemoaned these people's lack of civic energy on important issues—no Wilcox County public library, little aid to Black education—he had genuine respect for their high-level discussions about Mozart and Monet occurring monthly at the Camden Culture Club, a group of women of both "Cockolorum" and "Non-cockolorum" lineage. He felt similarly about the Camden Book Club, a group of well-educated men chiefly of "Non-cockolorum" origins systematically focused on books well reviewed in the *New York Times*.

Among such educated whites Kennedy seemed particularly taken with John Paul Starr, who lived in a massive, Doric-columned mansion on the outskirts of Camden, "White Columns." His father was the noted local physician, Lucius Ernest Starr, who moved from Chilton County, Alabama, to Wilcox in 1879. His mother was Molly Tepper Starr, whose father, Samuel Tepper—heir to significant portions of the estate of famous English watercolorist, Joseph Mallord William Turner—acquired "White Columns" from a financially stressed Felix Tait. After education at Alabama Polytechnique Institute (future Auburn University), Paul married the former Birmingham debutante, Lois Arnold. The Starrs had a daughter with long-term mental illness. Yet they lived a modern life. They traveled widely. An ARP deacon and energized reader, Paul was an innovator in agricultural practices, especially regarding the new enterprise of raising beef cows. To Kennedy, despite his big-house upbringing, Paul Starr was a "non-cockolorum": he had no antebellum Wilcox plantation background and, despite considerable wealth, had an unpretentious personality. Yet Kennedy and Starr's close friendship could know strain. On several occasions he urged Starr to put his money and modern energies behind development of a Wilcox public library. Always the same response: "little or no support for the idea . . . a lot of books in some of the big old houses but the people who could make a public library are not interested."[15]

The most well-read of these publicly passive, if well-educated, whites lived in the shadows. His name was Francis Esten Purifoy. He was the eccentric brother of Clyde Purifoy Miller. After college in Auburn, he moved to Birmingham in 1906 and worked as a chemist at US Steel. Back in Camden by the mid-1920s, he lived in a room on the west side of the Millers' home on Clifton Road. Esten had one big love; he bought her an engagement ring. When she jilted him, he gave the ring to his mother and never again considered marriage. He was prone to automobile wrecks and to bingeing on vanilla ice cream until nauseated. His photographic memory regularly permitted him to conquer the *New York Times* crossword puzzle, Kennedy noted, "with an *ink* pen." Out of the night he might appear uninvited at the back of Lottie Beck's home and knock on the Kennedys' door. His appearances frustrated Mary's trying to get Mary Conway to sleep.

Still, Esten had inherited a lot of land and even in the Depression could afford any book he saw advertised in the *Times*. Many the night he and Kennedy settled into hours of smoking and talking about books. "Tonight I lent Esten [James Stephens's 1930 translation of the late first-century CE classic] *Satyricom of Petronicus*. He lent me [Edgar Lee Masters's] *The Spoon River Anthology* (1915)." To the constant dismay of Clyde and John Miller, Esten was "an occasional member" of the KKK, though its leaders had to keep him in the dark about key clandestine activities out of his habit of broadcasting who might be scheduled for a flogging. Kennedy wondered if Esten took *Spoon River* to Klan meetings; he thought it "a real possibility." Later, Esten Purifoy shot himself dead.[16]

Kennedy's late 1928 and early 1929 reflections upon white-on-white behavior—aggressiveness as well as passiveness—led him to a new topic: feuding. This in turn guided him to broader conceptual reflections about the origins of most Wilcox whites, the "Scotch-Irish." These investigations seem to have emerged from such readings as Constance Skinner's *Pioneers of the Old Southwest* (1920), Henry Jones Ford's *The Scotch-Irish in America* (1915), and Charles Knowles Bolton's *Scotch-Irish Pioneers* (1910)—all works that were in Kennedy's library at the time of his death. For example, he underlined Skinner's comparison of "character" among Highlanders and Lowland Scots, the latter the predominant seedbed of the Ulster-Scot/Scotch-Irish. "In contrast to the Ulstermen [who were addicted to] whole freedom," Skinner wrote, "there were no highwaymen . . . in the Highlands. . . . Theft and the breaking of an oath . . . were held in such abhorrence [among Highlanders] that no one guilty of them could remain among his clansmen."

Moreover, during early 1928, while completing the Wilson essay, Kennedy focused upon strains of his hero's own Scotch-Irish identity. His diary notes on reading—not just referencing books but referring to specific page numbers within—reveal him enticed by William Allen White's *Woodrow Wilson* (1924), especially these lines: during his "unwhipped cubdom," the young adult Wilson exhibited "the urge to make . . . private sentiment public sentiment [and] to impose . . . upon [others]"; he often "wrangled with . . . meat and drink"—and certainly was "no 'grind' or textbook addict . . . the Scotch-Irish of it!" Yet, one might infer, Wilson the Scotch-Irishman progressed. In 1903, before the New England Society of New York, the new Princeton University president gave a well praised speech, "The Puritan." This address—reprinted (as Kennedy stipulated in his notes) in *Selected Literary and Political Papers and Addresses of Woodrow Wilson* (1927)—reveals Wilson's relatively sophisticated comprehension of strengths and weaknesses in his own Scotch-Irish lineage; and, as acclaimed Wilson scholar Arthur Link much later would write, it demonstrated as well Wilson's self-conscious notion of "the American as Southerner." For in analyzing the American character, even if reflecting what some modern commentators urge as over-stereotyping of "Scotch-Irish," Wilson focused on the frontier Scotch-Irishman's "unrest . . . adventure [and] unregulated ambition" as something that had to be offset by the New England Puritan's "discipline . . . order . . . polity . . . restraint . . . moral principle"—lines Kennedy carefully noted.

In short, as he launched into his assessment of Depression-era white behavior, Kennedy was armed with—and no doubt motivated by—a range of historical and literary insights about Scotch-Irish behavior, certainly current for *his* times. And, considering his adulation of Wilson, he might even have seen himself as an extension of the uplifting Wilsonian Scotch-Irish "model": reformed, educated, enlightened, Social Gospel–driven—though, as one of a later era, Kennedy held a view of Black people that quickly eclipsed Wilson's noted nineteenth-century paternalism.[17]

In December 1929, a wrenching narrative of racial violence had Kennedy turning to this Scotch-Irish lens. He and Mary went to dinner at the Miller Bonners'. Joyce and Bill Jones were there, too. At the table the senator held forth on far-ranging episodes of violence in the county. By this time, Kennedy knew to what extremes such accounts could go. Spring of the previous year, for example, he had gotten a full dose at Taylor's Barbershop as "the best men" talked over the recent California murder of a white girl by a man whom the group assumed to be Black. "Some wanted to mutilate and drag him behind an automobile. But death did not satisfy their idea of Justice. . . . 'He should be tortured at length . . . kerosene . . . No, I'd take my rusty Barlow and I'd fix him. . . . I'd work on him proper . . . ' The Wilcox bourgeoisie . . . believe that torture is fitting . . . their sense of Retributive Justice is part and parcel of their killing instinct . . . a blood-thirsty . . . barbarous strain . . . strong across south Alabama."

But there at the table Bonner brought it all closer to home: no target of a (possibly) Black person in California, but, for sure, Black people in Wilcox.

A renowned storyteller, particularly of the grotesque, he took some time setting the scene. Here is the short version.

In 1880, sixteen-year-old Bonner "stood guard with a rifle at the courthouse with other young fellows [having] orders to keep Negroes from voting." In that way, the "Yankee-Republican control finally came to an end," and local whites reasserted their influence over Wilcox politics. Twenty-seven years later, in 1907 (some six years after Alabama's Black Belt elite and urban-industrial leaders used wholesale corruption to orchestrate the segregationist Constitution of 1901), Miller Bonner was a Camden attorney. A graduate of the University of Virginia and the University of Alabama law school, he professed deep respect for "due process and the rule of law" and despised whites "shooting Negroes like rabbits." Yet as a staunch segregationist he also was "riding high on the new Constitution" of 1901. "The Democratic Party's leadership at that time included many of Wilcox who worked long" for this final "restoration of white rule." Since 1902, however, it had been young Bonner who "ran Wilcox's Democratic executive committee."[18]

More to the point, that December of 1907 the well-wired Bonner had just departed a private law practice with his brother, William Joel Bonner, to take "an appointment as one of several Wilcox solicitors." As his first case, the new solicitor "decided to prosecute a white man who shot a black man as if he were a rabbit." The defendant was the twenty-three-year-old future sheriff of Wilcox, Fleet Tait, only recently an overseer of sharecroppers at the McLeod plantation in Coy and at this stage a Wilcox mail carrier. Tait had done the deed—and did not deny it. There was no provocation by the unarmed Negro. "He had never shot a Negro," Bonner continued. "So, he went out and shot one." Perhaps Tait also was trying to develop his reputation before entering politics and law enforcement. At any rate, "it happened less than a mile down Clifton Road directly in front of the house of Fleet's aunt, Lottie Tait Beck." At the exact moment of the shooting, "Miss Sallie Hart was departing Miss Lottie's. She witnessed the killing." Despite the historic white code of passive silence on such matters, Bonner sought to prosecute Tait for "first-degree murder—unbailable," though apparently he was not put in jail.

Bonner "was not optimistic about a conviction." "A good many years before 1907, Old John Fails, father of Mrs. H. N. Jones and Mrs. P. E. Jones, killed several Negroes. . . . I don't know really how many Old John killed," Bonner said, "one he killed in the road . . . a few miles from town and left him there. . . . Negroes, you know, are superstitious about such deaths and did not move the body for a while." No prosecution. "But at the time [1907], recently a Black's Bluff man"—Bonner did not recall his name—had "blown the top off a Negro's head, from the eyes up," and no prosecution. Then recently Dr. Warburton Jones had "killed a Negro . . . shot him in the back . . .

in Joseph N. Miller's law office where he died"—with no prosecution. And, recently, too, "Frank Beck, across the river . . . killed a Negro who had bought a piece of land he wanted . . . and thought the best way to settle it would be to kill the Negro. He got his gun. Then he got his little boy of ten or twelve years and they rode [on horseback] out to the field where the Negro worked and before his little son Frank Beck shot the Negro dead." (That night Kennedy noted: "Mr. Bonner can't understand how a man would take his son out to see him kill a Negro.") No prosecution. "So," Bonner continued, his "case would be an ice breaker . . . the first time in Wilcox's history that a white man [would be] charged with murder for killing a Negro."

Since the Fourth Circuit Court judge, B. M. Miller, was out "on the circuit" hearing cases, the case moved to "arraignment with a justice of peace," standard protocol (with county approval) per Alabama's 1907 criminal code. At that hearing, however, Miss Sallie, the eyewitness, failed to appear. Confronted with a corpse but no witness, and nobody willing to say where the witness might be, the justice of the peace dismissed the case. The day after dismissal, Fleet's father, Charles Edwin Tait, approached solicitor Bonner on Broad Street. "I respect you for doing what you thought was your duty," he said. "I just don't agree it was your duty." The story concluded: "That same day Miss Sallie reappeared."[19]

Of course, the case was an "icebreaker" only in terms of the charge—not the outcome. "The clan held firm—attack repulsed," Kennedy later wrote. And with Miss Sallie's no-show, the code endured. Yet even with this outcome the case caused "a fifteen-year feud within the clan between Miller Bonner and Fleet Tait." During those years Bonner became one of the most powerful senators in Alabama history, Tait one of the most powerful "High Sheriffs" in the state. Both were dominant figures in Wilcox and in roles crucial to the county's development. And they did not speak. Same for the Hart family; they would not speak to Miller Bonner for his having tried to get Miss Sallie to testify.

Granted, nothing documents that Bonner's telling of such violence and feuding revived Kennedy's digestion of his earlier readings about Scotch-Irish behavior. But even had he heard of such horrible violence before, he indeed saw in this episode a "Scotch-Irish solidarity" activated by "outside" attack, as well as a Scotch-Irish proclivity for extreme violence alongside inner-clan "feuding," far later the subject of debate in modern scholarship.[20]

If Kennedy noted no other case in early Wilcox where whites broke rank with other whites on a racial violence issue, visceral white feuding persisted and indeed was much in front of him every day. He took particular note of "High Cockolorum" feuding. In some cases, here were people with the money, the education, and the power to change local behaviors—in Kennedy's mind, the wherewithal to model full Christian behavior and grow a better community. Instead, they fought within.

Take the Bonner-Miller feud. Miller Bonner married Benjamin Meek Miller's niece, Sara Pressly Miller. Here were two of the most prominent South Carolina ARP families of Wilcox. When Kennedy's church door opened, Bonner and Miller were there. In the late 1920s Bonner was already a fixture in the state senate. Miller had risen from circuit court judge to associate justice on the Alabama Supreme Court with gubernatorial ambitions, ultimately satisfied. Still, longstanding disagreement over land and law practices constrained the two men to speak only when professional life required. They stared at each other in ARP session meetings. In public they launched diatribes against one another on wide-ranging political issues. As Kennedy noted, "J. M. Bonner says he has been practicing law in Camden for twenty-six years and Meek Miller has not set foot in his law office [at the corner of Broad and Planter streets], nor vice versa."[21]

Jones family feuding was even more extreme—not the South Carolina ARP Jones family, but descendants of a Virginian whose father was president of the Virginia senate when Thomas Jefferson was governor. In 1844, John Cargill Jones moved from Prince Edward County, Virginia, to Wilcox. He developed an expansive cotton enterprise while practicing law in both Virginia and Alabama, and serving in the Alabama legislature. He was raised an Episcopalian. But some Great Awakening Baptist minister coming through Camden convinced him to embrace the Baptist church. His was a strong conversion. With his wife and children remaining active parishioners at St. Mary's Episcopal Church, in 1850 he left lawyering and politicking—if not planter life—to become a revered minister at Camden Baptist Church.

In the years immediately following the Civil War, some of Reverend Jones's children maintained the family's refined, if deeply conservative, Old Virginia aura—notably, educator-politician Richard Channing Jones and physician John Paul Jones. But another of Reverend Jones's sons, Edward Nathaniel Jones, headed in a different direction. Though a well-educated attorney and married into the Tait-Beck family, the pistol-packing hothead exuded anything but refinement. Indeed, John Miller told Kennedy that "Colonel Jones" (nothing indicates he served in the military) could be an easy target for opposing attorneys knowing of his temper. Another, equally fiery Camden attorney, Peter Horn, especially enjoyed challenging the colonel's honor. In 1894, at the rear of his law office across from the courthouse, Horn opened the town's first bank, the Camden Bank. When it went under the next year, Jones successfully sued Horn on behalf of depositors: the start of a feud.

On Friday, January 22, 1897, as the two opposed each other in a case tried at the Wilcox courthouse, Horn began his opening remarks with a slur on the character of Jones. John Miller did not recall precisely what was said, but it sent Jones into a rage. Horn responded in kind. The next day, Camden full with Saturday's late-morning shoppers, the two confronted each other on the north side of the courthouse. Shortly, Jones shot Horn. According to the *Montgomery Advertiser*, "the ball [entered] the mouth and [came] out in the neighborhood of the ear. [Though shot] Mr. Horn . . . grappled with Mr. Jones, and it was then that Mr. Dick Jones, son of the colonel, came upon the scene, and thinking it was his father who was shot, pulled his gun and fired, the ball entering the rear of [Horn's] head." For some twenty days, esteemed surgeon Luther Leonidas Hill kept Horn alive in his Montgomery infirmary. On February 20, 1897, however, Horn succumbed. The paddlewheel steamer *Nettie Quill* returned his body to Camden for burial.[22]

It was not just the "abject violent feuding" that registered with Kennedy. It was the "local tolerance for it." John Miller recalled no legal action taken against either Jones. The *Montgomery Journal* later confirmed this. It also noted that a February 24, 1897, resolution praising the "honor" of recently deceased Peter Horn—developed for the Camden bar by barristers Richebourg Gaillard, Benjamin Meek Miller, and Thomas L. Cochran, and published in the *Wilcox Progress*—made no mention of Horn's cause of death or of who killed him. It only wished Horn success "at that supreme bar where we all must sooner or later appear."[23]

A few years later, Kennedy returned to his key question about the Horn shooting: why its passive acceptance? He found a possible answer in Miss Cochran's recollections as to why Wilcox whites so disliked the leading Reconstruction Yankees of Camden—notably, William Henderson, John Russell Liddell, William L. Bruce, and Albion Morgan: "they would not fight . . . they were cowards, every one of them." In business and civic life, they navigated strategically, if at times manipulating tax laws and foreclosures to acquire property at severe discounts. Though such behavior delivered financial success, it also gave them opportunity to be civically engaged—to grow the community, when the Old Guard worried about their plantations and debt, and not about the town. Still, in Miss Cochran's mind that was beside the point. She said they were hated—could not even find "a local woman to marry"— because of their "not fighting—they did not fit in and seemed uppity."

By now convinced of "the Scotch-Irish [people's] long friendship with fighting . . . words, fists, guns, knives" and seeing them as a people for whom "no change . . . no change . . . [was] their premise for living," Kennedy now had a clearer view of why Peter Horn's ascent to that "supreme bar" above resulted in no charges against his killer: the whole episode—feuding to killing —had blessings of an ancient code, an "old behavior." Even so, Kennedy appears to have lacked the full historical background on the Yankees for his behavior prism to do its full work. Every one of these Yankee Reconstruction Camdenites may have come from "up North," but they also were but two generations removed from sophisticated families of the Scottish Highlands: Liddells, Bruces, Hendersons, Morgans.[24]

Among the sons of physician John Paul Jones was attorney John Paul Jones Jr., who stuck with the old-line aura. In 1901, he spearheaded the advent of the railroad; according to the *Wilcox Progressive Era*, his leadership "connected Camden with the outside world." But two others, Thomas Warburton Jones and J. Heustis Jones, seem to have received some of their Uncle Edward's genes. Both became Camden physicians; Warburton trained at Tulane University, Heustis at Columbia University—no doubt the first Columbia-educated physician to specialize in 6:00 a.m. goat-watching parties.

From at least 1914 through 1931, when Warburton died, the brothers feuded over patients and inherited property. Not speaking was only part of it. Regularly, they threatened to kill each other. Despite their mother's constant efforts at family disarmament, they went to work each day covered over with pistols. Should Warburton, for example, have Heustis "cornered in front of the courthouse," Heustis always was ready. Artfully, Kennedy recorded, he had "a custom-made holster strapped on his back between coat and shirt" which permitted "his right hand to reach behind his head as if to swat a mosquito on the back of his neck and then to come down fast with a firing thirty-two caliber revolver." Usually, such confrontations wound up with one challenging the other to a duel, which somehow never occurred.

One internecine Jones feud, however, came severely close to an actual killing. It involved a third-party relative. As John Miller told Kennedy, one day Heustis was walking on the side of the road toward his downtown office. He came face to face with Warburton's son, Paul. Heustis threatened to kill his nephew if he did not "give way." Out his office window, John Miller heard and saw all this unfolding. At 8:00 a.m. he pulled Heustis into his office and lectured him on who had the right to walk where. At 1:00 p.m. Miller finally escorted Heustis out his door with the doctor promising he understood that "each [white] person had a right to half the road." Kennedy's conclusion: "This is a strange place."

Much like the attorney-feuding of Colonel Jones and Peter Horn, the Jones physician-feuding easily crossed family lines to engage non–family members, notably the Bonners. As Kennedy recorded, "Dr. Ernest Bonner told me of a Negro who needed surgery. Dr. Bonner could do the surgery, but he needed a second doctor—Dr. Heustis Jones—for help with anesthesia. But Drs. Jones and Bonner hate each other. . . . They compete over patients and everything else. . . . So, there was no anesthesia and no surgery. The Negro died."[25]

As the Depression worsened during the winter of 1929–30, and Tait stresses resurfaced, Kennedy gained a revealing glimpse into feuding with "broken aristocracy" families. Historically, as Bertram Wyatt-Brown documented, antebellum planter elites settled their honor problems with dueling—or threats thereof. Early Tait life included at least one such instance. Violent family feuding was more the behavior of nonelites. With their postbellum downward mobility, however, Tait family members showed little hesitation to embrace the middle- to lower-class ways of settling their honor problems.

Ren and Mary long had heard Lottie Tait Beck shouting on the other side of the wall. They could tell it was not about Catholics; they suspected something related to property. Unknown to the Kennedys—later, Miller Bonner explained all—it turned out the noise they heard was but continuation of a seemingly "timeless Tait feud," and, indeed, regarding property.

Lottie's older sister, Mary, married William Rufus King Beck. When Lottie entered into courtship with his brother, James Tait Beck, Mary tried to disrupt the romance. She "did not want Lottie to marry—so that she might inherit all of the Becks' grand home at the decease of the two brothers." But in 1885, at age thirty-six, Mary's husband suddenly died. While Mary continued living in nearby Walnut Bluff, where the family had been for years, Lottie and husband, Judge Beck, lived on in the Camden home. When Judge Beck died in 1906, though each Tait sister inherited a half-interest in the Beck home, without consulting her sister Lottie added the apartments and kept the resulting revenue. Over Mary's regular protests this situation persisted for the next twenty years. Finally, as Depression stresses fueled the feud to breaking point, Mary hired a lawyer—Miller Bonner. He was to get her an equitable division of the home and its property. Lottie hired someone whom she knew would return fire—Benjamin Meek Miller.

At church Miller Bonner told Kennedy his "client would succeed." At church Meek Miller told Kennedy his "client would succeed." Litigation commenced, and a trial date was finally set for spring 1930. Meanwhile, Mary ignored her attorney's advice. She demanded that Lottie immediately give her major pieces of furniture as well as Vice-President William Rufus King's dueling pistols, spurs, and cufflinks. No one challenged Kennedy's having the walking cane. All liked him, plus he bought coal for the house.

Lottie refused to discuss Mary's request. So, just before noon on New Year's Eve, 1929, Mary brought in reinforcements: her sister, Rosa Tait McDaniel, and her sister-in-law, Mabel Jones Tait, wife of Sheriff Fleet Tait. It happened in the main living room. The Kennedys witnessed nothing: Mary had taken Mary Conway for a visit at the Clark Jones home; having been up reading most of the previous night, Ren was sound asleep in the apartment bedroom and never heard the escalating voices, or what came next. Several days later Miller Bonner gave him the gory details.

Lottie "knocked Mrs. McDaniel to the floor." This was not that difficult. Complaining of back pain from a recent fender-bender auto accident, the previous day she had prevailed upon Dr. Bonner for sufficient morphine to keep her "loopy" for several days. Still, "when she got up Lottie knocked her down again [so that] she hit her head on the door post and was almost knocked out." Next, Lottie "seized Mary by the hair and beat her head against the door post. . . . Then she threw Rosa over a chair. With an idiotic smile on her face Lottie [then] ordered her visitors to get out of her house." Wisely, they did.

Still, despite intensely bad feelings on all sides—lawyer detesting lawyer, clients engaged in near fatal combat—the case never went to trial. Bonner and Miller managed to communicate enough to work out a settlement whereby the house would be sold "eventually" and proceeds would be divided between the two sisters. Still, according to the agreement, on January 23, 1930, "Miss Lottie had to give up much of her furniture to her sister . . . [and] some of W. R. King's relics." From their furnished apartment Ren and Mary "lost in the transaction one marble topped table, a washstand, three straight chairs, and a fine large mahogany framed mirror that hung over the mantle"—minor losses considering the Depression deepening every day.[26]

On the other side of the wall from Miss Lottie the Kennedys struggled on for one more year. Relief finally came in February 1931. They moved into the renovated manse, a two-story wooden cottage at the corner of Broad and Whiskey Run Road, three blocks from the ARP church. The first floor offered a full kitchen, dining room, and "parlor" (living room), plus a bedroom with half-bath converted to "the preacher's study." Overnight, literally, the "preacher's study" became Kennedy's inner sanctum—with a nine-by-twelve rug, two floor lamps, a naked light bulb hanging from the ceiling, cushioned rocking chair, daybed, large office desk with wooden swivel chair, and wall-to-wall bookcases filled with works of history, philosophy, and literature—volumes "roughly sorted by topic, not size or color." The second floor had three bedrooms and a full bathroom. Much to the wife's glee, the parlor offered a wood-burning fireplace. Much to the husband's glee, the study offered a smaller, coal-burning fireplace. Out back a garage hosted the remains of a chicken coop (soon to be revitalized) and an eighth-of-an-acre yard—ample for a vegetable garden. Long awaited and indeed inviting. Throughout that brutally cold move-in day, however, eighteen-month-old Mary Conway tenaciously clung to her mother's skirt, intimidated by the spaciousness. She repeatedly demanded the family return to Miss Lottie's apartment—not exactly what mother and father had in mind.[27]

They lived on about $1,600 a year: $1,200 in ARP salary, $100 in individual congregational gifts, and, beginning September 1931, $300 from Mary's getting a part-time Bible-teaching position at Camden's white elementary school. This income level did not permit a car—a constant source of frustration for grocery shopping, county-wide meetings, and distant pastoral calls. "Begging a ride" and having "someone send for me" would be part of their lives for a long time to come. At least one Black minister had a car and "did not charge for a ride."

Yet there were happy times, too. If, back in June 1928, before marriage and Mary Conway, Kennedy was all cynicism as he observed local feuding over prospective sites for a new bridge over the Alabama River—Taits and Cooks pushing their Clifton Ferry site versus the Miller's Ferry site—in November 1929 he noted how enjoyable it was going in "Joe McMoore's rented car with Mary and the baby and seeing the new bridge out in the water at Miller's Ferry." Likewise, on December 6, 1931, a six-month courtship between Sam McNeill and Mary's sister, Dot—they had met the previous Christmas when twenty-one-year-old Dot visited in Camden—resulted in marriage. With Sam remaining a deputy sheriff, and Dot becoming a teller at Camden National Bank, the two quickly became well blended into life at Broad and Whiskey Run Road. But likely nothing gave Kennedy more happiness than Mary Conway's developing fascination with "God's different creatures"—turtles, snakes, stray dogs and cats; the proud father welcomed all. At four, however, she had a "faith moment" well eclipsing the Earth-bound.

> February 2, 1933 . . . A bright warm morning. I was in the backyard with my baby . . . She was swinging . . . under the big oak tree and talking to herself. She said, "Someday I will climb up this tree and go up into the sky where God is. I'll say, 'Hey, God!' He'll say, 'How did you get up to this place?' I'll say, 'I climbed up the tree from Camden, and I'll have two little angels to play with, please.'" THAT is genuine religion.

Beginning in September 1934, the same happiness revolved around the birth of their second daughter. If her eyes were a shade off, they still named her Margaret—for Grandma Muddie.[28]

Poignantly, despite such nurturing and relative security, Kennedy's devotion to Christian Socialism and neo-orthodox Christianity never let him feel removed from the ravages of the Depression. Quite the opposite. The worse the Depression, the more severe his critique of the relatively well-off white Christians around him, so focused on their own "piety" and "salvation" and "property" and so unfocused on the profound tragedies unfolding in Wilcox and all over America—and shortly overseas, too. Repeatedly he asked, "What would Jesus say?" His intensity sprang from both religious and secular sources.

Increasingly, he awaited the mail bringing the current issue of the *Christian Century*. Here, at least, he could read the words of others who favored a Social Gospel Christianity connected to interdenominational efforts—Protestant "unionism." At the same time, more and more he showed disappointment about those of his own flock and well beyond who stuck to the old-time evangelical "piety and salvation" approach to Christianity. Kennedy, of course, had grown up with that approach. Ever since Princeton, however, he followed the broader neo-orthodoxy. His most articulate expression of where he stood in the Depression, especially regarding Half Christianity, remains in a draft essay—never submitted for publication—that he wrote in the summer of 1933. An excerpt: "Of social justice . . . economic exploitation . . . political corruption, of the depression . . . unemployment . . . starvation . . . entrenched privilege . . . bloated riches, of all the festering sores—social, economic and political . . . the [evangelical] knows nothing. . . . The Christian religion must always be personal, mystical . . . offering the individual salvation of the soul. But that is only half of the message of Christianity. The other half is the call to build social and economic structures that are informed with the spirit and teachings of Jesus."

His understanding of American history fed off this faith view. As yet again evidence of the Republicans' failure to exercise measured, balanced leadership on behalf of the average citizen and the poor, he focused on systemic effects of the policies of the perennial US secretary of the treasury in the 1920s, Andrew Mellon. In response to President Wilson's domestic reforms, Mellon advocated radical deregulation of the economy. Get government out of regulating business so corporations will make more money. Then they will pass along their good fortune to the American workforce through higher wages and more jobs. In short, the Republican Mellon promised top-down prosperity to all.

Years later, in the 1980s, Kennedy called this Mellon's "Great Trickle Down Hoax." He admitted that as far as he knew, Mellon never actually used the phrase "trickle down." And that led to his holding forth on its true origins among a few sarcastic lines in William Jennings Bryan's famous 1896 "Cross of Gold" speech; and how satirist Will Rogers finally hatched the precise combination of words—"trickle down"—in derisive description of Hoover's continued deregulation of the nation's economy and the horrors it would cause. To Kennedy, however, that the actual words did not originate from Republican mouths in the 1920s was irrelevant. The "Trickle Down Hoax" did exactly what Mellon and other Republican leaders wanted. Return the nation to the Gilded Age and to the Robber Barons' manipulation of government and to the rich getting far richer, with no regard for the poor. It also caused the stock market crash and the Depression. Unsurprisingly, this Christian

Socialist read most of the major works of historian Charles Beard and used them in his sermons.[29]

Of course, Kennedy's "trickle down" thesis as the sole cause of the Depression overlooks other factors, such as technological unemployment, high tariffs, World War I debt, vagaries of agricultural life, materialism, and the credit craze. But when confronted on "trickle down" being only one of the causes of what he called "the Republicans' mess," he exhibited uncharacteristic irritation. "No. Everything else lined up under 'The Trickle-Down Hoax.' Around here [in Wilcox] most big landowners came out fine. There also were those who got out of it [the mess] with the war [World War II]. But most people—bad off to begin with—just never got out of it unless they left." In short, for him the late 1920s and early 1930s saw "the Hoax" and "the Republicans' mess" merge with the historic irresponsibility of many Wilcox whites: "broken aristocracy" in confluence with self-centered "piety religion" and Scotch-Irish feuding, violence, passivity, and lack of civic energy. And the result was a most un-Christian place, ironic considering its self-image. Although the term "Half Christianity" had not yet emerged, its gestation was well under way.

State and local politics of the Depression era only added to his intensity. In the Alabama governor's race of 1930, Benjamin Meek Miller—a pillar in Kennedy's church—ran on an anticronyism and anti-Klan platform. Here, Miller's religion could have been an issue, just as it could have been for the far-ranging politics of Miller Bonner. ARPs placed overwhelming priority on matters of individual piety and salvation, leading many to live disengaged from secular matters, domestic and international—to Kennedy's constant discouragement. Yet synodal "policy" only asserted "no politicking from the pulpit": individuals do as they please. And, as ARP historian Lowry Ware has detailed, over the years many ARPs had been politically active—from secession and Confederate politics up to the 1928 presidential race. Even if Hoover drank whiskey, in that campaign he carefully presented himself as the "dry" candidate, and most ARPs openly voted for him. So, Benjamin Meek Miller's 1930 campaign clearly demonstrated that ARPs could engage secular, earthly matters when it suited them.

Early on, no doubt emboldened by declining KKK membership, Miller said he would not permit a single Kluxer on the state payroll. If that sold well through some of Wilcox, it obviously did not among KKK voters statewide—still a force of perhaps 60,000. As the election neared, Miller felt the need to pivot. "The rank and file . . . in the KKK is fine men, good democrats . . . and do not endorse the Klan rule of government or politics." Kennedy understood the pragmatism involved. But despite the unfolding Depression, Miller also ran as a "financial conservative": lower taxes and smaller state bureaucracy.

As anticipated, he ran, too, as a "dry." Unlike many Wilcox "drys," he meant it. During the campaign, his long embrace of prohibition gathered even greater commitment as his son, Camden lawyer, Ben Miller Jr., degenerated through what the public thought was a losing battle with alcoholism, though—according to Kennedy—cocaine addiction enabled through Dr. Ernest Bonner's sales was even more his ruin than alcohol.

In the general election Meek Miller faced Birmingham lawyer Hugh Locke. Defrocked by the Alabama Democratic Party for supporting Hoover in 1928, Locke ran as the candidate of the recently created Jeffersonian-Democratic Party. He was as complicated as Miller. Though known to be pro-Klan and antibooze, Locke nevertheless had support among some anti-Klan voters and "wets" considering his "dry" position as more talk than substance.

Still, the Black Belt–Big Mule axis controlling Alabama's Democratic Party was worried about the "Klan state" image Alabama incurred under the leadership of outgoing governor Bibb Graves. It was bad for business. So, the axis threw its dominant power behind Meek Miller. Statewide, the Camdenite beat Locke by some 60,000 votes. Although many in Camden found Miller pompous, and some quietly criticized his harsh treatment of Negro sharecroppers on his extensive plantation across the Alabama River near old Midway, Wilcoxons gave their native son 1,309 votes, Locke 167. Because of the ARPs' relatively tiny numbers—and less so their piety orientation—Meek Miller thus became the first ARP in the nation elected to a state governorship.

Privately, Kennedy worried about Miller's conservative economic agenda resulting in more of the "hurtful hoax" perpetrated by national Republicans. Yet, believing Locke to be pro-Klan, and anticipating Locke's economic agenda to be just as conservative as Miller's, he voted for this mainstay of his church. Miller asked his preacher to swear him in at the January 19, 1931, inauguration. Kennedy did it.[30]

The crisis politics of the times wound up smashing Meek Miller. In an efficiency move, he eliminated numerous state jobs. When this damaged enforcement of prohibition, the "drys" and the Klan labeled him a hypocrite. At the same time "wets" labeled him inefficient for not dropping prohibition and garnering tax revenues off legalized booze. Then there was the factor of Kennedy's dear Camden friends, John and Clyde Miller. When Governor Miller named his distinguished cousin and attorney, John Miller, to be judge of the Fourth Circuit, "drys," "wets," and the Klan nailed him for "cronyism." These attacks only intensified when his wife, Otis, died and the governor asked Judge Miller's wife, Clyde, to assume hostess duties at the governor's mansion.

In some respects, Governor Miller showed a lot of courage. Despite having been the circuit judge who declared the previous Alabama income tax unconstitutional, in the Depression he tried to salvage the barely funded Alabama public schools and potholed highways by pushing through modest tax increases—including a progressive income tax. In turn, the Black Belt–Big Mule axis condemned him to political death for being a "turncoat." Of course, none did more to encourage such a label than his arch Camden feud rival—his cousin and fellow ARP, state senator Miller Bonner. Another episode among the legion of Scotch-Irish helping to defeat each other.

Caught in this vortex, Meek Miller then failed on his self-proclaimed hallmark of fighting "Judge Lynch" and the Klan. During early stages of the infamous Scottsboro trial—on which we will hear far more from Kennedy—he failed to send in the National Guard to block Klan activities, making the crisis even worse. In the middle of the Scottsboro trial, the alleged murder and rape trial of Willie Peterson, in Birmingham, gave Miller a chance to show his courage. When the final testimony of the arresting policeman said Peterson could not have committed the crime, and the supposed victim—a Mountain Brook, Alabama, white woman named Nell Williams—constantly changed her story, Governor Miller overruled the guilty verdict and granted Peterson a limited-time clemency. But when the clemency time ran out, he bowed to white conservative pressure and sentenced Peterson to life in prison. Miller also failed to send in the Guard to protect against a publicly anticipated lynching of a Black man in Brewton. The Klan mob proceeded to torture the man, then hang him. Yet when Brewton's Black citizens seemed on the verge of violent protest, Governor Miller dispatched the Guard to quell the Black crowd.

Meek Miller knew better than to run for reelection. Whether or not the majority of Wilcox whites would stick with him out of loyalty to a friend and relative never got answered. He knew the statewide Black Belt–Big Mule axis would not support him. He returned to his Camden law practice and to farming his extensive north Wilcox lands with sharecroppers. In 1944, at age eighty, he died, Miller Bonner bashing him right down into the grave out of their ancient, petty feuds over politics, law cases, and property lines. Beyond Bonner, locals had mixed feelings for him. Kennedy's friend, Frank Dexter: "He [did] noth'n' for our community. These roads we got in his administration were federal relief projects, except for one State road he built through his plantation across the River." Yet Charles Dobbins Jr. remembered him as "a kindly man . . . with strict moral code. . . . Camden people held him in great respect."[31]

While the Depression had Kennedy distraught over Republican policies and persisting Wilcox behaviors, it also focused him on certain elements of ARP orthodoxy. He was convinced that the ARP Synod's resistance to change—resistance to taking full-throated pulpit stands on behalf of the unfortunates in the Depression era and other stands letting it join the modern secular world—limited its appeal and therefore its congregation sizes and funding. Long-term tensions over how to fund Erskine College and Seminary, he felt, made his point. His own lack of a car to tend his flock did, too. Granted, he was not alone in wanting an ARP Synod of active social engagement; John H. Buzhardt, Gilbert Gordon Parkinson, Robert M. Stevenson, Ernest Neal Orr, Ebenezer Gettys, and a few others were his allies. And occasionally synod would establish some program to raise individual awareness of lynching or anti-Semitism. But focused chiefly on individual piety and salvation, overwhelming ARP numbers remained either opposed to such efforts or uninvolved.[32]

In May 1930, he received short-term relief from this depressing ARP scene. He attended a Rural Preachers Institute at Vanderbilt University. Alabama Episcopal bishop William G. McDowell nominated Justice Jones to attend and urged him to bring along Kennedy. Back in September 1929 Kennedy and McDowell had met when McDowell, at Justice Jones's invitation, presided over a Union Service at Camden's St. Mary's Episcopal Church. Funded by the Rockefeller Foundation, the weeklong Vanderbilt program gave participants access to Henry Edmonds of Birmingham's Independent Presbyterian Church and other noted liberal preachers of the South. With the exception of his early Chautauqua experience in Missouri, Kennedy had stayed clear of such liberal groups. Only local, immediate-impact organizations, such as the Wilcox County Red Cross, appeared to draw him. Undoubtedly, this proclivity also served his private reading and writing time, hard to protect for the organizationally active. Yet Kennedy made an exception for the Vanderbilt initiative. He needed the change of scenery, and he enjoyed the company of Justice Jones.

While he found Edmonds's message "scintillating," other instructors—who "talked too much"—were boring or without much real-life experience in social change. (In 1941 Kennedy would draft an essay on this experience with "windjammers" and "pontificators," but never submit it.) Still, it was good for him to be with other preachers of social action. In Justice Jones's words, " We [who attended the Vanderbilt meeting] were to use our pulpits and local contacts to solve [the] problems Negroes and others were having with poverty and unfair treatment—all Christians working together." There even was a short course on "conflict resolution" in small southern towns. Still, when the seminar ended, it was back to another kind of behavior.[33]

And right away this hit him in the face. For four days in April 1931 the ARP Synod met in Camden and Oak Hill, the first time since 1907. The *Montgomery Advertiser* and *Wilcox Progressive Era* covered logistics and social life down to what delegates stayed in whose homes and what they ate . . .

and did not drink. At the opening session, Governor Miller—introduced by Kennedy as "the first ARP governor in the United States"—gave a rousing welcome. From there, however, things went downhill fast, at least for the host preacher.

On the second day, with an impassioned speech, "Things That Grieve Me," Kennedy urged the synod to begin a series of conversations on how ARPs might find common ground with other Protestant groups so as to coordinate more assistance for the ever expanding numbers of starving people. Julian Miller, John Buzhardt, William Boyce Hemphill, Ernest Neal Orr, and a few other liberal ARPs responded with enthusiasm. Still, after "considerable rancor," there on Kennedy's home turf—and with his father, Ike, present—delegates overwhelmingly voted down his proposal. Among the delegates from his own Camden, Marion Junction, and Oak Hill churches, he received one vote—the vote of Bill Jones. Just to make sure Kennedy got the point, after the vote Miller Bonner—Jones's uncle—pulled him aside for this flat statement: "Even if Synod were to approve [what Kennedy proposed], Camden ARPs never will." The old-time emphasis on individual piety and salvation, not social action on behalf of others (except of one's own congregation), and the historic ARP "policy" against ministers getting involved in "politics" remained solid as ever. Here was a blow, even if one he expected.[34]

Back in December 1929, Kennedy had succeeded Bill Jones as chairman of the Wilcox County chapter of the American Red Cross. Three years later, schools functioned month by month often with teachers unpaid, but even more acute were sharecropper problems—cotton prices were at six cents a pound. Regardless of the synod's recent rejection of his Social Gospel ecumenicalism, Kennedy refused to give up on ecumenical Red Cross pleas to raise money for cropper relief. He targeted his congregants whom he knew could afford to give. Perhaps he remembered that in 1927 his similar plea for change—on school funding for Black children—used numbers and dollars. And it had gone nowhere. At any rate, this time he employed exclusively what his flock professed to hold so dear, the Bible and University of Alabama football. Beneath the surface, it was a plea from a neo-orthodox Christian Socialist notably lacking key tenets of Calvinism.

He titled his November 1, 1931, sermon, "On Aristocracy." It revolved around the Apostle Paul and Philippians 3:5–7, which makes sense from one standpoint, if not another. As a Jew, Kennedy explained, Paul had elite, if you will, aristocratic credentials; he gave them up to convert to Christianity. After explaining how the word *aristocracy* derived from ancient Greek civilization, where it meant "rule by the best," he extrapolated on pros and cons of aristocracy. First, if the elite and powerful—"the best"—help both the "bourgeoisie" and "proletariat" below them, as indeed happened in ancient

Greece, aristocracy has reason to exist. But if aristocracy focuses chiefly on self-aggrandizement, aristocracy really is not aristocracy at all—only a wealthy plague on society. Second, assuming some "legitimate" versions of aristocracy, he saw five types of "Earthly aristocracy" where people were recognized as "the best": "Wealth," "Brawn," "Arts," "Intellect," and "Blood." He urged, however, that one born into these types of aristocracy had no reason to feel superior. It was just their humble good fortune (no mention of predestination). For example, the 1930 University of Alabama football team "beat Washington State at Pasadena [in the Rose Bowl] 24 to 20 . . . artists in their specialties" whose "aristocracy value" derived from their "brawny" luck.

The aristocracy of wealth was more complicated. He read aloud what noted Virginia historian Thomas J. Wertenbaker had to say about aristocracy in the Tidewater/tobacco region of eighteenth-century Virginia. Only three families "derived from English houses of historic [aristocratic] note" and three more came from "the minor [English] gentry." Virtually no aristocrats created America. To Kennedy, this called into serious question assertions of a pervasive aristocracy of white "blood or race" recently urged by Madison Grant in *The Passing of the Great Race* (1921), despite some taking the book as evidence of "no better type of rule." Then, moving up to the nineteenth century, he read aloud passages from historian U. B. Phillips's new book, *Life and Labor in the Old South* (1929). Here, in at least the pages Kennedy read, Phillips profiled cotton planters as clearly not aristocratic. New money (less than three generations old) and virtually all lacking a sense of social responsibility beyond family matters made them little more than "Cotton Snobs." Still, as he next read from Charles and Mary Beard's *Rise of American Civilization* (1927), these Cotton Snobs "quickly assumed the cultural guise of the English aristocracy." And the wealth of this mythological aristocracy—the "mythological cavaliers" of southern "antebellum days—rested on slavery [and] at present it rests upon the labor of free men, white and black . . . [who] at least . . . are not called slaves."

The scene set, Kennedy now moved to what he wanted the well-off in front of him to understand, not to mention his sales pitch for Red Cross donations. Currently, Camden's best shot for a legitimately exalted group was "the Aristocracy of Crap Shooters" out front of the courthouse. Virtually all others considered aristocrats, whether by themselves or others, actually were not aristocrats and never had been. Cotton Snobs? Probably so. Christian cotton snobs, doing little more than carrying a Bible and coming to church? That, too.

Yet they still could become legitimate aristocrats thanks to two additional classifications of aristocracy, far eclipsing all others. For these two types of aristocracy, Kennedy explained, ancestry and inheritance and indeed current material wealth were irrelevant. It was all a matter of how one treated Wilcox's "bourgeoisie" and even more its "proletariat." One could become an "Aristocrat of Character" by living daily life according to Christ's standards of humility and service to others. Being a Christian was not a prerequisite; one could be an "Aristocrat of Character" without even believing in the historical Jesus. Still, to get to the topmost rung of aristocracy, the "Aristocracy of the Kingdom of God," as the Apostle Paul did, one had to be a full Christian focused on words of God and Jesus while also helping the most needy at every possible opportunity. By doing this, one joined Paul: "Paul saw a vision of Jesus and promptly gave up everything that he possessed in this world . . . to become an Aristocrat in the Kingdom of God." Kennedy now concluded: "May God lead each of us to see more fully Paul's vision and to follow Jesus as he did, saying: 'But what things were gain to me, those I counted loss for Christ.'"

Granted, to get to his point Kennedy pushed the limits on Paul, who sacrificed high status as a Jew to become a Christian but was no model for Christians crashing barricades to help the poor. Kennedy also overstated Phillips's critique of the Cavalier myth; while Phillips used "Cotton Snob" just as Kennedy said, the historian was blatantly contradictory with a last chapter extolling the high-level "gentry." Even so, Kennedy's history lesson demonstrates his evolving views on aristocracy as well as on Christianity. Regardless of their self-image, from Old South to New, he believed Wilcox's "aristocrats" only had been Cotton Snobs. Hence, a "broken aristocrat" was a Cotton Snob with no more wealth—angry and insecure about that loss and filled with aggression and pretension.

Even so, by superimposing his own aristocracy nomenclature on the historians', Kennedy left open possibilities for a "broken [mythical] aristocrat" to become a real one—of the highest order. This revolved around his bifurcation of Christianity. From Princeton, Russellville, and early Wilcox days he had a neo-orthodox devotion to both the individual piety/salvation tradition and the Social Gospel approach. But now, in late 1931, horrors of the early Depression in the Black Belt forced him to prioritize these components. That morning he was confrontationally oblique: after all, he wanted to raise money. But in many ways he still was clear. Those who focused on the words of God, Jesus, and the Bible, and piety and salvation, *plus* acted daily on Social Gospel responsibilities toward those less fortunate, were complete or Full Christians destined for the Aristocracy of the Kingdom of God. But those who did only the first, without regular Social Gospel action—Half Christians, by implication—were not. He remained silent on where such Half Christians would land after death. Though succeeding years would see him elucidate other elements of Half versus Full Christianity, he never clarified the hereafter element. Still, even by 1931 he had anticipated some of the "captive theology" critique that noted scholar of southern religion Samuel S. Hill Jr. would offer some three decades later in explanation of how and why many white southerners professing to be Christians stuck by segregation.

These larger reflections aside, at the end of that day, November 1, 1931, inside Kennedy only one thing seems to have resonated. In response to his eloquent, multilayered message, he got nothing from his congregants: no comments of any kind—no praise, no rejection—and, more to the point, no increase in Red Cross giving. He plodded on.[35]

As the 1930s unfolded—the Depression deepening and the election of 1932 seeing Hoover replaced by Franklin D. Roosevelt—the Wilcox scene only worsened. Kennedy showed any number of signs of quitting. But he did not. And one of the reasons he did not lies in a behind-the-scenes shift. Up through the time of the Crash, he had not taken his heretical message to a larger public—to life beyond Wilcox. He had kept his criticism inside Wilcox. In the early 1930s, however, he decided to go public. He moved out into the realm of public attack by submitting his thoughts for publication.

6

Attack

During their arduous courting days, Ren repeatedly told Mary he liked "to write." Neither her assertion that reading and writing gave him headaches, nor the ill-fated Woodrow Wilson essay, had quelled this urge. Beyond the intimate hand-scripted thoughts in the diary and well-orchestrated sermons, the keys on the Royal beckoned.

No doubt other factors worked on him, too. For all the reasons some devout Christians arise to offer spoken testimonials—some in restrained voice, others in whooping and speaking in tongues—his writing could provide concrete and open witness to his Social Gospel Christian concerns. Out of guilt and frustration, through writing he also could attack with a different strategy. The God Mandate of actually changing people in the immediate sense had proven in the main impossible. But if he shifted to the longer term approach of becoming less a commander "of the heavenly host" and more an Old Testament–style prophet "in the wilderness," he might avoid the feeling of outright defeat and still get something done. If so, he resembled some three hundred other southern neo-orthodox preachers, mainly white but a few Black, associated with the Fellowship of Southern Churchmen (FSC)—people like Will Alexander, Benjamin Mays, and Howard Kester.

Yet two factors likely explain why Kennedy did not engage with the FSC. Out of his extreme individualism, he had no interest in such organizations. Too, virtually all FSC members came from the upper South, where "white over Black" never had been as absolute as in the lower, predominantly cotton South. Hence many FSC members believed "moral suasion" could develop a Social Gospel Christian "fraternity which transcended racial or class distinction." As a tiller of Black Belt fields, by contrast, Kennedy had found little reason to be optimistic about such strategy.

Still, on his own, through writing he could lunge out from his encirclement of defeated Black Belt ministry and strike a well-crafted blow against the behaviors so tormenting him. Indeed, even if his writing changed no one, he would still have written it. And perhaps that could elicit from God a modicum of patience about his other failures. If not, at least there was the probability that such work would provide psychological relief. As the Georgian Lillian Smith, author of *Strange Fruit* (1944), confided to friends, she derived "therapy" out of "writing about . . . racial fear and hatred" in the South. Kennedy likely did too—fleeting perhaps, but still helpful in reviving him for those tough, unproductive rows God wanted him to plow.[1]

An intriguing metaphor helped usher in this major turning point in Kennedy's life. Since the final weeks of December 1930, back at Miss Lottie's, between midnight and 4:00 a.m., he had been pondering the word *yaupon*. Indigenous to the lower southeastern United States, it refers to a holly bush given its name by Creeks and Choctaws. Today, some spell it *youpon*. Too much of the robust black tea made from its leaves—which so many Confederate soldiers had to turn to as a coffee substitute—purged the digestive system into agony. Yet its shiny green leaves and red berries made for artful decoration around the foundation of a house. And one such Wilcox home, the Tait family's "Youpon" mansion at Canton Bend, had his intense focus.

Not long after arriving in Wilcox, Kennedy spent an evening at "Youpon." Though he found it "pretty shabby compared to its likely grandeur of Old South days," he also found its history a significant window into Wilcox. An Englishman, William J. Mathews—well-heeled from a Haitian sugar venture—departed the Caribbean in the mid-1830s to start over with cotton and slaves at Canton Bend, soon amassing an even greater fortune. By 1845 he had constructed a heralded Wilcox mansion, called "Mimosa." A firebrand secessionist, Mathews invested heavily in ill-fated Confederate bonds. His fortune essentially lost, after the war his descendants hung on with sharecroppers. But in 1899 they finally gave up and sold "Mimosa" to a wealthy former New Yorker who lived in nearby Catherine, Alabama, Myron Boynton. It is not clear if Boynton changed the estate's name to "Youpon" or if this came in 1902 when Boynton sold out to Frank Shropshire Tait, great-grandson of the baron of antebellum Wilcox, Charles Tait. Kennedy's memorable visit to the place came in early January 1929, a month after Frank Tait died and as the "Yaupon command passed to his widow, Maggie, and first son, [twenty-two-year-old] Julian Marsh Tait." As the Depression came on, Kennedy emphasized, "the shabby place became downright pathetic." Kennedy did not live to witness the stunning restoration of "Yaupon" (or "Youpon") after Tait descendants sold to the Rutherford family of Mobile in 1999. Then the home quickly became yet another revitalized antebellum structure on a Wilcox scene increasingly the destination point for devotees of historic architecture. For Kennedy, "sad Yaupon" always was the compelling metaphor for Black Belt whites' downward spiral as they refused to adjust to the end of slavery and other realities of history.[2]

Of course, William Faulkner also found a literary metaphor in a Native American word. In January 1929 he published *Sartoris*, initiating the world to a fictional Deep South place he called "Yoknapatawpha"—derived from two Chickasaw words, *yocona* and *petopha*, with the combined meaning of "flat land split by flowing water." Here was his fictional location for writing about the town of Oxford and the county of Lafayette in Mississippi. Five Yoknapatawpha novels later, in *Absalom, Absalom!* (1936), Faulkner even provided a map for these iconic places.

Yet nothing suggests that "Yoknapatawpha" motivated "Yaupon," nor that Faulkner's "Sartoris" family of degenerating aristocracy influenced Kennedy's notion of "broken aristocracy," nor indeed that Faulkner's "Snopes" family catalyzed Kennedy's more bizarre and rapacious characters. The diary shows no Faulkner experience before or during his creation of "Yaupon." While he could have seen *New York Times* reviews of Faulkner's early novels, that is about it. Not until the 1935 Thanksgiving holidays did he have his first full Faulkner experience through reading *Sanctuary* (1931). Then, between December 31, 1936, and January 7, 1937, he consumed *Absalom, Absalom!* (1936).[3]

Sometimes "Yaupon" was an entire county, at other times the central town of that county. Though similar in topic and, occasionally, in insight to Faulkner's work, stylistically Kennedy's writings were a world apart from the Yoknapatawpha series and never approached its epic significance. Unlike Faulkner, too, Kennedy left no maps of his Yaupon County or Yaupon Town. Yet, in some ways, his "Yaupon Tales" do for the Scotch-Irish of the Black Belt what *The Canterbury Tales* did for late medieval England. He provides far more than a "parson's tale"; he gets to the squires, the millers, the friars, the knights—pretty much all Geoffrey Chaucer's "types," and then some.[4]

"Yaupon" began to take form during the late hours of Tuesday, December 1, 1930. A month later, at 2:30 a.m. on Tuesday, February 4, 1931, he completed "Notes from Alabama on Homo Africanus." In five fictionalized conversations written with local dialect, this piece depicts whites and Blacks in the sharecropping culture of "Yaupon town," clearly drawn from what Kennedy had experienced since coming to Wilcox.

The initial tale concerns a Negro on trial for murdering another Negro; it includes a thinly veiled reference to Gee's Bend. As the jury deliberates in the courthouse, two white men across the street at the barbershop ponder the outcome. Here is the core: "The head barber: 'That . . . lawyer pulled a new one on me. Said a nigger had character. I never thought of that befo'.' A man named Jim . . . getting a shave: 'I ain't never seen no nigger what had character.' Jim made his generalization from vast experience, for he lived in Allen's Bend where there were three white families and five hundred Negroes."

Set at "Yaupon Drugstore," the second vignette also treats a Black-on-Black killing. "First customer: 'It was just a nigger's woman matter. Ella was Son's woman. But . . . she was prankin' around with another man. . . . ' Second customer: 'Well, I guess it means the electric chair for Son.' First customer: 'Naw, suh . . . he'll . . . be worth a heap to the State . . . on the highway befo' he dies.'"

The third conversation occurred in front of "Yaupon National Bank." "It was Saturday afternoon in Yaupon . . . Old Alexander Dussenberry [president of the bank]: 'Those damn niggers,' he said looking up from his ledger. He rushed out: 'What you niggers think this is? Act like you own the street . . . block'n the door. . . . Move along, now. Move along now.'"

The fourth involved a new preacher in Yaupon "profoundly interested in the metaphysics of the economy of the Black Belt." He visits a member of his congregation long involved in this economy, "Mr. Amos Reese . . . a big cotton farmer [who also had] a general merchandise store . . . established principally for . . . advancing supplies to his tenants." "'From the first of March until mid-fall when the crop was being gathered and sold,' Mr. Reese explained, he 'supplied his tenants.'" He marked up his merchandise "33 1/3%" plus charged interest. If his tenant had a bad crop and could not pay off what he had borrowed after selling in the fall, his debt to Mr. Reese got rolled into the following year's "advance."

> "It's a good system," said Mr. Reese. "I furnish a house, a mule, tools, fertilizer, seed, food and clothing. The Negro takes these and makes a crop . . . At the end of the year we divide up fifty-fifty on the proceeds . . . It is fairer to the Negro than to me. He risks nothing but his labor. I risk a considerable investment . . . Sometime I believe it is the Lord's own plan for Negroes here in the South." . . . The old wife of an old cropper knocked at the screen door. "Mas Amos, please let me hab five dollars dis week." . . . "You see," Mr. Reese explained to his preacher, "I advance her . . . I am entering five dollars here against Mary, but I could make it ten or twenty-five dollars. She can't read or write and would never know the difference . . . They are just children, especially the older ones."

The manuscript concludes with a one more furnishing-office conversation. "Mr. Renfro Jackson was considered a hard man in Yaupon. 'Niggers are animals,' he said, . . . '[and] niggers have no souls' . . . Doctor Blair knew all this."

"I come to see you about one of your niggers, Renfro . . . Willie Mc-Cracken's boy, Op . . . blocked bowels . . . looks like he's going to die . . . Let me take him to Mobile to Dr. Joyce . . . It'll cost you about fifty dollars . . . Dr. Joyce won't charge him, then ten days in the hospital."

. . . . "Old Willie owes me $535," Renfro replied . . . Doc, let nature take its course. They come out just as well in the end."

Kennedy's fulsome correspondence provides no sign that he sought publication of "Notes from Alabama on Homo Africanus." Rather, he seems to have written it as an experiment, feeling his way along. Likely, too, he was not quite ready to lunge out publicly.[5]

Five months later, in late July 1931, he tried a different topic and different tone, backing away from the "Yaupon" metaphor. "Alabama Feels Mr. Hoover's Prosperity" consists of eighteen typed pages of straight journalism reflecting Kennedy's extensive experience with citizens not acting to solve problems. It begins with the onset of the Depression in Alabama and the mantra of President Herbert Hoover and other Republicans: "everything will be alright" so long as we stay true to trickle-down economics. Kennedy then shows the opposite is happening. The "bloc" [Black Belt–Big Mule alliance] is defeating Governor Miller's emergency steps to keep schools open. While the drought is killing corn and beef, despite the drought—normally good for cotton—prices and the boll weevil are killing cotton. Both planters and croppers suffer dramatically. In Birmingham the steel mills are grinding to a halt. This leaves "the [city] people desperate and pitiful," sending many back to the farms, where there also is nothing. Yet Alabamians seem unable "to act to change things." "Conservative and orthodox in religion, politics, and economics . . . there is little evidence that they question the divine role of the economic system. They are praying that business will improve."

He submitted the piece to the *New Republic*. Back came a form-letter rejection. This could have resulted from his conclusion: a melodramatic flourish about "redistribution of wealth," springing from utopian strains in his Christian Socialism, which clashed with his otherwise terse, hard-hitting analysis. The plethora of such state-level profiles coming from left-leaning journalists of substantial reputation probably worked against him, too. Still, here is a compelling account of the onslaught of the Depression in Alabama. It offers stark contemporaneous criticism of "Black Belt–Big Mule" power by a white living in Alabama's Black Belt. It also profiles the extreme religious fatalism partially responsible for Alabama's dysfunctional citizenship in the Depression era and for years to come. "Alabama Feels Mr. Hoover's Prosperity" deserved broad readership in the 1930s and still warrants reading today.[6]

Something Kennedy had been working on since the summer of 1931 may have softened the sting of the *New Republic* rejection. Under the ruse of writing a Centennial celebration piece for Camden, he had been developing a profile of white behavior in the town. Over the next year he dabbled with it—original research, interviews, multiple rewrites. Finally, he sent it to Grover Hall at the *Montgomery Advertiser*—six pages of double-spaced typescript. Hall said he wanted it. Then he "sat on it." At last, on December 15, "1932 Camden's Centennial Year" appeared in the *Montgomery Advertiser*. This was two weeks shy of being late for the Centennial, though "if it had been late it would not have mattered," Kennedy later recalled, because "there had been no celebration at any point—nobody cared."

Kennedy began the article with a straightforward description of the town's emergence as an extension of British Isles culture. Then he briefly probed Wilcox's geology before profiling the evolution of a Black Belt "culture" with "slave-owning aristocrats." Out of this past, most whites in and around contemporary Camden were a self-conscious "anachronism." They cared not what the world beyond Wilcox did or said—so long as they were left alone. They liked their insularity; inside it they "lived life as an art not as a business."

Here, barely beneath the surface, was more than an invocation of the essential Scotch-Irish persona—"leave me alone." Much like so many other liberal southern intellectuals of the era, as John Edgerton shows in *Speak Now against the Day* (1994), Kennedy also used a knife as sardonically sharp as the one he just had observed in H. L. Mencken's *Prejudices, Sixth Series* (1927). Indeed, although he was miles apart from "the Baltimore Bomber's" racial conservatism and fascism, distaste for FDR, and anti-Semitism, he would gravitate to Mencken as an unknowing mentor in sardonic style, especially regarding southern "aristocracy." Kennedy said that Camden whites "live[d] life as an art." The "artful" ways of white Camden, indeed, included an "indifference to history." Granted, they were alert to certain forces of history—invasion, antiques, and ancestors. Otherwise, they were essentially ahistorical and "decadent"—living as if they were "still in a slave-owning society." They had no interest even in their own Centennial. In this context he seemed hard pressed to profile responsible, contributing citizens. He finally focused on Emmett Kilpatrick.

Most locals who read this piece told him they liked his depiction of their "cavalier" approach to life. They also thought his treatment of their race views to be fully accurate. Indeed, in the name of Camden boosterism, the *Progressive Era* even found a way to reissue the piece as a separate pamphlet. It printed 200 copies; they were gone within four days.[7]

Meanwhile, *New Republic* had circled back around. Despite the earlier rejection, editors thought Kennedy had potential as a contributor, and asked if he could do something on agricultural poverty in the Depression South. Frank Tannenbaum and a few other high-level writers already had provided initial treatments of this crisis. Shortly, the noted agrarian poet, John Crowe Ransom, would publish "Land! Answer to Unemployment," in *Harper's* (1932), followed of course by James Agee's heralded *Let Us Now Praise Famous Men* (1941). *New Republic* understood the significance of the unfolding story. It asked if Kennedy could do a short, pithy overview of the southern cotton culture and the Depression. The article would run with several other solicited essays under the general heading of "The Cotton Kingdom: 1931." He pounced. After a week's further research in data provided by the Extension Service of Alabama Polytechnic Institute, in one late night/early morning session (December 4–5, 1931) he wrote "Six Cent Cotton, A Southern Tragedy." It appeared in the December 16, 1931, issue.

Kennedy began with the core monetary problem across the South: cotton that brought an average of $215 a bale in 1922 brought an average of $27.50 a bale in 1931. The drop to $27.50 a bale translated into just six cents a pound—one huge tragedy. For all types of labor—sharecroppers, renters, and small-scale landowners—costs far outstripped proceeds. But the cropper was the worst off. The average cropper was a man with a wife and two children—a one-mule, one-plow operation. Kennedy calculated finances based on annual production of six bales. At six cents a pound in 1931, the cropper grossed $165. The landowner got one-half, leaving the cropper $82.50. But then the owner subtracted from that amount the cropper's costs for fertilizer, seed, and whatever other "advanced" supplies—coffee, sugar, flour, clothing, tools, equipment—the cropper had to have to get through the previous year. The cropper was left with a shortfall of up to $300, rolled over to the following year as a debt to the owner. To ease his tragedy, the cropper had only two options. If he used no fertilizer for 1931, the owner, of course, subtracted less. If his row crops—corn, peas—did well, he might sell some at twenty-five cents a bushel. Minus these slight possibilities, in 1932 "he will starve or steal . . . perhaps he will do both."

Kennedy then assessed other elements of the "system." He stated that renters and small-scale owners came out not far behind the cropper. *New Republic* had wanted a "straight facts" presentation. But editors gave him slack on one sardonic statement. "Psychologically [the small landowner with a mortgage] is in worse condition [than the cropper] for the possible loss of home and farm. . . . The tenant has nothing to lose but his life."

He then moved to the large landowner, "the man." He prefaced this assessment with the point that across the South—except for the Mississippi Delta—most planters had severely reduced cotton cultivation due to long declining prices. Then he explained owner finances for a 1,000 acre, sharecropped plantation of Wilcox County that "made money" in 1931. The planter had only half of his 1,000 acres in cultivation of any type. In 1931 this produced 150 bales, 75 of which went to croppers. At $27.50 per bale, he grossed $2,062.50. Then Kennedy backed out the planter's expenses: bank interest, $50; taxes, $150; seed, $150; deficit for tenant advances, $300; fertilizer (limited use), $200; tools and equipment, $200; livestock and feed, $300; miscellaneous, $200. These totaled $1,500. He netted $562.50 for the year—his income to support a family of five for 1931. This was $2,000 less than his family's living expenses. For 1932 he hoped the bank could keep him going. Yet this was unlikely. With six-cent cotton, no owners paid back loans. For 1931, banks rolled over loans instead of foreclosing; the collateral for the planters' loans—the land—sat there worthless. So, the following season banks would have far less money to loan. Indeed, as the banks' own indebtedness increased, the South in 1932 and 1933 could see a whole new rash of bank failures.

All this led Kennedy to two conclusions. First, "six-cent cotton is a southern tragedy in its social and economic consequences. It may prove to be as devastating for the southern financial structure as was the Civil War." Second, out of the white South's historic experience with cotton—the low-wage labor system and the addiction to fabulous wealth producing ideological resistance to change—the Black Belt South "will continue to grow cotton in spite of the tragic autumn of 1931." Over time, he missed it on cotton. But in place of cotton, substitute other extractive agriculture dependent on low-wage, low-skill labor, and he got it all too right.[8]

Encouraged by his words appearing in this esteemed national magazine, by late January 1932 Kennedy pitched a following piece to *New Republic*, tracking the southern cotton scene for a mid-1932 report. "Proceed." Over the next seven months he worked on it, while also researching and writing the Camden history article. Again, agricultural economists at Auburn provided much of the raw material. "Tightening Up in the Cotton Belt" appeared in the August 10, 1932, issue of *New Republic*.

Actually, it was conceived as "a report" similar to "Six-Cent Cotton," entitled, tentatively, "Crisis in the Cotton Belt." But the piece wound up differently. Three months out was the 1932 presidential election: the incumbent Republican Herbert Hoover versus the Democratic challenger, Franklin D. Roosevelt. So, he chunked the financial report approach and played off the election season to smash the Republicans.

Without mentioning Hoover, he profiled Republican requests for farmers to stay the course with the Agricultural Marketing Act, which essentially asked them voluntarily to reduce cotton planting so that scarcity would drive prices back up. Then he reviewed statistics known well to any Wilcox planter. In 1928, the South produced 34.6 million bales of cotton; in 1931 that number was 8.9 million. In 1928, southern cotton brought eighteen cents a pound; in 1931 that number was five and a half cents. The Republicans' Agricultural Marketing Act had not worked.

By the end of 1932 things would be worse. With increasing numbers of out-of-work southerners leaving cities for the country, where there was at least dirt for growing vegetables, landowners had virtually free labor, resulting in greater planting of cotton. Granted, much of this happened without expensive fertilizer; the South-wide yield would be about three-fourths the averages over the last five years. Combined with a glut of cotton in warehouses worldwide, however, this yield would see cotton prices decline still further by year's end. Much of the 1932 cotton, he predicted, would go unsold. And what was sold would likely go at between four and five cents a pound.

Behind the economics lived a complex human story. Kennedy gave Wilcox as an example. Recently, he had calculated financial indexes for an average Wilcox cropper family—a man and woman, with two children—working an average of 300 days a year, even more if weather permitted. They tried "to live on [an average total cash expenditure] of forty cents a week . . . with an average maximum *yearly* cash expenditure [of about] $19.20 [2020 value of $290.92]." This got them "three and a half pounds of meat [normally "fatback"] and a peck of meal" per week for the whole family. Three things let some survive: a vegetable garden—thanks to seeds given by the Wilcox County Red Cross (where Kennedy continued as director); firewood from the surrounding woods, usually stolen; and berries from the swamps along the Alabama River.

Wage hands had it "better." In 1928, a Black wage-earning male who worked cotton and corn made on average fifteen dollars a month, plus a month of rations for his family. By mid-1932 the going rate dropped to eight dollars a month, or twenty-seven cents a day, and no rations for anyone. If he managed to work 300 days this year, his annual cash income would be at most eighty dollars. But he had to pay rent or, in rare cases, a monthly mortgage note. That took him down to sixty or seventy dollars: little to feed people on and nothing for health care. Women and children might help chopping cotton at thirty cents a day. But this was seasonal work—maybe fifty days a year.

Then there was "the store." For the second time in a year he did all but identify the store setting as Gee's Bend. "The writer knows of a river bend community that has a population of 2,000 Negroes and five whites." In 1932 Black wage hands in this bend made "thirty cents a day"—a maximum of ninety dollars for the year if they worked 300 days. However, white owners did not pay in cash. Wage hands got their pay through "trade at the local store," which two of the white families owned. "The store's prices" often ran 15 percent to 20 percent higher than Camden or Alberta prices.

As for white landowners, again using Wilcox as an example, they made up 13 percent of the county's total population. Of that group, 5 percent dominated Wilcox farming. They owned the bulk of the cotton-farming land. "They are broke . . . they cannot pay any more than forty to fifty cents a day for labor." Some paid far less. "Some [are] ruthless men criminally exploiting their tenants this year."

Kennedy closed with two dry comments about the whole South. First, although "according to his accustomed standards of living, the landlord is worse off than the tenant . . . actually his standard is still far above that of the tenant. [Yet] his is future is more uncertain than that of the tenant": the tenant still lives on the soil; "the white, his master, merely owns it." Second, from bankers to owners to croppers many rural southerners are dependent on cotton. If it is "three-cent cotton in the fall [of 1932] . . . widespread bankruptcy and starvation" will result. "Probably it will mean riots and bloodshed. Perhaps it will mean the end of the era. The fourth year of the Republicans' 'Abolition of Poverty'"—what President Hoover hypocritically promised if there was but greater individual initiative in America—"continues to tighten up in the cotton belt."[9]

If this transformative—going open, publishing—stage of Kennedy's life emerged from his pent-up anger and sorrow about the Wilcox scene, it surely resulted, too, from the failure of Republican economic policies and how that led to Franklin D. Roosevelt's victory in 1932. Ever the political partisan, Kennedy's reverence for the Democrat Wilson easily transferred to the Democrat Roosevelt and his "first 100 days" of New Deal relief programs to ease the pain of the Depression. Poignantly, what Kennedy wrote about these times underscores something about journalists. For virtually all the successful ones, some compelling human drama serendipitously swirls through their lives. They grab on. And they must stay grabbed on—not always easy for someone of eclectic interests. "It could be war, revolution, pandemic, or some big social movement," according to retired *New York Times* editor, Howell Raines. Regardless, the good ones intuitively grab on. "Over and over they write about it—riding it hard up into the world of publication and impact." And that is a crucial framework for Kennedy's next writing about the Depression years. On May 15, 1932, a singular, low-profile tragedy in Wilcox emerged into a volcanic human drama forever recorded in the history of the Black Belt and the Depression. Though Kennedy had followed this developing story, now he grabbed on to it as never before.[10]

Some eight miles due north of Camden there is a big bend in the Alabama River. Over the eons periodic flooding of the river provided the northern side of that bend some of the most fertile alluvial soil in Alabama. In 1815, a monied fifty-five-year-old North Carolinian, Joseph Gee, who had initially settled in Clarke County, bought from the US government some 10,000 acres of this bend land—at the time still part of the Mississippi territory. Instantly the bend became known as "Gee's Bend." His relatives would inherent the broad tract and farm it with even more slaves. For a while, rising cotton prices made them rich, like a few other families with less imposing enterprises in the Bend—Camdenites such as Irbys, Spurlins, Carsons, and Lairds. In 1845, however, poor management of this wealth had the Gee descendants pass their land, house, and slaves to a rich North Carolina relative, Mark Pettway, to whom they owed a small fortune. Pettway added still more slaves and then passed it to his relatives, who ran the plantation up to 1895, when they sold to a Greene County, Alabama, planter, Duncan Dew. By this time, of course, descendants of Gee and Pettway slaves were sharecroppers.

In 1900, one of Dew's rich friends, Judge Adrian Van de Graaff, made him an offer he could not refuse. The noted Van de Graaff-Jemison family of Tuscaloosa took over. At the height of the myth-laden "prosperity" of the 1920s, while their descendants used an overseer and sharecroppers to make nominal efforts at growing cotton on the place, they seemed more eager about using the Bend for hunting and fishing with Tuscaloosa friends. For their Black cropper community, as Harvey Jackson relates, "it was a place unlike any other in America . . . some were Pettways, but [quoting a Gee's Bend descendant] 'some was something else but they signed their name Pettway.'" They got food, clothing, and supplies from "advancing merchants" either in Camden—via a rough-hewn ferry—or in Catherine and Alberta, some eighteen miles to their north up a dirt road. They were poor, but life was stable; among whites they enjoyed virtually uniform respect as hard-working, efficient, and responsible farmers.

Of course, with the 1929 Crash, things changed. By November 1931, as the Depression kept deepening, cotton was at five cents a pound. Despite Black Benders' strong reputation for productivity and money management, advancing merchants finally gave in to the plummeting price of cotton and the boll weevil, and not only stopped advancing but foreclosed on their "chattel liens"—sharecroppers—in the Bend. They took away plows, livestock, vegetables . . . whatever might help with their own debts. One of these advancing merchants, however, was the exception. And in this way the Benders' sole remaining furnishing agent, in Camden, became "the man." From December 1931 forward he was the lifeline, north across the Alabama River, for at least a hundred families—some seven hundred people of the Bend.[11]

His story is complicated. As much as Benders and their descendants down through the years remembered him as "the man" and as "a good man . . . [who] treated Negroes fair and fine," and Camden whites remembered him as "a regular church goer . . . a decent and gentle soul," other older whites and Blacks of the area told the opposite: "mean . . . bad . . . hurt so many." A short foray into historical memory solves the riddle and, even more, provides a crucial understanding of the noted Gee's Bend tragedy and Kennedy's grabbing on.

For years "the man" has been identified as "E. O. Rentz." And Ephraim O. Rentz certainly existed. Originally from Stuttgart, Germany, the Rentzes were one of seven German immigrant families—mostly Catholic—who moved to Wilcox in the 1840s to try fruit-growing. Those endeavors were no more than modestly successful. By 1914, Ephraim Rentz had a dry goods store in downtown Camden where he was well recognized as a sharecropper furnishing agent as well as a cobbler. But the truth is, Ephraim was not "the man." He went to his grave on April 20, 1924; when Gee's Bend exploded, he had been dead six years. "The man," it turns out, was his brother, Robert Lee Rentz, six years his junior, who ran the business after 1924. And in the oral lore of Wilcox County, Robert got merged with Ephraim, by locals and scholars alike.

In contrast to Ephraim, even as a young man Robert was a pillar in the Camden Presbyterian Church—a Sunday school teacher of twenty years, "one of the youngest elders ever," ultimately "Ruling Elder," and a leading, if often frustrated, Social Gospel voice in Wilcox. The Benders who actually dealt with him, chiefly household heads, saw him not just as "the man" but "the good man." Despite the Depression and his own heavy financial losses, and despite his extreme fatigue as a person with acute kidney failure, he kept advancing them. He knew they had nothing else.[12]

But Robert Rentz was not alone. As head of the Wilcox County Red Cross, Kennedy not only had been orchestrating the free-seeds-for-vegetables project in the Bend, but by early December 1931 had organized a group of six whites, including himself, to do more. They focused on Benders who already had been "closed out"—that is, foreclosed upon. Of these five other whites, none was more important to Kennedy than W. J. (Bill) Jones, Wilcox school superintendent. Since 1929, he and his wife, Joyce, had been delivering what aid they could muster to Bend croppers. In the Red Cross effort Jones had the money role, raising cash gifts, difficult at any time but even more so as the Depression deepened. Another was Bennett Houser Matthews. A descendant of South Carolina Dutch-Scots, a native of Dutch Bend near Autaugaville, Alabama, he had been in Camden since 1907 as owner of Matthews Hardware Store. Successful, civically engaged, indeed, a former head of the Wilcox Red Cross, he had the job of raising noncash gifts, such as food and clothing, for closed-out Benders. In that effort, Robert Rentz was his righthand man.[13]

Important, too, was Edward L. McIntosh. Grandson of Grampian Hills settler Svene McIntosh—distant descendant of one of the most civilized clans of the Scottish Highlands—Edward went to Vanderbilt University then medical school at Emory. As Wilcox County health officer, he long had been "making rounds" in the Bend and seeing patients at Pleasant Grove Baptist Church. In the Red Cross campaign, McIntosh worked with Jones and Rentz on fundraising. The little money they turned up came mostly from McIntosh's appeal—the "word of the doctor"—in approaches to members of the Camden Presbyterian Church, where McIntosh also was a longstanding member. Crucial to the developing Gee's Bend story, too, Robert Rentz was married to Dr. McIntosh's sister, Harriet Louisa (Lula) McIntosh.[14]

Mary Emma Harris, who later married businessman Stanley Godbold, rounded out Kennedy's "Red Cross Six." Product of two wealthy plantation families—McDowells and Harrises—she was the Alabama College–educated Wilcox County social worker. In early 1931, she started with family demographics and other information gleaned from the Wilcox County school system to create a group portrait of the Benders—household heads, families, children. Her files not only estimated how many would die from starvation as closeouts continued with no help, but also documented the ongoing aid distributed to Benders by Kennedy's group. Since the group met periodically at Kennedy's home, Harris's extensive data—"boxes and boxes"—stayed in his garage. Still, how much money they actually turned up and exactly how they spent it, and on whom, remains unclear. Sadly, in late 1986, not long after Kennedy's death and with the Wilcox Red Cross no longer functional, the boxes mistakenly went to the county dump. Still, Wilcox interviews done in the late 1930s and again in the 1970s, plus memories of Kennedy and Jones, converge on one point. They "helped some," if "nothing close to what was needed."[15]

At some point between May 3 and 5, 1932, Dr. McIntosh told his sister, Lula, to take her husband to "the Selma Hospital." Robert's kidney failure had become critical. There on Sunday, May 15, at 1:00 p.m., he died. He was sixty-seven. The next day Camden held a big funeral. Rev. C. A. Campbell presided at Camden Presbyterian; Kennedy assisted. That night Kennedy noted in the diary: "Funeral of Mr. Robert Lee Rentz. A Presbyterian. An elder in the church. One good man."[16]

Throughout the spring and summer of 1932, sixty-six-year-old Lula did her best with Robert's business. This included "advancing" the croppers in the Bend. Still, she had no business management experience. And the more she dug into her husband's records, the more debt she found: one more Black Belt business dying from five-cent cotton. Sometime in September she decided her survival depended on foreclosing in Gee's Bend. She turned the process over to a man who had "done it before," Kennedy recalled, one "Joe Wallace . . . originally from up around Brent [adjacent to Centerville, Alabama].

He had been a [sharecropper] overseer in Wilcox" for some time—the same Joe Wallace who slaughtered the purple martins and the stray dog at the Wilcox Hotel in early 1928 and dabbled in bootlegging. During October and November, Joe Wallace closed out all Benders on the Rentz accounts. Kennedy's group continued with what direct aid they could muster, at times getting distribution assistance from the Alabama National Guard.[17]

As this story unfolded, Kennedy grabbed on. In ten nights of late October and early November 1932, he wrote a piece titled "November Morn, 1932"—a Yaupon story merging insights from "Tightening Up the Cotton Belt" with barely fictionalized narrative of early stages of the closeout. At center is a Black sharecropper named Zeke Allen who lives north of Yaupon town near the river with his wife and two children. Kennedy does not say "the Bend." It is obvious.

Cotton is picked; Zeke produces only a bale and a half rather than his required three. So, the owners of the land, the Van de Graaffs, take it all due to a debt from last year. Yet Zeke thinks he can support his family through the winter because he has vegetables, two cows, some chickens, and two pigs. "No flour, sugar or tobacco," but nobody is going to starve. However, he owes a three-year accumulated debt of $250 to "a furnishing merchant in Yaupon." (Kennedy does not mention by name either the deceased Robert Rentz or his widow, Lula Rentz, who would die in October 1934.) Late in the morning the merchant's "close-out boys" arrive in three wagons.

If the leader of the raid also is nameless, he is described as a "fat red-faced white man with a pistol and four Negroes." They clear out virtually all the vegetables, even sweet potatoes still in the ground, plus all visible tools, equipment, and livestock. One of the cows is in the swamp. The leader: "Zeke, where's that other cow?" Zeke: "Naw, suh, I an' got no mo'." The leader: "Listen you black bastard, don't you lie to me. I'll be back in the morning for the other cow and the rest of those taters."

The merchant only gets $100 out of both raids. Because of his remaining $150 debt, Zeke goes into "involuntary bankruptcy." The family of four now faces winter with no food, no home, and just a few "summer clothes—thin, rotten, ragged . . . and no shoes." "Maybe God or the Red Cross will help."

Kennedy wrote this with Black and white Yaupon dialect reined in from the dialect of "Homo Africanus." If the concluding sentence—"God or the Red Cross"—comes off as flat and simplistic, the piece still is strong in its starkness. Neither *New Republic* nor *Christian Century* took it. No doubt they wanted more of an edge on the tone as opposed to "just the facts," as riveting as the facts were.[18]

Disappointed, Kennedy let go of the most compelling story around him. He moved to an all-white Yaupon tale. Written in January 1933, "Cremation" tells of a heavily indebted, poor white deciding to "ride the rails" to a better life. Well outside of town he teams up with an equally broke college professor. Undoubtedly modeled on Emmett Kilpatrick, the professor drives the poor white crazy quoting Shakespeare. The cacophony of Shakespearean and poor-white language is novel. In an attempt to hop a slow-moving train, the professor keels over from a heart attack—dead. Fearful of having his escape from Yaupon debtors complicated by "who killed the professor," the poor white deposits the body in an empty wood-framed church and sets the whole thing afire. Another train slows on the steep grade. He jumps on, heading down the rails to a Depression life beyond Yaupon. Despite the intriguing interplay of language, it is a weak piece. Nothing suggests that Kennedy submitted it.[19]

Through late winter and early spring of 1933 Red Cross work and ARP matters dominated Kennedy's days. But in early May he tried again. He produced two stories set outside the Black Belt. Again, he focused on uneducated whites. "Bill Dickens" is the story of a courageous door-to-door vegetable hawker in Conecuh County, Alabama. People buy his vegetables either to shut him up or because they enjoy his banter. At best offering local color but with no compelling plot, the piece went to the file drawer.[20]

In early June he wrote "Willie Watson." As a product of South Carolina, Kennedy knew the mill-town scene. His parents in North Carolina also sent him newspaper clippings telling of the Depression's effects on mill workers, much like Wilcox sharecroppers. In mill worker Willie Watson's case, two years of unemployment leads him to kill himself with a Colt .38. Kennedy's vivid description of Willie's funeral—the contrast between a rich man's funeral and a poor man's—is compelling. Much like "Bill Dickens," however, the story never moves beyond its Depression setting and strong local color. Indeed, Kennedy seems to have lost focus on his main point. The world increasingly heard tales of white Wall Street executives jumping off tall buildings as a "solution" to their Crash losses, which turned out to be more unfounded rumor than reality. But amid this Kennedy thought the world needed a reminder that Depression-desperate poor folks, Black and white, suffered mightily, too. At any rate, to the file drawer.[21]

Yet he was getting stronger. With each new effort the key components—compelling story, terse tone, effective dialogue, vivid if concise description—found refinement. He just needed to get them all together in one piece.

Despite continued tinkering with the Gee's Bend story, in late May 1933 he grabbed for the already infamous Scottsboro case, involving nine Negro youths falsely accused of raping two white women in Decatur, Alabama. The case had moved to retrial. Wilcox was like everywhere else in the South: Black and white people followed the case day by day. And out of such local conversations Kennedy crafted a Yaupon vignette on white reactions set in the "gallery" of a small Yaupon store. Despite a range of conservative white opinions—reflecting Kennedy's "killing" and retributive justice themes as well as the paramount fear of whites losing control—he reveals their convergence on one perception: Negro as threat. Here are excerpts.

> Barber: "The [electric] chair is too good for them son-uh-bitches . . . oughta be burned with slow fire . . ."
> Old Man: "If they had been lynched we wouldn't have had that uprisin' in Tallapoosa County [Camp Hill] last fall . . ."
> Lawyer: "You couldn't convict a white man on the evidence offered in that Decatur trial . . . But I am afraid that the United States Supreme Court is finally going to send back this case on the grounds that there were no negroes in the jury. When that happens . . . it'll . . . put niggers on the jury and the first thing you know they'll be wanting to vote . . ."
> Barber: "Slow fire is what I favor . . ."

Stark, pithy, honest, and distinctively aggressive, the piece warranted the sardonic title Kennedy gave it, "One Point of View." In his June 28, 1933, submission letter to Bruce Blevin, *New Republic* editor, he admitted: "The sketch is little more than a literal transcript of conversations I have heard in recent weeks regarding the Scottsboro case." Blevin rejected it with a standard "does not fit with our current needs" statement. *New Republic* already had published on Scottsboro. But there could have been other reasons for the rejection. Kennedy wrote it as a play script with all dialogue, no narration. Limited narration would have given it more cohesion. It also is possible that a high-level publisher of 1933 would have found its grotesqueness, while accurate, to be unnecessarily inflammatory. The manuscript was more the start of something, rather than a finished work ready for publication.[22]

Meanwhile, moving on from Scottsboro—to which he would return—Kennedy finally grabbed back onto the Bend story. Unlike "November Morn, 1932," he excluded the role of "the furnishing merchant." As he later said to any number of journalists and social scientists, "I do not blame that lady [Mrs. Rentz]. She had no choice." In 1983, he expanded: "Those [Gee's Bend] people were victims of history—how far back do you want to go? . . . If you want to place blame, place it on slavery and sharecropping. Blame it on the people who had the power and ignored these abuses. Blame it on Republicans for the mess they created—their greed gave us that Depression which made the tenant's problems so much worse . . . *All of that.*"[23]

Titled "The Face of the Poor," this Yaupon story gives a Bender the chance to tell the world what he thinks has happened. The scene is drawn directly from the front steps of the ARP manse on Broad Street in Camden, or Yaupon town. A peddler knocks on the door. He is "six feet in height, slightly stout, light brown in color, a small moustache upon his lip, intelligent eyes. . . . You knew this man had a story to tell. You knew instinctively the misery, despair, the desperation of his spirit."

This peddler says he's selling eggs at ten cents a dozen. The man asks where he is from. "Gee's Bend," comes the reply.

> Man: ". . . that's where they closed out so many folks last fall. Did they get you?"
> Peddler: "Capt'n, they gettin' me now. Tak'n' everything I got . . . Ol' man Welch tell us we could keep our mules and cows and plows and four barrels of grain. But he done changed. He sho' God done changed . . . They come an' git my cows and mules and plows yestiddy . . . White folks, I'm tellin' you. The Lawd gonna even this thing up one day . . . Us ain't askin' nobody to give us nuthin'. Us just askn' for a chance to farm. But we can't farm without mules and plows and a little corn and [fatback] meat."

The peddler has a large gunnysack with him—packed full. The man inquires of its contents; the peddler says it is his last food—a bushel of corn he is taking to be ground into meal.

> Man: "What are you going to do this winter when you eat up that bushel?"
> Peddler: "God knows, white folks."

That last phrase—"God knows, white folks"—holds the point of the vignette. A basic, if tragic, conversation on a wrenching subject reaches a perplexing dénouement. Unlike Kennedy's earlier conclusions, mostly literal, this one challenges the reader subtextually. Is the peddler counting on God to will white folks into helping him and others through the winter? Is he saying, this winter my life—my whole family's life—ends and it is the fault of white folks? Is it the first of these, but failing that, the second? This is potent storytelling. In pondering "'God knows, white folks,'" the reader further engages the complex tragedy at Gee's Bend.

No doubt smarting from *New Republic*'s last rejection, Kennedy submitted "The Face of the Poor" to *Christian Century*. Charles Clayton Morrison took it immediately. Here would be the first published depiction of the Gee's Bend tragedy. Because the Depression included so many horrific human predicaments, despite *Christian Century*'s relatively large American and transatlantic readership, the piece garnered little attention. Still, "The Face of the Poor," published on June 21, 1933, marked a threshold in Kennedy's writing. That was the day he finally birthed "Yaupon" as a published idea.[24]

Yet again diverted by eclectic interests, he failed to follow up. By June 1933, President Roosevelt's New Deal had a Civilian Conservation Corps (CCC) camp seventeen miles south of Camden in the lumber mill town of Vredenburgh. Here, some three hundred young and out-of-work white Alabamians lived in quickly constructed huts while working on reforestation projects. The New Deal provided them food and thirty dollars a month apiece, as well as the opportunity for Sunday morning chapel services. US Army chaplains organized such services and enlisted local ministers for the preaching. A military chaplain approached Kennedy for help. What happened thereafter Kennedy wrote up and sent to *Christian Century*. In "Military Interlude," published on September 3, 1933, he explained how he identified himself to "the Captain" as a "Christian-Socialist" and offered to go to the camp "and give the boys a little socialism" and "a sermon against war." "After all, it is in the New Testament." "The Captain" responded: "'Sir, I really believe you are trying to make sport of me. . . . I do not understand you at all." One can only surmise that Charles Clayton Morrison ran the piece to show fellow Christian Socialists how much work they still had to do. In the process, too, Kennedy let *Century* readers know he remained part of the fold—for the time being, at least.[25]

Even further removed from sharecropping and the Bend, he experimented with a non-Yaupon story set at the Oak Hill home of Sam and Matt Boykin, where Bill and Joyce Jones spent every weekend. In September 1933, Joyce's brother, Edward (Edgar) Sadler Carothers—a political science professor at the University of Alabama—brought home a faculty colleague . He was a New Yorker, a Jew, a philologist, and a psychic. Ren and Mary were invited to dinner. Drawing on the after-dinner conversation on the front porch, Kennedy created a fictional conversation profiling social tensions between the two worlds of 1930s Tuscaloosa: its backward, Old South, nineteenth-century "town world," where many of the rich and educated either tolerated or openly supported the Klan, and its progressive, twentieth-century, "university world" including any number of northeastern Jewish intellectuals. It was a compelling topic, yet weak writing pervaded the piece. To the file cabinet. Still, two years hence, a notable Tuscaloosa tragedy would return him to these same "town" and "university" comparisons, and his writing then would be more up to the cause.[26]

Meanwhile, *Christian Century* got him back on track. In mid-October 1933, it asked for a follow-up on the Depression in the Black Belt. Between Thanksgiving and Christmas, he did initial drafts, finishing it between 10:00

p.m. and 2:00 a.m., December 31–January 1. Completing "Note on Cotton" was his New Year's "celebration."

Here is Yaupon fiction probing the "decadence of agricultural capitalism" in the Black Belt amid New Deal programs designed not just to help farmers survive the Depression but to boost farm profitability over the long term. Abuse of the programs—cheating—was rampant. To profile such greed and deceitfulness, however, Kennedy focused on a small-scale white planter with a conscience. The story opens just like the actual event behind it. At the Yaupon drugstore the preacher encountered one Wilson Jeter, whom he had known for some time. Mr. Jeter no longer could afford to smoke "store-bought" cigarettes. He lit a rolled "Hoover dust" and began to unload on the preacher.

In 1914, Mr. Jeter had inherited 350 acres of cotton land, and ever since had farmed it with eight Negro cropper families—"successfully." In December 1929, still foreseeing no long-term problems, he borrowed $2,400 from Union Life Insurance to buy a new car and get his son started at the University of Alabama. But the Depression deepened—and cotton proceeds continued to plummet. Like the cropper, Jeter saw his debts mounting. He wound up owing not just $2,600 to Union Life but also $250 to "the Yaupon bank" and $3,500 to a local mercantile and feed store, Wilson & Wilson. Shortly, all of them "called" on their money.

With a lawyer, Mr. Jeter managed to hide some of this indebtedness. Then, even though his total property was worth considerably under $3,000, the lawyer showed him how to borrow money from two New Deal farm revival programs: $3,000 from the Federal Land Bank and $1,300 from the Farm Credit Administration. Though deceitful, his loan applications won approval. With that money he negotiated a scaled-back, $2,100 payoff of the Union Life debt. But as he and the preacher sat there in the drugstore, he had not yet paid it. If he did, he would have only $1,200 remaining to pay off both the bank and Wilson &Wilson. And they refused to negotiate. "It ain't right . . . Wilson & Wilson . . . have probably made $10,000 off me . . . but they ain't no worse than the bank.'"

Caught, and feeling guilty about his deceitfulness, Mr. Jeter finally decided on another course. He would return "the 'Government money'" and "'tell Union Life and the bank to come get [his farm]. If there's anything left, Wilson &Wilson can have it. God knows where I'll go or what I'll do. . . . [But] let 'em come and get it.' Mr. Jeter spat on the floor."

This is not profound. But *Christian Century* wanted exploration of the Depression in the Black Belt. And Kennedy clearly saw the New Deal as opportunity for the deceitful as well as the deserving. Just as important, "Note on Cotton," published January 14, 1934, in the *Century*, got him refocused.[27]

From late January to early March, he focused on the relationship between Black sharecropper poverty and white business morality by reworking his earliest Yaupon effort, "Homo Africanus," profiling a planter-merchant, Amos Reese, and an old sharecropper, Mary. Verb tense moved from past to present. A few amorphous places became concrete. The first version left vague the precise location of the conversation between the narrating preacher and the planter-merchant. The revision clearly placed the conversation in "the stuffy little office at the rear of his store." The first version implied Mary to be a cropper; the new one had "Mary and a grandson down by the river cropping a small piece of land." He increased Mr. Reese's markup on goods at his store from "33 and 1/3%" to "50%." Initially, he had Mr. Reese charging undefined "interest" as sharecroppers' debts rolled over. He strengthened this to "8% or more."

The first version certainly depicted sharecroppers locked into a feudalism in which money never changes hands and debt just endures. Still, he amplified this—describing how Mary could only "spend" proceeds from her share of the cotton crop as credit in Mr. Reese's store. Likewise, the first version depicted Mr. Reese's white Christian rationalization for this greed. Negroes are "'like children,' he said, 'we have to keep the books for them.'" Since Negroes could neither read nor write and had no capital—only their own labor—the "system is good." In fact, Mr. Reese pronounces, it could be "the Lord's own plan for Negroes here in the South." Hence Kennedy's sarcastic descriptive, "the metaphysics of the Black Belt economy." But the revisions intensified Mr. Reese's enthusiasm. Overly eager, he repeated, "The system is good," "I do not know of a better system," and "I don't take advantage of them." To this defensive assertion, Kennedy also heightened the preacher's sardonic reaction: "I would think so . . . a carefully evolved system."

By contrast, Kennedy left unchanged one of the simplest, yet deepest, elements of the vignette. Mary addressed the planter-merchant as "Mas' Amos"—not "Mas' Reese." This decision has a backstory. In the Black Belt of the 1930s—to an extent even today—Wilcoxons of all hues could show respect for nonfamily members they "trusted" through calling them by first names preceded by appropriate formal titles. "Mr. John," "Capt'n Bob," "Miss Eva," "Dr. Ken," "Cuh'nu'l Jasper." Whites did this to whites, Blacks to Blacks, Blacks to whites. But in a segregated society, whites to Blacks was another matter. A white might use "Uncle Lloyd" or "Aunt Sue" when addressing an older Black known affectionately and trusted. More rare was a white addressing a Black as "Mr. Bob."

Still, if a Black person lived outside the white person's affection circle yet well inside his "trust" circle, and the Black had age on the white, "Mr." might well be part of the white's addressing the Black. As late as 1997 the most revered carpenter and old-house restorer in Wilcox County was a fifty-four year-old Black man. Many saw him as "the wood artist." Here, he can be known as "John McGinnis." No educated white Wilcox teenager—rich or not, indeed, using "nigger" or not—dared call him anything but "Mr. John." Not just to his face but to others, Black and white. "Nope, we're doing it this way. That's what Mr. John said to do."

Such was the deep tapestry of language woven out of personalism and race in Alabama's Black Belt. Of course, the tapestry had dead-serious social implications. Parallel to the Black Belt white's "rage to explain"—storytelling—ran an equally strong tradition of nonspecific oral communication regarding power. Titles such as "Mr." or "Aunt" easily might reflect a counter, subconversational message about authority and trust. Think of one exchange of words conveying two simultaneous conversations. Kennedy had this mastered. He had grown up with it in Newberry and Abbeville counties. The Scotch-Irish of those counties brought it to Wilcox. All around him, daily, he experienced it.

It evolved into a key strength of his writing. In the original version of the furnishing-store vignette, Kennedy let Amos Reese speak to Mary with kind words and soft tones. He called her "Aunt Mary." Mary in turn addressed him as "Mas' Amos." Fortunately, Kennedy did not change this when he revised. The "Mas'" instead of "Mr." is obvious—a carryover from slavery days. But her also calling him by his first name suggested the two not only had known each other for a long time but had "trust" in their relationship. Still, in view of what Kennedy revealed about the actual financial arrangement between the two, we may ask: was their "trust" true? and even more, should there have been "trust"?

Put it another way. Though Kennedy was certain Amos Reese misused Mary and her grandson, did Amos Reese understand this? Had his racial paternalism merged so thoroughly with his skewed Christian values that he was oblivious to his transgressions? Kennedy saw him as hypocritical. But consciously? unconsciously? Had he sinned? by omission? by commission? And how, inwardly, did Mary view him? As a good man? a bad man but a practical necessity requiring such a one-sided deal?

These dilemmas formed the core of Black Belt "bookkeeping." Here, Kennedy blended his newfound device of ambiguity with his intuitive feel for what social scientists call "symbolic interaction" in deep South communication. As a result, to digest such engaging stuff at the furnishing store leaves one no choice but to remember what Kennedy wanted remembered: the complex history leading to the human tragedy of sharecropping in Yaupon and other, real-life Black Belt counties. Since 1930 he had taught himself a lot. The "Homo Africanus" sketch now evolved sardonically to "Book

Keeping." He dropped it in the mail. With no revisions *Christian Century* published it on March 28, 1934.[28]

Right away the *New Republic* took note. The *Century* had allowed him 1,300 words for "Book-Keeping"; *New Republic* now offered him 1,320 words for another cotton belt update. "What's Happening in the Cotton Belt," his most extensive national article so far, appeared in the April 18, 1934, issue.

He began by reminding readers of FDR's actions designed to help the cotton South: the 1933 Bankhead-Jones Act for crop reduction as well as relief and jobs with the Federal Emergency Relief Act (FERA), the CCC, the Works Progress Administration (WPA), and the Civil Works Administration (CWA). Then he weighed results of these steps. Paying farmers to reduce cotton cultivation—thus restricting supply and increasing demand—indeed raised cotton prices. They moved from five cents a pound in the depths of 1932 to ten or twelve cents a pound in late 1933. He also noted relief money now going to small-scale landowners, broke before the advent of crop-reduction benefits, as well as to sharecroppers no longer able to farm.

But in this relief he also saw long-term complications. No structural changes were occurring. "Remove federal relief and acreage control and the cotton country would at once sink [back into] primitive conditions of life and society." Most knew this. But most farm laborers as well as "landlords" increasingly "had confidence that the federal government will be there to take care of them." Indeed, his Christian Socialism now showing some cracks, Kennedy saw this as an ominous sign not just for the Black Belt but for all of American agriculture. Would capitalism and laws of supply and demand never again be deciding factors? Would most rural landowners become dependent on a quasi-socialistic economy—government subsidies, government manipulation of market—despite their hypocritical protests to the contrary?

Kennedy also saw systemic problems on the racial front. In the cotton belt, where most croppers were Black, many white landowners cheated their croppers on the federal crop-reduction money. This only increased racial stress. Similarly, federal jobs programs offered wages impossible for most Black Belt businessmen and farmers to match. Again, given that most Black Belt labor was Black, this severely worsened race relations in cotton areas. And long-term implications were awful.

Broad-based racial progress in the Black Belt, he thought, only could derive from interracial politics. But whites vehemently opposed this. Interracial politics represented one more in a long line of threats to their core values: not only to be isolated and autonomous, but themselves, the white minority, to be in full control of the Black majority. To block interracial politics, they wanted race relations polarized. And they had a sinister way of achieving this. To keep whites pitted against Blacks, they publicly urged that federal relief pay for croppers would defy "the sacred law of supply and demand, 'ruin the niggers,' and afford aid and comfort to the Communists." Of course, the flip side of such sinister behavior was for landowners to keep raking in their own federal relief dollars through the crop-reduction program, and if that furthered the racial divide, so much the better.

For the National Urban League's *Opportunity: Journal of Negro Life*, both the short- and long-term implications of "What's Happening in the Cotton Belt" were frightful; the journal longed for what Kennedy thought would not happen, a reasserted Populist Party strategy of Black and white downtrodden rallying to create a "new" political movement. Much later, Gilbert Fite and other historians profiled Kennedy's vivid description of extreme Black poverty: "Homes without a match or a cake of soap . . . naked children." But this article also is striking for Kennedy's prescient historical perspective on the New Deal—*as* the New Deal unfolded. Back in January he had told his college friend, Washington, DC, attorney, Andrew M. Hood, that FDR "must go further to the left." But while Kennedy said that, he also recognized the double-edged sword of the New Deal's transformative implications for government and economics. In May 1934 commencement speeches to Black students and faculty of Snow Hill Institute and white students and faculty of Wilcox County High School, he explained how "liberals" supported government expansion explicit in the developing Tennessee Valley Authority (TVA), while "conservatives . . . like Alabama Power" resented its "encroachment on free enterprise." This debate, he said, profiled how much "we are living in a . . . day of transition . . . and new ideas"—where he, personally, was a "liberal." Yet in "What's Happening in the Cotton Belt" this "liberal" also underscored an oft-told irony: the conservative consequences of liberal reform. For all their need in defeating "the bony hand of hunger," New Deal agriculture policies would intensify systemic problems of race and economics.

Given all that, nevertheless, in concluding "What's Happening in the Cotton Belt," he was pleased to note that FDR advisor Harry Hopkins had just completed a meeting in Atlanta with southern relief workers. They talked about revising the Bankhead-Jones Act to increase productivity and independence among Black farmers—people like the Benders. To the Wilcox liberal, this held the specter of much needed structural change.[29]

On April 16, 1934, the *Selma Times-Journal* protested. "Mr. Kennedy draws a . . . wholly unrepresentative [portrait]. . . . The southern negro tenant can boast of . . . as many of life's blessings as he could in any recent period in the South's history." On April 23, it printed Kennedy's response: "Sir, if you will come down to get me in your automobile and pick me up we will go over into Gee's Bend on the Alabama River and I will prove the truth of the picture I presented. And there are hundreds of Gee's Bends."[30]

Fueled by the Selma paper's manipulative myth, he plunged into a Yaupon follow-up—a more personal portrait of how Negroes lost out despite the New Deal's best intentions. With restrained dialect, it had a Black woman, "Cora Belle Jones," calling at the home of an old Yaupon County scion, "Capt'n Bendell." She was not a cropper. Capt'n Bendell let her and her son, Eugene, rent one of his shacks for $1.25 a month. They were months behind in rent. He was patient.

The government cut off Eugene from his WPA work because he had malaria and couldn't work. Cora Belle asked Capt'n Bendell for money to take Eugene to the doctor. Severely damaged, too, by the Depression, Bendell could not help. "He owed the butcher, and the tax collector and the lone $5.00 bill his right hand crumpled in his trousers' pocket as he talked must run him until the bank relented and gave him another loan."

Bendell advised Cora Belle to go the doctor anyhow. The doctor said he was broke, too. He needed cash to treat people. Still, if she got the director of the Yaupon relief office to promise payment, the doctor said he would treat Eugene. Bendell visited the director on behalf of Cora Belle and Eugene. The director said he was out of federal money to pay doctors. Bendell pressed him. Ultimately, the director promised to take another Black—a healthy one—off WPA work and redirect that money to the doctor to care for Eugene. The doctor gave Cora Belle an appointment for Eugene. But "Eugene died before the doctor comes."

Here was a sorrowful vignette out of daily life. It showed that, however humane some whites were, and despite significant federal government effort, the Black poor's problems of money and health care were so rooted in a past of slavery and sharecropping that they would not be solved with the current version of the New Deal. The article itself also was rooted in intimate reality. The nonfictional Cora Belle Nettles worked one morning a week in the Kennedy home. Her son had malaria from road work in the swamps up near Miller's Ferry. By the time Kennedy got the federal relief office in Camden to approve a doctor's fee—and, without Kennedy's prior knowledge, eliminating aid for another Negro—the son died. This ode on the death of Cora Belle's son appeared in the *Century* on August 8, 1934, under the title "Before the Doctor Comes"; when she died in November 1967, Kennedy gave a eulogy.[31]

If this ode revolved around pathos and concrete personal tragedy, in his next piece he returned to the abstract and metaphorical, and possibly to a grudge. Unlike his previous explorations in literary device, while Kennedy conceived this article in his usual solitary nocturnal sessions, a tiny set of Wilcoxons, increasingly appreciative of his now open attacks, provided curious midwifing. And out of this odyssey was born, too, what might be called the Wilcox Roundtable.

His renewed exercise in the abstract, oddly, started with baseball. In 1928, Black Belt baseball—long of hamlet and church leagues, Black and white—surged forward when the Bloch family, originally of Camden, launched a new team for the Southeastern League, the Selma Clover Leafs. The Blochs sent Kennedy season tickets, gratis. Initially, he was elated; via rides with Sam McNeill and Clark Jones, he rarely missed a game. But that enthusiasm proved temporary.

In 1933, as national journalism and New York publishers increasingly depicted the Depression South as the most backward place in America, some Black Belt leaders associated with the Selma Chamber of Commerce divined that this distinction was "bad for business." So, rather than advocating structural solutions to Black Belt problems, they joined with the *Selma Times Journal* to change the geographical descriptive "Black Belt" to something locally known as "successful" and "pleasant." Playing off the more lively, successful brand of the "Clover Leafs," not to mention the verdant green of some clover and the vibrant ruby-red of crimson clover, they initiated a campaign to evolve "Black Belt" to "Clover Belt." Here was the type of marketing "solution" to social problems birthed by the emergent Madison Avenue mentalities of the 1920s and not coincidentally the type of spin used by Republicans to peddle the lie that their extreme deregulation policies had not helped cause the Depression.

Ultimately, the pervasive opposition to *any* change harbored by most white Black Belters doomed the shift to "Clover Belt." But amid the campaign, in August 1934, Kennedy found a "Clover-cause" endorsement by the *Selma Times Journal* "the most sinister" of responses to the Depression, as well as pointing to even deeper flaws in Black Belt life. Indeed, this editorial ultimately provoked him to new thought about the lack of conscience among certain Black Belt elites—something initially surfacing in his Camden centennial piece.[32]

In three early August sessions, he drafted a profile of these self-styled "aristocrats" as an extension of "Old South civilization." Despite the end of slavery and the advancing growth of southern cities and industry, in 1934 the Black Belt remained overwhelmingly their realm—one of agriculture, poor Black labor, and large tracts of land owned by a wealthy few. Despite all the problems of cotton, they stuck with it, occasionally "diversifying" with another extractive enterprise—harvesting pine trees. While their wealth base was in the countryside, these "southern gentlemen" continued their "Old South" influence over significant appendage towns, notably Selma, Montgomery, and Mobile.

If neither "intellectual" nor "liberal," these "aristocrats" nevertheless were shrewd and "phlegmatic" (unfeeling) in protecting their control. They lived as a distinct racial minority. Still, they stayed in power with "brilliantly formed political alliances," allowing them to manipulate city, county, state, and indeed federal government policies. Intellectual honesty mattered not to them. Money and power were their strengths. Easily they railed against "government" while using "government" to their own financial benefit. Blowhards for democracy and free enterprise, they practiced the opposites. And they despised change. Most even rejected the superficial step of changing their area's name from "Black Belt" to "Clover Belt," not out of offense at its manipulative motivation, just that it represented change. Their history as a cotton kingdom with slave labor at the bottom and white elite at the top—adorned by the myth of the Cavalier South—provided a potent sense of self for these "phlegmatic" modern-day "cotton-snobs."

He then finished off with the same sharp razor he wielded in the 1932 Camden essay. These "aristocrats" live in a "civilization" best defined as "art." Their "art" is uncaring of realities beyond their realm. "They are the antebellum South with automobiles, bathtubs, electric lights, tenant labor.... [They] are an anachronism splendidly indifferent to opinion of outsiders.... When [Black Belt culture] passes[,] one of the most civilized sections of the country will have passed." They alone in America are not subject to "the virus of American standardization." Their values descend from the cotton-plantation values of their "sturdy Scotch-Irish and English" forebears, similar to such values wherever in the world cotton thrived. They live off another man's labor. They want "maximum enjoyment" for "minimum effort" on their own part. And they want to be left alone.

A Black Belt aristocrat—or wannabe—could read these words as an agrarian-elite manifesto, smile smugly, and raise a bourbon highball to the brethren. One not so oriented might peek between the lines and find incisive ridicule: the unreality, hypocritical behavior, and false sense of security making up the artistry of "Black Belt aristocrats." Pivotal words such as "civilization," "virus," "standardization," indeed "art" then reveal their sardonic flip sides.

At Kennedy's request, Emmett Kilpatrick—on university holiday and at home in Camden—read this first draft. Kilpatrick thought his friend "devoted too much energy to orchestrating an intrigue of ambiguity and not enough to a frontal attack.... Listen Kennedy, some people will think you have forgotten Gee's Bend and become one of these moronic rural [Fugitive] romanticists." Whether enjoying the ambiguity—or using it for slight cover, or both—Kennedy rejected the suggestion.

Recent readings also encouraged Kennedy to think he was onto something. When he and Justice Jones attended the Vanderbilt Institute for Rural Preachers, in May 1930, they sat in on a session in which Birmingham liberal

Henry Edmonds contrasted the Vanderbilt agrarians—over in the English department, just across the campus from Vanderbilt's divinity school—with those who saw the South so differently, the Chapel Hill liberals. Edmonds read passages from a recent issue of *Social Forces*. He talked about Howard W. Odom's sociological vision for moving the South beyond its retarding rural traditions and mythologies.

Based on his "Record of Reading," here likely was Kennedy's introduction to these opposing designs for the southern future. After the Vanderbilt trip he read Odom's *American Epoch: Southern Portraiture in the National Picture* (1930). Then in early 1934 he read the agrarian "manifesto"—The Twelve Southerners' *I'll Take My Stand* (1930)—as well as William Terry Couch's *Culture in the South* (1934), comments on the modern South by a wide range of liberals and conservatives. Although he found reinforcement from the Chapel Hill liberal viewpoint, he also found the conservative opinion—which Emmett wanted extracted—important to explore for purposes of contrast.[33]

On the night of September 7, 1934, a lot closer to home, he seems to have encountered still further reinforcement for his subtlety. It happened this way.

As he had passed the draft to Kilpatrick, Kennedy had extracted a promise: Emmett would "keep his mouth shut" about the piece. Well, the vociferous one could not. In "some detail," recalled the Kennedys' next-door neighbor at the time, "Emmett described it to me, and I was taken by the whole thing." After much urging, in fact, the neighbor suggested Kennedy come to her house for dinner along with some well-read friends—"all [of whom] he knew"—for him to get further feedback. "Reluctantly," Kennedy agreed.

This lady on the other side of the hedge was thirty-three-year-old Viola Jefferson Goode Liddell. Only three months earlier had she married Will Lithgow Liddell, descendant of Highlander Scot "Reconstruction Yankees" and owner of the massive, white-columned structure next door to the Kennedys' home. The new Mrs. Liddell had a storied heritage. Her father's Goode family included noted Virginia tobacco farmers intermarried with the Jeffersons of Monticello. Her mother's Gaston family traced to the Duke of Orléans and the highest level of sixteenth-century French society. Since the late 1830s, her plantation family had anchored the northern boundary of Wilcox, at Gastonburg. Before marrying Will, she had been a divorcée with one child, teaching English at the white high school in Camden. Before that, in 1920, she had graduated as a star literature student from Judson College, at Marion—some fifty miles north of Camden in Perry County—and entered into a short-term marriage with Oxford Stroud, also of the Gastonburg area. When she married Will, "there was inside [her] far more than a glowing ember" about becoming "a writer." As a businessman and farmer, Will "had not an aesthetic bone in his body." But that August 1934 he was smitten with his new, beautiful wife and fellow Presbyterian—they had met at church. And "if [she] wanted to write, [he] wanted her to write." Will's commitment never wavered.[34]

The invitation list for Viola and Will Liddell's "Kennedy dinner gathering" included Helen Burford Lambert, a Judson graduate descended from the nearby Rock West Burford family, which had been among the few wealthy, English-stock Virginia and Georgia planters to settle Wilcox. The list also included Lena Miller Rogers, a member of Kennedy's church and whose marriage to J. D. Albritton would be performed by Kennedy in February 1935. While Helen cautiously voted for FDR, Lena was a New Deal enthusiast whose loyalty survives her to this day via the photo-portrait of John F. Kennedy on the Albrittons' living room wall. Lena's sister-in-law, Clyde Purifoy Miller, also came. This dear friend of Kennedy was nevertheless "lukewarm, at best" on FDR.

Also on hand was Mary Emma Harris—the Wilcox social worker instrumental in Kennedy's Red Cross outreach in the Bend—as well as her husband, Stanley David Godbold, a lawyer, banker, musician, art collector, and civic leader. Stanley was a conservative Democrat already shifting away from FDR; Mary stuck with FDR. There, too, was Emmett Kilpatrick, whose "broken word" had given rise to the event. In early August 1934, less than a month before the "Kennedy dinner gathering," he had returned to Alabama for the job at Troy State Teacher's College; he now weekended in the Camden home he had inherited. Since "long before Will," Viola had known Emmett as "eccentric"—his "left index finger sporting an oversized amethyst ring." As for his drinking, Viola had experience in getting the "serious conversation out of him before he got too far along, for after that he was too dominating to be enjoyable."

Finally, the evening included the Harvard-trained psychology professor who ushered his old friend, Kilpatrick, through the door at Troy, Robert Hugh Ervin. Like Kilpatrick, from Troy he regularly returned to Camden where his brother, cattleman Samuel James Ervin Jr., still lived in the inherited antebellum showplace, "Countryside." Although Irvin supported FDR, his greater passion was famed American psychologist John B. Watson and his breakthrough 1920s concept of "behavioralism." "As much as Emmett talked about himself," Viola later recalled, "Hugh talked about behavior"—his ideas about "behavior and the human personality."[35]

With Mary Kennedy begging off, the group of ten gathered on Saturday night, September 7, 1934. After dinner, Kennedy read his draft of "Black Belt Aristocrats." Watsonian behavioralism, the New Deal, the "Clover Belt," Gee's Bend, Kilpatrick's dissent from his comrade's double-entendre obliqueness: no doubt some of these, if not all, were brought to bear on the manuscript. But there is no way to be sure; "much discussion followed" is the only record of the discourse. Still, the evening is documentably significant in that it *occurred*. Even more, it occurred again and again—normally about four times a year—for the next two decades. At times it focused on a book all had read, including John Watson's *Behavioralism* (1922). More often it discussed a Ren Kennedy manuscript or, further out, one of Viola Liddell's. A few sessions had guest intellectuals or artists. Call it Viola Liddell's Wilcox Roundtable. And the question Kennedy had asked himself after that buoyant night some seven years earlier at the Dexters' place, when he first met Emmett, now had been answered. Despite torments and tragedies of race and poverty, and Red Cross challenges, Viola's group showed him that, after all, Wilcox offered white people who were anything but "broken aristocrats."

As for "Black Belt Aristocrats," undoubtedly bolstered by this first meeting at Viola's, and convinced he indeed had the writing "right"—that is, that Kilpatrick was wrong—in late September Kennedy submitted it to the journal Henry Edmonds had read from at Vanderbilt: Howard W. Odum's *Social Forces*. According to Alabama journalist Gould Beech, who did a Rosenwald fellowship in sociology at Chapel Hill in 1937, the staff in the Social Science Research Institute had clear memory of how Odum "jumped on" Kennedy's compelling idea that the Black Belt was as much an "idea" as a "place." After circulating it among advanced students, Odum fast-tracked its publication in the October 30, 1934, issue. As far as southern change went, *Social Forces* stood as the foremost journal in America. Kennedy's was the lead article in that issue.[36]

On October 19, Kennedy received advance copies of the issue. By return mail he asked the *Social Forces* staff to mail offprints to close friends. Kilpatrick asked for more. Enthralled over the "Clover Belt" reference, he mailed one to the *Selma Times Journal*. The paper reacted . . . in print. It was stunned at Kennedy's assertion that in Selma there "still abide [an] inertia and . . . reactionary devotion to the past." Kennedy opted not to respond.

Wilcoxons rushed to buy reprints available at the Camden drugstores, the *Progressive Era* office, and the Selma Stationery Shop. Most applauded his portrait of the current Black Belt, perversely echoing that "Cavalier" pride voiced over his Camden centennial piece. Comrades of the Roundtable, of course, had other reasons for praise. For his broadside to the Black Belt's religion, race, politics, and economics, Kilpatrick touted Kennedy as "our Dixie heretic, our Scotch-Irish heretic, though really the local population could care less about [his] heresy." Indeed, except for the *Selma Times Journal*, dissenting voices remained quiet. And Kennedy's ministerial popularity kept growing.[37]

No sooner had the *Social Forces* piece appeared than *Christian Century* asked for an update on the New Deal and sharecroppers. Encouraged by the developing Bankhead-Jones Act, Wilcox's "heretic" went to work on a piece titled "Ox Farmers." He explained how the Reconstruction Finance Corporation, Civil Works Administration, and Public Works Administration "put food into empty stomachs . . . kept people alive . . . but did not rehabilitate individuals or families." He described the whole operation designed to change this: from the national Office of Rural Rehabilitation Programs to the state-level Rural Rehabilitation Office to the county-level Relief Office. He described the types of sharecroppers who might qualify for participation. Those with a good track record for managing property and money might get government-acquired acreage and startup housing, food, shelter, clothing, tools, even large steers for plowing. Locals called them "oxen," they were so big. Those lacking such experience might qualify for living in a government-owned and government-managed "collective farming" facility and over time get the experience to move to the ownership program. He saw the program not just as "the most constructive relief measure . . . attempted," but "the most interesting social and economic experiment the South has ever witnessed, if it is actually carried out." For this innovative plan, he congratulated FDR for "running with the hares and holding with the hounds, at which sport the president is admirably a master."

At the time he wrote this sentence, in early November 1934, Kennedy could not have known that those "informed conservative . . . Black Belt aristocrats" he had portrayed in *Social Forces* worked through the Farm Bureau to reduce the program at the congressional funding stage. They had no problem with receiving federal aid for themselves. But it was "communistic," "pinkish . . . cries of Moscow" for croppers to get it.

The Century liked the topic and wanted a Renwick C. Kennedy article. But it did not want a summary of the program. Newspapers had already covered that. At least it was not a form note. He took a deep breath and did what they said: "Rev. Kennedy, get back to the face of the poor."

In two days, he rewrote "Ox Farmers" as Yaupon fiction, starting with re-creation of the Gee's Bend raid in the fall of 1932. In his Red Cross trips to the Bend, he had talked with still others about how it all came down and had made careful notes on what they said. From this fund of striking detail (undoubtedly stored in boxes in the garage), he wove the story of one of the Bend croppers, fictitiously named "William Boatright." "Mr. Wallace" was the fictitious landowner—stand-in for the real-life Hargrave Van de Graaff. "The Wilsons" were the foreclosing furnishing-merchant family—the Rentz family.

For the first time he gave details on Mr. Wilson's advancing-business estate: $40,000 in debt due to accumulated unpaid advancing bills by sharecroppers countywide. For the first time, also, he explained how this single attack on Mr. Boatwright deepened the pain for *all* croppers on the 8,000-acre Wallace place who were raided as part of the same two-month closeout sweep. In the past, "collectors" or "raiders" closed out one or two cropper families. The Bend community—tight-knit compared to most cropper communities around the South—always had helped the hurt ones get through the winter. But when the fall 1932 raid hit every Wallace cropper, this could not happen. As a result, "sixty-five families"—"368 people"—had nothing to survive the winter but a "handful of peas . . . which the raiders generously left." During the winter of 1932–33, the Wilcox County Red Cross plus Mr. Wallace kept them from starving to death. By implication, at this stage, Kennedy appears to have viewed Mr. Wallace as a white landowner wanting to help the Benders despite his own finances having been decimated by the Depression—the same way he viewed the Wilson heirs.

At any rate, by summer 1933 things looked up for William Boatright and others. With arrival of RFC money, they "dug ditches" and "built roads" at thirty cents a day—limited to three days of work a week. And in December 1933 the CWA arrived with food and more pay for the road and ditch work at thirty cents an hour—"the highest wages of William's life at that time." That work, too, had limits of three days a week. But the supply of flour and meal was steady. Finally, in June 1934 "William's godfather, the government, made it possible for him" and two hundred other croppers in the county to do what they wanted to do. They did not want handouts. They just wanted to farm. And farm they did with Harry Hopkins's Rehabilitation Program. To emphasize accountability in that program, Kennedy ticked off William Boatright's documents in the county relief office. It was public information: a list of food and supplies he received; Mr. Wallace's waiver of rent—neither William nor the government had to pay; the government's lien document on his crop to cover supplies and food; and biographical information on William Boatright and family.

Wealthy whites of the county, however, were not happy with the government intrusion. They saw it as a blend of "Reconstruction and Communism." They pressured fellow whites not to lease to the US government program. Out of this opposition, Kennedy predicted, over the next three years the new Bankhead-Jones Act program would need to back off from leasing and, instead, buy the land from Mr. Wallace and others. Then, assuming William Boatright had a track record for responsible management, the government would move him into his farm as "owner," the cost of the property to be paid back over time from his crop production.

Again, Kennedy had no way of knowing how Capitol Hill cuts would limit successes of this bold plan. All he knew was that in late 1934 hardworking William Boatright's children had less hunger and his own "face" occasionally smiled with pride. Boatright wanted to be a productive farmer. This now was possible. *Christian Century* liked the rewrite. On November 14, 1934, it appeared as "Rehabilitation: Alabama Version."[38]

Kennedy's angst over the hurtful hypocrisy of Black Belt aristocrats—"cotton-snobs" and "broken"—continued to grow. In early December, he attacked their political and social alliances with bigwig industrial counterparts in Birmingham and Mobile, that he earlier had called "the bloc" and historians later would call "the Alabama Axis." If a long-time sporting love, baseball, proved the catalyst for the *Social Forces* article, another one, football, incited this next Yaupon attack.

It was not exactly any football game. On November 10, 1934, Bill Jones and his brother-in law, Edgar Carothers, took Kennedy to Tuscaloosa for Homecoming. They watched the University of Alabama smash Clemson 40–0. Don Hutson, Dixie Howell, Young Boozer, and Riley Smith dominated. A student named Paul Bryant played, too. For a man who touted himself as "the greatest Alabama football fan ever to come out of South Carolina," one would think this had to be a magical moment. Not so.

As a political science faculty member with a part-time administrative role in alumni affairs, Carothers wrangled invitations for the three to attend President George Denny's pregame luncheon at his majestic home on University Boulevard. Denny used such settings to mix a few high-profile faculty members with heavy-hitting moneyed supporters of Crimson Tide football: Black Belt planters and lawyers, doctors, and corporate leaders from Birmingham, Montgomery and Mobile. Noted journalism professor Clarence Cason was "on show." Carothers introduced him to Jones and Kennedy. Other than that conversation, however, the Wilcox three did not find much they liked.

After all, here were rich conservatives who did all possible to defeat Governor B. M. Miller's taxes-for-schools plan. Here were the people who bought new tractors off federal money tied to crop reduction, then blasted New Deal aid to Gee's Bend farmers. Here were the protectors of what Kennedy later called "The Slick Scam of the Real and Un-Christian Alabama Tax Code," that is, keeping Alabama taxes low while vigorously pursuing federal monies, that is, tax dollars paid by people in other states. Here were the people who had told the Alabama National Guard to shoot striking laborers. More to the point, since Armistice Day (November 11) fell on Sunday that year, Denny had arranged for a World War I veteran and major general in the Alabama National Guard to offer "After Lunch Remarks."[39]

The following Sunday night, Kennedy's mental notes about these "remarks" poured into the Underwood. Out came a fictional vignette. The major general chose to address labor union strikes and the threat they posed to Alabama life. After bearing down on unions as agents of communist conspiracy and "'the enemies within,'" he promised this deeply conservative audience that "while... private properties are no longer safe... the Army is ready." "After the applause," however, "an amazing thing happened. A big man rose... [and said] 'Mr. President... When [the speaker] intimates [that] we maintain the Army... to protect our property against the masses of our people, I wish to dissent. The people don't want our property. All they want is a living, and in some ways we must give them a living instead of turning the Army loose on them.... When the few use the Army against the many to protect their entrenched privileges, they have lost their country and are doomed.... Justice and human rights and numbers and the Christian religion are on the other side." "The luncheon broke up in dismay." Of course, nobody actually arose at the president's luncheon to lecture Black Belt aristocrats and Big Mules on "justice and human rights and numbers and the Christian religion." "This," Kennedy concluded, "is a fairy story."

These protesting words made it to the English-speaking Social Gospel Protestants on both sides of the Atlantic who read *Christian Century*, which published "A Fairy Tale" on December 19, 1934. Yet, while it undoubtedly resounded well with *Century* readership, and offered temporary balm for the author's Christian Socialist soul, it had doubtful impact on the well-imbibed Tide fans who trained across America to see Alabama beat Stanford, 29–13, on New Year's Day, 1935.[40]

The new year of 1935 turned out just as strong for RCK's publishing as the previous year, even if all seven pieces were in the *Christian Century*. The February 27 issue carried his "Quality in Reserve Corps," his sardonic reaction to conversations with US Army Reserve chaplains at CCC camps. All four of his conversationalists were southerners; talk revolved around rising fascist regimes of Germany and Italy, and the possibility of the United States becoming involved in another world war. Although the implications of that subject would plague Kennedy into the grave, here, in his initial written profile of white Americans and fascism, he already understood the long-term essence of it. In straight reporting—no Yaupon fiction—he recounts hearing these comments: "I was always a great believer in blood... a wop is always a wop, a nigger always a nigger... [and] I'm going to tell you the solution [to] the wops and the Jews... put them on ships and start them back where they come from and when you get them to the middle of the ocean sink the ships." "Now those Germans [of World War I] almost whipped the world... good stock... it's race and blood that counts." Quite a forecast for World War II and the American experience beyond.[41]

In April 1935, the *Century* showed him returning to a more focused expression of this sentiment as reflected in new developments in the Scottsboro case. Two months earlier the US Supreme Court had ruled that the guilty verdict for Haywood Patterson and Clarence Norris—two of the nine Negroes accused of raping the two white women—was in fact unconstitutional. Just as the earlier Yaupon drugstore talk had predicted, it was unconstitutional because no Negroes were in the pool of jurors selected to hear their cases. This violated the US Constitution's provisions for "equal protection under the law." Norris and Patterson, the Court ordered, were to be retried in Alabama with a jury-selection process that did not exclude Negroes. Meanwhile, they were remanded to Kilby prison in Montgomery.

Midafternoon on Monday, April 8, 1935, Kennedy "loafed" at Clark Jones's drugstore. On hand were Miller Bonner, still in the state senate; Edward Walker Berry, president of Camden National Bank; Ervin Dunn, seed salesman; Bob Smith, jeweler; Willie Sessions, electrician; Arthur Capell, twelve-year-old son of a planter; Ernest Bonner, physician; and Clark Jones. All were "old Wilcox" except Berry. As a well-educated banker from a moneyed background up in DeKalb County, he married into the Goode-Gaston family and represented those interests in the 1905 creation of the Camden National Bank. By 1935, he was president of that bank. Tenure, marriage, and money long since had stifled his hill-country roots; he now was a well-placed white Black Belter.

That they talked so openly about Scottsboro in front of Kennedy—all knowing his views on Negroes and with a twelve-year-old boy on hand—tells much of the "art" of cultural isolation and its impact upon public white conversation. That night Ren summarized what he had heard. "[When] I asked, 'What would be the effect of putting a few Negro names in the jury box?,' Miller says, 'Then we'll have niggers indicting white men. That won't do.' Berry says: 'Let them vote and serve on a jury and we would have to get out and turn over the county to them.'"[42]

Two days later Kennedy wrote a vignette called "Scottsboro Shadow." Into the Yaupon drugstore conversation he wove the trial of a white man accused of brutally killing a Negro cropper. The murder may or may not have been based on fact; at the least, it emulated much of what Kennedy had heard that was indeed factual. It begins with an "Alexander Pruitt" deep drunk on "Pensacola Rye," what locals called a premium northwest Florida moonshine—proof normally exceeding 170—available down at Rachel's. "Alexander was forty years old and had never killed a nigger though there were more niggers in the county than rabbits. . . . As Alexander got drunker and drunker his reasoning became clearer and clearer. He knew a dozen . . . fine men . . . looked up to in the county because they had killed one or more niggers. . . . But he, Alexander Pruitt, had never killed even one. . . . He would change that. He would go out and kill himself a nigger."

True to his plan, early that afternoon and propelled by still more

Pensacola Rye, Alexander stumbled out behind his home. There, Long Son Gilman and Simon Jeter bent to the ground picking cotton. The Black croppers knew to keep their heads down and work. When Alexander got drunk, he always came out to rant at them, then stumbled on back to the house. So, as he approached yelling, they kept their heads down and feverishly picked. Alexander walked up behind Long Son and placed his .38 revolver down at the back of his head. "The bullet smashed Son's brain and came out his left eye." Simon ran away, dodging Alexander's drunken shots.

Shortly, a deputy arrested Alexander at his home. His friends paid the bail and told him not to worry. A trial would occur, they advised, but there would not be any problem. Unworried, as his court date approached, Alexander planned to defend himself. A simple matter. But a prominent attorney made him do otherwise.

"Twenty years ago," the attorney counseled Alexander, "when I was county solicitor I prosecuted the first white man [Fleet Tait] ever tried in this county for killn' a nigger. I made enemies of the man and his whole family. The jury turned him loose." The attorney continued. "I also prosecuted the first case [of a white murdering a Black] that ever got a conviction. The jury gave the man [punishment of] $25.00. . . . But it ain't that way now. . . . You're likely to get anything up to ten years." Alexander was stunned. "Good, God, man," the attorney exclaimed, "you shot that nigger in the back of the head. . . . You ain't got no defense except he was a nigger. The only chance you got is for me to pack that jury with members of the American Legion and then plead insanity for you."

With Alexander paying $200 up front, the lawyer took his case. Sure enough, local Legionnaires—white World War I veterans—dominated the jury. The defense attorney explained to them how Alexander came home from the war traumatized. He took to heavy drinking trying not to remember the horrors he had witnessed. He did indeed shoot the Negro. But when he did it, he was mentally incapacitated as a result of the sacrifice he made in service to his country. After thirty minutes the jury said, "Not guilty."

Late that afternoon on the street one of the jurors told an old friend what had happened. "I felt like we ought to have given that fellow ten days and a $50.00 fine just to give him something. If it hadn't been for Scottsboro he'd ah gotten something, too." "'Yes, that's right,' said the other. 'Ain't no white go'n up for killn' some nigger as long as those niggers is still breath'n in Kilby prison.'"

In this "other face" of "Yaupon," Charles Clayton Morrison saw savvy comment on reverberations of the Scottsboro case—reverberations later pointed up by historian Dan Carter—and several similar to Kennedy's fictional case. *Christian Century* published "Scottsboro Shadow" on April 10, 1935.[43]

Less than a month later Kennedy returned to the rehabilitation scene in Gee's Bend. He employed Yaupon dialogue and a mixture of fictional and real names. Otherwise, the piece was straight factual, based on several visits he had recently made to the Bend with county agents overseeing federal relief. In this sense, "Roosevelt's Tenants" is an early 1935 update on the Gee's Bend project.

The reader joins Wilcox's white relief agent, a fictional "Miss Ella," for an auto tour of several Gee's Bend locations. She heads down a dirt road to a cluster of new, if rustic, pine houses in a settlement called Sodom. Miss Ella stops at the house of (nonfictional) Clement (Clem) Petway, a distant descendant of slaves owned by Virginian Mark Pettway, who in 1845 acquired the 10,000 acre plantation from relatives of Joseph Gee, the North Carolina planter who started the white settlement of the Bend in 1815. Miss Ella wants information to qualify Petway and his family for federal aid beyond materials recently provided for constructing the house. He is off working, so she interviews Clem's wife, (nonfictional) Cherokee Parker Petway. She is twenty-seven years old, and she and Clem have seven children.

The interview reveals that ever since the fall 1932 "raid," the Petways and some others around them have remained with virtually no food, plus no plows and no mules. New Deal relief has helped them with a house. Otherwise, the bureaucracy somehow has missed them. Miss Ella aims to document this and present the Petway case to the state relief office in Montgomery. She is not sure she will succeed. "We already have a thousand families in the county on relief," she tells Cherokee, "[and] we are not supposed to take on more [but] you sho' needs to be on." As the interview concludes, Clem appears with apologies for having been off at work. Miss Ella: "I like your new house, Clem. You sure built a strong house." Clem: "Thank-ee, Missus." Miss Ella: "But you oughta have some food in it." Clem: "Ya'mam. Us 'sho' ought." Miss Ella and her rider head on to similar appointments in the Bend.

Published in the *Century* on May 5, 1935, "Roosevelt's Tenants" demonstrated how many like Cherokee and Clem—people subjected to furnishing-merchant raids—were yet to be helped despite massive New Deal efforts and certainly aid by some Wilcox whites. That's the "update." Yet it also remains compelling for its detailed description of the Gee's Bend setting and of the tragic stoicism of the Petway family.

The article had an inadvertent result of higher public note. It eventually got New York photographer, Arthur Rothstein, focused on Cherokee Petway. Some two years after the appearance of Kennedy's article, Rothstein photographed Gee's Bend. The world then saw Cherokee and others in the *New*

York Times. Much later, many also came to appreciate Cherokee Petway for her quilts—the artist and the art teacher.[44]

So far, Kennedy's various writing efforts had focused on issues of class and caste in the Depression South. What he published, however, seemed limited to poor rural Black people needing a changed South and the large number of southern rural white people either not wanting change or unwilling to advocate it. This left assorted white citizens and professional-level Black citizens particularly in his purview for published analysis.

In early spring 1935 his publishing focus turned to a progressive, educated white man, as well as to poor whites, with a fifteen-page essay on the rising career of his distant cousin, Erskine Caldwell. He laced it with his own college memories of "the quiet cynic" of Erskine College. "Drinking liquor, shooting craps, playing poker . . . even a bit of wenching. . . . Erskine belonged to [the] element [that] didn't give a damn. . . . Silence was his chief quality." Kennedy also showed considerable pride in his cousin's father, Ira Sylvester Caldwell, a courageous Social Gospel ARP preacher of Georgia and South Carolina, offering stark contrast to the rank-and-file ARP ministry, not to mention the ARP Synod.

Foremost, Kennedy focused on Caldwell's *Tobacco Road*, published just two years previously, in 1933. He applauded Caldwell's telling the truth about the hardships endured by poor whites in Depression-era Georgia. He also appreciated the straight talk about poor white people's racism toward Black people. He found the graphic language and sexual directness of Caldwell's stories vital to a realistic account, one that might have impact on public policy. "None of [Caldwell's] books are allowed in the Erskine College library," he wrote. "His alma mater is not 'fond' of him, and the writer [is] not fond of Erskine [College]."

When first crafting this piece, Kennedy was in very much of a publishing mood. Yet nothing shows he took it before Viola Liddell's Roundtable, nor does his correspondence suggest its submission. The riddle of its file-drawer destiny likely is answered with a suddenly changed focus. News of profound personal tragedy out of Tuscaloosa returned him to concerns earlier articulated in the manuscript "Psychic" and in the article "Fairy Story."[45]

On the night of Wednesday, May 8, 1935, University of Alabama journalism professor Clarence Cason committed suicide in his Union Building office. On May 9, Kennedy read of this in the *Montgomery Advertiser*. For ten days, while awaiting his copy of Cason's new book, *90 Degrees in the Shade*, to arrive at the Selma Stationery Shop, the tragedy kept sinking in. At 9:40 p.m., Sunday, May 19, he began drafting "A Southern Suicide." By 11:59 p.m. he had completed an eight-page typescript—a Yaupon fictional vignette exploring why Clarence Cason shot himself.

Two people had permitted Kennedy to follow Cason's writing career leading up to *90 Degrees*. University of Alabama political scientist Edward Sadler Carothers knew Cason socially and professionally. So did Carothers's cousin, Richebourg McWilliams, the man who had given the "Hitler Report" on the Oak Hill front porch less than a year earlier. Through a Birmingham writers' group, The Loafers, as well as their mutual friendship with James Saxon Childers—McWilliams and Childers were faculty colleagues at Birmingham-Southern College—Cason and McWilliams had become casual friends. Kennedy also had read Cason's recent feature writing in the *Birmingham News* and the *New York Times*, and had talked "writing" with him, briefly, when they sat next to each other at President Denny's football luncheon the previous fall. So, though not one of Cason's friends, Kennedy had a reasonable grasp of Cason and his depiction of southern problems. He had looked forward to reading Cason's current project. His interest was especially piqued by the *Montgomery Advertiser*'s recent interview with Cason in which the author described his upcoming book as a "psychograph of the South—a paradox of unrest in a land of contentment."[46]

Out of that background, Kennedy conceived "Southern Suicide," a psychograph of Cason himself. The story unfolds at night in rocking chairs on the front porch of the Yaupon Hotel. A Yaupon lawyer with moderate views—modeled on Stanley Godbold—discusses Cason's suicide with a close friend. The colleague is a Yaupon County native home for the weekend from "the university" where he is a professor. In persona, the professor seems to be an amalgam of McWilliams and Carothers. The professor's voice, however, is clearly Kennedy's. After talk of the professor's knowing Cason, and much mulling of Cason's career, the conversation turns to two other southern writers the professor has recently read: Erskine Caldwell and T. S. Stribling. Compared to Cason, the professor urges, these two are significantly more confrontational about flaws in southern life. The professor also reflects on Edward Arlington Robinson's poem "Richard Cory"—about a man who shot himself dead, for no known cause. At last the lawyer asks the question, "So, why do you think Cason did it?" From stilled rocker the professor answers: "[After] he toned down the book [*90 Degrees in the Shade*] . . . in his soul he thought that it wasn't an honest . . . piece of work and . . . yet he still thought he said too much. His state of mind was not going far enough to satisfy his own sense of honesty and truth, but going so far that the Old Guard would be upon his neck as soon as the book was published. . . . Think about him brooding and fretting . . . sensitive soul . . . until he couldn't be rational. So, he shot himself in the head."

That "cause" is not what President Denny told the press. He emphasized Cason's suspected "health problems" and "recent depression." Even so, today

Kennedy's contemporaneous analysis remains the consensus on why Cason killed himself.

Just as revealing are the story's implications for Kennedy himself in the mid-1930s. Despite being "southern white liberals" in the heart of Dixie, he and Cason were different men in different settings. If Kennedy could be diplomatic, he also could hit hard: unvarnished attacks on gross violence, "befallen aristocracy," Christian hypocrisy, reasons urging a changed southern white behavior. Indeed, Kennedy could hit this hard and still have friendships with numerous members of the Wilcox elite who, while conservative and generally in disagreement with his positions on race and politics, liked him socially and may have shared his disdain for the Klan.

By contrast, in Tuscaloosa Cason normally offered himself as the diplomat, and many received him that way. So comfortable was the university with Cason, indeed, that it exhibited him as a social star—and used him for schmoozing at fundraisers in Alabama's most conservative professional culture. Cason's book would be no Blitzkrieg on the white South. Instead, it would emphasize "climate"—heat and humidity—as the nonthreatening cause for many of the South's "problems" and cast lynching as an "aberration" rather than something more endemic to white southern life. Despite Cason's extraordinary skills as a stylist (and perhaps because of them), he remained the diplomat "less interested" in southern change, to use his own words, "than in talking . . . about the region." Still, Cason knew that much of "white Tuscaloosa"—including the most educated and rich—either had acquiesced to or quietly supported recent, high-profile Klan aggressions in their community. And so despite his diplomacy Cason appears to have thought that this same elite would turn on him when *90 Degrees* came out due to a few overtly confrontational lines, such as his reference to "fascism."

Such differences in tone and substance between Kennedy and Cason no doubt can be traced to their different backgrounds. Kennedy's parents did not live as southern elites. Yet his grandparents and great-grandparents on both sides clearly had been well-positioned, upcountry South Carolinians and pro-Confederacy planters with slaves and later with sharecroppers. Among Wilcox white people Kennedy therefore had the reputation of coming from "the right people." And ironically this in turn provided him social securities in criticizing "the right people" around him.

In contrast, Cason had emerged from in between: his personal roots were neither in antebellum cotton plantations nor in "poor white" life. Up in St. Clair and Talladega, counties of east-central Alabama well removed from the Black Belt, his paternal grandfather as well as his father were country doctors in an era well preceding the wealth of modern city-based physicians. They treated pellagra patients in the rural South's barter economy. Patients who managed to pay them at all rarely paid with money; they paid with a few eggs, a basket of collards, or a Mason jar of buttermilk—basket and jar always returned. More to the point, in a town like Tuscaloosa, where deeply ingrained Lost Cause mythologies made conception behind white columns the ultimate measure of white worth, Cason's "in between" hill country origins—anchored in neither culture, rich nor poor—could have made him socially insecure, especially if otherwise his personality tended toward brittleness.

And oversensitivity indeed seems to have been part of Cason's persona, further elucidating how he differed from Kennedy. Several of Cason's close colleagues, notably Chapel Hill's William Terry Couch and Birmingham-Southern College's James Saxon Childers, regularly worried about Cason's overreacting to social unpleasantries around him. He seems to have had no inner mechanism for dealing with them. On "southern problems" the more Cason wrote, the more he worried how readers would react. Yet, while Kennedy had excruciating moments of self-doubt on his path to marriage, he seemed unthreatened by conservatives not liking his advocacy of southern change. The more he wrote about southern problems, the more balanced and productive he felt, and the more he wanted to write. So when it came to sensitivities about serious southern commentary, the two men likely were polar opposites.

Because Christianity played such a profound role in Kennedy's life, it is worth speculating, too, on how God figured into differences between these two liberals. Cason grew up in a devout Baptist family and, on his way to a career in journalism, enrolled in a St. Louis theology school—for one term. Still, nothing indicates that his liberalism sprang from religious faith. It came from his secular self, brittle though it was. It was different for Kennedy: always in the back of his mind was his felt Mandate from God. Though he generally steered clear of organized reform groups, he never worked fully "alone": he had God. When his sermons and writings about southern change did not bear fruit—which was most of the time—he still had the Almighty beside him telling him that what he had done was right and just, and to keep working. In this way Kennedy had little chance of finding himself in Cason's terminal bind. He pressed on—at least for a while.

On June 1, 1935, Kennedy's copy of *90 Degrees in the Shade* finally arrived at the Selma Stationery Company. After reading the book between June 3 and 6, he made only a few technical revisions to "Southern Suicide." Late that month, he read "Southern Suicide" aloud to the Roundtable. Viola Liddell remembered the session as "one of our most solemn . . . we all knew about Cason but most agreed the manuscript could be more than it was, including Ren. But I do not recall hearing any more about it." The "final" typed version shows his name and address at the bottom of the last page, as if prepared for submission. Yet Kennedy's detailed correspondence records reveal nothing about submission. For sure, into the file cabinet—a piece inadvertently as insightful of its author as of the man he portrayed.[47]

In the summer of 1935, Kennedy returned to a more familiar target and the one of such concern for Cason: southern white conservatives. With no Negroes in the jury pool, the US Supreme Court returned the Scottsboro case to Alabama courts. Now, with the case even more a matter of southern white paranoia, Kennedy reworked the earlier rejected "One Point of View" as "Alabama Dilemma."

His explanation of white fear remained the same. Yaupon white citizens gathered in the barbershop across from the courthouse accurately saw the presence of Black people on juries as leading to an end of the only Black Belt they knew. Yet he heightened the white stress with an exchange about "communist lawyers" entering the Black Belt to agitate Negroes over denial of their rights. Those at the drugstore note what communist attorneys so far have done with the Scottsboro case; they fear Wilcox is next. He also deepened the complexity of the dialogue on the "dilemma." The lawyer says he could go along with Black people having "business rights"—for nobody should be cheated—but only up to the point at which "business rights" do not evolve to "social and political rights." The lawyer holds out hope that the Alabama legislature will revoke "comity" for out-of-state lawyers. That at least will blunt the attack by outside "communist lawyers."

The local electrician wanders in. He asks how Alabama governor Bibb Graves could possibly have sided with the US Supreme Court on the question of Black people in jury pools, considering he came from the Black Belt—from Hope Hull, in Montgomery County. Poignantly anticipating a nationwide white reactionism of the early twenty-first century, another reflective citizen suggests that more Negroes being in the Northeast could ease pressure to change the South. If Yankees were "in our fix," living as a numerical racial minority, they would "understand" and quit pushing for change. A banker finds the conversation to be useless polemics. Black jury service will usher in Black voting. "Open the door and they'll be votin' and either we gonna start kill'em that day or we gonna clear out and tell'em to take the county." With those rewrites Kennedy sent "Alabama Dilemma" to *Christian Century*, where it appeared on July 10, 1935.[48]

He returned to the same white dilemma in "Sedition Bill." Having drafted it in early August 1935, a few weeks later Kennedy read a revised version to Viola's Roundtable. The "Sedition Bill," then working its way through the Alabama legislature, sought to stifle criticism of the Black Belt–Big Mule agenda. Instead of commenting on the manuscript, Emmett—"a tad in his cups"—launched into a "jag he was on": assessing the "character" of leading citizens of Wilcox, "self-avowed Christians one and all," according to which of "the Seven Sins" (gluttony, avarice, and so on) influenced each the most. Stanley Godbold finally got the group back on track by asking whether Kennedy had thought about using "Christian sin" in his "Sedition Law" manuscript. After all, members of the legislature all "considered themselves Christians." Kennedy said no. As current owner of the *Progressive Era*, Godbold continued to show grave concern. "If not sin . . . what about the Constitution?" The bill proposed significant punishment for anyone criticizing state, county, and local laws in Alabama—even current elected officials. Though Godbold was anti-union, he saw the bill as a frontal attack on press freedom. The group adjourned.

Shortly, Kennedy rewrote his Sedition Bill manuscript as a Yaupon drugstore conversation. He modeled "the editor" on Stanley Godbold, the "state senator" on Miller Bonner, and the "state representative" on Daniel G. Cook. "The teacher" appears to be an amalgam of Wilcox high school instructors. Same for "the preacher"—a blend of several deeply conservative, white Wilcox ministers. Over the next month the Roundtable went over several more drafts. Ultimately, Kennedy added what happened to the bill: Governor Graves vetoed it. *Christian Century* published "Sedition Bill" on October 23, 1935.

This final version represents Kennedy's first published hint of his concerns about white Half Christianity aligning with fascist totalitarianism, subtle though it is. "The editor of the *Yaupon Daily Democrat* made a strong editorial fight to keep his paper free of the restrictions of the [Alabama sedition] measure. . . . The editor could not understand why so many otherwise intelligent people favored a law that might have come out of Germany. . . . At the drugstore, the editor set himself the task of learning the reasons."

> Senator: . . . I voted for the bill because of the nigger situation. . . . Two yellow niggers from Chicago made speeches to a whole mob of our niggers . . . The niggers are gettn' more restless every year.
> Preacher: . . . I am for the Sedition Bill. As for the bill curbing the freedom of the pulpit, the pulpit has no business discussing anything that could come under the terms of the bill. The pulpit is to preach the gospel . . . not discuss social matters.
> Teacher: I want a law that will keep un-American teachers out of our school rooms. . . . The founders of our country were intelligent men and their ideas are intelligent enough for me.
> Editor: They were also guilty of sedition in the American revolution.[49]

Over the next month Kennedy's focus returned to Yaupon County Black folks. For the first time he examined a Negro archetype neither poor nor illiterate, in a piece based on the life of one William Green Wilson. Son of slave parents who lived near Chase City, Virginia, after education at Pennsylvania's Lincoln University and theology training at Allegheny College, Wilson came to Camden in 1905 as a missionary educator sponsored by the northern-based United Presbyterian Church (UPC). For some thirty years he was principal of Camden Academy, on the hill just south of town—one of the six UPC mission schools for Black students in Wilcox. On May 28, 1935, Wilson died of cancer. The following day Kennedy attended the funeral in the school's auditorium. That night he went to the diary: "Several Negroes spoke. Also, W. J. Jones, Wilcox County superintendent of education, and I made short talks. Burial was on the campus . . . a good man, a Christian, a friend of mine." For three months after the funeral he then drafted and redrafted what he had to say about the life of his "good friend." Both in style and in message this evolved into one of his most elegant Yaupon fiction manuscripts.

Kennedy had one William Hill Hunter in the role of Reverend Wilson; biographical information on Hunter correlates precisely with Wilson's. The vivid picture of Camden Academy reeks of irony. "It stands upon a commanding hill . . . would have been a fine site for a southern mansion of the magnolia-and-wisteria style. [But] long ago a white man and a Negro were hanged by the law on the brow of the hill and no [white] ever cared to build upon Hangman's Hill." Reverend Watson, principal at another one of the county's Black mission schools, presided and gave each of the other five principals their turn at eulogizing. "The county superintendent of education [also] spoke for three minutes . . . [and] the pastor of one of the white churches . . . spoke for five minutes." Then Kennedy concluded: "On the hill where he lived and worked . . . the body of William Hill Hunter rests. Two pine trees watch over him. . . . The crowd broke up. . . . As the [whites] walked down the hill to their cars one merchant said to another: 'Hunter was a good nigger. He'll be missed.' 'Hunter was a good nigger,' the cashier said to the bank president. 'Hunter was good nigger,' the doctor said to the third merchant. 'Hunter was a fine nigger,' the white woman said to her child. 'Hunter was a good man,' the superintendent of education said to the preacher."

Toward the end of Kennedy's drafting process, the Roundtable critiqued the piece. Discussion apparently centered on the cultural isolation Wilson experienced as an educated Black man in the Black Belt. From that, Kennedy extended the story beyond the knot of white people walking down the hill. This benediction probes Hunter's tough existence. Despite being "good," he had "the tragic isolation of the educated Negro who lives among privileged white people and underprivileged Negroes. . . . Cut off by race from one group in the community and by his own culture from the other, he lived alone." "Isolation" appeared in *Christian Century* on November 13, 1935.

Of course, profound residuals of such "isolation" continued. From the perspective of 1985, Black philosopher Cornel West could speak of "the grim predicament" of life in "an isolated and insulated world." Yet by 2004 William Green Wilson's own Duke-educated granddaughter, historian Cynthia Griggs Fleming, evolved West's insight—and Kennedy's—with the book, *In the Shadow of Selma*, profiling Wilson's life and that of many other educated Black Wilcoxons as segregation grudgingly gave way to civil rights.[50]

To finish out 1935, Kennedy retargeted whites whom he considered among the most hypocritical in the racist system so responsible for his friend's significant if tragic life—and among the most sinister. Over the past five years he had learned how certain members of the American Legion—World War I veterans—played crucial roles in the Klan-controlled jury pools used to maintain Wilcox's dual justice system. His articles had addressed these unconstitutional conspiracies as well as the dirty work some veterans did as National Guardsmen for conservative interests wanting machine guns to block labor union strikes and civil rights demonstrations. In "The Great Peace Celebration," published by the *Century* on December 4, 1935, he condemned yet another facet of the "Legionnaires' plague": their overtly wrapping white control in the American flag and simultaneously running roughshod over Woodrow Wilson's noble vision for world peace.

At the end of World War I, President Wilson had set aside an "Armistice Day" to celebrate "the peace." At the same time, veterans of the American Expeditionary Force formed the American Legion to advocate for veterans' benefits and patriotism. Like many veterans' groups nationwide, however, Wilcox Legionnaires shrewdly used Armistice Day (November 11) for different purposes. In the name of "Armistice" they applauded all wars fought by Americans, with special adulation for Confederate veterans, and they sold American flags to civic clubs with proceeds often going to illegal beer at the local Legion hall. At "Pineville"—the fictitious name Kennedy used for Pine Hill, in western Wilcox—the choirmaster at First Baptist handed out song sheets; all sang "It's a long Way to Tipperary," "Over There," "Let Me Call You Sweethearte," and "Dixie." Next came four Confederate veterans, "each nearly ninety [and] one with yellow braid," who spoke their "brief, feeble words." Then the congressman spoke: "'Mr. Chairman, veterans of the Confederate war, ladies and gentlemen . . . seventeen years ago the big guns ceased to roar on the western front . . . the German army was about to engulf all that is beautiful in this world [but it is now] a new day.'" "And [in this new day] the South must get its rights, all of its rights. . . . I challenge the judgment of history—there has been no greater heroism than that of the Confederate soldiers coming home to ruin, starting over again. They builded back their temple. . . . Lord, God of hosts, be with us yet, lest we forget . . . lest we forget."

Here, in Kennedy's mind, was not just a problem of veterans' groups and politicians using patriotism as an instrument of social control: through "Lost Cause" worship of the Confederacy, white people's control of Black people might be maintained. It was the additional problem of many other white people opting to do nothing about this. "'I thought [this] was going to be a peace program,' the fat man said to his angular wife. 'I don't know,' she said. . . . 'People have always fought wars and I reckon they always will,' the fat man continued. 'Yes, I reckon they will,' said his wife." True to fiction technique, Kennedy leaves the reader to ponder the implications. But historian Charles Reagan Wilson spells it out: "The dream of a separate political nation died among most southerners with Confederate defeat. . . . [But] gradually replacing the political dream was the cultural dream, and as the latter took hold Southerners found that they could honor the American political nation if it honored the Southern civilization."[51]

That was it for 1935, seven published articles: a "good" year from the standpoint of openly attacking, if another "bad" year for the behaviors he wanted changed. From one perspective, the following year would be far less productive. He would try another poor-white piece comparing economic depression and psychological depression—a tenant farmer suicide. Provocative concept, weak writing: to the file drawer. Yet this and three stronger articles were anything but his main focus in 1936. During that year two other developments arose. One ran the risk of gutting his attack, the other advancing it into a whole new realm.

7

More Attack

The new year of 1936 started off as repeat from the previous year. Kennedy returned to the cotton culture so instrumental in William Green Wilson's "good" and wrenching existence. Appearing on April 8 in the *Century*, "Mr. McClintock and His Tenants" was yet another Yaupon update on cotton lives amid the changing Depression. William Lowndes Yancy McClintock—not modeled on any single Wilcoxon—was the wealthiest man in Yaupon County. He had a mercantile business, thirty-five tenant families, some 2,000 acres just for cotton—either cultivated or in the New Deal no-plant-for-money program—plus 400 head of cattle, as well as pine trees and lumber. He avoided the informal title of "Colonel"; he did not need it. The name his parents gave him had ample cachet. He went instead by "Yance."

Yance's bookkeeper reviewed his 1935 balance sheet. On cotton alone: "You done fine. We cleared $6000. It's the best year we've had since 1928." And for good reason. By early 1936 New Deal programs and international cotton trends had moved the price of cotton back to twelve cents a pound. What inconveniences Yance had had three years earlier were history. He now had "two sons attending the first class country club university . . . two cars . . . [and] a well-satisfied pathological love of food" that indeed ran through the family. The wife "hopelessly struggles to disguise her fat body [by spending] enough money to clothe a whole plantation of tenants." Yance has a $70 fur coat, plus three other overcoats, "imitation silk underwear that sells for $2.50 a pair . . . and a trick pencil [that cost] $5.00." Mrs. McClintock "says her rugs cost $2,500, 'which is a very large amount for rugs in Yaupon.'" Yance likes "$1.50 steaks."

The 1936 life of "Eph" was different. As one of Yance's tenants, Eph was modeled on the real-life Ephraim (Eph) Evans. Kennedy's financial records show his giving Eph Evans fifty cents for food on November 22, 1933, and again on March 1, 1934—fifty cents being twenty cents more than Eph got for a day's work on an RFC road project. Kennedy did this because "in the late winter there comes a time when you can see [his children's] bones. [Eph's] family lived on the pellagra diet of corn bread, sorghum molasses, and sweet potatoes." "Eph had never eaten a $1.50 steak in his life."

Sam Campbell was another of Yance's tenants. Even in the winter Sam's "two small children wore only cotton dresses and nothing more above or beneath." Willie Gilder was likewise a tenant on the McClintock place. "Willie has no cook stove. His wife cooks on the open fire . . . [the children] sleep on a mattress on the floor . . . made of feed sacks sewn together and stuffed with moss."

The spring 1936 update for cotton and its people? At twelve cents a pound Yaupon County cotton was on the way back. The Agricultural Adjustment Act (AAA) money flowed into planters' bank accounts. But for croppers things seemed pretty much the way they were in 1928.[1]

Of course, Kennedy could not have known that cotton would go over twelve cents a pound before 1936 ended only to fall back to nine in 1937. He could not have known that FDR's efforts to make croppers more autonomous and self-sufficient actually would affect few. In late 1936, hope glimmered—and he changed to another angle on "scarcity." For five years he had been writing about cotton scarcity in driving cotton prices back up as well as tragedies of scarcity in the food, shelter, and clothing of croppers. Now he took a third approach: environmental scarcity and—still unbeknownst to his readers—its implications for "God's little creatures."

This article unfolded on a white man's front porch just outside Yaupon town. Talk revealed uneducated whites faced with starvation embracing prescient environmental concerns. In the Depression, the poor had no choice but to get what they could off the landscape of Yaupon County—berries, plums, deer. But an old white farmer, Will Robinson, observed that some poor folks destroyed things unnecessarily. "'I knowed a nigger that killed a hunnert 'possums last winter. He et a heap of 'em and give 'em away and thowed 'em away. He just loved to kill 'em' . . . 'Hit ain't only niggers,' said his friend Johnston. 'White people and niggers both done near about killed out everything in this country. They ain't no ducks now.' . . . 'They ain't even many robins here in the winter now,' said Will Robinson. . . . 'I heared Pete Hutcherson was poisin'[n] birds this year on account of some crows pull'n' up corn." Next came environmental effects of New Deal agricultural policy. "This here cotton poisin'n'[for the boll weevil] is killn' a heap of birds . . . bees . . . frogs . . . and lizards too. . . . People is bent on destroyn," said old man Mock. The recent uptick in the lumber industry had their attention, too. "'They ain't doin' nothin' but ruin'n the woods,' said Johnston. 'Them mill people just ruin the woods. . . . Everything is gittin' destroyed. . . . God's little critters ain't got no chance agin shotguns, traps and poison . . . no more long leaf pine . . . the world's gettin' to be a poor place to live in."

So, despite the New Deal's efforts to save "the land," knowingly and unknowingly it collaborated with traditions of hunger, killing, and extractive agriculture in man's continued assault on "God's world." If the economy improved, with some having less starvation, that assault even could be greater. On November 4, 1936, under the title "Waste," the *Century* brought out this melancholy note. It was Kennedy's first published piece addressing poor white people as well as the environment. Within the next year, Gerald Johnson would publish *The Wasted Land* (1937), garnering far more attention than Kennedy's article, but also with a different, arguably less prescient, message. Johnson addressed the dichotomy between the South's abundant natural environment and the tragic status of its poor and starving people. No writer of the era had greater concern for the poor and starving than Kennedy. But in "Waste," Kennedy focused on the environment for the sake of the environment. Here stood an unnoticed "bridge" between Progressive Era approaches to "conservation" and late twentieth-century "environmentalism."[2]

Kennedy's journalism for 1936 closed out with a return attack on the American Legion. The year before, the Legion's extensive grassroots lobby had pushed Congress to prioritize veteran bonuses in updating the Adjusted Compensation Act (ACA). As part of this strategy, Legionnaires attempted to turn Armistice Day into a day of bonus check rallies. Kennedy had followed press coverage leading up to rallies in Wilcox and personally observed the Pine Hill event. By the following year, Congress had passed the "bonus bill" over FDR's veto. Funds were immediately available to World War I veterans, instead of the original 1924 design of paying them out gradually up through 1945. For those who had served overseas, the cash value was $1.25 per day up to a maximum of $625. For those who did not cross the ocean, the cash value was $1.00 per day up to a maximum of $500.

Kennedy was beside himself. Veterans who went to battle and came home maimed unquestionably deserved the bonus. But of the 4.8 million who had served in the military, nearly half (some 2.4 million) never even left the United States. They should not be getting the bonus in view of everything else the nation faced. And it was even a greater wrong for those around him to get the money if they also received significant federal money in the AAA crop-reduction program. The more he thought about the situation, compared to the way Gee's Benders and other croppers were treated, the angrier he got.

"Legion Audit," appearing in the *Century* on December 16, 1936, unfolded in the Yaupon County town of Pine Valley (Pine Hill). On November 11, 1936, the Pine Valley American Legion held its first Armistice Day celebration in the new armory built by the WPA. One "Thomas Jefferson Lincoln" commanded that post. He was a "businessman." Though he had a public "Rabelaisian way of hail-fellow-well-met . . . , those who knew him best preferred his bond to his word and were dubious of the bond." During the war he was a buck private who never left Fort Gordon. He liked to be called "Colonel Jeff."

"To the 300 gathered there in the armory Colonel Jeff proclaimed 1936 as the best ever year for the American Legion. 'We at last and finally received the bonus.... There were those who opposed our aims ... but it was a matter of inevitable justice.... Our next great objective ... is a system of permanent pensions ... the government must take care of its old soldiers who risked their all for it.'" In the audience "the newspaper editor sat next to the preacher. Editor: 'These fat healthy ones who never got any further than Jersey City ... if that's patriotism, I'm a suckling mule.' Minister: 'Their fanaticism, intolerance and selfishness ... my nostrils detect a stench.'"[3]

These three articles, however, were not his main focus for 1936. All around him southerners produced books. Some were like Margaret Mitchell and Lyle Saxon, offering new angles on Lost Cause romance. Others—notably Faulkner, Thomas Wolfe, T. S. Stribling, Gerald Johnson, Erskine Caldwell, and, a few years later, Wilbur J. Cash—focused on the flaws of southern life and the myths behind them, a genre that came to be called "Southern Renaissance." In this latter group, though less highly regarded, was Birmingham's James Saxon Childers, whose novel about interracial friendship, *A Black Man and a White Man in the Deep South*, was published in 1936. So, while topics and styles and quality varied, here indeed were southern books published by big-name New York houses. And despite the Depression—indeed, perhaps because of it—a lot of people found the money to buy them and read them.[4]

That prospect increasingly was Kennedy's goal. His journalism gave him a national profile among *Christian Century* readers; offers for new pastorates were around the corner. But in some ways that was like preaching to the choir. His message was not having the impact he wanted. So, his focus turned to book writing. In fact, during 1936 he started to write two books at once.

One built on "Yaupon." To his earlier Yaupon sketches, published and unpublished, he added five more. "Roosevelt Hall" profiled the ambition of Black students at Snow Hill Institute. "Note on Trapping" treated the understandable defeatism within poor whites. "Clean Feet" probed the link between hopelessness and alcoholism among poor whites. "Solace of the Poor" focused on continued sorry health care for poor Black people despite other New Deal efforts. In short, he looked for ways to weave all the Yaupon material—and more to come—into a book about consequences of "decadent white behavior in the Black Belt."[5]

His second book manuscript harkened to his first year in Wilcox. Recall that no sooner had he arrived in Alabama than he was called to do periodic "meetings"—six- to ten-day revivals—in the Red Level area in Covington

County, to the south of Wilcox. Those continued at least once a year throughout the 1930s. So all along, while he wrote about Black Belt white people, Kennedy tinkered with a theme he first called "The People on Pigeon Creek," based on life along a stream meandering southerly from Butler County into northwestern Covington County on into Conecuh County, where it merges with the Sepulga River.[6]

Meanwhile, the journalism proceeded. In 1937, he did a short, hilarious piece for *Christian Century* about a local American Legion chapter sponsoring a patriotic speaker who, it turned out, was a con artist from a circus. He drafted three more Yaupon fiction pieces. One profiled the far lower wages planters paid white laborers versus Black laborers—and why. Another showed the hard life of the relatively few white tenant farmers of the Black Belt. "Forty-two Dollars" showed the effect of white poverty on white ignorance. No sign of submissions. He probably did them for the novel.[7]

That year, too, a young Manhattan photographer already on his way to fame, Arthur Rothstein, did a photo shoot of the Benders. It remains one of the iconic collections in the history of American photography. He came to a meeting of the Roundtable at Viola's, but he and Kennedy had no one-on-one time together. Another New York visitor was different. He immediately hit it off with Kennedy.[8]

This young Columbia University researcher, Robert Sonkin, was a speech analyst and language-and-culture social scientist. He appreciated the Roundtable gathering and, even more, the events of the next day, when Kennedy took him across the river and introduced him to the Petways and others. The friendship worked both ways. Sonkin brought Kennedy up to speed on the latest research models used in analyzing dialects and accents. Together, they made notes on the Benders' practice of adding the letter *o*, for example, to differentiate two Benders who had the same first name, as in "Tom" versus "Tom-o." From this Kennedy got new thoughts on why Pigeon Creek whites gave their children names that were bizarre by conventional standards. Well into the 1960s, as Sonkin became a major figure in speech analysis, the two stayed in touch.[9]

Likewise, in August 1937 a *Birmingham News* feature writer, John Temple Graves II, came to Camden to research a story on the Bend. With strong interest in publishing Rothstein's photographs of the Bend, the *New York Times*—which did not yet have a bureau in the Deep South—contracted with Graves to provide accompanying text. Though this Princeton graduate later would find the New Deal too liberal, and bolt with the Dixiecrats, at the time he was generally supportive of FDR's efforts to address rural poverty. Written in Graves's well-honed style, "The Big World at Last Reaches Gee's Bend" appeared on August 22, 1937, in the *New York Times* Sunday magazine. The physical isolation of the Bend, the crisis caused by the "bust up" of 1932–33, the Red Cross aid, the stages of US government intervention leading to the February 1937 plan to purchase land that Benders subsequently could buy from the government—it was all there. Graves also offered cameos of three prominent Benders: John Henry Miller ("the Plantation Man"), who talked well with white folks; Little Petway ("The Tribesman"), a taciturn authority figure; and Patrick Bendorff, a successful farmer.

Though Graves's research took him to some of Kennedy's early 1930s writings, he strangely did not seek to contact Kennedy, although the latter was in Camden at the time of Graves's visit. Yet Graves did interview Robert Sonkin, as well as Wilcox sheriff Reg Albritton. In the article Graves vaguely referenced Kennedy as "the Camden minister who first called attention to Gee's Bend." But then he dissented from Kennedy's description of the Benders as "superior" to other Wilcox Black people. Kennedy's was a potent interpretive point deriving from the diverse African origins of Wilcox Black citizens, and an idea pivotal to the whole Gee's Bend drama. Yet the *Times* did not ask Graves to clarify his dissent, much less insert the name of the man who urged it, indeed, the man who first got the "Big World" beyond Wilcox to even look at Gee's Bend—Ren Kennedy. Likewise, a few of Graves's descriptions are unartful paraphrases from the writings of the man whom Graves did not mention by name. Still, "Big World" provided a high-profile historical summary. It led to greater public awareness of Rothstein's photography and the Benders' plight. And it proved a useful rallying point for future, generally well-intended agendas for helping the Benders.[10]

A month before "Big World" appeared, no doubt aware of what the *Times* had coming, *Christian Century* asked Kennedy for an update on the Bend. The *Century* saw the US government's buying land and reselling it to Benders as a big development. But neither the *Century* nor Kennedy, nor the *Times*, could have known the even bigger story quietly unfolding at the time. As historian Wayne Flynt has explained, the Farm Bureau—led by Alabamian Edward A. O'Neal III—working quietly through Alabama's senator, John H. Bankhead II, "waged constant war" to redirect New Deal money away from projects such as Gee's Bend and into the pockets of large-scale white farmers. Preoccupied with writing two book-length manuscripts, Kennedy still agreed to send *Christian Century* "something." "Life at Gee's Bend" appeared on September 1, 1937, some twenty days after Graves's article appeared. Straight journalism. No Yaupon.

While Kennedy took the reader through the evolution of the crisis, he also gave detail lacking in Graves's article. He explained how four white landlords owned the Bend and how the Van de Graaffs' 7,500 acres fitted into the pending government-purchase plan. He also got concrete on croppers of the

Van de Graaff place as of mid-1937: 64 cropper families totaling 456 people. Perhaps irritated by Graves's assertion, he amplified the uniqueness of the Benders, as "another civilization" and "an Alabama Africa" and "a tropical spell," to capture the isolated cultural purity of these people. With clearer detail than Graves had provided, he explained the stages of government intervention leading up to the land-purchase plan. He quoted from Ed-O Pettway, Alf Moseley, and Patrick Bendorf, reflecting people getting "up on their feet again." What markedly separated the piece from his previous Gee's Bend vignettes, however, was his treatment of the 1932–33 "bust up."

In his early 1930s writings, Kennedy mainly focused on how the Rentz business kept "advancing" the Benders when nobody else would. Despite carrying huge Depression-era debt, Rentz alone did not cut them off and go collecting. In the context of the times he was an admirable man. As for the raid, in the early 1930s Kennedy saw the widowed Mrs. Rentz in a horribly indebted bind, which ultimately caused her to foreclose; her mistake was not hiring people to do it in a more compassionate way. In the 1937 "Life at Gee's Bend," however, this changed. He wrote: "The family was utterly ruthless in settling the estate." Perhaps over the last two years he had discovered more about the finances. Perhaps he had learned more about who said what within the Rentz family. Perhaps he found that at least one of the Rentz sons told the collection gang to do exactly what they did. Certainly, going in and out of the Bend, as he had been doing since the early 1930s, Kennedy heard even more stories of the harshness of the "bust up." At the same time, Kennedy's new Bend piece reflected no change in his great admiration for *Robert* Rentz— except possibly an increase in respect. Years afterward, when any number of people interviewed Kennedy about Gee's Bend, he backtracked to "*after* [italics mine] Mr. [Robert] Rentz died his family was in a bad situation and had little choice."

Despite his careful separation of Robert from the "bust up," Kennedy's 1937 descriptive phrase "utterly ruthless" emerged as the standard published characterization of the entire Rentz family, not just the collection agent. This had to have been facilitated by the well-known personality of Robert's brother, E. O. Rentz, and the public's confusing the two. Even more, if an array of writers and even the Wilcox public could confuse these two brothers, despite Ephraim's dying ten years *before* the "bust-up," two points jump out. First, *Robert* Rentz was a businessman who acted with what he and Kennedy considered a "Christian conscience." Second, the raiders did horrific things to the Benders. But with the loss of Kennedy's Red Cross records, and barring new information, the rest of the story remains forever murky.[11]

From January through September 1938 writing the book about Covington County whites took up most of Kennedy's attention. Back in September

1934 he had made a first start on the project—a twenty-page short story, "Episode in Alabama." Drawn from early notes as well as recent attendance at a revival near Mt. Sanai, the story focuses on a poor white preacher with two specialties: differentiating between "tracks" of rattlesnakes and copperheads, and shelling peas on the ground, then fighting two old roosters for the bounty. Such ventures continued through the good offices of ARP preacher Joseph L. Pressly, who had a church at the train juncture of Red Level, in Covington County, and an assortment of home missions throughout Covington and Escambia counties. Pressly regularly leaned on Kennedy for guest preaching as well as meetings. Kennedy enjoyed it, though Mary mocked the "pay."[12]

Pressley's "fertile field" was actually isolated pockets of farm life—chiefly people of Scotch-Irish origins out of Georgia and South Carolina. But Covington's soil was anything but Black Belt. Just north of the Florida line, its soil was the transition from the southern Red Hills to the piney woods. Corporate pine tree growing was yet to arrive in Covington. So, with few exceptions, here were poor white people praying that the next flooding of creeks somehow would spare their subsistence plantings.

Kennedy constantly compared Wilcox and Covington. Though no more than one-third of its 907 square miles offered nutritious soil, Wilcox had a fulsome history with King Cotton. In 1860 Wilcox's whites numbered 6,795, its Black slaves 17,797. The same year Covington's 853 square miles hosted 6,149 whites but only 800 Black slaves. Even factoring in Wilcox's Red Hills life, the two counties offered stark contrast.[13]

With the major exception of their harsh racism, Kennedy appreciated Covington's people for much the same reason he liked their preacher—personal humility. But their abject isolation from twentieth-century life also fascinated him. Whenever he visited, he came away with long diary entries on their food, housing, recreation, and speech habits—in effect, ethnographies by an untrained cultural anthropologist. After he recorded lengthy dialogues, he asked Pressly for analysis and interpretation. As he moved this project to a book-length manuscript in 1937, "Pigeon Creek" morphed to fictional "Fish Creek"—not to be confused with Baldwin County's Fish River. Otherwise, "The People on Fish Creek" remained exactly as he saw them, including their actual names. The manuscript ran some 300 handwritten 5 × 8 inch pages; the typed version did not survive.

Kennedy saw "Fish Creek" life as inseparable from geography. "Most of the land was rolling sand hills. . . . Fertilizer had to be used to make a crop . . . [but] profits got swallowed up by his fertilizer bill. . . . If a man had fifty dollars left at the end of the year, he felt it had been a good year." Unlike poor Blacks in Wilcox, many of these poor Scotch-Irish of Covington once owned their own land. But the cycle of advancing, bad crops, and economic downturns—accentuated by bad farming soil—brought their living standards down toward the life of Black Belt croppers. In short, as the Depression came on, most people of Fish Creek tenant-farmed and had next to nothing. Here is how that happened.

"Because of debt the Federal Land Bank, lumber companies and banks of Red Level and Andalusia came to own most of the land along the creek." Still, "the land was so cheap it was not fundamentally important who owned it." Given these hard realities, "Fish Creek people actually preferred to be tenant farmers. They didn't have to pay taxes." Fatalistically Christian—many Baptists and Methodists, some ARPs, and but no Old School Presbyterians—they accepted their circumstances and focused on what pleasures were free.

And there were some. Kennedy was fascinated by a laconic poetry permeating their daily lives. "The people on Fish Creek . . . never bothered to write down their poetry, but in their way of life . . . it crept out every day. 'A deer,' said Sam Hood, 'is jest natcherly made fer gettn' away from here. He's built for leavin'. . . . He's like a buzzard's shadow slippin' through the woods.'"

Their poetry also appeared in carefully concocted first and middle names of children in large families. "Dave Hill's masterpiece . . . was . . . Willie May, Jewel Gray, Bessie Ray, Edith Fay, and Elsie Gay." Carson Hood did the same with multiple syllables: "Allie Maybelle, Lola Voncelle, Mamie Estelle, Rebecca Moselle, Alabama Odell." "Lucian Smith told me if Carson had another girl he was going to name her, 'Goto Hell.'" Families were not territorial about unique names. "There were several Ovaries and Lavinias, Voncelles and Ovelmas." Male names further stretched the imagination: "Pleasant (Plez), Phone, Alto, Baalarn, Zimri, Cuvee, Jesker, Welcome, Blueford, Cumi . . . and Below."

If "unlettered," their life of the mind still included genuine sophistication about hunting and fishing. Take Will Robinson, "a lean, grizzled, grey man of 65 wearing . . . faded overalls . . . the poor white. . . . The stranger might conclude . . . human draught animal. . . . But the stranger would be wrong. His mind was incapable of appreciating an intellectual dogma but was extremely sensitive to the Great Spirit or whatever it is that is back of Nature." And that unlettered aesthetic also performed fine indoors. Consider Eugene Mitchell:

> The only thing Eugene Mitchell needed to make him happy was someone to listen to him talk. His mind was a trough for useless information and in the course of 50 years not one drop had sloshed out. . . . Six years under his monologue froze the genial current of [his son-in-law's] soul. . . . [When] the old man died . . . [the son-in-law] enjoyed the funeral more than any he ever attended. . . . He put up a tombstone . . . with a quotation from Solomon on it: "a fool is known by the multitude of his words."[14]

Yet clearly Kennedy found some of their "poetry" not that at all, but just simple "frontier humor" in the genre of Mark Twain. One particular episode from Covington County remained on his tongue for the rest of his life. Reverend Pressly recently had buried a man he knew to have been both mean and antiliteracy. He was not an ARP; he just needed burying. And it happened in a small family plot out in the woods under an oak tree. Notably, with the exception of the Bible, the man saw reading and writing as a source of much of what was wrong with civilization. Yet about a week after the funeral, the man's three adult daughters established a time for a conversation about his tombstone inscription. When Pressly, it turned out, had some urgent reason to return to South Carolina for a week, he asked Kennedy to fill in for him, including the tombstone counsel.

"We want a good tombstone for Daddy," the eldest daughter led off. "But we need help on what to put on it." In response, Kennedy suggested any number of biblical passages, none of which seemed to resonate with the three in front of him. So he threw out one or two from Shakespeare. Back came looks of puzzlement. To move things along, he cut right to his strong conviction about funerals. "Since the deceased is, well, dead, tombstones are for the living. Choose an inscription that helps *you* in your time of bereavement." Though the daughters said they understood, they still seemed stuck. The afternoon growing long, Kennedy next offered up the ever useful: "A Good Man." At that, the second oldest daughter blurted out, "But Daddy wasn't!" Softly, Kennedy said again: "Remember, tombstones are for the living; and, anyhow, Rev. Pressly said your father could not have cared less about what words you choose. So as long as it's the truth, the choice is up to you." After a significant pause, the youngest daughter queried: "Don't most people put something about God on there?" Kennedy nodded yes. After a short huddle the three emerged, eagerly, with their passage: "Daddy—Not a good man, by God."

For reasons we soon will see, Kennedy never worked this encounter into his writing. Yet for years afterward, given the slightest opportunity, he used the vignette in conversations about funerals. Here was his first articulation of record about something he felt strongly about. Tombstones are for the living.[15]

At any rate, through such Covington observations Kennedy observed causes and consequences of cultural isolation—the same notion explicit in the life of Black educator William Green Wilson, but with a different angle. Many people of Covington settled where they did between 1815 and 1820 *because* it was isolated. Never mind its harshness. The Black people of Gee's Bend, by contrast, did anything but choose where they landed. But what race and physical removal did to the Benders, poverty did to Covington's poor whites. With their acceptance of life the way it was, their integration into the twentieth century looked bleak even if they wanted something different.

Broaden the comparison, and he saw something else. Obviously, the roots of cultural isolation among Black Belt planters were so different from those of the Benders and the Pigeon Creekers. Each day options for change were available to the planters. They just did not want it. Kennedy's notes reflect these and many other comparisons. Foremost, he gained considerable insights into Black Belt aristocrats by looking at the other white life in Covington. Still, he thought he had two manuscripts publishable independently—separate from the comparisons.

In October 1937 he mailed off the manuscript of "The People of Fish Creek"—a book about poor isolated whites trying to survive the Depression. The Macmillan Company said no. Shortly after, Charles Blanchard at Little, Brown and Co. showed some interest. He kept the manuscript for six months and got several on his staff to react. In the end back it came, another no: "We liked the authenticity and realized that many of the sketches are written with artistry. Nevertheless, there is a certain monotony and lack of warmth."[16]

But Kennedy's sardonic perspective persisted. During the summer of 1938 he wrote a centennial celebration history of the 136-member Camden ARPC. On September 1, 1938, it appeared in the *Progressive Era* and was subsequently reprinted by that paper for independent sale. Though meticulously researched, as a commemorative piece it nevertheless could have been perplexing for his more analytical congregants. By tone and vocabulary, it seemed dominated by his own inner psychology about where he lived: "No prospect" for growth.[17]

Meanwhile, all through 1938 he rebuilt the Yaupon book—drafting more and reacting to suggestions for changes offered by members of Viola's Roundtable while the group otherwise was preoccupied with *The Report on the Economic Conditions of the South* (1938), the much publicized report by the Roosevelt administration documenting the South as "the Number One Economic Problem" in America. As Kennedy deduced from the Little, Brown rejection, whether "Yaupon" or "Fish Creek," his vignettes needed slightly more distance from the real-life people who prompted them—without diminishing concreteness and starkness. Not easy. His researching and writing a history of the Camden ARP Church right in the middle of all this added to the problem: in a few cases the characters were the same.

Meanwhile he kept adding new vignettes to "Yaupon." "The Whipping of Lester Carloss" probed the conscience of a planter from an old family whom many in Yaupon considered a "liberal" on race. Modeled at least in part on Kennedy's friend, Paul Starr—Starr did not have an antebellum Wilcox plantation background—"Mr. Barclay" agonized over "proper punishment" for a mildly "retarded" black sharecropper's son who stole a few items from his house.

Another one, "Bird Hunt," traced a conversation between planters and their business-executive guests from the city. As they shot quail, they talked about out-of-work people around them as if they were widgets. Here, Kennedy does not use the word "bloc," as he did in "Black Belt Aristocrats." Still, he delivered a scathing attack on the heartlessness of the Black Belt–Big Mule alliance so powerfully defeating modern progress in Alabama. "Don't think about them," said the vice president, "just go after that next covey." Kennedy's antihunting biases were apparent; these people terminated workers the same way they shot quail. Pragmatically, he kept that connection muted. An unleashing of his proto–animal rights sensitivities would have weakened his political and economic message. The *Century* published "Bird Hunt" in its December 28, 1938, issue.[18]

It also got several more straight journalistic reports out of him. In the May 11, 1938, issue he provided yet another, even bleaker update on cotton and the Depression, "Is It the End of Cotton?" After rehashing the fall of cotton prices and various efforts of the Farm Bureau and the US government to increase prices through controlling production, he said point-blank: "Results are discouraging."

After five years of various "controls" in the United States, three things stood out. First, the world cotton market had a glut. Second, the American share of both cotton production and cotton exports had declined significantly. A removal of controls would see southern cotton selling at three to four cents a pound rather than the 1938 price of about eight cents a pound. But continued controls further diminished the role of southern cotton in the world economy. Stuck in a box. "The agricultural South" lived on with "subsidies from the federal government, [and] poverty just increases year to year." The cotton belt had welfare farming at every level. Even if this had helped some landlords, the New Deal had done anything but rescue the cotton belt's masses.[19]

On June 8, the *Century* carried his equally depressing outlook for jobs resulting from the bleak cotton-belt economics. "W.P.A., Here We Come!" was classic Yaupon. Two weeks earlier he and Bill Jones had attended graduation exercises at the high school of Snow Hill Institute. Kennedy changed a few names, replaced Snow Hill with Rose Hill, and recounted the graduation of the twenty-five seniors. "I sat on the front row with the white superintendent . . . and a white woman on the board. . . . [The twenty-piece student orchestra led off]. I said [to Bill], 'Cotton field Negroes playing a Schubert serenade. . . . The white schools do not make a better showing. . . . There's not an orchestra in any white school in the county.'"

As for the white woman with them, this was Martha Patton Simpson. Here was the daughter of Ramson Overton Simpson, of nearby Furman. Protégé of Booker T. Washington, he had provided major support for the

Black native of Snow Hill, William J. Edwards, to begin development of Snow Hill Institute modeled on Washington's Tuskegee Institute. For this and other acts of relatively liberal racial behavior, Simpson lost many white friendships. But daughter Martha embraced her father. On inheriting most of his wealth, she continued his commitment to use it to the good of others.

Among the student speakers at the Snow Hill commencement was one Kennedy called "Isaiah Samuel Young." He addressed "Some Aspects of Rural Economics and Social Life . . . an intelligent [talk] on what he learned at the school about scientific farming." "Isaiah said he looked forward to the day when he and his neighbors would have farm incomes of $1800 a year." Next came the commencement address by a Tuskegee Institute faculty member. Though "bitter" about "the loss of traditional Negro jobs to poor whites," he urged "leadership among Negroes" to overcome "farm tenancy, ignorance, and unscientific farming." Realistically, what future did these graduates have? Despite the courage called for by the professor, Kennedy was not optimistic. After Snow Hill, "Isaiah may make $300 a year as a tenant farmer. . . . A few of the graduates will go on to Tuskegee . . . or Fisk. And what then? . . . The dice are too heavily loaded against them. It is a hard matter for a white man in the depression to make a decent living in the rural South. It's almost impossible for a Negro. WPA, here we come!"[20]

Even so, he was encouraging in an update on the Gee's Bend project, "Life Goes on at Gee's Bend," appearing December 14, 1938, in the *Century*. Because of the Farm Security Administration work, begun in 1936, life was a lot better for the 100 Negro families—650 people—living in the 11,000 acres of the Bend. Reasonably good roads now led to the ferry landings. In place of tenant "shacks made of pine poles, mud daubed," and lacking window screens, Benders increasingly lived in new homes they bought through forty-year mortgages from the federal government. The three- and four-room structures were made of "sawed and planed wood" and had glass windows, built-in screened porches, and roofs with actual shingles.

They had neither electricity nor indoor water. But near clusters of homes they had access to hand-pump wells and sanitary toilets. Their food situation was good as far as vegetables went; it had been a rainy season. This meant, however, that cotton proceeds were down. The FSA had erected a schoolhouse, a new church, and a clinic staffed with a resident nurse. A doctor came at least once a month for two days of appointments. The FSA also created the Gee's Bend Cooperative. This offered a cotton gin and a commissary. The Benders managed it.

Kennedy praised the work of FSA project manager W. A. Cammack and resident engineer R. P. Yount. He mentioned the foreclosures but said nothing about the Rentz family raid of 1932–33. He admitted that "some white people [in Wilcox County] say [the project] is ruining the niggers, not only in Gee's Bend but all niggers in the county." He could have mentioned that many of these same white people readily accepted federal government assistance for farming. But this time he did not. Overall, he saw the "fascinating experiment" as off to a good start—"transformation" to go on for some time. On reading the piece, his good friend, Stonewall McConnico, had a different twist. McConnico was not one of the whites who resented Gee's Bend, but he still was skeptical: "I do not know how much longer [the government effort at] Gee's Bend will go on . . . give it a chance and we shall see."[21]

Kennedy's focus on books continued in 1939. He drafted more Yaupon storylines, ready for dialogue. The simplistic hypocrisy of whites ridiculing Blacks and government aid, reactions to further developments in the Scottsboro case, friendship between white and Black preachers, local political corruption and local Baptists, the limited worldview of most Black Belt Baptists compared to some urban Baptists, the difficult future of farming in the Black Belt—these idea pieces went to the file for "the Yaupon book." He also completed "Peter DeSoto," his new archetype Black Belt leader. In the Depression, the family of Captain DeSoto "hung on, essentially useless in the greater world but well fed, well clothed and with two cars. To the ultimate defeat of themselves and everyone around them, they wouldn't turn loose to let better things happen." Yet one of the 1939 Yaupon pieces intended for "the book" he also sent to *Christian Century*. It appeared in the May 17, 1939, issue. And it created what he forever called "The Jolt." More than hinting at why his regular focus on southern Baptists had intensified, it had been awhile in the making.[22]

Back in October 1934 Rev. John Dobbins departed Camden Baptist Church. He was replaced by Eldridge Waldo Roark, a Maryland native who came to adulthood in New Orleans. In contrast to Dobbins, the new minister had deeply conservative views on race, more in line with what deacons of the church wanted. After all, several of the deacons were Klan leaders, and the church had approved a Klan rally on its property. Kennedy did not describe Roark as a member of the Klan. Yet, against the backdrop of the Scottsboro case, he believed Roark regularly used his pulpit and his tall stature, good looks, and magnetic personality to attack the idea of Negroes serving on juries and voting, and saw how this might shape the future of Wilcox County—clearly a minority white county. Kennedy attributed Roark's message and that of some other Baptist ministers to an intensification of racial tensions throughout Wilcox during the summer and fall of 1938. A decade later, the cultural anthropologist Morton Rubin was in Camden researching Black Belt life and went further: Rubin found Roark "a charismatic man [and] an expansionist, one who would say most anything to expand his flock."[23]

Out of that background something awful occurred. On the night of Tuesday, September 6, 1938, a Negro named Jonas Martin broke into the home office of Edgar Pritchett, the planter whose land he tenant-farmed just south of Camden. Martin stole thirty-five dollars and a .38 Smith & Wesson revolver. The 200-pound Martin long had held records for cotton picking. Attention he got for such accomplishment, however, only deepened his resentment over how little he received from such feats. Local whites and Blacks knew him as "an angry man"; he had assault records in a neighboring county. He stole the money and the pistol, and took off. Pritchett called Sheriff Reg Albritton, who put his deputy, Goode Tait, on the case.[24]

All this fitted into a complicated scene of descendants of old planter families and law enforcement. Thirty-four years old and great-grandson of US senator and federal judge Charles Tait, Deputy Tait seemed destined to follow in the footsteps of his brother, Felix Tait III, who was sheriff from 1923 to 1927 and unable to succeed himself because Wilcox at the time had the wisdom to bar sheriffs from repeatedly successive terms, a prohibition ceasing in 1939. After high school graduation in 1930, Goode Tait sold used cars in Camden and Texas before getting on as Camden's town marshal. In 1936, Reg Albritton—from an old Snow Hill family—became sheriff, succeeding his father, Lee Albritton. The new sheriff then promoted Goode Tait to deputy. But this promotion was only to the junior deputy position. He would report to the senior deputy, one Columbus P. (Lummie) Jenkins.

Jenkins's grandfather was a noted Episcopalian and antebellum planter and physician; Jenkins's father, a Wilcox sheriff from 1913 to 1917. After a 1927 graduation from the Wilcox County High School, Jenkins headed straight to Nashville for a six-month course on auto mechanics. No sooner had he left home, however, than the position of Camden town marshal opened up. He took the post. Nine years later, when his first cousin, deputy Thomas Jenkins Jones, died from gunshot in the line of duty, Lummie Jenkins moved from town marshal to deputy. That is how Lummie Jenkins came to be Goode Tait's immediate supervisor in 1938.

Like most things Deep South, all this had a religious twist. By the mid-1930s, with the exception of Lummie Jenkins—sometimes a Baptist, at other times an ARP—these law enforcers regularly attended Camden's ARP church. Even some of the Tait lawmen had forsaken their family's long history with Methodism, going back to the friendship between Sen. Charles Tait and American Methodist Episcopal bishop, Francis Asbury. So, Kennedy's life had its complications, not just feuding lawyers and physicians, but old-family descendants claiming their hereditary and "understood" roles in Wilcox law enforcement.[25]

The day after the robbery, Wednesday, September 7, Deputy Tait went to Martin's house to question him. Tait could not find him. So he put out the word that the law wanted to talk to him. The next morning, Thursday, the fugitive emerged from woods along the Miller's Ferry Road. He flagged down a Trailways bus. The bus driver knew of the search. He stopped at Henderson's Store in Miller's Ferry and called Sheriff Albritton's office. The Trailways bus moved off again. But shortly Deputy Tait drove up behind the bus, and the driver pulled off at a fish camp on the river "for a cold Coca Cola."

As the bus came to a stop, Jonas Martin broke through the door and ran for the woods. On foot Tait chased him. Folks milled around the bus waiting for the deputy to bring him out of the woods. After thirty minutes they heard two shots. Nobody came out of the woods. They called for more law and spread the word. Sheriff Albritton, two state troopers, and a posse of Wilcox whites soon found Deputy Tait: dead, shot in the face.

The next day, Friday, September 9, Sheriff Albritton announced a $300 reward for anyone turning in Martin and expanded the search with a Camden posse led by the sheriff himself and Deputy Jenkins. This was augmented by eleven Alabama state troopers and two Negro inmate-trustees with bloodhounds. Reports varied on origin of the trustees and the dogs: some said Kilby Prison in Montgomery, others "a prison in Meridian." Regardless, troopers knew them as effective "dog-boys"—managers of bloodhounds.

As the search commenced, Sheriff Albritton told a reporter for the *Tuscaloosa News* that the posse were "responsible men." He expected "no trouble in the event the posse captured the negro." The Baptist minister, E. W. Roark, was prominent in the posse. An experienced hunter, Roark carried his own semi-automatic shotgun loaded with buckshot.

At first the search produced no fugitive. But the following morning, Friday, September 9, some thirty miles northward in Perry County, near the hamlet of Felix, Jonas Martin sought food at the house of a Black sharecropper named Joseph Williams. The father quietly told the son to go get the law. State troopers, posse, Reverend Roark, bloodhounds, and "dog-boys" soon encircled the tiny farm. Jonas Martin bolted from the house. One report says he made it to a cornfield, another says it was a sugarcane field. At any rate, they ran him out of the field. In interviews with the *Birmingham News* and the *Anniston Star*, Deputy Jenkins said that "Frank (Buck) Porter, a life-term trustee . . . reported [that] the fugitive 'showed fight'. . . . [So] Porter opened fire when the fugitive made a motion indicating he had a gun." That first shot reportedly hit Martin in the right arm. He kept running, it was later told, until one of "the [other] dog boys" brought him down with a load of buckshot to the back.

For public viewing they took Jonas Martin's body back to Camden to the steps of the jail behind the courthouse. It lay there for several hours. Kennedy was on the scene. "Some kicked on it," he noted, "like a dead animal." The minister from Antioch Baptist Church—a Black church founded during Reconstruction—and a few friends took the body away for burial.

That same Friday afternoon, Joseph Williams received the promised $300 reward, and Kennedy did the funeral for Goode Tait. That night Kennedy told the diary: "Buried Goode Tait this afternoon, a decent Christian man, a good friend and a member of my church." On, Monday, September 12, the *Anniston Star* quoted Deputy Jenkins as saying, "In no way [could the killing of Martin Jonas] be called a lynching." The September 15 issue of the *Wilcox Progressive Era* covered Goode Tait's death with little reference to the chase for "his assailant" and no mention of what happened to "his assailant." Same for the *Tuscaloosa News*.[26]

Although any number of Kennedy's sermons over the next several months can be read as showing that his mind was on this event, none of them specifically referenced it. As was his habit, he undoubtedly just listened for more details—for the truth—as he loafed at the barbershop and the courthouse square. Likewise, the war in Europe was expanding. If that preoccupied him on its own, it also profoundly influenced his view of the Jonas Martin killing. For example, on Friday night, January 13, 1939, a penetrating conversation occurred up at Oak Hill, where Joyce and Bill Jones now lived full time taking care of Sam Boykin—his wife, Matt, having died six months earlier. That evening the Joneses hosted an Oak Hill dinner-and-book-discussion night. Ren and Mary were the only Camdenites included. Kennedy's diary notes from that night permit reasonably concrete reconstruction of the table talk.

The book for the night was Eva Lips's *Savage Symphony* (1938), telling of Jewish persecution in Nazi-controlled Germany. With the Jonas Martin killing still on everyone's minds, conversation moved swiftly to a comparison of persecution suffered by German Jews and American Negroes. Then it moved to racial discord in Wilcox and the overwhelming issues of law enforcement.

Whites were a distinct minority, all agreed, but assisted by the historic lie of white superiority over Black, they had the power. How deep and pervasive was the Negro's general fear of the white-man's power? How did that sometimes result in Negro fugitives shooting it out with white officials? How did Wilcox's generally violent behavior factor into killings and law enforcement? For sure, out of these dynamics numerous Blacks died from lynchings and other transgressions void of due process. And what about white law enforcement officials killed due to a racially polarized event? Over the previous thirty years, white law officials killed trying to arrest Blacks included Dallas County deputy sheriff (native of Camden) George F. McNeill (January 26, 1915); Wilcox deputy sheriff Thomas Jenkins Jones (January 1, 1936); and now Wilcox deputy sheriff Goode Tait (September 7, 1939).

The evening concluded with a question for the group: "If I were part of a minority, whether numerical-minority or power-minority, and I were consistently subjected to violence"—referencing both Jews of Europe and Blacks of the American South—"would I have the courage to fight back?" There is no record of what Kennedy said at the table, nor the others. But that night back in the manse in Camden, after summarizing the table conversation, he confessed to the diary: "I don't know."[27]

With these thoughts anything but gone, during January, February, and early March of 1939 Kennedy worked feverishly on revisions to "The Yaupon Tales" as well as the "Fish Creek" project. At the same time, he critiqued Richebourg McWilliams's prospectus and early chapters for the Martin Van Buren Jones novel. Now married and an associate professor of English at Birmingham-Southern College, McWilliams responded well to Kennedy's direct appraisal: "The prospectus needs to go more to the point of the proposed book." With appropriate changes made, Kennedy wrote a strong, lengthy endorsement to the Rosenwald Foundation for McWilliams to get a year off from Birmingham-Southern to finish the novel. In late March, Kennedy finally moved on to his own two projects. Although he had had no contact with T. S. Stribling, celebrated north Alabama author of *The Store*, he was taken by that novel and Stribling's other work. Again, he rolled the dice. He mailed "The Yaupon Tales" as well as "The People of Fish Creek" to the New York house publishing Stribling—Doubleday, Doran. They said they would take a look.[28]

Meanwhile, in mid-April—the seven months since September having barely diminished Camden street talk about Goode Tait and Jonas Martin— Kennedy started to write about the two killings. It would be an additional Yaupon tale. He changed Jonas Martin's name to "Adam Gilmore." He called Goode Tait "the sheriff." He couched the sketch in the context of something he had addressed several times before: how ongoing reverberations of Scottsboro exacerbated white fears about Black people serving in jury pools and their voting and, ultimately, white people's loss of control over Yaupon. More broadly, he explained, because of white minority status, and out of "history, racial feeling, self-interest, and human nature," the whites had long ago decided that adherence to "white supremacy" was their only way to exist. "White supremacy" took precedence over all "questions in their minds about justice." He then took the reader through basic facts of the case. He did not question that Adam Gilmore shot the sheriff. But the killing of Adam Gilmore was another thing. The sardonic tone laid it out: "A man hunt is a fascinating scene. The posse—half of the members cowardly and terrified, the rest as intense as bloodhounds—gets a savage thrill from it. . . . The technical distinction between shooting a man down and lynching him is not clear."

Kennedy obviously concluded that Jonas Martin did not attack the posse and the law, resulting in their shooting him "for cause." Instead, he concluded, the man ran. Then they shot him rather than arresting him and bringing him in for trial. Kennedy did not say who—or how many—shot "Gilmore." Though he undoubtedly heard of thirty-six-year-old Monette Curtis—a Camden night watchman and Klan member—"street-bragging" about having fired the shot that brought down Martin, Curtis's well-known proclivity for exaggeration (likely a function of insecurity stemming from a childhood of public ridicule for being a stutterer) may well have made Kennedy doubt the Curtis story, even if his comrade, Bill Jones, heard the story from Curtis's lips and believed it. Still, without naming names, fictionally or otherwise, Kennedy pointed up the oddity of the main Baptist preacher in town being present at the killing, shotgun in hand. And anthropologist Rubin, who visited Wilcox a decade later to interview locals about Black Belt daily life, and who spent many hours with Kennedy, remembered: "Kennedy believed that [Baptist minister] Roark . . . encouraged the killing of that black man." Likewise, Kennedy emphasized in the article that "the sheriff's family" urged posse members that the Negro was to be killed, "not captured." And in a subsequent Yaupon piece, "The Liquidation of Mr. Smith," he dispensed with the sardonic literary question about whether it was a lynching and simply called this "a lynching." It was the Scottsboro influence. "Yankee lawyers and a jury with Negroes might interfere . . . more direct and simple to handle it in the woods." And then the acerbic conclusion: "All the white people in the county felt that it was a sad piece of business. Most of them felt that since it happened at all it was better that it turned out the way it did. Most of them disapproved of lynching and torture. Most of them also didn't want a legal trial." He titled the piece, "How It Happens." *Christian Century* took it with no revisions.[29]

Century subscribers often received their copies in the mail as much as ten days before book and magazine shops had them. Although "How It Happens" appeared in the May 17, 1939, issue, the magazine arrived in Kennedy's home mailbox on Tuesday, May 9. When he went to the box at noon something else was in there, too—a letter from Doubleday, Doran turning down both of his book manuscripts. That night, late, he wrote his friend: "Richebourg . . . I knew the odds were against me . . . my personal pride has suffered a little bit . . . [but] I still believe I can write a novel." Over the next week, however, that sting passed as "How It Happens" hit Wilcox "in the gut."

At this time, four other Wilcoxons subscribed to the *Christian Century*— Bill Jones, Stonewall McConnico, Viola Liddell, and Hugh Ervin. Before, as their issues were passed around to friends who might have agreed with a certain article, or not, Kennedy's pieces had generated little to no reaction, much to his continual frustration. This time it was different. Martha Patton

Simpson, Viola Liddell, and Emmett Kilpatrick publicly applauded the piece. Indeed, along with Bill Jones, Viola offered her copy for others to read. By the same token, "four or five" members of his Camden congregation—unspecified in the diary—"temporarily departed." While "distressed and angry," Miller Bonner was not one of them, nor was former governor Meek Miller. Still, even though Kennedy never said Roark shot anyone—only that he carried a shotgun loaded with buckshot, which no one seems to have denied—Baptists were especially angry about the article. What Kennedy so badly wanted finally occurred: the people around him reacted.

In June, he wrote to Charles Dobbins Jr., in an administrative post at Alabama College, that he was "still living, breathing ... and getting ... satisfaction out of having jolted the community." Several days later Dobbins replied: "I believe by sitting steady you'll come through with just a few scars." Even though Miller Bonner, then serving as legal advisor to Gov. Frank Dixon, again recovered—"That we will go to the end of the weary road as loyal friends neither of us has ever doubted"—"scars" seemed of little concern to him. In early July, on receipt of another letter from Kennedy, saying the "tempest" was about over, Dobbins wrote: "I can *understand* your satisfaction in having jolted the community. It was a genuinely healthy experience for all."[30]

Kennedy never forgot this episode. On May 9, 1942—and on May 9 for many years to come—he reminded the diary, "Anniversary of The Jolt." And in 1947, anthropologist Rubin would try to read into the episode something larger: "On reactions to that killing of the black man in 1939, well, that turned out to be the last Klan killing in the county"—granted, an assertion likely inaccurate with the unfolding of the 1950s and 1960s. So, whether the episode and Kennedy's high-profile coverage of it catalyzed the change of any white hearts remains difficult to judge. Yet "How It Happens" offered clarity on a related matter: differences between Cason and Kennedy. As far as confrontation goes, "How It Happens" well exceeded *90 Degrees in the Shade*. And the Wilcox heretic was ready for more.[31]

And that makes his looking around all the more complex. Not that he hungered to leave in the mid-to-late 1930s, but Kennedy's fulsome publishing brought any number of job opportunities elsewhere. A University of Alabama philosophy professor and Presbyterian minister, George Lang, figured prominently into these sub rosa developments

Throughout the 1930s and 1940s, Lang strategically advanced social reform and Protestant ecumenicalism within churches of the Deep South by serving as an informal "headhunter" for personnel moves connecting socially liberal preachers with churches wanting them—though not many did. His regular network included two well-known liberals, Birmingham's Henry Edmonds and Anniston's Charles R. Bell Jr., at Parker Memorial Baptist. It also included Atlanta's J. McDowell Richards, president of Columbia Theological Seminary. Considered by 1930s and 1940s liberals a "conservative" seminary for its theological orientation—a distorting label persisting into modern historical scholarship—it nevertheless produced any number of "conservative" pastors who embraced broad-ranging Social Gospel endeavors, just like J. McDowell Richards himself. Even though they had several mutual friends—not just Lang and Richards but also Charles Dobbins—Kennedy and Bell may never have met. But Kennedy clipped and saved Bell's prescient 1944 *Christian Century* article, "A Southern Approach to the Color Issue," urging an assertive Black-led civil rights movement. Lang and Kennedy, in contrast, had a particularly close relationship. On several occasions in the mid-1930s Kennedy guest-preached at Lang's home church, the First Presbyterian Church of Tuscaloosa, and far later at the new, overtly liberal University Presbyterian Church. Likewise, Lang provided several union services in Camden. Once he appeared side by side with Episcopal bishop, William G. McDowell—compliments of Rev. Justice Jones at Carlowville.[32]

Out of this nexus, in early 1939 Lang advanced Kennedy for the pulpit of Tuscaloosa's First Presbyterian. It is difficult to judge Kennedy's interest. Still, he agreed to be considered, only to be advised by Lang that it was "too late": their top candidate, Warner Hall, who had been waffling, took up the call. Lang immediately put Kennedy's name in for the pulpit of First Presbyterian Church of Montevallo. Again, Kennedy agreed to enter the search. He preached. His old friend from Camden, Charles Dobbins Jr., secretary (executive vice president) to Alabama College president Arthur Fort Harmony, weighed in nicely. And Kennedy got the offer, which included part-time instructional opportunities in philosophy and literature at the college. Just before the offer went public, however, Kennedy withdrew, implying that the salary was too low.

Lang kept going. Kennedy's name entered the search at the First Presbyterian Church of Birmingham. Too late: another waffler, North Carolinian Harold J. Dudley, decided to accept the call, only to stay a short while and be replaced by Edward V. Ramage, a product of Columbia Theological Seminary and, as Jonathan Bass has detailed, destined to welcome Black worshippers into the Birmingham First Presbyterian Church and play a major role in events leading to Martin Luther King's "Letter from Birmingham Jail." At any rate, at Selma's First Presbyterian Church it was the compensation factor again. Finally, there was the First Presbyterian Church of Norman, Oklahoma. Before the Presbyterian Club of the University of Oklahoma, Kennedy preached a sermon with the title "Jesus Was a Liberal." He also spoke on "The Black Belt Today" before the Norman Rotary Club. Rotarians liked him. Presbyterian students liked him. Presbyterian elders did not. No call.[33]

This "looking around" seems to have remained subterranean. Although that can be attributed in part to Lang's diplomatic skills, and Kennedy's too, it did not hurt that most successful ministers do a fair amount of guest preaching—good subterfuge. Camden and Marion Junction ARP leaders seemed unaware. For sure, there were no counteroffers or "retainer deals" in this period of Kennedy's career, as there would be much later. Indeed, as late as 1941, five liberal ARP preachers—still considering Kennedy a loyal ARP—publicly advanced him for a professorship at Erskine College. The job included editorship of the *Associate Reformed Presbyterian*. Only the president of Erskine College had a higher ARP profile. These liberals hoped Kennedy would provide a beachhead for a larger invasion of ARP traditionalism. Kennedy seriously doubted the conservative ARP Synod would go along, nor did he want the job. Nor would Mary have agreed to a move to Due West, home of Ren's early flame, Louise Guerard Kennedy—married to Ren's distant cousin, Selden Kennedy. Even so, "talk" about his candidacy proved further cover for his clandestine investigations beyond ARPism. And in the end, as Kennedy anticipated, the Erskine position went to his opposite: the arch-conservative, fierce opponent of alcohol, Rev. Calvin Brice Williams.

Obvious questions remain. Despite the God Mandate, was Kennedy serious about leaving Wilcox? Or was he more like an animal at bay, pacing to and fro, awaiting his own instincts and the changing circumstances before making his next move? Despite possibilities of a breakthrough over "The Jolt," did looking around—without actually leaving—provide relief, or reinforcement, from feelings of incompleteness regarding the Mandate? or regarding rejection on his two book projects? Much like "The Jolt," time would tell.[34]

At any rate, these looks outside Wilcox appear not to have diminished Kennedy's intensity about Wilcox life—personal, pastoral, writing. Indeed, a major consequence of his trip to Oklahoma was a new publishing opportunity. At the Norman Rotary Club meeting he met a man five years his junior— Savoie Lottinville, editor of the University of Oklahoma Press. A native of Idaho and Oklahoma whose education included stints at Oxford University (where he was a Rhodes Scholar) as well as the universities of Berlin and Munich, Lottinville was one of the most highly regarded university press directors in the nation. He was decades ahead of other university press leaders in publishing readable and marketable nonscholarly "crossover" books, not just to reach broad audiences but to generate income that could underwrite first-class, if financially unproductive, scholarly works. After carefully listening to Kennedy's talk on "The Black Belt Today," he invited Kennedy back to his office for some two hours of conversation. At the end, Lottinville asked to see "The Yaupon Tales" as well as "The People of Fish Creek."

On return from Norman, Kennedy plunged ahead with their plan. He crafted eight additional Yaupon vignettes: New Deal damage to the Black Belt landscape; Black Belt planters' increasing shift to welfare agriculture; cataclysmic effects of alcoholism and racism; the conservatism of rural Baptists; and, as the war expanded in Europe, Black Belt reactions to overseas fascism. By prior agreement with Lottinville, one of these he published in the September 25, 1940, issue of *Christian Century*: "Poll Tax," showing this as just another strategy for whites to try to hang onto control of the Black Belt. On January 6, 1941, he submitted both book-length manuscripts to the University of Oklahoma Press.

Kennedy shared his submission news with Viola Liddell. She had been writing hard herself on Wilcox topics similar to his, just without any quasi-fictional cover. Otherwise, he kept his cards closer than usual. No sign of mentioning his submission to other members of the Roundtable. The Oklahoma review process, Lottinville cautioned, took time—quite different from a New York process.[35]

Meanwhile, Kennedy had published in conjunction with ever-orchestrating Emmett Kilpatrick. In 1939, Marie Bankhead Owen, director of the Alabama Department of Archives and History, asked her friend whom she helped rescue from Russian prison, "Captain Kilpatrick," to be associate editor of her new state-sponsored journal, the *Alabama Historical Quarterly (AHQ)*. He would have responsibility for article selection as well as lobbying the legislature at budget time. While notoriously resentful of Reconstruction carpetbaggers in Wilcox, Kilpatrick was otherwise a cosmopolitan socialist who did not share what journalist Kyle Whitmire has profiled as Bankhead's "Bourbon Democracy" devotion to the myth of the Lost Cause. Still, Kilpatrick was beholden to Owen. And not only did he revel in the social cachet of her Black Belt–Montgomery realm, he also used it shrewdly. He could do most of his *AHQ* work out of his Troy State Teachers College office. Should he need to meet with Mrs. Owen herself, his 1938 Ford knew well the fifty-mile route northwest to Montgomery.

More to the point, Kilpatrick recruited Kennedy to the same cause. It was an odd move. In April 1939, when Kennedy saw a *Birmingham News* replication of the new State of Alabama Great Seal, designed by Mrs. Owen and profiling the Confederate battle flag, he wrote her about how much he disliked it. She acknowledged his letter, tersely. Far more, she and he were polar opposites on Alabama history. Likewise, while the *Century* paid $15 for 500 words, *AHQ* paid nothing. Yet, without compromising the two book manuscripts, Lottinville wanted Kennedy's name in publications for future marketing purposes. And Emmett kept pushing. "We need you badly, *mon ami*, to make Mrs. Owen's journal a success." He also promised that he—not Mrs. Owen—made final decisions on articles. "She just wants her name on the front—showing she is editor." And, indeed, Kilpatrick promised to pay Kennedy ten dollars out of his own pocket for every article of his the *AHQ* carried. So, all three—Owen, Kilpatrick, Kennedy—had their own agendas.[36]

During 1940 Kennedy sent Kilpatrick three pieces. Cleared with Lottinville, the first was an excerpt from the "Fish Creek" manuscript, called "Poets of Fish Creek." It ran in the spring 1940, issue of *AHQ*. The excerpt consisted of six pages on how these isolated people named their children. Drawn chiefly from elites of the Black Belt and the state's large cities, *AHQ* readership undoubtedly chuckled over "Rebecca Moselle" and "Alabama Odell" and "Phone, Blueford, Alto and Below." Marie Bankhead Owen liked it. So did Kilpatrick, who wrote Kennedy: "The article is better than a similar one by Mencken I read not so long ago . . . caviar to the vulgar! . . . some spice!" Frustrated on lack of progress with her own writing, Viola told Ren, "If one can't do such things one's self, it is good to have a neighbor who can."[37]

Even so, as soon as Kennedy received his copy, he had regrets. The humor came at the expense of the Pigeon Creek people and at a time when he was in no mood to poke fun at unfortunates. The downtrodden were on his mind, Alabama's and increasingly those of Europe. He "disliked the whole thing." His writing about these people worked in a book-length setting, he thought. Without proper context, however, the excerpt was "unfortunate public ridicule" of humble people—people he liked and appreciated. No doubt this also explains why he never wrote up the vignette about the sisters and the "by God" tombstone inscription.[38]

Next, the fall 1940 issue of *AHQ* ran an Alabama update of Kennedy's 1934 "Black Belt Aristocrats." He called it "Alabama Black Belt." After laying out his now standard definition of the Black Belt as "a culture—a way of life," he moved on to some new questions. He wondered if Black Belt culture had not endured, intact, more in Alabama than in Georgia and Mississippi. If so, he offered several possible reasons. One involved where the Union military did the most damage in the Civil War. Alabama's Black Belt experienced little of the hard Civil War destruction; the Yankee "torch was not applied promiscuously . . . and [the area] is not so cluttered with purple history." But Georgia's and Mississippi's cotton belts suffered more, and so perhaps were more open to change in the postbellum era. Likewise, he raised the specter of the last decade's mass-culture exposure—in fiction and film—to Georgia's and Mississippi's Black Belt. Prime example could be seen in *Gone with the Wind* (1936), which he read shortly after it appeared, and then saw its equally heralded 1939 film adaptation. To a national audience, if Margaret Mitchell's creation evoked "contempt" for an "untitled nobility," it also called for "sympathy"—which could invite new developments in Georgia. So far, Alabama's cotton belt had not experienced such exposure. He wondered if change in Georgia would be tied to such portrayal, real and mythologized, good and bad. Here was the provocative nub of a notion later described by James Cobb as "the Selling of the South," and, no doubt more immediately, a teaser for a possible new book on the Black Belt. Lottinville's hand can be neither denied nor confirmed.

Within that context, Kennedy next turned to the man at the top of the 1940 heap in the enduring Alabama Black Belt—the big landowner. As in the 1934 piece, a first or uncritical reading of Kennedy's words makes one think the writer is engulfed in contradiction: he praises and then criticizes what he praises. But beneath the literal is a sardonic Menckenian critique. Here is "a Gentleman . . . a scholar . . . a Christian" whose "graceful life" springs from his belief that "the Lord made the land for him to own and for someone else to work." He is "civilized"—at least by the standards of "feudalism." An Alabama Black Belt "Gentleman" looks with condescension on "all poor whites," while feeling loyalty to Negroes who stay in "their place." "A Negro out of place [and] demanding civil liberties and civil rights," however, "[receives] the lash . . . or death."

Then, with the same double entendre, Kennedy moves to the demise of the cotton plantation and the "Gentleman." Since 1931 his journalism and fiction had traced the travails of the cotton belt—its human as well as cost-accounting predicaments. If further mechanization, cattle and pine tree endeavors, government funding, outward migration, and then finally the civil rights movement would finish it off, from the perspective of 1940 Kennedy sees the old plantation system already prostrate on the canvas and not about to come up with the count. And this has big implications for the historic "Gentleman" of the Black Belt. Instead of the "Gentleman" being "artfully" uncaring, indeed "cavalier," as Kennedy depicted him in 1934, the "Gentleman" of 1940 is "either arrogant or timid in the face of [the change], but in either case . . . defensive." The happy anachronism of 1934 had evolved to a brooding, decidedly unhappy anachronism in 1940. Still, despite defensiveness, the "Gentleman's" contorted view of other "Gentlemen" persists. "Ingrained hatreds" and "perverted personal dislikes"—Scotch-Irish feuding—dominate the "Gentleman's" inner circle. Let that circle come under outside attack, however, and ranks close fast: "a friend is always right, even unaccountably he be a liberal or a sheer freak." Far inside this critique are autobiographical clues as to Kennedy's own Black Belt life. As a heretic inside the contorted circle, his acceptance sprang from the same behaviors denying him ministerial success. Over time, these clues would emerge as guideposts for a soothsayer.

Meanwhile, one is left to ponder what alchemy Emmett Kilpatrick brewed up to get such a Menckenian critique of postbellum Alabama published in the journal of the *grande dame* of the Lost Cause. Perhaps Mrs. Owen just focused on the praise and ignored the critique, the way much of white Wilcox did in 1934. One wonders, too, if Kennedy would have conspired with Kilpatrick had he known what historians later found—that Marie Bankhead Owen's brother, US Rep. John H. Bankhead II, quietly had redirected a goodly portion of FDR's Black Belt sharecropper aid to his rich friends among the Black Belt "Gentlemen." Yet one thing is for sure. "Alabama Black Belt" was only an hors d'oeuvre among the alchemies yet to appear on the Kennedy-Kilpatrick menu.[39]

Kennedy sent Kilpatrick one more article, "Alas, Poor Yorick," profiling different levels of Black Belt funerals. But for the remainder of 1940 and on into 1941 Kennedy was engaged in shifting to Yaupon and World War II. This had little to do with Depression recovery. Those Black Wilcoxons deciding not to head north for the war industry jobs remained mired in the old, segregated ways, while many white people around them felt the benefits of recovery in timber and cattle endeavors and receipt of federal money to leave fields unplanted. In some ways it was a new economic scene. In other ways it was not. And, in Kennedy's mind, the God Mandate about white behavior remained as needed as ever. Hence his shift had less to do with Black Belt behaviors and more with the lens through which he viewed them. Hitler's grotesque aggressions yanked America out of the Depression; they also forced a bigger view of the South and race.[40]

8

ALL-OUT WAR

In the mid-1930s only a small contingent of Americans—some Jewish leaders and civil rights advocates as well as some East Coast FDR Democrats—placed a moral priority on stopping the fascist slaughter of Jews, Poles, Chinese, and Russians. Most Americans, including the majority of liberal Protestant leaders, wanted no part of "foreign wars." Even Charles Clayton Morrison, editor of the *Christian Century*, shifted to interventionism only in December 1941 after the Japanese attack on Pearl Harbor. And if Morrison's one-time colleague, Reinhold Niebuhr, had a similar response to Pearl Harbor, this was not without last-minute reservations.[1]

Kennedy was different from most of these Protestant leaders. Though he came from the same 1920s Christian Socialist pacifist isolationism Morrison and Niebuhr did, by 1934 when he met with Richebourg McWilliams on the porch at Oak Hill, it was for more than a tumbler or two of Old Forester and a good story. Badly, it seems in retrospect, he wanted that "Hitler Report" as he struggled inwardly over the best strategy for him, personally, to confront fascism. Unsuccessful in combating it in Alabama, he at least was tempted to look beyond. If "beyond" extended to overseas, where Nazi horrors exceeded racial atrocities in the American South, might this alleviate his bind with God? Could attacking racial fascism abroad somehow refocus America's struggle with the same problem at home? This was complicated. And over time, just as Kennedy's Christian Socialism gave way to certain realities of the New Deal, it had even more adjustments ahead regarding World War II.

For a good many years Kennedy's Wilcox critiques had drawn from high-level literary thought—from socialist Scott Nearing's *Where Is Civilization Going?* and Sinclair Lewis's *Main Street* to wide-ranging neo-orthodox writings in *Christian Century*. All along, this menu also had included antiwar literature, notably Charles Clayton Morrison's *The Outlawry of War* (1928), Erich Remarque's *All Quiet on the Western Front* (1928), and Alabamian William March's *Company K* (1933). These fed his long-developed perspective on outcomes of World War I. Granted, Kennedy never stopped admiring Wilson, and in the mid-1930s, as Europe reeled back toward war, he saw renewed need of a Christian American influence. Even so, as a noninterventionist pacifist, he also seemed stymied by only hoping and praying.[2]

His sermons reflected this significantly chastened Christian idealism about world affairs. During the mid-1930s he regularly told ARPs of Wilcox that "poor decisions" after World War I helped cause "the rise of Hitler." In treaty-making at Versailles, England and France ran roughshod over Wilson's pleas for balance. This, he urged, "delivered a Germany raped and depressed—fertile ground indeed for a demagogue." As Hitler gained full control of Germany and Benito Mussolini tightened his grip on Italy, he preached that Europe worsened daily out of the 1918–19 failure of Christian wisdom and compassion. When Nazis took the Rhineland, Austria, and Czechoslovakia, he granted that Hitler was "a ghastly tragedy" and "a degrading" force for civilization, indeed a "false prophet." But should the United States enter the war? No. The Bible said Jesus considered killing a "sin," which Kennedy applied to "war killing," despite the ARP Synod's historic emphasis on individual salvation and piety, and less so on government policies. In short, honestly and openly—and at times in open conflict with his own denomination—he was stymied on an appropriate US response to overseas fascism. As with the *Christian Century*, he urged fellow Christians to pray for "renewed humility." But for neither the *Century* nor its neo-orthodox comrade in Wilcox did prayer offer the sole answer. A "reasserted Christian humility" was only a crucial first step toward finding an appropriate solution to the European crisis.[3]

As he practiced and preached this approach, however, his thoughts also were elsewhere. Ever since the 1934 "Black Belt Aristocrats" article, increasingly Kennedy had depicted an "axis" of wealthy planters and big city industrialists and other professionals using demagogic tactics—chiefly fear of Black people and communists—to manipulate the general white citizenry into supporting state and local political agendas to the sole financial benefit of those two interest groups. He also had portrayed less powerful whites—low- and middle-class business people and professionals, including some lawmen and World War I veterans—as "nationally self-righteous" grassroots implementors for the axis program. Members of the Klan and the American Legion handled the lynching, flogging, rigging of jury pools, and wrapping of reactionary agendas in the American and Confederate flags. Indeed, beginning in February 1935, with "Quality in the Reserve Corps," Kennedy cameoed the racial view of the German Axis and its henchmen in a transatlantic context: the Alabama white man said: "Yes, I hold to . . . Hitler's theory of Aryan superiority . . . it's race and blood that counts." And by 1938, reflecting on Eva Lips's *Savage Symphony*, he showed even more concern about a Hitler-style racial fascism reflected in white people controlling the Black people all around them.[4]

Yet even before that 1938 discussion—"in the middle of the 1930s, not long after the front porch 'Hitler Report'"—he posed a question to Bill Jones, which the superintendent never forgot. Jones was a veteran of the World War I American Expeditionary Force and forever mourned what German forces did to the people of France. To him, fascist expansion in Europe during the mid-1930s called for immediate US military intervention. And he said so regularly to his dear friend, at this stage still the Christian Socialist pacifist. Finally, Kennedy replied: "Bill, why not Alabama first?" At the time, as Robert Brinkmeyer has explained in *The Fourth Ghost* (2009), a select group of white and Black southerners addressed connections between fascism in the American South and German fascism ravaging Europe. Kennedy appears to have seen this nexus around the same time, perhaps even before Clarence Cason articulated it in the *90 Degrees* chapter, "Fascism—Southern Style." Yet while Cason's analysis of southern fascism, based chiefly on Mississippi and Louisiana observations and a few on Alabama's Tom Heflin, suggests sole demagogues as the core of the matter, Kennedy's implies a systemic and institutionalized phenomenon, involving two powerful interest groups functioning at different levels of white society and not dependent on a single politician. At any rate, both Kennedy and Cason were some six years ahead of the more noted probing of southern and European fascism by Wilbur J. Cash in *Mind of the South* (1941). And poignantly, as Kennedy struggled over the "right" thing for America to do regarding European fascism, inside him—not expressed in sermons at this time—was an awareness that the evil "over there" also was "here."[5]

As late as Sunday, September 17, 1939, with Hitler assaulting Poland, Kennedy told his Camden congregation: "I will never endorse this war, nor our entrance into it, nor—should we enter it—the conscription of our young people. I hereby pledge my refusal under any circumstances to become a propagandist for the supreme sin of the [human] race—war." Indeed, on October 22, 1939, to Roosevelt's providing munitions to England, he said it all again. Despite being a strong New Dealer, he proclaimed: "We must stay out. This is a European war. . . . War settles nothing."[6]

Then everything started to change. On November 30, 1939, the Soviet Union—at the time aligned with Germany—invaded weak Finland. This event had dramatic impact on American journalism. Since the start of Hitler's atrocities on Jews, the *New York Times* had placed such news at the back of its paper. Owned by the Jewish Sulzberger family, the paper apparently did not want to appear "too Jewish" with a national readership as well as any number of high-ranking American officials and financiers not lacking in anti-Semitism. But with Finns under attack, the *Times* now had a non-Jewish issue to gradually increase front-page coverage of all Axis evils, including news on the killing of Jews—a profoundly pivotal development. If there was one turning point in American public opinion leading to increased acceptance that US intervention might have to occur, this arguably was it. No anti-Semite, indeed far from it, Kennedy the devout *Times* reader responded to the fuller war coverage.

On December 17, 1939, he approached his Camden pulpit armed with new clippings from the *New York Times*. "England and France . . . are fighting . . . our battle. . . . We should help them with materials . . . [although] I am convinced that it would be folly for us to enter the war as a belligerent." At the same time, while the antiwar sentiment did not leave his reading menu, more and more he focused on what he called "Hitler reading." He paid careful attention to war coverage in the *New York Times* and also what appeared on Jewish massacres in the *Montgomery Advertiser*. His reading of Ernest Hemingway's probing of fascism, "Fifth Column," in *The Fifth Column and the First Forty-Nine Stories* (1938), and Lips's *Savage Symphony*, only reinforced what the newspapers said. His is shifting continued.[7]

On April 21, 1940, up at Marion Junction and with Hitler invading Norway, he preached that "the German barbarians must be stopped or this world will not be safe for anyone." On Sunday, May 5, he gave the commencement address at the Wilcox County High School. Unperturbed about the crowd of conservatives before him, he started off: "Jesus was a liberal. He opposed one group oppressing another." He challenged graduating seniors not to go forth and become "conservatives and fat and happy" and "just make money." They should become "liberals like Jesus." They should "oppose the oppressors of the day." On Sunday, June 2, at Camden in the morning and Oak Hill in the afternoon, and with Rotterdam recently destroyed by the Luftwaffe, he preached on "The Beast of Berlin." "Hitler is an odious affront to the dignity of man. The world must be free of him, at whatever costs to those of us in the surviving free nations. . . . You cannot be tolerant of a mad dog."[8]

By July 10, 1940, his views had evolved yet again. That Sunday in the Camden pulpit he addressed Roosevelt's new national defense bill. "Let us pass this bill, [and] if materials of war are not enough let us give men [to England]. . . . Hitler is the anti-Christ." As the Battle of Britain proceeded on September 15, he moved even further. He went from "if" England needs us to "it now seems unlikely that gallant England, left to face this onslaught alone, can defeat them."

In September 1940, the German-Italian-Soviet pact formalized alliance with Japan. The same month Roosevelt activated the Selective Service, drafting men ages twenty-one to thirty-five. On October 20, from his Camden pulpit, forty-year-old Kennedy strongly supported "our young men [registering] for military service." "I regret that I am beyond the age limit," he continued, "but if we do enter this war, as I believe we will, I give you my pledge here and now that I will volunteer as a chaplain."

His evolving thoughts almost had reached conclusion. In October 1939 he was an ideological Christian Socialist pacifist and noninterventionist. One year later, in October 1940, he was not. He urged US intervention in the war and planned to be part of that effort. His activist Christianity ran off and left his Socialist pacifism. For him, it was the Full Christian's mandate to help England defeat the lying fascists of Germany.

Then, on November 6, 1940, *Christian Century* published Adam Alles's "Forces That Produced Hitler." This piece took Kennedy's pro-interventionist thoughts to final conclusion, if not as Alles might have intended. A second-generation Russian immigrant who studied at the universities of Strasbourg, Berlin, and Paris before completing the PhD in philosophy at Yale, Alles was an ordained Congregational minister teaching at St. John's College when he unloaded on scholars then having a field day explaining why Hitler's fascism was emerging in Germany. He summarized their explanations: misused, the Treaty of Versailles obliterating Germany's economy; America's refusal to "liquidate Germany's war debt"; long delay of German acceptance into the League of Nations; the Depression and unemployment; Hitler's "unscrupulous use of power"; and German capitalists' not opposing Hitler but instead thinking they could manipulate him to their benefit. Then Alles urged what they had missed: the role of religion as a once cohesive force in Western life.

The Reformation, wrote Alles, had achieved a badly needed realization that Western man was not "cleric bound." The resultant emphasis on men and women reading the Bible permitted the Judeo-Christian tradition a continued cohesive role in Western life. Yet, another major transition in Western culture, the early twentieth-century emergence of Darwinian thought, had a major downside for Western life. For all the amazing gains in science, industry, and medicine it facilitated, by encouraging the rejection of the biblical text it had unleashed long-term deterioration of the very binding force—the Judeo-Christian culture—encouraging its rise. Indeed, as that deterioration found reinforcement in "English empiricism" urging that men and women were born with a "blank mind" and hence subject to wide-ranging behavioral influences—rather than instincts bestowed by God—millions of westerners gradually moved to a point of feeling there was no overarching authority or cohesiveness in their daily lives. As a result, they were left hungry for some replacement form of authority and order. More to the point, Alles summed up, the standard scholarly explanations for Hitler's rise all were true. But they were just the starting point for understanding the immediate secular circumstances faced by Western humans in crisis. Fate brought Hitler into this chaotic time; in place of no cultural order or cohesiveness and against a backdrop of crisis, Hitler offered a fascist order and many Germans lunged for it. Yet it was not just Hitler, as destructive as he was; it was this perverse need for societal order that brought him on.

The nonspiritual person might point up any number of cracks in Alles's thesis. Still, if one takes his notion of the role of religion in purely anthropological terms—and cultural anthropologists long have asserted connections between cultural cohesiveness and shared spiritual life—Alles's critique offers a remarkable parallel to what any number of modern intellectuals have said (with much scholarly approval) regarding the relationship between societal insecurities and acceptance of extreme forms of order, notably those embracing aggressiveness and violence.

Kennedy's reaction to the Alles article resembled these later insights about insecurity and order through aggression—but also with one significant contemporaneous dissent. Well-attuned to race and fascism before reading Alles's piece in the second week of November 1940—an article so important to him that he remembered many elements of it as late as 1983—he believed that Alles did not explicitly address racist elements of German fascism and wrote off new social science thoughts about "behavior as part of the problem." Hence, to Kennedy, Alles missed a central point: the breakdown of Western spiritual cohesiveness "opened the door for even more aggressive behavioral urges among western white people." And out of this reaction to the piece, Kennedy's dichotomy of Half versus Full Christianity shortly reflected enhanced clarity. With no explicit Social Gospel theology as a countervailing spiritual influence, an old style "Holy Joe," Deep South Bible Belt Christianity—with its historic absolutes of white people dominating Blacks and a theology focused chiefly on individual piety and salvation" facilitated a white person's attraction to racial fascism. It provided "order" attuned to ancient ethnic stereotypes.

Since the Depression, ARP synodical developments had made this problem even harder to confront. Their "Whole Gospel" commitment had evolved from a "Committee on Reform" to a "Committee on Social Regeneration." But for the overwhelming majority of ARPs, according to Lowry Ware and James Gettys, this outreach to solve secular ills normally was restricted to alcohol and lack of piety—much to Kennedy's persisting dissent in meeting after meeting of the synod. To him, indeed, ARP "Social Regeneration" represented a diversion from—indeed, a big obstacle to—genuine embrace of social responsibility, that is, "Whole Gospel" evolving dramatically to genuine, activist social responsibility. In these thoughts, nothing in ARP records shows Kennedy using the terms "Half Christianity" versus "Full Christianity." The terms gradually evolved within his most private thoughts until the last ten years of his life when, retired from active ministry and plain worn out, he seems to have been more open with them. As for "Holy Joeism" versus "Social Gospelism"—that is another matter.

On January 1, 1941, a week after Roosevelt's "fireside talk" on America's need to be "an arsenal for democracy," from the Camden pulpit Kennedy said point-blank that America should be *more* than an "arsenal for democracy." "America should declare war on Germany." On January 6, 1941, FDR used a congressional address to articulate even more forcefully the ultimate American goal. It was not just peace in the world. It was an environment of "freedom": freedom of worship and of speech, freedom from want and from fear. The following morning's *New York Times* carried much of the "four freedoms" speech. Kennedy clipped the core paragraphs and put the tiny piece of paper in his wallet, what he later called "the ideas essential for defeating fascism." That tiny, folded clipping had big-time travels ahead.[9]

Now, return to Kennedy's Yaupon writing. In the two weeks following FDR's "Four Freedoms" address, this compulsively self-analytical Wilcox preacher cogitated on what had happened to him—the Royal clicking as he thought. He took the role of a Yaupon minister, "Rev. Jim James." In the fall of 1933 Reverend James was "pacifist-inclined." But he became "swept along by the war" until he had to face "the dilemma of supporting his doctrine that all war is sin or of supporting England and France" in their fight against Hitler. So, he chose war for his country and for himself. This article, "Pulpit Diary," *Christian Century* published on January 29, 1941—some eleven months before Pearl Harbor.[10]

He kept writing. On July 23, 1941, *Christian Century* brought out his article on sharecroppers and the war. It revolved around the developing draft policy. By 1943, with the United States well into the war, the Selective Service took Black citizens. But the initial draft policy of 1940 excluded Black people, chiefly out of the War Department's "understanding"—provided by powerful US congressmen from the South—that they were "inferior," plus the recognition that giving them advanced training with weapons might be a problem once peacetime returned. Still, a good two years before the change to drafting Blacks, the War Department accepted Black volunteers. In "Volunteer" Kennedy portrays one such Black cropper, "Joe King." The Yaupon recruiter was happy to get him; he had received few volunteers of any color. And the planter, "Mr. Wilson," a small piece of whose land Joe King's parents sharecropped, also seemed eager about the development. "There ain't nothing much for you to do here. [But] you'll have a big time in the Army, son. And maybe you can help us out here at home . . . send[ing] us a little money every month." In Yaupon a pernicious "understanding" prevailed. Mr.

Wilson had to release Sam from his family's cropper responsibilities for the local draft board to accept him, even as a volunteer. With that leverage, the planter cut a deal with Sam about his army pay. If 50 percent of what Sam sent his family each month went to Mr. Wilson, he would "advise" the local draft board that Sam was "o.k." for volunteering. Sam wanted to serve. And thus, as historian Pete Daniel documented for LaFayette County, Mississippi, did the white man in the big house—the white man with direct influence on the draft board—capture yet another federal dollar that might have eased the life of a cropper family.[11]

On Sunday, December 7, 1941, Kennedy was not scheduled to preach. He had preached November 23 in Camden and was scheduled for the Marion Junction church on December 14. So, as was their habit with such "off" Sundays, on the morning of December 7 he and Mary and the children went either to the Methodist or the Presbyterian service. From the perspective of 1983 he did not remember which one they attended that morning. Yet that afternoon, he clearly recalled, on their new Philco radio he was listening to the Giants-Dodgers game when about 1:30 p.m. the broadcast suddenly switched over to the announcement of the bombing of Pearl Harbor. Shortly, he walked the ten minutes to the town square. There, the "quite large Philco radio" mounted in a first-floor window of the courthouse for Alabama and Auburn football provided play-by-play of far greater consequence. "Negroes and whites . . . mingled around and listened and talked." With dusk he walked back up Broad to home and listened more to the attack news.

Two nights later he started a Yaupon vignette, "December 7, 1941." Here is the short version. That morning, whites of Yaupon town heard one of four sermons, none "remotely address[ing] the horrible condition of the world." The well-off moved from church to big Sunday dinners; those who did not go for a ride enjoyed heated conversation about what New Year's Day would bring. For on that day, the Cotton Bowl in Dallas would pit Alabama against Texas A&M. Nine families from Yaupon town were headed for Dallas. Then "about 1:30 it happened. In thirty minutes most of the radios of Yaupon were screaming the news." At times Wilcox people can be "blatant and contentious." But that afternoon they seemed uncommonly "quiet, very troubled, tight-lipped . . . amazed but not hysterical." Some went to the courthouse and milled around the radio. "Services in the churches that night meant little. Preachers preached on what they had prepared days earlier."[12]

With "December 7, 1941" in the file for the book, Kennedy pressed on with something well stuck in his craw. Back in June 1941, with George Lang's encouragement (and financial assistance), Kennedy had attended another ministers' institute at Columbia Theological Seminary in Atlanta. In July he wrote up his reactions. "In a world going to pieces the school concentrated upon religious education. Twiddling one's thumbs for two weeks over religious education in the desperate summer of 1941! . . . No one had much to say about democracy or Nazism or communism, about war, poverty, labor . . . or anything else . . . but religious education." "Christmas 1941" never went beyond initial draft. In early November he returned to it, then again set it aside. Still, the thrust of it emerged at Marion Junction, December 14, when Kennedy preached on "Responsible Living"—meaning the need for Americans to help those overseas and join the army. He pulled no punches. "If you can live responsibly"—the central message of Full, Social Gospel Christianity—"it is really unimportant whether you live to 69 . . . or 85 . . . or whether you die young." Onward Christian soldiers, whether Full Christian or not: all were needed.[13]

Some Wilcox men, of course, were too old or in too poor health or too illiterate for the draft. Mobilization saw many of these, and Wilcox women, too, take off for Mobile and Pascagoula for the new shipbuilding jobs or make the forty-minute drive to jobs at the new Craig Air Force Field in Selma. But for "boys from Wilcox" heading to the military, the Trailways bus station in downtown Camden, two blocks south of the courthouse, became one of the poignant places of the era. Five Wilcox "boys" flunked the physical; within a month they were back at the bus station. For others it was basic training and then overseas. Those who never came back numbered thirty-four. When families got the dreaded letter, word spread fast. Kennedy rented a car and went consoling—no matter the color, the money, or the faith.[14]

Still, his last Camden service before Christmas, on December 2, did not waver. Of course, he started with Luke 2:11, "For unto you is born this child." Then he got down to the crisis at hand. Despite being wealthy and privileged, some before him would be dead this time next year. And considering that, he asked, "if you had to preach a [Christmas] sermon this . . . [year of] 1941, when all of the world is at war, when men everywhere turn their backs on Christ and on His teachings, what would you say?" Some five hundred words later, here was his answer, especially for those who might not see another Christmas: "Do at least one generous thing for somebody, white or Negro, who *cannot* pay you back. 'Do it unto one of the least of these.'"[15]

On March 10, 1942, responding to new draft-age guidelines, Kennedy had just registered with the Selective Service when he finally got news from Lottinville. The Oklahoma press would not pursue "The People of Fish Creek." Yet it had continuing interest in "The Yaupon Tales." No commitment—but a strong possibility. Kennedy was encouraged and determined to keep drafting more chapters for Lottinville's eye.[16]

This would not be easy. As 1942 unfolded, his life became a vortex, brought on mostly by him. Besides his two churches, he directed three Wilcox committees—the high school PTA, the Committee for the Finnish Relief Fund, and the War Bonds Committee. With Viola Liddell's major assistance, the PTA work was not taxing. The other two, however, required extensive countywide travel. For visits in Camden, a former member of his congregation, the Mobile physician William C. Jones, sent him $41.36 to buy a "Victory" bicycle at Matthews Hardware Store, a purchase immediately christened "Vic." Bill Jones, Mary Carter Tait, and Roundtable members drove him to more distant appointments. The Finnish cause did not resonate with Wilcoxons. He had to take out a ninety-day note at Camden National Bank just to have $115 to send to Alabama Power's Thomas W. Martin, chair of the Alabama committee. Yet the War Bond cause succeeded, notably among Wilcox Black citizens responding to a poster with Joe (The Brown Bomber) Lewis—still only eighteen—urging participation.[17]

Kennedy's writings on Gee's Bend and Black Belt aristocracy also kept bringing distant intellectuals to his door: John C. Heinrich, a Presbyterian social worker–missionary from Philadelphia and author of the recent London-published book on racial discrimination, *The Psychology of the Oppressed* (1937); Dadeville, Alabama, native and Chapel Hill–trained anthropologist Olive Stone, commencing field studies in the Bend; historian Glenn Nolan Sisk, doctoral candidate at Duke writing on race and economics in the Black Belt. All three wanted visits to the Bend with a Kennedy narration. He accommodated them, and Viola Liddell hosted them for Roundtable dinner and talk.

Likewise, two white "Northern Presbyterian" (PCUSA) missionaries, "Misses Hornsby and Barnhoeff," came to teach at Camden Academy, living on the campus with several other, Black teachers and hosting Reverend Heinrich for a week. With the proclamation that all three were "communists and spies" (which they were not) and "non-believers in the bodily virgin birth of Jesus" (which they were), the Baptists' Reverend Roark whipped up a public outcry about their presence. Unbeknownst to his boss, Sheriff Lummie Jenkins, Chief Deputy Sam McNeill advised his preacher brother-in-law, Kennedy, that the three had every reason to fear at least some type of Klan reprisal. Under cover of darkness, Kennedy and Bill Jones moved them to the Selma bus station, from where they departed Alabama.

And right in the middle of this, in the summer of 1942, four of Kennedy's liberal ARP colleagues launched yet another effort to merge the ARP Synod with the Southern Presbyterian (PCUS) Church—asking that Kennedy not only join in, as he had done before, but push for a local merger of Camden Presbyterian with Camden ARPC. Kennedy supported his comrades, but he knew the effort was futile. ARPs voted a resounding no. Regardless, Viola Liddell pushed Camden Presbyterian toward the merger. And when it came to a congregational vote, overwhelmingly negative, feelings were so hard that she likely would have quit Camden Presbyterian had it not been that the church had long been supported by the Liddell family.

As this happened, Kennedy's Camden and Marion Junction congregations revolted against his implementing "Day Light Savings Time," or "War Time," designed to advance war industries and preparedness. They did not want the change in service times. Noting in the diary, "These people just do not give a damn about the war!" he refused to back down. Service times changed for the duration of the war. "Wartime in Wilcox"—at least on these counts, if not exactly going after fascism—added another draft chapter to a promising book manuscript. Still, he confided to the diary, "I am tired . . . not enough hours in the day." Then his typewriter broke—four days in Selma for repair. And what long had been a single cocktail with Bill Jones perhaps once every two weeks, without Mary, evolved over seven months to several "slugs," often three times a week, with Bill; and then to "several slugs" several times a week not just with Bill Jones but "at home" in Mary's presence.[18]

Yet the life of the mind still got serious attention. The year of 1941 saw publication of two of the most significant books ever written about the American South: William Alexander Percy's *Lanterns on the Levee* and Wilbur J. Cash's *Mind of the South*. With the passing of large plantation life, Percy saw educated elite leadership in the South replaced by newly monied people of less depth and sophistication, leaving himself open to criticism about acceptance of racial views of the old elite. By contrast, Cash maintained that the old elite amounted to little more than a mythical aristocracy, with the South always led by relatively shallow, greedy men on the make. Because of his hectic schedule at this time, Kennedy did not read these well-reviewed books until September 6-20, 1942; first he took on *Lanterns*, then immediately consumed Cash's book. Since the early 1930s, he had been both agonized and mesmerized by the very behaviors profiled in these books. With his schedule at this time, however, he left nothing to indicate how he would have compared himself to Cash and Percy.

But one might infer. As a man who believed he had an overt God Mandate, he likely was different from both writers. Yet he also shared a lot with them. No doubt he was emotionally closer to Percy's views; he always saw Beth Eden as evidence of the *possibility* that at least some plantation aristocrats, even of Scotch-Irish origins, could be compassionate and educated and grow with the times. Still, his view of most southern whites around him—violent, anti-intellectual, prone to feuds and clannishness, and some awash in a mythological sense of self—was closer to Cash's, not to mention Cash's chief promoter, Mencken.

So much for speculation. Instead of leaving a reaction, even as he read these books, he plunged ahead on two more Yaupon pieces. "By-Product of

War" shows Wilcox's labor force headed to the Pascagoula and Mobile shipyards with the higher federal pay standards. It was intended for "the book," he told Lottinville. But "for the $15" he also sent it to the *Century*, which finally brought it out in July 1943. Another piece profiled Black poverty continuing in Yaupon. Granted, yesterday's sharecroppers now sent back money from the shipyards, cotton prices pushed twenty cents a pound, and lumber mills whirred with wartime demands. Yet Yaupon still had a lot of destitute people. Most large-scale planters had shifted to mechanized farming. Smaller landowners preferred the free government money that came with not having acreage in cultivation. Either way, this "new system" of Black Belt agriculture, spurred by what the late Morton Sosna termed "the virtual orgy of war-induced [federal] spending . . . [and] the biggest boom in American history," counted out what little the cropper once had. Kennedy called the vignette, "Coat." Essentially autobiographical, it derives from his giving a destitute Black former sharecropper a coat in mid-winter. It focuses on the receiver—not the giver—with the "coat" but a metaphor for so much more. It is nuanced, disciplined, terse, yet emotive. He had learned a lot. Again, "for the $15," *Christian Century* got this one, too, appearing a year later.[19]

Meanwhile, on January 16, 1943, he opened the letter he did not want. The Oklahoma press director, Lottinville, pled that Kennedy understand the difficulties of university press publishing in wartime. Undoubtedly, there were paper, funding, and personnel shortages—ironically, factors so different for Boston and New York houses booming with wartime books. Still, Lottinville held out hope. He had submitted the manuscript to attorneys and ensured there were no problems with "privacy issues" regarding the many real-life Wilcoxons at the root of Kennedy's stories. The Yaupon manuscript, he concluded, had "much to recommend it . . . and if I can find a way to bring it into the list sometime in the future, I will be glad to make that effort. If, however, you prefer to have it returned to Camden, please let me know." While this was profoundly disappointing news for Kennedy, it still left a clear crack in the door. Yet in the tumult of the era that crack rapidly lost meaning. Kennedy never asked that the typed manuscript be returned. Though he would continue to use "Yaupon" in journalism, the handwritten "Yaupon Tales" manuscript went to the file drawer, with the diary forever moot on feelings that must have gone into the drawer with it.

Still, Kennedy's immediate past and future actions cast a good bit of light on those feelings. Two weeks before Christmas 1942 he was keynote speaker for the annual holiday banquet of the Camden Exchange Club. His was not exactly a holiday message. "In the last war Wilson had great plans for world peace. But ruthless European diplomats and a Republican Congress refused to let the U.S. have much part in creating the post-war world. But now we have another great world leader in Franklin Roosevelt. . . . I resent bitter attacks on him by so many today. . . . I would regret seeing him replaced by some cheap reactionary political hack who belongs in the last century. I marvel at the cold fury with which so many hate Roosevelt. . . . We can go back to fighting among ourselves when [the war] is over . . . but we need to be a united nation under Roosevelt for now."

In short, when Lottinville's letter arrived, Kennedy already was "in the war" with Roosevelt. And that speech was but the overt secular strain of his commitment. Spiritually, he still felt a Mandate for helping the downtrodden—and for converting self-avowed Christians to do more on their behalf. With no outward wallowing over the apparent fate of "The Yaupon Tales," as never before he moved forward on that Mandate and its activist social commitment.[20]

The greatest of America's "Greatest Generation" were the ones killed defeating the enemy in World War II; the establishment of a second tier of greatness is another matter. Surely in that mix should be those who were so morally outraged about the era's violent racial fascism that they urged US intervention in World War II *before* Japan's attack on Pearl Harbor—before war was a defensive necessity. That became Ren Kennedy.[21]

An April 1942 sermon makes this clear. Two months earlier, the *Atlanta Journal* had run a feature story on the war views of one Marion McHenry Hull. J. McDowell Richards clipped it and sent it to Kennedy. A well-educated Atlanta physician, Hull founded the Atlanta Bible Institute and served on the Committee of 100 Fundamentalists. He also was a fundamentalist preacher in his own right and authored numerous books about the Bible. In the *Atlanta Journal* interview, Hull gave a chapter-and-verse breakdown on how the Bible forecast the rise of Hitler and European fascism. Since he believed the *only* solution to the European war was the second coming of Jesus, however, he found talk of US intervention useless. As for Hitler's being the "anti-Christ," he said there was no way to know without overt intervention by God and Jesus.

Of course, Kennedy had his own beliefs on the inerrancy of the Bible. And he assuredly believed in prayer and considered the war as mankind severely damaging God's world. But he viewed detailed biblical forecasting of modern human events as being "too Baptist like" and awaiting the Jesus solution on Hitler, "the anti-Christ," as blatant fatalistic irresponsibility. Indeed, he occasionally encountered similar sentiment among white Wilcoxons. To the woman on the street who asked him if she was not offending God by praying that the Allies would defeat Hitler—after all, was it all not in God's hands?—Kennedy said, "No, you should pray." So, after reading and outlining for more than a month, during the night of March 3 and 4, 1942, from 11:45 p.m. to 4:50 a.m., he wrote down his own views on God, fascism, and the war:

twenty-five (4 × 9 inch) handwritten pages. He then asked Bill Jones to critique it. There remains no record of Jones's reaction Still, several weeks later, on April 9, when the new preacher at the Oak Hill ARPC, Calvin Smith, was scheduled to be off, and Kennedy, too, from the Camden church, Jones had Kennedy fill in at Oak Hill and give "the war sermon." That Sunday morning, out of an Oak Hill congregation of seventy-two, sixty-five were on hand.

In that soft and syncopated voice, he started off with Psalm 46. "Be still and know that I *am* God; I will be exalted among the nations, I will be exalted in the earth." From there he puzzled anyone listening. From the Psalm he moved to passages from Ernest Hemingway and William March, and then to this:

> In war you kill. . . . To war nothing whatsoever is sacred and anything at all may be violated. . . . I have preached sermons . . . denouncing war as the supreme collective sin of the human race. . . . I do not retract them [because] what I preached was true. . . . [Yet] all the while the war drew steadily nearer. . . . It is your dilemma and mine, and there is no easy way out of it. . . . I support this war for two reasons. First, it is an inexorable necessity. . . . We and the rest of the nations have made the world [to be] patterned after the selfish will of man . . . clogged with injustices and evils, social, economic, political, racial, religious. . . . This war is not God's Will. [But] it is His Judgement coming inexorably upon men in consequen[ce] of their violation of His spiritual laws. Second, the State [i.e., US government] is waging the war . . . not the church. And I am a citizen of the State. . . . Jesus Himself said, "Render under Caesar those things that are Caesar's, and unto God those things that are God's." . . . The State guarantees to the church and its members the right to . . . practice their religion. The guarantee carries with it certain responsibilities to the State. Second, [US entry into the war] violates Christianity. But the alternative promises to violate it still more. Therefore I choose between the two evils and support war.

So, even though he was a contradictory Christian if not a contradictory citizen, Kennedy would be "still" and calm knowing that God would accept him. For God would prevail regardless. Here was something modern. Reality meant contradiction, even for a devout Christian. Reality meant the end sometimes justifying the means. Reality meant that for a Christian to act responsibly in the secular world, that Christian at times had to side with sin. Here was the opposite of Hull's conservative Christian fatalism. Here was neo-orthodox Christian activism fully comporting with the spirit, if not exactly the geography, of his God Mandate.[22]

On Sunday, August 2, 1942, just after Camden church, Kennedy asked senior elder Miller Bonner to support him for a leave of absence to join the military. Bonner agreed. Shortly, a joint meeting of Camden and Marion Junction elders made it official, plus stipulated that Mary and the girls could stay in the manse. Despite several years of sub rosa flirting with other denominations, on October 30, he mailed his request for a chaplaincy recommendation to the ARP Chaplaincy Approval Committee, at Due West. A week later he received a letter from President Grier at Erskine College: "You may count on me personally, and, I am sure, our committee as a whole will give your application for chaplaincy a very hearty and strong endorsement." Behind the scenes it was not quite that smooth. Though Kennedy's looking around had not gone public, one conservative on the committee long had been his strongest critic on ecumenicalism, unionism, and social activism—and also his drinking alcohol. He was capable of letting these views shape reaction to Reverend Kennedy becoming "Chaplain Kennedy." But Paul Grier delivered. He, James Presley, and William Boyce strongly supported Kennedy's candidacy, and the other—conservative editor of the *ARP*, Charles B. Williams— voted "un-opposed."[23]

On December 1, Kennedy took the train to Atlanta for meetings with various committees of the Chaplaincy Corps. He was taken aback by how much up-front cash, five hundred dollars, he would have to lay out for uniforms and personal supplies—and how much of this the army would not reimburse. Finally, he asked for help: his brother Richard, who was a Charleston dentist, and Dr. William C. Jones, he who had funded "Vic," sent checks totaling four hundred dollars. Camden and Oak Hill ARPs wrote checks for the other hundred. Early in the afternoon of Friday, February 26, Bill and Joyce Jones crammed the four Kennedys and Ren's gear into their blue Plymouth sedan and drove to Montgomery. After a farewell supper at The Elite (pronounced, "E-lite"), at 6:50 p.m., the Scotch-Irish heretic—still an ARP—headed off to war on Southern Railway No. 36.[24]

On Tuesday, March 2, Kennedy arrived at the struggling Harvard Divinity School, leased by the US military for chaplaincy training, where he checked into Room 47 of Perkins Hall. He noted the presence on campus of any number of Black chaplain candidates; in 1942 the army had desegregated its Chaplaincy School, though segregation in the units would continue for another six years. In his room, he found a letter waiting on his desk. Surely, memories of that first night in the Wilcox Hotel, back on November 17, 1927, came rushing back. Before he left home, Mary had laid down the ground rules for wartime communication: she wanted a lot. Beside hers was an "Army letter" about "the Army Chaplaincy." Although chaplains were only to "speak for themselves, not for the Army," they also were to put aside "denominational theology" and preach "faith group" generic—Protestant, Catholic, Jewish. In short, his thirty-day return to the Ivy League was to be a lot different from heady times at PTS in the 1920s with J. Gresham Machen, Lefferts Loetscher, and Charles R. Erdman. Ren Kennedy was in "the Army."

At the age of forty-three and a weight of 143 pounds, he not just survived but enjoyed the early morning exercise regimen. The same for classes on "map reading"—especially lectures on how light and sound travel at night. The "religious education" offered by army chaplains over at the Divinity School was something else. He understood the army's desire to minimize "soldier incapacity due to venereal disease." Yet he found the lectures on sexual abstinence an unrealistic Catholic influence in the Chaplaincy Corps as well as reminiful of "standard Baptist fare" in Camden—"useless," in his estimation. For the required "hand-written lecture on Sexual Morality," he argued that "the evil of sex is to take advantage of unknowing people," most of all "the children who may approach you." The Catholic chaplain teaching the course gave him only a "satisfactory." It was the lowest grade he received on written work required in the program. Over the next three years of military life the essay still wound up a required part of his army repertoire—and, in his mind, always "useless."

On a snowy Saturday morning, April 3, he graduated from the Chaplaincy School in a ceremony at Saunder's Theater. On his jacket they placed the bars of a first lieutenant and a chaplain's cross. He then headed for Boston to board the train for San Luis Obispo, California. Here awaited his "Army home"—the 102nd Evacuation Hospital.[25]

Like other officers moving through Stateside assignments, Kennedy had choice about how he got to California. Rather than Boston to Chicago, then straight on to the Pacific coast, he selected the slightly less direct route . . . through Alabama. He overnighted with Mary at the Whitley Hotel in Montgomery. Hugh Dale drove her over. As requested, Mary brought along a thick folder of some fifteen sermons Kennedy thought more useful than what he had picked up at Harvard. That night they "went over money." For starters, he would get $257 a month—a $47 increase over his Wilcox civilian income. He could expect more. But for now he would send home $140 per month. The next morning Joyce and Bill arrived at the Whitley with Mary Conway and Margaret. The six drove to the train station, and Ren departed. After overnighting at the Monteleone Hotel in New Orleans futilely "looking for Faulkner," he headed "westward."[26]

"SLO" was what military people called San Luis Obispo, California. As he arrived that April the army was creating the 102nd Evacuation Hospital. It would be one of some seventy evacs to see action across the Pacific, European, and North African theaters. Seven months into training exercises, the unit was retargeted from the Pacific to Europe. It then spent December 1943 through February 1944 training for winter conditions at Goffs, California, in the Mohave Desert. Prescient winter training.

The 102nd consisted of thirty white physicians and thirty-three white nurses. It also had some 225 white "boys and men" to ensure that its thirty tents, equipment, and medical talent stayed highly mobile in trucks and jeeps—and, on rare occasions, trains. Ideally, the outfit would follow some six miles behind a given front of US artillery and infantry advancing across Europe. At 10:00 a.m. and at 3:00 p.m. Kennedy offered Sunday services. In between those hours, he gave individualized services to patients and "guys in the stockade"—"more receptive to God if . . . free cigarettes accompanied preaching." The patient who most impressed him was one Vasco Hale, a Black officer with all-Negro units of the 93rd Infantry, training nearby. In a combat exercise a private mishandled a grenade, resulting in the 102nd surgeons having to "remove one [of Hale's] arms . . . and the other hand" and "both eyes [were] blown out." From counseling Hale in post-op Kennedy went to his diary: "Hale . . . fine . . . and brave." But years later—as Hale turned into a celebrated advocate for equal treatment of Black veterans— Kennedy's memory focused on something else: "After the surgery, white boys on either side of him asked to be moved. I blocked that."[27]

As in civilian life, a weak military "leader" easily can avoid responsibility and conflict by "delegating" a problem. This was especially the case in an evac where a weak commanding officer, despite being a physician, if not a surgeon, might not want to "manage" strong-willed surgeons. Fortunately, Kennedy's age and his experience with organizational management and conflict resolution— inside ARP life as well as in small-town existence generally—made him a quick study for both the spoken and unspoken "orientation" he received about "Army ways."

Within two weeks of his appearance at SLO, the 102nd commanding officer (CO), a career army doctor, Col. Carleton D. Goodiel, began to use him to address discord among officers and enlisted men alike. This could be downright mercurial. In April 1943, Sterling College, in Kansas—an institution with strong ARP connection—awarded Kennedy an honorary doctorate, in absentia. Immediately, Goodiel talked up his chaplain's new title: "*Doctor* Kennedy, our chaplain from Princeton." Though Kennedy did not care for the attention, he quickly grasped Goodiel's strategy of heightening the chaplain's abilities as a conflict-reducer. Seven months later, in December 1943, the profile got another boost. Goodiel promoted Kennedy from first lieutenant to captain. The CO's "termatoid" way soon had the 102nd increasingly approach "Doctor-Captain-Chaplain Kennedy" with all their army problems, keeping Goodiel well removed from personnel disputes.

In mid-March 1944, the 102nd trained across America to Camp Kilmer, New Jersey, in preparation for its April 6, 1944, crossover from New York harbor to England. Overseas, especially after they were truly "in the war," Kennedy's informal authority grew even more. With Goodiel smugly isolated from many problems, Kennedy assumed a de facto leadership role well beyond the duties of chaplain. He also became an integral element in the officers' poker games—and even more their "bug juice" sessions.[28]

"Bug juice" urges special note. One making such a cocktail normally started with grain alcohol from the pathology tent. Then he added whatever other alcohol happened to be around: rum, gin, vodka, bourbon, cognac. Then, in went something with sugar—Coca Cola, 7-Up, or canned juice (orange, grapefruit, or pineapple). The 102nd's detachment commander (DC), twenty-three-year-old Dan Laws, from Elizabethton, Tennessee, served as chief orchestrator of bug juice sessions. Many a time did Laws "call" a session with bizarre written invitations showing stick-man characters well lubricated on bug-juice, if not passed out. As an Erskine graduate, Kennedy never had experienced "fraternity life." Now he did. Still, much like a first-year state university student filtering "what it's like" in Christmas holiday chats with his parents, in not one of some thirty surviving war letters to Mary did he mention "bug juice."

At a bug juice session in the fall of 1944, in Belgium, Laws decided it was past time to rebaptize the chaplain out of due respect for his *real* role in the 102nd. For months, Goodiel's remoteness seemed more and more a problem. He was not in command. Kennedy had come to Europe to wage all-out war on racial fascism; his unit, with neither leadership nor "readiness," was not up to this tall order. On many days Kennedy had to serve as the shadow CO. Recently, the chaplain had implored the CO to lecture officers on treating enlisted men with more respect to help solve serious morale problems in the ranks. Goodiel would not. So, Kennedy did it . . . boldly. "Quit pushing them around," he told the officers in a staff meeting. A few of the surgeons griped about the whole scene. But most understood the message; they respected Kennedy for interceding. And shortly afterward the inner sanctum of officers who gathered regularly for poker-with-bug-juice concurred. On cue from Laws, they baptized Kennedy, "The Pulse."[29]

A jeep played a pivotal role in The Pulse's war life. As a chaplain, Kennedy had assigned to him a Willys MB jeep; he took possession of it in England on June 22, 1944. Although his physician-brother, William, had left his new Buick in Camden on his way overseas for field-hospital service, and Kennedy had driven it a few times before selling it, this jeep was "his" first, long-awaited "car." It even came with a driver, Pfc. Roland Rhynus, a Seventh Day Adventist conscientious objector from Freeport, Maine, who promptly named the jeep *Alabama*, and had the motor pool splash that name in white across its front, just below the windshield. Halfway through the war "a doctor" stole *Alabama*—never seen again. Laws and Rhynus expeditiously produced *Alabama II*—another jeep MB with replicate signage across the front.[30]

More to the point, travels in "my Jeep" delivered Kennedy to some of the most horrible things in the transatlantic world. How did this Christian, so committed to US military action as a necessary evil for the defeat of fascism, react to the sordid sorrow he saw all around him in Europe? How did his preoccupation with what he considered the fascism of the American South shape his reactions to the fascism of Europe? How did this Black Belt heretic, so devoted to logic and order, react to the greatest clash of armies and deathly horrors known to Western civilization? In essence, what did the war do to the pulse beneath "The Pulse"?

After unending schedule changes at Southampton, the army decided not to send the 102nd to Normandy until after the initial invasion. It would be part of a following "fresh wave" of evacs. So, after a "crossing over" party on the night of July 5—with "scotch, gin, and wine" and where a nurse, Amy Erickson, "taught [Kennedy] to dance," all unreported to Mary—the 102nd finally crossed the Channel and disembarked at Utah Beach on July 18, some thirty-six days after D-Day, June 6. From there they swiftly moved southeast into the Cotentin peninsula and the war.[31]

Actually, as war goes, things at first went well. Even with the Battle of Saint-Lô sending evacuees to their tent complex at Picauville, Kennedy had interesting times. One afternoon he and Rhynus took *Alabama* to nearby Surtainville to collect laundry the 102nd's physicians sent out to local homes. As they returned through a tiny intersection, they encountered none other than Kennedy's brother-in-law from Camden, Sam McNeill. Back in Camden, Sam and Dot lived a ten-minute walk from the Kennedys, and they were regular parts of each other's daily lives. But in the European theater, of course, neither had any idea where the other was. Sam just happened to be at Picauville on a short leave from tough fighting as a gunner on one of Gen. George Patton's half-tracks.

Thrilled to offer *Alabama*'s rolling hospitality, with Rhynus driving, Kennedy "took Sam in my Jeep" for a tour of Picauville and the 102nd Evacuation Hospital. They then returned him to his buddies who had been conveniently delayed with "liberated cognac" just outside Surtainville. As they parted, Sam advised that it was just a matter of time before Patton had him heading far north. He asked his brother-in-law to be on the lookout for a pair of L. L. Bean Maine Hunting Shoes—leather tops, rubber bottoms. Kennedy promised to try. In his next letter home to Freeport, Maine—home of L. L. Bean, Inc.—Rhynus said he would give it a shot, too.[32]

Then there was the visit to one very big house—far bigger than any white-columned "big house" of the American South. In August, to support the Battle of Brest, the 102nd moved to Ploudaniel, westward in Brittany. It set up in tents facing the sixteenth-century Château de Trébodennic. Kennedy had watched Goodiel make several social calls to the iconic site. So, one Sunday afternoon he decided he would do what he often did on Sunday afternoons back in the States. Go calling.

In the twilight he walked up that hill and sounded the iron knocker on the massive wooden door. To the owner, Louis Croc, he explained that he was Ren Kennedy from Wilcox County, Alabama, USA. He was just dropping by to say thank-you for the use of the pasture. And he apologized for not coming by earlier.

Monsieur Croc invited him into the *grand salon*. They sat with his wife, Christine, his sister, Marguerite, and his twenty-six-year-old nephew, Pierre Louboutin—sophisticated people and English speakers all. "Fresh pears and a bottle of Calvados" facilitated "a pleasant" two-hour visit in front of the seven-foot-high stone fireplace and bookshelves. Booze, books, a slowly burning fire: by now, Kennedy's kind of place.

That night Christine Croc chronicled the visit in her diary. Kennedy had listened to tales of the château's construction in 1584 and of the Germans' recent occupation of it—until *one* week before the 102nd arrived out front. He learned of the way Monsieur Croc hid Resistance fighters in tiny rooms of the château; "the last place they would look." He heard of other Resistance leaders not so fortunate. He heard particularly of famed Ploudaniel civic leader Aimé Talec, who never returned from the Bergen-Belsen prison camp. In essence, that adventuresome walk up the hill provided Kennedy not just a civilized evening in Europe but one enduring cameo in citizenry courage—fighting racial fascism.[33]

Of course, such adventures and others in Paris late in the war were but a tiny part of the story. The unhappy far outweighed the happy—and had far the greater impact.

Four days into France, at Picauville, on July 25, Saint-Lô fighting sent them "a flood" of patients. He wrote Mary, "Ambulance after ambulance . . . surgeons working day and night . . . there are two shifts [twelve hours on, twelve off]. . . . The boys [are] exhausted when they come in from lack of sleep and with pain . . . don't have much to say [but are] patient and brave. It was so bloody."[34]

And from there things got worse. By August, as Allies pushed the German infantry out of the Cotentin peninsula and readied for Saint-Malo fighting, the 102nd was sixty miles southwest across the peninsula at Saint-Pair-sur-Mer. Sunday evening, August 6, Kennedy was observing surgeries. A 102nd ambulance brought in French civilians hurt in a grenade accident two miles west at Sartilly. Though repeatedly warned not to touch stray grenades left by the Germans, a ten-year-old boy picked up one. On a parent's instant instruction to put it down gently, the boy dropped it—not gently. The explosion sent several pieces of shrapnel into the left arm of eleven-year-old Marie-Thérèse Provost. It sent the mass of the shrapnel into the upper body and head of twelve-year-old Bleuette Bindel.

When the girls arrived at the 102nd, the physicians already were treating twelve other children injured in similar incidents as well as injuries from accidental strafing by Allied war planes. Many of these died. Marie Thérèse survived; to this day severe scars show on her left arm. But Bleuette died right there on the operating table.

That night Kennedy turned in, sad and frustrated. He thought about his own two girls at home, Mary Conway and Margaret. He tried to fathom what he had said in "The Church and the War." "To war nothing whatsoever is sacred, and anything at all may be violated." No longer was this just a compelling idea. It was felt pain—visceral and personal.

With a break in the patient load, Goodiel approved his chaplain for a half-day of exploration. He needed a diversion from the pain of Bleuette's death. The plan failed miserably. Kennedy and Rhynus took *Alabama* westerly through just liberated Avaranches and back along the coast to Saint-James. There, in an otherwise bucolic countryside they drove into one massive, temporary cemetery for US casualties: "125 bodies [lay] on the grass . . . [placed in] mattress covers . . . [ready] to bury."

His earlier agonies suddenly merged into a singularly overwhelming "bad" feeling. Beyond the bodies out in the bay stood the sixteenth-century Mont Saint-Michel—one of the greatest historic sites of Europe, which had been spared the fascist bombs through a most unholy deal between Nazis and the papacy. Normally, he would have rushed toward such a thing. Instead, after giving it a "glance," he instructed Rhynus to head *Alabama* on back to Saint-Pair. There, "I go out and lie on grass."[35]

Later, in September, the 102nd convoyed the seven hundred miles north to Belgium and Luxembourg. At first they set up in a modern and luxurious sixteen-building facility just outside Bastogne. Here, originally, was an educational operation for Hitler's German Youth Movement. As the war progressed, however, regular German soldiers moved in. Recently, advancing Allies had forced them to flee—just three days before the 102nd's arrival. Kennedy moved into his posh Nazi dorm room, then took *Alabama* into central Bastogne for sightseeing. After two weeks—during which Kennedy wrote into the diary detailed descriptions of the facility—the 102nd moved again. Fortuitous. Three months later, out of this precise location—the German

Youth Movement facility—there began the epic, bloody Battle of Bastogne, with 2,000 KIAs (soldiers killed in action) just for the 101st Airborne alone.[36]

On departing Bastogne, Kennedy's unit moved some twenty-five miles southwest to Château de Roumont, just outside the village of Ochamps, in Belgium. They were told to wait until the war caught up with them. Such a break should have provided The Pulse some interesting relief. After all, it was not just a break from the violence. It was a break to live in the huge, sixteen-bedroom "hunting lodge" of Belgium's foremost industrialist of that time, Baron Evence von Coppée, of Brussels. Winter was not too far off. The "lodge"" even had its own furnaces—with fuel—and two kitchens. Officers had comfortable beds. The place had its own chapel. Here was luxury rivaling the Vanderbilts' Biltmore estate in Asheville, North Carolina.

There at Roumont, in late October, Kennedy received a letter from Sam. For sure, now, Sam knew his half-track unit would be in northern Europe by midwinter. The Bean boots would be crucial. And since Roland Rhynus had not heard back from Freeport, and *Alabama* travels were yet to turn up a pair, Sam urged, "I understand officers can get them through quarter m[aster] pretty quick.... Get me a pair of 9 1/2 E boots ... twelve or fourteen inches high.... Let me know the price so I can send you some money." Kennedy replied in the negative on the quartermaster front. Even with Dan Laws's help, the boots were not to be had. Still, raised in an east Tennessee family of avid hunters, Laws advised that Château de Roumont was within easy drive of the historic center of European hunting, Saint-Hubert, Belgium. Thrilled in writing Sam of this new prospect, two days later Kennedy took *Alabama* to Saint-Hubert. Instant victory—if a used pair. Off the boots went to Sam through the army mail ... wherever Sam was.[37]

Yet waiting for the war to catch up with the 102nd also had its downside. At Roumont, bug juice flowed as never before. Drunk officers broke furniture. Drunk officers ordered "a few of the men" to roll beer kegs up and down the majestic marble stairs—chipping and marring them in ways visible even today. Though physicians and other male officers had assigned beds on one floor, the nurses on another, what the army still calls "sexual fraternization" went rampant. In short, though anything but a prude, Kennedy saw discipline and structure evaporating. Should the war deliver a sudden group of 200 patients in a twenty-four-hour period, he saw lack of structure resulting in unnecessary loss of life. "The doctors stayed either drunk or hungover." This was not the way to defeat Hitler's racial fascism.

More than ever he counseled Goodiel that the only officers staying focused and disciplined were "the Jewish ones." Since SLO, Kennedy had considered Lt. Joe Rutenberg and several other Jewish officers to be the 102nd's "brain team ... I like them, and [they] regularly come to my services."

Rutenberg had been transferred, but the others were still there at Roumont: "our stability." Otherwise, most officers regularly "drank too much" because of "personal problems" back home, which they felt powerless to influence— "divorce or death of a family member." The "powerless problem" also led some physicians and nurses, professionally attuned to feeling powerful, to "over drink" after several months of not being powerful enough to save certain lives. Several surgeons, too, "drank far too much just so they would be considered alcoholics"; they wanted out so as to get home to "their civilian practices." Yet most of all it was "the idle time" at Roumont that had more of them drinking "far too much." As he urged on Goodiel, "Few [physicians and nurses] read or have intellectual interests"—one of the many who did not being the CO himself. Take newspapers and magazines, for instance. Kennedy received forwarded subscriptions to *New Republic* and *Christian Century*. And friends from the States regularly mailed him entire issues of the *Los Angeles Times* and the *New York Times*, especially if they included searching analyses of Hitler, fascism, and American war aims. When he tried to share these among doctor and nurse colleagues, however, with few exceptions all they wanted were "the comics and the sports page."

Minus intellectual interests, not to mention concerns about defeating fascism, physicians and nurses were dependent on patients to stay occupied. With breaks in the war they had few of them. So they drank excessively, slept around, and entertained themselves by ordering "the men" to run stupid errands for them—even berating them to their faces. In turn, as Kennedy had noted since before departing the States, the unit continued to have "little cohesion and little realistic chain of command." "Much chicanery, politicking . . . battle for control of organization . . . 102nd racked by dissension . . . and morons running it." To Kennedy, this was chaos. Repeatedly, he tried to get the CO to establish some regimen. Goodiel did not. A good leader desperately needed to replace this "old regular Army officer of moronic incompetence," he confided to the diary. And, it turns out, The Pulse read it all too right . . . and yet wrong, as the 102nd's greatest call to action lay just ahead.[38]

In November, as Patton's hard fighting pushed on northward through Metz, France, forecasting a huge battle in the Ardennes forest, the 102nd found itself relocated to a structure closer to the anticipated front. It moved to a large, modern educational facility in Ettelbruck, twenty miles north of Luxembourg. Germans had converted the Ettelbruck Agricultural College into a soldier rehabilitation center. The 102nd moved in right on the heels of the fleeing German soldiers and patients. And the Roumont pattern continued. Bug juice flowed. Discipline was a joke.

The night of Monday, December 11, however, brought a sudden change to the chaplain's worries. At supper the Red Cross nurse, Flora Jane Bromley, advised she had a telegram for him. When he finished eating, he went to his office for open counseling hours, but mainly he just awaited the message: he knew what Red Cross messages did; he just did not know who this one did it to. Finally, at 10:00 p.m. "she brings . . . [in the] radiogram." It was from his sister-in-law, Dot McNeill, back in Camden, "saying that Sam McNeill was killed in action in France on November 15 . . . the saddest news I have ever received," he told the diary. "It leaves me sick at heart."

Granted, Kennedy never had been as close to Sam as to a few others back home, especially Bill Jones. Sam was more of "a man's man . . . a devout hunter, fisherman, a deputy sheriff." He did not share Kennedy's obsession with the life of the mind. But the in-laws still held great affection for each other. Plus, though a Negro fugitive had killed Sam's father, Sheriff George McNeill, Sam still had moderate racial views. His deputy sheriff record included acts of kindness toward Negroes. Many Negroes trusted him. Ren admired Sam for this.

From England to France, Ren and Sam generally did not know where the other was. Yet forwarded correspondence from others in Camden let them have news of each other. And in other ways, too, the war actually brought them closer. Sam's "man's man" tone gave way to something deeper. Recently, he had written Dot—a letter she sent to Ren—that "how many Germans you've gotten will be more a secret [after the war] than something to brag about. . . . The man who really does these things is not going to talk so much." Then the strangeness of war brought them together in July at that intersection of country roads in Lower Normandy. They had several hours of "good catch-up talk"—war talk, sharing news from home, and the all-important matter of the L. L. Bean boots. Although Dot had written Sam that she had struck out on them, Ren managed to find them and put them in the mail to Sam. But none of that mattered now. The Germans had killed Sam. As Kennedy recalled in the early 1980s, here was "one more Wilcox deputy sheriff killed in the line of duty"—granted, "a different line of duty" at least geographically—and "the deputy sheriff we needed most to become head sheriff in Wilcox. Such a good man. He could have been such a good and historic force."[39]

Four days later, on Saturday, December 16, 1944, just before daylight, Germans launched a carefully planned surprise counteroffensive to the US First Army's push through the Ardennes. The Battle of the Bulge was on. Six miles back from the initial battle, the 102nd had the full engagement of a field hospital, plus an evac, with German artillery hitting all around the hospital. Early the next day Kennedy recorded how it was going. "Hospital flooded with casualties . . . bad ones . . . over 200 admissions . . . many chest wounds." By nightfall "patients [were] all over the halls."

Around midnight, Goodiel received word that in the next twelve hours, if not sooner, the enemy would overrun the facility: he should relocate immediately to Spa, Belgium, some seventy miles north. Kennedy went again to the diary. "[We] have orders to move 8 am tomorrow. . . . Rhynus and I load the chaplain stuff on the trailer. All patients evacuated this PM except 35 non-transportables [still being operated on]. Laws, Meads, Mills and [fifteen] enlisted men will remain with them."

Chaos now ruled. Just as the convoy of patients was pulling out, Goodiel received word that German soldiers were taking Spa. Some of the 102nd drivers got the message to head instead for Huy, Belgium, seventy-five miles northwest on the Meuse River. But Goodiel did not get the message to others. "Our group simply was not used to getting clear orders and following them," Kennedy later recorded.

Over the next *three* days various elements of the 102nd rolled into Huy. German planes strafed one of their convoys carrying patients. No one killed. Other vehicles with Goodiel and his chaplain followed. Toward the end of the third day yet another segment of the 102nd appeared. It had been captured by Germans. But when they found the convoy carried no surplus fuel—what the Germans wanted—it was freed. Two days later, the morning of December 21, Dan Laws and his two ambulances of "non-transportables" arrived. They had no choice—either redefine their patients as "transportable" or see them dead. Surgeons Mills and Meads had treated them in the hurtling trucks. All thirty-five survived.

During that three-day period some four other US Army medical units also arrived at Huy. They occupied numerous old buildings, including a convent and a whorehouse. Because the 102nd was the only unit—whether evac, field hospital, or medical group—able to move its equipment and staff intact, it was assigned the space of Huy Normal School. From there, the 102nd had the lead role in this Battle of the Bulge "medical center." By the morning of December 20, the 102nd was partially functional. In the first *hour* 299 casualties arrived.[40]

Today, the Huy Normal School is a multipurpose public complex. No historic marker stands out front to tell what happened there during the Battle of the Bulge. But indeed there should be. What happened there remains unmatched in the annals of US military medicine. Of the 19,000 American casualties at the Bulge, some 4,700—25 percent—received treatment at one evacuation hospital: the 102nd. And of those 4,700 only 100 died while patients of the 102nd. On Christmas Day alone, the 102nd treated 667. In short, despite weak leadership by the 102nd's CO—Goodiel was relieved of command on December 28 and replaced temporarily by Col. John F. Blatt from 44th Evac and then on January 8 by a senior surgeon from the 9th Infantry,

Col. John Woodruff—the unit's extraordinary medical talent delivered. And what happened to the Wilcox County preacher during this greatest clash of armies in modern history? During this potent moment in military medicine? A lot.[41]

The morning of January 11 a US pilot shot down by Germans arrived at the 102nd, that is, the "parts of him" which medics could retrieve and place "in a bucket." Word of this spread rapidly through the unit: "the parts of the pilot they brought in in a bucket." Even among some physicians the resulting morale issue eclipsed adrenaline. Three days later, Sunday, January 14, Kennedy's service went to John 14:6 with hopes for an offsetting message: "And Jesus said, 'I am the way, the truth, and the light.'" But it is unlikely that many of the 250 who heard him preach that day thought about something other than "the parts" and "the bucket." Similarly, on January 21 he drew from II Timothy 4:7: "I have fought the good fight and I have kept the faith." He figured a "distracted attendance of 143."

Throughout these eleven epic weeks, however, the 102nd's chaplain did far more than preach. One-on-one counseling with the ever incoming patients had him in the wards thirteen to fifteen hours a day. Among these "brave and uncomplaining boys" were identical twin brothers from Delta, Alabama (near Anniston), Millard and Willard Lumpkin. Back home they not only "shared headaches" but also corner jump shots on the high school basketball court—jump shots so identical the coach never could tell which brother was shooting. As sharecropper's sons they had to quit school after the tenth grade to take work at a pipe foundry in nearby Oxford, Alabama. Then, upon turning eighteen, they joined the army. Eventually, army life had them on the European front as part of the noted 83rd Infantry, 33Q Regiment, Company G.

On Friday, January 5, 1945, at 7:30 a.m., Willard took shrapnel wounds to the stomach, chest, and limbs. At the same time, ten yards to his left, Millard received shrapnel wounds to his right leg. Millard helped a medic carry Willard the seven miles to a field hospital. From there an ambulance moved them to the 102nd at Huy.

That evening, as the surgeons worked feverishly on Willard, Kennedy counseled Millard while a nurse carefully removed metal fragments from his leg. Twice during that procedure Kennedy checked on Willard. He shielded his brother from certain details; he did not tell him, "Vic Mills removed packing [applied by medic] to Willard's chest and two [sic] quarts of blood run out." But he told him honestly of the gravity of the "sucking chest wound." Mills finally emerged with little hope. When Kennedy took Millard in for a visit, they found Willard lingering on heavy doses of morphine. Well after midnight the chaplain got to his diary: "Willard died at 12:30 am [January 6, 1945]. Sgt [Leonard] Reichlin shaves him, combs his hair, puts him on the table with blanket over him, face exposed—looked nice. I take Millard in to see him and say prayer.... The mother, Mrs. Ethel Lumpkin, Rt. 2, Delta, Alabama. [Willard will be] buried at Fosse, Belgium."

The next day Kennedy brought Millard a pencil and a piece of paper. Together they wrote a letter for Millard to send his mother. "Dear Mother . . . Willard died Friday night. It seems I cannot do without him but someday I hope to meet him. . . . He lived 17 hours after he was hit. . . . Captain Kennedy from Camden, Alabama, was there with us in the hospital. It was hard to give him up but we had to do it. He was put away nice. I will get by some way."

Willard's "sucking chest wound" was just one of the horrors Kennedy regularly noted in the diary. "Evisceration of abdomen," "paralyzed diaphragm," "scrotum 1/4 testicle," "bore two holes in skull to pick out shattered bone," "walk-in with side of face blown off," "blast entered anus and blew him apart inside," and of course, "the parts of the pilot they brought in in a bucket"—these and many others were but the written record of war's horror. And as these horrors continued over the next two weeks, increasingly his notes on them were accompanied by distinct editorial comment: "this insane business keeps going on," "this horrible war," "men suffering and dying around here . . . it gets more and more sickening." Then on January 19 his focus changed.[42]

That day Kennedy got a response from a written request he had made on where "the Army" buried Sam McNeill. "The Army" reported he was buried at Limey, not far from Metz, in northwestern France, where the army had leased space for temporary graves. This was where Patton's men had fought so hard on their push toward Luxembourg and Belgium. On the morning of January 23, the new CO, Colonel Woodford, approved Kennedy for a three-day leave. With the temperature at zero Fahrenheit and roads covered in two feet of snow, Kennedy and Rhynus headed off in *Alabama* to find Sam . . . and how he died. It was Huy to the Metz area. They overnighted inside barbed-wired German POW camps. When they finally got to Limey, they were told, instead, that Sam's body was at another, temporary grave site outside the neighboring farm village of Noviant-aux-Prés. They headed there. On return to Huy, on January 26, here is what Kennedy mailed Dot via Mary about Noviant-aux-Prés.

> I . . . stayed out there by the grave with Sam for a half hour just thinking about him and talking to him. I had no flowers in this terrible winter over here. But I cut a small evergreen limb from a fir tree and placed it and a copy of the Gospel of John opened at the 14th chapter on the grave, and weighted them down with a lump of frozen snow. . . . I learned that Sam was killed in action on November 15 [1944] at a place called

Béchy, southwest of Metz . . . from mortar shell fragments, wounds in head and chest. It is probable that Sam was killed instantly . . . was never conscious after being hit, and if he had to die I am glad it was that way for I have seen the terrible suffering of so many of the wounded . . . Sam is not sleeping there alone. There are 5800 other American boys sleeping there with him. And there will be more.[43]

On the 102nd's last Sunday in Huy, January 28, 1945, its chaplain preached a tough sermon, sardonically titled, "Victory!" He began with a reading of Matthew 3:8: "Bring forth therefore fruit . . . [worthy of] . . . repentance." After such a reading, on the heels of Bulge horrors and losing—then finding—Sam, one might anticipate this Social Gospel preacher to move to the message often drawn from that passage. Despite all our sorrow, let us not forget that only God got us through this, and out of our indebtedness to God we must do good deeds for our fellow humans. Not so. Instead, in a seeming disconnect—as if he could not say what he often had said following that passage—he shifted to hard implications of all-out war on Hitler's racial fascism. He had written it out on two sheets of paper, and alongside those he had that small, folded clipping from the *New York Times* he had been carrying in his wallet: the one that described the opposite of racial fascism, FDR's "Four Freedoms." Here is the core of his disconcerting message.

> Our hopes on entering the war [focused on a] world federation, the end of imperialism, [the] rebirth of freedom. [But] what has the war done for our [own] country? The slaughter and crippling of 1,000,000 [U.S.] soldiers. . . . And what has war done for Europe? Freed it from Nazism and Hitler but not freed it from fear, want, savagery, tyrannies, and despair. [After the war] . . . Germany will be the prize. If Britain's sphere [fails to balance] . . . Russia's, there could be a communistic government in every State in Europe in ten years except Scandinavia, Switzerland, and the UK. . . . [So] the war [after all] does not give us a better chance to rebuild the world. [It is] better that we had started that in the 1920s.

Kennedy's analysis was not far off the mark of a coming Cold War of Soviet totalitarianism pitted against a Western alliance of at least rhetorical commitment to the Four Freedoms. Of course, similar if more refined prescience was about to be articulated by any number of notable Soviet-watchers in America, especially US diplomat George F. Kennan. Unlike Kennan's relatively clinical prognostications grounded in history and social psychology, however, Kennedy's message seems to have been triggered by his emotional reactions to the ironic futility of the current war. Ravages of "the war"—Vasco

Hale, Aimé Talec, Bleuette Bindel, "parts of the pilot," the Lumpkin brothers, Sam for sure, and thousands upon thousands of others, not to mention a segregated army where white US soldiers in the 102nd wards requested to be bedded next to German POWs rather than alongside fellow Black US soldiers—had taken their toll. Not since November 1927, when he sought help from John Calvin and God, had Kennedy been so slumped in the corner. And he stayed there for a while. Indeed, the following day the "return to sender Army mail" brought him one devastating box, "the pair of boots I sent to Sam." And the next day, January 30, 1945, when Mickey Rooney and Marlene Dietrich entertained the 102nd, Kennedy's "down" appraisal: "Rooney . . . looks like a bum . . . Dietrich . . . a hag."[44]

By mid-March 1945, the 102nd operated out of the Kurhaus Hotel, at Bad Neuenahr, Germany, just north of Bonn, tending to casualties from the Remagen Bridge battle. *Kurhaus* translates roughly into "place where you are made to feel better." Adjacent to the hotel bubbled up warm springs visited by many a European tourist before the war. Of course, the war shut down the spa. Though the remaining luxury of the place provided a modicum of physical relief for Kennedy and his comrades, what he increasingly called the "downs" of the war hardly let up.

He expected the many casualties the 102nd received from Remagen Bridge fighting. But he did not expect to walk into a Kurahaus ward a few seconds after a German girl was pronounced dead from choking in her own blood and vomit. Although a 102nd nurse was supposed to have been with her, she was next door in a suite adjacent to the girl's ward with "a group of visiting brass . . . colonels . . . getting drunk with their women, their nurses." Perhaps a *Kurhaus* for some.[45]

In April, they set up in tents at Gera, forty miles from the Czech frontier, to deal with the manifold issues of Germany's gradual liberation—final fighting and freed POWs (prisoners of war). There Kennedy chanced upon a patient, a staff sergeant named Joseph C. Frownfelter, of Sedalia, Missouri, who had been part of the maneuver resulting in Sam's death. As Frownfelter talked, Kennedy jotted notes; those notes survive. And that night he took the matter to the diary. Sam's half-track and three jeeps with machine guns volunteered to move out ahead of their group to reconnoiter a battery of German artillery on a road east of Béchy, France. The enemy guns were in the woods—well camouflaged. Out of nowhere German 88s and mortar fire hit Sam's half-track. Instantly, the others of Sam's unit moved up. A brutal fight ensued. It was two hours before medics could get to what was left of Sam's half-track. As driver of one of the rescuing half-tracks, Frownfelter was with the medics when they finally could function on the site. He insisted the medics could do nothing for Sam. "His entire back was blown away." As hard as this was, Kennedy wrote Dot of the conversation—confirmation that Sam died quickly, no suffering. He left out the words, "His entire back was blown away."

At Gera it was chaos beyond Roumont. Woodford lost control. Bug juice flowed "like the Meuse." Doctors went to surgery hungover. One drunk private accidentally shot another drunk private. Still another drunk private fell off a truck and was killed in the following traffic. "Three of our truck drivers [ran] over 3 liberated Hungarians, killing one, breaking arms and head of another [then] pulled .45 on warrant officer" arresting them. Kennedy did the funerals. Despite no combat, the chaos and death continued, further eroding his morale. FDR's death did not help matters: "I wished he could have lived to win the war and make the peace."

Kennedy felt "disorder," he confided to the diary. Besides the constant noncombat violence, "our boys" were involved in so much crime. Released POWs straggle in from brutal conditions and "just die on the street." "The dead are often robbed" of shoes and blankets, "and likely as not by US soldiers." When Mary wrote for Dot asking about recovery of Sam's watch, which she had given him as a wedding present, it was the same point. "The dead are often robbed by our own soldiers"; Dot "should not expect" to have Sam's watch returned. Nothing documents that a US soldier stole Sam's watch. Kennedy's assessment, however, evolved from the "Inventory of Personal Effects" he found for Sam at the Graves Registration office in Noviant-aux-Prés. His notes survive. The inventory included "3 photos, 2 keys, 1 ring—silvered colored—broken, 2 pen knives, 1 wallet—brown." No watch. In late April, his sense of history made him undertake a four-day "*Alabama* run" to Buchenwald, which had been liberated on April 12. His "down" continued: "'They entered by the gate and left by the chimney,' said a captured SS officer, and . . . lampshades [were] made of human skin."[46]

Adolf Hitler's suicide on April 30 led to VE Day (Victory in Europe) on May 8. At the back of his tent Kennedy held a "peace service." Some 200 attended, a record for his wartime services. But despite the "right music"—"Faith of our Fathers"—"everyone was quiet and afterwards immediately returned to what they had been doing for days." "Lt. Roy Crooks from North Carolina dies from truck wreck—hit by drunk [US Army] soldier in another truck."

In mid-May it was on to Giessen, Germany, thirty miles north of Frankfurt, and much the same disturbing behavior. "I watch [Lawrence] Dickey for two hours do postmortem on Sgt Raymond Aclin." An Arkansas soldier who died after a motorcycle crash, he was "drunk, rides motorcycle standing up, waving to girls, shouting Heil Hitler." There, too, he encountered sexual assault. It was not really new for him. Back at SLO, Goodiel had him counseling a second lieutenant on legal charges he would face for raping a private's wife who was visiting her husband before he went overseas. In Giessen, however, six "men" of the 102nd found themselves accused of raping two local girls, ages fourteen and eighteen.

Woodford assigned Kennedy to interrogate the accused. Chaplain's duties can vary. Courts-martial ultimately sent five of them back to the States with dishonorable discharges for "vague involvement" in the matter. One of them, however, twenty-two-year-old Marion Brown from McGehee, Arkansas, "with a complex personality," explicitly confessed to attacking both girls. He maintained the other five constantly accused him of being homosexual. All were drunk. They said he had to prove his heterosexuality by having sex with the girls, whether the girls wanted sex or not. With the other GIs' assistance, he assaulted them. In the stockade, two days after his confession, "somehow [he] stole a pistol" from a guard and "shot himself in the heart . . . [and] died within fifteen minutes."

Immediately, Kennedy held a funeral for Brown. His body went to a grave in Margraten, Holland, where it remains today. Kennedy then urged the CO to hold an officers' meeting on how to avoid future tragedies of this type. Woodruff did so. Kennedy's photograph of the meeting survives, with a note on the back saying what it is. The chaplain spoke, too. If no record remains of his words, it is not hard to imagine what was on his mind. On at least five occasions different COs of the 102nd had used him in counseling soldiers admitting to homosexuality before—according to army policy—they were "sent home" on a "CDD," Certificate of Disability Discharge. And the diary reveals he had counseled at least four others of the 102nd "accused" of homosexuality. Brown was not one of them.

Late that afternoon, Kennedy wrote one difficult condolence letter. He had to tell Brown's wife that, while the army classified her husband's death as "a non-combat death, in the line of duty," "sooner or later you must know . . . something else." But he did not tell all. "He had become involved in some difficulties. Apparently, they preyed upon his mind to such an extent that he chose to end his life. . . . Sgt. Brown often spoke to me of you, and of the baby who I understand he never saw. . . . May God bless and comfort you in this bereavement." After mailing it at the Red Cross office, he and Dan "got plastered with Bug Juice." He gave Mary a brief summary of the Brown matter; no reference to "plastered."[47]

By this time, his physician-brother, William, was in Dachau. He had served with the 10th Field Hospital in North Africa, Italy, and France before assignment to the 16th Evacuation Hospital just outside Dachau. Not knowing of William's specific assignment, just having the Dachau-vicinity address, in early June Kennedy and Rhynus headed off in *Alabama II* with a four-day pass. He found William housed in a former SS officer's room next to one of the subcamps that made up the Dachau complex. In his three nights there, he heard of the horrors William found as one of the first US physicians to enter the complex: "so many Jews on the threshold of death from typhus and starvation." Of the 35,000 prisoners there when William arrived, 18,000 remained, 4,000 of them requiring constant medical attention, with "25 to 30 dying per day." William showed him the "death houses—the furnaces." William kept saying, "I didn't save enough. I just didn't save enough." While Ren wrote Mary two long, clinical letters about visiting the camp and, sardonically, the beautiful countryside around it, all he said about William's reactions was "he is doing fine." But what Kennedy saw never left him, nor did William's deep remorse.[48]

As the 102nd moved through a series of demobilization locations, zigzagging toward an ultimate departure out of Marseilles, France, it had virtually no patients. This permitted Kennedy to sleep long hours and return to one of his long-time passions: losing himself in books. Konrad Heiden's *Der Fuehrer: Hitler's Rise to Power* (1944) helped explain to him why it all happened. He also read Stephen Crane's *Red Badge of Courage* (1895), Lillian Smith's *Strange Fruit* (1940), and Thomas Wolfe's posthumous *You Can't Go Home Again* (1940). What the *Kurhaus* had failed to provide, reading and rest began to deliver. In August, granted, it was not books that made him hardly notice the US bombing of Hiroshima and Nagasaki, Japan, and then VJ Day on August 15; he was deeply involved in another case of a GI raping a young German girl, and "a boy from Mississippi, drunk, driving Jeep—almost killed." "The Army . . . it does so many bad things when it is not actually fighting."

Still, the restful zigzagging of his unit continued for two more months, and the reading and resting too, and with that the gradual return of his precombat mentality. When he was not reading, he started writing a history of the 102nd Evacuation Hospital. One can plot his resurging state of mind through the changing language in different drafts. In the mind of The Pulse, a futile war gradually moved to another reality—"the defeat of Nazi Fascist Germany." Surely, his morale moved up yet another notch, if in a bittersweet way, when he opened a perfectly punctuated letter from his eleven-year-old daughter, Margaret, bringing the most glorious of bulletins—"tonight there are 7 million crickets and tree frogs making music"—and so different from youth lives he had agonized with over the last year. Finally, in late October, at Calas—down near Marseilles—he threw himself into Somerset Maugham's new novel, *Razor's Edge* (1944). This depicts war trauma after the Treaty of Versailles, and it did not take him "down." The day after he finished it, on November 1, Dan Laws brought big news: "We have been assigned to a ship, the *USS Sea Porpoise*." Bedrolls and footlockers packed, the two war comrades attended a "last night in Calas" party for officers of the 102nd Evacuation Hospital. Details unrecorded.[49]

On November 3, at 4:30 p.m., the ship eased out of Marseilles. It carried 2,700 troops. For the next ten days it sloshed along at its maximum of 18 knots. On Sunday, November 11, as they left the Mediterranean and headed for the Azores, Kennedy gave his last army sermon. He preached on "Humility, Not Hubris, in the Post-War World." "A few" enlisted men attended. No officers. And "no one listened." Still, he was up and running again.

Blessedly immune to seasickness, Kennedy spent most days at sea on deck stretched out in a chaise lounge. Wrapped in two wool blankets, he made further refinements to "A History of the 102nd Evacuation Hospital." As the *Porpoise* pushed on, the story got better and better, especially as his eyes periodically left the manuscript to move to "my watch."

Notably, this was not the "fine Elgin" pocket watch he had had from Erskine days. It was a wristwatch. Ever since the World War I era, when soldiers returning from the fronts of gas and barbed wire extolled the greater efficiency of the wristwatch over the pocket watch, wristwatches were increasingly the fad. Throughout the 1920s and 1930s, Kennedy had resisted. But on departing the Harvard Chaplaincy School for SLO he finally capitulated. Out of $250 the army refunded him on uniform expenditures, he went to Melinick Brothers in Boston and bought a "fine Lathan military watch." He was told it was "worth $60—[he] paid $30." In a three-day period, he returned it twice for "tuning"—"a wristwatch *should* keep precise time." After that, however, he wore it throughout the war and indeed until the day he died.

Always having felt a sense of precise time to be a bedrock to sensible living, how reinforcing for him, now—on the deck of the *Porpoise*—to track the crossing of time zones on a course heading him home. November 11: "Turn watch back one hour again tonight; have retarded watch one hour on Sun., Mon., Weds. Thur. and Sat. nights—five times." And the story of the 102nd kept getting better. November 12: "Retard again tonight, sixth time." The *Porpoise* had entered the Eastern time zone.[50]

On Tuesday, November 13, the 102nd unloaded at Staten Island, New York. By the next morning they were asleep at the barracks in Camp Kilmer, forty to a room. The chaplain slept six hours. After "a good steak dinner" in the officers' mess, he telephoned Mary about his arrival plans in Montgomery. Then he got a haircut before heading for beer and talk with buddies. That night, on returning to his bunk, "noisy bastards" all around him prohibited sleep. So he just lay there fiddling with sentences in "The History of the 102nd Evacuation Hospital." The next morning he and Dan ate a farewell breakfast; the conversation was not easy. For the next thirty-eight years, Ren and Dan (who was destined for the University of Virginia law school and a noted practice in Elizabethton, Tennessee) called each other on New Year's Day. But they never again set eyes on each other.

As the train chugged southward, Kennedy pondered an old reality, one he and Mary had written about at least six times during the war. On his leaving the army, the family income would go from $4,000 a year back down to where it was in early 1943, just $2000. And they were dead set on college for Margaret and Mary Conway. So, when he mustered out at Fort McPherson, in Atlanta, he signed up for the US Army Reserve with promotion to rank of major—an extra twenty dollars a month. Every dollar would count.[51]

On Monday, November 19, 1945, at 9:30 a.m. Central time, Southern Railway No. 37 pulled into Montgomery. Off stepped the khaki-clad preacher. He looked like the veteran he was: 1st Army patch, Bronze star, battle stars for northern France, the Battle of the Bulge, the Rhineland, and central Germany. Yet beneath the pride this introspective man undoubtedly felt something else. The khaki, the jacket insignias, and indeed the Lathan spoke to a profound accomplishment: a confounding and often tragic accomplishment, but one still permitting him to do something meaningful on behalf of his God Mandate. Though it had taken all-out war, he had played a concrete role in defeating racial fascism—at least in other countries.

Sam's widow, Dot, drove Mary and the girls to meet him. By Trailways his trunk followed. That night in Camden, Bill and Joyce Jones joined the family for sandwiches. Adrenalin finally caved to exhaustion. Before early bedtime with Mary, The Pulse slipped off to himself in the study to tell his diary one complex thing: "Home, again."[52]

The grave monument of Rev. John Renwick, Cannon's Creek Cemetery, Cannon's Creek, South Carolina. Photo by Michael Bedenbaugh.

Black-robed Renwick Kennedy on the steps of Camden Associate Reformed Presbyterian Church, Camden, Alabama, c. 1956. Photo by Hugh C. Dale Jr.

Camden Associate Reformed Presbyterian Church, Camden, Alabama, 2017. Photo by Susan McWilliams.

Prosperity Associate Reformed Presbyterian Church, Marion Junction, Alabama, 2017. Photo by Susan McWilliams.

Bethel Associate Reformed Presbyterian Church, Oak Hill, Alabama, 2008. Photo by Susan McWilliams.

Mary Moore Kennedy, c. 1938. Photographer unknown.

Richebourg Gaillard McWilliams, c. 1936. Photographer unknown.

William Junius (Bill) Jones, c. 1963.
Photographer unknown.

William Green Wilson (front row, second from left) and teachers of
Camden Academy, Camden, Alabama, c. 1916. Photographer unknown.

Viola Jefferson Goode Liddell, c. 1945.
Courtesy of Will Liddell.

Emmett Kilpatrick, c. 1958. From the Troy
State College *Palladium: 1958*. Courtesy of
Wiregrass Archives, Troy University-Dothan.

Renwick Kennedy and Capt. Daniel M. Laws III, Picauville, France, 1944, on emerging from an extended "bug juice" session. Photo by Roland Rhynus.

Bleuette Bindel, Saint-Pair-sur-Mer, France, August 1944, dressed for school and only a few weeks before she was killed by a hand grenade. Photographer unknown. Courtesy of the late Yvette Bindel Gilbert.

Kennedy and his Jeep *Alabama II*, at blown-up Bastogne, Belgium, March 1945. Photo by Roland Rhynus.

Martha Patton Simpson, c. 1933, in front of Simpson family home, Furman, Alabama. Alabama Department of Archives and History, Photographs and Picture Collection, Mary Lee Simpson Negative Collection, Q91349.

Kennedy and new members of the Camden Associate Reformed Presbyterian Church, 1961. Kennedy and (left to right) Carey Cole Falkenberry, Haden Jones Gaines, Martha Lee Jones, Jane Shelton Dale, Roy Patterson Bonner, and Marvin David Falkenberry. Photo by Hugh C. Dale Jr.

J. Jefferson Bennett, c. 1963. James Jefferson Bennett Papers, Hoole Special Collections, University of Alabama Libraries, Tuscaloosa.

Kennedy as a Troy State College literature professor, 1953. Photographer unknown.

Sarah Ann McDaniels Woods, 1995, at Holy Cross Lutheran Church, Camden, Alabama. Photo by Udell Holmes. Courtesy of Veronica Woods.

Part II

TORMENTED PRAGMATIST, 1945–1985

The postwar world gave Ren Kennedy periods of optimism and hope: coming home from war and thinking America might deal with its own racial issues the way it had with Europe's and Japan's; his children growing into educated, modern adults; new developments in his professional life bringing significant increases to family income—easing his wife's long financial insecurities.

Yet these years also had him on a roller-coaster, winding up where all of them ultimately do: down. Even by 1948, he knew his prewar Social Gospel hopes about race and fascism and white blasphemy, especially among fellow Scotch-Irish, were more than in trouble. Granted, with the 1950s and 1960s, despite the civil rights movement encountering massive white resistance, occasional developments in state and national politics rekindled at least some of his old neo-orthodox drive. But these often turned into fleeting moments—some dashed by extreme tragedy. Likewise, his developing leadership role at nearby Troy State College increasingly revealed the public persona of no more an idealistic man. In some ways he seemed the real-life version of Jack Burden in Robert Warren's epic novel, *All the King's Men* (1946), with Governor Willie Stark just replaced by Kennedy's "cousin"—Governor George Wallace. Yet that oversimplifies Kennedy. For beneath such public pragmatism were daily struggles for this privately persisting neo-orthodox Christian.

9

"Home, Again"

On Sunday morning, November 25, 1945, Reverend Kennedy mounted the pulpit at Camden ARPC. A packed house awaited. Compared to his 1942 "The Church and the War" sermon, he spoke with a decidedly secular voice as he gave an extensive report on his wartime life—"the best there is human nature... and also the worst... hunger, death, depravity." He concluded with a profession: "I do not know what the war has done to me." From there on, he entered upon his odyssey through the postwar era—years that eventually answered the potent question behind that forthright profession.[1]

This era offered him good things. Right away, Camden ARPs raised his yearly salary from $1,700 to $2,000. Marion Junction ARPs moved his part-time pay from $300 a year to $500. Throw in Mary's part-time, Bible-study instruction at Camden elementary, plus his stipend for Army Reserve, and an average of about $300 a year in outright gifts by congregation members, and he could predict a 1946 income of around $3,500—just short of his World War II army salary. Daughter number one, Mary Conway, was a sophomore at the Wilcox County High School and already talking about going to Erskine College. Daughter number two, Margaret, was three years behind her.[2]

Before the war, recall, he had pedaled around Camden on his bike, "Vic." And for pastoral visits or committee meetings out in the county, he had had to beg someone for a ride or rent a car from a member of his congregation—out of his own salary. Indeed, for that 1934 visit to Oak Hill for "Richebourg's Hitler Report" he had had to rent Miller Bonner's 1930 black Chevrolet sedan. So, if his 1946 salary was not enough to begin a college fund for the children, it possibly might be enough to address something for which he had long felt pressing need: a car.

A year back in Camden, in November 1946, Kennedy caught a ride to the army's surplus center south of Atlanta. For $398 he drove away with Willys Jeep No. 132991, a 1942 MB model, carefully noted in his "little black book" not far from the Elgin wristwatch numbers. It was a replica of *Alabama*

II, but *Alabama III* was not to be. His daughters christened it *Jeep.* Poetic bridge from wartime to peacetime, the ARP preacher *driving himself* in *Jeep* instantly became a celebrated part of the Wilcox scene.[3]

Meanwhile, the writer in him surged forward, if at first toward a different quarry from before the war. Even by mid-December 1945 he had put finishing touches on his "History of the 102nd Evacuation Hospital" and mailed it off to "the US Army." Members of the 102nd wrote him for autographed copies. Out of cost considerations (they did not offer to pay), he politely directed them to the Veterans Administration. It was not until mid-1948 that their letters and phone calls filled with "bug juice" stories finally tapered off, though the Wilcox version of "bug juice"—"shots" of hard liquor—did not.[4]

Then, as if he had never written the upbeat 102nd story, he unleashed a series of broadsides on American soldiery. Well beyond anything he ever wrote about race or poverty in the American South, his first such postwar attack remains his most recognized and controversial journalism.

All through New Year's Eve, 1945, and well into the following morning, the keys of the Royal came down hard. The "courage," "numbers," and "superb machines of war" American soldiers brought to Europe, he granted, proved a decisive factor in the Allied victory. But this did not mean that average American soldiers understood why the war had to be won, or even that they cared to understand. Repeatedly, this showed up in the way enlisted soldiers and officers alike, male and female, treated "average" citizens of Europe. Many of them acted "vulgar," "arrogant," "loud," "noisy," "boisterous," "undisciplined," "sexually immature," "drunken," "fat and well fed," "selfish," "obscene," indeed "odious," "disgusting," and "primitive." Any "decent" woman "feared" them. They stole from European civilians. They stole from each other. More to the point, just at the time when the United States needed to help mount an anti-Soviet strategy in Europe, because of these actions "from England to Germany they have had enough of us."

With the sardonic title "The Conqueror," he sent the piece to *New Republic.* It was declined. He next sent it to *Christian Century* and got an immediate acceptance. It appeared in the April 16, 1946, issue. Kennedy's copy came to the house on April 17. In view of the victory celebrations across America, Emmett Kilpatrick—home in Camden for the weekend—was "amazed" that even the *Century* took it. Regardless, three weeks later "The Conqueror" was a phenomenon all its own. Even *Time* and *Newsweek* carried excerpts.

Personal attacks on Kennedy poured in, from, among others, some twenty US soldiers still on duty in Germany. They asked: "Are you proud of yourself? We so-called stupid GIs are just as ashamed of your article as you are of us." Still, as a *Time* editor wrote Kennedy, favorable reactions to his critique far outweighed the attacks. William H. Danforth, chairman of the board of

Ralston Purina Company, reported that he had served in World War I and saw the same thing: "Your article stirs me to the depth." He urged that Kennedy write again on how to confront the problem. Likewise, World War II veteran, Frank Trinder, of Babson Park, Massachusetts, advised: "Many times during my tour [in the European theater] I felt ashamed of the uniform I was wearing." Lee Hand, yet another new veteran, wrote from Battle Mountain, Nevada: "The average American is a conceited prig.... It's too bad a uniform does not improve a man's character."

In short, chiefly because of the *Time* and *Newsweek* coverage, Ren Kennedy was among the first to focus America's reading public on this pressing postwar problem. Indeed, in his 1966 classic, *The Crucial Decade—and After*, Princeton historian Eric Goldman credited Kennedy with the prescient question: "Could the United States pull off the new world role it was assuming [in the Cold War]"? Goldman called on his readers to think long and hard about the message from "Renwick C. Kennedy, certainly no alarmist newspaperman but an army chaplain out of small-town Alabama who was home after twenty months in Western Europe."[5]

Unsurprisingly, the *Christian Century* editor, Paul Hutchinson, wanted more. In "How Good Were the Army Chaplains?" appearing June 1946, Kennedy blasted "the Army" for letting Archbishop Francis Joseph Spellman of New York use his Washington, DC–sanctioned title of "U. S. Military Vicar" to skew management of the 8,000-member Chaplaincy Corps. Combined with the normal Southern Baptist reluctance to do anything ecumenical, Spellman's intrusive arm left other Protestant chaplains and the Jewish ones—the majority of the corps—"on their own" to try to foster what "the Army" itself had called for: "non-denominational" services as well as general chaplain behavior. Unfortunately, any number of Catholic-haters read the article as Kennedy's attacking Rome and sent him an assortment of papacy-conspiracy theories, the last thing Kennedy sought. Indeed, in the following decade, when elders of Camden Presbyterian Church refused to let longtime church member Susan Cherry Ervin be married in the church to a Catholic, Connie McKelvey, Kennedy's much-publicized dissent from Camden Presbyterian's stance stretched logic when he even declined an invitation for the eventual back-up plan—a Presbyterian wedding ceremony at the Ervins' stately home, "Countryside." Too, he not only endorsed but encouraged John and Clyde Miller's granddaughter, Marian Perdue, when she decided to leave ARPism for Catholicism: "If you have done what you felt you should do, then it was right for you to do it."

Next, he sent the *Century* one on US soldiers and stealing, "To the Victor Goes the Spoils," out in July 1946, asserting that the Army "tacitly accepted" looting. With censors doing little, soldiers simply stole and mailed the loot home through parcel post. Many enlisted men stole guns and knives; indeed, "there must be very few binoculars and cameras left in Germany." Officers stole on a bigger level, from entire collections of leather-bound books out of Belgian châteaux to sedans out of German garages. "Recently a sergeant from the [European Theater of Operations] called at the office of the governor of Alabama and presented him with a sword from Munich, once the property of Ludwig, mad duke of Bavaria. The sword now rests in the Alabama Department of Archives and History. And this state that still curses Yankees for looting the South!"[6]

This article, in turn, led to an expanded analysis of how the war profiled American military life as a window into American character. In "Brass Hats," published in the *Century* on October 2, 1946, Kennedy granted the army had some high-quality leaders. But "so many of them were mediocre . . . inefficient, stupid, worthless, brutal, or thoroughly evil. . . . Their intelligence and culture were the scorn of Europeans. . . . Their abuse of privilege . . . often a scandal." How did this happen?

During the war Kennedy had seen young "citizen-soldier" officers as more efficient than older career-army officers. But this did not mean the younger ones treated European civilians with greater responsibility and sophistication. Too often the new officer "out-Heroded Herod." At core, this problem stemmed from the army's nonconcern with character. "Let [the officer] do his job efficiently; that is all the Army requires . . . [with] no concern about a man's morals or religion . . . drunkenness, profanity, vulgarity, promiscuous sexuality, coarseness, brutality, looting, abuse of privilege and out-right dishonesty are not qualities of a gentleman." He went further. Such behavior had "roots deep in present-day corruption of American life," and during the war the army offered that behavior not just acceptance but mobility and clout. This boded poorly for the future of American culture—at home and abroad. Indeed, within the year Kennedy followed up in the *Century* with "G. I. Gravy Train," showing how that same corrupt character had many— certainly not all—veterans grossly abusing the generous educational, job, and housing benefits offered them by the Veterans Administration.[7]

One of the major family magazines of America, *Better Homes and Gardens*, took note of Kennedy's writing and asked him to weigh in on what Congress was considering: an extension of the draft (which of course Congress eventually passed). Would this be "good" for "your son"? Kennedy pulled no punches. "Unless it can be shown conclusively that military training [and compulsory service] is essential . . . [to] national security," he urged, "arguments for it are vicious and false. . . . At an immature and impressionable stage . . . [your son] is plunged into a rough life, liberally sprinkled with rude associates . . . petty autocrats . . . stupid, unworthy exemplars."

In short, just like noted theologian Reinhold Niebuhr, on behalf of building a better America—one strong enough for the international challenges ahead—the Wilcox preacher wanted a deeper, more sophisticated homefront culture, except in this article he did not couch this in terms of "Christian" character, as Niebuhr often did. To get this, Kennedy pled for parents not to send their sons to the debasing influences of US military life unless it was a national emergency. The letters he got in response were a balanced mix. The check he got from the magazine ran $150—his largest writing check ever, and a badly needed start-up for the Kennedy college fund.[8]

Alongside this critique of the US military, Kennedy's racial preoccupations appeared muted—if not gone. In early January 1946, he picked up two special orders at the Selma Stationery Shop. Immediately, he plowed into Gunnar Myrdal's landmark sociological study, *American Dilemma* (1944). Although this was a searing portrait of American segregation, it actually offered hope. If far more whites were made aware of the Negro's horrific status, Myrdal concluded, the gradual elimination of segregation—de facto and de jure—was possible. Unlike the throngs who read Myrdal, no doubt, Kennedy then turned to another new book, Walter Van Clark's *A Christian Strategy for the Global World* (1945). Executive director of the National Council of Churches, Clark in many ways echoed what was now preached by Reinhold Niebuhr, as well as by the devout Presbyterian, delegate to the United Nations, and future secretary of state, US senator John Foster Dulles. The emergent Cold War necessitated a Western Christianity united in advancement of Western economic and social institutions. Kennedy's diary does not articulate how these readings marinated in his mind. While their big points represented nothing he had not already thought about, and indeed written about, perhaps, combined, they reinforced his ideals in some way and made him more skeptical in others. At any rate, they were inside him as he moved forward into postwar race relations.

On Friday, February 15, 1946, he was scheduled to preach a morning convocation for the Black students of Miller's Ferry School, nine miles north of Camden, which was sponsored by the Presbyterian Church USA (PCUSA). Since this was before the advent of *Jeep*, his commitment of course was conditional on "a ride." D. F. White, Black minister at another PCUSA school in Prairie, had the assignment of coming to Camden in his car to take Kennedy to Miller's Ferry and returning him home afterward.

That night in the diary Kennedy noted two things about the day. He preached to "175 Negro school children"—a far larger group than most white groups he normally addressed. And on the way back to Camden, Reverend White talked about "race relations." "He says Negro soldiers are [coming home] then leaving, some going back to the Army." When Kennedy asked for more, Reverend White replied, "The Negro's life is like a bird's. Some trouble arises. He gets shot. No one ever does anything about it. [Plus] whites won't sell land to Negroes here in Wilcox." In other words, despite the cataclysm of World War II and Negro soldiers' fighting valiantly to defeat racial fascism—and some Black veterans heading to the North and Midwest and to California for decent jobs—Black Belt race relations in 1946 had changed little from those of 1941.Here was concrete illustration of Myrdal's findings. But whether the sociologist's recommendation that vast publicity of the problem might change this was another matter.

Within the year, Kennedy's thoughts clarified. The same month, February 1946, as his Miller's Ferry visit, his liberal ARP colleague in Charlotte, North Carolina, Ernest N. Orr, implored him to reconsider his earlier turndown of an invitation to come to Bonclarken the coming August for a "forum ARP radicals are organizing" to try again for a changed synodical position on ARPs being more engaged in the pressing secular issues of the postwar world. Kennedy thought it useless. Still, Orr prevailed with the hope that at least 300 would attend and the promise that Kennedy's only role—not requiring any substantial preparation—would be a talk comparing the recent works of Myrdal and Clark. Indeed, the diary reflects limited preparation, not even a roughed-out set of remarks. It only tells he had an audience of "thirty-five" and the "stand pats" refused to budge—the synod adopting nothing.

Even so, from the perspective of 1984, Kennedy recalled that he went to the forum to support his liberal colleagues, and that indeed he urged what he long had urged, but even more so, as Clark proposed, because of the Soviet threat. He called on ARPs to join an "ecumenical union" of Christian activism to eradicate the poverty and dislocation of war-torn Europe, which offered such opportunity for Soviet expansion. But he had a caveat about Clark's "Christian strategy." Drawn from his own Cold War writings, and reinforced by Reverend White and sociologist Myrdal, Kennedy said that "the same racial prejudice standards to which western Christianity and Allied governments held Nazi Germany must be applied to the United States, too. Or any thought of either one of those—or both—having real impact on the Soviet Russia, and in fact the world in general, is for naught."

If his recollections were correct, therefore, by the summer of 1946 Kennedy still held to his prewar idealism and God Mandate vision—only "updated" to account for the Cold War. Yet this idealism was chastened. Much as his 1930s Christian Socialist pacifism and isolationism had been chastened, and then forced to change, by the dilemma posed by Hitler, so did his immediate postwar hopes have quite a journey ahead.[9]

At any rate, assuming that uncertainty had Kennedy stymied in the summer of 1946, it is not surprising what he took on next. In July, just before heading for Bonclarken, he received a letter from the liberal Alabama newspaperman, Gould Beech, proposing that he become a regular columnist for the *Southern Farmer*. The Chicago millionaire liberal, Marshall Field, recently had purchased the journal, and had hired a former New Dealer from Alabama, Aubrey Williams, to publish it out of offices in Montgomery. The two knew what was coming: in the approaching congressional elections of 1946, Republicans would take both houses. And they saw a coalition between poor white farmers and poor Black farmers as the vital shot at helping President Harry Truman fend off the coming Republican assault on many of the New Deal reforms. Hopeful of being more successful than the Populist Party of the late 1890s, Field and Williams believed a National Farmers Union could advance this cause. And they turned to Beech for help.

Out of his anti-Klan work at the *Montgomery Advertiser* and the *Anniston Star*, Beech enjoyed a strong reputation among crusading southern liberals. More recently, he had worked part time in James E. Folsom's liberal gubernatorial campaign. In speech after speech—crafted by Beech—Folsom cast himself as a neo-populist sympathetic to civil rights and opposed to the Farm Bureau and other political arms of the Black Belt–Big Mule alliance. More to the point, Beech had followed Ren Kennedy since 1934, when *Social Forces* published "Black Belt Aristocrats." But he undoubtedly focused more on his fellow Alabamian after *Time* and *Newsweek* created such a stir over "The Conqueror." Likewise, Kennedy's strong Christian message and World War II soldiering afforded the National Farmers Union some protection at this time of right-wingers, including many in the Farm Bureau, increasing attacks on social liberals like Williams and Beech for being "communists" or "big spenders."

Southern Farmer was a monthly. Beech wanted Kennedy in every issue at ten dollars an article. But he made it clear that "the times"—the national as well as southern attack on liberalism—necessitated Kennedy's remaining "folksy," not confrontational. On behalf of the Southern Farmers Union, they would handle the sharp attacks on national Republicans and on the Black Belt–Big Mule Alliance closer to home. Kennedy said fine, he would "calm the satire" in his voice and "just try to get people who have never worried much about anything other than their own salvation to understand that true Christians should get involved just as Jesus did."

Williams and Gould's passionate disagreement over the 1948 Democratic nomination saw Gould leave *Southern Farmer*. After failing to get a job in public relations at Troy State (then called Troy State Teacher's College), he took a position with a Houston, Texas, radio station. Kennedy then reported directly to Williams. That worked fine as well. He told Williams how much he admired Field for "being a very rich person who wanted to help others" and went on to explain that, though he had never met the man, he felt a "distant bond" to Field out of the marriage—a marriage Kennedy had performed in 1927—between Field's nephew, Blake, and Miller Bonner's daughter, Marlow. Beyond the "corporate," too, each ten-dollar check for an article would pay for a week of Mary Conway's food at Erskine College.[10]

Month after month he delivered the softest Christian messages on pressing secular issues. If he could not reach most of his own denomination, perhaps this ARP heretic could show the light to some other traditionalist Christians. "Can the Christian Faith Work on a Seven Day a Week Basis?" True Christians "feel bad when they see human need, and they want to help." Who currently needed help because of hunger? "They may be white people or Negroes or Mexicans or Jews." They also were "the millions . . . of Europe and Asia." Reach outward, my Christian friends, and help your neighbors. Well short of calling out Republicans for dismantling the New Deal, he just wrote that Jesus stood for people taking care of each other—and politicians should do what Jesus did.[11]

Alongside his oblique messages in *Southern Farmer*—perhaps because of them—Kennedy's psyche never fully left his old direct liberalism. In early January 1947 he drafted "Southwind," straight journalism portraying the postwar South approaching a fateful crossroad. Recently, Alabamians had rejected Birmingham lawyer James E. Simpson and his "vicious . . . race baiting . . . [to block] [Lister] Hill [returning] to the Senate." Georgians "abolished the poll tax and gave free rein to [their] liberal governor, Ellis Arnall." "Florida [kept] Claude Pepper in the Senate." "Senator Dennis McKellar [of Tennessee] started to speak an occasional tolerant word for the T.V.A." In South Carolina, Sen. Ellison (Cotton Ed) Smith was "retired from public life and died." Not only had "Negroes voted in unprecedented numbers . . . [but] even in the darkest Mississippi a few enlightened voices were to be heard." Yet some recent gubernatorial elections were reason for worry. In Alabama, the winner was Jim Folsom—"a clown" if a "liberal" clown. Was the "clown" sustainable? Kennedy omitted to note that an informal Democratic Party organ, *Southern Farmer*, from which he regularly derived small checks, strongly supported Folsom's election—indeed, that his immediate boss, Beech, was the architect for much of Folsom's campaign. At any rate, other places were more foreboding. In Mississippi and Georgia, victories went to "swash-buckling demagogues," Theodore Bilbo and Eugene Talmadge. "Both [were] publicly committed to intolerance, racial bigotry and narrow sectionalism."

The "forward looking" of the South, he went on, could view Bilbo and Talmadge as "typical of nothing . . . except the bottom of American life." Or, despite hints of something better in congressional elections, they could be worried about "the turmoil in the South [being] really just one thing—the race issue." Replete with sharp contemporaneous insights, "Southwind" remains but a first and rough draft. Yet it also indicates that, while he helped Williams and Beech with their low-profile political strategy, a more profound concern still weighed heavily on Kennedy. Would the successful attack on Europe's racial fascism be repeated in America? In the summer of 1947, Selma native Nat Welch—a young Chapel Hill graduate currently working in Montgomery who had read not just Kennedy's *Southern Farmer* pieces but his *Christian Century* articles—wrote Kennedy: "What I marvel at is that you are a man who has dared to preach the true Gospel of Jesus Christ in the Black Belt of central Alabama." Surely, Kennedy wondered if, over time, such sentiment would prevail over that reaching up "from the bottom of American life."[12]

The late 1940s saw other opportunities come Kennedy's way, too. Like his preacher friend, after the war Emmett Kilpatrick stayed on in the Army Reserve. And in March 1947, Lieutenant Colonel Kilpatrick—fluent in French and Spanish, and functional in Italian and German—received orders to spend the upcoming summer at Fort Riley, Kansas, in an advanced school for intelligence officers. This meant his normal summer classes at Troy State would need covering, especially with the influx of veterans supported by the GI Bill. After much juggling of faculty schedules, the net result was that the Department of Languages and Literature, over which Kilpatrick presided, would need help in English composition and English literature. And as only the conniving Kilpatrick might have done, he convinced long-time Troy president, Charles Bunyan Smith, that Ren Kennedy should fill in for him.

Kennedy had zero college teaching experience; he did not even have a master's degree in English. He had a bachelor's in English from Erskine College, a bachelor's in divinity from Erskine, a master's in theology from Princeton, two terms of graduate study in philosophy at Princeton, six weeks of "Army Christianity" at Harvard's Divinity School, and an honorary doctorate from Bryson College in Kansas. So, by today's standards, Kennedy's *entrée* to Troy would have to be called yet another "Good Ole Boy" deal.

And Kennedy lunged for it. It was not just "the dilemma" on the social reform scene and his need for college money. He was in a "soul-searching mood in the late 1940s," recalled an old friend, Charles Dobbins, "and likely would have applied for Ph.D. work in literature at either Princeton or Chapel Hill had he had any money and a wife willing to move. Not long after the war he read Richard Wright's first book [*Uncle Tom's Children* (1938)]. His mind was so eager—everything literary interested him." Troy prospects eased his angst. Likewise, recall that before the war Kennedy had been approached by other churches; he did not discuss this with elders. Still, during the war, word of it gradually made the rounds in preacher circles and ultimately got back to Camden and Marion Junction ARPs. With savvy strategy, his elders—dominated by Millers and Bonners—viewed the Troy overture as a way of keeping the minister they so valued. Despite grumbling by some in the Camden congregation, they not only approved Kennedy's Troy plan, but kept him on full salary and full manse use, *plus* placed $500 into a special savings account at Camden National Bank with hopes of growing the fund to help him buy a "real car." In short, elders gave Kennedy "a retention package" hard to beat. That, combined with Mary's now working three-quarters time as a Bible teacher at Camden elementary, placed the Kennedy family's 1947 annual income at $4,300.[13]

So, the summer of 1947 was busy. His weekends had him preaching in the Camden and Marion Junction ARP churches, running the Wilcox Red Cross, writing for *Southern Farmer* and *Christian Century*, and working hard on an article blasting the culture of "unnecessary hunting." He long had resented killing for sport in Wilcox as further evidence of his "lust to kill" theory about Black Belt Scotch-Irish. (In early 1948, when the article finally came out in *Outdoor Life*, Kennedy received muted death threats from across the nation, and "some Wilcox hunters" deliberately ran over two of the Kennedy family dogs, "Eightball" and "Stray Dog," as they were sleeping in the gutter in front of their house.) Obviously, too, that summer he was a husband and a father of two girls—Mary Conway due to enroll at Erskine in September 1947 and Margaret, who was dating actively, announcing she would be headed to the University of Alabama "where it is just more fun."

Then, after such busy weekends, on late Sunday afternoons—pastoral calls completed—he and *Jeep* headed the ninety miles back to Troy, landing at a rented bedroom and bath in the home of Mr. and Mrs. Arthur Parks, 718 Three Notch Road, South. All week he taught, two sections of English composition and two of English literature, unfolding over two concentrated terms at $250 per term. Nothing suggests that Mary objected to such weekly absences; indeed, they permitted her unitary decisions on all dating. Even more, though she always had worries about money—stemming from her father's severe losses in the Great Depression—much like his war income, Kennedy's Troy work helped ease her fears. And by war standards his absences were short. Plus, theirs had never been a marriage of intimate soulmates. The only dissent came from Ren's father, still senior ARP minister in Mooresville, North Carolina, who worried: "You may be driving your engine too hard—and I do not mean your Jeep's engine. Son, take the counsel of an old man who loves you, and slow down." The son, of course, did anything but that.[14]

On Friday, August 15, Troy's double summer session wrapped up. Kennedy received a check for $500; "$200 of this went to expenses." At commencement he donned the "doctor of divinity gown and hood" given by Bryson College and marched in the faculty procession. He long appreciated such regalia. The ARP Synod strongly rejected preachers wearing robes, a painful reminder of what Anglicans and Episcopalians wore—and what they stood for far across the Atlantic: the "Killing Time." Still, Kennedy long had admired the robe worn by his close friend and fellow racial liberal, Justice Jones, Episcopal priest at Carlowville. To wear a commencement gown only further whetted this envy. It gave him, he told the diary, "a degree of liberation." Poignantly, two days later, on Sunday, August 17, he donned this same gown for services at Camden ARPC, and did so for the remaining thirty years of his Sunday-preaching life—salve for a heretical spirit.[15]

Much earlier in 1947, well before Kennedy took the Troy job, he encountered one of the most intriguing people ever to visit the Black Belt. And as their friendship developed, through this visitor Kennedy began to reveal even more about his private contortions about race after the war.

This visitor was the earlier mentioned twenty-four-year-old Boston Jew and World War II veteran, Morton Rubin. With GI benefits, he pursued the PhD in cultural anthropology at the University of North Carolina, Chapel Hill, supervised by John Gillin, distinguished anthropologist attached to Chapel Hill's Institute for Research in the Social Sciences. The Rosenwald Foundation funded Gillin to support doctoral students studying "subcultural variations" within postwar southern social change. Rubin had the assignment of studying a southern county with strong antebellum plantation experience.

In great part because of Kennedy's earlier *Social Forces* article on the Black Belt, Gillin suggested Rubin consider Wilcox County for his dissertation. Rubin could have gone to Marengo or Perry to find a more cohesive "plantation county" from the standpoint of preponderance of Black Belt soil and a multitude of big cotton ventures. Still, on Gillin's belief that large-scale planters had dominated Wilcox regardless of their being a relatively tiny portion of the white population, and because Howard W. Odum, Rupert Vance, and other UNC social scientists considered Kennedy "good entree for a Jew from Boston," he had Rubin focus on Wilcox.[16]

In mid-February 1947, Rubin spent two days in Camden working on a proposal and making contacts. At the end of the visit Kennedy took him to look at a furnished apartment in the back of a house at 205 Clifton Road, two blocks west of downtown Camden. After leaving Miss Lottie's in the late 1930s, Bill and Joyce Jones had leased it for occasional weekly use as they tried to live part-time in Camden and part-time in Oak Hill. But recently they had decided that Bill would start commuting every day from Oak Hill. Kennedy thought it a "perfect fit" for Rubin.

Rubye McWilliams—known as "Miss Rubye"—owned this place. When her husband, Will McWilliams, died suddenly in 1934, she found herself not just elected to fill his position as Wilcox County tax collector, but reelected for the next twelve years, when at sixty-three she bowed out. She lived there on Clifton with her husband's unmarried sister, Eleanor McWilliams, and her brother, Dave McWilliams, a retired high school Latin teacher. All three were born and bred Scotch-Irish Baptists, the brother and sister grandchildren of noted Baptist preacher of Alabama's antebellum frontier, Miles Levi McWilliams.

Miss Rubye's deceased husband had a lot of the great preacher's "fire," not to mention streaks of his violence, if not quite so extreme as that of the great preacher's youngest son, Enoch McWilliams. In 1895, Wilcox sheriff Stonewall McConnico finally had to shoot down Enoch—dead—out of his uncontrollable drunken "dirk fighting." By contrast, in only three ways did Dave and Eleanor resemble Reverend McWilliams. They "feuded pungently," in Kennedy's words, especially with Miller Bonner for whom they had enduring resentment over his having represented the "wrong side" in a dispute over property inheritance. They also were devoted to the Baptist Church. And they made constant professions of being "dry"—and Dave and Miss Rubye actually were. It must have taken a great leap of faith for Rubin to move into the home of these relatively reformed, small-town, Southern Baptist, Scotch-Irish prohibitionists, especially when northeastern Jews visiting the Deep South quickly found themselves labeled "racial liberals" and "communists just like lawyers at the Scottsboro trials." Still, the visit ended with the young anthropologist feeling good about the plan to rent from the soon-to-retire Miss Rubye.

Rubin returned to Chapel Hill to work on his proposal. With last-minute nervousness about how his student would be received, Gillin decided on another "site visit," not just in Wilcox but in the McWilliams home. On Monday, June 9, Kennedy was in his study at the manse preparing for summer teaching at Troy, when Gillin showed up on his front steps. After an hour's talk, the two took off in *Jeep* for an afternoon of Wilcox touring. A long visit with Rubye, Eleanor, and Dave wrapped it up.[17]

Back in Chapel Hill, Gillin gave Rubin the green light. By June 26, he had checked in at the Wilcox Hotel, recently acquired by the Sadler family, and awaited the Joneses' final exit from the McWilliams apartment. A local high school teacher on summer break, Lillian Jones, was helping out on the hotel's front desk. She gave Rubin a room right next to where Kennedy lived in 1928 before moving into Miss Lottie's. That summer Lillian Jones also wrote part time for the *Progressive Era*. With considerable interest in Rubin's project, she interviewed him right there in the lobby before he even moved his suitcases upstairs. Two days later the *Era* carried her front-page article on Rubin, including a plea that people of the county open up and talk with him. His goal, she urged, was not social reform—just "description and analysis."[18]

A month later Rubin moved in with "the Baptists." After brief competition with businessman Peyton Burford, who wanted to use his car to move the guest, Eleanor's "sharp tongue and salty comment" prevailed in sending "a mule cart to the hotel to pick up me and my things," Rubin later wrote. As a twentieth-century Bostonian, here was "my first ride on a mule cart . . . interesting . . . animal strong." He was to pay thirty dollars a month. This included breakfast with the family. "Dinner" (midday) and supper (leftovers from dinner) normally were offered gratis if he happened to be on hand. It also included his use of a small office in a building Miss Rubye owned just off the town square. That first night he entered into his Field Notes—meticulously typed notations still preserved in the Southern Historical Collection at Chapel Hill—a detailed sketch of the McWilliams home. Then a short editorial: "I am going to like it here."

And things stayed that way—for a while. Bill Jones remembered, "Mort became part of the [McWilliams-Jones] family." And when interviewed in 1983, right before he retired from a faculty position at Northeastern University in Boston, Rubin recalled, "They took me in. . . . I was a member of the family. Dave died [at age eighty-one] while I was there," right there in the house at 5:00 p.m. on October 5. That afternoon Kennedy had stuck by the radio—the World Series. When he got to the house, "Morton Rubin says the McWilliams home has been like Grand Central Station." Later, after all had gone, Miss Eleanor, Ren, and Mort had wine on the porch—while the "true dry, Miss Rubye, was in the kitchen." Two days later Rubin wrote in his Field Notes: "I was a pallbearer" at the service of Dave McWilliams at the Baptist church.[19]

As the doctoral student cranked up his research, Kennedy of course was headed to Troy. Through the remainder of the summer of 1947 they saw each other occasionally on the weekends. Rubin reported on various observations and interviews: despite no legal alcohol, white men "drink freely in all-male settings, American legion—normally, no alcohol in mixed company"; different people drinking whiskey while "driving [him] around the county"; "Exchange Club [business leadership] openly hostile to new businesses except those inclined to maintain the historic low wages for manual labor"; "many [whites] really don't want to work in a profession, just inherit . . . everyone . . . men and women . . . talk of inheritance of land"; perceptions of Ren Kennedy and Viola Liddell as "the liberals"; so long as participants are "local," "politics" revolve less around "liberal versus conservative" or "problems needing solved" and more around "personalities and family feuds"; at high school "football practice," coach's instruction focuses on success through "individual violence" rather than "success through team work"; "Camden siren sounds at 8 pm on Saturday night—all Negroes must be gone from town."

Further, "younger women are more liberal than older women or men . . . several of the younger women know Howard W. Odom's name" from studying "social work at Auburn" with another Chapel Hill social scientist, "Herman Johnson." Among these "younger women" was Lower Peach Tree native Dorothy (Dot) Watson. A twenty-two-year-old graduate of Alabama College, she became a noted Red Cross social worker in Montgomery and Birmingham. In view of Exchange Club opposition to new businesses, Rubin found her interview fascinating. "Dot engaged to a Berry [son of former bank president] who is in law school [at] U of Ala. . . . Won't practice in Wilcox. Says most [young, educated whites] leave—parents want children to advance, encourage leaving for better positions." If these comments were accurate, they reflected a unique perspective among Wilcox white leaders of the postwar era: though they saw every reason for their children to leave Wilcox because of its lack of broad-ranging professional opportunity, they resolutely opposed change in the county.[20]

In late August, with Troy summer school over, Kennedy had additional time for the engaging visitor. Rubin requested a visit to "The Spot," a roadside eatery thirty miles north of Camden at Safford, just inside the Dallas County line where alcohol was legal. Recently back from Fort Riley, Emmett Kilpatrick took them in his Ford, along with Viola Liddell. Established during the Depression by Viola Liddell's sister-in-law by her first marriage, Laurine Stroud, this noted log cabin advertised "real [good?] steaks" and a "genuine live parrot from South America," which welcomed each new party with, "Hey, Ba-bee!. Have unutha on me!" On that night, at least, a scrawled note at the top of the mirror in the men's room politely pled: "If you think you're gonna vomit, please go out back. The Mgt."

After appropriate time for the Boston intellectual to adjust to his new surroundings, dinner conversation at The Spot turned to one of Kennedy and Liddell's pet projects. Wilcox County was one of the few in the state without a public library. As its county seat, Camden was not lacking for well-off and well-educated people. Rubin chimed in: "Why did Camden not seek a public library in the early part of the century when Andrew Carnegie gave away millions to help towns build libraries?" Kilpatrick noted, "Selma did [for Dallas County]. . . . Union Springs did [for Bullock County]. And Judson [College] got one for Marion [in Perry County]." Much later that night, back at Miss Rubye's, Rubin's field book received this: "People here won't get together and act, as in other communities. [There is strong] individualism and lack of coordinated town planning. [They can't work together because] people here have short tempers and they are long on remembering."

Here was fodder for a Scotch-Irish critique. Here also was a seminal discussion, it seems, leading to Liddell, Kennedy, and a preacher soon to arrive at Camden Presbyterian, John Henry (Jack) Bogie, finally marshaling the necessary forces—including Kilpatrick's connections to Marie Bankhead Owen—for Camden to have by 1949 not just a public library but something destined to be what Kennedy considered, in 1984, "the best managed public thing in Wilcox." And likely in 2023, too.[21]

The Liddells also hosted a dinner gathering for Rubin. Conversation geared up over Rubin's question, "Who is liberal in Camden?" Will Liddell fired the opening volley: "I am conservative, my wife is liberal, and Kennedy is radical." Kennedy agreed with the first two assessments. But he dissented from Will's depiction of him. "Radical" likely fitted him prewar. Now, in the late 1940s, "liberal conservative," he urged, was the better descriptive for him. The evening ended without appropriate clarification.

Still, clarity emerged over the coming months. Viola Liddell told Rubin, "[Kennedy] has a conscience and writes things that outrage certain people ... the article about the lynching [of Jonas Martin] caused a lot of trouble." Kilpatrick advised Rubin that one "good barometer of 'liberal' was the vote on the Boswell Amendment," giving Alabama voter registrars broad discretion in judging a would-be voter's knowledge of the US Constitution and openly designed to eliminate voting by Black citizens. From that, Rubin's research turned up: "Kennedy, Liddell ... Bill Jones, E. O. [Osborn] McKay ... [Helen Burford] Lambert and Kilpatrick ... intellectuals and non-conformists ... all voted against the [Boswell] bill," despite a big majority of Wilcoxons voting for it. Then a comparison of Kennedy and McKay. Until recently pastor at Camden Presbyterian, and replaced by Bogie, McKay—a Morriston, Florida, native and graduate of the University of Florida and Atlanta's Columbia Theological Seminary—was as liberal as Kennedy. Rubin recalled: "[He] did not like the way most whites depend on the Negro ... maybe more liberal ... did not like most whites." Indeed, after three years in Camden, McKay departed on his own because of the racial climate.[22]

In the coming months, Rubin captured Kennedy alone in his home study for several lengthy interviews. The book Rubin ultimately published out of his dissertation research, *Plantation County* (1951), makes modestly effective use of this material. And Rubin never mentioned Kennedy's name—as was his practice for all interviewees. But from his private Field Notes, here is the fuller version. "[Kennedy] is tired of narrowness of [the] town but [he] figures city [life] would be as bad. . . . His congregation [is] fairly tolerant [of him]. [It] has grown to expect his outbursts. [He] delivers balmy sermons for several weeks, then delivers one on social problems. . . . [He] says he is no radical but a conservative liberal. . . . He believes all educated [white and Black people] should be able to vote and serve on juries. However, in this area he sees no likelihood of [white acceptance of] reform. So, short of dispersal [that is, far greater out-migration of Negroes than already occurring], he doesn't know a solution to the race problem."

Still, Rubin found Kennedy seeing a few limited signs of change. According to Kennedy, "last year a county committee of women led by... Mary Godbold, welfare worker ... organized a clinic to assess needs of Wilcox's crippled children." It was scheduled for the Masonic Lodge. But when Masons found that Black kids would appear, they blocked the event. Mrs. Godbold went to her minister, Herbert Hill, at the Methodist Church down the street, and rescheduled the clinic for several weeks later in his church. "Colored kids could be there." The Masons protested again. But "Hill upholds the women, almost getting into a street fight with the men" who wanted it blocked there, too. The event occurred.[23]

Kennedy also believed the increasing numbers of automobiles throughout the county gradually altered sexual habits among young white males. Before the advent of cars, they regularly preyed on Negro teenage girls—both rape and sex for slight pay. With automobile dates replacing Victorian chaperoned dates on the front porch, however, white boys increasingly had their first sexual experiences with white girls, their dates, in cars. Black girls were less victimized.

Still, "the horrible habits" had not vanished. Indeed, on October 11, 1947, Kennedy told Rubin that over the past week "2 white boys beat up and raped a Negro girl" on the outskirts of Camden. The Negro girl, it was said, "sassed" the boys. "Turns out they got the wrong girl." "White community strongly condemns ... [but] colored community" says it is "a common occurrence [and] newspaper will never mention it." The incident returned Kennedy to a 1935 social visit to neighboring Uniontown where he could not escape one "white-columned Patricia Pitt Yarborough." As he related to Rubin, she obviously had no problem with white men abusing Black women. Indeed, her formula for a "good house servant was ... that they have ... light skin ... white blood ... [and she was] so proud of her two housemaids because they have Pitt blood." Again, on such abuse of Black women, Kennedy believed some change had occurred compared to the 1930s—just not nearly enough. Rubin's interview with the new Presbyterian minister, Bogie, confirmed this assessment. "I have seen young men in their twenties—one married, one not—go into the Negro section at night and come out Sunday morning."[24]

In February 1948, Rubin moved on to research with the school superintendent, Bill Jones. In most ways Jones "expresses liberal southern view ... that Negroes want equal rights and services [and that] Truman's civil rights plan is essentially right." He believes "Negroes should have the vote, but questions whether anybody should vote—black or white—if not educated ... as more are educated, more should vote. . . . However, he sees little or no chance of majority whites accepting this or any other change." By now, this was unsurprising for Rubin: "Same as Kennedy."

The disparity between a dramatically improved racial climate in Europe—with the Allies' defeat of fascist Germany and Italy—and the lack of improved racial climate at home clearly had muted the tiny liberal fire of Wilcox. Even if the US government under Truman managed to marshal the necessary attack on segregation, which seemed more doubtful every day, there remained the sheer statistical reality of Wilcox's "black numerical majority," which Kennedy and Jones had focused on in the 1938 discussion of Eva Lips and fascism. Postwar out-migration of Wilcox Black people would have to increase dramatically beyond the late 1940s split of 70 percent Black and 28 percent white. Indeed, this was only 2 percent fewer Black people than Wilcox had had at the height of slavery in 1859. Otherwise, significantly compounded by educated white people telling their own children to go elsewhere—which they did—the county's future would be a function of its continued Black majority. And, just or unjust, with fears of Black majority rooted in nineteenth-century slave revolts, most white people—whether consciously or unconsciously—considered that an enduring demographic formula for "no change." They had to stay in control.[25]

After researching in Wilcox from June 1947 to March 1948, Rubin focused on one last "observation opportunity" before departing Camden. On the southern city limits of town a local eatery, The Journey's End, offered hamburgers and hotdogs on the main level and a jukebox and dance floor in the basement. White high schoolers flocked there after football and basketball games. One Saturday night in late March, Rubin cajoled Kennedy into taking him "to watch the younger set's dating practices on the dance floor." Things did not go as planned. He and Kennedy had not been seated in the basement corner for more than five minutes when somebody put a dime in the jukebox and punched the number for "Just Because." The song had been around since the mid-1920s as an incipient country-rock tune popularized by The Shelton Brothers out of Reilly Springs, Texas. And it was "workable if not ideal" for the late 1940s jitterbug. Still, the disc that came up in the jukebox, it turned out, was not the Shelton Brothers; it was the new, celebrated 1948 version recorded by Frankie Yankovic—a face-paced accordion version ideal for the polka, not exactly the Wilcox craze in 1948. Dancers immediately left the floor. To Kennedy's shock, Rubin then strode to the other side of the room and asked one Sarah Brice Armstrong to dance, the twenty-five-year-old graduate student taking the fourteen-year-old through basic steps of the polka which he likely had learned as a soldier in occupied Germany. "Sara Brice picked it up real fast . . . followed him and then got it down and did great," recalled her carefully observant friend, Betty Gaines. At conclusion of

"Just Because" Rubin returned to a smiling Kennedy in the corner. "That's it—all through working for the night," Rubin pronounced. "Let's leave right now before I go back out there." They did, as a still beaming Kennedy added, "We did not come here for you to hop around with a young member of my church and direct descendant of a great ARP preacher [John Miller], one whom, I can assure you, did not dance."

Back in Chapel Hill, Rubin spent another year writing the dissertation, earning his PhD in May 1949. From there he did a postdoctoral stint as a United Nations researcher in Israel. Then he spent several years on the faculty of the University of Wisconsin, Madison, before landing for good back home in Boston at Northeastern University. In 1951, while still in Madison, he published *Plantation County* through the University of North Carolina Press. Kennedy always maintained he could have chosen a "fuller plantation county" than Wilcox. Yet he thrived on his friendship with Rubin, and the book remains a classic. In the early 1960s Rubin returned to Camden for more research; that visit was a lot different from his mule cart, "Hey, Ba-bee!" and polka sojourn of the late 1940s.[26]

Just as Rubin exited Wilcox in early 1948, Wilcox insights of a different genre surfaced. Back in March 1943, recall, Savoie Lottinville wrote Kennedy the discouraging letter about "The Yaupon Tales." Despite this defeat, as he headed to the army's Chaplaincy School, Kennedy gave Lottinville's contact information to his vivacious and smart next-door neighbor, his Roundtable comrade, Viola Liddell. As a student at Judson College, in neighboring Marion County, she had been a writing star. By the early 1940s, though she had placed a few articles with respected magazines, her focus was a book about the rise and fall of King Cotton in the Black Belt as told through the experience of her own Wilcox family, centered at Gastonburg. Still, when Kennedy returned from the war, he found Liddell had sent Lottinville nothing.

Liddell was worried that her folksy style worked against her serious message about the need for racial and economic change. During early 1946 both Kennedy and Kilpatrick critiqued chapters. Ultimately, the entire Roundtable helped her see that what she thought was a weakness was indeed a strength: keep it a "folksy tale" about, truly, real life—"sort of like *Huck Finn*," added Kilpatrick. More poignantly, the Roundtable also helped her find resolution on "final changes [to the manuscript] about Negroes and white people." As she later recalled, she would not advocate for "change in race relations the way President Truman and most of us wanted . . . those changes [toward desegregation] might work in other places, but here [in Wilcox] white people would not go along. . . . Things would just get far worse. . . . No, Dr. Kennedy did not fully agree. He said I should be more direct about what I thought was right and separate that from what I thought was possible. But I did not think I could do that, *at that time.*"27

Still, Kennedy telephoned Lottinville to see if he were still interested. He was. She sent it. And on January 29, 1947, Liddell received Lottinville's response: "much interested," though some changes were needed to "avoid litigation." Through the winter and spring of 1947 she proceeded with revisions. In June, barely arrived in town, Mort Rubin read the revised version, with title changed from "Father Was a Family Man" to "With a Southern Accent," something Lottinville felt to be more marketable as well as heightening the book's inherently "disarming truths." Rubin found the manuscript "a treasure of information and attitudes about southern change."28

On Saturday, March 20, 1948, *Southern Accent* hit the stands. One of the most perceptive reviews appeared in *Phylon*, a journal founded by W. E. B. DuBois and focused on American life from a Negro perspective. Thomas D. Jarrett wrote the review. At the time this Black Tennessean, World War II veteran, and University of Chicago doctorate taught literature at Atlanta University, where *Phylon* was published. Jarrett found Liddell "vivid" and "honest" in telling of the Black Belt whites' "dislike of new things . . . and fear of change." She "sees the handwriting on the wall and know[s] that [the whites'] day, as a chosen few, is about up." Still, he believed Liddell herself had not taken "the full trip down the road to de-segregation"; she had not endorsed desegregation, plus she "clung to certain stereotyped concepts of Negroes."

Lottinville mailed Liddell a copy of Jarrett's review. Immediately, she showed it to Kennedy "at the [holly] hedge. . . . Neither [she] nor Ren disagreed" with Jarrett, she recalled in the mid-1980s. "Honestly, as I think back, I should have said in the book that the sort of changes [Dr. Jarrett] wanted were just and Christian. That was truer to my own feelings. . . . On the other hand, 'darky' and other words some did not like in the book were the words used by the people I wrote about. Whatever. I wrote what I wrote."29

Yet that private backstory bore little resemblance to *Southern Accent*'s national reception. Of some twenty-five reviews from outside the South, only those in the *Toledo Blade, Christian Science Monitor*, and *Newark* (NJ) *News* criticized the book for devoting too much attention to description of Wilcox problems and having insufficient focus upon solving these problems—notably racial problems. Otherwise, national and southern-based reviews generally praised Liddell's lucidity regarding southern change. One depicted the book as "none of the moonlight and magnolias found in *Gone with the Wind*," while in the *New York Times* it was the progressive southern voice "at its best."

Granted, book reviews are not designed as referendums on pressing societal issues. But if the totality of *Southern Accent* reviews are considered alongside a twenty-first-century retrospective on the civil rights movement, it is hard not to see further reflection of a fact disheartening for both Kennedy and Jarrett, even if such discouragement took them to different places. Regardless of what Truman and the national Democratic Party sought, large portions of white America—including most whites of the "Greatest Generation" and overwhelming numbers of white southerners, veterans and others— did not place a priority on major changes in American race relations the way it had happened in Germany. In sad, if inadvertent, poetry, indeed, the *Christian Science Monitor* review, by noted critic Bucknell Eubanks, wound up in the same May 19, 1948, issue devoted to the frustrated civil rights movement, including notably an article titled, "South Shuns GOP Compromise on Racial Issue Draft Bill."[30]

Back in Wilcox reactions only further underscored Kennedy's take on what was happening. Throughout the remainder of 1948 and on into the following year, rumors told not just of certain white Camdenites suing Liddell for the way she portrayed their backward families, but of her being fired from her job teaching English at Wilcox County High School and angered citizens buying up copies at the Selma Stationery Shop and the Camden drugstore, and burning them. Along with Kilpatrick, Kennedy scoffed at such words: "All untrue . . . no facts support. . . . Few, if any, cared about what she said about Wilcox race relations. They were going to oppose change regardless. . . . Maybe some were miffed about not being mentioned kindly in the book, but that was about it. Most were unaffected." As for Kennedy himself, he found the final draft sent to Lottinville "good," even if he would have been "more direct" about prospects for change in race relations—and even if he were being just as nonconfrontational in *Southern Farmer*. As Liddell's project gained momentum, his diary reflected encouragement and congratulations, and the final product a "very good history of her family and the times." And she recalled, "Soulmates at the hedge, we were."

Indeed, two years later, she wrote to Kennedy in Troy about her transformation since the book appeared. She wished she had been more confrontational. "Alas and alack . . . I [always have had] a desire not to hurt anyone— which of course is a sign of weakness. . . . [But more recently] I have put one foot over the fence and, lately, I have about put the other over, and I feel better." Even so, as late as 1983, despite philosophies on writing about race more attuned to one another, Kennedy still showed minor sensitivity over who "ultimately delivered the fine Black Belt book." It was not the two Ivy Leaguers—"not [himself] and not your father [Richebourg McWilliams] . . . it was the woman from Judson. . . . [Yet] her book was different from what would have been in our books."[31]

Not that Kennedy's serious writing about white southerners came to a full stop. "Ecumenity at the Grass Roots," appearing in the February 1948 issue of *Christian Century*, had his satirical criticism once again focused on Gee's Bend. As he related *sans* names, during 1946 and 1947 he, along with Viola Liddell and Mary Godbold—representing Camden ARPC, Camden Presbyterian, and Camden Methodist, respectively—sought to develop an interdenominational educational and nurse-staffed clinic facility in Gee's Bend. Two worries motivated this effort. Local FSA managers were selling hunting rights to whites—rights that should have gone with the Benders' new property ownership. The church group feared such corruption would spread to other Bend endeavors, ruining what had been a reasonably successful effort to grow self-sufficiency in the increasingly post-sharecropper world. Likewise, since early 1946, when long-time Bender physician Edward L. McIntosh, of Catherine, went into semiretirement, the only physician seeing patients in the Bend was Camden's J. Paul Jones. But he recently had stopped going there; he said he would return when the "government" increased his rate of reimbursement. Kennedy saw this as an "odd request" from a well-off physician with "a monopoly" on health care in the Camden area. Still, he and others of the church alliance saw prospects of no health care at all in the Bend if the "government" failed to come up with more money. When Camden's Baptists reported they already had plans to deal with these Bend problems, the other three churches proposed joining them for, at the time, the Baptists lacked both funds and staff.

The Baptists told the alliance to back off. According to Kennedy's article, their rationale was the often ballyhooed premise that "Negroes are just naturally Baptists." Kennedy's group acquiesced. Still, by January 1948 the Baptists had turned their attention elsewhere; their outreach in the Bend folded. Instead of something of "ecumenity" and something badly needed, Kennedy concluded, the Bend now had yet another void. Fortunately, some nine months after Kennedy's article appeared, the "government" met the terms Dr. Jones wanted, and for several more years he returned to spending one day a month in the Bend, not what Benders needed—but there are times when 25 percent of something is better than zero percent of nothing.[32]

Kennedy also had two pieces in *Christian Century* that indeed addressed desegregation, at least up to a point. In May 1948, "No Where to Go" gave a Yaupon fiction account of Black Belt whites and the approaching 1948 presidential election. President Truman's call for desegregating certain key elements of American life had many unwilling to return the Democrat to the White House. They were not about to vote Republican, either. They feared a Republican in the White House would resurrect a Reconstruction-style racial activism. Nor would they support Henry Wallace on the Progressive ticket; he was "soft" on communism. And Norman Thomas, the Socialist, was out of the question. As for a southern-based splinter group, Kennedy doubted it could get much traction. Despite Miller Bonner and other local southern-rights advocates pushing a separatist plan, Kennedy predicted that many educated white voters even of the Black Belt thought this would be a throwaway vote: the southern anti–civil rights position would not carry a national election. In Kennedy's mind, these whites had "No Where to Go." In short, despite returning from the war acutely attuned to racial fascism— defeated in Europe, persisting in the United States—and the lack of sufficient Negro out-migration for Black Belt whites to be willing to consider change, his self-declared "liberal conservatism" held a thread of hope for an element of common sense among certain whites that, possibly, might provide a beachhead for changing the US racial scene.[33]

Then, a month before the 1948 presidential election, *Christian Century* published his update on this quandary. "The Cracker Boy's Vote," again using Yaupon conversation, unfolds out front of the Wilcox County courthouse. A "po' white boy" advises more educated whites of his plans to vote for the Democratic nominee. After all, his family always has voted Democrat. The others explain he cannot do that. Truman is "for lettin' the niggers vote." "The boy liked niggers but he wasn't much for having them vote." A week later the boy was back at the square to announce he was voting for the Republican, Thomas E. Dewey. The courthouse crowd replied that just as "people of Yaupon do not throw dead cats into churches . . . they do not vote for Republicans." Another week and the boy advised he was supporting Henry Wallace. The others nixed that, too: a vote for Wallace is like a vote for Norman Thomas—"a vote for Joe Stalin." They recommended Strom Thurmond—"a great statesman . . . the Dixiecrat . . . the man to vote for." Two days before the vote, all met again under the trees at the courthouse. Since Thurmond could not win, the "po' white boy" reported that he was "goin' squirrel hunt'n" on November 2. "And before the day was over seventeen of the other whites told him they were going with him."

On Thurmond's inability to win in 1948, of course, Kennedy proved correct. And his depiction of the southern white quandary lives on in William E. Leuchtenburg's noted work, *The White House Looks Back* (2005). Still, Kennedy missed the mark regarding how whites around him would vote, something of profound impact on the remainder of his life.[34]

The year 1948, indeed, turned into a defining time for him. In the three years since returning home from the war, Kennedy saw President Truman use executive authority to desegregate the US military and federal workforce and try to guide the nation toward a federal antilynching bill and extension of the Fair Employment Practices Commission. East Coast liberals and Black veterans and a few southern whites supported this agenda. But for the vast majority of Alabama whites—many of whom had gone to Europe and helped defeat Nazi fascism—the national Democratic agenda was a stab in the heart of white control. Though Truman's executive-authority desegregation steps had not included public education, Miller Bonner toured the Black Belt, preaching: "I have seen a race war coming since I was in college in the early 1900s, and Truman's program will lead to that race war, with white students killing any nigger who tries to go to a white college." On that incendiary note, indeed, Bonner was elected to be a delegate to the Democratic National Convention in Philadelphia and proceeded to help organize the Dixiecrat walkout leading to Strom Thurmond's official nomination at the Dixiecrat convention in Birmingham.

Like Bill Jones, Kennedy did not vote in the 1948 election because Alabama's Democratic Party had refused to put Truman's name on the Alabama ballot—the only state in the nation to do that. On the night the votes were counted, Kennedy was in his Troy apartment listening to radio reports of how everybody else had voted. Despite Thurmond's southern support, as Kennedy predicted, the South Carolinian turned out to be no national threat. And Kennedy went to bed seeing Truman with a possible chance of beating the favored Republican candidate, Thomas E. Dewey. The diary: "Truman surprisingly strong. Wish Truman could win." The next day, with the announcement of Truman's upset victory, following afternoon classes Kennedy met Emmett Kilpatrick and Hugh Ervin for beer at the Conecuh River filling station, a favorite beer-drinking spot for Troy faculty. All being liberal supporters of Truman, many an amber bottle went up to honor "Harry! Whom we *would* have voted for!"

Yet that elation lasted only "about a week." "Once I was back in Camden for a few weekends and heard what people were saying about Truman and those Yankee Democrats . . . [and] read the reports on how different people voted," the growing reality of what had happened "quickly dawned." More than 95 percent of Wilcoxons—1,162 white people—voted for Thurmond. Just 1 percent—14 voters—went with Dewey. Ren Kennedy, Bill and Joyce Jones, Emmett Kilpatrick, Hugh Ervin, and Viola Liddell did not vote. Oddly, after all "the Republicans" had done to her father, Mary Kennedy voted for Dewey. Neither the Prohibitionist nor the Progressive candidate garnered a Wilcox vote. And these margins were echoed across every Deep South state but Georgia, which barely went for Truman. With digestion of all that, the caution and wonderment Kennedy had confided to Rubin—and the grasping at the slightest hope for common sense he held out for some whites—morphed into full-blown intellectual resignation, not to mention spiritual and emotional depression. All he could do was privately mock Miller Bonner's 1948 role as "Heroic" and describe a postelection speech in Camden by the noted Birmingham Dixiecrat, Albert Stapp, by using Stapp's own self-depiction: "nigger-hating."

Spiritually, Kennedy went to war in yet another fight pitting Full Christianity against racial fascism; through such a contest not only could the evil be defeated but in the process he could show God that, after all, he was good on his commitment. Intellectually, as the sophisticated reformer, he went to war out of hope that a victory against European fascism would leave the conscience of America no alternative but to do the same thing at home. Only partially, of course, would these goals appear to have been met: Hitler indeed was defeated, and with Ren Kennedy playing a role. Still, when his vaguely hopeful "Home, Again" collided with the Dixiecrat movement, it was another matter. Rather than desegregation, the vast majority of white Alabamians, and no doubt others, were fixated on only one racial formula for the postwar era—the one from before the war.[35]

Kennedy's shifting views—hope, tentative hope, caution, defeat—encourage speculation beyond him. To use Kari Frederickson's clear words, "by all accounts the Dixiecrats' play for political power failed. . . . [Yet] the Dixiecrats led the exodus of Black Belt whites from the solid [Democratic] South . . . [and] provided an outlet for white anxiety and the first tentative steps toward significant and lasting regional change,"—that is, the ascendancy of a dominant, socially reactionary Republican Party in Dixie with considerable support from Republicans across the nation. Yet, beyond growing anxiety about practical challenges to white control posed by the New Deal and the war, according to Kennedy's experience at least, a long-growing ideological factor could have helped drive this surging white conservatism.

Strains of racial fascism—belief in the rightness of one racial group controlling another through violence, political and economic institutions, and law—may have reinforced the practical implications of power and money in southern white politics of 1948. Down through history this ideology had been articulated by intellectual, political, and business leaders. Even more, it had prevailed as an unarticulated element of white popular culture—especially religion—in both passive and aggressive forms. And to Kennedy all this found reflection in the war effort.

To him, the average American soldier turned a blind eye to defeating Hitler's racial fascism. No overt fascist by Nazi standards, this soldier still had anything but a focus on the cardinal Allied war goal. Indeed, of those white Americans who went to the war, regardless of the ballyhoo of patriotism, Kennedy believed, they went for one or more of these reasons: the reality of the draft, the adventure, and the consistent army income, vastly better than whatever could be scrounged in the Depression. Once overseas, Kennedy found, most of the rank and file proved good at what they were ordered to do: erecting tents, driving trucks, and killing for the good of Allied tactics, often indeed with great bravery—or, in the case of doctors, nurses, and medics, saving lives. For the vast majority, however, patriotism and the defeat of fascism were not on their minds.

After the war, granted, historians now know that some white GIs—including a handful of southerners—supported the growing American civil rights movement out of their newfound respect for Black soldiers' courage on the front. Yet, as Kennedy urged, after the war, while whites of the Greatest Generation overwhelmingly focused on "the victory," they seemed virtually moot on its core significance: the defeat of Germany's racial fascism. Nor, just as during the war, did they show any interest in the profound racial goals implicit to the Four Freedoms and the Atlantic Charter pertaining not just to Germany's racial fascism but, if well digested, to racial fascism in America. Instead, they were part and parcel of what Kennedy observed (and historians now have documented): whether passive-aggressive or rankly outspoken, the dominant numbers of white people were supportive of protecting the "color line." And this provokes thought about 1948.

As part of the war effort, the US government marshaled a sophisticated and large-scale campaign to "sell" to its citizens the profound values of the Four Freedoms and the Atlantic Charter. The effort failed. It had little, if any, impact on what appeared to be the proto-racial fascist values across a broad swath of twentieth-century white America. Among southern senators, notably, these reactionary values stood out in the drafting of the UN charter and its subsequent Senate support; well attuned to worries back home, in committee meetings these senators felt compelled to block any human rights language giving the United Nations an angle on encouraging their region's desegregation. Of course, this same feeling, if even more strident and open, spurred white anxieties about the questionable future of white control in politics of 1948. Again, this was most notable in the Deep South with its density of Black people. But, as Kennedy projected, with the twentieth century's continued unfolding, not to mention the early twenty-first century, it was well beyond the South where such proto-fascism so profoundly moved out of the shadows.[36]

Whether valid prescience or not, and 2023 America lends it credence, for Ren Kennedy this was anything but academic speculation. To him, the Full Christian, it was the firmly deduced truth. In 1948 he had little choice but to think as both historian and soothsayer—that blended burden of the educated conscience, Christian or not. As he philosophized in 1984:

> After the election [of 1948] . . . after the Dixiecrats and the election and then insufficient congressional support for civil rights. . . . I could not believe most white Alabamians would support desegregation anytime soon . . . the majority of white Christians around here [in Alabama] were

not about to change their hearts about the Negro any time soon. And from what I experienced with all sorts of Americans in the war . . . many not from the South. . . . I believed this uncivilized behavior also was well beyond the South. The question was—could the more civilized Americans defeat them [racial conservatives]—the way we did overseas [in Germany], though, of course, not through force of arms . . . unless . . . necessary. Today [1984], I am still worried about that . . . regardless of the [Supreme] Court decisions and [1960s] civil rights laws.

Nothing indicates Ren Kennedy had poll data behind this thought, either in 1948 or 1984. But such data confirms his worry. In March 1948, Gallup found that of the 63 percent of Americans who had heard of Truman's civil rights initiatives, only 33 percent—not just of southerners but all Americans—said it should be implemented. And down deep in the data was the fact that some 42 percent of Americans did not even believe lynching should be made a federal crime. To the question, "Is this what you meant, a minute ago, when you said 1948 was your 'rendezvous with reality'?" he replied: "Yes. Right. And [rendezvous with] 'blasphemy,' too."

And so was revealed what "the war did" to Ren Kennedy. It delivered to his Mandate one final and concrete benchmark for civilized and indeed Full Christian behavior—defeating racial fascism in America. As he saw himself surrounded by failure, could the Mandate survive? Could his intellectual and spiritual idealism endure? Or, if the "cracker boy," after all, knew where to go, would it not be the Mandated heretic who wound up with "nowhere to go"?[37]

10

Somewhere to Go

A secular serendipity, it turned out, determined where Kennedy went next. In March 1948, just as Viola Liddell's book came out, Emmett Kilpatrick came home to Camden for a long weekend "to celebrate Viola." Over drinks at his home on Bridgeport Road, Kilpatrick confided to Kennedy that he was not doing a good job as chair of Troy's Department of Literature and Foreign Languages. Administration bored him. Veterans poured in—"there is just so much to do." He also confessed embarrassment about occasionally not showing up for an 8:00 a.m. class—a department chair, mind you. Too, there was the more immediate matter of his need to spend the summer of 1948 with the Army Reserve.

But there also was something up his sleeve. He told Kennedy he wanted to keep his full-time Troy department chair salary and "just travel more." Indeed, recently he had ingratiated himself with Wallace Malone, board chairman of the First National Bank of Dothan. The Great Pan-Africa Road Race—Cape of Good Hope to Casablanca—was being planned for the early 1950s. Kilpatrick was in the process of convincing millionaire Malone that he should compete and of course spring for Emmett's going along. So, Kilpatrick may have had serious concerns about his job performance, and fully trusted in the noted efficiency of comrade Ren, but this grand adventurer who had survived Russian prison right after World War I also longed to return to action. The key, the conniver believed, was moving Kennedy into the unlabeled role of vice-chair of Troy's Department of Foreign Languages and Literature, effective summer 1948 and continuing through the 1948–49 academic year.[1]

As Kilpatrick concluded his alchemy in Troy, word reached Camden that the Montevallo Presbyterian Church was trying again to hire Kennedy. The job likely would include a part-time appointment in English at adjacent Alabama College; key members of that faculty remained active in that church. So, it was a savvy add-on retention strategy when the Camden and Marion Junction ARP elders jumped to approve Kennedy's return to commuting between Troy and Camden. To facilitate the arrangement the Hugh Dale family sweetened the pot by adding $1,000 to the earlier $500 "Kennedy Car Fund." Still, Kennedy's negotiations with Roland Cooper's Chrysler dealership, in Camden, only could bring a new Plymouth down to $1,599.13. This left him about a hundred dollars short. To make the deal go through, and then some, Oak Hill ARP Jacob (Jaki) Harper quickly paid Kennedy $525 for *Jeep*, $187 more than he had paid for it. Quite the different look from *Jeep* (dents in both front fenders, one functioning taillight), the shiny black 1948 Plymouth had a hard top, four doors, seat covers, even a push-button radio.[2]

For those twelve months, May 1948 through May 1949, besides pastoring at Camden and Marion Junction on the weekends, Kennedy served as a temporary, full-time Troy faculty member. As Kilpatrick's "assistant-chair without portfolio" (Kilpatrick's words), he offered five courses per semester—three English compositions, two literature surveys. Spring term of 1949 he also offered one advanced literature class on Friday nights at Troy's Daphne facility, on the eastern shore of Mobile Bay. Troy paid him $345 a month. After taxes he took home $275 a month, half of which went to Troy living expenses. Yet he also remained on full ARP salary. For 1948–49 he earned a total of about $5,300 (equivalent to around $65,000 in 2022). In the Kennedy family—with Mary Conway on partial ("minister's child") scholarship at Erskine College—things were looking up. The Princeton graduate finally had made it to the bottom rung of the American middle class. And the workable formula for pragmatic marriage he and Mary had embraced since the late 1920s easily accommodated this extended commitment to weekly absences.[3]

In Europe, Kennedy had proven brilliant at navigating among key officers of the 102nd Evacuation Hospital and managing drunken surgeons in the midst of the bombs and machine gun fire. This experience proved vital in his Troy work. Too, on discovering the east Alabama populist roots of Troy president Charles Bunyan Smith, and his genuine idealism about education improving the lot of average Alabamians, Kennedy naturally fostered common ground with the leader. Had education not catapulted Kennedy and his own family beyond the backward ways of some of their frontier Scotch-Irish brethren?

Again, Emmett purred. In August, back from his army stint, he suggested Kennedy ask Smith for advice on his new writing project: postwar attitudes among first-year college students in the American South. Troy students provided his "sample." In the article Kennedy "granted a few morons—playboys . . . athletes," but most he found likable. Hardworking and self-reliant, indeed, on racial matters they stood "far better than the average state politician." Smith liked that race part. Kennedy also addressed their idealism. Most of the students would graduate "idealistic, brave . . . the promise of American life . . . still real for them. . . . Our future is not hopeless in the hands of our freshmen," a conclusion resulting more from political considerations than true thought. His original draft included the caveat that their "idealism" likely would not last long, undoubtedly a reflection of his own experience. At Emmett's suggestion, however, he cut that from the final draft; Emmett knew Smith hoped those "ideals" would stand the test of time. It appears that Kennedy made the edits with nary a squirm. *Atlantic Monthly* rejected the article. But in September 1949 "Freshmen Are Alright" appeared in *Christian Century*. Kennedy quickly dropped off a copy at the president's office with a note of appreciation for his assistance. Kilpatrick's manipulation looked for its next target.[4]

When the inevitable downturn in veteran enrollment forecast a budget that might well dash Kennedy's chances for the entire 1949–50 academic year, Kilpatrick instructed Kennedy to write letters to Smith's friends regarding employment elsewhere. They went to Hubert Searcy, president of Huntington College in Montgomery, and to Brooks Forehand, chair of the English Department at the University of Alabama. Return letters from them indicated their enrollments were tapering off, too—but not before Kilpatrick had shown carbon copies of Kennedy's inquiries to President Smith and gotten Smith's promise that Kennedy could return to Troy for 1949–50, temporary but still full time. With that encouraging news Kennedy transferred his Army Reserve endeavors from a Montgomery unit to one in Troy. This now delivered $25.65 a month, and covered rental of his apartment at the home of Mrs. Betty McBride, 218 Walnut Street. Upbeat and proud, Kennedy wrote Mary Conway, still at Erskine College, "Your Pop stays busy. But it is not a bad way to live. Keeps your Pop out of devilment, or out of additional devilment. He has the time only for a limited amount of devilment."[5]

It is hard to believe Troy life did not take a toll on Kennedy's ARP endeavors, but elders seemed happy. It was not just new pews in the sanctuary and a new organ at Camden ARPC. It was the new Sunday school annex, resulting chiefly from Kennedy's appeals to Lucy McDaniel Spiva. Sister-in-law of Rosa Tait McDaniel, survivor of Miss Lottie's violence in the Tait family feud of 1929, the early widowed Mrs. Spiva had found it best to live in Atlanta with her husband's relatives. But, having grown up in Camden ARPC, she attended Kennedy's services several times a year and wrote big checks for the church in memory of her parents—her father having been the esteemed Camden physician John McDaniel, one of the founders of Camden ARPC. Dedication day for the McDaniel Memorial Annex, January 16, 1949, brought Kennedy singularly good feeling. "Today was one of the best days in the history of this church," he told the diary. Construction projects were a lot easier than changing hearts.[6]

But being a preacher plus an Army Reserve chaplain, of course, also included the sad events. In January, Camden native Private First Class (PFC) Marvin McKinley was among the first Wilcoxons killed in action in Europe to be brought home for interment in Camden. In Europe, Kennedy had devoted almost as much effort to locating McKinley's body as he had to locating Sam McNeill's. In full military dress, Major Kennedy presided over the service at the Camden Cemetery. Then came PFC Willard Lumpkin, of Delta, Alabama, just outside Anniston. At the Battle of the Bulge, Kennedy had sat in the pyramid tent beside Willard's brother, Millard, as 102nd surgeons tried to save him from severe shrapnel hits. He later helped Millard write his mother about Willard's death. In Troy, Wednesday, April 6, Kennedy arose one hour early—5:00 a.m.—hoping Kilpatrick remembered to cover his classes. He drove from Troy to Lineville, near Anniston. He had a two-hour conversation with Millard, his mother, Ethel, and his sister Maudine. Out loud Ethel read the letter Kennedy helped Millard write that horrible January 7, 1945, at Huy, Belgium. Again, in full military dress, Major Kennedy then presided over Willard's 1:00 p.m. military funeral. By 7:00 p.m. he was back in Troy. Kilpatrick *had* remembered.[7]

And then came PFC Sam McNeill—Kennedy's brother-in-law, blown up while driving one of Patton's half-tracks." Somewhere between Atlanta and Camden, Sam's "box" went missing. Kennedy's response harkened to 1944: "The Army!" Normally stoic and strong, his widow, Dot—despite having remarried two years earlier to Montgomery florist, Duke Paterson—"just fell apart." Finally, on Saturday, April 23, 1949, beside a huge floral arrangement of a half-track provided by Dot's husband, Major Kennedy laid Sam to final ease in the Camden cemetery.[8]

Despite his more tangible endeavors in Camden and Troy, some of Kennedy's other preoccupations continued, if more abstractly than earlier. He wrote another piece for *Christian Century*, "The More the Merrier," criticizing Protestants competing with Protestants for church membership, if with less ridicule than earlier. More important, in early August 1949, he agreed to a wide-open interview with a Washington-based reporter for the *New York Times*, Phillip Cabell—of Virginia's historic Cabell family—who was writing a feature story on Deep South racial and economic change. Whether Viola Liddell's book prompted the *Times*'s interest in Camden is not clear. Still, when he visited Camden, Cabell clearly had read *With a Southern Accent*, and his article in the August 28, 1949, Sunday magazine, "Camden, Alabama: A Case Study," probes many of the themes both Liddell and Kennedy had pursued: How an "Old South" Black Belt place was, and was not, adjusting to modern America.

Cabell found Liddell just like her book: "charming" and "candid." He found the new mayor, thirty-six-year-old automobile dealer and cattleman Roland Cooper, energetically focused on new business development. And he found sixty-year-old Miller Bonner—formerly state senator, chief counsel to the governor's office, and most recently unsuccessful candidate for the Alabama Supreme Court—determined that Wilcox would never desegregate. But foremost Cabell quoted Kennedy. There, in the parlor of the ARP manse, Cabell asked how the "South's crumbling feudalism" would influence ideas about "the Negro Problem" and specifically "desegregation." As he answered, Kennedy's "lean, earnest face showed his perplexity" as he articulated old thoughts and new, with clear, if unintended, implications for a surging twenty-first-century racial reactionism well beyond the American South. "The white man is a minority here. He lives under the fear . . . that the masses will rise up—or what is worse, be lifted up—and take that power . . . away from him . . . and there will be violence. . . . So the white man here is afraid . . . for his prestige, for his property, and for his way of life. . . . That makes for a terrible conflict in his soul which he tries to rationalize by a sort of [religious] puritanism on the one hand and a dogmatic racialism on the other."[9]

Since the 1930s Kennedy had been focused on sources of insecurity—numerical minority as well as power minority—that evolved into white-control behaviors ranging from subtle customs to abject violence. In Wilcox he saw the numerical majority factor at work, in Germany the financial power factor, both leading to fascist aggression. Indeed, this behavior helped frustrate his Mandate. With the exception of mulling over Protestant puritanism in Woodrow Wilson's sense of self, however, puritanism in southern white racial views was new.

Granted, "guilt" over not measuring up to God's standards—puritanism—made it to America most obviously via the Puritans of colonial Massachusetts. Yet, if less openly articulated, it also came full bore with Scotch-Irish Protestants, especially Presbyterians and most notably ARPs. And on race it could work both ways. Grotesque treatment of Black people—slave or free—could make some whites feel guilty about violating basic tenets of Christianity and motivate them to be racial reformers, such as any number of New England whites and a few of the South. As Fred Hobson has shown, such guilt could lead to a spectrum of "racial conversion." Yet the vast majority of southern whites long had personified the alternative dynamic of racial guilt. Feeling the guilt—yet focused on getting right with God not through changed racial behavior but through individual salvation and piety—they pragmatically reaped financial and social benefits of "racialist" labor, from slavery and sharecropping to segregation.

Before the Civil War, this bifurcated influence of Christian guilt on racial behavior had been articulated by a tiny circle of preachers and intellectuals—mostly racial reformers associated with abolitionism. With the Depression and World War II, prompting another wave of racial reformism culminating in the postwar civil rights movement, the duality of white Christian guilt received even more currency. Among those southern whites to articulate it, to greater or lesser degrees, were novelist Lillian Smith, minister-activist Will Campbell, and literature professor James McBride Dabbs. Kennedy's expression of the idea well presages Campbell's and Dabbs's. Like Smith's, however, Kennedy's appeared immediately in the wake of the 1948 surge of white conservativism. Indeed, in *Killers of the Dream* (1949), Smith's confession seems to sum up not just Kennedy's full critique of puritanism but also his construct of Half Christianity and white Black Belters' turning to the puritanism of the Old Time religion as moral and ethical anesthesia. In her early years in Georgia, Smith recalled: "I learned it is possible to be a Christian and a white southerner . . . to believe in freedom . . . and practice slavery. I learned it . . . by closing door after door until one's mind and heart and conscience are blocked off from each other and from reality."

A coterie of liberal to radical white and Black southern preachers expressed similar Social Gospel thoughts in concert with the Fellowship of Southern Churchmen, numbering close to six hundred in the late 1940s. People like Howard Kester sought to "nurture, nourish and evoke a consciousness . . . alternative. . [to the] perception of the dominant culture around them . . . [so that] a new future can be believed in and embraced."

At any rate, after explaining the guilty-puritan Christian dynamic, Kennedy told Cabell something that must have required two swallows before it came out of his mouth. Or maybe not. Maybe it was his reeling pragmatism. Maybe he said it for President Smith and for the advancement of his own job at Troy State Teacher's College. He offered: "More and more [white] people [in Wilcox] are coming to recognize . . . drastic changes in our system are inevitable." Oddly, Cabell showed no evidence of pushing back on this point. He just quoted Kennedy's disconnected note of encouragement. And clearly some read Kennedy's words not seeing the disconnect. Shortly, he received a letter from a Presbyterian minister in Pennsylvania, Marcellus Nesbitt, who took Kennedy's statement that change is coming as encouragement for him to "stop worrying about the South since her own great liberals are now speaking out."[10]

Even so, this published interview caused as least as much locally whispered criticism of Kennedy as did the "the jolt" he provided Wilcox over the Jonas Martin death. It was not so much the puritan critique. His flock long had ignored his pleas for more Social Gospel Christianity. It was his comment about race change. No longer were white liberals and Black activists limiting their agenda to ending Judge Lynch; they were pushing desegregation.

Likewise, with the escalating Cold War of 1949 and 1950, "communism" and race change had an even deeper connection than in the 1930s. For FBI director J. Edgar Hoover and Wilcox's Miller Bonner, the new racial liberals even more fit the bill for "communist." Bonner never personally broke from Kennedy. Indeed, he and other conservative ARPs continued to want him as their preacher. But after the Cabell interview, a certain amount of cloistered Camden talk referenced Kennedy as "pink." In February 1950, Viola Liddell advised Kennedy of small-talk she had recently encountered at a Camden women's club meeting: when "I told them, if you were a communist so was I.... I got a pretty shocked silence and a change of subject."

Even so, the "puritanism" analysis in the interview resonated well with at least one white Alabamian. Among those who apparently encountered it as reprinted in the *Montgomery Advertiser* was Montgomery public relations specialist, Carl Griffin. Brother of Georgia governor Marvin Griffin, Carl had moved to Montgomery when his wife, a niece of Alabama governor Chauncey Sparks, was asked to be Sparks's official hostess at the governor's mansion. In a letter to the editor in the *Advertiser*, Griffin urged that "reprints of [Kennedy's interview] be distributed to all colleges, civic clubs, women's organizations and professional groups [in Alabama]." While Griffin's racial views appear to have been different from those of his arch-segregationist brother, his suggestion that Kennedy's comments get wide consideration went nowhere.[11]

By February 1950, President Smith had confirmed Kennedy's full employment for summer 1950 through the summer of 1951. Simultaneously, Kilpatrick was implementing his plan. For summer 1950 he had a visiting professorship at San Marcos University in Guatemala. Then, for the first four months of 1951, he would be on leave without pay, compliments of Wallace Malone and the Great Pan Africa Road Race. In his absence, Kennedy would be more than behind-the-scenes manager. He would be official acting department head.[12]

On the more philosophical front, his Christmas sermon for 1950—the year he himself turned fifty—showed his continued Cold War preoccupations only heightened by the new nuclear threat. He worked off of William Faulkner's recent Nobel Prize speech, delivered in Stockholm, Sweden, just fourteen days earlier. What is on man's mind today? "Not being blown up," urged Faulkner. Even so, Kennedy managed to circle back to race—and more cogently than he did with Cabell. While we are waiting to see if we will be blown up, we still have before us "the race problem." And today, a "self-consciousness of colored people" grows worldwide. It is accompanied by "a gradual disappearance of the myth of white superiority. The white man's rule seemed firm to [Rudyard] Kipling as the century turned; there are only a few belated minds who do not see today that it is over." Yet the succeeding caveat still had him virtually paralyzed. "These [belated] minds are still found in places where it is possible to do great damage." He had distanced himself from the Mandate. But secular reasons for that distancing remained right in his face.[13]

In May 1951, Kilpatrick returned from the six-month Africa adventure. Though he and Malone had not won the race, Kilpatrick had worked with Kennedy to create a "victory celebration" for him—"just for finishing." It got off to a rough start. Kilpatrick had been back in Alabama no more than two days when he learned that Troy art professor Martha Jane Ballard was departing for the University of Florida. Over the last few years, according to Kilpatrick, she had proposed marriage to him—twice; he declined, but he still had strong attachment to her. And her leaving threw him into an emotional tailspin. Kennedy delayed his press releases and rescheduled a series of speaking engagements. Four days later, however, the great adventurer took a week's victory lap through south Alabama civic clubs and high school assemblies, compliments of Troy funding and Kennedy chauffeuring—and indeed Kennedy's distributing Troy student recruitment literature at every opportunity.[14]

The next month, with the Korean War expanding, Kennedy wrangled his way through an army physical in Montgomery and converted his status from "Reserve" to "Active Reserve Chaplain/Major," at twenty dollars more a month. But he did not just attend the monthly meeting. Within the year he would bury more dead soldiers, such as "Sgt. William A. Barker, a Negro, 18 yrs old . . . at Village Springs . . . on 20 miles north of Birmingham . . . cemetery out in woods, on hilltop . . . with firing squad, eight enlisted men." Yet, as in World War II, his loyalty to the military did not preclude his being analytical about it. The same week his change of status came through, he published a *Christian Century* piece, "They Never Had It So Good." As if to echo Faulkner's thoughts in his Nobel address, it was immoral stupidity for the United States to expand its anticommunist intervention from Korea into China simply for the sake of "megalomania" and dollars. That expansion risked a third world war, with nuclear armament.

Down at the Conecuh River filling station and bar, colleagues bought him beer in celebration of the article. Psychologist Hugh Ervin, historians Auxford Sartain and Eugene Sterkx, English professor Janette Stout—they bought beer just to hear him hold forth on Truman's courage in dismissing that "tin-horn, racist Dixiecrat," Gen. Douglas MacArthur. They bought him more beer as he recounted how he had recently taken Kilpatrick to Vaughn hospital, in Selma, after Kilpatrick's drunk driving landed him in a deep ravine on the Pine Apple-to-Oak-Hill highway, breaking two ribs and "totaling" his Ford; and how he had then connived with Kilpatrick to spring him from the hospital—"against doctor's orders"—with wrapped ribs and "slight morphine . . . nothing to rival what happened at the [Battle of the] Bulge."[15]

In short, it appeared as though failed Mandate and the war had chanced to deliver Kennedy to a new life—somewhere to go. It was not just the classroom and the students. It was Troy's environment of free ideas and non-Victorian social life with faculty colleagues—easily and in the open, not cloistered behind small-town doors. He had fallen in love with university life. And it, seemingly, with him. Mary seemed more than comfortable with the changes so long as she did not have to leave Camden—so long as she did not have to be in modern life on a regular basis and the extra money kept coming. In fact, Mary even resigned herself to their younger daughter, Margaret, recently crowned "Homecoming Queen" at Wilcox County High School, dodging the strict life of Erskine and heading on to the University of Alabama. Kennedy had other reservations about Margaret's college wishes: he considered the University of Alabama "the largest private social club in the state" and wanted Margaret to meet "more people of a higher quality than those who descended from self-styled plantation aristocrats." But the father capitulated, too. The only quid pro quo was that Margaret do a "transition semester" at Troy, not too far removed from her father. That summer of 1951 she sailed through English composition classes while regularly borrowing the keys to the Plymouth, occasionally even getting gas money. Worries about Margaret's future social circle aside, the Kennedys' life looked good.[16]

It was at this high moment in early August 1951 when he found out. This was when Kilpatrick told him that, after all, President Smith lacked the money to renew him for the 1951–52 academic year. Devastated, he vented to Mary, "Emmett needs me here and he knows it." This normally supra-analytical man seemed unable to focus on the fact that the rush of veterans was winding down; colleges and universities in Alabama were cutting back.[17]

A fall and winter of revived optimism and self-respect, if fewer ideals, devolved quickly to a summer of disappointment and fear. The years 1946 to 1951 had seen him move from a pummeled idealist to a start-up pragmatist with more money. He now had to find another way to get money for Margaret's UA enrollment. He now had to make sure Mary Conway's 1951 graduation moved swiftly to a job at Camden National Bank—another income for the family. And he had to readjust to full-time Camden life minus the comradeship of academia. In some ways, the resulting hole was even bigger than what he felt when departing the 102nd; his Troy comrades actually read books. Now, "Nowhere to Go" applied not just to the Alabama reform front but to his own daily front.

As he turned in summer grades that August, his heart was heavy. He moved his "teaching books" from his office to the trunk of the Plymouth and drove to Camden. A month later, still hurting, he vented even more in writing a short story about his "rise and fall" at Troy. It is called "Fog in August." Writing the piece may have provided short-term psychic relief. But its poor conception and poorer dialogue, despite its great title, garnered quick rejections from *Yale Review*, the *English Teacher*, and *Southwest Review*. Into the file, permanently.[18]

In early 1952, fellow Wilcoxon Hugh Ervin sought to ease Kennedy, writing that he hoped his Troy departure would be "temporary" for "I miss your cryptic comments on the monumental angels—and monsters—of Wilcox County." Still, in the regular family circular letter, Kennedy submitted honestly to his seven brothers and sisters that not teaching at Troy "has put me in the poor house again.... Mary Conway is working at bank... but is in a lot of weddings. They have cost me $350. I have had enough of all this." As fall gave way to Christmas, he remained "down." Morton Rubin's book, *Plantation County*, appeared in November 1951. It created quite a stir in Camden as citizens tried to determine how he had used their interviews (the published work included no names). The Roundtable asked him to lead a discussion of the book. He declined. Hugh Ervin—product of multiple Wilcox antebellum plantation-family lines, including the Taits—tried to engage him analytically: "[Rubin's] economic survey is revealing and pragmatic. If read by the real actors in the County, it could be of benefit.... You come through in glowing color.... Emmett did likewise... My brother [Samuel J. Ervin, Jr.] came through truthfully.... Viola was robbed of the color of her identity.... The Taits got what was coming, but of course they are like all families... a little of everything." Then Viola personally pled. And he declined again.

Still "very down" in August 1952, he wrote close friend Jack Bogie, who a month earlier had departed Camden Presbyterian Church to "demit" from the clergy and live in New Orleans. After congratulating him on his "courage," Kennedy reflected on himself. "At this late stage in life I do not want out [of the ministry] ... [but] I have a high degree of pure cynicism about it.... Write to me. We must meet over a full bottle again."[19]

Granted, when Oak Hill ARPs suddenly found themselves without a full-time preacher at Bethel, they offered Kennedy the position on a temporary, part-time basis at $850 a year; and he jumped at it (they later eliminated the "temporary" condition). But the financial pressures only increased with spring and summer 1952. Mary Conway announced "starry-eyed" plans for a July marriage to recent UA graduate from Atmore, Lawrence Edward (Dickie) Dickinson. His mother, Helen, was a Wilcox McConnico—one of Kennedy's favorite families. But the wedding would be expensive. In the end he staggered on, with his physician-brother, William, in Charlotte, volunteering a "donation" of $500 and Camden National Bank loaning him another

$500. On July 31 he married Mary Conway and Dickie there in his Camden church. Off she went to Atmore and to a noted career as a public school teacher. Along with her went her monthly check that had been helping the family adjust to no more Troy.

Kennedy returned to his pre-Troy schedule of reading and writing between 11:00 p.m. and 4:00 a.m. This meant six hours of sleep, and then breakfast around 10:00 a.m.; a day of visiting congregation members and dealing with other church matters; early evening social engagements and late supper; Saturday and Sunday afternoons with sports on the Philco radio; Thursday night sermon preparations; Sunday mornings Camden services; and Sunday evenings Oak Hill services, except once a month when he was in Marion Junction on Saturday nights and Sunday mornings.[20]

During the spring of 1952 he made several weak starts on articles. Nothing worked. Then, upon the early July invitation of *Christian Century*, he managed a straight journalistic piece entitled, "Why Churches Do Not Unite"—meaning Protestant churches, with ARPs as a thinly disguised case study. It was hard-hitting. The racists were the only honest anti-unionists. Others strutted around spouting "doctrinal differences" to camouflage their hypocritical hearts. They were "selfish and fearful." Mergers would cost some preachers their jobs, some elders their status and prestige, some family members the pride of saying their grandfather helped found the church. He saw all of the opponents as "feckless." They put themselves before Christianity's expansion—a problem-solving social force in desperate need everywhere. Letters poured in. Among regular *Century* readers they were uniformly positive. From others they ranged from sanely negative to vicious.[21]

Momentarily buoyed by reactions, Kennedy tried a new fiction project. Back in January 1952, a horrible tragedy barely was averted at Powell Skinner's place near Snow Hill, just east of Camden. In early June, he researched it well beyond the original newspaper write-up. A white well-digger, John Bell, was in the final stages of digging a 125-foot-deep well when the walls caved in on him. He was buried alive at the bottom, just his head and arms above ground. After a seven-hour ordeal a Black well-digger, David Andrews, brought him up—alive. The day after the event Andrews was in front of the Camden Courthouse. Two of Bell's white friends approached him. They tipped him with what currency they had in their pockets, $16.50. Andrews then returned to his shack seven miles east of Camden, walking. No road went to this shack.

In late June Kennedy retold this story as Yaupon fiction. He titled it, "The Well-Digger." The actual names in the manuscript remained, undoubtedly with the plan to disguise them for publication. If a first draft, it almost was his old self: passionate about racial injustice yet sardonic, concise, restrained, and with superb Black and white southern dialects. Viola Liddell suggested several places where the piece needed tightening. Instead, he mailed it off explaining the name changes he planned. *Reader's Digest* swiftly declined. It was one of his best. It just needed a few more nights of refinement. And it went to the file drawer. His will to finish it was not there. He badly needed Troy. And he badly needed a better America.[22]

In September 1952, at home in the early evening, Kennedy answered the phone. It was Emmett Kilpatrick. For a moment they chatted about the upcoming presidential election; the Democratic governor of Illinois, Adlai Stevenson, with his vice-presidential running mate from Alabama, Sen. John Sparkman, had little chance of beating the World War II hero Republican nominee, Dwight Eisenhower. Then the call shifted. On at least one front, it took Kennedy where he wanted to be—if only out of tragedy.

In 1945, Kennedy's Wilcox County friend, Edward (Edgar) Sadler Carothers—the UA professor and New Deal administrator who had brought the psychic to Oak Hill and helped Kennedy meet Clarence Cason—departed Tuscaloosa to become assistant to the president at Troy State Teacher's College, with chief responsibilities for the rapid expansion of off-campus academic and service programs. Product of another Kilpatrick maneuver, Carothers's move to Troy proved happy and successful for all. Still, there in Troy the lifestyle of Carothers finally caught up with him. He was thirty-eight years old, 5 feet 8 inches tall, and weighed 235 pounds. He also was a smoking, eating, and cocktailing machine. By the early fall of 1951 he kept an apartment in the same home Kennedy did, and Kennedy's diary tells ominously of his friend's increasing pain in the abdomen and chest. Finally, Carothers acceded to Kennedy's taking him to Selma's Vaughn Hospital. Though Selma physicians focused on heart problems, they lacked the specificity of diagnosis to initiate surgery and recommended further diagnosis at the Johns Hopkins University Hospital. Carothers went to Baltimore. And there, on October 15, 1951—after four hours of emergency surgery—he died. Kennedy saw his comrade's massive corpse into the ground behind Oak Hill's Bethel ARPC.

Carothers's death left a serious hole in Troy. Not so much the off-campus operations as the politics. Whenever President Smith made a money trip to the state legislature, he took Carothers along. In the late 1940s and early 1950s, the historic Black Belt power on Goat Hill may have been diminished. But it was far from gone. Smith was a Wiregrasser—a Crenshaw County native. Most Black Belters in Montgomery never trusted him for his populist upbringing. But Carothers knew just about all the politicians from the old cotton counties. It did not matter that he was "liberal." It did not matter that he was an open critic of the Klan. It did not matter that in private social settings too much alcohol invariably moved him to hilarious ridicule of "the utter stupidity of John C. Calhoun's concept of the secession," climaxed with, "the man was just a nut!" It did not matter that he often vacationed at a nudist colony in south Florida. All that mattered was that he had the right cotton-county genes and that he was educated—University of Alabama, Harvard—and that he was charming. In short, the Troy president used him as his "professional Black Belt schmoozer" to offset his own Wiregrass roots. As Smith wrote Kennedy shortly after Carothers's death, "I had long ago decided that he was more valuable going about doing and saying kind things to people than in being efficient."[23]

So, with Carothers barely in the ground, Maestro Kilpatrick again went to work. It took a while for him to get Smith to see the light. But he indeed did. That was what the telephone call was about. Long story short, beginning fall term of 1952—with ARP elder approval—during the week Kennedy was back in Troy yet again, living in the same apartment and serving as part-time English professor, *plus* by 1953 director of field work (off-campus programs), director of financial aid, director of student employment, and director of publications and public relations. At that time, the word *lobbyist* rarely appeared in university life. Yet "political operative" undulated through virtually all of Kennedy's nonclassroom functions. He had two half-time secretaries and a less-than-half-time student assistant. Never mind the workload. All it took was intelligence, long hours, hard work, and political skill.

In so many ways this was like returning to the role of combat chaplain in an evac. Recall that during the war fellow officers of the 102nd had nicknamed Kennedy "The Pulse." He read people well and got results when nobody else did. He brought home many good things in addition to that "fine Lathan wrist-watch"; fighting Nazi racism let him return with the well-honed management skills of organization, efficiency, finesse, and potent work ethic. And, now, in August 1952, as the Mandated if pessimistic idealist rapidly embraced a conscientious pragmatism, The Pulse was about to apply these skills to another type of fascist front: Alabama politics during the civil rights movement.[24]

Remember, before the war he had tackled a white Wilcox culture of predominantly Scotch-Irish foundation and, by his perception, Scotch Irish "behavior." Now, in the early 1950s—and for over a decade to come—he found himself face to face with an Alabama state government likely more diverse in white ancestry than Wilcox's yet with a Scotch-Irish factor still at work. The rich and powerful people controlling these politics knew well the art of manipulating the backwardness and insecurities of other Alabama whites, including significant numbers with Scotch-Irish sensitivities. Poignantly, Kennedy found no difference between predominant white "behavior" on race and Christianity among Wilcoxons and the "behavior" of those running Montgomery. Those elected were to use lies and intimidation—and violence where necessary—to block any threat to the privileged and rich of white Alabama.[25]

The new job had significant financial implications for Kennedy and his family. For 1953, his combined church and Troy incomes ran $10,500 ($109,000 by 2022 standards). This is deceptive. Although he had "made it" to the upper level of the middle class in postwar America, that was only by working the equivalent of two jobs or a total of some seventy-five hours a week.

Still, the family finally felt some relief. In a complicated way this was especially so for Mary. She had had an early life with all the benefits of her father's status as an executive with International Harvester. She also had a strong educational background, including a sophisticated social life in college. Yet, according to her daughters, despite fundamentalist Methodist influences of her youth giving her "a particular inclination for dressing dull, truly unattractively," "the severe losses" her father experienced with the Crash of 1929 also made her "long for money, especially nice furniture." "She never fully got over that," recalled daughter Margaret, "even though [her father] recovered better than some." So, while Mary dressed "dull" the remainder of her life, Kennedy's increasing income still provided her a much-needed sense of material security "she had not known since [her early twenties] at the start of the Depression."[26]

After one semester back, Kennedy found himself moved up to the battle front. The state legislature and the state board of education launched an investigation of President Smith for significant unauthorized expenditures related to a new student center and other buildings. For 1952–53 the state budgeted Troy at $500,581. "Contrary to law and Board regulations," the *Montgomery Advertiser* explained, Smith had exceeded this by $14,921.

But a treacherous subtext also underlay these investigations. State superintendent William R. (Bill) Terry wanted Smith removed from his job. As a Demopolis-born Black Belter with UA education and an honorary doctorate from Birmingham-Southern College, Terry detested the east Alabama populist liberalism so prominent in Smith's leadership of Troy. At Columbia University Teachers College, in New York City, compliments of the Rockefeller fund, Smith—a Brundage native—studied with any number of noted intellectuals associated with the original Charles Beard liberals. Foremost, George Counts instilled in Smith a deep appreciation for teachers to "organize." Because conservative political blocs, effectively unions, opposed higher taxes for education and certain social changes, urged Counts, educators had no choice but to do likewise: organize unions to advance progress.

More specifically, Smith strongly supported the Alabama Education Association (AEA). "Yes, it is a union," he was known to say among friends, "but it was a union created by necessity to offset another union—the big landowners of the Black Belt, the Farm Bureau, and the industrialists of the cities." In Montgomery circles he had a reputation as a closet desegregationist. Granted, in the early 1950s the AEA was far from the powerhouse it became by the early 1990s. Still, it had "enemy" written all over it in the eyes of the Black Belt–Big Mule axis, of which Terry was a part. In initial meetings with Terry, Kennedy found him "bitter" against Smith. With the attacks on Smith during the 1953–54 academic year, the Troy president needed all the political help he could get. Where better to get it than from a shrewd strategist with trusted Black Belt connections? In personal visits with principals and county superintendents known for closeness to given members of the legislature, Kennedy urged phone calls to Goat Hill. Tell them Smith has learned his lesson about careful budget management. Tell them Smith still has much to offer. He pled the case before David Walker Hodo, state finance director (whose son, William Hodo, served on the state board), and Jake Jordon, state budget officer. He visited with an old Wilcox friend, Charles Dobbins, now owner/editor of the weekly *Montgomery Examiner* and a key member of the state school board. He took Smith with him to Union Springs to get the aid of state board member Byron B. Nelson. He cranked out news releases profiling Smith's many accomplishments as Troy's president. No help from the *Birmingham News*, so committed to the axis. But the *Anniston Star*, *Montgomery Advertiser*, and *Examiner* assisted. They lauded Smith's past leadership and urged his misdeeds as serious but unintended oversight.[27]

Equally important, after serving as chief attorney for Governor Frank Dixon and making an ill-fated run for associate justice on the Alabama State Supreme Court, in 1950 the venerable conservative Miller Bonner returned to his old seat in the Alabama Senate. The Dixiecrat may have been sixty-four and anything but the force he once was. But he felt renewed muscle when, in the fall of 1953, his long-time preacher and friend—if exact opposite on politics—Ren Kennedy asked for help.

Bonner not only had the old connections; he had membership on the Senate's Judiciary, Constitutional Amendment, and Education committees. In November, Kennedy even took Smith to Selma's Vaughn Memorial Hospital, where the senatorial lion was recovering from a broken pelvic bone resulting from a bad fall—the pastoral visit serving an overt political agenda. Bonner would not survive a 1954 challenge from Camden mayor Roland Cooper. Yet during two crucial years, 1953 and 1954, Bonner's personal loyalty to Kennedy eclipsed his old Black Belt–Big Mule proclivities to "gig education"— that is, to stymie its funding and denigrate many of its progressive leaders. Time and again Bonner appears to have made phone calls to old friends in the House about going light on Smith.[28]

Even more, Bonner leaned on his son-in-law, forty-one-year-old Samuel Martin Englehardt Jr. Although this arch-segregationist often has been profiled as a product of an elite antebellum cotton-through-slavery life—an image he promoted—his background was not quite that. In 1819 his German immigrant great-grandfather, a tinsmith named John Englehardt, arrived in Alabama. By the time he fought for the Confederacy, he had a hardware store in Montgomery and a small farm in southern Elmore County. In 1920, his son, Samuel Martin Englehardt, gained access to planter life through marrying Annie Floyd Pinkston, daughter of James and Hattie Pinkston, who lived on a cotton plantation at Cross Keys, in Macon County. In the late 1850s, the Pinkstons had some 6,000 acres and 40 slaves. Yet even that was a relatively small operation by the astounding scale of slave ownership in antebellum Macon, where one planter had 868 slaves and, among the 116 largest slave owners, the average number of slaves owned was 70. By the late 1920s Sam Englehardt had moved from a Montgomery grocery business to Shorter, in Macon County—some five miles from Cross Keys and adjacent to Tuskegee—where he worked for his father-in-law managing sharecroppers and a cotton gin.

From there, financially bolstered by his grandparents, young Sam Englehardt Jr., born in 1912, indeed followed in the footsteps of his Black Belt contemporaries with deeper Old South credentials—a secondary education at Chattanooga's private McCallie School and college at Washington and Lee University, where he was a leader in the Old South–rooted Sigma Alpha Epsilon social fraternity. Back in Montgomery, selling insurance and serving as city treasurer, on September 5, 1935, the twenty-three-year-old Englehardt married Bonner's second daughter, Sara. This despite Miller Bonner's worries about the "non-gentlemanly tattoos on [Sam's] right forearm" and warnings from his Wilcox comrades that "Sam always will be more than rough around the edges"—pressing his classification as a neo-Bourbon "aristocrat." Kennedy performed the ceremony at the Camden ARPC. If Englehardt clearly understood he had married into a historic ARP family and supported his wife's loyal membership in Kennedy's church—with their children baptized by him—he remained the proud Baptist he always had been.

Englehardt's first major political step was the 1950 election to represent Macon County in the state House. And for the next three decades he would be known as one of the most racially conservative white voices, not just in that county but in the entire state and indeed in America. Just four years after his House election, and only months after the 1954 *Brown* decision, Englehardt joined forces with Dallas County legislator Walter Givhan to establish the Alabama chapter of the [White] Citizens Council of Alabama, a national-level group only recently founded in Indianola, Mississippi, to defeat desegregation.

Still, like his father-in-law, Englehardt could put his personal relationship with Kennedy ahead of his considerable Black Belt–Big Mule loyalties. While a member of the House Education Committee, Englehardt worked that group on Smith's behalf. Even more than the Bonner son-in-law factor, he had precocious clout as a rapidly rising star of white massive resistance. This only grew when the election of 1954 had him moving on to the Macon-Bullock Senate seat. Even more, though the 1958 election denied him the lieutenant governorship, that election still saw fellow segregationist John Patterson ascending to the governorship, and out of that Englehardt not only wound up director of the State Highway Department but also executive director of the Alabama Democratic Party.[29]

The 1954 elections also delivered an end to the long-time political career of Sen. J. Miller Bonner. By a 475-vote margin, he lost his reelection bid to Camden mayor Roland Cooper. Shortly after the election, rumors spread through Wilcox that Bonner's trouncing resulted in his having a nonfatal heart attack. Kennedy's diary denies that. Instead, short-term depression put Bonner in bed for a while. This election, however, represented Wilcox change in more ways than personalities. Neither college-educated nor a native of Wilcox, Cooper grew up in Baldwin and Washington counties and started Camden life working in a gas station. Ultimately a dynamo in business, as mayor he focused far more on growing Camden commerce than on worshiping white columns. Still, many of Kennedy's Old Guard Wilcox friends got over those drawbacks because Cooper was cunning. Shortly, he was known as "the Wily Fox from Wilcox." Even more, he was half Miller Bonner's age and aswirl with energy. Though Bonner was a rank, if well-spoken, racial paternalist, in the polarized environment following the *Brown* cases, Cooper's strident, less educated racial conservatism had even more appeal among the majority of Wilcox whites.

More to the point, throughout the mid-1950s Kennedy used these archsegregationists to save the closeted desegregationist, Smith—strange bedfellows indeed. On November 19, 1953, while Bonner was still in power, the House Education Committee did no more than "censure" Smith and "punish Troy" with increased budget oversight. Though the college "was agog," Kennedy noted, the original, Terry-drafted resolution slamming Smith for "overt obstinacy" and intended "deception"—the resolution that could have led to Smith's firing—never emerged from committee. Smith kept his job. Even when Smith again overspent his budget by some $20,000 in December 1954 ("same sins as before"), yet again he survived after several visits among Kennedy, Bonner, Terry, and state finance director Hodo, plus some Englehardt phone calls. And more. With Kennedy's assistance, over the next two years Englehardt helped Smith get Troy funding for another building.[30]

The "Protect Smith" project overlapped with other, more high-profile politics within the State Department of Education. In May 1954, the Alabama Democratic primary, still tantamount to a general election, included choosing a new state superintendent. By law Bill Terry could not succeed himself. First elected superintendent in 1946, Austin Meadows sought a return to the job. Prospects of Meadows succeeding Terry offer a key window into the times and Kennedy's struggle with Alabama politics.

Terry was different from Meadows. Well before *Brown*, the specter of desegregation had Terry's State Department of Education strategizing for continuation of the old racial absolute. And in February 1954, four months before the Alabama Democratic primary vote and the US Supreme Court's issuance of *Brown*, he tried to get the AEA's thirty-member legislative committee—including all county superintendents—to endorse a resolution opposing any would-be Supreme Court mandate for public school desegregation. For this period no records of the State Department of Education survive. But Kennedy's diary and a smattering of journalistic coverage, as well as AEA documents, provide at least a partial reconstruction of this meeting. Having coordinated with Terry, Bullock County superintendent Robert J. Lawrence proposed adoption of a "hold the line" resolution: "The abolition of segregation is repugnant to the concepts of our people and contrary to long-standing customs and traditions of Alabama and our sister states. Therefore, we join those in Alabama and other states who believe as we do in doing everything possible to preserve segregation in our schools."

When Terry moved for adoption, however, Wilcox County's superintendent, W. J. (Bill) Jones, moved the resolution be tabled and that a "substitute motion" take its place, a motion to *support* desegregation should the Court call for it. Jones did not say this "substitute" had been drafted the day before with the substantial aid of his and Miller Bonner's favorite preacher, Ren Kennedy. He just read it, adding that while he was doubtful about a successful desegregation process in Wilcox, there always was a chance the Court's expected approach might succeed in his county. And if so, this was much to everyone's benefit. Out of such logic, he urged there be no opposition to the Supreme Court's anticipated decision. Decatur superintendent Walter Jackson seconded the Jones motion.

One-third of the AEA's Legislative Committee—chiefly school superintendents—decided to "hide"; those ten "did not vote." But twenty did. And Jones's motion passed, 14–6. Here was a significant, heretofore untold chapter of moderate white action in the Alabama civil rights narrative. And it originated in Wilcox, from where just the year before Senator Bonner—Bill Jones's uncle—had sought, if fruitlessly, to privatize all of Alabama's public schools rather than comport with the expected Supreme Court decision.

Beyond Jackson, the following superintendents and AEA officers supported the Jones substitute: John Bryan (president of Talladega School for the Deaf and Blind); R. E. Moore (superintendent of Cullman City Schools), P. B. Carter (superintendent of Eufaula City Schools), Mary Ruth Holleman (teacher at Birmingham's Phillips High School and AEA vice president), Laura Gaines Sprott (teacher at Troy High School and AEA president), Mrs. R. L. Self (superintendent of Jacksonville City Schools), and C. P. Nelson (superintendent of Pike County Schools). Those who joined Terry and Lawrence in opposing the Jones motion—that is, in favoring the "hold the line" for segregation resolution—included P. G. Mize (superintendent of Alexander City Schools), Vernon E. St. John (superintendent of Opp City Schools), Julian Newman (superintendent of Athens City Schools), and S. Reece White (assistant superintendent of the Alabama State Department of Education).[31]

For sure, Kennedy was in Montgomery that day. After the vote he and Bill Jones met for lunch. "Bill exhibited great consternation," Kennedy told the diary that night. Though "he felt he had no choice," he also knew major fallout lay ahead. They decided a letter to the editor of the Wilcox paper, *Progressive Era*, was the only shot Jones had at ameliorating this reaction—and that was a long shot. Over the next two days writing it proved difficult. Even if he knew most Wilcox white people would not accept school desegregation, Jones was unwilling to renounce his personal belief that integration of schools was morally right. Yet he also felt a responsibility to keep his job; if he wrote the letter from his moral standpoint, the county school board would have no choice but to replace him with someone far more conservative, making matters even worse. And he also felt a moral responsibility not to make things worse. Out of this moral dilemma, the letter to the *Era* required a literalist strategy—and misrepresentation.

Black citizens and white citizens in the same public school system in Wilcox, Jones wrote, was not "workable." Yet "any resolution taken by the [Montgomery] group [to oppose integration of the state system] would have no bearing whatsoever on the Supreme Court's decision" and "agitation" would just make things worse in Wilcox. The letter also said—surely Jones knowing it was not true—that "thinking people, both white and black, are agreed that segregation of the schools is the only practical . . . plan in our county."

As Jones and Kennedy feared, the letter solved nothing. Clearly, it was not what Wilcox Black people wanted to read. It also smacked of "enemy" to many whites, locally and statewide, who supported more the stance of Jones's uncle, Miller Bonner: segregation was "right" and "must always be." Wilcox's long-time probate judge and KKK leader, Jesse McLeod, led the conservative counterattack. Ever mindful of not losing one vote in the next election, he let fellow Camdenite Laura Lee Moore, known for her Tuesday Literary Club, sign the letter to the editor sent to the *Era* labeling McLeod's longtime foe Bill Jones the ultimate sinner: "an integrationist." Locally, of course, McLeod's disguise was no more effective than his consistently too-short Klan robe, always revealing his skinny legs; few indeed were the Wilcoxons who did not know that Laura Lee Moore was his sister-in-law. Still, many beyond Wilcox did not. And, aided by Miller Bonner, the McLeod-Moore letter quickly went statewide through the magazine *Alabama*, political mouthpiece of the Black Belt–Big Mule alliance with editorial offices in Birmingham's Massey Building.

On April 2, 1954, Superintendent Terry sent Jones a perfunctory congratulatory note on his "completing . . . thirty years as Superintendent of Wilcox County Schools." But that hardly reflected more genuine reactions. The sentiment McLeod and others whipped up delivered five white-hooded Klansmen to within ten feet of the front steps of Jones's Oak Hill home, skinny-legged probate judge front and center. For five minutes they assailed him with shouts of "Nigger-Lover!" Then, life—such as it was—moved on, with fifty-nine-year-old Jones keeping a loaded double-barreled twelve-gauge shotgun beside his bed and seventy-eight-year-old McLeod assuming White Citizens Council leadership in Wilcox and Dallas counties. As for the subsequent relationship between Jones and his uncle Miller Bonner, in 1979 Jones recalled, "Yes, he [Miller Bonner] knew Ren helped me with it, and neither one of us told him otherwise." For another decade Jones continued as Wilcox superintendent—a Black Belt white man fearing assault not by Black people but by other Black Belt white people. And, with one notable exception, in this vortex his preacher-comrade was right beside him.[32]

Regardless of the Jones resolution, as the Supreme Court's *Brown* decision got closer, state superintendent Terry regularly warned Black principals about "agitating" and advocating "the subversive propaganda organizations" (that is, the National Association for the Advancement of Colored people [NAACP]). By contrast, as the most formidable candidate to succeed Terry, Meadows stood as one of the new breed of educational leaders fostered with modern doctoral training at Columbia University Teachers College, through the Rockefeller Foundation's General Education Board (GEB). Here was the same program Smith had attended. Still, like Smith, in 1954 Meadows was sympathetic to desegregation yet maintained a public stance of pragmatism.

At that time Meadows did not favor an Alabama education system embroiled in a paralyzing fight over civil rights. Yet he also advocated the Columbia Teachers College mantra of teachers forming unions to defeat groups traditionally opposed to increased funds for improved public education. He supported the growing Alabama Education Association. So, just like the "Save Smith" efforts, the "Elect Meadows Project" used quiet diplomacy to challenge the long-time Black Belt–Big Mule opposition to change.

Throughout March, April, and early May of 1954, on President Smith's orders, Kennedy advocated Meadows's election, not to mention Jim Folsom's return to the governor's office. One of Kennedy's targets was community leaders he encountered in his student recruitment travels. The University of Alabama and Auburn University dominated recruitment of white students in the state's large urban areas—Huntsville, Birmingham, Montgomery, Mobile. Other schools, mainly state teacher's colleges, served north Alabama and west Alabama. So Kennedy regularly visited in high school towns of Macon, Barbour, Houston, Geneva, and Bullock counties, as well as Covington, Escambia, Butler, Crenshaw, Monroe, and Wilcox counties. Before leaving one of these towns, he used private visits with high school principals and teachers to advocate Austin Meadows's strong character and leadership ability.

He also visited with influential bankers, lawyers, and business owners—raising money for Meadows's campaign. Far more than "a bag man," he wrote, placed, and paid for "radio spots" urging Meadows's candidacy. Surely, in this politicking of Alabama's State Department of Education he was not alone. But he was remarkably good at it. Compared to advancing unity among Protestants, or turning ARPs into Social Gospelers, advocating Meadows was more than doable. And in the end, this pro-Meadows activism—assisted by the liberal Jim Folsom's winning the Democratic primary race for governor, effectively being elected governor—allowed Meadows to defeat the four other candidates. Education advocates were upbeat.[33]

A week after Folsom's primary victory, of course, the US Supreme Court decreed in *Brown* that "separate but equal" was unconstitutional. And a year later, on May 31, 1955, fearing extensive violence if white southerners were not given at least a chance to tailor the implementation on their own, the Court added the clarification that segregation in public schools would end with no more than "all deliberate speed." Civil rights advocates screamed hypocrisy. Southern white conservatives saw an opportunity to stall . . . forever. The US Justice Department hoped that gradualism somehow would work.[34]

As Alabama's political environment now went from bad to wretched, so did prospects for enhancing elementary, secondary, and postsecondary education in Alabama. Here, just four out of ten white citizens and only one out of ten Black citizens had more than an elementary education. After the May 1954 *Brown* decision, potent white massive resistance saw Governor Folsom back off from the liberal rhetoric of his first term. For a while Meadows followed suit. Still, they continued pressing on several other reform fronts. Folsom pushed through tax increases for an astounding "farm to market" road-building program as well as reorganization of the state docks at Mobile, not all that difficult out of their abundant possibilities for kickbacks to legislators. He also expanded old-age pensions. But more money for education was another matter. Not only would this take another tax hike, but everything related to education was shackled by race.³⁵

In 1955 the total state appropriation for education was funded through taxes at $87 million. Meadows and the 1,800-member AEA joined forces with university presidents finally to convince Folsom that the following year's allocation should move to $123 million—yet another tax hike. Rather than increased education monies, however, the legislature and its controlling corporate interests were preoccupied with defeating implementation of *Brown*. If that decision led to racial equality, it would erode Alabama's cheap labor and what it permitted—high business profits. The governor's education proposal had tough sledding ahead. Quickly Kennedy found himself involved.

Again, official records for the Alabama State Department of Education are gone. The same for the papers of Austin Meadows. Yet Kennedy's diary suggests that a clear set of directions went out from Meadows to Smith together with other presidents of state teachers' colleges and county superintendents. Meadows called for a full-court political press on the state legislature. Those directions then went from Smith to Kennedy.

At this stage the preacher from Wilcox became one of three higher education "public relations" figures (lobbyists) to help AEA officials deliver a massive pro-education demonstration to the front steps of the state Capitol. After orchestrating an "overnight" AEA membership drive at Troy, on June 29 he bused Troy faculty and students to Montgomery. The group pled its case for more appropriations in several key offices. They hit Rep. Andrew Love (Pat) Boyd of Troy. They hit the newly elected senator from Macon-Bullock, Englehardt. And they hit the newly elected senator from Wilcox, Roland Cooper. As Kennedy ushered Troy students into Cooper's office to plead for the education money, he regaled them with tales of Cooper's Chrysler mechanics keeping *Jeep* on the road before it retired to Jaki Harper's pole barn in Oak Hill, and more recently of Cooper's dealership selling Kennedy another new Plymouth—"at a good price." This political operative stuff was complicated.³⁶

Ultimately, the well-orchestrated press on Goat Hill was one among several factors leading the House Ways and Means Committee to pass modest increases in education funding. This moved elementary and secondary teacher salary averages to around 80 percent of the national average. Yet total per-pupil expenditures in the state remained a drastic problem in the eyes of Kennedy and other education advocates. In 1955, Alabama's education leaders still found it impossible to keep up with growing national standards for educational funding. Anything further had to involve an increase in corporate taxes. And, it turned out, under Folsom this was not to happen.

The governor pushed a tripartite reform package: more worker rights to unionize, extensive constitutional reform, and reapportionment. Such reforms could spell the end of the Black Belt–Big Mule axis in Montgomery. The axis attacked by blocking the tripartite package as well as increased corporate taxes for education. Folsom counterattacked by rechanneling patronage deals. It was ugly.[37]

As this unfolded, a Walker County native from a poor coal-mining family, Otis James (Joe) Goodwyn, had just been elected to the House as a representative out of Montgomery, where he practiced law. As his first step among many on behalf of funding education, Goodwyn developed a strategy for going around the corporate tax blockage. He proposed a constitutional amendment. It would authorize a modest graduated tax on adjusted gross incomes, applied to individuals and corporations alike. But it required a "vote of the people." In retrospect, Goodwyn's plan was poorly conceived; it lacked political strategy to get "the people" behind it. Still, Kennedy's after-hours student recruitment visits across south Alabama now focused on the importance of the "Goodwyn Amendment."

He held private meetings. Unlike the secret Meadows election campaign, he spoke before Rotary, Kiwanis, and Civitan groups. Wherever he recruited students, he took in small donations from AEA-affiliated teachers (virtually all), depositing the funds in a "Goodwyn campaign account" at Farmers and Merchants Bank in Troy. The money bought newspaper and radio spots. "I write four-page speech on Goodwyn Bill for a farmer to read to be tape recorded for radio." "I attend Future Teachers Association meeting at 7:00 pm and give them 1000 cards to distribute to students in re. School amendment." "Take radio script from Meadows re. Goodwyn Bill to radio stations in Opp, Andalusia, Troy, Ozark, Geneva, Elba."

In Montgomery he took the message to politicians from Troy: Sen. Ben Reeves and Reps. Gilmer Barrett and Pat Boyd. They promised public endorsement of the amendment and delivered. He also visited with politicians whom he had gotten to know first at "college nights" across his student recruitment turf. These included senators Ralph Jones of Monroeville, Tully Goodwin of Florala, George Little of Eufaula, and Richmond Flowers of Dothan. While the others equivocated, Flowers—the Senate floor leader—promised to talk it up.[38]

What about Wilcox connections—Cooper? Englehardt? Generally supportive of whatever happened to be the Black Belt–Big Mule goals, they strategically remained on the sidelines. So did Wilcox representatives Sam Nettles Jr. and Gregory Oakley. Indeed, Kennedy told President Smith that in this case his Wilcox connections would not "break ranks." They were all too glad to stay quiet and have the issue "simply" and inadequately "put to the people." In late November, over lunch at the Whitley Hotel, Charles Dobbins and his well-wired Montgomery friend, the politically moderate attorney, Truman Hobbs—son of Alabama congressman Samuel Earle Hobbs—told Kennedy the Goodwyn Amendment's chances for succeeding were "dubious" at best. On December 8, 1955, their depressing prediction came true. By a 5–1 margin, "the people" voted down the Goodwyn Amendment.

"All [the] school people [are] discouraged," Kennedy noted after the defeat. Yet the project had quite the opposite impact on Kennedy's own profile. Back in late March 1955 his dynamic advocacy of the Goodwyn amendment resulted in fellow higher education public relations experts and lobbyists electing him president of the Alabama College Association of Public Relations. UA's hard-hitting governmental affairs star, J. Jefferson Bennett—in historian Dan Carter's words, the key "cloak and dagger" operative in desegregating the University of Alabama—proposed him to the association and worked it through. This is to say that in four years, as Alabama politics moved from bad to awful, Kennedy's postwar life assumed a new vibrancy thanks to vicissitudes of his previous life as well as strong mentoring by one just as interwoven with pragmatism and idealism as Kennedy himself: Jeff Bennett.

Kennedy sensed his new strength. He even sought to use his rising clout to make President Smith more confrontational. He urged him to organize other Alabama college and university presidents behind one bold move. Instead of cutting their prepared budgets to conform to these harsh realities, they should continue expenditures as planned. And when they ran out of money, they should simply cease functioning—close the doors. Maybe that would make the point. Smith decided to try it. But the strategy soon fell flat. As an omen of many future efforts for Alabama higher education to function cohesively, Auburn president Ralph Draughon and UA president Oliver C. Carmichael refused to cooperate. With their clout—and free football tickets—they figured they could cut a deal with key legislators to find the money for their own campuses. The two big campuses would sell out the little ones. And so they did. Yet still they got no increase. Through the summer of 1955 Kennedy's reaction was "there is just no money."[39]

"There just is no money," again, because desegregation and the white massive resistance it engendered—despite the federal government's intentionally going slow—paralyzed politics necessary for funding Alabama education. In November 1955, the hyped racist reactions to Folsom's hosting the Black New York congressman, Adam Clayton Powell, led many of the governor's supporters in the legislature to back off. In turn, Folsom sought distance from desegregation. In December 1955, the Rosa Parks event developed into the yearlong Montgomery bus boycott. In February 1956, the Black student chosen to test *Brown v. Board Education* at the University of

Alabama, Autherine Lucy, found herself barred from the institution. Folsom did little substantively to guide his state through these crises. Odds are the racist White Citizens Councils (WCCs) would have advanced their massive resistance anyhow. But Folsom's seeming withdrawal effectively, if unintentionally, aided and abetted them. Indeed, fear of the future engendered by WCCs opened up room for even more fear. White politicians earlier concerned about doing good in Alabama—but who wanted power and its money far more than doing good—decided to manipulate Alabama's ever so easily manipulated white racial fear to enhance their control. On the near horizon stood John Patterson. And just beyond him awaited George Wallace.[40]

It is interesting to ponder whether Kennedy grasped all this. Throughout the late 1940s and 1950s, while he abstractly endorsed the rightness, indeed the Full Christianity, of desegregation, he was just like the Wilcox superintendent, Bill Jones. He did not think it fully possible. He did not expect a change in white hearts, much less whites relinquishing control. After chaos and violence and far-ranging negative effects on government, things would remain the same. Did he take the events of the mid-1950s as confirmation of his caveat? If so, considering his deep concerns about fascism at home and abroad, did he get one of the cardinal ironies of Alabama in the 1950s? Did he comprehend that, after some 6,000 white and Black Alabamians heroically died in the bloody defeat of fascism in Asia and Europe, just ten years later most white Alabamians emulated the very way of life causing these Alabamians to die? Cautious speculation suggests he did, and that this Full Christian's distant hope remained.

In March 1953, thirteen months before the *Brown* decision, *Christian Century* published Kennedy's hopeful piece, "While the Supreme Court Ponders"—a Yaupon-style short story, indeed the last time he used the "Yaupon" metaphor. It evolved from a reading assignment he gave a Troy English composition class. The assignment was an essay by Texan Aubrey Burns, titled "Segregation and the Church." First appearing in the spring 1949 issue of *Southwest Review*, where Kennedy had sought to publish, the piece worked off of Gunnar Myrdal's *American Dilemma* to urge the essential un-Christianity of white churches nationwide not adamantly advocating desegregation. Racism, Burns held, was the polar opposite of the teachings of Jesus Christ. After reading the essay in advance, students entered into an open classroom discussion of it, and then wrote an out-of-class essay reacting to both Burns's argument and the class discussion.

On collecting the essays, Kennedy went from grading to something he had not done in years. From 10:00 p.m. to 3:00 a.m. he wrote. He re-created the class discussion as a portrait of the range of reactions to desegregation among middle-class white southern college students—all this while the

Supreme Court pondered a decision in *Brown*. One of the students, Wilcoxon Marie Lawler—a member of his congregation—he cast as "from Yaupon."

From pros and cons of admitting Black people to white churches, he moved the vignette to the admission of Black students to Troy. The most conservative to the most liberal viewpoints found expression. Tempers came close to flaring as one young female—"a blond with a sharp tongue"—constantly attacked segregationists for being "hypocritical Christians." Yet most seemed to agree on one thing. White citizens' attitude of superiority over Black people was a "learned behavior." It was humans influencing humans, not something God ordained. And if this were true, editorialized the professor, transformation of attitudes might be possible—a premise, of course, foundational to his own frustrated God Mandate in Wilcox. Had life on a college campus influenced Kennedy to rethink his long-held caveat? Was cautious optimism—or maybe just "possibility"—creeping in? If so, this fits with how he ended the discussion. Just before the bell sounded, he called for a vote. "How many of you would be willing to admit Negroes into this college and go to school with them? The vote was nineteen ayes and twenty-one noes."

Cautiously, he now saw a chance of better odds for southern white change than he had faced in 1928, 1938, or for sure 1948. And several days after appearance of "While the Supreme Court Ponders," President Smith placed it "on reserve" in Troy's library. Proud of Kennedy, and of the desegregation sentiment among his students, he used "hall talk" to diplomatically suggest people go read it. Reinforcing.[41]

Still, this was not nearly enough to return him to his prewar idealism. Further reflecting on reactions to the article, not to mention the desegregation crisis oncoming like a runaway train, in June he wrote his siblings a kind of message he rarely did at this stage of his life: a straight-talking, nonspoofing philosophical commentary. "The normal state of human life . . . is turmoil . . . [and] combat. That is not a complaint . . . just a factual observation." Here was hardly the Victorian's "Be Ready in the Morning" message so idealistically urged at that Wilcox High School commencement of 1927.[42]

Yet later that month Kennedy received more encouragement. He reported for two weeks of Army Reserve summer camp at Fort Rucker, an hour's drive south of Troy. The night he returned to Troy, here is what he told the diary about military desegregation: "There is no more segregation in the Army. . . . Negro sergeants and officers are over white boys. Negro officers in the mess. I ate with Negro officers and their wives in the officers' club . . . they seem to be having no trouble with it."

Seven months later, in early October 1953, this well-restrained hopefulness found still more reinforcement. Though it elicited the ire of many legislators and caused "a terrible public relations mess" for him and President

Smith, the Troy student newspaper, *The Tropolitan* (for which Kennedy was faculty advisor), carried a lengthy story on student views of desegregation. Kennedy encouraged it. The writer was one of his best English majors, Margaret Key. The editor-in-chief was another, Peggy Austin. Their admittedly non-scientific poll turned up majority support for desegregation. Here is a sample of what they quoted. Remember, these quotes came from white students—the only kind Troy had at the time.

—Bob Williams (South Carolina): Under the assumption that this country is predicated on Christian principles, I cannot see any reason for segregation . . . [But] if the people of this country refuse [to support desegregation] it is our government's duty to discontinue its vast propaganda . . . and tell the people abroad the truth. . . . Tell them we are prejudiced.

—Margaret Craft (Andalusia, Alabama): In light of the fact that America is supposedly the leading democratic Christian nation of the world, I think there should be non-segregation in our colleges and universities. However, I do not think the different races should be compelled to attend the same school when they can attend schools of their own.

—Tom Ellison (Mobile, Alabama): The Negro, especially in Alabama, has been denied equal opportunity in education. . . . I am opposed to segregation in the schools. . . . It is un-Christian. The Gospel of St. John tells us that we are to love one another as Christ has loved us.

—Gordon Maddox (Graceville, Florida): [Negroes] should be allowed to attend any college they prefer. . . . After all, what is the purpose of having our Constitution if all citizens aren't allowed to enjoy its provisions?

—Harvey Murphy (Enterprise, Alabama): The time will come when we will have de-segregation . . . [and] I believe I could adjust to the situation as I lived with Negroes while I was in the service [in Korea]. . . . A person should not be judged by his color.

—Kirby Snow (Springfield, Missouri): I believe if adequate facilities for the advancement of Negro education were established all over the United States, the Negro would be satisfied to go to his own school.

—Tommy Duck (Bay Minette, Alabama): This issue of racial segregation will become insignificant in a few generations because of intermarriage producing a hybrid type of people. But for the present, what license does have a society have to deprive an ostracized group of equal educational advantages?[43]

While that article profiled Kennedy the sympathetic observer, in early April 1954—a month before the Court ruled in *Brown*—he became the adamant advocate. *Christian Century* carried his "Alabama Book Toasters," a straight journalism critique of the reactionary right's manipulation of communism to attack integration. On the last day of the 1953 Alabama legislative session, in coordination with state superintendent Bill Terry, one of Jefferson County's legislators, real estate executive James Bryant Morgan (not to be confused with Birmingham mayor James W. Morgan), introduced a bill to require "labeling"—though it was never clear by whom—of every book used in Alabama's public education, elementary through university. If there was the slightest hint of "Marxist socialism"—and ever since the Scottsboro case this meant advocacy of Black civil rights—the teacher assigning the book could be fired. In that last day's flurry of activity, Act 888 passed the Senate 20–0 and the House 62–1. Only the thirty-one-year-old Mobilian, Robert Bernard Wilkins—graduate of Spring Hill College and the University of Alabama law school—voted no. Though relatively moderate on race, Democratic governor Gordon Persons was sympathetic to McCarthyite sentiment of the Republican right and went along with it.

Shortly, the *Montgomery Advertiser, Anniston Star*, and *Tuscaloosa News* told readers what had happened. As the Tuscaloosa paper put it, the act was nothing more than "a nervous tic from [an] orthodox fathead." Likewise, the president of Auburn University, Ralph Draughon, urged the nonfunctional nature of the law: a million dollars or more would be required to "label" all the books just in Auburn's library alone. Finally, in the name of "academic freedom," an ad hoc statewide group of professors, led by liberal faculty of the University of Alabama medical school and extension center in Birmingham, filed legal papers to strike down the act—hint of a future Birmingham several shades different from what Kennedy had observed.

"Alabama Book Toasters" appeared a month before Alabama's Fifteenth Circuit Court, in Montgomery, rendered its judgment on the faculty group's suit. Kennedy diplomatically steered around Superintendent Terry's involvement. Yet he urged that Representative Morgan's "imbecility" was anything but surprising. Morgan represented the dirty, uncultured steel city of Birmingham, with "citizens ... divided into ... the bourgeoisie and the workers. The latter yearn to be bourgeoisie, the former yearn for culture and do their best to buy it." The current "imbecility" out of Birmingham, he concluded, could be traced to "a book toaster," if not a book roaster. Even more, it was classic "McCarthy mentality, the kind of thing . . . done in Communist-controlled countries." So, Kennedy still could muster satirical social criticism. He could address the obvious connection between racially motivated Dixiecrats and McCarthyism. And certainly he was pleased—indeed surprised—when, on May 10, 1954, the deeply conservative presiding judge of Alabama's Fifteenth Circuit Court (Montgomery), Walter B. Jones, somehow saw fit to strike down the Terry-Morgan law.[44]

Buoyant about "Book Toasters," Kennedy remounted his pulpit in a letter to brothers and sisters. "What we need in the White House is another Franklin Roosevelt or Harry Truman. I fear that McCarthy, the American Hitler, will be our next president." Three months later he was still going strong. On Sunday morning, August 23, he blasted McCarthyism from the Camden pulpit. He titled the sermon, "The Phony"—a term he later applied to George Wallace and Ronald Reagan. Years earlier he had developed no qualms about running roughshod over the ARP ban on getting "political" in the pulpit. In that spirit, before the ninety-four gathered that morning, he started off reading Matthew 23:3. He explained it as a lesson about the Scribes and the Pharisees and misrepresentation and manipulation. Then he bore down. From this passage "one idea stands out clearly: Jesus had no use for the deceiver . . . the hypocrite . . . the phony." After an exhaustive description of the un-Christian nature of these three archetypes, he offered an example of one person who exemplified all three of them: Sen. Joseph McCarthy. Indeed, the only two people in history who could be compared to the un-Christian "phoniness and demagoguery of McCarthy were possibly Adolf Hitler and Benito Mussolini." Surely Kennedy's was one of the few white voices from the Black Belt to utter such words.[45]

Still, throughout this period the pragmatic strategist in Kennedy did anything but disappear. The diary reveals tones ranging from flat stoicism to edgy cynicism: "Today [I go] to the [State] House to watch filibuster blocking reapportionment"; "White Citizen Council rally at [Montgomery] Coliseum today"; "Last year . . . Alabama had Phenix City [murder of Albert Patterson], and now has Autherine Lucy . . . count on Great State of Alabama to entertain nation"; Wilcox's "Bruce Henderson gives segregationist speech [in ill-fated gubernatorial run] . . . depressing"; Montgomery's "Judge Walter B. Jones gives . . . [segregationist] Memorial Day speech . . . sorriest speech I have heard in a very long time." And though he wrote his siblings that "no, the Negro boycotters [in the bus boycott] never shoot at me," he also told them that failure to bring about civil rights changes sooner or later could result in violence similar to Black people revolting against white African control as described in Robert Ruark's recent *Something of Value* (1955), which he had just read.[46]

Here also was the environment in which he worked. It was so different from his classrooms or the manse study or indeed the beer table with friends at the Conecuh River filling station. In 1954, President Smith again overran his budget by $17,000, relatively minor by later standards but significant for Troy State Teacher's College in the mid-1950s. This left Smith, not to mention his institution, again vulnerable to the machinations of controlling conservatives of the legislature. With Smith "squirm[ing] and flush[ing]," Kennedy handled it with phone calls to Sam Englehardt.

Likewise, on Sunday, March 17, 1954, two months before *Brown*, he was at home in Camden packing for the return to Troy. Out of the blue, one Clara Hard Rutledge knocked on the front door This was one of Montgomery's leading white integrationists and friend of noted New Dealers Clifford and Virginia Durr. Kennedy had heard of her but never met her. After a thirty-minute conversation in his study, she departed, not having convinced him to join the Montgomery chapter of the Southern Regional Council.

Though the diary describes Rutledge's visit, it is moot on Kennedy's reason for refusing to join up. One only can speculate. He never had been attracted to such groups: fairly or not, he considered them little more than a setting for strutting egos to preach to the converted. But even more, out of his new pragmatism, membership in a high-profile liberal organization might damage his politicking on behalf of more funding for Troy.[47]

Then, some three months after *Brown* came down, his cynicism about the future of desegregation showed in reaction to a conversation at Albritton's drugstore in Camden. There, he encountered sixty-six-year-old Miller Bonner talking about the role of his son-in-law, Sam Englehardt, in developing new plans for Wilcox's chapter of the White Citizens Council. At this stage—before the Civil Rights Act of 1957 and Eisenhower's efforts to enforce desegregation at Little Rock—Wilcox's was a relatively weak chapter. But Bonner still saw the WCC as potentially counterproductive. If its protest of desegregation involved violence, all it achieved was drawing increased federal attention on Wilcox. Bonner was like so many whites counting on "the stall"—as Kennedy later recalled—and "the whole thing sooner or later . . . blow[ing] over." Shortly, Kennedy's lack of optimism continued out of another local encounter. The thirty-nine-year-old president of Camden National Bank, Leslie Johnson, telephoned him, upset about being elected a Camden WCC officer when he did not even want to be a member. "What should I do?" Kennedy did not mince words. "You are opposed to the White Citizens Council. You do not belong in it. Just get out." Johnson did not.[48]

While it is not possible to say Kennedy comprehended all the subtleties of these trying times, by his actions it seems clear he grasped the essentials of where he stood. He grasped that Troy students and faculty gave him a glimmer of hope on desegregation—no doubt subliminally encouraging whatever elements remained of the Mandate. But it was just that: a glimmer. Otherwise, his doubt about significant successes with southern race change prevailed. Indeed, when *"Brown 2"* came down, in May 1955, with the Supreme Court applying the brakes of "all *deliberate* speed" to the desegregation process and at a time when the state of Alabama added "Heart of Dixie" to all its automobile license tags, it was with a pragmatically distant voice that he told the diary: "Supreme Court decision . . . desegregation as soon as feasible."[49]

This could not have been easy: a severely muted neo-orthodox, God-Mandated hope—idealism—coexisting alongside strategic, if conscientious, pragmatism. Most days the pragmatism won out. Still, from these dueling mentalities must have resulted guilt and stress capable of rising to torment. Kennedy was like so many of the 102nd Evac surgeons. Much as their powerlessness to counter life's realities in the war—the lives they could not save—led them to excessive alcohol, so was Kennedy drawn to drink out of his inability to resolve "the American dilemma" in the deepest South. Before going to the war, he moved from occasional to modestly regular consumption of alcohol. By the mid-1950s, his imbibing with colleagues at the Conecuh River filling station went from "a couple of beers" to "three or four" to "six"—regularly—plus just before bed a shot or two of vodka or gin, plus an occasional nip in the car in the evening driving from a last appointment back to the apartment or on a Friday afternoon returning to Camden. In another spoofing letter, he came close to confessing to all this in an April 1960 message to his siblings. On "the frailties" of many professed Christians around him, he wrote, "I have become tough and do not let it worry me. On the other hand, what do you think has driven me to the use of morphine, opium, and marijuana?"

As his consumption changed, so did his vocabulary. In the diary, "slug" evolved to "nourishment," and then "nourishment" to what he had picked up from evac life, "commodity." But that is deceptive. Despite having virtually limitless officers' access to alcohol, much of it provided gratis by the Army, just like cigarettes, Kennedy's wartime consumption never broached alcoholism. Indeed, he regularly warned comrades of its threat, and his war notes in the diary show, with few exceptions, a person wary of his own consumption and exercising caution. It was not the Allied war against European fascism that led to the escalation; it was the home-front theater against fascism—Alabama's and America's—that ultimately got him. While he was not an alcoholic in the mid-1950s, he appeared headed there.[50]

Yet, to think that Kennedy's drinking in the 1950s portended a reduced life, even a slowed pace, is off the mark. He was not just a dynamo as a Troy leader. His mind continued to find nurture with the most challenging new books: J. D. Salinger's *The Catcher in the Rye* (1951), William Faulkner's *Intruder in the Dust* (1948), Ralph Ellison's *The Invisible Man* (1952), Sloan Wilson's *The Man in the Gray Flannel Suit* (1955)—just to name a few. He also published several compelling pieces in *Christian Century*, one on the winding down of postwar prosperity in the South, one on the evils of big-time college football, and another on the Cold War as chaos.[51]

Likewise, he stayed the witty, supra-partisan Democrat. As the presidential election of 1956 came on, he chided his Republican siblings about reelecting Eisenhower—a man with "a midwestern peasant personality" addicted to "golf and vacations," with a secretary of state, John Foster Dulles, reminiful of a "misguided missile." He even gave them a dose of his old Mencken-style humor. In August 1955, the Republican National Committee mailed nationwide a letter expressing modest support for desegregation. In response, Kennedy wrote his brothers and sisters, asking how they could support reelection of a president devoted to "Republican radicalism" so committed to "our grandchildren going to school with colored children." As for him, "it is hard for an old Black Belt conservative like me to stand all this Eisenhower Republicanism." On the verge of the election, still, he dropped the spoof. "Ike will win the election, I fear, but I shall vote for the two sterling Democrats, Adlai Stevenson and the Tennessee senator, Estes Kefauver . . . who refused to sign the [Southern] manifesto" opposing public school desegregation endorsed by every other Deep South congressman. And when Eisenhower won, despite Democrats retaining control of both houses of Congress, it was: "The world is going to hell in a hack . . . very sad situation."[52]

He was the same in Wilcox life. The diary reflects constant engagement with daughter Margaret as she graduated from the University of Alabama, took a teaching job in Pensacola, then married a Marine Corps aviator, Wilbur Ausley, of Geneva, Alabama—no "Black Belt aristocrat." It shows the same about Mary Conway and Dickie and their growing family, and indeed about a spate of family deaths—his father and Mary's father both in 1950, his mother's a year later. The same indeed for church life. Beyond enhancement of church facilities in Camden, when Oak Hill ARPs had their centennial celebration, Kennedy found it "very fine," writing carefully crafted press releases for statewide media. And shortly, when Oak Hill ARPs failed to tax themselves to meet annual congregational tithes to Erskine College, he quietly took out a bank loan and paid the tab himself. Still an active clerk of the ARPs' Tennessee-Alabama Presbytery, a role he had had since 1927, he even exhibited less angst over the synod's continued rejection of Protestant unionism and reluctance to encourage vigorous Social Gospel outreach. As for alcohol, at the ARP's Bonclarken Conference Center, in Flat Rock, he stayed "off campus" at the adjacent Johnson's Motor Court, where he could enjoy a cocktail or two. Outspoken conservative ARPs condemned his drinking as only further indication of his going against the grain of long-standing ARP practices; he ignored them.[53]

In short, America's first postwar decade ultimately offered Ren Kennedy somewhere to go. Amid convoluted ironies of ideals and pragmatism, it offered material and professional ascent alongside deep personal regrets, with potential for something seriously debilitating. Yet as the 1950s gave way to the 1960s, Kennedy remained a man of many strengths—intellectual and spiritual. And he would need them all for what lay ahead.

11

The Limits of Ascent

President Smith again overspent Troy's budget. And, again, Kennedy and Meadows ultimately saved him. But while Kennedy lobbied to save Smith, word of Smith's renewed vulnerability leaked out. "Embarrassed profoundly" about their president, Gene Sterkx joined Hugh Ervin and Emmett Kilpatrick in launching a quiet campus "campaign" for the state board to replace Smith with an acting president—Renwick C. Kennedy. This was still a time when Alabama politics could reflect the personalism of family and friends trumping ideas and ideology. So, it was not surprising for Kilpatrick to approach Miller Bonner about enlisting Sam Englehardt for the envisioned "coup d'état" at Troy. Though that would take time, more immediately, Kilpatrick managed to get students editing the *Palladium* to dedicate the 1957 yearbook to Kennedy—big photo, words of praise, gravitas. Sterkx beamed. Even when it became clear that Smith's career would survive the crisis, faculty talk of Kennedy's ascendancy continued. And curiously the "Kennedy for President" move—Sterkx's words—appears to have had no adverse effect on Kennedy and Smith's working together in Troy's most trying political challenges yet. The Pulse's "academic life" seemed to be evolving to something well beyond Kennedy himself.[1]

In Alabama's May 1958 Democratic primary, the AEA channeled support to the two-term state legislator and probate judge from Barbour County, George Wallace. He had proven to be a strong education advocate, especially regarding money for trade schools and veterans—white people as well as Black. Granted, at the 1948 Democratic National Convention Wallace had criticized pro–civil rights stances of the party when many southern white liberals—Ren Kennedy included—applauded Truman's race agenda. Still, Wallace remained "a Democrat" who steered clear of race-baiting Dixiecrats. Deftly, Meadows began to assemble his developing AEA machine to support Wallace the "liberal" instead of his key opponent in the primary, the "conservative" John Patterson. President Smith jumped to support Meadows's quiet plan, assigning Kennedy the operational side of Troy's agenda.[2]

At this particular stage, as odd as it seems in retrospect, Kennedy considered Wallace's racial views roughly in line with those of the noted civil rights liberal and Emory University historian, Bell Wiley. Back in November 1955, at a Memphis meeting of the Southern Historical Association (SHA), Wiley used his presidency of the organization to help foster a forum on how best to "bury" Jim Crow. Historians C. Vann Woodward and James Silver, plus novelist William Faulkner and the Black president of Morehouse College, Benjamin Mays, were among the many who spoke. Gene Sterkx attended that noted SHA session and talked with Wiley afterward. More to the point, Sterkx returned to Troy uplifted over Wiley's passionate if vague core message: despite potent backlashes, desegregation could indeed succeed if white and Black southerners, together, made it work. Dubious about that happening, Kennedy was nonetheless curious—possibly encouraged—over Sterkx's suggestion that Wiley be invited to present his ideas at Troy.

And the timing was right. Recently, acting on long-time urging by Hugh Ervin and Emmett Kilpatrick and more recently by Kennedy himself, President Smith had orchestrated renaming his institution "Troy State College"—dropping "Teacher's" to signify the institution's full liberal arts "college" mission. This would be a boon to student recruitment as well as a symbolic step toward a broader intellectual environment useful in faculty recruitment and retention. As part of this change, Smith's pride and joy was a new Troy State College Visiting Lecture Series already to include an address by Will Durant. Kennedy had Smith issue an invitation for Wiley to lecture at Troy in October 1957.

That fall, before a packed Troy auditorium, Wiley pled that the "the South has an optimistic future if it musters the will to be more inclusive . . . and embrace desegregation." Yet at Troy as elsewhere he also emphasized two keys to this agenda. He called for no further federal intrusion with arms, just southerners getting on board and doing it. He also hoped desegregation could avoid insertion of ill-prepared Black students into traditionally white southern higher education. This he saw as the ultimate offense to Black people—a sign that higher education leaders considered them inferior and unable to equal the secondary school achievement of white students, a thought Wiley took to his grave in 1980. His speech won "resounding applause."[3]

Out of this perspective, indeed, as 1957 gave way to 1958 Kennedy came to place Wallace in the same category as people like Bell Wiley: people favoring desegregation with caveats. Of course, as we now know, Wallace's Folsom-style economic populism of the 1950s did not extend as much to race as Folsom's did. Wallace probably wanted Black citizens treated better in the context of segregation—but nothing much beyond that 1930s white liberal agenda. Still, at that time Kennedy and other liberals contrasted Wallace's words with the shrill racist cries of many Dixiecrats. Fearful of the future, and hungry for a reasonable person to rally around, any number of southern white liberals saw Wallace as a moderate New Dealer they needed to support. The very person who sought Kennedy's membership in the Southern Regional Council, in fact, Montgomery's Clara Rutledge, pragmatically looked at Wallace's key opponent, John Patterson, and supported the "Fight'n Judge from Barbour County," as indeed did the NAACP. Then there was the added touch of personalism. Kennedy believed he and Wallace shared a Scotch-Irish kinship; both had deep roots in the noted Laird family of the Carolinas and from there back to Ulster Plantation and the Borderlands—a connection Wallace would be apprised of shortly. The image of Wallace not just as distant relative but as a well-evolved, enlightened Scotch-Irishman, much like Kennedy himself, resonated with the Troy lobbyist.[4]

This image of Wallace as an agent of change obviously benefited from its contrast with John Patterson's rank conservatism. As Alabama attorney general, Patterson had coached Sen. Roland Cooper and the Wilcox Board of Registrars on how to get around a US Civil Rights Commission request for Wilcox voting records by submitting these records instead to a grand jury—where their confidentiality was guaranteed. Patterson also had "noninvestigated" the bombing of Martin Luther King's Montgomery home, supported the University of Alabama's not registering a first Black student, Autherine Lucy, and promised to close down public education in Alabama rather than comply with desegregation. The fact that the Supreme Court rejected his antiboycott strategies, in *Browder v. Gayle* (1956), made him all the more popular with racial conservatives, especially Klan members. And, of course, Patterson's opposition to any "new taxes" for public education cemented his backing from the Black Belt–Big Mule alliance.[5]

In that polarized context Meadows stayed clear of publicly aligning with any candidate. Still, behind the scenes he took a strong stand for Wallace. Like some others in Meadows's State Department of Education chain of command, Kennedy got directions to raise donations from AEA members. With the cover of his public relations role at Troy, however, his role well exceeded that of "fundraiser." Montgomery's WSFA television personality, Catherine Wright, asked for his assistance in an on-air sampling of student political views. After quiet coordination with Wallace's publicity director, Frank Tennille, Kennedy sent Wright three pro-Wallace Troy students—Marie Lawler, Carol Hutton, and Carol Hicks. On May 4 those efforts and many similar ones statewide helped Wallace survive the eleven-candidate gubernatorial primary election.

In the primary runoff the politics became even tougher. On May 15, lobbyist friends Jeff Bennett and Ren Kennedy joined a meeting in Montgomery with Meadows, Smith, and seven others: the three other teacher's college presidents (Jacksonville's Houston Cole, Florence's Ethelbert P. Norton, Livingston's Delos P. Culp), plus Auburn president Ralph Draughon; the new UA president and Bennett's boss, Frank Rose; Alabama State University president A. C. Trenholm; and the new Alabama College president, Howard Phillips. After much soul searching about race and chaos in Alabama, they agreed the state's education funding, as bad as it already was, remained too vulnerable for them to attempt any unified effort in the runoff politics. Yet it is doubtful that any of these leaders sat on the sidelines. For sure, Meadows's State Department of Education and its teacher education colleges did not. The day after that meeting Smith received directions for Kennedy to keep up his quiet fundraising through AEA channels. He did. Of course to no avail. In the June Democratic primary runoff, Patterson "out-seged" Wallace to victory, which in "one-party" Alabama meant winning the governorship.

The day before that final vote, and anticipating how it would go, Kennedy informed his siblings: "Wallace's loss will be a bitter blow for me." Certain of more sibling chides about their brother's supporting "liberal Wallace" over Patterson, he concluded the letter with another backhanded shot. This one had unknowing prescience. Wallace will lose, he explained. But if he *were* elected "[he] will ... preserve the Southern way of life [and] keep the colored in their place."

Still, the night following Patterson's January 19, 1959, inauguration Kennedy had a more somber and direct comment about Alabama's racial scene. He attended Patterson's inaugural events. As he reported to his brothers and sisters, he saw "No Negroes. . . . Four years ago when . . . Jim Folsom was inaugurated about half the spectators were Negroes. We have a bad racial situation in Alabama, and it gets worse." Poignantly, as Kennedy wrote that, the 1962 "Wallace for governor" campaign already was gearing up. And Wallace's plan—emulating Patterson's—would do everything *but* improve that "racial situation."[6]

On June 24, 1959, despite campaign promises to the contrary, Patterson acceded to AEA and higher education pressures, and convened a special session of the legislature to get new monies for education. Here was one convoluted effort. To prepare for an ill-fated run for lieutenant governor in 1958, Sam Englehardt had resigned from the leadership of the Alabama White Citizens Council. But he still had clout as the new director of the State Highway Department; indeed, it was out of Englehardt's strong support for Patterson that Englehardt got the Highway Department job. With Smith's approval, Kennedy went to Meadows with an angle. On the assumption that the State Highway Department would continue as one of the mother lodes of corrupt money in Alabama, he would get Englehardt to use his leverage of approving highway construction projects to persuade members of the House to support increased taxes for education. And, according to Kennedy, Englehardt played ball. Still, most of the Black Belt–Big Mule axis opposed tax increases necessary for Patterson's education effort and made sure the House members they controlled—most of them—rejected the bait. Indeed, just as they had treated Gov. Meek Miller back in the Depression, they now turned against Governor Patterson despite his racial conservatism. After all, they were accustomed to getting most of what they wanted, not just some of it. Most Wilcox politicos both in and out of office joined in turning on Patterson—the "turncoat" who decided, after all, that more education money was necessary. None was more vociferous than former senator Bruce Henderson. But retired Miller Bonner and his son-in-law, Sam Englehardt, were different. Out of Englehardt's abiding appreciation for Patterson's arch-segregationist stance—and no doubt reinforced by his father-in-law's devotion to Kennedy—Englehardt stuck firmly with Patterson.[7]

Indeed, worried about a sustained Black Belt–Big Mule opposition, Patterson began working through Englehardt to resolidify his conservative base, using strategy after strategy to block integration: more white massive resistance. He managed at least a temporary ban against NAACP work in Montgomery. He made no serious effort to pursue those responsible for blowing up the Montgomery homes of Black civil rights activists E. D. Nixon and Ralph Abernathy. And when, in the waning days of his governorship, "Freedom Riders" entered Montgomery in buses to test court-ordered desegregation of interstate transportation, he did little to block their being attacked by an angry mob. He told the State Board of Education to expel from Alabama State College Black students who protested segregated eating in the Capitol cafeteria, and they did it. Even so, Patterson never fully recovered the support of the Black Belt–Big Mule alliance, leaving the sea of chaos sweeping over Alabama's education and other public priorities getting rougher and rougher each month.[8]

Kennedy longed for the next election and what Meadows—and Smith, too—anticipated to be the modern, thoughtful New Dealer, George Wallace. His hope grew as the Wallace movement gained strength. On July 30, 1958, Smith had Wallace on the Troy campus for an assembly program. He did not talk about civil rights, just about making Alabama courts more efficient. Afterward any number of Troy State "liberals," including Kennedy and Sterkx, had coffee with him. Here, Kennedy told Wallace of their mutual heritage. The governor's great-great-great-great grandmother, Mary Laird, back in Abbeville County, South Carolina, was Kennedy's distant cousin. "Politely interested" in that tidbit, Wallace connected more with Kennedy's briefly recalling his wartime visits to "the birthplace [Berkenhead, near Liverpool,

England] and death place" [Cherbourg, France] of the *Alabama*, the Confederate war ship built by our distant cousin, a Scotsman named [John] Laird."

By November, a far larger pro-Wallace liberal crowd gathered in the Troy Student Center to watch the midterm election returns for Congress. "Democrats sweeping the country," Kennedy told the diary. And he could not pass up another backhanded shot to his conservative brothers and sisters: "I feel greatly concerned over the record Democratic victory [in Congress]. This deprives me of the pleasure I found in attacking the Republicans."[9]

Still, he remained realistic about any similar swelling of moderate-to-liberal ranks in Alabama, notably Wilcox. In January 1957, powerful conservatives in Camden Presbyterian Church ran off its minister, John Calvin Chestnutt. Aligned with more liberal strains of Presbyterianism, this young Georgian had suggested every now and then that some Black people might want to attend Camden Presbyterian. Viola Liddell and a few other congregants protested Chestnutt's fate. They liked his liberal message and appreciated his Boy Scout leadership in the community incorporating many a hunting and fishing venture. But to no avail. Chestnutt then moved to Montgomery's Trinity Presbyterian, where much the same thing happened. But from there he helped found the more open Westminster Presbyterian Church in Montgomery before becoming executive secretary of the PCUSA for Alabama. Long after departing Camden, however, he regularly returned for deer and turkey hunting with the Liddells and dinner with the Kennedys.

Indeed, in that first year after Chestnutt's departure, on at least three occasions he returned for long visits with Kennedy—searching conversations about what was possible, and not, for a Social Gospel minister in the Black Belt of the late 1950s. There is no record of what precisely they concluded. After one of these discussions in early September 1958, however, a little of Kennedy's old verve—harkening back to his "Aristocracy of the Kingdom of God"—seems to have come over him. Kennedy's ARP flock was not responsible for what happened to Chestnutt in Camden. But, in preparing his sermon for Sunday, September 7, he seemed so taken with the Presbyterians' lack of Social Gospel spiritualism that he vented to the ARPs. He titled the sermon "When the Books Are Opened," drawing on Revelations 20:12: "and the dead were judged out of those things which were written in the books, according to their works." "Now, we believe that we will be saved by faith," he explained, "but apparently we will be judged by our works. . . . It may be that some people who claim to have faith will have it proved that they did not by what the record shows." Indeed, "it may be that some humble Christian will have a higher place than some missionary. . . . Or that some person of another color will have a higher place than a white man or woman. . . . Each of us writes a record by the way we live every day. . . . Whether you are sincere or phony . . . you write the record by the way you live." Relatively nonthreatening. But also clear.

In the spring of 1959, a similar crisis developed over Chestnutt's replacement, a recently ordained minister named B. Clayton Bell, son of noted China missionaries and a graduate of Wheaton College and Columbia Theological Seminary. Though a theological conservative, for the times Bell still was a racial liberal attuned to evangelist Billy Graham's incrementalist approach to race change, which included compliance with *Brown*. In Camden, Bell regularly asked why God's church doors could not be opened to Black people should they wish to walk through. Openly urging the University of Alabama and Auburn University to admit Black students, he offered notable praise for tentative steps at desegregation within the Westminster Fellowship of Auburn's First Presbyterian Church—known for joint services with Methodist students from nearby Tuskegee Institute.

Terminated in late April 1960, Bell moved on to churches in Birmingham and Dothan, Alabama, and Rome, Georgia, along the way marrying Billy Graham's sister, before establishing a noted theologically conservative Presbyterian church in Dallas, Texas. According to Kennedy, "several prominent Camden whites led by Viola—people who did not like Bell's theology yet applauded his position on race"—traced Bell's termination to Sam Englehardt's telling Camden Presbyterian leader Fred Henderson, son of Judge William Henderson and brother of state senator Bruce Henderson, that Bell was "a serious liberal threat on racial matters." Kennedy's editorial comment—"sad knifing."[10]

Local reaction to Bell's firing, Kennedy found, also fit with certain Camden "opinions" that World Peace Foundation researcher Alfred O. Hero Jr. found in Wilcox in July 1960. On recommendation by fellow Bostonian Morton Rubin, Hero chose this county as one of several for researching the attitudes of "rural cosmopolitans"—educated, well read, well-traveled—for what would become his noted work, *The Southerner and World Affairs* (1965). That Hero came from an old Louisiana sugar and rice plantation family, about twenty-five miles north of New Orleans, did not hurt his ability to get prolific interviews among this Wilcox set.

After his initial meeting with Kennedy, on Saturday afternoon, July 9, Hero headed to Fred Henderson. Hero found Henderson polite and open in conveying strong support for massive resistance on race change as well as a resolutely isolationist foreign policy. Next, Hero talked with the young lawyer Jo Robins Bonner, Miller Bonner's nephew. They hit it off: Bonner had completed his law degree at George Washington University, where Hero did his doctorate in political science. Bonner regularly read the *Manchester Guardian* and the *New York Times*. He liked Franklin D. Roosevelt and John F.

Kennedy. A pragmatist on race, he figured desegregation was coming. He hoped it could be peaceful.

Kennedy also guided Hero to his literary comrades—the Roundtable. The researcher found Emmett Kilpatrick "far to the left of John Kennedy," "favoring recognition of Communist China" and opposed to "reactionary leaders" at home and abroad. He found Viola Liddell to be much like Kennedy. She agreed with most editorials in the *New York Times* and was comfortable with the level of conversation in the *Atlantic Monthly*. She was convinced that South African apartheid was "suicidal." She favored broadening the voter base of Wilcox—Black as well as white people—and generally supported desegregation. Yet she worried about the negative effects of uneducated people voting and insufficient primary school backgrounds for Black students to succeed in a modernized, racially blended Wilcox high school.

Annie Brice Bonner, Miller Bonner's second wife, took that reservation much further. She told Hero she regularly read the *New York Times*, the *Sewanee Review* and the *Virginia Quarterly Review*. And she "still ... read some Latin and Greek," too. Still, she saw no bright future for healthy democracy owing to the way new "technologies" (television?) created "a mass mentality" easily manipulated by "demagoguery" committed to liberal reform.

According to Kennedy—not quoted in Hero's book—the researcher found "Miss Lena" Albritton "just wanting peace in the world and nobody hurting anybody and seeing the need for desegregation." Hero also found Stanley Godbold smart, conservative, informed, despite holding nominal membership in the White Citizens Council. He interviewed Hugh Ervin as well, but no record remains. Whether Hero interviewed Mary Godbold remains unclear. Like Kennedy's Red Cross records, Hero's research notes did not make it to an appropriate storage place, much less to an archive—only to the garage behind his family's Louisiana plantation house—and they do not exist today.

In short, among his sample of well-educated Camden whites, Hero found a range of views. Some were "liberal"; most were not but still sophisticated and informed. Out of the firm belief that "it just will not work," however, none of them seemed comfortable with immediate and across-the-board, federally enforced desegregation. And Fred Henderson and Annie Brice Bonner opposed any approach to desegregation. This Deep South planter's son, Hero, also took careful note of local reactions to Sam Englehardt. Despite white Black Belters providing unmatched support for Alabama's WCC, among those Hero interviewed, "pretty much all did not care for [Englehardt] because of his White Citizen[s] Council activity." The only exception was Fred Henderson—descendant not of slave owners but of northerners who helped free the slaves. Yet if that were not irony enough—which Hero apparently missed—arguably the most "liberal" of those he met in Camden was the one with the most current working relationship with Englehardt, the pragmatic Kennedy.[11]

Indeed, on September 16, 1960—three months after Hero departed Camden—something happened in Camden that elucidates the Kennedy-Englehardt relationship as indeed more than ironic personal relationship. On that night Englehardt hosted a small dinner party to honor his eighty-one-year-old father-in-law, Miller Bonner. The honoree welcomed the gesture, but his declining health necessitated that the event occur in his Camden home.

As specified by the honoree, the guest list was restricted to Bonner's "old close friends." These included four well-known Black Belt liberals: Hugh Ervin and Bill Jones, still "FDR Democrats"; Emmett Kilpatrick, an open socialist but normally voting Democratic in national elections; and Ren Kennedy, once an open Christian Socialist but long since an "FDR Democrat." Beyond Englehardt, the conservatives included Walter B. Jones, a noted white supremacist, son of "Bourbon" governor Thomas Goode Jones and judge of Alabama's Fifth Judicial Circuit; John S. Tilley, a Montgomery lawyer and popular "Lost Cause" historian of the Old South; R. F. Hudson, owner of the *Montgomery Advertiser* and known for firing Charles Dobbins and other journalists critical of Alabama Power's political influence; T. B. Hill Jr., a Montgomery lawyer and devotee of Jefferson Davis; and Thomas W. Martin, an Alabama Power executive and historic leader of the Black Belt–Big Mule alliance. Massey Wilson—former Alabama attorney general, one of the last living members of the 1901 constitutional convention, and political mentor for Tom Martin—was invited too. But on a pastoral call to Oak Hill, where the ninety-year-old Wilson lived with relatives, Kennedy found him too frail for such an outing and, as expected, he declined the invitation.

For the big night Kilpatrick had requested and of course received the assignment of chief orator, that is, reading a three-page resolution congratulating Bonner on his long and productive life. For two weeks before the event all the invitees critiqued and revised this document, first drafted by Kennedy. As indicated by the multiple versions with sardonic marginalia (in Kennedy's papers), this was not easy; the final version had to praise Bonner for traits unanimously considered "true" by this broad spectrum of political views. But they finally got a consensual document. After dinner Kilpatrick arose. Since Miller Bonner now was deaf, Sam Englehardt handed his father-in-law a written copy to follow along with Kilpatrick's oratory. What came forth was anything but another Kilpatrick show. Englehardt had extracted a solemn pledge for "a tame Emmett," one of the few instances of his ever delivering structured, nontheatrical "truth." That no alcohol was served out of respect for the honoree's "honorable dryness" undoubtedly helped account for his discipline. The core: "Mr. Bonner hates liquor, and can express his hatred of it fluently and in detail and at length. . . . He is a dedicated conservative, rejecting . . . all liberal philosophies. . . . His own theology is Presbyterian—Calvinistic, Augustinian and indeed Pauline."

The setting, of course, was more evocative than the formal remarks. Here were powerful conservatives and noted liberals joined in upper-class white fellowship—classic Black Belt. But even more revealing stood Kennedy's diary entry that night: "Very good steak . . . but . . . [with] people who have been left behind by the times." Indeed, Tom Martin, who had to miss the gathering owing to a last-minute conflict, shortly wrote Kennedy that he considered the venerable old Bourbon, Bonner, "one of God's noblemen." Yet, it turned out, "left behind by the times" wound up having less to do with conservative versus liberal—what Kennedy undoubtedly meant—and more to do with conservative versus conservative.[12]

By 1962, the US Fifth Circuit Court of Appeals, in New Orleans, would have ordered that Wilcox voter registration records back to 1958 be made available to the US Civil Rights Commission. Shortly, the fact of overt racial discrimination in Wilcox would become publicly documented. The same year the Supreme Court made the Old Guard even more "left behind." The Court's decision in *Baker v. Carr* stipulated the unconstitutionality of Alabama, or any other state, avoiding reapportionment of numbers of state senators and representatives as the centers of population changed. Out of these and other legal blows, the Black Belt–Big Mule influence over Alabama further declined, as did the clout of White Citizens Councils and other elements of massive resistance. Yet none at the Bonner party could have fully anticipated these developments and the politics they would impact, least of all that someone not invited to the Bonner celebration—George Wallace—would revitalize the losses of these earlier conservatives.[13]

On that complex note let us return to the concrete scene. In September 1959 President Smith finally announced his retirement effective May 1960—though it turned out he did not leave by that date. His announcement surprised nobody. Thirty-nine years was long enough; the last five he barely survived. As the State Board of Education went to work on choosing a new president, the Emmett-Hugh-Gene troika geared up. Still, in late October 1960, as Montgomery and Troy conversation focused incessantly on the search, Kennedy told his comrades to stop pushing his name. The political environment for getting better support for education—ultimately, the only key to a better Alabama—had more than a few glimmers of hope. He did not have to be president of Troy to play a role in this progress. After all, Wallace was in the wings.

Yet all three of these Troy faculty members felt strongly about Troy's recent change of status from Troy Teacher's College to Troy State College. At the helm they wanted someone with a broader background and intellectual interests. Kennedy understood. State Board of Education member from Tallassee, Byron B. Nelson, already had told Kennedy that Austin Meadows's successor as state superintendent (he could not succeed himself), Frank Stewart, wanted Smith's job. So the troika's concerns rang true. Without mentioning Nelson or Stewart, Kennedy nevertheless asked again that they stand down on advocating Renwick C. Kennedy. They instead should focus on someone with more experience—fearless Jeff Bennett.[14]

Though at times too undiplomatic, Jeff Bennett worked as chief lobbyist for the University of Alabama. He had grown up in Fairhope, where his Kentucky-born parents moved for teaching jobs, his father ultimately serving as principal of Fairhope High School. On graduating from UA with a bachelor of science degree in business, young Bennett served in World War II as a Marine and fought at Guadalcanal. Immediately after the war, he entered UA's law school, graduating at the top of his class in 1949. After brief private legal practices in Birmingham and Fairhope, he took a faculty appointment in the UA law school. By the time of the first attempt to desegregate the University of Alabama, the Autherine Lucy case of the late 1950s, he was assisting UA president Oliver C. Carmichael on navigating race change—a difficult role due to Bennett's being more committed to desegregation than Carmichael was, not to mention most of the UA board. By 1959, in short, Bennett worked aggressively, if often behind the scenes, for a modernized Alabama.

Kennedy first met Bennett while working the legislature. As combat veterans they easily connected over horrors of the Battle of the Bulge and Guadalcanal. Kennedy also knew Bennett from rounds of vodka martinis at The Club in Birmingham, where the Alabama College and University Public Relations Society often convened. Over the martinis they discovered their mutual admiration for Gould Beech as well as their similar thoughts comparing the difficulties of desegregation with problems of unionism among Protestants. Bennett grew up in tiny St. James Episcopal Church in Fairhope. He remained an avid Episcopalian, and from that early influence long had favored greater coordination of liberal social action among all Protestants. Back on July 20, 1959, eating lunch at The Elite in Montgomery, Kennedy asked Bennett if he would take the Troy presidency should there be a "clear path available." Bennett demurred. On August 20, again at The Elite, Kennedy pressed. Bennett said, "Possibly, yes."[15]

Of course, things did not come down quite that way. After the Christmas break, in mid-January 1960, Superintendent Stewart planted a few comments in the press indicating he indeed planned to be a candidate for the Troy position. Educated at Jacksonville Teacher's College and Auburn, Stewart had a formidable politicking background: Anniston school superintendent, Cherokee County school superintendent, administrative assistant to Meadows, assistant state school superintendent, strong AEA advocate—until recently all he had lacked was a degree allowing people to call him "doctor." And in 1959 Auburn solved that problem by awarding him an honorary doctorate. He wanted the Troy job, which included a large home and a $12,000 salary—$2,000 more than the state superintendent's. Understandably, Bennett stayed in the wings. And Kennedy tried to as well, despite the Troy troika's wanting otherwise.

At Kilpatrick's suggestion, Miller Bonner—though deaf and aging fast—began a back-channeled lobby for Kennedy as Troy president. On January 23, 1960, Bonner wrote his daughter Sara (Sam Englehardt's wife): "Tell Sam to get John Patterson's attention on Renwick C. Kennedy to be president of Troy.... While Dr. Kennedy is not and will not become an active applicant, he is willing for you [Sam] to let Governor Patterson know [of his interest].... Remember, he baptized you [Sara], and all your children."

Ideological segregationist Sam Englehardt went to work for pragmatic desegregationist Ren Kennedy. He made the calls to the governor. When Kennedy found out, while he did not try to reverse Englehardt's actions, he carefully informed Bennett. On July 26 the two schemed in the coffeeshop of the Stafford Hotel in Tuscaloosa. Bennett reiterated his interest; Kennedy apparently indicated that some still supported him, though his priority was with Jeff's candidacy. On September 14 Bennett telephoned Kennedy in his office to reassert his interest because his contacts advised, "'Governor [Patterson] is against Stewart." To Kennedy this rang true. With Kennedy present, a March 1960 State Board of Education meeting focused on the lack of money for desperately needed teacher pay raises. There, over Governor Patterson's strong objections, Stewart marshaled the votes to pass a resolution "to pay teachers in full for the time they teach and to close [the schools] when [the] money is gone," a step ultimately proving unnecessary when Patterson's pared-back education bill finally found approval. With Stewart vulnerable, Kennedy was even more strongly behind Bennett. Yet if Bennett dropped out, there still was support in some quarters for Kennedy himself to become an active candidate. Obviously, prospects of his being president of Troy—which could be turned into a serious leadership platform in the state—now had "The Pulse" rethinking his future.

The flip side of Jeff Bennett's lack of diplomacy was his impatience with foot-dragging. After the war he never ceased being the Marine ready to charge the next hill. "I just always had to get on with things," he recalled years later, crippled with phlebitis, down on Bay La Launch at his Old Orange Beach retirement cottage. And, as Montgomery hunkered down on white massive resistance, the Troy presidency search became so prolonged that Bennett began telling Kennedy he was losing interest. So when Frank Stewart officially added his name to the chaotic search, that did it. Bennett's "silent candidacy" ceased.[16]

In early November 1960, Kennedy quietly advised the troika of all this and agreed for Emmett to return to Sam Englehardt and Miller Bonner, and now Senator Roland Cooper, too, for strong-arming Governor Patterson on his behalf. Yes, indeed, these usual critics of the Black Belt–Big Mule axis—Kilpatrick, Sterkx, Kennedy—wanted a traditional Black Belt leverage applied to Patterson: Kennedy was to be Troy's president, not some "State Department of Education person" like Stewart. On November 28, Kennedy capsuled all this for his siblings. "I am engaged in a dark and devious political undertaking relative to being president of this college."

One would think Englehardt's support permitted Kennedy a significant pragmatic angle. Englehardt not only was State Highway Department director, but also, with Patterson's thumb on the process, he recently had been chosen executive director of the Alabama State Democratic Party. On February 19 Englehardt joined Roland Cooper in calling on Patterson. Results were encouraging. "If Gov . . . gets 2 more votes for me on the State Board," Kennedy told the diary that night, "he will put me in as Troy president." So, on March 10, 1961, Kennedy confirmed newspaper accounts of his candidacy and formally submitted an application for the job, as required by state law. Yet the State Department of Education lobby—including many AEA contacts with whom Kennedy was close—carried the day. On March 21, 1961, a 3:30 p.m. radio newscast brought the news. With Governor Patterson's public endorsement, Frank Stewart would be the next Troy president.[17]

Though the troika reported, "No joy in Troy over Frank Stewart's election," Kennedy responded with aplomb. Immediately he drove to Stewart's Montgomery office to work with him on an institutional press release. The next day, March 22, he had Jeff Bennett call Stewart with the word that Kennedy had made formal application for the position only because he was "drafted"—with his own serious reservation.

Aplomb continued. That same day, March 22, Bennett telephoned Kennedy with what he *thought* explained the outcome. The board decision was close: likely the deciding influence came from Tuscaloosa state senator Edwin Weber (Skid) Skidmore—a prolabor attorney, member of the Southern Regional Education Board (SREB), and opponent of the Black Belt–Big Mule axis—who weighed in for Stewart in return for state adoption of certain secondary school English and Communication Arts textbooks in which Skidmore's family had a substantial financial stake. "I didn't have much of a chance against that . . . ," he wrote his siblings, "but I cannot prove it." Nor can Bennett's "intelligence" be considered anything more than an undocumented rumor he heard in Tuscaloosa circles. More to the point, Kennedy kept his mouth shut on the Skidmore rumor and went to work for Frank Stewart.[18]

On April 19 Mary Kennedy took the early bus from Camden to Montgomery. There, at the Sahara Restaurant, she helped her husband host a Troy leadership dinner party welcoming Frank and Margaret Stewart. Kennedy invited the Smiths. They declined. That same month Austin Meadows again won reelection as state school superintendent, replacing Stewart. Kennedy saw a workable team. On June 15, according to the diary, "I visit with Frank Stewart for one hour. We talk frankly. I tell him of some problems he will face—three deans, science departments weak, the hierarchy, etc." Still, implications for what he noted after the Miller Bonner dinner—for the Old Guard "the times have passed them by"—must have been far clearer now. The Black Belt's political power, which long had benefited him (despite his visceral criticism of it), he no longer could count on for doing deals in Montgomery.[19]

As federally enforced reapportionment and an ever growing AEA continued the decline of Black Belt influence, a set of deaths symbolically punctuated this transition in Alabama life. On March 29, 1966, with Ren Kennedy presiding, the ninety-six-year-old Bourbon, Massey Wilson, entered the ground behind Bethel ARPC. By two years Wilson had outlived his acolyte in the dark art of Alabama oligarchy, Tom Martin. Then, after several strokes beginning in 1965, on New Year's Day 1968, at 2:45 p.m., death came to another one of Wilson's best students, eighty-nine-year-old J. Miller Bonner. On Wednesday, January 3, with some 200 present, Kennedy buried him in the Camden Cemetery. That night in the diary Kennedy distilled what he had withheld at Bonner's earlier home fête. Though "an old friend," Bonner went to the grave "stubborn . . . egotistical . . . selfish . . . if a Christian believer." Consistent with his own definition of the word, Kennedy could have amended this to "Half-Christian."[20]

Beyond those changing horizons in Camden, Montgomery, and Troy, of course, loomed the larger national political setting: the *other* Kennedy candidacy, John F. Kennedy's. In primaries leading up to the 1960 presidential election, key national Democratic candidates—while aligned vaguely with racial reform—refused a big endorsement. They would not openly support President Eisenhower's employment of the US military to enforce public school desegregation and what many expected the Republicans' key candidate, Richard Nixon, to do as well. Many southern whites, accordingly, stayed in the Democratic fold. They generally liked Texas senator Lyndon Johnson and Massachusetts senator John F. Kennedy. They also might support the senior Democratic statesman of Illinois, Adlai Stevenson—though, having failed twice to get his party's nomination, he said he was available but would not campaign.

Of these Democratic "racial moderates," the noted governor of Mississippi,

James P. Coleman, especially liked John Kennedy for his equivocating on implementation of the 1957 Civil Rights Act designed to enforce the *Brown* decisions. Though he voted for the bill, Kennedy did not support efforts to move the bill around the Senate Judiciary Committee, chaired by the archconservative senator from Mississippi, James Eastland. Kennedy also did not support changes in Senate cloture rules to cut off southern filibusters. For these reasons, John Patterson and indeed George Wallace—if less so Sam Englehardt—seemed pro-JFK.

Early on, however, Ren Kennedy supported Stevenson. As he chided his Republican siblings in April 1960, "It is now time for the sterling gold-plated Democrats to get together behind that great statesman and scholar, J. Adali Stevenson . . . the smartest of them all." Yet as the primaries unfolded, still-influential Eleanor Roosevelt urged Stevenson to get more fully into the campaign and be stronger on civil rights. And when he did not, she publicly switched to young Kennedy. The Wilcox preacher followed suit.

Ren Kennedy's diary as well as his letters to siblings reveal that a JFK endorsement from that iconic American liberal, Eleanor Roosevelt, greatly influenced him. As always, too, Kennedy remained glued to the *New York Times* and other high-level journalism. Between July 1953 and July 1960 the *Times* increasingly waxed eloquent about JFK, including five in-depth profiles of him in the Sunday *Magazine*. The *New Republic* did the same in six major pieces. *Time* and *Newsweek* were similarly enthusiastic. *Look* and *Christian Century*, too. Poignantly, little of this coverage explored JFK's racial views, perhaps reflecting how national-level journalism was attuned to the mass of white Americans' reticence about an all-encompassing civil rights movement. Instead, these newspapers and magazines focused on JFK's general social progressivism, his determination to defeat the spread of communism, and his personality—wit, intelligence, charm, Harvard education.

Not long before the general election, however, JFK telephoned Coretta Scott King showing concern for her husband, Martin Luther King Jr., being jailed while protesting in Georgia. And JFK's campaign manager, his brother Robert, subsequently used Kennedy contacts to help get King out of jail. The *New York Times* gave this positive coverage. Ren Kennedy noticed the development, later recalling its impact on public opinion as "similar to the way the *Times*' coverage of the Soviet invasion of poor Finland had an influence on how Americans looked at getting into the [second world] war." If this could be overstated poetry, he also recalled that the incident resulted in worries among white racial conservatives as well as strong Black voting for JFK in the election—no overstatements. At any rate, led on by Eleanor Roosevelt and the *Times*, the Kennedy from Wilcox County, Alabama, jumped on the bandwagon of the Kennedy from Massachusetts.[21]

The evening of July 13, 1960, he and Emmett Kilpatrick drank gin and tonics while watching these political developments unfold on Mrs. Carter's new 12 inch television set. Late that night Kennedy noted that Kilpatrick felt a little "out of sorts . . . cranky." Earlier in the day he had strolled around the campus telling of his plans to retire "at the end of upcoming fall term." Kennedy believed his old comrade felt upstaged by everyone's focus upon possibilities of John F. Kennedy's nomination. By the night of July 15 they had watched the Democratic National Convention do its dramatic thing. And Kennedy then believed Kilpatrick was adjusting to his "lesser priority." "Well," Emmett queried humbly, "is it now Kennedy for Kennedy?" Indeed it was.

Ten days later the two gathered again in front of Mrs. Carter's television for the Republican convention. Ren Kennedy: "Nixon mouths many platitudes. I will vote for Kennedy." On the night of October 19, 1960, they yet again gathered for drinks with Mrs. Carter to watch the Kennedy-Nixon debates. The diary for that night went right to it: "Kennedy is better." It was the same scene on November 3 with Nixon talking in South Carolina: "Nixon is a phony. . . . Hope Kennedy beats him."[22]

Down in Troy, Alabama, when the final counting seemed a day away, Kennedy turned in, noting: "John F. Kennedy well ahead when I go to bed." The next morning, despite the continued vote counting on the presidential election, Troy priorities had to shift. Kennedy had press releases in both the college paper and the town paper announcing the upcoming retirement of Emmett Kilpatrick and inviting all to the campus for "Kilpatrick Day, November 9, 1960" and the awarding of a special gift to the honoree—his office typewriter.

That afternoon, returned to the office after the Kilpatrick event, Kennedy got the radio announcement: "The Minnesota votes mean Jack Kennedy has won." Resurgence seemed in order. By 5:00 p.m. he and Kilpatrick were full blast at the Conecuh River filling station. "Commodities aplenty." Gene Sterkx rolled in about 5:45 p.m. Shortly thereafter in came some of Emmett's other old friends—Hugh Ervin; plus superintendent of Troy City Schools, Roy Thaggard; Troy State's treasurer, Clay Stabler; and the history department head, Trapp. Someone raised a brown bottle: "To Jack!" Then, after an awkward pause, "And to Emmett!" One historic day.

In short, Troy's old guard was departing. Kennedy was not going to lead the place, but with the other Kennedy headed for the White House, he still seems to have had a surge of renewed hope—perhaps idealism—about what he might get done at Troy aided by a new shot of FDR liberalism. As he wrote his brothers and sisters, "I voted for Jack Kennedy . . . [who] has courage and honor and intelligence and is going to make a good president. . . . He will not try to run the country like the citizens of Wilcox County, Ala., . . . nor any of the old Southern Bourbons."[23]

On New Year's Eve, after talking on the phone with Dan Laws, Kennedy told the diary, "1960—a very good year." After all, he was providing for his family. A man whom he understood to be a New Deal Democrat, John Kennedy, was about to be inaugurated president. And another he considered a New Deal Democrat, George Wallace, was moving forward to change Alabama. Even if Protestant unionism remained beyond the pale, American reform might again find its way to the front burner. At *home* racial fascism might yet be addressed.[24]

As the early 1960s unfolded, other things lifted Kennedy, too. Camden ARPs permitted him to buy the manse at the northwest corner of Broad and Whiskey Run Road. The Kennedys finally had a home of their "own"; by August 1965 even the mortgage was retired. Likewise, finding modernization too intruding on historic Monroeville, "Hollywood types" secretively overnighted at Viola and Will Liddell's while scouting Camden for filming *To Kill a Mockingbird*. In Camden modernity was less a problem. For the trial scene its antebellum courthouse looked promising. So too the Female Institute. Harper Lee even popped in for a quick secretive look. By the time of this site visit Kennedy had read Lee's book—finding it "good"—but the Liddells kept their secret so well that prospects of filming in Camden did not even make it across the hedge until early January 1962. With similar low-profile assistance from Viola Liddell, and Kennedy, too, socialist-activist-anthropologist Olive Stone returned to Wilcox to initiate a study of how New Deal planning did and did not improve life in Gee's Bend. Bored in retirement, Emmett Kilpatrick moved "Phoenix-like" (Kilpatrick's words) to acquire the chairmanship of the Department of Literature at Presbyterian College in Clinton, South Carolina. The Erskine College board tapped Kennedy as its vice-chairman. And always the joyous receiving of new church members—Hayden Jones Gaines, Jane Sheldon Dale, Roy Bonner, and other children of long-time ARPs.[25]

Still, as the 1960s unfolded, other things were anything but good. Kilpatrick bombed at Presbyterian College. Just two months into the job he wrote Kennedy, "I am too old for this. . . . I can't see how it will end well. . . . And my eyes failing." As Thanksgiving break approached, he wrote again: "Je n'en puis plus" (I cannot go on). Officially resigned from "this ill-fated misadventure," he moved to Clearwater, Florida, to live with a nephew for a year. Then, returned to Camden, he fought futilely to save his "primal longleaf pines" from an eminent-domain strategy to build the Camden bypass. September 1968 he died—age 78. Then there was the filming foil. Apparently because of the heat and humidity in Camden, the movie people opted for a fake, air-conditioned set on the back lot of Universal Studios in Hollywood for the making of Harper Lee's movie, released in December 1962. Too, Olive Stone returned to UCLA to write her "sequel to Gee's Bend"—but did not; when she died, the bulk of her notes found the same fate as Kennedy's Red Cross records and Hero's interviews. And Ren's daughter Margaret's husband, Wilbur, went off to the abyss of Vietnam as a Marine Corps aviator.[26]

Of course, these local and family issues of good and bad paled beside others of the era. Despite initial optimism by people wanting change, the renewed and revised New Deal—what JFK called "The New Frontier"—never made it to completion. Two weeks beyond his inauguration, the civil rights movement saw nine Black students in North Carolina going to jail for protesting restaurant segregation. At the same time the horribly botched Bay of Pigs invasion went down.

Every now and then problems abated. Right out of the FDR playbook, the food-stamp initiative, urban renewal, and the Peace Corps came into being. Then, way beyond any FDR imagination, Alan Shepard accomplished a suborbital space flight, followed by JFK's dramatic announcement about reaching the moon. Still, on entering the White House, JFK showed neither strong personal commitment to civil rights legislation nor an initial willingness to push the racial agenda on conservative southerners in Congress for fear of losing their support on other issues, just like FDR. Yet the young president evolved—fast. Beginning in late May 1961, Freedom Riders and Black voting protesters encountered brutal violence. In response the administration began shifting to a pro–civil rights stance. But simultaneously, as the spring of 1961 gave way to summer and fall, President Kennedy found himself out-strategized by the USSR in the further partitioning of Germany, ultimately seeing erection of the Berlin Wall. A tumultuous time . . . and far more to come.[27]

Throughout all this, Ren Kennedy stuck with Jack Kennedy. His loyalty inadvertently assumed an added, deeply personal tone in August 1961, thanks chiefly to one James Bonner of Camden, Alabama. That month, Ren's old friend Mort Rubin returned to Camden. He had maintained a lively correspondence with four or five Wilcox families and in 1953 stopped by Oak Hill for supper with Joyce and Bill Jones. But in late July 1961 he returned for serious research. How much transformation had occurred in Wilcox County since the late 1940s? Since the Supreme Court ordered desegregation? Those were his questions.

In one sense much change had occurred. In the late 1940s, Rubin made close friends, never felt vulnerable, and accomplished a great deal. This time banker-turned-insurance salesman Bonner and a few other white Wilcoxons offered something different. Rubin moved into his old digs—the apartment at the home of Rubye McWilliams. Then he went downtown to the barbershop to start his interviews. There, James Bonner began to harangue him for being a Freedom Rider, communist, and general troublemaker. Ren Kennedy had chatted briefly with Rubin after he settled at the apartment. But Kennedy was due back right away in Troy. They made plans for a good catch-up conversation on Wednesday, August 16—when Kennedy thought he could be back in Camden with considerable time to devote to his friend.

As that date approached, however, Troy State College president Stewart had Kennedy in urgently scheduled meetings to build a stronger AEA lobby for the next legislative session. So Kennedy had to cancel plans for departing Troy that Wednesday. Meanwhile, the Boston scholar's work moved on beyond the barbershop to still more difficulty. Rubin described these problems in the revised edition (1961) of *Plantation County*. He gave more detail in a 1984 interview in Boston. And Kennedy and Bill Jones later filled in some gaps.

In essence, Rubin received repeated physical threats in Camden. James Bonner called on state senator Roland Cooper—in town managing his car dealership—asking to have state troopers arrest him. "Is that not what you do with a known communist?" Bonner asked Cooper. The senator instantly called over to the State Department of Public Safety in Montgomery. At Cooper's request, director Floyd Mann checked his list of Alabama's "known communists," and reported back that Rubin had not made the list. In fact, anticipating some "stress" in his research, in advance of his visit Rubin had written Mann of his plans and advised that he was a World War II veteran as well as a member of the Army Reserve in Massachusetts. To Mann, he emphasized he was "not a Freedom Rider." It remains unclear if Mann told Cooper this—or if he reminded Cooper that state troopers normally were not sent into cities with local police forces. But Mann clearly told Cooper that Rubin was no communist.

Still, bolstered by Fred Henderson and Pine Apple bank president Byron Hale, Bonner and several others would not let up on Rubin. So on his second day in town Rubin borrowed a car "through Rubye McWilliams" and drove to Montgomery for further communication with Mann. "I wanted someone in authority to tell these people to leave me alone so I could work," Rubin recalled in 1984. In Montgomery, Mann advised him to be cautious. Clearly, to some locals he was "a communist Freedom Rider." Yet nobody had broken the law. Whether he told Rubin that Camden police and the Wilcox sheriff had key jurisdiction also remains unclear.

That night Rubin returned to Camden. The next day he kept on with interviews, and the next day, too. "Heckling and impolite gestures" increased. Earlier in the week Sheriff "Lummie" Jenkins was out of town; that was why Bonner went to Cooper. On the sheriff's return the day after Rubin's

Montgomery visit, Bonner tried again on Rubin's arrest, this time approaching the sheriff. But the arrest never occurred. Rubin never knew if that was because Jenkins truly had no "cause," or for some other reason, perhaps some communication between Mann and Jenkins.

If pleased not to be "in the vulnerable place of the Wilcox jail," Rubin continued to receive "public unpleasantness . . . escalating unpleasantness." Finally, on Friday morning, August 18, Bill Jones navigated his old friend into the safety of the superintendent's office, adjacent to the courthouse. They concluded that Rubin was "in serious danger of being beat up or worse." On the superintendent's call for assistance, Kennedy canceled his last meeting and departed Troy around 2:00 p.m. Rubin stayed put. Two hours later Kennedy joined them in Jones's office.

The scene was ripe for violence—not the fake violence that might have been recorded on film at that very time and location if the "Hollywood types" had opted for Camden. But real-life violence. And in that context, it is important to remember that, if not W. J. Jones, Kennedy himself was a physically active man. In college he had played halfback on the Erskine football team—offense and defense. In the war he completed all basic training, including the noted "ten-mile hike with a forty-pound backpack," and unlike some officers, he had carried his own seventy pounds of gear as the 102nd disembarked at Utah Beach. Up through his early fifties he could spurt across the outfield to snag a fly ball. And in the summer of 1961, at age sixty, to be ready for fall fires he still split green oak logs with a double-faced axe. Yet ever since Princeton he also was a pacifist and indeed one opposed to "killing"— not just people, even squirrels. The chaplaincy role in the war had permitted him to confront racial fascism and still be true to this personal creed. Would this physically strong, well-coordinated pacifist still be that way in downtown Camden in August 1961? Would he follow in the antebellum footsteps of abolitionist John Brown, resorting to violence to advance his cause regardless of consequences to himself? Or in the equally historic Gandhian footsteps of Martin Luther King Jr., pushing forward nonviolently, again, regardless of consequences to himself? What would he do if Rubin's attackers invaded the superintendent's office?

To this day that question remains open. From Bill Jones's office, Kennedy telephoned Roland Cooper in Montgomery and asked for a state trooper to transport Rubin to the Montgomery bus station. Several hours passed, and no trooper appeared. Cooper maintained he had made the call, which both Kennedy and Jones always doubted. Months earlier, after communication with US Attorney General Robert Kennedy over violence in Birmingham and Montgomery, Floyd Mann demonstrated clear sensitivity to the vulnerability of Freedom Riders or those suspected of being such. In view of this, plus Mann's earlier contact with Rubin, it is plausible that at this stage Mann would have waived the protocol regarding local law enforcement and at least sent a state trooper to help, if Cooper had called. At any rate, after two hours and with "four or five men pacing around out front of the office," Kennedy and Jones "walked out the front door straight through the crowd" and placed Rubin "into the back seat of [Jones's] car." Five minutes later they delivered Rubin down Clifton Road to the Rubye McWilliams home.

That night, at Kennedy's renewed request, Cooper said he called for a state trooper to pick up Rubin on Saturday. But, again, no trooper. Despite a seemingly peaceful scene out front of the McWilliams residence, just before noon on Sunday morning—he was not scheduled to preach—Kennedy telephoned Cooper yet again. No trooper. Finally, on Monday, August 21, about 9:00 a.m., with Kennedy having sat out front of the McWilliams home all Sunday night in his own car, a state trooper pulled up. Kennedy instructed him to take Rubin wherever he wanted to go. As it turned out, this was to "a Jewish family he [Kennedy] knew" in Selma. Tricky business, for Selma Jews were anything but uniformly pro–civil rights. Far later neither Kennedy nor Rubin could recall the family's name. But both were clear on one thing. It was not noted Selma segregationist Sol Tepper. At any rate, after quietly overnighting in Selma, Rubin began making his way home to Boston.

Back in his Troy apartment that night of August 21, Kennedy unloaded on the diary with one potent assertion: "The Rubin incident is an obscene blasphemy." *Blasphemy*: for Kennedy—the Full Christian—that meant a direct affront to what Jesus said in the Sermon on the Mount, "All things whatsoever ye would that men should do to you, do you even so to them," a core tenet for real Christians often paraphrased as, "Do unto others as you would have them do unto you."

At any rate, Kennedy's anger gradually subsided. Although "the Rubin incident" always underscored for this Social Gospel Christian the virtue in JFK's increasing support of civil rights, a month after Rubin's departure, Kennedy wrote his brothers and sisters this analysis: "I think [JFK] has done a pretty good job so far, considering the fact some of the problems he faces seem to have no solutions." While he stuck with JFK, the encouragement he felt about social progress right after the election now had cracked. By October 15, he would preach from Job 3 on how "no solutions" to problems of "needed change" often generated an attitude Jesus considered "not forgiving" and contrary to Christianity– more a sermon to himself, no doubt, than to those out front.[28]

And the cracking continued. As Rubin returned to Boston, Black voter registration encountered white violence all across the South. On television JFK announced he wanted Congress to pass a law desegregating hotels and restaurants. Then bombs destroyed two Black churches in Georgia, and two people died in Ole Miss violence as the first Black student, James Meredith, registered. Shortly, the third world war almost started over the Cuban missile crisis. And the president used his executive authority to ban racial discrimination in federal housing projects. Much change. And southern white congressmen finally knew, for sure, that the current occupant of the White House was a "turncoat." Again, for Ren Kennedy, the hopes of late 1960 and early 1961 seemed to be exploding just as rapidly as they formed.

On May 10, 1962, in writing his brothers and sisters about the continued Black boycott over voting rights in Tuskegee, he still mustered support. But he was so unsure. "The bitter battle has been going on to get all qualified Negro voters registered to vote. And some day that will happen. . . . [However] in Wilcox and Lowndes counties no Negroes vote."

Likewise, an invitation from the Troy history faculty, in July 1962, returned Bell Wiley to the Troy campus for another update on "The Changing South." In his own words, here is Kennedy's 1984 recollection of what Wiley said, remarkably close to passages in Wiley's speech files and notably close to Wiley's posthumously published essay, "American History and Racial Understanding."

> Full de-segregation needs to occur across the South . . . the process should not include admitting Negroes to all-white high schools or universities until Negroes have the appropriate background to succeed. . . . It is the moral and legal responsibility of whites to provide the quality of public education needed for Negroes to have a chance to catch up because whites capriciously put them in the spot they currently are in; if this is not done, but desegregation proceeds . . . in many places public classroom life will founder and whites will turn to private schools, which means the most crucial foundation of American growth, public education, will not be working in many places of the nation. Then all lose.

And from the perspective of 1984, what did Kennedy think of Wiley's predictions? "Very good but nothing I did not know." Of course, history is still trying to sort out the relative wisdom of Wiley's approach.[29]

As the southern white backlash against JFK expanded, Wilcox's Kennedy stayed steadfast with his FDR soulmate in the White House. On Sunday, November 18, needing to deposit some checks when the bank opened the next day, Kennedy postponed departure from Camden until late Monday morning. At 9:00 a.m. that Monday in the Bank of Camden he approached a teller, "Mrs. Perry." "She says she wishes she could change my name—a political [anti-JFK] joke. I hold my tongue. But I should have slapped her in the face." It was the same feeling on December 17, 1962—if from a positive angle. He joined Mrs. Carter for JFK's extensive televised review of his first two years in office. Kennedy's appraisal: "Excellent."[30]

Then came 1963. George Wallace finally moved into the governor's mansion, with his "segregation now, segregation forever" inaugural speech forecasting one horrible year. Martin Luther King Jr. shrewdly moved his demonstrations into Birmingham—where he knew his nonviolent tactics could result in a fight, television cameras whirring. Arrested, he produced the famous "Letter from Birmingham Jail." His subsequent "Youth March" caused a rollback of some of Birmingham's historic segregation code, but not without trouble from Bull Connor and the police dogs. A subsequent desegregation demonstration at Florida State University, in Tallahassee, led to use of tear gas and more than two hundred arrests.

All of which led up to June 11, 1963. On this date, in Tuscaloosa, Governor Wallace of course did his "Stand in the School House Door." Then, as previously orchestrated by him and Robert Kennedy, he moved aside for Black students to register at the University of Alabama. That night, with Deputy Attorney General Nicholas Katzenbach still in Tuscaloosa, JFK went on national television. He affirmed his commitment to public higher education desegregation and indeed upped the agenda by asking Congress to pass a bill desegregating not just public education but also public accommodations—restaurants and hotels.

The next day Reverend King could not believe what JFK had done. Southern white congressmen could not either and prepared to filibuster JFK's bill into oblivion. Down in Mississippi whites murdered Black civil rights worker Medgar Evers. And protests continued across the Black Belt South—involving much of Wilcox—as Black and white civil rights activists pushed hard on Black voter registration. June 1963 was cataclysmic.[31]

And the whole thing—from January through June 1963—put Ren Kennedy in a tailspin. Here was a historic seven-month period in American history. Yet his normally compulsive private writings covered little of it. And what they did address came off as short and vacillating. On Wallace's infamous January 14, 1963, inauguration speech, Kennedy wrote his siblings: "a rabid segregationist speech" followed by the hopeful "[Wallace] has had a lot of pressure to go slow on segregation extremism, and he probably will." On April 3, again to his siblings, came a reaffirmation of contemporary Democratic liberalism: "[I am raising my grandchildren to be] 100% Franklin D. Roosevelt, Harry Truman, and John F. Kennedy Democrats." Then, on June 11, 1963, after Bull Connor's police dogs, King's "Letter from Birmingham Jail," and Wallace's "Stand in the School House Door," he returned to his backhanded sarcasm with his siblings: Wallace is "brave." That was it. He had hunkered down . . . silent, even to the diary. If he still was loyal to JFK and civil rights, there were so many chances, and so many failures.[32]

Then arrived August 28, 1963. Southern whites in Congress had JFK's civil rights bill tied up in filibuster. Reverend King offered his unsolicited assistance in getting it through with a massive desegregation demonstration on the mall in Washington, DC. Some 250,000 US citizens, Black and white, heard his dramatic "I Have a Dream" challenge. It was a call for change, not later but "now."

That day JFK's actual timidity in politics guided him away from the mall and toward a small black-and-white television in the White House. This alone thrilled the president—the would-have-been historian privately marveling at an iconic moment in Western culture. One witness maintains the president's "knuckles turned white" on the banister he gripped while watching King talk. Afterward, on a spontaneous decision, he hosted King and his lieutenants in a White House reception as a powerful expression of presidential appreciation—and, far more important—of presidential engagement. Beyond the abstract and the intellectual, JFK's *emotional* commitment to civil rights, and Robert F. Kennedy's too, now seemed real.

And the other Kennedy down in Alabama responded. Although long before 1963 Ren Kennedy had evolved beyond the Victorianism of his youth, through much of his pre–World War II adulthood he remained sufficiently "post-Victorian"—not fully "Modern"—to have visceral reactions, some indeed torturous, to the chaos inherently accompanying major change, personal as well as societal. Yet for the most part he apparently had learned to "manage" these reactions by writing. As it has been for legions down through history, writing—or something else creative—was his "therapy" for getting through troubled times. Still, by the early 1960s he wrote mainly press releases and business correspondence, rarely the searching fiction or essays that had eased his earlier angst. So, with the horrors of 1963 in his face, this "post-Victorian" seems to have turned inward, clamming up even unto himself, perhaps an unavoidable transitory step before returning *either* to an outwardly missionary idealism *or* to an inwardly cynical pragmatism. More to the point, he likely was in this clammed-up limbo when in August it happened. Whether it was King's March on Washington and the heralded speech, or JFK's enthusiastic response, or both, right afterward it happened. He shifted.

Much like John Kennedy himself, Ren Kennedy began to embrace the more radical goals of King's civil rights revolution. The diary, August 28: "Spent eight hours [in Troy Student Center] watching t.v.—the Negro civil rights march in Washington, D.C. Very Impressive." The diary, September 2:

"[In Camden] watch three-hour television show on civil rights story. Very good." Letter to siblings, October 21, just a month after National Guardsmen desegregated Birmingham City Schools and Klansmen blew up four young girls in Birmingham's Sixteenth Street Baptist Church: "There must be a united front to return John and Bobby to Washington for another term." To him, the Kennedys represented sophisticated, assertive, peaceful steps to confront the racial fascism of America's home front—bold action grounded in Full Christian ideals, indeed an explicit assertion of all Jesus represented.[33]

Despite persistent white resistance to the civil rights revolution, JFK's momentum continued to grow with the peaceful solution to the Cuban missile crisis, the Partial Test Ban Treaty, and a large-scale "War on Poverty." The president's reelection campaign moved into high gear. In Ren Kennedy's view, the attack on domestic fascism was moving full speed ahead. But, of course, then came November 22, 1963, when Lee Harvey Oswald assassinated the president at a Dallas campaign event.

Though stunned, Ren Kennedy remained reflective. During the war he had cradled the body of a child assaulted by a hand grenade, said a prayer over a pilot whose parts came to him in a bucket, touched Dachau lampshades made of the skins of Jews. In Wilcox he regularly had heard church bells ring in the Negro section after another lashing, and he had witnessed fellow citizens kick the corpse of a lynched man. To this preacher-writer-academic-politician, violent evil was nothing new.

Still, the Dallas assassination deeply saddened him. The diary, midnight, November 22, 1963: "After [lunch] I returned to office . . . Mrs. [?] Hanson tells me President Kennedy has been shot. I turn on radio. He was shot by an assassin in Dallas, Texas, at 12:30. Died 1:00 pm. . . . Radio reports all afternoon. I listen in office. [Then] I listen to car radio all the way to Oak Hill re. murder of John Kennedy. A fine man. No. 1 Citizen of the World. Able, brilliant . . . a leader."

That Friday night back in Camden he imbibed no slugs, a most uncommon thing. The next morning, after talking on the phone with Frank Stewart about a Troy memorial service for JFK, he did what most Americans did. He stared at the television. Around 3:00 p.m. he walked uptown; it was Saturday, and many would be milling around the courthouse, and he might be needed. He was not. The first small group he bumped into was "white men I knew—and all I heard was happiness over the death of the nigger lov'n' Catholic. Same should've happened to Al [Smith] in '28." For sure, Wilcox also had white people, not to mention Black, utterly distraught by JFK's death. But that is what he encountered that day at that place. Quickly he walked back home to the comforting television tones of Chet Huntley and David Brinkley.

Back in Troy late Sunday afternoon at Mrs. Carter's, he returned to the television and the breaking news about Jack Ruby's shooting Oswald. Then at 9:30 a.m. Monday some 750 of the Troy State and surrounding community attended the JFK memorial assembly with Ren Kennedy at the podium.

> God, we commend unto Thy mercy his family in their great sorrow, and especially the two little children bereft of a father and the gentle woman who is his widow. Give them Thy comfort and peace and sustain them in their great sorrow. . . . We also pray for those few persons who rejoice in his death. Have mercy upon their souls and remove their hatred from them. . . . We thank Thee for the life and services of Thy servant [John F. Kennedy] who was so foully murdered. May the giving of his life to his country not be in vain. . . . Help our nation in this time of crisis and change. May that which has happened bring our people a new dedication to our historic principles of freedom and religious faith and moral integrity and decency.[34]

This never left him. November 26: "Kennedy's death and funeral—the saddest thing I have ever known," words heretofore reserved for Sam McNeill's horribly violent death in the war. For his Christmas sermon—given at Marion Junction on December 8 and three weeks later at Camden and Oak Hill—he tried hard to convince himself of a Christmas spirit: "If we listen carefully we may be able to hear above the scream of the jets and the roar of the rockets and the murder of a president . . . : 'For unto you is born this day in the city of David a Savior, which is Christ the Lord. . . . Glory to God in the highest, and on Earth, peace, good will toward men." The same on December 11. He wrote his siblings that John Kennedy "was smart, young, vigorous . . . in the midst of all the major things."[35]

In view of the "nigger lov'n' Catholic" comment he encountered in front of the courthouse, it is understandable that Kennedy saved a notable newspaper clipping from this tragic time. Two days after JFK's assassination, Daniel (Dee) Albritton—whom Kennedy had baptized at Camden ARPC and who at that time was a doctoral candidate in physics at Georgia Tech—wrote his family about how he felt. His mother, "Miss Lena," sent the letter to the *Atlanta Constitution*, which published it on December 5. "After the first few minutes of shock and utter disbelief wore off we wept for our dead president. . . . How we hung to the smallest shred of hope that he would not die! . . . Can I say to [my son] Dannie that I have worked my utmost to eliminate the hatred that causes this and other horrible deeds. I must admit I think I have failed to speak out. . . . Perhaps in this inexplicable tragedy we find a purpose." Here was more than public grieving and sage thought and indeed Full Christianity from a unique element of Kennedy's own Black Belt ARP flock. It was much needed solace for the preacher himself. Still, unlike his relatively easy adjustment to limits of his own ascent—comprehending the ironies of Black Belt power in the Age of Wallace—it was the more catastrophic and tragic limits of John F. Kennedy's ascent against the backdrop of American history, and the harsh fact that all this was *not* "inexplicable," that gave him such torment.[36]

12

WALLACE'S TROY

JFK's assassination returned Ren Kennedy to his post-1948 mentality. Not that he rejected JFK's successor, Lyndon B. Johnson. He seemed generally supportive of LBJ's expanding the New Frontier into the Great Society. And as a Troy administrator he soon worked closely with Johnson's numerous federally funded education programs. Mustering some of his old Menckenian sarcasm, indeed, he even wrote his Republican brother Richard, an archconservative Georgia dentist who had managed to escape the World War II draft, "If we just can get [Georgia governor] Lester Maddox and George Wallace teamed up together . . . we can . . . bring in a NEW GOLDEN AGE: . . . every man a king . . . colored and white lov[ing] each other, a pension to everyone . . . and cause people to forget LBJ's imperfect Great Society." And despite a son-in-law piloting sorties across Southeast Asia as KIA numbers increased daily, he also went along with US involvement in Vietnam. South Alabama's devout Rooseveltian liberal was not among those early on to question Washington's Cold War misconceptions.

Still, from late November 1963 to the election of 1964, giving Johnson a presidential term on his own, Kennedy left no record of a single enthusiastic assertion about LBJ himself. His private thoughts, earlier so resonating with JFK enthusiasm, now addressed virtually nothing the *New York Times* and national television news profiled as Johnson's personal liberalism. The November 1963 address to Congress calling for fulfillment of Kennedy's "New Frontier" legacy; the May 1964 speech at the University of Michigan articulating the "Great Society" program; the July 1964 signing of the new Civil Rights Act; the August 1964 signing of the Economic Opportunity Act: no mention of the president himself. Only Johnson's well-publicized crudeness captured his attention. Back in 1959, still the proto–animal rights advocate, Kennedy had published an article in the *Montgomery Journal* excoriating a Troy State night watchman for "assassinating" a stray dog that had adopted the campus. Undoubtedly, this sentiment was somewhere in his brain when he told his old friend, Richebourg McWilliams, "The man from Texas who picks up his dog by his ears cannot compare to our revered Yankee from Massachusetts." Liberal or not, LBJ's hard persona paled beside that of the cultured JFK, whose speeches "were the essence of high oratory and historical profoundness." Though McWilliams heartily concurred on the LBJ-JFK comparison, he urged that Adlai Stevenson "even surpassed JFK as a public orator"—to Ren Kennedy's extended dissent.

Still, in his voting record Ren Kennedy's general affirmation of Johnson's political actions seems apparent. As the 1964 presidential election unfolded, with some whites around him increasingly interested in the Republican conservative Goldwater and far more the "unpledged Democratic electors" scheme the Alabama Democratic Party cooked up to effectively ban LBJ from the Alabama ballot, Kennedy wrote in a defiant, if futile, "electors pledged to the Democratic Party," later telling the diary: "No [Barry] Goldwater for me!" He was pleased with Johnson's landslide White House victory in November; he was pleased that Democrats expanded their majorities in the House and the Senate, permitting the federal government's continued backing of the civil rights revolution.

Yet, out of reaction to that revolution, 1964 still witnessed the massive resistance counterrevolution against Black people's rights begun by the Dixiecrats and expanded even more as white southern Democrats gradually departed the Roosevelt coalition for the Republican Party. From Alabama four "Goldwater Republicans" took seats in the House: Jack Edwards, Bill Glenn Andrews, John Buchanan, and Jim Martin. The only remaining Alabama "FDR Democrats" on the Hill were senators Lister Hill and John Sparkman, and representatives George Andrews, Armistead Selden, and Bob Jones.[1]

That ever growing counterrevolution indeed forecast Ren Kennedy's work environment in his last decade at Troy. Privately, he never again felt a liberal passion the way he had in the presidencies of FDR and, so briefly, JFK. And in public he lived as the pragmatic politico. Yet even his secret and subdued liberalism remains remarkable in view of how George Wallace and race dominated the scene.

Return to 1962. That year, despite Wallace's having used his position as a circuit court judge to stymie any number of federal initiatives to increase voting by Black people and despite his incendiary racial rhetoric, most of Alabama's public education advocates supported Wallace for governor. So did the NAACP. Stewart and Meadows were a visceral part of this effort, with Ren Kennedy helping ensure AEA donations for the cause. Wallace prevailed through a large primary field and of course in the runoff went on to defeat the more racially moderate Ryan DeGraffenried. And he got the Troy lobbyist's own vote.

This was after JFK's election yet before Ren Kennedy's transitory return to racial justice optimism in the late summer of 1963. In the early 1980s he recalled: "Once in power, I thought back then, Wallace would just do what Hugo Black did—move to a better position on race." And this would result in just what Alabama needed: a "New Deal" George Wallace. That the death of JFK, object of Wallace's intense public scorn (if at times private respect), occurred as Wallace delivered dramatically on more funds for Alabama education, including a new, multicampus two-year college system, only further complicated thoughts of those awaiting his race pivot.

Rather than making the pivot, of course, Wallace turned his attentions to challenging Lyndon Johnson for the Democratic presidential nomination by bashing Johnson's civil rights endeavors. Granted, Wallace eventually dropped out of the presidential race, and in the 1964 presidential contest Ren Kennedy voted for LBJ. But as 1965 approached, Kennedy seemed caught in an unarticulated bind: JFK was dead; LBJ was not JFK; and each day George Wallace became ever more the segregationist.

Maybe, after all, Ren Kennedy again had nowhere to go . . . except to work every day. His "distant cousin" seemed also a distant, if common, strain of Scotch-Irish: Wallace was smart, educated, and, much like Kennedy, knew well the historic voice and sensitivities of most Scotch-Irish. Yet, unlike Kennedy, he used the resultant skills to manipulate his fellow Scotch-Irishmen's fears, and those of many other American whites, to advance his own power. Indeed, despite several cute public statements denying he was a fascist-style leader, more and more each day he was. Wallace sought full control—of everything, certainly including Alabama higher education. As he soon would tell Alabama's education leaders, "If you agree to integrate your schools, there won't be enough state troopers to protect you." Two modern Scotch-Irishmen: one shrewdly fascist-oriented, openly advancing the countermovement to the civil rights revolution and helping block the type of race changes that came to Europe from also coming to America; the other, his "distant cousin," wanting exactly the opposite, yet holding a far less powerful position and, with little reason to think he could find success, working at the most subterranean and pragmatic levels.[2]

With that as a work environment, two days before the announcement of Frank Stewart's selection as Troy president, on March 21, 1961, Kennedy had picked up campus rumors that Stewart had had a mild heart attack. Stewart started in his new job, and that spring nothing more surfaced. On August 31, 1963, however, Stewart self-admitted to the Troy hospital. He complained of horrible chest pains and headaches. Kennedy drove him home on September 6. Everything seemed okay. On September 17 Stewart did not come to the office—"feeling bad." Six months later, on March 20, 1964, Stewart headed to Montgomery's Maxwell Air Force Base for a strategy session on Troy's overseas military base programs. Kennedy could not attend; he was at presbytery in Fayetteville, Tennessee. Late that Friday afternoon Stewart had a stroke. He was admitted to the base hospital.

The next morning a telephone call apprised Kennedy of the situation. By Sunday afternoon he made it to Stewart's hospital room. "Severe stroke [and brain hemorrhage]. Breathes only with a machine. Condition apparently hopeless. I am sad. Not a bright college president but a good man." On Tuesday, March 24, at 10:20 a.m. Frank Stewart died. The next day Kennedy conducted a memorial service on the campus, and the day after, a funeral in Stewart's hometown of Centre—200 miles north of Troy.

The night after the funeral he got back to the Troy apartment at 9:00 p.m. At 9:15 the State Board of Education member from Dallas County, Cecil Perdue, called to thank him for becoming acting president at Troy State College.[3]

Board member message or not, Kennedy's appointment proved at best a questionable rumor. After a day of silence from the State Department of Education, on Thursday, March 26, at Sterkx's urging, Kennedy met with him, history head Trapp, and treasurer Stabler to connive on how to have a "search" for a real university president—not one drawn from "purely local political ranks." A capable man indeed, state superintendent Austin Meadows, wanted the job. Still, because they did not see him as "an intellectual leader"—and he was not Ren Kennedy—Sterkx and company wanted Meadows blocked. Sterkx, Stabler, and Trapp divided up the State Board of Education members and started making calls. Their telephoning continued over Easter weekend, not only a "dark and devious" escapade but a seriously risky one. Kennedy the nondeclared candidate seemed anything but timid.

Meanwhile, for one reading the *New York Times* and watching the evening news, as Ren Kennedy was doing, there not only was the reality of JFK's being dead, LBJ's not being JFK, and George Wallace's not being anything close to a New South liberal. Big events kept coming. Jack Ruby went to prison for killing Lee Harvey Oswald. After a slug-match Congress passed the Civil Rights Act of 1964. The people of the United States approved the Twenty-fourth Amendment abolishing poll taxes in federal elections. George Wallace campaigned in Wisconsin for the Democratic nomination to be president of the United States, challenging LBJ. US military deaths in Vietnam moved up to around 350—but a fraction of what it would be three years later. And amid all this, regardless of further diminished Black Belt leverage, Ren Kennedy yet again pursued the possibility of public university leadership. Troy, Alabama, was aswirl.[4]

On April 9, the State Board of Education met. It could not agree on the next move at Troy. Eight days later it reconvened, naming an interim executive committee: Dean of the College George Robert Boyd, Treasurer Clay Stabler, and the Science Department head, William (Bill) T. Wilks. Superintendent Meadows did not put Kennedy on the committee because "some Board members—two Wiregrassers and a Black Belter"—had advised that they considered Kennedy a top candidate.

While Meadows also retained interest in the permanent job, his candidacy would not go far. Back in 1956, in an earlier stint as state superintendent, he had refused to cave in to White Citizens Council pressures to block the Black Nobel laureate Ralph Bunche from speaking at Alabama State University. More recently, while he had sent letters to Attorney General Robert Kennedy urging him to back off on some of the federal site visits to Alabama, he also made high-profile speeches urging the wrongness of "Freedom of Choice" as an alternative to desegregation—what Bill Terry, now a professor of education at private Athens College in northwest Alabama, was pushing for the Wallace machine. To Meadows, "Freedom of Choice" would bring an end to public education in Alabama. In fact, despite statements in 1954 and 1955 indicating support for segregated schools (which likely tracked with Folsom's shift back in that direction), Meadows recently had gone up to the point of almost saying: cooperate with federal desegregation orders. All this made him highly suspect in Wallace's eyes.

Shortly, the reality of that era prevailed. All that really mattered was what George Wallace wanted. He chaired the State Board of Education and, unlike most previous governors, at will he micromanaged the board to his political benefit. And he indeed found Meadows anathema—no obvious fealty, and no strong words, much less actions, of opposing desegregation. With Wallace's opposition confirmed, Meadows withdrew from the Troy competition. "Cousin" Kennedy could get no clear feedback on Wallace's view of him, however, and let his name stay in the "silent candidate" hat.[5]

Meanwhile, the chaotic 1960s got even more so. On Monday, May 11, 1964, Cecil Gaston beat up two white civil rights workers on the steps of the Wilcox Hotel. They were Presbyterian ministers from up East. Kennedy was devastated—"pathetic, awful." He joined Bill Jones in "working a few Camden offices," asking why local authorities refused to take legal action against Gaston. Nothing happened. Likewise, Wallace's lack of big success in Wisconsin returned him to Montgomery for soul searching. Would Wallace continue in the Democratic presidential primary?

In late June Wallace came charging back out of his corner: he would continue. As for his "shift on race," which Kennedy no longer expected, Wallace just talked more about "encroachment of federal authority"—code words for desegregation designed to make himself more palatable to perhaps a third of white America, folks who were not supportive of civil rights though many, notably nonsoutherners of the "Greatest Generation," were unwilling to say so in the open. Before Wallace's campaign team departed for the Midwest, on the morning of June 23, the governor sent one Ralph Adams for a walk-around visit to Troy State's campus. Everybody then knew; late that afternoon Senator Cooper telephoned Kennedy: "Yes, Adams has it." For Ren Kennedy the final limit on his own ascent now was clear—it was George Wallace. Yet aplomb generally would prevail. Immediately, he wrote Wallace that Troy was in good hands with the current leadership committee should Adams be needed elsewhere for a while longer.[6]

At that time Ralph Adams was a full-time law instructor and assistant dean in the Air University at Maxwell Air Force Base, with rank of lieutenant colonel in the US Air Force Reserve. He also served as paid director of Alabama's Selective Service—a 1962 Wallace appointment facilitated through the JFK administration. Still, Adams's more engaged life was as political advisor and constant companion for the would-be US president from Alabama. Native of Samson, just south of Troy, Adams graduated from Birmingham-Southern College in 1937. After a World War II stint as an Air Corps navigator in the Pacific Theater, he took his VA education money to UA's law school. In April 1946, while in law school, he ran for a seat on the Alabama Public Service Commission. That failed. But by August 1946, law school completed, he got his law school roommate—one George Wallace—to approach Wallace's great Barbour County benefactor, Gov. Chauncey Sparks, about an appointment as a judge in the Tuscaloosa County Inferior Court. This clicked. Then Wallace helped him get the more lucrative job of staff attorney—and ultimately deputy director—for the Alabama State Department of Insurance. In short, few indeed had their mobility so connected to Wallace. Even so, honing command skills of Air Force officers and processing Vietnam draftees were not exactly what Sterkx and company had in mind when they envisioned credentials of "the next university president."[7]

Despite Adams's "walk-around" Wallace remained focused on his own presidential run. He let Troy wait. It really did not matter. The Black Belt boys no longer controlled. He did. Plus, the new president of Troy traveled with him in his Midwest campaign. He could take his time going public with Adams.

Two months passed. Finally, on August 3, 1964, Wallace told the Alabama State Board of Education to send out a press release identifying Adams as Troy's new president. Immediately, Adams went on the State payroll as the $18,000 a year Troy president. It would be a "little while," however, before he got to the campus. On August 28, not having reported for his new job, Adams telephoned Ren Kennedy to explain his need for help on two little matters.

According to the diary, Kennedy did not mention his own silent candidacy in the convoluted presidential search—only that he would help.[8]

The "help" Adams needed turned out to be considerable. First, Frank Stewart's wife, Margaret, refused to move out of the new, $100,000 home that went with the Troy presidency. Back on April 24 the three-person Troy executive committee had sent her a letter indicating she had to be removed from the premises by May 31. She replied she had "no plans to move" until a successor was ready to move in. Kennedy understood: she was "either off her beam or mean—or both." (Margaret Stewart even went to court—futilely—to claim her title as president of the Alabama Genealogical Society.) And Kennedy was not at all surprised to learn from Adams what she pled to Governor Wallace: those who would evict her from the president's home were "liberals, bolder and bolder every day."

Second, Governor Wallace wanted Adams to have a doctorate. While Adams had an earned law degree, this was still some fifteen years before the UA law school, following national trends, changed the "LL.B." to "J.D." (Doctor of Jurisprudence). Grandson of a doctor and well-attuned to the authority Alabamians gave to that title, whether medical or otherwise, Wallace needed people to call his man "Doctor." Adams had been counting on UA for an honorary doctorate, "but Jeff Bennett won't do anything to help me." After all, Wallace had blocked Bennett's candidacy. At Adams's request, Kennedy wrote Wallace what Jeff Bennett told him to say: "These matters take time, as much as a year or more." But Kennedy added his own comment, "You [the Governor] may be able to make this work out sooner." And that happened. Adams's conferral of degree made it to UA's August 1965 commencement— an Honorary Doctor of Laws for one Ralph Adams.

Mrs. Stewart's eviction finally worked out, too. Two days after Adams's call, Kennedy had her under way . . . without force. The cincher was Kennedy promising to tell Adams she needed a spate of paid speaking engagements before various chapters of the John Birch Society. She wanted the money to help fund her run for John Sparkman's seat in the US Senate. She actually went on to challenge Sparkman on grounds of being "soft" on winning the war in Vietnam. Even if he had supported censure of Sen. Joe McCarthy, few in Washington could beat Sparkman's Cold Warrior voting record, and he easily survived Stewart's attack as well as those of more substantive conservatives. Indeed, just as he eased Stewart out of "Adams's house," over in Wilcox Kennedy was helping raise campaign money for Sparkman.[9]

Adams's credentials firmly (almost) in place, and Mrs. Stewart theoretically bought off and living on the family's farm back in Cherokee County, the new Troy president and his wife had moved in by the time he started work on October 1, 1964. His arrival delay, it turned out, had far less to do with the Selective Service, an honorary doctorate, and Mrs. Stewart than with his being a logistics coordinator in the Wallace presidential campaign. Kennedy fully understood: "None of this bodes well for the future," he told Bill Jones, and none of this related to what Troy State needed to be doing, "changing Alabama for the good." Still, the soon-to-be "Doctor" moved forward.

His first morning in the president's office, Adams advised Kennedy to spread the word: until the "Doctor" title actually was anointed, people should address him as "Colonel." The next day he had Kennedy send a color photo of himself and George Wallace to a framing shop in town. Reproduced "in the hundreds," they were to be spread throughout the campus—which Kennedy made happen. Next, the Colonel overruled a special faculty admissions committee and admitted to Troy a severely weak student who was son of a State Board of Education member who was also a big Wallace supporter. Finally, President Adams confided to Kennedy that he could get him the rank of "Honorary Colonel" with the Alabama State Troopers. Politely, Kennedy declined. On Friday afternoon, five workdays into Adams's presidency, down at the Conecuh River beer joint historian Sterkx brought down the house: "Lenin is not dead after all!" Little did they know. Of course, October 1964 also saw Wallace back in Montgomery. With LBJ's moving on to a landslide victory over Goldwater, this meant that Colonel Adams had at least a few years to be Troy's president—before Wallace, so encouraged by the Republican showing in the South, reignited his own presidential quest in the form of the cooked-up American Independent Party.

Despite that bizarre first week, actually, Kennedy soon found encouraging signs in Adams's presidency. Adams formed faculty committees to strategize for expanded arts and sciences programs at TSC—and acted on many of them. He also used his military contacts in growing TSC off-campus programs. To the Fort Rucker programs begun in 1951 (to become TSC/Dothan), he added joint endeavors with Montgomery's Maxwell Air Force Base, which by 1965 morphed into TSC/Montgomery—a new campus welcoming military and nonmilitary alike. With Governor Wallace's power wand, indeed, by 1967 Adams would have TSC removed from the purview of the State Department of Education and given its own autonomous board, unsurprisingly staffed with a strong contingent of Wallace backers. Even on the desegregation front per se, though Kennedy found Adams deeply conservative, the new president also could be forcefully pragmatic. First, some context.[10]

In spring 1957 a young Black man from a sharecropping family on the outskirts of Troy applied for admission to TSC. He received no response. A precocious acolyte of Martin Luther King Jr., the student considered Troy's response a turndown. At King's encouragement he strongly considered filing suit, though in the end he decided not to, fearful of reprisals against his family. That student was the future civil rights icon and Georgia congressman John Lewis. Kennedy's papers reveal nothing about Lewis's application. Two years later, in April 1959, a month before President Smith retired, campus rumors told of a Black student being admitted to TSC for the following fall. As director of student recruitment—but not admissions—Kennedy had no firsthand knowledge of "the event." But he soon discovered it to be a case of a Black student writing a letter of inquiry about admission. Under orders from Governor Patterson, Dean Boyd sent the student a polite advisement of the availability of his desired program at all-Black Alabama State College in nearby Montgomery. Then, in June 1960, a young Black woman walked into the Troy registrar's office. At the time Kennedy was acting director of admissions. A clerk in the registrar's office telephoned Kennedy asking how to handle the matter. He was on the phone. By the time he called her back three minutes later, the Black woman had explained she was looking for the Pike County Teacher's Credit Union, temporarily housed on Troy's campus.

Yet TSC had early desegregation on an ancillary front. President Harry Truman's executive order desegregating the US Armed Forces had Montgomery's Maxwell Air Force Base and related US government military enterprises in Montgomery racially mixed by the late 1940s. So, in January 1965, when Troy State signed a contract with the US Department of Defense, cementing plans for joint Troy-Maxwell programs, desegregation at Maxwell was long a *fait accompli*. Not that it sat well with many Montgomery white people, but a few of Maxwell's Black airmen even had supported Rosa Parks and the 1955 bus boycott.[11]

Now to Troy's main campus in the mid-1960s. For matters not carefully monitored by the Southern Association of Colleges and Schools and persistently inquiring journalists, Governor Wallace sought to employ demagogic micromanagement of public higher education in Alabama. He was never as successful as he wanted. According to Frank M. Johnson Jr., then judge of the US Fifth Circuit Court of Appeals, and who ultimately prevailed in curtailing some of Wallace's legal strategies for resisting desegregation Wallace failed in strongarming Alabama's college and university presidents to sign a document providing for "control by the governor of all state-supported institutions of higher learning." Likewise, Joseph F. Volker, vice president of UA's Birmingham campus, generally protected highly sought-after medical and dental school acceptances from Wallace's regular efforts to push for admission of relatives of his big supporters. And UA's Frank Rose, who helped defeat Wallace's route of university autonomy, played the governor as hard as Wallace played him, even on desegregation. Still, in the mid-1960s Alabama's teacher education institutions could be putty in Wallace's hands because of their being part of the State Department of Education, which Wallace controlled. And with his long-time crony, Ralph Adams, at Troy State, that institution (not separated from the State Department until 1967) set the pace in assisting Wallace's higher education intrusions.

Here, staff jobs were Wallace's regular grist. In February 1965, for example, he wrote Adams to place one Alice Dent—Montgomery native and daughter of Bill Hunt, a longtime close friend of Wallace—in the position of registrar on Troy's Maxwell Air Force Base campus. She already was registrar at the main campus in Troy. But, the governor explained, "She doesn't like this." The job "required [her] working two nights a week." When Adams said there was no such position at Maxwell—the registrar on the main campus served all—Wallace told him it was time for there to be a Troy registrar at Maxwell, adding, "And keep this confidential." The same for student employment. In August 1965, he advised Adams: "My cousin, Brent Wallace, who went by to see you the other day came by my office. I want you to get him a job at the college—look after him. And let me hear from you." Then in December 1965 Wallace told Adams to award his ever loyal lieutenant governor, James B. Allen, the title of "Honorary Dean of Troy State College." According to Ren Kennedy, here was part of a multiple-front strategy Wallace had to boost Allen's press coverage in preparation for his eventual run for the US Senate seat to be vacated on the upcoming retirement of Lister Hill. Yet, as confided to the diary, Kennedy classified the move in one word: "Stupid."[12]

But such intrusion also applied to pure academics, if at times with less success. A professor with joint appointments in Speech and English, Janette Stout Rosenburg, openly lambasted Governor George Wallace in various campus settings, including faculty meetings of the English Department, of which President Adams's wife, Dorothy Kelley Adams, also was a faculty member. According to Kennedy, Rosenburg subsequently was quoted on campus as having said that "Wallace is a racist dictator," and she probably had a "strong hand" in a student petition (garnering some 680 signatures out of a student body of 2,313) sent to the state legislature calling for Adams's removal. After Wallace instructed the legislature to ignore the petition—which it did, according to Kennedy—he told Adams to get rid of Rosenburg, even though she was tenured. Bypassing Dean Boyd, Adams immediately instructed Speech Department head Wallace L. Waites to make this happen. Still, with counsel of an attorney and private lobbying by Kennedy—a great admirer of Rosenburg, Kennedy had eagerly accepted her request to preside over her marriage in 1953—the termination ultimately did not occur. Pivotal to Kennedy's lobby on Adams was that he and Wallace already were involved in other highly publicized freedom of expression cases, leading to Troy being censured by the American Association of University Professors.

The most notable of these was the Wallace administration's conflict with

Vietnam veteran and editor of Troy State's student newspaper, the *Tropolitan*, Gary Dickey. As one who shared Rosenburg's view of Wallace, and also known for running editorials comparing Wallace negatively to the more progressive Frank Rose, Dickey quickly gained a place on Wallace's hit list. Dickey was well aware of the "Adams Rule," as apparently promulgated by the governor: that nothing critical of Wallace would be published by any Troy organ. He also had been warned by the *Tropolitan*'s faculty advisor, Wallace Waites—the same department chair pivotal to the Rosenburg case—that Adams wanted Dickey to write about "hunting dogs in North Carolina instead of Governor Wallace." Sensing even more a story, Dickey proceeded to publish the front-page headline, "Lament for Dr. Rose," and beneath it over a blank space the word "censored." Immediately, Adams told people Waites was so irate with the front page that he "fired" Dickey on the spot, which Waites told Kennedy was an absolute lie. With Dickey still in the editor's position, apparently, Adams then went to Wallace and asked that the State Board of Education request him as president to expel Dickey. And indeed, that board—Wallace's board, and on the verge of separating from Troy State—gave Adams the cover of doing just that. Upon receiving his notice of expulsion, Dickey finally got his story, a strong First Amendment case. With legal counsel of Montgomery attorney Morris Dees, later founder of the Southern Poverty Law Center, Dickey ultimately prevailed in federal court as Judge Frank Johnson wrote the landmark higher education opinion: "A state cannot force a college student to forfeit his constitutionally protected right of freedom of expression as a condition to his attending a state-supported institution." Judge Johnson reinstated Gary Dickey. This *cause célèbre*, with statewide press coverage accompanied by the Troy Faculty Senate's publicly censuring Adams, took Kennedy to these private thoughts: "Campus upset and disturbed—90% of students and 95% of faculty against Adams . . . [who] feels lonesome and uncertain . . . fried real good [by Wallace] . . . yet still thinks he has the right to censure student newspaper . . . a fool." Indeed, as he wrote in his memoir, *Retrospect: An Autobiographical Reveille and Taps* (1995), Adams never stopped believing his actions in the case were legitimate and justified.[13]

In the midst of all these Wallace-control maneuvers, Kennedy understood the reality he faced regarding Troy's compliance with desegregation. Again, "Lenin is not dead." But he also had found that Adams's fealty to the governor did not preclude his being strategic with Wallace. And out of these complicated relationships Kennedy ultimately found an angle on voluntary desegregation of Troy State that both Adams and Wallace accepted.

In spring 1965 Kennedy attended several meetings in Birmingham sponsored by US Department of Health, Education and Welfare (HEW). They were focused on the immediate availability of federal student-aid money, *provided* there was institutional nondiscriminatory compliance with Title VI of the Civil Rights Act of 1964 no later than August 31, 1965. In turn, Kennedy repeatedly hammered Adams on all the federal money they were not getting because of being noncompliant—no Black students. From his Selective Service and Maxwell experiences, Adams was no novice on federal funding. He told Kennedy to apply for the federal money anyhow. As part of that process Kennedy began to identify Troy students who qualified financially for the federal aid; by May he reported to Adams he had thirty, if all white. Adams told him to submit the application. On or around June 1, Kennedy reported back that Troy's application—as expected—had gone nowhere: rejected in the first round of evaluations.

Accordingly, on June 3, 1965—no doubt according to plan—Adams wrote Wallace that Troy's remaining noncompliant with Title VI would cost the institution some $285,000 in federal student loan money. While "we could ride out this storm," Adams advised Wallace, "the [more] critical matter is the [federal] dormitory loan," also dependent on a degree of desegregation, to be acquired from the Housing and Urban Finance Agency (HUFA)—on the verge of being replaced with the Department of Housing and Urban Development. Adams did not specify the exact amount of the HUFA loan. But he nevertheless urged, "The money is critical because we need to get started on [the final application] within the next few days in order to have it [the dormitory] ready for occupancy for September, 1966."

Undoubtedly Wallace got the point. Within two weeks Adams had told Kennedy to recruit one or two Black students, with their studies to commence in the second summer session of 1965. He did, and the students enrolled as planned. In early July Kennedy advised Adams that Troy's resubmitted application for federal student assistance was accepted—not thirty, as originally planned, but sixty-eight students immediately would have work-study jobs. Carefully, Kennedy kept from Adams that he had arranged for Jeff Bennett to contact Frank Rose about telephoning a good friend high in HEW ranks with a sympathetic word about Kennedy's difficult situation and the need for Troy's application to find approval as a path to immediate desegregation. According to Kennedy, Rose made the call. How George Wallace would have reacted to news of Frank Rose apparently helping desegregate Troy State is not hard to fathom. By mid-July Kennedy also told Adams that he had captured National Defense Education Act (NDEA) funds for forty more Troy students.

Kennedy's remarks before an Erskine College board meeting help confirm the timing of these developments. On July 29, 1965, to that board Kennedy referenced "over a quarter of a million dollars in federal student aid for which we [Troy State College] have been approved." So, it appears that

Troy's signing the compliance forms and beginning to admit Black students occurred in the first two weeks of July 1965. Still, Troy's 1965-66 academic year must have included no more than a few Black students. For Kennedy's diary received big racial news in the early summer of 1966. Still serving as director of financial aid as well as director of off-campus programs, he helped bring twenty-two Black in-service teachers—graduate students from south Alabama—to the TSC campus. With federal financial aid they enrolled for an on-campus graduate seminar. They lived in a dormitory and took meals with all other students in the college cafeteria, smoothly. Yet it apparently was late spring of 1967 before a Black student showed in Troy State College's student yearbook. And it was the summer of 1969 before Adams finally acquiesced to Kennedy's wanting to place in Troy recruitment literature photographs of Black and white students joining in campus life.[14]

This placed Troy's official desegregation in the middle of what happened in four-year undergraduate education at previously all-white institutions across Alabama. At the University of Alabama, of course, the first successful Black student enrollment occurred in June 1963. Other public campuses gradually followed: for fall term 1963 the barrier came down at Florence State College and at UA extension centers in Birmingham and Huntsville. That same fall in Mobile the UA extension center formally became the unsegregated University of South Alabama. In January 1964 Auburn University desegregated. Jacksonville State College made the change for fall term 1965, Livingston State College for fall term 1966. Though signed off as "compliant" in 1967, Alabama College (to be the University of Montevallo) enrolled its first Black student in September 1968.

As for baccalaureate-level private institutions, in 1954—just before issuance of *Brown*—desegregation came to the Jesuits' Springhill College in Mobile. But Alabama's other private colleges awaited the cover of the large public institutions. Finally, in September 1965 the change came to the Methodists' Birmingham-Southern College, Athens College, and Huntingdon College. Two years later the Baptists' Samford University (previously Howard College) and Mobile College (now the University of Mobile) technically desegregated. It took until September 1968 for the Baptists' female-only institution, Judson College, to desegregate. Over in Due West, South Carolina, Erskine College's desegregation followed the same 1965 timeline as Birmingham-Southern College and Furman and Vanderbilt universities. But Erskine College had its own special Kennedy drama, which sheds further light on the Troy story.[15]

With Erskine, Kennedy found himself in an especially awkward situation created by the ARPs' bedrock reverence for individual congregational autonomy. Right after passage of the Civil Rights Act of 1964, Kennedy used a sermon before all three of his congregations—Marion Junction, Camden, Oak Hill—to explain that the law certainly could not force desegregation of private religious denominations such as the ARP Synod or its congregations, nor could it force desegregation of Erskine College and Seminary. But he emphasized that some ARPs indeed were bothered by "racial discrimination in God's house." For example, the Ora, South Carolina, church where he was baptized, now welcomed Black worshipers to services. Even if many ARPs were not worried about such discrimination, however, the point remained that "Erskine's faculty recruitment and access to federal funds would be severely damaged by non-compliance." He concluded by reading excerpts from two recent articles: one, in the *Christian Century*, reported progress the PCUS was making with desegregation; the other, of his own authorship and entitled "The Church Looks at Itself," appearing in the *ARP*, predicted a highly questionable future for ARP congregations as well as Erskine College if ARPs failed to engage modern life.

All to no avail. Shortly, the Oak Hill, Camden, and Marion Junction ARP congregations passed resolutions opposing Erskine's compliance with the act and promised to take up the slack with increased individual giving to Due West operations. Privately, Kennedy saw these resolutions as "useless." They were not going to change the course of history. Nor, based on a notoriously laggard giving record—excepting a few congregants—would his people write more or bigger checks. Since before World War II, Erskine's fundraising campaigns had often resulted in Kennedy making "quota" by paying for at least half of their "due" with a Camden bank loan, which he personally paid off over time. Indeed, so low were his expectations for giving—for anything, even to the Sunday-morning collection plates—that he recently had drafted a pithy Yaupon piece, no doubt intended for a "comments" section of the *Christian Century*, including these Menckenian lines: "[Because] the minister forgot to take the offering, at the end of the service one of the deacons confronted him—'We can't operate this way; we got to have collections.' On Monday the minister gave the deacon $20 to make up for missing the collection, to which the deacon said: 'Let's not take up anymore collections. You just bring us the $20 every Monday morning. We come out ahead that way.'"

But their adamancy would not let up. Bill Jones somehow wound up an elected Bethel ARPC delegate to synod. Point-blank he told the Oak Hill congregation that he would support desegregation compliance at Erskine College regardless of how his brethren felt. Shortly, another vote saw his cousins politely replace him with a noncompliance representative. Polite or not, Kennedy noted, it "put Bill in a mental state."

On May 31, Kennedy wrote "J. C. Harper, R. F. Lane, and Jno. T. Moore"— of Oak Hill, Camden, and Marion Junction congregations, respectively, and all of whom he suspected of having applied for and regularly received federal aid out of the extended version of New Deal agriculture subsidies—saying, "I am against [your] position on refusing Fed aid to Erskine." To the diary he described this communication as "a good gutsy letter." He then went off to the June 1965 ARP Synod at Bonclarken, bound by ARP policy to "vote" according to the ("useless") position of the congregational resolutions. As he had done so often since the war, he stayed not at the standard ministers' quarters at Bonclarken, but "off campus" at nearby Johnson's Motor Lodge. Here, he mixed bourbon highballs for his few imbibing ARP colleagues. When word got to him that a particular conservative lambasted him behind his back for being a "whiskey-drinking liberal," he confronted the person with the same upbeat tone he used on his prohibitionist sisters: "In the Bible, while there are warnings about drunkenness, it also is true that alcohol was drunk from Genesis to Revelations, and Jesus Himself provided wine for that festive occasion . . . in Gallilee. . . . It is a matter of perspective."

Though he voted the way his congregations instructed, Kennedy spoke assertively about the advantages of compliance as he had experienced them at Troy. And by a vote of 130 to 80, the ARP Synod ultimately approved a report favoring compliance at the college and seminary. Synod also encouraged individual congregations to accept God's house as a place to practice the equality of humanity. Still, it left final decisions about welcoming Black people into ARP church services as something to be determined by individual ARP congregations.[16]

In response to these synod developments, in early July Kennedy's three congregations jointly authorized expenditures of "up to $100" to be used in mailing and travel expenses necessary to help defeat "compliance" at the upcoming Erskine board meeting. At that July 29, 1965, meeting, Kennedy had the high-profile role of vice chair of the board as well head of the board search committee to select a new president of Erskine College and Seminary. Once again—true to his congregations' mandates—he cast a noncompliance vote after speaking strongly for compliance. Adamantly, he highlighted not just the way Troy's federal funding had increased with compliance, but profiled a procompliance resolution signed by a majority of Erskine College and Seminary faculty. In the end, procompliance board members prevailed, 24–10. Shortly, Erskine College and Seminary desegregated under the leadership of the president whom Kennedy's committee had recommended: Joseph Wightman, a British infantry officer in World War II who completed a history doctorate at the University of South Carolina before working up through the ranks to the post of academic dean at Erskine.[17]

Typical of his general postwar distance, the big exception being his late-developing JFK enthusiasm, Kennedy digested both Troy and Erskine desegregation the same way he continued to react to civil rights sorrows in Wilcox and Dallas counties: emotionally distanced and with little hope. "Ironic business," he told the diary. "I don't worry much about these matters," he wrote his siblings in April 1965. "Eventually, Negroes will get the laws for what they want . . . and it is time . . . [but] it will be far longer for them to get real acceptance [by white people]." Indeed, some thirteen months later, after desegregation of Troy State permitted acquisition of significant federal funds for the institution, facilitating continued erection of new buildings and "College Drive" being renamed "George Wallace Drive," Wallace had the legislature pass a resolution condemning and rejecting the original HEW desegregation guidelines necessary for public schools to acquire federal funds as an unconstitutional intrusion into Alabama life. After having sat in the gallery for the whole charade, the night afterward Kennedy distilled what he had witnessed. He knew Wallace understood the coded racial buttons to push to keep demagogic control over Alabama. But he did not scream out. Analytically, he just noted, "Except for Wallace control, the resolution accomplishes nothing."

The same tone characterized his comment—or lack thereof—on other developments of the mid-to-late 1960s. As 1964 gave way to 1965, and Congress began debate on what would become by August 1965 the Voting Rights Act, Reverend King sought to encourage Congress to get this right, at last, by orchestrating voting rights demonstrations throughout the South. Although Birmingham was the strategically targeted place for demonstrations leading to desegregation of public accommodations in the Civil Rights Act of 1964, in King's plan key Alabama Black Belt counties were the right places for whirring television news cameras in the voting rights campaign. Lowndes and Wilcox counties had not one Black voter. Moreover, Dallas County offered the strong-willed sheriff Jim Clark, who—more than Wilcox's cagey "Lummie" Jenkins—could be counted on to resist with force, playing the sucker role Bull Connor had delivered in Birmingham.

Still, Kennedy stayed hunkered down. For the February and March 1965 demonstrations in Camden, he made the flat diary note: "Negro demonstrations in Camden." On March 7, 1965, when horrible "Bloody Sunday" unfolded on Selma's Edmund Pettus Bridge, he offered the terse comment, "Race riots . . . expected blasphemy." On March 25, 1965, when Klansmen murdered white civil rights activist Viola Liuzzo, on the Selma-Montgomery highway, no comment. On April 16, 1965, when the *Alabama Journal* reported that over the last several days "twelve Wilcox Negroes" had been registered to vote, he rendered nothing. The same silence prevailed after Phillip Winters and many other Wilcoxons lost substantial funds—and Bill Jones half his already scant retirement money—in the January 1967 failure of the Bank of

Pine Apple. These losses, one would think, might have recatalyzed old worries about Wilcox "behavior." Bank president Byron Hale—among those so adamantly opposed to Mort Rubin's return—stole much of the bank's assets in a sordid case involving longtime feuds, cooking the books on stock sales, fabricating loans to Black people who could neither read nor write, indeed hiding money beneath a "hog parlor." But Kennedy seemed little affected. Perhaps the most stunning sign of his cocooned life came from a dramatic racial showdown in front of Camden Academy where Bill Jones was at center stage.[18]

Actually, considering the times, the Camden Academy incident evolved out of relative calm. On Saturday, April 17, Kennedy, home from Troy for the weekend, agreed to join Jones in a meeting with three white Presbyterian ministers. They were "not from Alabama," and Jones understood they were encouraging Black high school students of Camden Academy to participate in voter registration demonstrations. To these three, notably including a Californian seminarian, John Golden, the superintendent, explained that for more than decade he knew his county had skirted compliance with school desegregation and for far longer the registration of Black people for voting. He said that he personally favored compliance with federal law on both issues. Even so, he continued, Alabama State Department of Education regulations required all students to attend classes a specified number of days a year. For this reason, seniors who missed many class days out of participating in protest marches would find themselves unable to graduate. Then both Kennedy and Jones urged the ministers to encourage student demonstrations only after school hours and on weekends. The ministers, again, notably Golden, said they understood. That night, Kennedy recorded "reasonable, productive meeting." But, it turned out, someone failed to convince a Black civil rights activist named Ralph Eggleston, also from California, that this was the agreed-upon course.

The following Monday, April 19, with Kennedy back in Troy, Jones got word that Eggleston and others were about to lead students out of school for a march. Jones went to Camden Academy to underscore the consequences according to State Board of Education regulations. Eggleston confronted him. Things went ugly. Eggleston got up in his face, Jones later recalled, and told him the students were going to march anyhow and also boycott school, regardless of what he (Jones) said. At that point Jones slapped Eggleston, later recollecting, "I lost control—that was obviously a stupid and wrong thing to do" and "exactly what he [Eggleston] wanted me to do." That night Jones telephoned Kennedy, whose total diary note on the episode was a clinical: "Bill upset about incident at Camden Academy." Nothing more.[19]

Nothing more, ever, despite potent implications. The same Alabama school superintendent who urged compliance with *Brown v. Board of Education* and who long had wanted Black citizens to vote wound up slapping an out-of-state civil rights activist, which in turn got the superintendent what he *wanted*: compliance with *Brown v. Board of Education*. For out of this episode noted Birmingham civil rights attorney Orzell Billingsley signed on to fight the legal battle to desegregate Wilcox schools. And in 1974 the US Fifth Circuit Court of Appeals finally rendered its judgment in *U. S. v. Wilcox County Board of Education*. Full desegregation would occur immediately. But only in a legal sense did this occur. Most white students wound up in all-white private schools, poorly funded and equipped. Just as Bell Wiley predicted, nobody really won. Though Kennedy and Jones turned out to be "right"—and so badly had wanted to be "wrong"—Kennedy never again referenced the Jones slapping incident.[20]

And that is pretty much the way it continued. On August 6, when LBJ signed the Voting Rights Act putting long-awaited enforcement teeth in the Fourteenth and Fifteenth Amendments, Kennedy noted: "Long since time for Negroes to vote." On August 20, when a special deputy, Tom Coleman, gunned down white civil rights activist Jonathan Daniels at Hayneville, the Lowndes County seat forty-nine miles northeast of Camden, Kennedy left no comment. And the same for the 1965 opinion of the US Fifth Circuit Court of Appeals protecting Lonnie Brown, a Black Wilcoxon, from white reprisals over his voter registration activism. "Gruesome" was the total description he gave the continued demonstrations in Camden. He offered no commentary on Black citizens exercising their new vote when, in 1966, they almost elected Furman storekeeper Walter Calhoun as a replacement for Sheriff "Lummie" Jenkins, in a vote of 3,460–2,738. And "very good" was his total verdict for President Johnson's 1966 State of the Union address pledging even stronger support for civil rights.

When, in 1968, Wallace ran for president under the banner of a third party, the American Independent Party, it was yet again the same. Long sensitive about US military veterans wrapping themselves in patriotism while being silent about—even worse, downright supportive of—what he considered the racial fascism explicit to segregation, Kennedy might possibly have emerged from his cocoon had he known that Wallace, who had tried pulling political strings to evade military service in World War II, responded to 1968 California hecklers calling him "fascist" with such patriotic assertions as, "Hey, I was killing fascists when you were still in diapers." But that was not known at the time.

From February 2, 1968, when Adams tipped him off that Wallace indeed would charge out of his corner again and take on both parties, on through the end of the 1968 election cycle Kennedy generally stayed focused on Adams's being away from the campus helping with the campaign and "not being president." Only once did Kennedy go significantly further. With an insight partially shared by Republicans of 1968—and far more in the future—he wrote his brothers and sisters: "If Negroes and others burn down enough cities next summer [of 1968], [Wallace] may get further than you might think . . . not a good thing for the country." That did not happen. Still, Wallace had "a racket . . . he runs because he makes so much money out of it." Otherwise, Kennedy generally stayed hunkered down, especially in public. President Wightman asked him to give Erskine's 1968 baccalaureate sermon. Out of Ephesians 5:15, he preached on "Redeeming the Time"—making the most of your life because when you die, God's judgment of you will derive from the "book" your life has left. But his sermon encouraging those seniors to go forth and do "good works" on behalf of others, not just do Bible reading, made not even a veiled reference to the civil rights front. For he long since had lost his expectations that they, and others like them, actually might engage this front.[21]

And yet, just as on the battlefields of Europe, even in the darkest days there were times when he eventually reached for light. In the depth of that home-front "down," he and Bill Jones set in motion something that did not reach the public eye until much later and is little recognized even to this day. It calls for another zoom across Wilcox time.

In the 1960s, twenty miles east of Camden in Furman, there still lived one Martha Patton Simpson. Her father, recall, was the noted Snow Hill merchant and planter, Ramson Overton Simpson; her mother, Elizabeth Ann Gulley of the nearby Gulley plantation. Theirs was an Old South cotton-and-slaves wealth. Yet all through the 1920s and 1930s R. O. Simpson was known far and wide for his "liberalism." He was no advocate of desegregation. But he clearly sought a better life for Black people.

The son of one of his sharecroppers, William J. Edwards, wanted to go to Booker T. Washington's Tuskegee Institute. Simpson made modest contributions toward his going. Then on Edwards's graduation, Simpson essentially funded Edwards to work with Booker Washington to create a small replica of Tuskegee in Wilcox, to be called Snow Hill Institute. In the process Simpson became a confidant of Booker T. Washington and of national philanthropist George F. Peabody, too. Ultimately, Simpson served on the board of the Tuskegee Institute and traveled with Washington in fundraising trips to New York City. Booker T. Washington saw Simpson as rare among southern whites supportive of Black education; he appeared at ease in Manhattan's interracial social life.

After graduating from the University of Alabama as a strong Kappa Delta sorority member, Simpson's daughter, Martha Patton Simpson—who never married—picked up where her father left off. She inherited most of the family wealth, and she spent it helping people. Bill Jones grew up fascinated with Ransom Overton Simpson and his family; his second summer as a Rosenwald fellow at Columbia University, Jones wrote a research paper on Simpson family efforts at race change. In Kennedy's first several years in Wilcox he quickly absorbed why Jones so respected the Simpson family. Like her father, Martha Patton Simpson's racial liberalism was chiefly of a 1930s strain. Yet occasionally she took on projects found more often in the 1960s and beyond. Here was one of them.[22]

In May 1965 Ren Kennedy was "down" . . . but not out. Despite depression about school desegregation ever actually working, he tried a "Hail Mary"—or, one might say, a "Hail Martha." He went to Furman to visit his friend, who was by this time seventy-nine years old. He asked if she would leave her substantial fortune to the education of Wilcox children—of all colors. Maybe some way, somehow, this could help.

Many the time Martha had told Ren and Bill, "'I have no children of my own . . . but then maybe I do. Maybe all the children of Wilcox are mine.'" So, as Kennedy recalled in 1984, that May morning she answered in "the language of a true aristocrat—unassuming, straightforward, certainly no self-adorning tones or words." "Softly," as he described it, she said, "Yes, I will."

The next Sunday, heading back to Troy, Kennedy stopped at Oak Hill to give Jones the big news. At that time Jones could use some. The slapping incident had occurred just three months earlier. Because of the bleeding ulcers, plus his being two years beyond retirement age and just worn out, he had tried to retire for a year leading up to the episode. With the slap, finally, the State Board of Education agreed to quit pressuring him to stay. By late March 1965 a Monroe County educator, Guy Kelley, took over as Wilcox superintendent; he was Jones's opposite on race and exactly what Jones and Kennedy had feared back in February 1954. So as Kennedy came up on the porch that Sunday, he encountered his comrade still in the throes of deep regret about the way his career wound up. Uplifting news—Jones indeed could use some.

Kennedy advised Jones of "Martha's gift to Wilcox." The two began to sketch out "the plan." A decade earlier, Martha Simpson had written Jones, "You have shown courage and vision in promoting better educational opportunities for the Negro youth of our county, thus encouraging interracial understanding." Now, over the next six months, Jones made repeated visits to Martha Simpson and her lawyers to work out details. And two years later, on May 5, 1967, the lawyers entered the documents into her will. Martha Simpson's fortune went to "The Martha Patton Simpson Educational

Foundation." A nephew, wanting the money, launched a prolonged challenge to the document, but the will proved air-tight.[23]

Zoom forward. It is hard to say how Kennedy and Jones would have reacted if they had lived to see what happened. In the late 1980s, with the Simpson endowment having grown to the required level, the foundation began disbursing funds. All of Wilcox's young people—regardless of color, wealth, or high school attended—could receive substantial aid to attend any type of postsecondary education for which they otherwise qualified. This could be technical school, junior college, community college, four-year college, medical or law school, public or private. (It did not matter so long as the institution had appropriate accreditation.) And that led to more.

Martha's cousin Allerae Wallace (no kin to George Wallace), who lived on a plantation southeast of Snow Hill at Allenton, was taken aback by possibilities for the Simpson Foundation. When she inherited her husband's large timber and cattle holdings, she created the Wallace Foundation, doing pretty much what the Simpson Foundation did. Then another old Wilcox white family, the Farishes—the same family that provided the founding director of research at Colonial Williamsburg, the Harvard-trained Hunter Farish—did the same thing. In short, as of 2023, when all three funds are combined, there likely is no county in America with more local private monies per capita to assist residents pursuing higher education. Over four hundred of them a year get such assistance—many getting full support owing to extreme lack of family resources.

If, in one sense, Kennedy's 1965 "Hail Martha" move delivered beyond all expectations, in another it did not. The county with the stunning level of aid for higher education also remains one of the most depressed in the nation. Today it has growing tourism tied to its beautiful landscape, historic architecture, and arts and crafts (notably Gee's Bend quilts). But it lacks the jobs that can only derive from economic diversification and what might deliver that: reasonable property taxes; rational, openly developed county policies; and foremost a majority of citizens committed to electing honest county officials—stubborn negatives indeed. Most motivated and smart Wilcox high school graduates—of all colors and financial backgrounds—take the money and go away for education, never to return to work and live in the county and help change it.[24]

Back to the earlier reality. While Kennedy saw at least one ray of long-term hope in Martha Patton's gift, he glimpsed another in 1968. Back in November 1967, Minnesota's senior US senator, Eugene McCarthy, decided to challenge incumbent LBJ for the 1968 Democratic presidential nomination. With a vigorous attack on Johnson's pro–Vietnam War stance, McCarthy called for US withdrawal from the tragic quagmire of Southeast Asia.

That, plus Johnson's relatively poor showing in the New Hampshire primary, opened the door, in March 1968, for New York's new US senator, Robert F. Kennedy, to enter the presidential primary as well. Ren Kennedy responded: "Young Kennedy . . . a fine, intelligent man," all too ready to persevere with the Rooseveltian way of his older brother. When LBJ subsequently decided not to run for reelection, Ren Kennedy felt renewed optimism about RFK and America, little knowing—like the rest of the nation—what lay ahead.

On April 4, 1968, James Earl Ray assassinated Martin Luther King Jr. From several Troy television sets Kennedy followed the whole unfolding tragedy, including RFK's involvement. The day of the shooting RFK—less than five years beyond his brother's assassination—was scheduled for a campaign rally in Indianapolis. As he arrived, the predominantly Black crowd had not yet heard of King's assassination. As Frye Gaillard has written, "remarkably, in this era before the cable news/internet cycle, they did not know that King had been shot. It fell to Robert Kennedy to tell them." RFK chucked the rally speech and announced the shooting. Then he delivered to the stunned group one of the greatest impromptu calls for racial progress in American history.

One day later, April 5, far back on page 33, the *New York Times* published R. W. Apple's coverage of all this. Apple managed to replicate RFK's quoting the ancient Greek dramatist Aeschylus, whose works the New York senator had encountered through the many writings of classicist Edith Hamilton. "Even in our sleep," RFK quoted from the great Greek, "pain which cannot forget falls drop by drop upon the heart until in our despair, against our will, comes wisdom through the awful grace of God"—something RFK knew a lot about. Apple then quoted RFK's own words: "I ask you now to return home to say a prayer for the family of Martin Luther King . . . and to say a prayer for our country . . . and for understanding and . . . compassion." Would that the *Times* had given Apple the space to reproduce more of this address, where RFK emphasized Aeschylus's belief that civilization could advance only if sufficiently wise people never gave up, no matter what, on two moral imperatives. They must persevere in seeking to "tame the savageness of man." And they must never cease efforts to "make gentle the life of this world."

Ren Kennedy, the Scotch-Irish preacher-politico, became entranced by the way RFK spontaneously connected timeless, classical thought to the modern tragedy of King's death. He clipped Apple's article and the one in the column next to it reporting on Governor Lureen Wallace's fight against cancer while her husband, George, pursued his third-party presidential campaign. Granted, modern scholarship has challenged some of Hamilton's translations from the Greek. Still, Ren Kennedy's own copies of Hamilton's books—over the previous thirty years he had bought them as they were published—show penciled underscores of much of what RFK quoted, including words omitted from Apple's reportage. In that these are the only lines underscored, it appears that Apple's article returned him not just to Hamilton's work but perhaps even to his learning at Erskine and Princeton as he reflected upon King's killing and Robert Kennedy's sensitive wisdom.

And, of course, the awfulness continued. In the diary he noted the wrenching television coverage of King's funeral, followed—unbelievably—by coverage of the assassination of RFK on June 6 in Los Angeles. After that, privately appalled at Wallace's anti–civil rights campaign, he wanted George McGovern to get the Democratic nomination. When Hubert Humphrey captured it, instead, Ren supported him. But he remained "down." On November 22, ten days after casting his futile anti-Nixon vote, he wistfully noted, "Fifth anniversary of JFK's murder." Based on what Republicans had seen in Wallace's appeal, not just in the South but nationwide, the Nixon era was on . . . with what historians call the "southern strategy."[25]

More localized events elicited a different reaction. In 1968, one of LBJ's Great Society programs, Volunteers in Service to America (VISTA), initiated major social service programs in Gee's Bend—including medical care. In times past, such a development would have had Kennedy's undivided attention. Not now. A "Camden doctor"—no clear identification survives—irate about loss of patient income from Benders, reportedly plotted with Sol Tepper and Selma Klansmen to have the VISTA director assassinated. The plot failed. Simultaneously, numerous Black ministers in the county wanted VISTA workers expelled from what they viewed as their turf. Camden streettalk buzzed with this dangerous complexity. But Kennedy mentioned it neither in the diary nor in his voluminous private correspondence.

Likewise, in 1970 the former Camden mayor, Reg Albritton—uncle to the physicist Albritton whose JFK letter found publication in the *Atlanta Constitution*—garnered considerable Black votes and defeated Sheriff "Lummie" Jenkins. This ended the thirty-year reign of one powerful lawman. No mention in Kennedy's diary or letters. The same was true as Black Wilcox voters moved more and more of their own into key county offices, until by the mid-1970s the county government was majority Black.[26]

Instead, to reiterate, other than Washington, DC, developments, he seemed focused only on Montgomery and Troy. In 1966, since George Wallace was constitutionally barred from succeeding himself for a third term, in the gubernatorial race he ran his wife, Lurleen, instead. A broad field opposed her, but notably the ascendant north Alabama Republican businessman, Jim Martin. Kennedy followed orders and placed "Lurleen Wallace for governor" literature around the campus and town. Unknown to the Troy president, however, in the Democratic primary Kennedy voted for Richmond Flowers, the Alabama attorney general, who recently had won landmark voting rights cases before the US Supreme Court: *Baker v. Carr* (1962) and *Reynolds v. Sims* (1964), cases that continued the Court's striking down of segregationist vote control practices so effectively assaulted in 1960 in *Gomillion v. Lightfoot*. But in the Democratic runoff, Lurleen Wallace easily defeated Flowers. This did not surprise Kennedy. He knew his was little more than a quiet, symbolic vote for a Black voting rights advocate and against Wallaceism.

In the general election Lurleen Wallace also trounced Martin. Although Kennedy had no one to vote for in that election– and quietly did not vote—he still found himself embroiled in Wallace machine strategies. Just before the voting, a former student worker in his office who had moved on to editorial writing for the *Tropolitan*, Gregory Flynn, conducted a poll of TSC students regarding the Wallace-Martin choice. The poll showed Martin a big favorite. When this news appeared in the *Montgomery Advertiser*, crediting Flynn's work, George Wallace apparently hit the ceiling. First, according to Kennedy, he had President Adams telephone the *Tropolitan* faculty advisor and tenured department head, Waites, with this message: "If this type of thing happens one more time, you are fired." Waites then turned for help to Kennedy, who immediately went to Adams's office to talk about settling "the big row." Adams told Kennedy the solution was for him, Kennedy, to "fire Gregory Flynn." According to Kennedy's diary, he replied: "You cannot fire a student for politics, especially this one because he no longer works for me." Though Adams backed down, in protest of "the row" Flynn resigned from the staff of the *Tropolitan*.

The diary also shows Sterkx, Trapp, Janet Rosenburg, and numerous other faculty colleagues visiting regularly in Kennedy's office to gripe about Adams's making Troy State College an arm of the "Wallace for president" campaign. Over the past quarter-century these faculty and others had reflected a strong mix of political views—and far more liberalism than stereotyping normally gives a mid-twentieth-century university in southeast Alabama. Granted, President Smith was a goofy egoist, weak on budget management and easily manipulated by the likes of Kilpatrick. But he still was a serious intellectual and a college president with a social conscience. He represented a courageous blend of the best strains of Wiregrass populism with the intellectual liberalism of noted Columbia University historian, Charles Beard. A rarity in Alabama. For a long time under Smith's leadership, most of the Troy faculty correctly believed their institution was helping move Alabama to the right side of history. That institutional commitment to an educated, responsible citizenry now seemed sidetracked, at the least, with a president devoting far more time to George Wallace's various aspirations than to leading Troy. And Kennedy shared their dissent.[27]

Increasingly, Kennedy expressed to his diary his personal rejection of the Wallace machine. On March 9, 1967: "Adams gets me to write 500-word letter of recommendation for Mother of the Year Award for Lurleen Wallace—waste an hour." On March 28: "George Wallace has lost every battle with Feds [including Troy's desegregation], but his constituency seems to like it." April 21: "Letter [in *Montgomery Advertiser*] by unknown [Troy] student ridiculing Governor's Day at Troy . . . sarcastic and clever." June 17, on Wilcox senator Roland Copper serving as Wallace's floor leader: "R. Cooper has warm heart and cold blood." In December, when the State Board of Education finally made it official that Troy State College now would be Troy State *University* with its own board separate from the State Department of Education—something Kennedy and close colleagues had wanted since the 1950s—his recent experiences at "Wallace's Troy" prompted this diary note: "Big assembly . . . 200 people celebrate in Sartain Hall . . . big doing . . . ALL A PHONY AND A FRAUD."

Too, he was fixated on rumors of Wallace's syphoning off presidential campaign donations for family members. "Wallace," he wrote repeatedly, "is a crook." Lurleen Wallace's death from cancer, in May 1968, elicited similar cynicism. The day after she died, President Adams seemed "more concerned about having to cancel a TSC baseball game" and a "Lettermen's concert" than the governor's death . . . just one more Redneck in a powerful job." He wondered if the widower felt the same. Albert Brewer's resultant ascendancy from lieutenant governor to governor, however, lifted him. He hoped Brewer could find reelection on his own, believing Brewer the "same class of leader as Frank Rose."[28]

That hope, of course, proved all too fleeting. As Brewer scholar Gordon Harvey has detailed, the new governor—an Alabamian who did indeed shift on race—offered thirty-three months of "New South" leadership: moderate and reconciling on race while strongly supportive of all levels of public education, plus tackling the state's historically pathetic "public ethics" and nineteenth-century constitution. But then Wallace ran roughshod over his promise not to challenge Brewer if he ran for a full term of his own. And in one of the meanest extended episodes of Alabama politics, culminating in a runoff with "a scared Wallace" painting Brewer as "a communist," "nigger loving" homosexual, Wallace prevailed in returning for a third term as governor. Throughout, Kennedy quietly stuck with Brewer, angry over Wallace—"scared" of being without power, "the phony," without a "new idea since John Patterson beat him . . . when he vowed never to be 'out-niggered again.'" Obviously unknowing of what lay ahead for Wallace, in February 1970 Kennedy wrote his siblings, "I think the state will be much better off with Wallace not as governor. I prefer he run for president [again] where he will be finished off." Shortly afterward to the diary: "I turn on t.v. at Mrs. C's. . . . Wallace on t.v. I turn it off." Likewise, much to Kennedy's private approval, in mid-April 1970 *Tropolitan* editors did a little roughshodding of their own. Despite repeated warnings by Adams, they yet again polled Troy students and reported they favored Brewer over Wallace, 52 percent to 31 percent. Though he left no record of reactions by Wallace and Adams, to himself Kennedy considered the students' work, "Good job."

Still, Wallace's victory left Kennedy anything but surprised over a new Gallup poll well publicized in the *New York Times*. It showed that across America, not just in Alabama, Wallace enjoyed substantial respect—in some places "ahead of the Pope." For today's historians, of course, this only forecast the further emergence of a modern, counterrevolutionary Republican Party and a more expansive, nationwide resistance movement. For Kennedy, it reinforced his long-held conviction—and certainly a cardinal, if often hidden, point in the Republican strategy—that many Americans did not want their government to confront racial fascism at home the way it had done some thirty years earlier in Europe.[29]

Notwithstanding all this, Kennedy the pragmatist managed to finish out his professional life with a substantial degree of public composure. Much as other American universities did in the mid-1960s, Troy State College expanded its upper-level bureaucracy. Between 1966 and 1968, owing in part to new federal monies and new programs they supported, Adams added four vice presidencies between him and his deans—all of them "staff" vice presidents with little to no experience in faculty governance and issues of academic freedom, and all with growing full-time "staff." Normal life evolved to top-down administration as the president bypassed "line" officers of dean and department head rank. Granted, since the 1950s and 1960s, Troy had expanded dramatically. But most of what Ren Kennedy once did by himself with a secretary and two student assistants became spread across—by President Adams's own count—"thirteen full time employees."

While these changes permitted Kennedy to move to a normal work week, they also had their downsides. By 1968, with the areas of financial aid and student employment having migrated to other administrative lines, he had the even more complicated life of reporting to the president on governmental relations (lobbying), to one vice president on his student recruitment endeavors, and to another vice president on public relations, plus reporting to the department head for Literature and Foreign Languages on his part-time teaching of English composition and literature. "The Pulse" adjusted. After all, "the Army"—even more, "the Army with surgeons"—had schooled him well on enduring the frustrations of organizational politics, and close to forty years trying to find Full Christians in Alabama had not hurt along these lines either. More to the point, here was the institutional home front from which he confronted the continued agonies of Alabama public education in the late 1960s and early 1970s.[30]

Kennedy did not have the benefit of the historical statistics. Yet he saw what caused them as events unfolded. As with the geologic Black Belt, it was all a function of the late Paleozoic era. Some Alabama counties did not get the "cotton card"—the loamy soil making for high-yield cotton and therefore high investment in slave labor. In those counties, where some 60 percent or more of the total population was white in, say, 1970, public schools normally made the transition to being racially mixed. Private all-white academies appeared not to dominate. Yet, as Kennedy wrote so many times before World War II, where the geology and resultant cotton culture produced a population with far fewer white people than Black—Black people overwhelmingly descendants of slaves—white citizens' acceptance of Black, and vice versa, was so different. Indeed, in counties such as Wilcox, for example, where the 1970 population was roughly 70 percent Black, desegregation produced perhaps an even greater racial divide than before.

In Wilcox as in other high-density Black counties, virtually all white people quickly moved to private "academies." This left public schools, now effectively all-Black, struggling to make up for a long history of substandard education, exacerbated by some principals and board members—Black and white—who were corrupt to the core. Likewise, out from under at least some state guidelines, yet minus a lot of state money, the new white academies now were freed to place even greater emphasis on football fields, less on science labs. Opened in the fall of 1970 with considerable backing from the Henderson family, Camden's own Wilcox Academy quickly captured a strong majority (significantly, not all) of the town's white high school students, only to agonize through the succeeding decades with significant financial and programmatic weaknesses.

As Kennedy noted both for Camden and for his broader student recruitment area, this produced many white high school graduates of mediocre skills and scores on national standardized tests, and who were hence unable to pursue certain higher education programs leading to long-dreamed-of careers. In many cases white parents rationalized these disappointments, if some of their own making, with embrace of George Wallace's well-honed con message. "If those people from the outside, the federal government, only had left us alone." Undoubtedly, this reverberated deep into the behavioral roots of many of Wallace's fellow Scotch-Irish. And it was premised on gross lying about—"rewriting"—history, always a seductive first step among those of even an inclination to fascism. Indeed, combined with the white victimization implicit in Wallace's message—further energized, arguably, by the shooting that injured him and necessitated his withdrawal from a second presidential campaign—all this resonated far beyond whites of Scotch-Irish origins to become a binding force in the post-1940s growth of white conservative thought in the South.[31]

Kennedy spent the early 1970s recruiting in this evolving environment. So many days wound up like this: "Today Phenix City and Hurtsboro... both of these [high] schools will be mostly Negro next year." And this: "To Louisville High School, 3 to 1 Negro, then to Clio High School, 50–50 Negro and white." He applauded the 1970 merger of the all-white Alabama Education Association with the all-Black Alabama State Teachers Association. Still, that merger—which, in Kennedy's opinion, saw Black teachers become far more active than whites—could do little overnight to alter the fact that so many Alabama high school graduates, regardless of color, were substandard in their educational achievement. Of course, some of the substandard whites had the advantages of monied, politically connected parents. Over Kennedy's head they landed in Troy the same way, Kennedy suspected, they avoided having to land in Vietnam: either "a phone call to Adams, the veteran, indeed the colonel," or one to the governor himself, apparently with reason to understand why some would want to dodge the draft.

Granted, over the years Kennedy rarely missed a legitimate opportunity to assist earnest Troy students from Wilcox. Camden attorney Donald M. McLeod recalled: "He obviously could work behind the scenes. One day I found a grant application in my mailbox... filled it out and turned it in and got a $500 tuition grant." But the "deals" to assist substandard students—notably, as Kennedy recalled, those with "families still contributing to Wallace's campaigns"—apparently prompted Kennedy to see Alabama's K–12 education through the prism of Wallace's counterrevolutionary political machine, Troy State University certainly an arm of it.

Before the war Kennedy had urged the Republicans' "trickle-down economics" as the sole reason for the Crash of 1929. With similar single-causation flaws, he believed Alabama's weak primary and secondary education resulted from the state's persisting de facto segregation. Despite Wallace's increase of education funding, Kennedy saw the students' weak profile going back to Wallace's "manipulation of a majority of Alabama white citizens with little or no social conscience.... Half Christians... resulting in the state's [persisting de facto] segregation in many of its schools." In this context, Kennedy left no record of labeling Wallace's impact as "fascist." If he had, according to Wallace biographer Dan Carter, this likely would have been inaccurate, for "Wallace had no deep ideological commitments... [he was] just a needy person who wanted desperately to be adored." Still, in Carter's view, Wallace's innately brilliant ability at "channeling and articulating views of his listeners" was a fact. So, by Kennedy's notion of Half Christianity and the way it opened doors for grassroots proto-fascist or fascist sentiment, his reading of the popular white voice Wallace consistently advanced, and which polarized race relations, lent credence to his critique of Wallace as a severely hurtful influence on Alabama's K–12 education.[32]

The 1970–71 academic year also saw Kennedy more and more leaving work by 4:00 p.m. Instead of following his longtime schedule of returning to the office after supper and working until 8:00 or 9:00, he often went from beer sessions straight to the movies, at the Pike County Theater, seeing films such as *Easy Rider* ("desultory, but interesting"), *Tick, Tick, Tick* ("race film and very good"), or *Joe* ("a dirty-language film but good story re. youth, drugs, failure of Establishment"). The Victorian South Carolina college student who softly reveled in his Elgin pocket watch had come a long way. Too, as the compulsion to hit the office by 7:30 a.m. eased up, his late-night reading returned: William Faulkner's *The Reivers* (1962; "not as good as his others"), Eudora Welty's *Losing Battles* (1970; "very good"), Joseph Heller's *Catch-22* (1961; "puzzling but good"), John Cheever's *Bullet Park* (1969; "not as good as Gene [Sterkx] said it would be"), and one he had had to skip over during the war years, Carson McCullers's *The Heart Is a Lonely Hunter* (1940; "sad and good").

He also drifted toward long weekends in Camden. Increasingly, he returned home by midday on Friday and did not leave for Troy until after lunch on Monday. He seemed even more attentive to ARP matters. He performed marriage ceremonies for Patricia Bonner, Bonnie Dean, and others who had grown up in his churches—his kind of weddings, where "nothing went wrong." He helped Juliette Harper write a campaign speech in her June 1971 winning quest to be elected treasurer of the ARP Synod's Young People's Christian Union. When she won, he even wrote a press release for the *Associate Reformed Presbyterian*. He chaired a stressful synod committee to determine who got what church properties as a few moderate to liberal ARPs, including some of Kennedy's own relatives in the Carolinas, looked to the PCUSA for more racial tolerance and modern Christian theology; or as some ARP churches just succumbed to reduced numbers of people living in the rural South.[33]

Meanwhile, in August 1970, not long after an exchange of letters with old friend Richebourg McWilliams on how their different careers had worked out—shortly, McWilliams would depart Birmingham-Southern College for a last stop at the University of South Alabama—Kennedy told Adams he was ready to hang it up. For two years the diary had paved the way: "I get real tired of the rigamarole here, but I guess we still need the money . . . didn't plan to stay this long . . . it's changed so much . . . not too much longer . . . too many people I don't know, now." On October 1, 1970, Kennedy would turn seventy. He told Adams a retirement date of June 30, 1971, would do just fine.

On hearing of this, Bill Wilks—now academic vice president—asked Kennedy to return to the English Department on a full-time basis for at least one academic year before finally leaving. For two days Kennedy pondered. Then historian Leonard Trapp dropped by to say Adams finally had decided he had had enough of his History Department chair speaking openly against Wallace; Trapp reported he would no longer be chair after the Christmas break. Adams would be replacing him with a Maxwell Air Force Base instructor in whom he had greater trust in toeing the Wallace party line, Duane Tway. Kennedy confirmed to Trapp that "Adams wants you to go" and later noted, "Trapp—a brave face, but is sick at heart," what could have been said for many of Troy's experienced faculty, secure in their jobs or not.

That talk, followed by news that Wallace and Adams were hiring the nationally noted critic of 1960s reformism, Max Rafferty, to be the new dean of Troy's School of Education, took Kennedy to his limit. He sympathized with Rafferty's attack on John Dewey's "progressive" approach to teacher education, a noted part of Rafferty's stint as state superintendent of education in California. But someone in Atlanta apparently mailed to Kennedy's Troy office a copy of the *Atlanta Journal-Constitution*'s recent Sunday magazine feature on Rafferty's move to Troy. Entitled "Comeback of a Left-Out Rightist," it profiled Rafferty's reactionary social agenda and politics as so compatible with the Wallace machine's. Shortly thereafter, Rafferty gave a Troy speech repeating his well-known condemnation of university students and faculty who openly protested "administration"—what Kennedy saw as a direct attack on Janette Stout Rosenburg, Leonard Trapp, Gary Dickey, Gregory Flynn, and other critics of Wallace and Adams. From that speech he "almost walked over to Adams' office and made [his] retirement retroactive to September 30, 1970." But on cooling down he managed to call Wilks and just decline his offer to stay longer. June 30, 1971, for sure, was his date to be gone.

Then he telephoned Jeff Bennett, who by this time had left a high-level Washington, DC, lobbying job to become chancellor of the University of the South (Sewanee). In that conversation, Bennett recalled, Kennedy said he viewed his "cousin's university" (Wallace's Troy) to be "'a sad thing' and that he was 'looking forward to being gone as soon as possible.'" Then, "he granted that Ralph Adams was a significant success as a hard-working builder of a campus and student enrollment, and I would add to that—George Wallace was the same on buildings. But it was the intellectual life they wanted inside those buildings that saddened him. He said Adams was an intolerant developer [and] . . . you can count on history to keep giving us more of those types."

The months moved fast. Kennedy felt good about the decision. "I smoke too many cigarettes," he wrote his brother William, and—borrowing a few lines from Mark Twain—"I take very little exercise and have been known to imbibe a little alcohol. . . . It's been a good formula for the past and should do me well in the future." After all his blood pressure "rest[ed] proudly at 119 over 82."[34]

As his end at Troy neared, on April 23, 1971, despite severe disappointment about Wallace and "hatred" (his word) for Adams, at his president's request Kennedy managed one last act of pragmatism. He wrote an adulatory "capsule history of Troy State University" for the *Tropolitan*, subsequently reprinted in the *Montgomery Advertiser*. Altogether, it tells an extraordinary story and should be read by one with justifiable pride in contemporary Troy University. But the piece also was extraordinary for what it did not say. In the 1930s he would have woven in the most sardonic criticism about race and Half Christian social conscience and the reactionary politicizing of a university. In April 1971 he elected not to go down that road. Wasted energy.

In June, for Kennedy's last two days, Mary was there in Troy along with Joyce and Bill Jones: two dinner parties "with *faculty* colleagues," then "an awkward retirement ceremony" in the Faculty Lounge with the president. That final night at Mrs. Carter's he worked through a bottle of Old Crow while they loaded the car. "To bed 10:40. High of 98 today. Tired . . . slightly drunk. . . . Troy over."[35]

13

Breakfast at Ren's

On Thursday, July 1, 1971, Kennedy awoke in Camden. After an hour in the garden he "unpacked the suitcase I have lived out of for twenty-four years" and integrated books and other "stuff" from Troy into his home study. He then downed two shots of vodka, ate a lunch of three cold barbecued spareribs, and took a half-hour nap. Midafternoon he walked to town, "loafed" at the courthouse, and then walked back. He had one beer, then "a good many gin slugs . . . no dinner . . . pondered not having had to see that Red Neck president today and not tomorrow either . . . bed at 11:00."

For a first day of retirement, perhaps, this might be understandable. If it became a pattern it was not all right—for anyone. And, in fact, it did. That is not right, actually. It already was a pattern, one that had been growing and growing for some time. That Camden voted "wet" on October 29, 1970, ending a prohibition dating back to 1907, had little to do with the pattern. Instead, it likely had evolved from a Full Christian's struggle with Alabama, America, and God.[1]

Far from the activist of old, Kennedy nevertheless continued for a while as a community leader and preacher—and much opinionated. He agreed to serve on an eighteen-member steering committee dispensing federal aid for indigent care, an offshoot of JFK/LBJ reforms not eliminated by Nixon. By 1975, correctly anticipating that the state of Alabama would not come up with the necessary match for the state to have uninterrupted federal money to assist with indigent care, he quietly made last-minute telephone calls for one particular Wilcox resident to get assistance for hospital care: Rosa Lee Pettway, sixty-one-year-old descendant of the noted Gee's Bend family, whose sorrowful story he had broken to the world. Likewise, while his synod attendance gradually tapered off, when he appeared he did his best to maintain his Scotch-Irish heretic confrontations with conservatives, using such favorite Menckenian lines as, "The Holy Spirit stalks the Land armed with a pitchfork and a bucket of tar." Long ago, Wilcox ARPs had adjusted to this. Unabated, their baptisms, marriages, and burials continued; increasingly he even buried those he had married and some he had baptized. And until 1981 he continued as clerk of the Tennessee-Alabama Presbytery—except for the war years a position he had held since 1927—and until 1983 also as clerk of the Camden ARPC session.

Still, on November 18, 1971, he wrote his siblings: "You get tired of a situation and maybe people get tired of you and it is not good to remain too long." In Wilcox that stayed beneath the radar. But it was not much of a surprise when, in January 1973, he advised ARP elders in Camden, Oak Hill, and Marion Junction that it was time to look around for his pulpit replacement. Though he could hang on for a while, the search for a new call needed to start. He urged their taking a look at a modern-thinking young preacher trained at Columbia Theological Seminary in Atlanta, Henry Lewis Smith. Instead, in May 1974, one Harold Richardson arrived as the replacement. Kennedy found him a good person and a highly regarded part-time high school English teacher at the new, private Wilcox Academy and for a while enjoyed traveling to synod with him. From the pulpit, however, this product of the arch-conservative Reformed Theological Seminary of Mississippi seemed to offer exactly what had caused Kennedy such agony. Richardson offered "rank . . . Hell-Fire and Damnation . . . Half Christianity . . . reeking with theological gore." Kennedy rarely showed up at church.[2]

Yet he remained well attuned to state and national politics. He was not surprised that George Wallace "borrowed" the new Troy dean, Max Rafferty, for wide-ranging campaign roles in his runs for president. On May 15, 1972, of course, Arthur Bremer shot Wallace while he was campaigning in Laurel, Maryland. Kennedy cut him little slack. "Wallace doing well but paralyzed in legs . . . had a pretty shabby record . . . too enthusiastically received" at the Democratic National Convention. In the 1974 Alabama gubernatorial primary, Kennedy voted for the young moderate Jere Beasley, though Wallace easily won. In the 1978 gubernatorial primary he fruitlessly voted absentee for the young progressive lawyer and lieutenant governor, Bill Baxley. However, he found the man who won, Forrest (Fob) James, to be a good governor. No, Kennedy did not support a Republican. Native of the east Alabama mill town Lanett and a former Auburn football player, civil engineer, and entrepreneur, James won his first term as a relatively moderate Democrat urging an Alabama moving on from its Wallace racism. It was only some twelve years later, with Republicans on a white vote juggernaut, that he won a second term as a state's rights Republican.[3]

The White House also kept his attention. In 1972, repulsed by "Nixon . . . the evasive one," Kennedy voted for the Democrat, George McGovern. When Nixon's reelection led to a national paralysis over the Watergate scandal,

Kennedy felt less distraught than confirmed. "Of course, he is a crook . . . he is a Republican." On the heels of a letter from two of his conservative sisters, saying they found Black people individually kind but "as a group right now they are a problem," Kennedy upped the ante: "As individuals certain Republicans are alright, but as a group they smell like Nixon." Gerald Ford's pardon of Nixon he found on balance "simply wrong," the work of a "hack politician . . . perhaps [Ford is] more honest than Richard I, but what we need in the White House is a good Democrat."

Of course, by the mid-1970s some Alabama whites stuck with Wallace for president, while others were part of the Deep South's growing Republican ranks and backed Ford in his 1976 election bid. Surrounded by such opinions, Kennedy vented to his brothers and sisters that he was not surprised to see Governor Wallace enter the Democratic presidential primary, where he actually would carry Alabama, Mississippi, and South Carolina. But Kennedy's perception of Wallace as a demagogue who could use proto-fascist language was not swayed by Wallace's recent efforts to seem less strident on race. The truth about Wallace's supporters, he advised, is that they are voting for a person who "believes we should have fought with, not against, Japan and Germany, in the last war." And as for Republican voters, because he long had criticized Republicans so openly, "some of my neighbors look at me as a snake lying in the grass waiting to bite the heels of their Republican children. What they don't comprehend is that some Republican children badly need their heels bitten."

So, the election in 1976—the Bicentennial year—was an easy choice for him. The Republican nominating convention was "dull," he thought, just a bunch of "old people" who paired the incumbent, Ford, with Robert Dole, certainly a respected veteran but still "a dull clod." Ren himself vigorously supported the Democrat, the "brilliant young southerner . . . my boy," Jimmy Carter. And when Carter won and Rosalyn Carter chose not to wear a fur coat at the inauguration, Kennedy found the whole thing "a magnificent show." Despite the tribulations of Carter's presidency and the tough odds in Carter's 1980 reelection bid, he did not waver. But it was more than Carter's being a Democrat and Ted Kennedy's "vigorous and stirring speech" carefully identifying Carter with the FDR/JFK/RFK liberalism that energized Kennedy. It was the Republican candidacy of Ronald Reagan. This returned him to what Reagan had done at the 1964 Republican nominating convention.

There, Reagan showed what Ren Kennedy called the "gross hypocrisy" of borrowing, without even appropriate credit, one of Franklin D. Roosevelt's greatest lines from his June 22, 1936, speech accepting the Democratic nomination: "To some generations much is given. Of other generations much is expected. This generation of Americans has a rendezvous with destiny."

Actually, most scholars credit FDR aide Thomas G. Corcoran with inserting that line in FDR's speech. But it quickly became synonymous with the liberal ideas of Roosevelt's presidencies. A former New Dealer, Reagan loved the drama of the phrase, and found no problem applying it to the opposite of what FDR espoused. Reagan pled that Goldwater's arch-conservative agenda—reversing much of what Democrats had achieved since the 1930s— was Goldwater's "rendezvous with destiny." Then, in the 1980 election, Reagan repeatedly used the line to advance his own candidacy as the corrective conservative. Again, in Kennedy's mind, this was not just irony but "gross hypocrisy." Of course, the mass of Wilcox whites—Alabama whites, too— professed great approval of Reagan's counterrevolution promise to dismantle policies of the Rooseveltian way—the New Deal, the New Frontier, and the Great Society—even though for the foreseeable future many of those with land quietly would relish the federal money they received for not planting certain acreage, a program implemented by Roosevelt and extended by subsequent Democrats. In 1981, Kennedy lamented to his siblings, "For eighty I am doing pretty well. But I feel very oppressed living under a Republican administration, and I cannot help but wish we had the Peanut Farmer [Carter] back."[4]

Ultimately, beaten down by the "phony baloney" of county, state, and national politics, not just local church life, Kennedy went through his last decade thinking more and more about simple human relations, which had their ups and downs, especially regarding race relations. Right after his retirement from Troy, he continued his longtime "*New York Times* ministry"—regularly taking a week's worth of the paper to different Black families in Camden. On one such trip, a rainy day in December 1971, he dropped off the papers at "a Negro home" where folks inside were making placards for the next day's boycott and marches downtown. On leaving, when his rear tires slid into a sloshy hole, four of the protest organizers politely suspended their preparations to push him out of the mud.

But things were more complicated than that. The diary for January 21, 1975: "To Foodland [grocery store in Camden] . . . [verbal] altercation with an obnoxious Negro woman." Eight days later he was even stronger. Some Negroes "are rude and hate white people . . . [and] I do not like them. . . . I am sorry I feel this way." Likewise, the diary and letters to siblings of the mid-1970s report him repeatedly voting by absentee ballot. This allowed him to avoid what often happened in voting lines. "Whites mumbled cursewords to blacks," he later complained, "and blacks did the same to whites— Rednecks all. Regardless of their color, they . . . whites and blacks . . . were like . . . mongrel dogs growling from their base insecurities." In July 1985 this stress still was fresh in his mind: "With the exception of a few leaders of both races . . . most people were frightfully lacking in sophisticated thought . . .

so under-educated.... As desegregation continued it could be hurtful, mean on the streets and in public buildings and stores. Connie [his daughter, Mary Conway] experienced some of this in Atmore [as a public school teacher] but it was a lot worse here [in Camden]."[5]

So focused was he on these down-the-street insults, indeed, that he paid little private attention to other local developments that would have had him privately vociferous in times past. He ignored the county's continued shutdown of the Gee's Bend ferry across the river, begun in 1963 to limit Benders' participation in demonstrations. He also showed little interest in two of modern Wilcox's most noted deaths and the resultant political developments. In 1969, murder ended the life of noted probate judge William J. Dannelly. Kennedy barely noted this high-profile story and the subsequent trial. Dannelly was replaced by Josiah Robins Bonner. Then, four years later, Bonner resigned due to ill health and died soon thereafter. Kennedy had deeply admired Bonner and had written him a "literary masterpiece" of a recommendation letter to Georgetown law school. He considered Bonner an enlightened, lifetime member of his congregation, and baptized his three children—James, Judy, and Jo. Still, although Kennedy buried Bonner, in the diary he hardly mentioned the unexpected death within one of Wilcox's noted families. Likewise, within days of Bonner's funeral, Roland Cooper resigned from the state Senate to accept Governor Wallace's quickly orchestrated offer of appointment as Bonner's successor. Again, Kennedy barely mentioned it. When Reg Albritton beat Cooper in the election of May 1976—amid high-profile accusations of Cooper's using his previous and current offices to go around state bid law and sell Chrysler trucks to the State Highway Department—it was the same. Just mentioned; no editorial.[6]

Only slightly more attention did he give the high-profile murder of the "Wily Fox." On Wednesday afternoon, April 30, 1977, at age sixty-three and no longer holding any public office, Cooper "checked out" a Black prisoner, Charles Lee Bufford, from the Wilcox jail. Here was a "time-honored" practice by which influential whites got cheap day-labor. By approved county practice—occasionally followed—the "fee" of some five to ten dollars went to the upkeep of the sheriff's office, not the sheriff's pocket. At this time the sheriff was forty-three-year-old Marion Maness, who grew up in Coy. After Cooper checked out Bufford, he drove him to his extensive vegetable garden on the river road. There is no record of what happened in the car. But at the garden, when Cooper apparently turned his back, Bufford used a hoe to strike several lethal blows to the back of his head. In Cooper's car, Bufford then drove to Selma, where police arrested him for driving through a red light. Convicted of burglary and murder, he was sent to death row. Still, as the venerable Black Belt journalist Amanda Walker has written, he subsequently was freed on grounds that certain elements of the Alabama death penalty law were unconstitutional (if not Alabama's use of capital punishment per se) and that evidence used in his conviction was illegally manipulated by authorities—as it was. At a retrial in Camden, in November 1981, the jury apparently thought "four years was enough for what he did." More to the point, despite the horror of Cooper's end, and Kennedy's having bought several cars from him, not to mention having worked Troy political deals with him, Kennedy's sole "eulogy" on the life of this noted segregationist leader and Wallace crony was the well-worn phrasing: "Cooper—warm handed but cold hearted."[7]

And that apparent detachment continued. In 1978, a Black man named Prince Arnold—a twenty-seven-year-old Alabama State University graduate and an insurance agent turned special education teacher in Wilcox—won the sheriff's election. Because of the 1937 decision to eliminate term limits on Wilcox sheriffs, thus giving Sheriff "Lummie" Jenkins such an extended tenure, Arnold proceeded to hold that position for over thirty years, garnering statewide law enforcement honors just as Jenkins did. Kennedy could not have known of this future. But on its own Arnold's election was a stunning symbol of change. In one brief sentence, however, Kennedy noted, "Prince Arnold elected sheriff," then signed off, "very good uneventful day." Shortly, in December 1978, "Lummie" Jenkins died in a Selma hospital. Again, it was simply, "Sheriff thirty-two years . . . the old-order passeth."[8]

For most of his final decade Ren Kennedy had Bill Jones with him. The retired superintendent remained quite a force and not always a good one. After his wife, Joyce, died in 1980, his steady imbibing got even steadier. Two days a week Jones drove the fourteen miles down from Oak Hill to Camden. He parked in Kennedy's driveway and entered through the back door. In spring and summer he brought a variety of fresh vegetables; in fall, collards. Year-round he also brought beer, gin, vodka or bourbon, or wretched sugary wine. From about 9:00 a.m. to 10:30 a.m. the two sat at the kitchen table having "commodities and grits." For special occasions it was "sausage, commodities and grits." But they did not just sit there and sip.

Bill Jones never was a regular at the Wilcox Roundtable discussions; most of those intellectual gatherings occurred on Saturday nights, and it took genuine crisis for Jones and his wife not to be in Oak Hill on weekends—and Bethel church on Sunday mornings. But during the 1930s and early 1940s Jones indeed was an avid discussant with the Camden Book Club, which met on Wednesday nights in Camden. Now, in the mid-1970s, he returned to books—with comrade Ren and the booze. Breakfast at Ren's.

From Kennedy's own large library they selected noted works. Kennedy had read them before, Jones not: Tolstoy's *Anna Karenina* (1961 edition), Shakespeare's *Hamlet* and *King Lear*, the more recent *Dr. Zhivago* (1957) by

Boris Pasternak. They subsequently tackled Henrik Ibsen's *A Doll's House* (1965 edition) before moving back a couple of thousand years to Aeschylus, Sophocles, and other ancient Greek authors. While these big thoughts about why humans do what they do eased their mutual agonies over life in Alabama, it came too late to curb the liquid ancillaries.[9]

In 1979, however, two things might have reversed their rapidly escalating consumption of "commodities." On the night of May 21, while working on details for him and Mary to take a two-week European tour, Kennedy suddenly was struck with excruciating abdominal pain. Mary got him to the Camden hospital, the next day to Vaughn Hospital in Selma. Diagnosed with extreme pancreatitis—undoubtedly from the alcohol—he stayed there for close to a month. The pain was so severe that when he returned to Camden, he had no recollection of his first ten days in the hospital. The European trip, however, was nonrefundable; he and Mary needed to be in London on July 16, and they were.

They returned August 8. Never having flown, Jones had no grasp of jet lag. So, of course, on August 9 he arrived at Kennedy's 9:00 a.m. sharp. Out came the vegetables. And that was all. "Grits" (and "sausage," undoubtedly in honor of the safe passage), but no booze. And that is the way it went for a while. Minus "commodities" they got back to their books, among them Rona Jaffe's *Class Reunion* (1979). Kennedy had read a review of Jaffe's instant classic, and it appears he thought it would be good for them to sample her women's liberationism from New York's Upper East Side . . . a long way from Wilcox.

Still, on September 4 Kennedy drove to Selma for a checkup at Vaughn Hospital, and on the way back, on the south side of the Edmund Pettus Bridge, he stopped "for commodities" at a package store—beer. And so resumed Breakfast at Ren's. And beyond. In October 1980 Ren and Mary caught another cruise, this one to Turkey and Greece. On October 18 they returned. On October 20 Jones eased down the driveway to the back door, commodities inside vegetables.[10]

On the morning of March 31, 1982, Kennedy had a stroke. He was at home in his study when it happened. Mary managed the situation well. After some four weeks in Vaughan Hospital, on May 5, he returned home— "truly . . . a clear head," daughter Mary Conway would recall, "his recovery . . . astounding." Off and on for the following three months, however, Jones's biweekly visits did not include alcohol. And nothing suggests Kennedy drank a drop without him.[11]

Back in 1979, after Mary had had a series of falls, Mary Conway and Margaret prevailed on their mother to hire the local health assistant, Sarah McDaniel Woods. An early member of Kennedy's *New York Times* ministry, the forty-seven-year-old Woods was the daughter of a Black sharecropping couple and grew up on Sand Island in the Alabama River, just north of Miller's Ferry. After education at the Lutheran school in Camden, she moved into a nurse assistant position at Camden's J. Paul Jones Hospital. From a strong reputation there, she departed to work on her own in home care for the local old and ill. Successful at this, she soon left the old Black shanty section of Camden to become the first Wilcox Black person to own an all-brick home. Though Margaret and Mary Conway felt fortunate indeed to line her up for their parents, the deal still took constant steamrolling.[12]

Mary did not care for Sarah. While Mary grew up both fearing and despising the KKK, recall that her views on both race and class were more conservative than her husband's. By itself, still, that was not the problem. The crux of the issue was Sara Woods's civil rights activism in Camden. In that brick home in 1969 she hosted Coretta Scott King. Ren Kennedy was devoted to Sarah Woods. So were his daughters. Well into the mid-1980s, when his assistant wanted two hours off in the middle of the workday to ferry folks to the polls, he overrode Mary's no with his own emphatic yes. In response Mary wanted to dock Woods's pay. Ren said no to that, and both daughters backed him up. On several occasions Sarah had car trouble and wanted to borrow the Kennedys' car for poll transportation. Mary said no; Ren said fine. It happened. By late 1983 Mary begrudgingly caved, if not without occasional outbursts.

Indeed, by 1983 Sarah Woods's role had evolved from health care assistant, 9:00 a.m. to 2:00 p.m., to full-time attendant, plus driver for the Kennedys and all that went with that, including being the acquirer of "commodities." Kennedy went out less, napped after lunch, and at night headed to bed by 9:30. Bill Jones continued to visit but only when brought by his cousin (via marriage) Becky Bonner, who lived in Oak Hill, a stone's throw down the Pine Apple highway. Still, Ren saw to the "commodities": "M. goes to church [Tuesday night] with Margaret Dale . . . and Sarah and I go for 'commodities.'"[13]

In this increasingly sedentary state it was sheer glee for Kennedy to discover one of his former Troy students, Thomas Lane Butts, as a potent preacher in Montgomery's First United Methodist Church with regular Sunday-morning television broadcasts available in Camden. Native of Bermuda, Alabama, just outside Monroeville, Butts preached a racially liberal message. Throughout the late 1970s and early 1980s Kennedy ceased even occasional church attendance in Camden and spent Sunday mornings "with Tom." But that ended abruptly, due to an upheaval in Butts's church. Though a star in the pulpit, Butts held racial views that never were accepted by many of his congregants or by certain other powerful preachers in the Methodists' Alabama and Northwest Florida Conference. In 1983, on accusations of sexual misconduct with a female congregant—proven to be contrived—and abuse of due process in the termination of an associate pastor admittedly guilty of sexual misconduct with a female congregant, Butts found himself suspended from Methodist pulpits for some two years. Irate, Kennedy led a group of some twenty Alabama ministers, most of whom were not Methodists, who continually wrote checks for "The Tom Fund" to help get him through these tough times. Butts's troubles finally ended when childhood friends Alice and Harper Lee saw to it that he was offered the pulpit of the First United Methodist Church of Monroeville.[14]

Butts's full professional recovery, not to mention his heralded, million-dollar slot machine bonanza at Atmore's Wind Creek Casino—money he then gave away—followed Kennedy's death. All Kennedy knew was that Tom Butts went through a lot of "unfair tribulations." Along with Ren's growing immobility and more problems finding a "non-medieval" ARP preacher for Wilcox, the sudden demise of "Tom's t.v. church" basically ended any regular Sunday-morning services for him, anywhere. Not that Sunday became "just another day" or that prayer ceased. Sunday remained "the Sabbath." And not only did prayer continue but a relatively new practice was added, praying for people on their birthdays—family members; World War II comrades Roland Rhynus, Amy Erickson, and Dan Laws; and indeed University of Alabama football coach Paul (Bear) Bryant. Still, during hours long committed to church he increasingly read. Not the Bible. But Thoreau's *Walden* and other classics, plus wide-ranging newer works: Evelyn Waugh's *Brideshead Revisited* (1945), Fawn Brodie's *Thomas Jefferson: An Intimate History* (1974), Henri Troyat's *Catherine the Great* (1980), and Richard Adams's *Watership Down* (1975). As daytime reading spread to other days of the week, the family did its best to shield him from guests while he was "in a book."

Still, on Saturday, April 16, 1983, there was a happy exception. That afternoon, as he was reading and Mary was out back in the garden, there came a knock on the front door. He put down the book and opened the door to find two white adults, Blake Field Jr. and Bettie Lou Albritton Falkenberry, asking if he would marry them. Since they were two of Kennedy's "special church members"—he had married their relatives, baptized both of them, and had long admired Field for the significant financial support he quietly gave Camden's Black churches—he performed the ceremony. This was his last wedding.[15]

A week later, on the night of April 23, 1983, Kennedy had "a small ache in stomach" that continued through the following day. Mary took him to the Camden hospital. That night he noted: "It may be another [bout of] pancreatitis, I am told. Not too bad yet." At any rate, a week later he and Sarah Woods went to the bank and stores; "I do not go in." The following day Bill

Jones was scheduled for Breakfast at Ren's, but phoned early to say "a stomach pain" would keep him from coming. Nothing seemed crucial.

On May 18 Kennedy and Sarah Woods went for a ride "by [Paul] Starr's turn-off and the airport. She let me drive for five miles." Again, things seemed stable. On May 21, a Saturday, he was clear-headed, indeed, enthusiastic for an interview. "Two and a half hours with Tennant McWilliams," he noted. "Many questions on tape recorder. Nap at 4:00 pm."

The night of Thursday, May 26, he noted he had "had pain in stomach all [the previous] night. Did not sleep . . . must cut down on alcohol?" Yet that very afternoon when "M. goes for walk . . . I drink can of beer," and despite stomach "generally hurting," not long after he went with Mary and others of Camden to attend the wedding of Mary Conway's daughter, Lee, in Atmore. It was a big turnout, with all the grandchildren, those of college age and young adults. "Good peach daiquiris at reception." The old verve anything but stilled, he wrote his sisters, "Champagne flowed like water, too . . . sorry for the prohibitionists among you."[16]

The stomach pain came and went. Into the 1983 Thanksgiving holiday he had "no pain. . . . I don't get better, but I don't get worse." None of Camden's ARP families stuck with him more than that of Hugh Dale. Hugh Dale Jr.—son of Hugh Dale so instrumental in Kennedy's original recruitment to Camden in the late 1920s—had driven Kennedy to his final synod and presbytery meetings in 1982, and over the last five years he also had been bringing meals to the Kennedy house at least once a week. That Thanksgiving of 1983 there they were again: when Mary declined their Thanksgiving dinner invitation—"Not up to it"—Hugh sent his daughter, Jane Shelton, to the Kennedy house with a complete turkey dinner for two, along with "a dozen—minus one—of Bonnie Dean Mitchell's deviled eggs." That night Kennedy noted how this kindness permitted a "quiet, pleasant Thanksgiving."[17]

Still, the diary started to telegraph what he was not actually saying. More and more, when Sarah Woods prepared his meals, he waited until she went to another room then fed a good portion of the food to his new pet, "S.D."—a mutt whom he had christened "Stray Dog." The earlier pain from the stomach had expanded to pain when he swallowed. The dog was an easy out.

Too, when he noted Auburn's 1983 Iron Bowl victory over Alabama (23–20), with Bo Jackson rendering an epic touchdown run as tornadoes skirted Birmingham's Legion Field, he recorded the score with tiny circles for degrees as if it were 23 and 20 degrees outside. And while he eagerly greeted the constant stream of old friends—Jack Bogie, Charles Dobbins, Gene Sterkx, his wartime assistant Roland Rhynus, and at least three nurses from the 102nd—his notes increasingly referenced visits by local women with their married last names omitted: Taylor Jones [Harper], Lena Miller [Albritton], and Snooks Jones [Gaines].

There also was the inevitable complication of the television remote: "Sarah, I can't find the remote," Mary Conway remembered his saying so anxiously. "Sarah, *please*, have you seen the remote?" "Yes, Mr. Kennedy, you're sitting on it." Yet during December 22–24, 1984, he still had ample focus to reread portions of Edith Hamilton's *The Greek Way*.[18]

And at least some drinking continued. In July 1984, "Jack Bogie and Roy McIntosh drop by for [bourbon] highballs." In November "Sarah does some shopping for me—beer, cigarettes, gin." Yet "commodities" likely tapered off during this period. Sarah Woods had assumed full responsibility for "empties," and only intermittently did she seem occupied with the task. Of course, there is also the possibility that Kennedy just quit noting the process as carefully as before. But this is doubtful. Everything Sarah Woods did he went out of his way to note, always concluding: "Sarah is wonderful to me . . . so good to me . . . a great comfort."

Through that summer and into the fall the barbershop was his major outing. Once a month, like clockwork, Sarah Woods drove him there. More than social life, it was the same concern about being neat and well-presented he had exhibited as a student at Erskine and Princeton and from the pulpit and through all those offices of Troy and Montgomery, and even as a combat zone soldier in Europe. This is telling. For much of the "Greatest Generation," the longer haircuts and scruffy appearances so stylish from the early 1960s to the early 1980s became a repulsive symbol for the nonconforming hippie ways of those times. Despite his fastidiousness, however, through old age Kennedy left no evidence of ridiculing new hair fashions, whether Afros or "Hippie cuts." Perhaps this is even more an indication of how he lived through the postwar era as a unique subset of the "Greatest Generation." Indeed, July 1984 found him glued to the television, excited about Gary Hart's Democratic presidential possibilities. And in August the old partisan could not help pronouncing Reagan's and Bush's convention speeches "so tedious."[19]

Kennedy seemed fully attuned to his inevitable end. Back in May 1976 he had told his sister, Margaret, that this senior member of the "Tribe of Isaac" had no wish to die, but he knew "it must come and I do not fear it." As the circle tightened, that tone evolved. Of course, a year later the second oldest of his siblings, William, died. Then in 1981 and 1982 brothers Leon and Richard did, too. On top of that, in September 1982 cancer took Elise Bonner Hickey. Kennedy saw this coming for more than six months, visiting her many times in Vaughan Hospital. Yet according to Mary Conway the "blow [to him] was still like losing a favored family member and he did not want to talk for several days after she died." As 1982 closed, he wrote his three sisters, "You have only one brother now . . . keep him for a while." And by February 1984 he had moved to "all my friends . . . are dying off. That is to be expected, but it leaves me lonely."[20]

His old comrade was in the same boat. Though he had suffered a slight stroke in August 1981, thanks to Becky Bonner, Bill Jones kept up his morning visits. Through April 1984 he did not miss a rendezvous. May started off the same, but on May 12, 1984, Jones called and "says he is not coming by . . . pain in stomach." Several visits to Vaughn left him missing in action for a while. Yet on June 18 there he came again: "Brings vegetables and bottle of wine," Kennedy recorded. "but stays only forty minutes. He can hardly walk." On September 3, 1984, Bill Jones suffered another stroke. Becky drove him from Oak Hill back to Vaughn. There the next day he died.

Since the mid-1960s, Bill Jones had been in and out of Vaughn with what Kennedy called "ruptured ulcer . . . bleeding ulcer." Then of course the strokes in 1971 and 1981. In recent years his cousin and brother-in law, Richebourg McWilliams, had addressed possible sources of these health problems. In January 1965, McWilliams wrote Jones: "If the attritions of your office have given you ulcers, and many a night of troubled sleep because of your innate sensitivity toward others, you should know that out of that same sensitivity came your strength, pitiably lacking in so many others." Then in June 1974 McWilliams wrote Jones of his difficulties "steering yourself through troubled waters [in 1954] when Uncle Miller [Bonner], whose political stands I always disliked, decided that, because his tenure of his Senate job was threatened . . . he would make an issue out of your vote [against school desegregation], as reported by that far-right magazine . . . and for your trying to keep politics out of the school system." In short, Jones's half-century-long struggles with racism and Alabama politics, agitated by a fat-laden diet and capped off by the desegregation crises of the 1960s and 1970s, all took a toll on his physical self. And, just as with Kennedy, it is hard to believe this toll did not lead him into excessive alcohol consumption. Jones was still alive in 1983 when Morton Rubin was asked if he knew his old friend had a serious drinking problem. He replied: "No. I didn't know that." Then quickly added: "Bill has a personality similar to Ren's . . . polite and diplomatic, outwardly, but in private philosophical, analytical, and worried . . . so worried . . . and often sad. And then there was the Wilcox bank [Pine Apple] fraud case where, just retired, he lost much of his retirement. No easy life."

Kennedy did not feel able to attend Jones's funeral, though Sarah Woods offered to take him. He just "was not up to it," Mary Conway later said. Undoubtedly old age was closing in. Several days later he mustered a note to his sisters: "Bill Jones died last week . . . one of my best friends for more than fifty years. I suppose you lose your old friends when you get older, but it leaves the world a more desolate place."[21]

Most in Camden knew that Bill Jones's death hit Kennedy hard. For his October 1 birthday, turning eighty-four, visitors flooded in with interminable spreads of food. But another downer offset the would-be festivities. That day his driver's license came up for renewal. In the morning, when Sarah Woods went to inquire about the procedure he should follow to get it renewed, Kennedy was effectively "non-renewed" out of his inability to appear at the courthouse. Remember, his struggles to live on an ARP preacher's income did not permit him to get a car until he was forty-three. And, of course, *Alabama I* and *II* actually were not his; they were the army's. But as he moved through the postwar years with larger income, he relished not just the succeeding Wilcox *Jeep* but in time new V-8 Plymouths, eventually with jet-plane wings, air conditioning, automatic transmissions, even pushbutton radios. Over the past year he hardly had driven the new Ford Torino. But the "non-renewal" hurt. It stabbed into his final autonomy. It took him "down." That night he watched a television documentary on John Kennedy's presidency. Nothing indicates whether this buoyed him or took him further down.[22]

The physical decline continued. Midafternoon, December 21, Viola Liddell slipped through the break in the hedge for a visit. At the back door Mary advised that her husband was too tired to see her. That night Kennedy noted, "Could not see Viola when she came by"—a first. For Christmas Day 1984 the family turned out—decorated tree, presents, big dinner, champagne. According to the diary, however, Kennedy's high point for the holidays that year was his receiving from Margaret a whispered, "Yes, Daddy," after he asked if she had slipped Sarah Woods a fifty-dollar Christmas bonus when Mary was not looking, and the next day when Mary Conway did precisely the same.

On January 2, 1985, Kennedy wrote his sisters, "I do not improve . . . and never will . . . the next thing on my agenda is income taxes . . . sorry for my typing errors." Indeed, by early February he had completed his taxes: $1,026.00 to the federal government, $187.15 to the state of Alabama. Sarah Woods drove him to the post office to mail the returns. On January 11 he wrote a long letter to his wartime comrade Dan Laws. On January 21, after a few phone calls, he gave the diary a complete retrospective on "the coldest winters in Wilcox," concluding that January 21, 1985, indeed was "the coldest since February 13, 1899." On January 27–29 he watched the television serial, *Robert F. Kennedy and His Times*. In May, Mary hit the ceiling over Sarah Woods wanting time off for voluntary "election official" work; Kennedy saw to it that she got the time.

Beyond navigating Mary, the empties, and the taxes—and reliving the 1960s assassinations striking down one advocate for racial justice after another—something else finally was right before him. At mealtime, swallowing became increasingly difficult. In early July physicians at Vaughn gave him the diagnosis: carcinoma of the esophagus. If Kennedy blinked there is no record of it. Old friends kept visiting, and so did a historian: "July 20, 1985—Tennant McWilliams visits for 1 hour and 15 minutes."

"He never discussed the cancer with us," Mary Conway remembered. Far more than their mother, the daughters had an innate appreciation of their father's complicated blend, an abiding concern for others despite deeply private ruminations. Yet they had no knowledge of the secret code in the diary, nor of what he wrote his brothers back in 1971: "The most deep-seated and personal worries . . . each of us have we keep to ourselves and that's the way it should be."

The countdown proceeded. Between July 30 and November 15 Kennedy gave the diary brief accounts of his esophagus shutting down—articulate, well punctuated, indeed graphic. On November 24, 1985, he made his last diary entry, in a shaky hand: "Routine Sabbath day. Nice weather. Clear, warm. Sunday papers. Bed 9:15 pm. 58 degrees." Mid-morning of December 4, after eighty-five years, those Muddie eyes shut for good.

The seventeenth-century Borderlands martyr, James Renwick, went to his end with violence and chaos, his bones like a stray dog's scattered and unidentifiable. Some three hundred years later—on December 5, 1985—and across a vast ocean, his likely distant cousin, Renwick Carlisle Kennedy, did the opposite. Before a large and respectful crowd the family buried him at Camden Cemetery in a plot and with a tombstone he had selected and paid for three years earlier, an occasion of sensitivity and order. Out of the purest of Borderlands blood had emerged one potently sophisticated Scotch-Irish heretic. Though silently tortured by the harshness of history and the blasphemies of Half Christianity, and the transgressions of many fellow Scotch-Irish, to his very end he still managed a quiet elegance.[23]

From where the Kennedys lived at the corner of Broad and Whiskey Run Road—today this is a vacant lot, city-owned, and with no signage—it is a five-minute walk down Broad to the Camden Cemetery. Kennedy's old church is directly across the street. This cemetery hosts some 1,550 souls, the earliest dating to the mid-1830s. Well over half of these tombs are for people whose families came from the Carolinas and before that the British Borderlands. Their monuments represent a stellar collection of tombstone literature: lengthy passages extolling the virtues of the dead—like all cemeteries, lies as well as truths. Biblical quotes dominate. But a broad range of English and American literature is in there, too.

In stark contrast stands Kennedy's monument. No flowery quote. No editorial. Just the basics:

Renwick Carlisle Kennedy, 1900–1985
U. S. Army, World War II
Pastor, Camden Associate Reformed Presbyterian Church, 1929–1974

If ever there were a moment for him to demonstrate one of his longtime preoccupations, it would seem, this was it. Tombstone monuments, Kennedy believed, are for the living. And the living should decide on their own what words, if any, might be appropriate. Even from the grave: fearless.[24]

Coda

What He Was

Robert Penn Warren once wrote, "What you do . . . in relation to other people" is the sole determinant for "what you are." As a defining barometer for human significance, this maxim out of moralistic existentialism may encounter dissent from the intensely spiritual. Yet all, likely, would credit the great poet-novelist with a profound expression on assessing human life, and incidentally comporting with crucial strains of Social Gospel Christianity. Indeed, when "what you do" is distilled alongside "in relation to other people," the many elements of Ren Kennedy's life merge into a compelling portrait of what he was. Parts of the portrait have strong definition. Others remain murky, if still evocative.[1]

Although he never lived in Scotland and Ireland, Kennedy spent a lot of time where the way of life of these places grew from frontier hamlets to potent transatlantic communities, South Carolina and Alabama. Even more, as a Renwick named "Renwick," likely descended from the family of James Renwick the Martyr, he was about as pure-bred a member of this Scotch-Irish "stock" as one might find. Still, his heretical relationship with many of these beginnings remains an ironic element in who he was.

Unusual among Scotch-Irish of South Carolina's upcountry, Kennedy came to adulthood under multigenerational family influences urging sophistication and humanist concern. In maturity he bore little resemblance to such egotistical Scotch-Irish hotheads as John C. Calhoun, George Patton, and George Wallace. The radical resentment of authority, romantic attachment to violence, and advocacy of Aryan superiority justifiably associated with many Scotch-Irish—though clearly not all—were his polar opposites. Down through the ages, wherever Scotch-Irish had goodly numbers, many ran roughshod over prudent thought and truth, and viscerally rejected change. One sensing this also knew the hot buttons to manipulate them. Many of them, so manipulated, played key roles in the rise of white massive resistance, which fought so hard to turn the tables on American reform: despite the defeat of racial fascism in Europe in World War II, support it at home.

Through his Yaupon tales, Kennedy committed much of his writing to what he considered to be these behavioral flaws and their resulting blasphemous transgressions. He did not live to see significant numbers—reportedly a majority—of Scotch-Irish nationwide again exhibit such ways in screaming cultlike adulation for US president Donald Trump, a key element in what likely should be called the second rise of massive resistance. But undoubtedly he would not have been surprised. Whether he would have railed from the typewriter and the pulpit, or just turned silently to the "bug juice"—or both—is another matter.[2]

Kennedy's Christianity reflected the same irony. His upcountry South Carolina roots within the Associate Reformed Presbyterian Church remain unrivaled as a transatlantic seedbed for traditionalist Lowland Scot Calvinism. His father's family and even more his mother's—with its seventeenth-century James Renwick connection—produced some of the area's most historic Scotch-Irish ARP ministers and congregational leaders. In that setting theirs was the orthodox Old Time theology: the hereafter, the literal accuracy of the Bible, individual piety and salvation, and separation of church and secular government affairs.

Still, as an adult preacher himself, Kennedy parted with some of these early influences. His precocious sophistication and intellect merged with ideas he encountered in and around Princeton Theological Seminary—modern thoughts about science, religion, and social responsibility. He embraced Social Gospel Christianity and subsequently found the Old Time theology's general rejection of it to be a major problem for much of the Christianity around him. Hence, it is only the most ironic of fates that spanned space and time to bestow upon this man the name of the great Borderland's Calvinist martyr, James Renwick.

Even so, contrary to his writing life, in both pulpit and community reform ministries, it seems that Kennedy strategically avoided public articulation of the relatively uncivilized ancestral origins of many of the white Christians in his ministry, which were, after all, his origins, too. Normally, he confronted their racial and economic conservatism and untruths with something of more common ground, biblical instruction on the words of Jesus. This was natural. His brand of neo-orthodoxy, if acknowledging hurtful effects of Social Darwinism, revered the evolutionary science behind modern health care and especially the developing social science field of behavioralism. But he never rejected such Old Time tenets as the Genesis explanation of human origins, nor did he reject individual piety and salvation as Christian essentials. To some, this combination reeks of contradiction. To him, the neo-orthodox, it was a spiritual mystery resulting from an abiding faith in God.

Out of that faith mentality, accordingly, he used the Bible to hammer away on his central message. If the Old Time tenets were practiced by *themselves*—with no Social Gospel complements applied to life before heaven—dramatic earthly human suffering remained unaddressed. This profoundly contradicted the preaching of Jesus and the Ten Commandments of God. As the diary and late-life conversations show, after long festering in him privately, the Half Christianity around him evolved to a major articulated preoccupation, in part owing to Adolf Hitler.

As his "behavioralist" perception of white authoritarianism, rooted in an essentially Freudian notion of white minority insecurity, merged with concern over Hitler, the "mad dog, the Anti-Christ," Kennedy's Half versus Full Christianity critique further crystallized. By the mid-to-late 1930s his thoughts on fascism were both similar to and different from W. J. Cash's. The noted journalist located roots of southern white fascism in a social psychology story of "ancient" and often "savage" addiction to authority periodically reactivated by rapid socioeconomic change challenging white people's control over Blacks. And nothing suggests Cash had moved from that social-scientific perspective when he committed suicide just before *Mind of the South* appeared in 1941. No less believing in the virtues of social science to explain "white numerical insecurity" as a source of "white aggressiveness," Kennedy nevertheless incorporated these behavioral insights into a neo-orthodox Christian worldview. To him, so long as what Cash called "ancient" insecurities among most southern whites went unaddressed—and that was Kennedy's God Mandate, to convert them—these whites were incapable of embracing a Social Gospel, or Full, or indeed *true* Christianity. As a result, with their historic authoritarian racial untruths unchecked, whether articulated or not, it was natural for them to gravitate to aggressive, indeed blasphemous, racism and even fascism—where in many ways they had been all along. In this way, Kennedy's dichotomy of Half versus Full Christianity assumed greater theological clarity. For the contemporary observer accepting Kennedy's critique, likewise, his thoughts on Half Christianity help explain how the first, southern-based massive resistance movement morphed. It grew into Newt Gingrich's and Donald Trump's larger, national-based second massive resistance movement, where an uncivilized, indeed primal, politics-is-war mentality likely reverbated even into hostility toward Democrat attempts to stem the deathly COVID-19 pandemic.[3]

Understandably, Kennedy's critique of the Scotch-Irish and Christians with little or no social conscience had political implications, further revealing the way he was. Not that he saw Jesus as an FDR Democrat. But he strongly believed "Jesus was a liberal" and said so regularly and openly. Too, his early adult devotion to Christian Socialism developed into an enduring commitment to the Democratic Party. In publishing he made no bones about this partisanship for "the party of FDR." Granted, just arrived in Wilcox in the late 1920s, he stayed clear of overt political discussion—true to ARP strictures. And his individual pastoral counseling and community ministry never knew political limits: from all religious denominations to all races, financial strata, racial viewpoints, genders, and sexual preferences. Yet with the Depression and World War II he found politics too vital to his Social Gospel message to stay quiet. In the pulpit he became known for ignoring synod policy and endorsing many Democratic endeavors, domestic and foreign.

Unsurprisingly, Alabama whites whom Kennedy most admired, and felt closest to, tended to be eager Social Gospel FDR Democrats—the socialist and atheist Emmett Kilpatrick the major exception. Still, in his last years, Kennedy appeared especially preoccupied with his "likes" and "dislikes" among the humanity around him, past and present. He worried he had not been sufficiently forgiving of those he had considered Half Christians. Yet he still was adamant about God's pecking order and equally eager to talk about it. In the 1930s, he recalled, only two white Wilcoxons stood as strong candidates for admission into the Aristocracy of the Kingdom of God: Robert Rentz and Viola Jefferson Goode Liddell. Of those two, early records show Rentz with greatest attention, though with the late 1930s and 1940s clearly Liddell gained his unqualified respect, indeed, "soul mate" devotion. By 1983, time's marination had significantly expanded his list to include Martha Patton Simpson, Bill Jones, and Lena Miller Albritton. All five, in his mind, were "Full Christians and Democrats."

Almost a year later, in March 1984, with a memory still reaching effortlessly to compelling parts of the past—if not to where the television remote was at that moment—he found himself asked: "On your idea of an Aristocracy of the Kingdom of God, what about Black people of Wilcox . . . some strong candidates?" His response: "It is not my idea. It's the *Bible's* idea. But, yes, of course. Besides Sarah [Woods], for sure . . . my good friends Joe Allen . . . Reverend [D. F.] Williams . . . that remarkable Mr. [William Green] Wilson . . . yes, as I understand it, you know, I think these qualify for the Aristocracy of the Kingdom of God, though of course that is not my decision. . . . It is such a shame that . . . except for Sarah . . . these good people could not vote."[4]

Unsurprisingly, beyond needs of their own church members, most of the whites around Kennedy rarely bonded with him over his broad Social Gospel ministry and certainly not his Democratic liberalism. Some of them also publicly condemned his drinking alcohol. Contrary to the "gothic small-town South" of Hollywood, however, many of these people still revered him. Front and center among such conservative white supporters, according to Charles Dobbins, were ARPs of Camden, Oak Hill, and Marion Junction. "Publicly gentle but privately brooding, [Kennedy had] racial values different from the

Millers and the Bonners. Yet they liked him because . . . he was erudite on the *Bible* and sophisticated and educated." On more general white reactions, Morton Rubin, ever the Chapel Hill social scientist, offered: "How has Kennedy existed in Wilcox? Despite his racial views and liberal Christianity, he has meshed with the folk culture . . . exuded oneness with the community. But this is not to say his racial views have been tolerated by the majority and powerful. For most of them, [his views] really are not tolerated at all. Inherent to 'toleration' is 'recognition.' These people have values, especially racial values, so deeply embedded in the Old South that Kennedy's viewpoint never has penetrated them. No 'recognition,' no 'toleration'—yet effectively still permitting his blending in with the folk culture."

Whether for those who tolerated him or those who did not, Kennedy's attention to individual personal needs added to his popularity: from grief counseling, to assisting college admissions, to ministering to Camden's well-known heavy drinkers with his professed (if unsubstantiated) antidote of cornbread soaked in buttermilk . . . here were deeply appreciated personal elements of his ministry. Still, far and above other reasons for his popularity was his regular employment of the literal Bible. Historically conditioned to be deaf to neo-orthodox/Social Gospel components of his Full Christianity message, they simply focused on his reading the revered words in a voice of Princeton gravitas, and admired him.[5]

In view of all this, to reiterate, the broad terrains of Black Belt life and indeed Alabama's, as well as the general ARP experience, revealed little change as a result of Ren Kennedy's hard work. Bible-toting and heavenly focused "Holy Joeism," as Kennedy called it, intricately woven into a tapestry of Anglo control and status quo economics, carried the day throughout Kennedy's lifetime and beyond. Regardless of the immensity of his Mandate, his essence therefore must include a stark fact. Even a more modest God Mandate still would have left him front-loaded for failure. And with so little impact, at some point one would think such an analytical person would have left. As probed in this book, however, despite options with pastorates of more Social Gospel orientation, Kennedy stayed on, struggling daily with defeat. Nor did he look outward for help when the help was out there. And this further elucidates the way he was.

From the 1920s through the 1960s recurring waves of reform moved across the South. Beginning with the 1930s some of the white reformers increasingly worked hand in hand with Black civil rights advocates. Early on some Black reformers urged the most systemic of changes. Along with them, whites generally evolved from advocating change within the context of "separate but equal"—increased education funding, no more lynching, tenant farmer rights—to reforms premised on the inherent impossibility of "separate but equal": equality in education and other public spheres, voting and office holding, and employment and housing. In varying degrees these reformers shared a lot with Ren Kennedy. Voraciously, he read what many of them wrote—from Richard Wright to W. J. Cash. He published a high-profile article in Chapel Hill's most noted organ for regional change, *Social Forces*. He helped professional social scientists as well as doctoral students with their Black Belt research. Futilely, he also submitted two book manuscripts to noted publishers of "southern change" literature, New York houses and one university press.[6]

But that was as close as he came to associating with the main structures of New South reform. Otherwise, he remained isolated from the movement. As he wrote Jack Bogie in 1952, "I live to myself, which is the way I prefer to live." Discrete, if overlapping, elements of his persona appear to have led to this isolation. Central was the individuality of his roots in Britain's Calvinist Borderlands. His childhood embrace of individual salvation and individual piety as crucial individualistic routes to heaven likely evolved into a strong strain of individualism within his secular self. A well-documented parallel of faith background inadvertently influencing secular thought is the connection psychologists have found between "lapsed" religious faith and a "guilt" complex affecting secular life. Another, even closer to home, lies with the well-explored Protestant ethic of individualism and the drive for material wealth. Should such speculation regarding Kennedy have merit, it is logical that neo-orthodoxy subsequently allowed him to embrace modern views of social responsibility toward the earthly "here and now" without sacrificing his deeply rooted individualism and his conscious sense of self as an individualistic "radical" or heretic.[7]

Likewise, beyond his youthful pattern of *leading* certain groups, rather than following, his marriage to Mary adds to this individualistic profile. The two had any number of incompatibilities; it took the Mary Mandate for the marriage finally to occur. His strident individualism added to their incompatibilities. Yet it also helped ease their being together. His hunger for late nights and early mornings alone in his study clearly met creative needs, but it also permitted avoidance of marital tensions. The same for his longtime employment at Troy, away from home. Indeed, only in her final two years as a widow—she died March 3, 1989—did Mary Moore Kennedy seem "somewhat lost without him."

In this light, it is reasonable to see his individualism influencing other major endeavors, notably his reform ministry. Granted, Kennedy's sense of self precluded being completely "alone." Whether in defeat or victory, he always had the Almighty beside him. Yet, irony of ironies, in a secular context this reformer who so intensely worked against the "Leave Me Alone" frontier ethic of his Borderlands brethren likely was most comfortable trying to change southern white behavior by "Going It Alone." He remained separate from the likes of Howard Kester and the Fellowship of Southern Churchmen, as well as from Herman C. Nixon and the Southern Conference for Human Relations. And, certainly, the God Mandate would have reinforced this: if targeting societal change, that Mandate nevertheless sprang from *one* man and his God.

Yet, the era of World War II ultimately saw Kennedy temporarily move beyond such strident individualism. His commitment to changing white southerners evolved to helping confront an international threat, racial fascism, of which white southerners were but a subset. His God Mandate guided him toward confronting German fascism. In the process he came to see an ancillary result of such a victory. Perhaps a US role in defeating Hitler would lead to an expansion of the national conscience such that the US government then would defeat southern segregation, too. At any rate, for the first time, to get significant secular assistance with his Black Belt mission, he took a major step beyond "Going It Alone." He not only urged US intervention in the war; he joined the US Army.

Unlike the mass of white Americans ultimately labeled America's "Greatest Generation," some southern white reformers, not to mention Black, actually focused on defeating German fascism. Apparently, however, it was a relatively small set of these sharing Kennedy's commitment to take the fight to the enemy—in combat. Such morally motivated citizen-soldiers included the Georgia civic activist most known for his future work with the Southern Regional Council, Harold C. Fleming; the future US senator from South Carolina, Ernest F. Hollings; the future Alabama higher education visionary, J. Jefferson Bennett; the future civil rights journalist and *St. Petersburg Times* editor, Georgian Eugene Patterson; the future state senator from Alabama, Joseph N. Langan; and the future federal judge from Alabama, Frank M. Johnson Jr. These men had brutal combat experiences similar to Kennedy's as well as considerable contact with Black US soldiers, both of which had lasting impact on their views about race and fascism and certainly desegregation. Yet among even these Kennedy was uncommon. He was the neo-orthodox chaplain and, perhaps not coincidentally, he wound up decidedly unoptimistic about postwar American change.[8]

After the war, despite writing about racial and other insensitivities of America's white soldiers, Kennedy started out hoping the US government would defeat racial fascism at home just as it had led in the defeat of Nazi Germany. Then "Home, Again" hopes collided with 1948. Virtually overnight he took the overt white racism of the Dixiecrat movement as the writing on the wall. Even if Dixiecrats lost the presidential election, he thought,

Dixiecrats showed American conservatives of both parties the significant potential for renewed racialist politics. Over the next three decades, despite notable reformers in their own party and implementation of major civil rights reforms, Republicans gradually realigned their message to encourage racial conservatives of the South and well beyond. Likewise, Democrats had their share of supporters for the developing Black-led civil rights revolution. Yet other Democrats and overwhelmingly those of the South embraced the postwar racial conservatism. Back came Kennedy's combat impressions of race. Clearly unaware that at least a few southern whites shared his views—the experiences of Langan, Hollings, and others would emerge later—he believed that except for Jewish officers from the Northeast most white US soldiers, despite being strong warriors, showed little to no regard for the courage of Black US soldiers, as well as little, if any, focus on defeating fascism. As those memories merged with potent residuals of the 1948 "down," his heart and mind moved to a place where he generally stayed for the remainder of his life. He had moments of thinking differently, notably from encouragement by John and Robert Kennedy's ultimate support for new civil rights laws. But the harsh reality always returned. At least one-third of white America did not believe people of color were their equals. And in Wilcox and likely much of the Black Belt this percentage surely remained far greater. It also produced a residual Black backlash of sad irony. At least in Kennedy's mind—certainly no universal opinion—those Black civil rights advocates who acted crudely only intensified counterproductive forces long established by surly white segregationists: Black or white, uncivilized "Rednecks all," for Kennedy, and a profoundly hurtful mix in an already difficult if still noble cause.

Here, the confluence of Kennedy's lifespan and locale undoubtedly added to his "down" and isolation. Despite enduring New Deal loyalties, the 1930s left him with long-term memories of failed change unavoidable as a filter through which he viewed the 1950s, 1960s, and 1970s. Likewise, daily he lived not only in "massive resistance" Alabama but arguably in the most *persisting* "southern place on earth," Alabama's Black Belt. Most other New South liberals had different living experiences: Atlanta, Charlotte, Jacksonville, New Orleans, Dallas, Nashville, indeed Birmingham offered beacons of change—and differing degrees of optimism. Too, those still focused on the bedrock historical issue of the legacy of slavery and persisting threads of racial fascism, as Robert Brinkmeyer distills in *The Fourth Ghost*, may have "remained haunted by long memories of anguish and guilt . . . [as the] shadow of Nazi Germany continue[d] to shape white Southerners' perceptions of their homeland." But they lived on through the latter third of the twentieth century finding modest relief in their firm belief that "Southern society [at least] has changed for the better." By contrast, Kennedy never did. Out of his evolving perception that Half Christianity often fostered racial prejudice and other blasphemies, he remained cynical about chances for pervasive change among the needed numbers of white hearts in the South and across America. Of course, such a broad prophecy awaits history's considered judgment. Meanwhile, it deserves focus, especially alongside the continuing decline of its natural antidote, a robust and institutionalized American Social Gospel Christianity.

In that postwar mentality, though still a minister, Kennedy therefore found himself a pragmatic and at times cynical lobbyist in Alabama politics. And in that role, his joining liberal groups—with which he never had been comfortable—seemed not just futile but defeating for his newly pragmatic endeavors in the eras of Patterson and Wallace. To help grow Troy State College, he had to cut deals with his polar opposites on race and society. From the outside looking in, some of these deals appear so mercurial as to question belief. Yet from the inside looking out, clearly they were understandable in a state political culture still rife with historic Black Belt subtleties. By the same token, on seeing a politically feasible opportunity to advance desegregation of Troy, the submerged Black Belt Social Gospeler quietly found a way to take full advantage. He did not expect his actions to change Alabama whites. He only hoped to help one small place in one small way. Not exactly the way he emerged from his conversation with God that May 17, 1927, in Room 22 of the Wilcox Hotel.

Renwick C. Kennedy lived much of the contorted experience that noted writer George Packer describes in *The Blood of the Liberals* (2000). Yet he did this not as a multigenerational experience. He did it in one sole lifetime. Not long after arriving in Wilcox, he came to feel powerless—a failure. Then arrived the God Mandate, bringing uplift and renewed drive. But private darkness during the Depression and war and afterward regularly returned, apparently drawing him to excessive use of alcohol. In so many ways after the war he came to mirror the very wartime surgeons he so carefully observed and counseled. Just off duty, sitting tormented on the side of the cot, head in hands: reliving every minute of the last twelve hours of blown-up guts and heads and chests and wondering why it could not be different, right now. More "bug juice."[9]

Yet Kennedy's essence also included many things besides a saga of faith and idealism ultimately going "down." Joys of fatherhood, excitement about writing, pastoral counseling of concrete benefit, indeed being an essentially honest, if shrewd, competitor in the regularly corrupt environment of Alabama politics: in daily life these could extract him from the larger saga and provide genuine happiness. And it appears something else more philosophical did, too, especially as his life wound down.

God was far from his only confidant. Literature was another. And in his last years he immersed himself in some of the greatest reading of all. The literature of ancient times and pre-Christian antiquity this Christian found stimulating, comforting, and useful. A half-century before the birth of Christ, the Greek dramatist Aeschylus urged civilized human behavior as an ethical and religious imperative. And, while the God of Ren and the Zeus of Aeschylus had their differences, over his last two decades Kennedy increasingly connected to the urgings of the old Greek. Here, in the roots of Western culture, he found solace and reason not to give up fully on the people around him.

Actually, this was less a discovery of Aeschylus and more a reunion. It all began with his studies at Erskine and Princeton. He then reread Aeschylus off and on his entire adult life. In the early 1950s, apparently after a protracted synod exchange on the practical virtues of a moral life, he and his ARP pastor comrade, Coot Love, entered upon extended correspondence on what the blind Greek poet, Homer, had to offer on how each of them would be remembered long after death. "You, Kennedy," Love concluded, "[will be remembered as one who] lived differently from the rest of us.... We feared what other fellows may think of us; [you] feared no man.... The only way ... [you were] like others was ... [you] had to die." Here was a remarkable commentary on human universalities. It also offered comforting words for the end of life.[10]

If nothing indicates Kennedy reread the letter in his final days—several months after his death it remained in a dusty manila folder of 1930s ARP Synod business—in 1986 daughter Mary Conway revealed that it still would have been a perfect fit with his mood. After all, the 7,000 books in his home when he died included pretty much everything the noted classics scholar Edith Hamilton ever wrote. Recall, he even underlined some of the words of Aeschylus that Robert Kennedy used in his impromptu plea after the assassination of Martin Luther King Jr. Mary Conway continued: "Until the stomach cancer finally stopped the energy of his mind, and this really did not happen until close to the end, the [ancient] Greek philosophy reading kept him in a reflective mood . . . let him be ready, consciously ready to go."[11]

Let us hope his final Greek readings led to private pondering on how his civilized individuality shaped his actions toward others, notably appropriate for a Social Gospel Christian focused on the blasphemy of racism and, by Robert Penn Warren's standards, the cardinal measure of the way he was. For in his own heretical ways and against overwhelming odds, Ren Kennedy of Wilcox County, Alabama, not only sought to "tame the savageness of man" and to "make gentle the life of this world." True to Love's forecast, he quietly endured the consequences—no small accomplishment for this pure Scotch-Irishman of the deepest South.

Appendix

The Writings of Renwick C. Kennedy

Manuscripts of Renwick C. Kennedy's writings remain in possession of Tennant McWilliams. Ultimately, these materials will join the Renwick Carlisle Kennedy (RCK) Papers in the Archives of Princeton Theological Seminary.

Nonfiction

"Alabama Black Belt." *Alabama Historical Quarterly* 2 (Fall 1940): 282–89.
"Alabama Book Toasters." *Christian Century* 71 (April 7, 1954): 428–29.
"Alabama Feels Mr. Hoover's Prosperity." Draft, 1931. Rewritten as "Rehabilitation: Alabama Version."
"Alas, Poor Yorik." *Alabama Historical Quarterly* 3 (February 1940): 405–15.
"Ancient Relic Found—Pine Stake Marked 1824 Roadway." *Alabama Journal*, April 28, 1957.
"Annals of the Cotton Belt." Draft, 1933.
"Are They Our Neighbors?" Part 1. *Southern Farmer* 107 (October 1946): 13.
"Are They Our Neighbors?" Part 2. *Southern Farmer* 107 (November 1946): 5.
"Are We Too Conservative?" *Southern Farmer* 108 (May 1947): 12.
"The Best Years of Our Life." *Southern Farmer* 108 (January 1948): 17.
"Black Belt Aristocrats." *Social Forces* 13 (October 1934): 81–85.
"Brass Hats." *Christian Century* 63 (October 2, 1946): 1179–80.
Camden's Centennial Year. Camden, AL: Wilcox Progressive Era, 1933.
"Can the Christian Faith Work on a Seven Day a Week Basis?" *Southern Farmer* 107 (August 1946): 12.
"Capsule History of Troy State University." *Tropolitan*, April 23, 1971.
"The Charity Rackets." Draft, 1971.
"Christian Living." *Associate Reformed Presbyterian*, July 19, 1967.
"Christmas 1946." *Christian Century* 63 (December 13, 1946): 1530–31.
"Christmas 1947." Draft, 1947.
"The Church Looks at Itself." *Associate Reformed Presbyterian*, June 7, 1953.
"College English Awakening." *Clearing House* 28 (November 1953): 157–58.
"Commencement Address, May 8, 1934." Draft, 1934.
"The Conqueror." *Christian Century* 63 (April 17, 1946): 495–97.

"Decadence in the South." Draft, 1948.
"Do Our Churches Fight Each Other?" *Southern Farmer* 106 (August 1947): 10.
"Do You Cast an Honest Vote?" Draft, 1947.
"Drought In the South." *Christian Century* 71 (December 1, 1954): 1459–61.
"Drunk." Draft, 1939.
"Ecumenity at the Grass Roots." *Christian Century* 65 (February 15, 1948): 238–39.
"Episode in Alabama." Draft, 1934.
"Freshmen Are All Right." *Christian Century* 66 (September 7, 1949): 1033–34.
"George Washington." Draft, 1932.
"The G. I. Gravy Train." *Christian Century* 64 (August 1947): 944–45.
"Give Up Hunting." *Outdoor Life* 101 (April 18, 1948): 17–22.
"Government in Private Business." Draft, 1939.
"Great Peace Celebration." *Christian Century* 52 (December 15, 1935): 1553–54.
History of the Associate Reformed Presbyterian Church of Camden, Alabama. N.p., n.d. [1938].
History of the 102nd Evacuation Hospital. N.p., 1946.
"How Good Were the Army Chaplains?" *Christian Century* 63 (June 5, 1946): 716–17.
"How to Buy a WAA Truck." Draft, 1947.
"In That Case." In Murray H. Leiffer, ed., *In That Case*. Chicago: Willett and Clark, 1938.
"Is It the End of Cotton?" *Christian Century* 55 (May 11, 1938): 591–92.
"James Bonner." Draft, 1976.
"Jeremiah Buys a Field." *The Pulpit* 22 (July 1951): 15, 18.
"John Is Going to Be a Minister." Draft, 1950.
"The Land Is Holy." *Southern Farmer* 109 (February 1948): 17.
"Letter from Chaplain (Capt.) Kennedy [on Life as a Chaplain]." *Associate Reformed Presbyterian*, March 15, 1944.
"Liberals Beware." Draft, 1940.
"Life at Gee's Bend." *Christian Century* 54 (September 1, 1937): 1072–75.
"Life Goes on at Gee's Bend." *Christian Century* 55 (December 14, 1938): 1546–47.
"Make Peace with Your Neighbor." *Southern Farmer* 108 (January 1947): 11.
"Military Training for Your Son?" *Better Homes and Gardens* 25 (October 1946): 33, 168.
"Minister's Institute." Draft, 1941.
"Mrs. Joyce Carothers Jones—Funeral." Draft, 1980.
"Neither Fish nor Fowl." Draft, 1939.
"New Southern Voice [Book Review]." *Christian Century* 66 (December 27, 1939): 56.
"Night in Decatur." Draft, 1934.

"99th Anniversary of the Presbytery of Alabama." Draft, 1941.
"Note on Erskine Caldwell." Draft, 1935.
"On Being Tolerant." *Southern Farmer* 108 (March 1947): 12.
"One Thursday Morning." Draft, 1939.
"Our Revival Meeting." Draft, 1933.
"Ox Farmers." Draft, 1934.
"Pests." Draft, 1946.
"Poets of Fish Creek." Draft, 1936–37.
"Poets on Fish Creek." *Alabama Historical Quarterly* 2 (Spring 1940): 44–51.
"Prosperity ARP Church, 1949–1972." Draft, 1972.
"Rehabilitation: Alabama Version." *Christian Century* 51 (November 14, 1934): 1455–57.
"Report on Standing Committee of Social Regeneration." Draft, 1941.
"Roman Stone." Draft, 1939.
"Samuel Johnson, The World's Greatest Conversationalist." Draft, 1948.
"Sedition Bill." *Christian Century* 52 (October 23, 1935): 1344–45.
"Six-Cent Cotton, A Southern Tragedy." *New Republic* 69 (December 16, 1931): 129–30.
"Southwind." Draft, 1947.
"Strength for Our Time." *Southern Farmer* 108 (September 1947): 16; 108 (October 1947): 16.
"They Never Had It So Good." *Christian Century* 68 (June 27, 1951): 765–66.
"Tightening Up the Cotton Belt." *New Republic* 77 (August 10, 1932): 337–38.
"To the Victor Go the Spoils." *Christian Century* 63 (July 31, 1946): 936–37.
"Trees." Draft, 1932.
"Two Weeks at Pressly Chapel and Salem." Draft, 1935.
"Veterans Make Good Citizens." *Southern Farmer* 108 (April 1947): 6.
"War." Draft, 1942.
"Waste in a Hungry World." *Southern Farmer* 108 (June 1947): 16.
"The Weakness of Protestants." Draft, 1947.
"The Well Digger." Draft, 1949.
"We Need to Think of This Life, Too." *Southern Farmer* 107 (December 1946): 1, 12.
"What Do We Read?" *Southern Farmer* 108 (November 1947): 17.
"What's Happening in the Cotton Belt." *New Republic* 79 (April 18, 1934): 266–68.
"What Woodrow Wilson Means to Me." Draft, 1925.
"Why I Gave Up Hunting." *Outdoor Life* 101 (February 1948): 24–25, 77.

FICTION
"Advancing Agent." Draft, 1935.

"Alabama Dilemma." *Christian Century* 52 (July 10, 1935): 917–18.
"All Men Speak Well of You." Draft, 1940.
"Angel and the Little Man." Draft, 1937.
"Before the Doctor Comes." *Christian Century* 51 (August 8, 1934): 1020–22.
"Bill Dickens." Draft, 1933.
"Bird Hunt." *Christian Century* 55 (December 28, 1938): 1606–7.
"Bookkeeping." *Christian Century* 51 (March 28, 1934): 423–24.
"By-Product of War." *Christian Century* 60 (July 1943): 865–66.
"Cherry Bounce." Draft, 1940.
"Christmas in Yaupon." Draft, 1941.
"Clean Feet." Draft, 1936.
"Coat." *Christian Century* 61 (February 1944): 175–77.
"Cotton Tenant Survival." Draft, 1937.
"Cracker Boy's Vote." *Christian Century* 65 (October 27, 1948): 1143–44.
"Cremation." Draft, 1932.
"Death in the Family." Draft, 1941.
"December 7, 1941." Draft, 1941.
"Face of the Poor." *Christian Century* 50 (June 21, 1933): 811–12.
"Fairy Story." *Christian Century* 51 (December 19, 1934): 1620–22.
"Family Plate." Draft, 1935.
"February the Eleventh." Draft, 1935.
"Flood in Harvest." Draft, 1939.
"Fog in August." Draft, 1951.
"Food." Draft, 1946.
"Forty-Two Dollars." Draft, 1937.
"Half-Back." Draft, 1939.
"Hector and the Alcohol." Draft, 1940.
"How Good Is Progressive Education." *Christian Century* 71 (November 10, 1954): 1366–68.
"How It Happens." *Christian Century* 56 (May 17, 1939): 641–42.
"I Have $1,000,000 to Leave." Draft, 1936.
"Ill Wind in Poland." Draft, 1939.
"Isolation." *Christian Century* 52 (November 13, 1935): 1455–56.
"Johnny's Bonus." Draft, 1946.
"Land." *Christian Century* 57 (February 1940): 213–15.
"Lawn." Draft, 1937.
"Legion Audit." *Christian Century* 53 (December 16, 1936): 1688–90.
"Liquidation of Mr. Smith." Draft, 1941.
"Military Interlude." *Christian Century* 50 (September 13, 1933): 144–45.
"The More the Merrier." *Christian Century* 65 (November 30, 1949): 1418–20.
"Mr. McClintock and His Tenants." *Christian Century* 53 (April 8, 1936): 533–35.

"Note on Cotton." *Christian Century* 51 (January 17, 1934): 87–88.
"Note on Trapping." Draft, 1936.
"Notes from Alabama on Homo Africanus." Draft, 1930.
"November Morn, 1932." Draft, 1932.
"Nowhere to Go." *Christian Century* 65 (May 26, 1948): 510–12.
"O, Southern Baptists." Draft, 1939.
"An Old Gospel Horse." Draft, 1935.
"One Point of View." Draft, 1933.
"Peter De Soto: Decadent Aristocrat" Draft, 1939.
"Piney Woods Bill." Draft, 1948.
"Pitcher." Draft, 1947.
"Poll Tax." *Christian Century* 57 (September 15, 1940): 1176–77.
"Psychic." Draft, 1933.
"Pulpit Diary." *Christian Century* 58 (January 29, 1941): 151–52.
"Quality in the Reserve Corps." *Christian Century* 52 (February 27, 1935): 272–74.
"Red Menace." *Christian Century* 54 (December 9,1937): 1526–27.
"Return to Yaupon." Draft, 1940.
"Roosevelt Hall." Draft, 1936.
"Roosevelt's Tenants." *Christian Century* 52 (May 8, 1935): 608–10.
"Scottsboro Shadow." *Christian Century* 52 (April 10, 1935): 476–78.
"Solace of the Poor." Draft, 1936.
"Southern Suicide." Draft, 1935.
"Tax Collector." Draft, 1940.
"Thousands and Thousands." Draft, 1941.
"Trapped." *Alabama School Journal* 58 (November 1940): 20–21.
"Volunteer." *Christian Century* 58 (July 1941): 931–32.
"Waste." *Christian Century* 53 (November 4, 1936): 1457–58.
"While the Supreme Court Ponders." *Christian Century* 70 (March 4, 1953): 253–55.
"While Thousands Cheered." *Christian Century* 67 (December 6, 1950): 1454–55.
"The Whipping of Lester Carloss." Draft, 1938.
"Why Churches Do Not Unite." *Christian Century* 69 (July 15, 1952): 825–27.
"The World's Most Generous People." *Christian Century* 64 (April 4, 1947): 525–26.
"WPA, Here We Come!" *Christian Century* 55 (June 8, 1938): 728–29.

Abbreviations

ADAH	Alabama Department of Archives and History, Montgomery
AH	*Alabama Heritage*
AJ	*Alabama Journal*
AOSR	*Alabama Official and Statistical Record*
AR	*Alabama Review*
ARP	*Associate Reformed Presbyterian* (magazine)
BN	*Birmingham News*
CC	*Christian Century*
EK	Emmett Kilpatrick
FSMCS	Field Studies in Modern Culture of the South, Southern Historical Collection, University of North Carolina, Chapel Hill
HWC	*The Heritage of Wilcox County*
INK	Isaac Newton Kennedy
JAH	*Journal of American History*
JCCJ	Joyce Clopton Carothers Jones
JSH	*Journal of Southern History*
KRF	Renwick C. Kennedy Research Files of Tennant McWilliams
KRF/B	Renwick C. Kennedy Research Files of Tennant McWilliams/Biographical
KRF/C	Renwick C. Kennedy Research Files of Tennant McWilliams/Chronological
KRF/T	Renwick C. Kennedy Research Files of Tennant McWilliams/Topical
LAT	*Los Angeles Times*
MA	*Montgomery Advertiser*
MCKD	Mary Conway Kennedy Dickinson
MKA	Margaret Kennedy Ausley
MM	Mary Moore

MMK	Mary Moore Kennedy
MR	Morton Rubin
NA	US National Archives, Washington, DC
NYT	*New York Times*
PCGD	Papers of Charles G. Dobbins, Special Collections and Archives, Auburn University Libraries, Auburn, AL
PLMD	Papers of Lisa McNeill Dobson, in her possession, Camden, AL
PMR	Papers of Morton Rubin, Archives and Special Collections, Northeastern University Library, Boston
PPVJGL	Private Papers of Viola Jefferson Goode Liddell, in possession of Will and Ruth Liddell, Montgomery, AL
PRCK	Papers of Renwick Carlisle Kennedy, Special Collections, Princeton Theological Seminary Library, Princeton, NJ
PRGM	Papers of Richebourg Gaillard McWilliams, in the author's possession, Fairhope, AL
PVJGL	Papers of Viola Jefferson Goode Liddell, ADAH
PWJJ	Papers of William Junius Jones, in the author's possession, Fairhope, AL
RCK	Renwick Carlisle Kennedy
RCK/AD	Ancillary Documents of Renwick C. Kennedy, in PRCK
RCK/C	Correspondence of Renwick C. Kennedy, in PRCK
RCKD	Diary of Renwick Carlisle Kennedy, in PRCK
RCK/RR	Reading Record, a compilation of books read by RCK (with dates read), compiled by the author and based on reading notations in RCKD and RCK/AD
RCK/S	Sermons of Renwick C. Kennedy, in PRCK
RCK/UP	Unpublished RCK writings, in possession of author
RCK/WFMR	Record of Weddings, Funerals, Members Received (with incidental notes), in RCK/AD
RG	Record Group
RGM	Richebourg Gaillard McWilliams
SF	*Social Forces*
STJ	*Selma Times Journal*
VJGL	Viola Jefferson Goode Liddell
WJJ	William Junius Jones
WPE	*Wilcox Progressive Era* (newspaper)

Notes

Overture

1. For more on views of Warren and other southern intellectuals—and on roots of fascism emphasized by Hemann Rauschning, Carl Jung, Sigmund Freud, and more recent commentators—see Robert H. Brinkmeyer, *The Fourth Ghost: White Southern Writers and European Fascism, 1930–1950* (Baton Rouge: Louisiana State University Press, 2009). See also Robert O. Paxton, *The Anatomy of Fascism* (New York: Alfred A. Knopf, 2004), 218; Isabel Wilkerson, *Caste: The Origins of Our Discontents* (New York: Random House, 2020), 270–71; Timothy Snyder, "The American Abyss," *New York Times*, January 9, 2021 ("post-truth"); Steven Pinker, "Why We Are Not Living in a Post-Truth Era," Skeptic.com ("post-truth in electoral politics"); Steven Pinker, *Rationality: What It Is, Why It Seems Scarce, Why It Matters* (New York: Viking, 2021); Neil Faukner et al., *Creeping Socialism* (London: Public Reading Room/Bookmark, 2019); Caleb Ecarma, "Tucker Carlson," Vanityfair.com, June 2021.

2. On the debate over "Christian fascism," no doubt begun by liberation theologian Dorothea Solla, see, for example, Chris Hedges, *American Fascists: The Christian Right and the War on America* (New York: Free Press, 2007); Todd Shy, Review of *American Fascists*, *Christian Century* 24 (April 7, 2007): 38–39; Walter Russell Mead, Review of *American Fascists*, *Foreign Affairs* 86 (March–April 2007): 171; and Peter J. M. Wayne, Review of *American Fascists*, *Journal of Contemporary International Affairs* 83 (July 2007): 828–30. Among the many assessments of Christian Democrats of Europe is Jan-Werner Müller, "The End of Christian Democracy and What the Movement's Decline Means for Europe," *Foreign Affairs*, July 2014. Also relevant to this discussion—if no soliloquy on Christian fascism—is Robert P. Jones, *White Too Long: The Legacy of White Supremacy in American Christianity* (New York: Simon and Schuster, 2020). Among other sources, the evolution of minority-white aggressiveness among antebellum southerners is traced in Jesse T. Carpenter, *The South As a Conscious Minority, 1789–1861* (New York: New York University Press, 1930). On the 2020 US Census data and contemporary white-minority social and political aggressiveness, see, for example, *The Guardian*, August 12, 2021.

3. RGM, taped interview with the author, Mobile, March 23, 1979; "William J. Jones," Rosenwald Fellowship Awards, Julius Rosenwald Fund Records, 1920–48, Armistead Research Center, Tulane University, New Orleans; WJJ and JCCJ, taped interviews with the author, Oak Hill, Alabama, November 21 and 22, 1979. All my interview notes are in my "KRF/B" papers unless otherwise noted. Completed in the 1970s and early 1980s, those original taped interviews survive only in the most damaged of conditions owing to my own storage of them. Still, transcripts and notes based on those tapes, along with notes for many other interviews (face-to-face and by telephone), do

indeed remain. The archives of the Birmingham Public Library include excellent, well-preserved taped interviews with Renwick C. Kennedy, William Junius Jones, and Joyce Clopton Carothers Jones. "Gee's Bend Project, Papers, and Photographs," Department of Archives and Manuscripts, Birmingham Public Library, Birmingham, Alabama. See also *WPE*, June 9, 1927, noting that RGM—at the time a young instructor of Spanish at the University of Alabama—was in Camden on Monday. Technically, Bill and Joyce Jones were not my aunt and uncle. After the death of his mother, Katherine Gaillard McWilliams, RGM—age five—and his father, Evander Tennant McWilliams, moved into the home filled with a blend of Clopton, Carothers, Harriss, Jones, McWilliams, and ultimately Boykin descendants. Here, RGM and Joyce were raised as "brother and sister." Subsequently, Joyce married another Oak Hillian, her second cousin (and also RGM's third cousin), William Junius Jones. Well into the twentieth century, for both Black and white people, and regardless of station in life, such was relatively common within the isolated pockets of family life stretching across the overwhelmingly rural and agrarian Black Belt, prompting loose usage of such words as *uncle*, *cousin* and *brother*. See, for example, Becky Bonner, comp. and ed., "Family Facts [Known to Joyce Carothers Jones]," 1967, typescript, 19 pp., in possession Tennant McWilliams, Fairhope, AL.

4. RGM interview, March 23, 1979.

5. Richebourg McWilliams, "They Were Seven," *Story* 6 (May 1935): 92–96. Whit Burley to RGM, February 4, 1935; Edward J. O'Brien to RGM, March 19, 26, June 6, July 11, 1935; Martha Foley to RGM, April 30, 1935, all in PRGM.

6. Aileen Kilgore Henderson, *Eugene Allen Smith's Alabama: How a Geologist Shaped a State* (Tuscaloosa: University of Alabama Press, 2011), 31, 37, 50, 65, 68, 70; Roland Harper, "Some Relations between Soil, Climate and Civilization in the Southern Red Hills of Alabama," *South Atlantic Quarterly* 19 (July 1920): 201–15; Roland Harper, *Resources of Southern Alabama* (Tuscaloosa: Geological Survey of Alabama, 1920): 14; Glenn N. Sisk, "Negro Migration in the Alabama Black Belt, 1895–1917," *Journal of Negro History* 17 (November 1953): 32–34; Glenn Nolan Sisk, "Alabama Black Belt: A Social History,1875–1915," PhD diss., Duke University, 1951; Ronald C. Wimberly et al., *The Southern Black Belt: A National Perspective* (Lexington: TVA Studies and the University of Kentucky, 1997); RGM interview, Mobile, July 9, 1983. On the clear argument that Wilcox was never covered over with majestic homes and endless cotton fields, see Daniel Fate Brooks, "The Mind of Wilcox County," MA thesis, Samford University, 1984.

7. RGM interview, February 24, 1979; RCK interview, May 21, 1983.

8. RGM interviews, February 24 and March 23, 1979; RCK interview, May 21, 1983; RGM, "Proposal for Rosenwald Foundation Fellowship," including writing samples of Martin Van Buren Jones manuscript; "Notes for [RGM] Autobiography," including character sketch of Martin Van Buren Jones; Maria Leiper to RGM, April 23 and 30, 1935, May 29, 1936, August 1, 1939, June 26, 1942; RGM to Edward C. Aswell, June 26, 1937; Aswell to RGM, July 13, 1937; Marian Ives to RGM, June 3, 1936; Harold Strauss to RGM, August 23, 1940, February 4, 1941, September 26, 1941, July 3, 1942; RGM to Robert Hillyer (draft/undated); Hillyer to RGM, December 1, 1938; Hillyer to RGM, January 12, 1946—all in PRGM. Death certificate: [Martin] Van Buren Jones, July 13, 1934, Alabama Department of Health Statistics (Montgomery). Disturbed by Eugene O'Neill's racism in casting the character Brutus Jones in *The Emperor Jones* (1920), RGM

initially sought to develop his Black Wilcox "Jones" character as much the polar opposite of O'Neill's, and "with no regional consciousness." But he "could not find Van's voice" through this medium; Van Jones's "consciousness" was inseparable from his region—the Deep South. RGM then reconceived Jones with a "regional consciousness" and tried to write his story as "a Black Belt novel." But finding "Van's voice" remained his problem. At the time, Edward C. Aswell and other Knopf editors—including Alfred A. Knopf himself—had growing focus on a new breed of southern writers, notably William Alexander Percy and Wilbur J. Cash. And Percy had urged Aswell to court RGM. But whether Knopf and Percy ever knew of RGM's problems with "Van's voice" remains unclear. RGM interviews, February 24 and March 23, 1979. On Knopf's courting of "new" southern writers, see James C. Cobb, *Away Down South: A History of the Southern Identity* (New York: Oxford University Press, 2005), 97–98, 160–65. On RGM as writing teacher see, for example, Howell Raines, "A Mentor's Presence," *New York Times Magazine*, July 20, 1986.

9. "Notes for [RGM] Autobiography," PRGM; RGM interview, March 23, 1979.

10. RGM interviews, February 24 and March 23, 1979, March 13, 1982, July 9, 1983.

11. "Mrs. Joyce Carothers Jones . . . Funeral, Sept. 2, 1980," draft, RCK/UP. All of RCK's draft writings are in RCK/UP unless otherwise noted.

12. In the 1950s and 1960s, while still living in Montgomery, writer Judith Paterson knew Kennedy well; Kennedy's former sister-in-law, Dorothy ("Dot") Moore McNeill, was married to Paterson's father, Duke Paterson. Judith Paterson confirmed my memory of Kennedy's appearance and speech, especially his accent as "a blend of Ivy League and Old South, something you hear less and less today." Paterson interview, May 12, 2012. See also Judith Hillman Paterson, *Sweet Mystery: A Book of Remembering* (Tuscaloosa: University of Alabama Press, 1996).

13. RCK and MMK interview, May 21, 1983; RCK interview, February 25, 1984.

14. Two of the most recent warnings about contemporary totalitarianism and fascism are Madeleine Albright, *Fascism: A Warning* (New York: Harper Collins, 2018); and Anne Applebaum, *Twilight of Democracy: The Seductive Lure of Authoritarianism* (New York: Doubleday, 2020). "Rationality inequality" is used to characterize Americans easily accepting lies and myth in modern tribalistic electoral politics, as given by psychologist Steven Pinker in "Why We Are Not Living in a Post-Truth Era." See also Snyder, "The American Abyss," urging today as evidence of a broad "post-truth era."

Chapter 1

1. For these and other Roman critiques, see Edward Gibbon, *Decline and Fall of the Roman Empire*, 2 vols. (London: Strahn and Cadell, 1783), 1:6–8 and passim. Though he maintains that some of the consequences dissipated over time, Vann explains the impact of the Protestant Reformation on Lowlander psychology and spirituality in *In Search of the Ulster Scots: The Birth and Geotheological Imaginings of a Transatlantic People* (Columbia: University of South Carolina Press, 2008), 25–46, 89. The "Leave Me Alone" characterization is mine.

2. James Renwick's life is detailed in John Howie, "The Life of Mr. James Renwick," *Biographia Scoticana* (Edinburgh: S. Bryce, 1781), 496–521. On Renwick's iconic death at Grassmarket Square, see especially James Grant, *Cassell's Old and New Edinburgh*, 2

vols. (London: Cassell and Co., 1822), 2:230–31; Brian J. Orr, *Testimony of the Covenant* (2010), available online at Lulu.com; Dane Love, *Scottish Covenanter Stories: Tales from the Killing Times* (Edinburgh: Neil Wilson Publishing, 2000). Transatlantic origins of *redneck* are treated in David Hackett Fischer, *Albion's Seed: Four British Folkways in America* (New York: Oxford University Press, 1989), 623. Current uses of *redneck* are discussed in Nash Boney, "Redneck," in *Encyclopedia of Southern Culture: Myth, Manners and Memory* (Chapel Hill: University of North Carolina Press, 2004), 255–60; and in James C. Cobb, *Away Down South: A History of the Southern Identity* (New York: Oxford University Press, 2005), 227–28.

3. Charles Knowles Bolton, *Scotch-Irish Pioneers in Ulster and America* (Boston: Bacon and Brown, 1910). In many ways James Webb's *Born Fighting: How the Scots-Irish Shaped America* (New York: Broadway Books, 2004) illustrates the Bolton profile reincarnated. The most focused non-Bolton profile, if not universally accepted, is Fischer, *Albion's Seed*, especially 754–82. But also see James G. Leyburn, *The Scotch-Irish: A Social History* (Chapel Hill: University of North Carolina Press, 1962), 3–119; Patrick Griffin, *The People with No Name: Ireland's Ulster Scots, America's Scots Irish and the Creation of a British Atlantic World, 1689–1754* (Princeton: Princeton University Press, 2001), 65–98; James McBride Dabbs, *Who Speaks for the South* (New York: Funk and Wagnalls, 1964), 204–16; and Alistair Moffat, *Scotland: A History from Earliest Times* (Edinburgh: Birlinn, 2017), 246–359. Likewise, in her classic, *Pioneers of the Old Southwest* (New Haven: Yale University Press, 1919), 1–30, Constance Lindsey Skinner differentiates the disorderly, often "bloody" mentality of Lowland Scot immigrants to America from the more orderly, if still violent, Highlander Scot immigrants. For analysis of the aggressive, disorderly Scotch-Irish archetype, see Bill Gilbert, *Westering Man: The Life of Joseph Walker* (Norman: University of Oklahoma Press, 1985), 21–28 (suggesting the Ulster experience made the Lowlanders even more violent and resentful of structure); and Karen F. McCarthy, *The Other Irish* (New York: Fall River Press, 2014). H. Tyler Blethen and Curtis W. Wood Jr., eds., *Ulster and North America: Transatlantic Perspectives on the Scotch Irish* (Tuscaloosa: University of Alabama Press, 1997), offers strong argument against over-stereotyping. Even more assertive in this vein is Warren R. Hofstra, *Ulster to America: The Scotch-Irish Immigration Experience* (Knoxville: University of Tennessee, Press, 2012). But see Kevin L. Yeager, "The Power of Ethnicity: The Preservation of Scotch-Irish Culture in the Eighteenth Century American Backcountry" (PhD diss., Louisiana State University, 2000); and Lynn A. Nelson, "Historiographical Conversations about the Backcountry: Politics," *Journal of Backcountry Studies* 2 (Autumn 2007): 1–10.

4. Ray A. King, *A History of the Associate Reformed Presbyterian Church* (Charlotte, NC: Board of Christian Education of the Associate Reformed Presbyterian Church, 1966), 238–39; Robert Lathan, *History of the Associate Reformed Synod of the South* (Harrisburg: By the Author, 1882), 70–71.

5. Fischer, *Albion's Seed*, 605–782; Leyburn, *The Scotch-Irish*, 184–256; Griffin, *The People with No Name*, 162; Walter B. Edgar, *South Carolina: History* (Columbia: University of South Carolina Press, 1998), 56–58; Robert Lee Meriwether, *The Expansion of South Carolina, 1729–1765* (Kingsport, TN: Southern Publishers, 1940), 133–35, 147–58, 169, 246.

6. *Renwick* etymology springs from different lines of linguistic development in the

British Borderlands. Although *wic* or *wik*, meaning "isolated place or village," seems to have remained constant, *ren* did not. In Umbria, in northwestern England, *ren* evolved out of *raven*, from which modern English gets its *crow*. There, as in adjacent Cumberland, *renwick* therefore meant "an isolated place [or farm] where crows live." Yet just to the north, in Dumfriesshire—in the Scottish Lowlands—*ren* meant "a small river or creek" (where crows lived?); and, connected to *wic*, or later *wik*, meant "an isolated place next to a creek." See Elson C. Smith, ed., *New Dictionary of American Family Names* (New York: Harper and Brothers, 1973), 423; George F. Black, *The Surnames of Scotland* (New York: New York Public Library, 1946), 689; Patrick Hanks, *Dictionary of American Family Names*, 5 vols. (New York: Oxford University Press, 2006), 3:185.

7. Thomas H. Pope, *The History of Newberry County, South Carolina*, 2 vols. (Columbia: University of South Carolina Press, 1973), 1:82, 239, 2:20, 304; Lathan, *History of the Associate Reformed Synod*, 159–379; "John Renwick," Ancestry.com. On the relationship between Rev. John Renwick and the martyr, James Renwick, despite substantial Edinburgh archival material on James, nothing suggests he had either wife or children. Still, in 2012–13, I sought a biological DNA trace on the relationship between James and John, the latter buried at Cannon's Creek ARP Church, Newberry County, South Carolina. That effort resulted in a dead end. The bones of James in the massive Edinburgh pauper graves remain scattered among thousands upon thousands of others' bones. The father of James apparently had siblings, and James's younger sister apparently married and had children, but there are no reliable records on these Renwicks, either. James Hogg to author, April 12, 2013, KRF/B. Unless otherwise noted, all correspondence cited in the notes is located in KRF/B.

8. Pope, *The History of Newberry County, South Carolina*, 1:131, 149–50, 2:342; "Renwick/Carlisle Home," *Newberry County Historical and Museum Society—Bulletin* (Fall–Winter 2005), 9–19; Margaret Renwick Fellers, "The Homes of William John Simpson Renwick and Mary Toland Renwick" (typescript [1972] in possession of Tennant McWilliams); Charles Carlisle interviews, May 15, June 6 and 8, 2007.

9. Michael Lynch, *Scotland: A New History* (London: Pimlico, 1992), 179–80; Charles Carlisle to author, June 14, 2007; Richard N. Kennedy Jr., interview, September 13, 2007; Pope, *The History of Newberry County, South Carolina*, 2:98, 100, 116, 225, 310, 342; RCK to INK, March 15, 1971.

10. Gavin Wright, *Old South, New South: Revolutions in the Southern Economy since the Civil War* (Baton Rouge: Louisiana State University Press, 1986), 16.

11. Pope, *The History of Newberry County, South Carolina*, 2:341–42; RCK to Folks [brothers and sisters], March 6, 1974; Julie Saville, *The Work of Reconstruction: From Slaves to Wage Laborer in South Carolina, 1860–70* (Cambridge: Cambridge University Press, 1996), 107–8, 176; *ARP*, November 29, 1899.

12. William Patton Kennedy's grandfather, Rev. John Kennedy, joined Rev. Thomas D. Clarke's pre-Revolution immigration from Ulster to Long Cane Creek, South Carolina. There, he married one of the many Ulster-origin Waardlaw girls, Leila. John and Leila's son, Edmund, with wife Jane Boggs, homesteaded near Long Cane Creek with their son, John, and his wife, Sara Devlin. The four took the place from log cabin and pigs to cotton plantation with slaves. Likewise, the Lairds, McLains, McCaslans, and Pattons made the voyage from Ulster to Long Cane Creek, and over several

generations, again, turned pig farms into modest cotton plantations. RCK to Folks, November 10, 1961; "The Kennedy Family Genealogy," undated typescript in possession of Richard N. Kennedy Jr., Atlanta; "The Life of Dr. I. N. Kennedy—A Scrapbook," in possession of Mary Conway Kennedy Dickinson, Atmore, Alabama.

13. J. Greg Carroll, *Abbeville County Family History* (Abbeville, SC: n.p., 1979), 101–3; *Sesquicentennial History of the Associate Reformed Presbyterian Church* (Clinton, SC: Jacobs Brothers, 1951), 169–70 (hereafter cited as *Sesquicentennial History)*; *ARP*, November 29, 1899.

14. On Calvinism, "Puritanism," Scotch-Irish Presbyterianism, and the resulting lack of social conscience, see James McBride Dabbs's analysis in *Who Speaks for the South*, 79–99. The basic steps in ARP and Due West development are in Lathan, *History of the Associate Reformed Synod*, 274–394; Maynard Pittendreich, *History of Erskine Theological Seminary, 1837–1976* (n.p., 1981), 1–30; Erskine Clarke, "Associate Reformed Presbyterian Church" and "Erskine Theological Seminary," in *South Carolina Encyclopedia* (Columbia: University of South Carolina Press, 2006), 34, 309; and Lowry Ware, *A Place Called Due West* (Columbia, SC: R. L. Bryan Co. for the Author, 1997), 1–108. On ARPs, slavery, and segregation, I remain grateful to Lowery Ware (Ware interview, July 8, 2007), especially on the incorrectness of Lathan's assertion that slavery had little impact on creation of the ARP Synod of the South. Erskine College's early enrollment never was large. For example, in 1840 it was 32; in 1860, 124; in 1882, 82; and in 1917, 120. The same small numbers characterize Erskine Seminary: 1837, 2; 1860, 3; 1863, 1; 1880, 5; 1882, 3; 1892, 11; 1900, 12. As for the context of these numbers, general ARP membership in 2008 totaled some 39,600; in the nineteenth and early twentieth centuries membership was approximately as follows: 1803, 2,500; 1839, 4,500; 1845, 5,000; 1880, 7,500; 1900, 10,000; 1920, 16,160. Lowry Ware and James W. Gettys, *The Second Century: A History of the Associate Reformed Presbyterians, 1882–1982* (Greenville, SC: Associate Reformed Presbyterian Center, 1982), 2–3; Edith Brawley to author, October 1, 2012, KRF/B/Brawley.

15. Ware, *A Place Called Due West*, 109–69, 253.

16. *Sesquicentennial History*, 168–70; *ARP*, March 30, 1892, May 3, 1939; "Kennedy Family Scrapbook," copy in author's possession; "Due West ARP Cemetery Directory," 59–60.

17. *ARP*, November 19, 1899, August 5, 1926. Also RCK to Folks, June 14, 1954; Mary Kennedy Todd and others to Family, October 31, 1951; Gladys Kennedy Hood to Mary Kennedy Todd, undated (1952?); Mary Kennedy Todd to Family, October 13, 1951. RCKD, May 5, 1928, October 1, 1953, June 17, 1978. "Prosperity [ARPC]"; *Sesquicentennial History*, 525–26. "Chart of Kennedy Children" drawn for me by Mary Conway Kennedy Dickinson, June 10, 2006, KRF/B/Kennedy; Elaine Owens Dickey, *Lincoln County: A Tribute to Our Past* (Fayetteville, TN: Dickey Publications, 1977), 119–221; Lincoln County Heritage Book Committee, *Heritage of Lincoln County Tennessee* (Waynesville, NC: County Heritage, Inc., 2005), 50.

18. *Sesquicentennial History*, 506–8; RCK to Folks, November 28, 1960 (copy), February 14, 1961 (copy); Ralph Erskine Blakley, *Memories* (Davidson, NC: Privately printed, 1992), 44. For a brief, moving obituary on Emma Elizabeth Renwick Carlisle, see *ARP*, August 20, 1930.

19. RCK/S/ 1940; RCK to Folks, August 16, 1956, September 4, 1956; MM to RCK, August 1, 3, 1926; and RCK interview, May 21, 1983. Shortly after getting news of the death of his grandmother, Mary Elizabeth Renwick Carlisle, RCK wrote her brother Richard (his uncle), the following: "I have been sad and depressed. . . . She is gone and it is hard to give her up. . . . She loved me and I loved her. . . . Some of the happiest days of my childhood were spent in her home . . . those Christmas times . . . and summers when as a little fellow I used to spend weeks there . . . she was one of the best friends I have had in the world." RCK to Richard C. Carlisle, August 14, 1930 (copy).

CHAPTER 2

1. Ralph Erskine Blakley, *Memories* (Davidson, NC: Privately printed, 1992), 44–46; RCK to INK, June 22, 1973 (copy); RCK, "Girl Scouts," RCK/S/1940.
2. The "Black Book" is in RCK/AD.
3. RCK, "Pulpit Diary," *Christian Century* 58 (January 29, 1941): 151.
4. RCK interview, May 21, 1983, February 25, 1984; *Erskine College Catalogue 1916*, 10–16; *Sesquicentennial History*, 169. The graded examinations are in RCK/AD.
5. Andrew Hood to RCK, July 30, 1930; RCK to Folks, October 31, 1954 (copy); RCK to INK, November 23, 1970 (copy), and November 29, 1971 (copy); RCK to Folks, October 2, 1977 (copy). *Erskiniana 1921*; Blakley, *Memories*, 56–58. Years later, when Kennedy had his first child, former Erskine teammates wrote him congratulatory notes affectionately calling him "Venerable." See, for example, J. K. Stuart to RCK, September 11, 1929.
6. RCK to Folks, November 23, 1970 (copy); RCK to Sisters, November 1, 1983 (copy). See also Wayne Mixon, *The People's Writer: Erskine Caldwell and the South* (Charlottesville: University of Virginia Press, 1995); and Caldwell's memoir of an early life with "ARPism," *Deep South* (New York: Weybright and Talley, 1966).
7. RCK interviews, May 21,1983, and February 25, 1984.
8. Student Records, College Archives, McCain Library, Erskine College; E. C. Stewart to RCK, August 28, 1921; *Sesquicentennial History*, 169.
9. *Sesquicentennial History*, 248–50, 267–68, 311–13; RCK/S/1921.
10. RCK/S/1922.
11. *Sesquicentennial History*, 173; RCKD, September 1, 1924; RCK/S/1923; RCK/WFMR/1923; RCK US Army "201 File"—copy in RCK/AD. RCK to Folks, July 16, 1923 (copy); E. D. Ellis to RCK, November 24, 1923; Karen Buck to author, July 7, 2006.
12. RCK/D, December 11, 1928.
13. On southerners in the Ivy League, see, for example, Michael O'Brien, *Conjectures of Order: Intellectual Life and the American South, 1810–1860*, 2 vols. (Chapel Hill: University of North Carolina Press, 2004), 1:27; and Glenda Elizabeth Gilmore, "Which Southerners? Which Southern Historians?" *Yale Review* 19 (January 2010): 56–69.
14. US Army RCK "201 File"; *Catalogue of the Theological Seminary of the Presbyterian Church at Princeton, New Jersey, 1923–1924*, 10; Kennedy, "Pulpit Diary," *CC*, 151; Arthur M. Byers Jr., comp., *Biographical Catalogue of Princeton Theological Seminary: Biographies of Alumni, 1900–1976* (Princeton: Princeton Theological Seminary, 1977); RCK interview, March 24, 1984.

15. James H. Moorhead, *Princeton Seminary in American Religion and Culture* (Grand Rapids, MI: William B. Eerdmans, 2012), 311–55, 366–69, 398; Edwin H. Rian, *The Presbyterian Conflict* (New York: Garland, 1988); David F. Wells, *The Princeton Theology* (Grand Rapids, MI: Baker Book House, 1989).

16. Moorhead, *Princeton Seminary*; Rian, *The Presbyterian Conflict*; Wells, *The Princeton Theology*. RCK Registration Information Sheet, Student Records, 1923–26, PTS Special Collections; MM to RCK, February 14, 1926; RCK interview, March 24, 1984. Some of the essays RCK wrote for Machen and Greene, with a significant body of his PTS class notes, are in RCK/AD.

17. RCK to Folks, February 3, 1924 (copy); RCK interview, February 24, 1984; RCKD, November 27, 1924, and December 28, 1928; Kennedy, "Pulpit Diary," *CC*, 151; *ARP*, February 2 and March 3, 1924.

18. Kenneth Henke to author, June 6, 2006; Karen Buck to author, July 6, 2006; RCK interview, September 9, 1984. Byers Jr., *Biographical Catalogue*; Andrew C. Reiser, *The Chautauqua Moment: Protestants, Progressives, and the Culture of Modern Liberalism* (New York: Columbia University Press, 2003), 136–38, 264–68, 284–85. Andrew Reiser to author, June 30, 2006. RCK's Chautauqua work also occasionally had him serving as purchasing agent—where cash transactions could leave him agonizing over the morality of co-mingling, in his coat pocket, Chautauqua funds with a few dollars of personal "tobacco money." He prayed over not getting the two funds confused. See RCK to R. E. Bendell, October 29, 1923 (copy); Bendell to RCK, November 6, 1923; Harry P. Harrison to RCK, November 16, 1923.

19. Sidney E. Ahlstrom, *A Religious History of the American People* (New Haven: Yale University Press, 1972), 938–45; Perry Deyo LeFevre, "The Chicago Theological Seminary: History and Christology in the Theology of Tillich, Morrison, and Reinhold Niebuhr" (PhD diss., Chicago Theological Seminary, 1946), 14–34, 57–93; Rolland D. McCune, "The Formation of the New Evangelism (Part One): Historical Theological Antecedents," *Detroit Baptist Seminary Journal* 3 (Fall 1998): 3–34; Michael Wightman Fox, *Reinhold Niebuhr: A Biography* (New York: Pantheon, 1985), 171–73, 192–206, 215–23. David L. Chappell's *A Stone of Hope: Prophetic Religion and the Death of Jim Crow* (Chapel Hill: University of North Carolina Press, 2004), 9–52, discusses how the "liberal" white viewpoint had to give way to a "prophetic" Black viewpoint in the evolving civil rights narrative, a fascinating mix of ideas helpful to one probing how "liberals" also prompted reactions within whites, turning them to neo-orthodoxy.

20. RCK interview, September 9, 1984. Christian Socialism receives general assessment in Charles H. Lippy and Peter W. Williams, eds., *Encyclopedia of the American Religious Experience*, 3 vols. (New York: Charles Scribner's Sons, 1988), notably the essays "Social Christianity" (2:917–31) and "Protestants and Reform" (3:1455–65). On the American South's experience with Christian Socialism, see Robert Hunt Ferguson, *Remaking the Rural South: Inter-racialism, Christian Socialism and Cooperative Farming in the Jim Crow South* (Athens: University of Georgia Press, 2018), though this subject as a regional phenomenon needs far more exploration.

21. Student Information Sheets, Student Records, PTS Archives; US Army RCK Personnel "201 File"; Byers Jr., *Biographical Catalogue*; RCK interview, March 24, 1984; Kennedy, "Pulpit Diary," *CC*: 151. Louise Guerard to RCK, June 30, 1923, October 31,

December 1, 1924. Louise Elliott Guerard ultimately married RCK's distant cousin, Selden Kennedy. Product of a noted ARP banking family in Due West, he owned a filling station in that town for some forty years and she taught in local schools. On the high-powered Guerard family—a significant source of ARP philanthropy—see, for example, "The Heidelberg House and Gardens" (copy in Archives, Bonclarken [ARP] Conference Center, Flat Rock, NC). The Guerard family narrative provides a useful case study of French Huguenot descendants intermarrying with Scottish Covenanter descendants, a key point in recent Scotch-Irish studies emphasizing the "blending" factor as reason for not over stereotyping.

22. RCK to Folks, May (?), 1954 (copy); MM to RCK, April 1, April 3, June 12, and August 14, 1927; RCK to MM, October 16, 1924 (copy), all in possession of Mary Conway Kennedy Dickinson, Atmore, Alabama (hereafter cited as MCKD Collection) and summary in KRF/C/1924/25; *Charlotte Observer*, April 30, 1946, November 19, 1950.

23. MMK interview, March 24, 1984; MM to RCK, June 24, 1926, March 9, 1927.

24. Student Information Sheets, Students Records, PTS Archives; RCK interview, March 24, 1984; Mrs. William Greene Benton to RCK, April 14, 1925.

25. RCK to MM, October 16, 17, November 2, 23, 1924, all in MCKD Collection, and summaries in KRF/C1924; RCK to MM, November 23, 26, 1924; MM to RCK, December 21, 1924.

26. RCK to MM, November 23 and 26, 1924.

27. MM to RCK, January 1, 7, and 8, 1925.

28. Howard Wheeler to the author, May 9, 25, 2007. Russellville's ARP Church no longer exists, but leaders of the Pottsville ARP Church aided significantly in this research.

29. Daniel Joseph Singal, *The War Within: Victorian to Modernist Thought in the South, 1919–1945* (Chapel Hill: University of North Carolina Press, 1982).

Chapter 3

1. *Sesquicentennial History*, 534–35. INK to RCK, May 4, 1925; Howard Wheeler to the author, July 5, 2006, and May 21, 2007 (including copy of Minutes of Arkansas [ARP] Presbytery, March 5, 1925, April 15, 1925, October 12, 1926, January 19, 1927, April 2, 1927, and May 5, 1927); RCKD, November 27, 1927.

2. *Sesquicentennial History*, 173; *Russellville Courier-Democrat*, November 27, 1925; *ARP*, October 10, 1925. T. H. McDill to RCK, September 26, 1925; MM to RCK, August 1, 1926; Joseph Lindsay to INK, September 12, 1925; Joseph Lindsay to RCK, October 22, 1930; A. N. Falls to RCK, September 9, 1926; E. D. Ellis to RCK, April 25, May 3, 1926; E. C. Stuart to RCK, February 10, 1927; RCKD, August 14, 19, 1926.

3. RCK interview, September 9, 1984. RCK's disappointment with the lack of sophistication of people around him is encapsulated in the marginalia he jotted on a clipping from the *Arkansas Gazette* (August 8, 1926), a poem-prayer about politics and bootlegging written by one of his Russellville congregants: "Written in Ark. by an Arkansawyer, with true Ark. genius and spirit." RCK/AD and copy in KRF/C/192.6.

4. Despite persistent stress in their relationship, during this year RCK and MM apparently wrote each other on average twice a week, debating their future as a married couple. Of this correspondence, while few of RCK's letters survive, virtually all of MM's

do, and they often repeat what was in RCK's last letter. For examples, see MM to RCK, January 17, February 10, 14, March 7, April 6, May 25, July 18, August 5, and December 12, 1926.

5. E. C. Stuart to RCK, June 30, 1926.

6. *Sesquicentennial History*, 194–95; A. B. Love to RCK, September 5, 1926.

7. *Washington Post*, June 26, 1921; *Washington Times*, January 14, 1922; *Anniston Star*, December 29, 1927. MM to RCK, October 9, 1926, and February 5, 1927. John Milton Cooper, Jr., *Woodrow Wilson: A Biography* (New York: Vantage Press, 2011), 585, 592. The various handwritten drafts of RCK's essay, "What Woodrow Wilson Means to Me," are in RCK/AD.

8. RCKD, December 3–7, 1925 (located in Reading Book 1925, RCK/AD).

9. *Sesquicentennial History*, 133–34, 169–70.

10. RCKD, December 3–7, 1925; and RCK interview, March 24, 1984, including a remarkable summary of touring with John and Clyde Miller—people to whom Ren would be forever devoted. For summaries of the lives of the Millers, consult *Wilcox Progressive Era (WPE)*, February 11, 1943; *Selma Times Journal (STJ)*, March 11, 1974; and *Heritage of Wilcox County (HWC)* (Clanton, AL: Heritage Publishing Company, 2002): 243–44. Robert Gamble, *The Alabama Catalog: Historic American Buildings Survey—A Guide to the Early Architecture of the State* (Tuscaloosa: University of Alabama Press, 1987), remains the definitive guide to noted antebellum structures in Wilcox County. But for detail on people connected to these structures, see Brooks, "Mind of Wilcox County," 133–58. See also Thomas Perkins Abernethy, *The Formative Period in Alabama* (Tuscaloosa: University of Alabama Press, 1990), 22 and passim. MR, June 26, 1947, and October 22, 1947, FSMCS (hereafter, unless otherwise noted, all references to Morton Rubin's Wilcox research are from this collection); James B. McMillan, *Indian Place Names in Alabama* (Tuscaloosa: University of Alabama Press, 1984), 4, 17; Alan Crozier, "The Scotch-Irish Influence on American English," *American Speech* 59 (Winter 1984): 310–31; Stuart Harris, *Alabama Place Names* (Huntsville: Strode Publishing, 1982), 80; "Swene [Svene] McIntosh," Ancestry.com; US Federal Census 1800; North Carolina State Census, 1781–87; *WPE*, August 29, 1901; *HWC*, 228–29. On other early white settlers in Wilcox, consult Brooks, "The Mind of Wilcox County," 1–8; *WPE*, November 14, 1935.

11. RCK interview, March 24, 1984. William James Fletcher, *The Gee Family* (Clarendon, VT: Tuttle Publishing Company, 1937), 92; Tennant McWilliams, "Wilcox County Slave Data: From Federal Census 1820–1870 and Alabama State Census 1820–1870 [With Incidental Comments on Nativity of Slave Owners]" (25-page data set, 2012, in possession of Tennant McWilliams).

12. RCK interview, March 24, 1984; Charles Hill Moffat, "Life of Charles Tait" (PhD diss., Vanderbilt University, 1946); John M. Martin, "William Rufus King: Southern Moderate" (PhD diss., University of North Carolina, 1956); and Daniel Fate Brooks, "The Faces of William Rufus King," *Alabama Heritage* 68 (Summer 2003): 14–23. *WPE*, June 29, 1922, includes a detailed account of property owners and homes in early Canton. See also Brooks, "Mind of Wilcox County," 24–25; *HWC*, 257–58; *Wilcox American*, September 28, 1977; Kathryn Tucker Windham, "They Call It Gees Bend" (undated typescript, Wilcox County Public Library), 2–3; Albert James Brewer, *History of Alabama*

and Incidentally of Georgia and Mississippi from the Earliest Period (Spartanburg, SC: Reprint Publishing Co., 1975), 577–78. Harvey H. Jackson III, *Rivers of History: Life on the Coosa, Tallapoosa, Cahaba, and Alabama* (Tuscaloosa: University of Alabama Press, 1995), 64–65, offers an insightful discussion of Prairieville as a cameo of the speculative nature of such river towns. Stuart Harris, *Dead Towns of Alabama* (Tuscaloosa: University of Alabama Press, 1977), 69, 98; "History of Prairie Bluff" (typescript, 1977, Wilcox County Public Library). On Tait clan origins in the Borderlands, see Fischer, *Albion's Seed*, 627; and "Charles Tait," Ancestry.com. On the term *Wilcoxon*—at times rendered *Wilcoxan* out of Americanized corruption—both the *Oxford English Dictionary* and Ancestry.com show *Wilcoxon* as the preferred spelling. The term's evolution from "son of William" to "Wilcoxon" as a family name and then to an adjective for "excessive obstinacy" can be traced in "Wilcoxon" as well as "Joseph M. Wilcox," Ancestry.com; and in Reynolds Webb Wilcox, *The Descendants of William Wilcoxson, Vincent Meigs, and Richard Webb* (Boston; New England Genealogical Society, 1998).

13. RCK interview, March 24, 1984; *HWC*, 109; Brooks, "Mind of Wilcox County," 7. The Alabama Department of Archives and History (ADAH) holds one 1840 issue of the *Alabama Herald*, published at Barboursville by William Gilmore and John H. Martin; it sheds no light on the naming issue.

14. J. Mills Thornton, *Politics and Power in a Slave Society: Alabama, 1800–1860* (Baton Rouge: Louisiana State University Press, 1978), 10–14; William Warren Rogers et al., *The History of a Deep South State* (Tuscaloosa: University of Alabama Press, 2018), 66–72; Charles D. Lowery, *James Barbour: A Jeffersonian Republican* (Tuscaloosa: University of Alabama Press, 1984), 123, 146, 196; Hugh C. Bailey, *James William Walker: A Study in the Political, Social, and Cultural Life of the Old Southwest* (Tuscaloosa: University of Alabama Press, 1964), 173, 87–92, 102–3, 141–42, 178–79; Harry Ammon, *James Monroe: The Quest for National Identity* (New York: McGraw Hill, 1971), 452–55.

15. Brooks, "Mind of Wilcox County," 29–31, 157–58; *HWC*, 6–7, 21–22; "John Daniel Caldwell," *Memorial Record of Alabama*, 2 vols. (Madison, WI: Brant and Fuller, 1893), 2:1034–35; P. D. G. Thomas, "Charles Pratt," *Oxford Dictionary of National Biography*, 20 vols. (Oxford: Oxford University Press, 1937–38), 16:285–88; *WPE*, March 24, 1924.

16. RCK interview, March 24, 1984. For a detailed history of the owners and operators of the Wilcox Hotel, see *WPE*, April 25, 1968.

17. RCK interview, March 24, 1984; Ouida Woodson, *Men of Wilcox: They Wore Gray* (Camden, AL: O. S. Woodson, 1989); *WPE*, February 6 and April 4, 1964. For an overview of Civil War and Reconstruction in Wilcox, see Clinton McCarty, *Reins of Power: Racial Change and Challenge in a Southern Community* (Tallahassee: Sentry Press, 1999), 32–62.

18. JCCJ interview, November 21, 1979, in which Joyce Clopton Carothers Jones (1900–1980), great-granddaughter of Martha Harriss Jones, recounts the story of Union soldiers visiting the house at the end of the war—stories told her by grandmother, Joyce Harriss Carothers (1847–1907), who had yelled from the rooftop, "The Yankees are coming!" For corroboration of the timeline and other components of this story, see *The War of the Rebellion: Official Records* (Washington, DC: Government Printing Office, 1897), Series 1, Part 1, 49:30; "[Military] Remembrances," Papers of Raymond Henry

Perry Jones, Special Collections and Archives, University of Vermont, Kingston; Frederick P. Dyer, ed., *Compendium of the War of the Rebellion*, 3 vols. (New York: Thomas Yoseloff, 1959), 3:1212–13. See also Becky Bonner, comp. and ed., "Family Facts [Known to Joyce Clopton Carothers Jones]," an eleven-page transcription (dated 1967) of a taped interview and in possession of the author; Joyce Carothers Jones, *Bethel's Shadow: Bethel Associate Reformed Presbyterian Church* (Oak Hill, AL: Bethel ARP Church, 1979), 21–22.

19. T. J. Lucas to Headquarters Cavalry Forces, at Vicksburg, June 22, 1865, in *War of the Rebellion*, Series 1, Part 1, 49:305; *HWC*, 3, 7–8, 96; "Memories of Zoroaster Cook," *Wilcox New Era*, January 24, 1900; Alice Foster Cook, "History of Camden and Wilcox County" [part 1], *WPE*, March 15, 1934; Brian Steel Wills, *The Confederacy's Greatest Cavalryman: Nathan Bedford Forrest* (Lawrence: University of Kansas Press, 1992), 310–17; William Warren Rogers, *Confederate Home Front: Montgomery during the Civil War* (Tuscaloosa: University of Alabama Press, 1999), 147. Construction and early ownership of the Wilcox Hotel are given in *WPE*, April 25, 1968. In 1900, contemporaneous observer Cook (cited above) placed the invasion "in April . . . late in the afternoon." But in talking with Kennedy on January 25, 1938, another contemporaneous observer, Helen Dexter, firmly recalled to him that Union troops arrived in Camden on a Sunday morning. "'Dressing for morning church, [she] first saw them out in the street [Clifton Road]" (RCKD, January 25, 1938). Dexter's memory comports with Union military correspondence in *War of the Rebellion* and various accounts of the last days of Forrest's cavalry.

20. RCK interview, March 24, 1984; Bonnie Dean to author, June 1, 2021; Betty Dale Williamson, "Hamburg Cemetery" (typescript, 1970, in possession of Tennant McWilliams); *HWC*, 115–16; Jones, *Bethel's Shadow*, 5–14.

21. RCK interview, March 24, 1984; Bonnie Dean to author, June 1, 2021; Betty Dale Williamson, "Hamburg Cemetery"; *HWC*, 115–16; Jones, *Bethel's Shadow*, 5–14; *Sesquicentennial History*, 352–55.

22. RCK interview, March 24, 1984; Bonnie Dean to author, June 1, 2021; Betty Dale Williamson, "Hamburg Cemetery"; *HWC*, 115–16; Jones, *Bethel's Shadow*, 5–14; *Sesquicentennial History*, 352–55; Jones, *Bethel's Shadow*, 15–26; "Joshua B. Grace" (1802–75)," Ancestry.com; *Montgomery Advertiser*, December 22 and 29, 1962.

23. RCK interview, March 24, 1984; Jones, *Bethel's Shadow*, 26–29; *Sesquicentennial History*, 151–52, 368–70; RCK, *History of the Associate Reformed Presbyterian Church of Camden* (Camden, AL: Wilcox Progressive Era, 1938), 1–5; Edith Brawley to author, July 2 and 7, 2014; RCK interview, February 25, 1984.

24. RCK interview, March 24, 1984; RCK/S/1926; RCK, *History*, 6.

25. RCK, *History*, 6; MM to RCK, January 6, 8, 31, February 14, 1926.

26. MM to RCK, February 28, March 7, April 1, 4, 25, 1926, and January 16, 23, February 15, March 29, April 20, 1927; *WPE*, April 4, 1942.

27. Clyde P. Miller to RCK, January 1, 1927; Hugh Dale to RCK, January 23, 1927.

28. RCK to Camden, Alabama, ARPC, January 1, 1927 (copy); Robert M. Stevenson to RCK, April 9, 1927; W. W. Orr to RCK, March 9, April 20, May 1, 5, 1927; John L. Boyd to RCK, April 30, May 6, 1927; MM to RCK, February 9, 24, March 1, 9, April 20, 22, 24, May 1, 1927; RCK to MM, May 4, 1927; RCK/S/1926; *ARP*, February 23, March 1, 1927; RCKD, November 28, 1927.

29. MM to RCK, April 26 and May 1, 1927; RCK/WFMR/1926–27.

30. MM to RCK, May 11, 1927; RCK to MM, May 15, 1927; RCK interview, February 25, 1984.

31. R. C. Grier to RCK, May 18, 1927; RCK interview, September 9, 1984, where RCK said: "Yes, I arrived in Camden a Christian Socialist."

32. *NYT*, October 25, 1925; MM to RCK, May 19, 1927; RCKD, July 15, 1927.

Chapter 4

1. RCKD, November 17, 22–23, December 8, 1927, October 10, 1928, and May 1, 1947; WPE, May 19, 1927; WJJ interview, January 5, 1983; MM to RCK, November 8, 1927.

2. R. C. Grier to RCK, May 18, 1927; MM to RCK, May 21 and 27, 1927.

3. *STJ*, June 1, 1927; RCK, "Pulpit Diary," *CC*, 151; RCK/RR/1926–27. Kennedy's vague and lofty solutions to the problems of Western culture may well have reflected the strategy of many leftists of the 1930s: staying clear of concrete solutions to protect the strategy of being fully on the outside while critiquing the inside. See John Patrick Diggins, *The Rise and Fall of the American Left* (New York: Harcourt, Brace, Jovanovich, 1973), 27–45, 93–210.

4. WPE, June 23, 1927; RCKD, August 14, 1926, through July 27, 1927; August 8, September 24, October 2, November 14, 22–23, 1927, December 27, 1929. "My mind works better at night" is from RCKD, May 3, 1929. On small-town baseball in the rural South, and its fascinating origins with Confederate veterans learning the sport as prisoners incarcerated in the North, see John E. Dimeglio, "Baseball," in Harvey H. Jackson III, ed., *Sports and Recreation*, vol. 16 of *The New Encyclopedia of Southern Culture* (Chapel Hill: University of North Carolina Press, 2011), 28.

5. On the matter of codes in the diary, when first seeing these in mid-1930s entries, I attributed them to Kennedy's recent reading of great mystery writers, such as Agatha Christie, Willard Huntingdon Wright, and Arthur Conan Doyle: he was entertaining himself. But the codes continued to appear intermittently for years after. And though I believe they were personal and significant, even with the aid of a high-level US Army intelligence officer trained in Cold War decoding, I never deciphered them.

6. MM to RCK, May 22, 26–27, June 2, 1927. For a detailed description of Kennedy's typical pastoral life in Marion Junction, see, for example, RCKD, August 11, 1927; and WPE, June 6, 1927.

7. Even after Kennedy moved to Camden, a Russellville nurse remained persistent: "Write to me real soon as I am so lonesome, and I always like to hear from you." Karleen McCord to RCK, June 2, 1927; RCK/MFMR/1927; *STJ*, July 10, 1927; RCKD, July 7, 1927.

8. WPE, July 7, 1927; *STJ*, April 4, 1971; MM to RCK, July 10–11, 1927; Cy Hood to RCK, July 7, 1927.

9. RCKD, July 15, 1927; MCKD interview, July 8, 1988; interview with MKA, June 27, 1989.

10. *Sesquicentennial History*, 150–51, 273–74, 392–93; MM to RCK, July 14, 1927. As a comment on the relative lack of a cotton/slave economy in Covington County, according to the *Federal Census 1860* and *Slave Census Covington County, Alabama* and *Wilcox County, Alabama*, Covington's 1860 white population totaled 6,000 and its Black

slave population, 462; while that year in Wilcox whites numbered 7,000 and Black slaves 17,797. For other aspects of early Covington County, see Wyley Donald Ward, *Early History of Covington County, 1821–1871* (Spartanburg, SC: Reprint Co., 1991); *Heritage of Covington County* (Clanton, AL: Heritage Publishing Company, 2003), See also RCK/WFMR/1927.

11. MM to RCK, July 16, 24, 29, August 7, 22, 1927; RCK to MM, July 29; RCK to Folks, November 18, 1975; RCKD, July 14, 1926–July 29, 1927.

12. Glenn Feldman, *Politics, Society, and the Klan in Alabama: 1915–1949* (Tuscaloosa: University of Alabama Press, 1999), 92–93 and passim; RCK interview, September 9, 1984 (he remembered only the year—neither the month nor the specific location). Lynching data on Arkansas in the 1920s—including at least nine killings between January 1923 and August 1927—are given in the online *Encyclopedia of Arkansas*.

13. Lynching Data for Wilcox County, Alabama (Tuskegee Lynching Records, Tuskegee University, Tuskegee, Alabama; hereafter cited as "Tuskegee Lynching Records"); RCKD, January 23, August 8, 1927; RCK to MM, August 8, 1927. The "hanged twice" lynching also was recounted to Chapel Hill anthropologist Morton Rubin, when he researched in Camden in 1947; a Black man named Andrew told him the story, as did probate judge Jesse McLeod. See MR, July 12, 1947.

My own father, Richebourg McWilliams (RGM), recalled second-hand encounter with two unrecorded lynchings in Wilcox. One occurred in approximately 1909, when he was eight years old, midway between Oak Hill and Pine Apple. There, one night in the Model T, he and his father, Evander Tennant McWilliams (my grandfather), encountered a recently burned cabin, embers still glowing. When his father asked men standing around what had happened, they said they had "burned a nigger inside." Despite his youth, RGM remembered the event in part because this was "the first and only time" he saw his father—a racial moderate for the times (if no "liberal") and "distinctly anti-God and anti-church" since his wife died in 1907—"put his head in his hands and muttered, 'Oh, Lord, God. Please, God. Please.'" Then, in 1919, home on Christmas holiday from the University of Alabama, where he was a student, late at night RGM drove his uncle, physician Samuel Swift Boykin, to Pine Apple to treat a patient—one John Franklin ("Poss") Melton. After treatment, Melton came out to the car and showed RGM a bullet. He recalled Melton saying, "Here, boy, you want to see this? It's one of the bullets we dug out that nigger up the road last night, after the fire [burned-up shack] cooled down." On the way back to Oak Hill, Boykin mentioned that Melton was a "mean man in an otherwise kind and well respected family." RGM interview, February 24, 1979; Robert A. Smith III and Frances Dudley Grimes, "History of Pine Apple, Wilcox County, Alabama, 1815–1985" (1990 typescript in possession of Tennant McWilliams), 11, 16, 41–43. For examples of the *Wilcox Progressive Era* covering relatively benign KKK endeavors, see *WPE*, March 5, 1925, October 15, 1925, July 8, 1927, and December 29, 1927. The Lillian Smith quote is from Fred C. Hobson, *But Now I See: The White Southern Racial Conversion* (Baton Rouge: Louisiana State University Press, 1999), 24. The loose, popular-culture usage of *behavior* is profiled in Bertram Wyatt-Brown's *Honor and Violence in the Old South* (New York: Oxford University Press, 1986), 61–62 and passim. For more on how *behavior* has played a pivotal role in the historiography of race and the South, see for example Cobb, *Away Down South*, 202–3.

14. Clippings from *Talladega Home*, July 19, 1927; *Anniston Star*, July 16, 1927; *Eufaula Citizen*, April 9, 1927, all in Tuskegee Lynching Records; handbill (small poster) bannered "July 1927 Camden," KRF/AD; RCK to MM, August 7, 1927. According to *STJ* (August 14, 1927), in this sermon Kennedy "openly denounced the recent floggings ... declaring they were cowardly and law-breaking and he deeply deplored them. A large congregation enjoyed his discourse." Two months after this sermon, Dobbins gave Kennedy a lecture on his own views about the Klan's strategies and goals. See RCKD, September 20, 1927. On Dobbins, see also Wayne Flynt, *Alabama Baptists: Southern Baptists in the Heart of Dixie* (Tuscaloosa: University of Alabama Press, 1998), 359.

15. RCK interview, July 20,1985; RCKD, July 23, August 8, October 3, 1927, July 24, 1928. The water-cooler letter is in *WPE*, December 29, 1927.

16. On Eleanor Elizabeth (Bess) Cochran and her family, see *HWC*, 9, 21, 45; *Livingston's Law Register* (New York: Published by Subscription, 1856); *Federal Census 1860; Slave Census Wilcox County, Alabama*. *WPE*, April 17, 1889, April 10, 1930, November 17, 1932, July 4, November 5, 1936, July 4, 1939, and September 26, 1940; RCKD, February 3, 1942. Far later, Emmett Kilpatrick told RCK that because of abolition the Cochran family's post–Civil War life had consisted of "two battles"—"one against death, one against life." RCKD, February 22, 1946. Bess Cochran died on October 8, 1947. She was the last of her immediate family; her younger sister, Sarah Louisa, had died the year before. Kennedy presided over Bess Cochran's funeral, noting afterward that "not one member of her [local extended] family attended the funeral." RCKD, October 11–12, 1947.

17. H. L. Mencken *Prejudices, Second Series* (New York: Knopf, 1920), provides one of the earliest high-profile attacks on a southern elite as "legitimate aristocracy," emphasizing the southerners' forced agrarian labor practices—whether slavery or sharecropping—as a strike against one's being a "true" aristocrat. No doubt harkening to the role of "aristocrats" of ancient Greece, in this critique the pivotal issue seems to have been whether labor was treated with *noblesse oblige*. Kennedy did not read Mencken's critique until 1929, but he likely embraced the same notion of aristocracy and labor in 1927, if not much earlier. See Fred Hobson, *Serpent in Eden: H. L. Mencken and the South* (Chapel Hill: University of North Carolina Press, 1974). To pursue Mencken's contact with Grover Hall, consult Daniel Webster Hollis III, *An Alabama Newspaper Tradition: Grover C. Hall and the Hall Family* (Tuscaloosa: University of Alabama Press, 1983), 29–31, 94–95. On the myth of "legitimate aristocracy" in early southern history, and the argument that large-scale cotton production worked counter to the development of legitimate aristocracy, see W. J. Cash, *Mind of the South* (New York: Knopf, 1941), 11–17; Rollin G. Osterweis, *Romance and Nationalism in the Old South* (New Haven: Yale University Press, 1949), 41–51; Carl Bridenbaugh, *Myths and Realities: Societies of the Colonial South* (Baton Rouge: Louisiana State University Press, 1952), 60–74, 98–99; and William R. Taylor, *Cavalier and Yankee: The Old South and American Character* (New York: G. Braziller, 1961), 74–75.

18. *WPE*, August 25, 1927; MM to RCK, September 2, 4, 17, 19, October 9, 1927. Warren F. Kuehl and Lynne K. Dunn, *Keeping the Covenant: American Interventionists and the League of Nations, 1920–1939* (Kent, OH: Kent State University Press, 1997), 34–35. Along with several early drafts, the twenty-page handwritten version of Kennedy's

Wilson essay survives in RCK/AD. See RCK interview, March 2, 1984; A. Scott Berg, *Lindbergh* (New York: Putnam, 1998).

19. RCKD, September 20, October 3–4, 7, 1927. On editor Grover Hall and the KKK, see Hollis, *An Alabama Newspaper Tradition: Grover Hall and the Hall Family*.

20. MM to RCK, September 25, 1927.

21. RCKD, September 23, October 2, 1927; RCK/S/1927; Rosa Young, *Light in the Dark Belt: The Story of Rosa Young as Told by Herself*, rev. ed. (St. Louis: Concordia Publishing House, 2014), 28, 34, 53–59, 71–85, 98–125, 144–45, 164; Glenn Feldman, *The Irony of the Solid South: Democrats, Republicans, and Race, 1865–1944* (Tuscaloosa: University of Alabama Press, 2013), 55; Hobson, *But Now I See*, 10, 17, 24. For larger state-level and beyond context of Kennedy's public education critique, see the impeccable study by Ira Harvey, *A History of Education Finance in Alabama* (Auburn, AL: Truman Pierce Institute for the Advancement of Teacher Education, 1989), 108; and Adam Fairclough, *A Class of Their Own: Black Teachers in the Segregated South* (Cambridge, MA: Harvard University Press, 2007), 204–8 and passim. See also Ancestry.com data on John Miller Bonner, William Junius Jones, and Jessie Taylor Bonner Jones.

22. RCKD, October 2, 1927, July 10, 1930; Lisa Dobson to author, February 12, 2013; John Henry Bogie to author, February 15, 2013; Ernest N. Orr to RCK, July 9, 1928. Feldman, *Politics, Society, and the Klan in Alabama*, 95; *HWC*, 8, 45, 65; *WPE*, March 26, 1942.

23. RCKD, October 3, 1927; RCK interview, July 20, 1985. On how the WKKK identified with a degree of "women's liberation," see Kathleen M. Blee, *Women of the Klan: Racism and Gender in the 1920s* (Berkeley: University of California Press, 1999). Glenn Feldman offers qualified dissent from Blee's approach in "Keepers of the Hearth: Women, the Klan, and Traditional Family Values," in Bruce Clayton and John Salmond, eds., *Lives Full of Struggle and Promise* (Gainesville: University of Florida Press, 2003), 149–80. For a more recent approach to women and the defense of segregation, see Elizabeth Gillespie McRae, *Mothers of Massive Resistance: White Women and the Politics of Massive Resistance* (New York: Oxford University Press, 2018), 23–108.

24. RCKD, October 3, 1927; RCK interview, September 9, 1984.

25. RCKD, October 3, 1927; RCK interview, September 9, 1984; MM to RCK, October 5, 1927; Ware and Gettys, *Second Century*, 349–50.

26. RCKD, October 7, 1927; Rose Herlong Ellis, "The Calhoun School, Miss Charlotte Thorn's 'Lighthouse on the Hill' in Lowndes County, Alabama," *Alabama Review* 37 (July 1984): 183–201; RCK interview, September 9, 1981. The story of Rev. Justice Smith Jones (1884–1962)—mountain man, barroom brawler, civil rights reformer, Episcopal minister—needs full telling. Certain educational and church records on him are in possession of Tennant McWilliams.

27. *ARP*, December 7, 1927; RCKD, October 14–15, 1927; *WPE*, October 20, 1927, February 16, 1928; MM to RCK, October 16–18 and 21, 1927; RCK/WFMR/1927–28.

28. MM to RCK, September 25, October 18, 1927; *AOSR, 1927*, 75.

29. RCKD, October 31, November 23, 1927; RCK interview, September 9, 1984; *HWC*, 315–16; "Selma Missions" and "Priests at Selma, 1910–1939," Archives of the Archdiocese of Mobile. RCKD, February 26, 1928; *WPE*, September 1, 1938, December 1, 1939; *HWC*, 202; WJJ and JCCJ interview, November 21, 1979; John Laurie

Dale Jr. interview, November 3, 2004; "Samuel Swift Boykin," Ancestry.com; Certificate of Death: Mrs. S. S. [Lodie] Boykin [January 4, 1914], Alabama Center for Health Statistics, Montgomery; Edward M. Boykin, *History of the Boykin Family, from Their First Settlement in Virginia, 1685, and in South Carolina, Georgia, and Alabama* (Camden, SC: Colin Macrae, 1876).

30. RCKD, September 23–24, 1927, November 23, 1928. Some ten years later Kennedy's portrait of Benjamin Meek Miller—down to starched collar and gold chain—found uncanny reflection in a photo essay on Miller, "Portrait of an Alabamaian—'Rugged Oak of Wilcox,'" *Alabama* (March 8, 1937), 8–10.

31. RCKD, November 12, 21, 24, 27–28, 1927. From March 28 to April 1, 1927, Kennedy read Sinclair Lewis's *Elmer Gantry* (1927) and from November 21 through 24, 1927, he read Lewis's *Main Street* (1920). RCK/RR/1927. See also Cobb, *Away Down South*, 78, 107; Sarah Newman Shouse, *Hillbilly Realist: Herman Clarence Nixon of Possum Trot* (Tuscaloosa: University of Alabama Press, 1986), 58–59; Herman C. Nixon, "Whither Southern Economy," in Twelve Southerners, *I'll Take My Stand: The South and the Agrarian Tradition* (New York: Harper and Brothers, 1930), 186–200.

32. RCKD, November 22, December 2, 1927, February 2, March 13, June 25, July 31, August 1, October 1–2, 1928; Lori Gruen, *Ethics and Animals* (Cambridge: Cambridge University Press, 2011); Gruen, "The Moral Status of Animals," *Stanford Encyclopedia of Philosophy* (Fall 2017 edition). Kennedy's animal concerns continued the rest of his life. During the Depression, he even refused to kill rabbits eating his garden lettuce. Once, in a moment of "horrible weakness" when conceding to Clark Jones's pressures to go hunting, he agonized for days: "I got ... no pleasure out of killing the squirrel. ... God knows I kill few of his creatures." RCKD, November 21, 24, December 11, 1928, February 1, 24, March 1, April 24, 1929. On southerners and hunting, see Wyatt-Brown, *Honor and Violence*, 120.

33. RCKD, November 26, 1927; MM to RCK, December 2, 1927.

34. RCKD, November 26, 1927; MM to RCK, December 2, 1927.

35. On ARPs' partial embrace of secular social-progress agendas—"Social Regeneration," "Whole Gospel," and more—and, despite this, the central point that individual salvation and piety, as well as many Victorian values, always were their priority concerns as opposed to people helping people, see Ware and Gettys, *Second Century*, 329–74. James McBride Dabbs's complicated racial conversion is lucidly analyzed in Hobson, *But Now I See*, 52–60.

36. MM to RCK, January 20, November 4, 8, 22, 27, 1927; RCKD, November 21, 24, December 2, 20, 23, 28,1927, March 14, 1928.

37. RCKD, November 12, 1927; MM to RCK, December 18, 20, 23, 27–28, 1927; RCK/S/1927. In 1911, Henry Plant opened the Selma Stationery Shop on Water Street in space recently used by photographer Edgar Cayce, later of international psychic fame. Throughout the 1920s and 1930s, Plant's shop enjoyed a Black Belt "literary salon" status. On the first floor, he sold stationery, typewriters, and a full range of Black Belt newspapers, plus major daily newspapers from Mobile, Montgomery, and Birmingham, as well as the *New York Times*. Upstairs he offered books—classical literature, history, fiction. Plant was most revered for expediting special customer orders for new fiction well mentioned in the *New York Times*, and RCK was a regular

customer. Anice Armstrong interview, April 8, 2009; clip from *Selma Mirror*, June [?], 1911, Newspapers.com.

38. RCKD, December 30, 1927, June 28, 1928; WJJ and JCCJ interview, November 21, 1979. On Emmett Kilpatrick's life, see, for example, *NYT*, January 1, October 19, 1921; *WPE*, May 17, 1956, October 3, 1968; RCK, "Veteran Troy Teacher Reviews Large Career," *STJ*, December 29, 1957. On Kilpatrick's presence at the University of South Carolina, see *WPE*, September 21, 1933; *Garnet and Black, 1929* (Columbia: University of South Carolina, 1929), 29; *Garnet and Black, 1932*, 214; and *Garnet and Black, 1935*. See also Kilpatrick-Latané correspondence in John Holliday Latané Papers, Series 3, Box 5, Archives of the Milton S. Eisenhower Library, Johns Hopkins University, Baltimore; and University of South Carolina Archives: Office of the President: William D. Melton, Box 4, 1923–26. On charges of his being drunk on campus and his resignation, see correspondence in University of South Carolina Archives: Office of the President: J. Ron McKissick, Box 4, 1936–37. Marie Bankhead Owen's long arm is addressed in Kyle Whitmire, "How a Confederate Daughter Rewrote Alabama History for White Supremacy," *Mobile Register*, February 27, 2022.

39. RCKD, August 8, 1928; MM to RCK, January 29, February 9, 26, 1928.

40. RCKD, March 13, 20, 21, 1928.

41. RCKD, May 5, 1928; MM to RCK, May 9–25, 1928.

42. RCKD, June 1, 7, and 12, 1928; *WPE*, June 14, 1928; MM to RCK, June 28, 1928.

43. MM to RCK, June 8, July 9, 30, 1928; RCKD, July 17–18, October 1, 26, 1928.

44. RCKD, October 1, 1928.

45. RCKD, August 28, 1928.

46. RCKD, October 1–2, November 26, 1928.

47. RCKD, February 26, November 26, December 30, 1928; *WPE*, June 16, 1938. In this context, he had other comments about Tait descendants. The night after he did the funeral for Frank Tait, another descendant of Charles Tait and who lived at "Yaupon," he recorded this: "Frank was one of the old-landed aristocracy, a descendant of the Old South. Taits once were high cockalorums in this section, though their glory is now departed . . . down at the heels, run to seed, broke, most of them at least, struggling for a living. . . . Frank had land but great debt. . . . A few years ago he did something with a check of a Negro who had been a soldier [in World War I]. It was a government check. . . . Nothing was done to Frank Tait." RCKD, December 15, 1928. Kennedy also leveled more criticism at Sheriff Tait over the types of people he befriended and defended. For example, in 1927, "Dallas County Sheriff J. E. Geddy turned a white man loose after he killed a Negro over thirty-five cents." The following year, "Geddy shot down a Negro man who was courting the sheriff's mulatto girlfriend. Though Geddy was guilty of first-degree murder," according to Kennedy—who witnessed the trial in Selma—"this evil man got a sentence of only five years—and Sheriff Tait went around Camden telling everyone what an unfair sentence his friend, Geddy, received." RCKD, February 13, 15, 26, 1928; MM to RCK, February 17, 1928.

On social degeneration and the "Southern Renaissance," most who have studied this genre of literature and history place its incipient beginnings at 1929, with appearance of Thomas Wolfe's *Look Homeward, Angel* (New York: Scribner's, 1929), and

William Faulkner's, *The Sound and Fury* (New York: Jonathan Cape and Harrison Smith, 1929). So, at least in this regard, Kennedy's 1928 private thoughts on intergenerational decline might be viewed as barely ahead of this major genre of published southern writing. See Richard H. King, *A Southern Renaissance: The Cultural Awakening of the American South, 1930–1955* (New York: Oxford University Press, 1980); and Cobb, *Away Down South*, 112–29.

48. RCKD, December 11, 1928. The long journey of Senator King's noted cane only got longer when it came into possession of Ren Kennedy. It was in his Camden household when he died in 1985. At his wife's death in 1989, it was mistakenly packed with many items of furniture bought by a local antique dealer, Betty Williamson. Subsequently, it was spotted behind the counter at Williamson's Oak Hill shop. From there it was returned to Kennedy's oldest daughter, Mary Conway Kennedy Dickinson, of Atmore, who in turn gave it to the Alabama Department of Archives and History. Jane Sheldon Dale, "William Rufus DeVane King" (undated typescript in possession of Tennant McWilliams).

49. MM to RCK, May 12, 1929.
50. MM to RCK, May 14, 1929.
51. MM to RCK, May 14, 1929.
52. RCKD, June 28, 1929; RCK to Maude Pressly, August 17, 1928; Maude Pressly to RCK, August 12, 14, 1929.
53. RCKD, August 8, 30, 1929; Maude Pressly to RCK, September 2, 1929.
54. RCKD, May 2, October 16, 1929, January 12, 1930; Clyde Purifoy Miller to MM, September 8, 1929.
55. Maude Pressly to RCK, October 18, 1929.
56. RCKD, November 15, December 30, 1929.

Chapter 5

1. William W. Rogers et al., *Alabama: History of a Deep South State* (Tuscaloosa: University of Alabama Press, 2018), chap. 27; Clinton McCarty, *Reins of Power: Racial Change and Challenge in a Southern Community* (Tallahassee: Sentry Press, 1999), 95–99, including a vivid description of Wilcox in the 1920s before any signs of a depression; and Wayne C. Curtis, *Establishing and Preserving Confidence: The Role of Banking in Alabama, 1816–1994* (Troy, AL: Wayne C. Curtis, 1994), 90–148. The Bank of Camden story is unique in the broader narrative of Alabama banking. After reopening on October 1, 1928, it operated with stability throughout the Depression, not one regular depositor losing anything—an exceptional Depression-era story. But there was a long-term trade-off. The bank's major rescue money did not actually derive from Wilcox; it came from Illinois entrepreneur, Peter Vredenburgh. In 1902, this son of a noted Union cavalry officer bought "an empire of land" on the Wilcox-Monroe county line and in the Pine Hill area. Two decades later he had developed the mill towns of Pine Hill and Vredenburgh, with railroad connections to Memphis and then on to the Midwest. In one sense the Vredenburghs were much like the Liddells, Morgans, and Hendersons—Union army veteran families who brought a certain business vitality to postbellum Wilcox. But the Vredenburghs' role also stands as a precursor to the later pattern of "outside" corporations controlling much of Wilcox property and using that wealth to connect with local

political elites to keep property taxes in the county among the lowest in the nation. Ironically, Peter Vredenburgh's son and namesake, a strong New Dealer, married Dorothy McElroy of Mississippi, who went on to become secretary of the National Democratic Party (1944–88) under her remarried name (Peter Vredenburgh Jr. died in 1956) of Dorothy McElroy Vredenburgh Bush. Because that role had her involved with a major Democratic agenda—progressive tax reform—one wonders what stance she assumed on tax reform in Alabama, notably in Wilcox and Monroe counties, from which her substantial inheritance appears to have derived. In short, if hard to quantify, the Bank of Camden's overnight revival of 1928 seems to have carried some systemic "associated costs." See *WPE*, September 27, 1928, October 20, 1966; RCKD, September 20–October 1, 1928; *New York Herald Tribune*, March 20, 1944; *New York Post*, March 24, 1944; *Congressional Record*, 102nd Cong., 2nd sess. (January 23, 1992), S217–18.

2. MM to RCK, November 24, 1927, March 20, April 8, 1928; John T. Moore to RCK, November 11, 1940.

3. *ARP*, July 4, 1928, June 5, July 10, December 4, 1929, July 16, 1930; RCKD, May 2, 10–12, June 16, July 30, September 22, November 27, 1929, May 28, August 1, 1930. Charles D. Griffith to RCK, March 29, 1928; A[rthur] J[ones] Ranson to RCK, May 2, 1929; I. N. Kennedy to RCK, August 7, 1929; Byron Dexter to RCK, August 1, 1930. MMK's joining Camden ARPC is documented in RCK/WFMM/1930.

4. Glen Feldman, *The Irony of the Solid South: Democrats, Republicans and Race, 1865–1944* (Tuscaloosa: University of Alabama Press, 2013), 66–86; McCarty, *Reins of Power*, 98–99.

5. On memories of "Republican cooperationists" during Reconstruction and the election of 1928, according to Bess Cochran—as recorded by RCK—white Wilcoxons most noted for courting business deals and political favors from "Yankee Reconstruction leaders" were descendants of antebellum Wilcox's richest planters: "Felix Tait . . . a McDowell, Sam Cook, Peyton Burford . . . John Pritchett, Dan Pritchett . . . people regarded by locals as Scalawags and never forgiven." Likewise, B. M. Miller advised RCK that "Old Sam Ervin—grandfather of present Samuel J. Ervin—should be on the same list, people who thought it better to cooperate with Republicans and have some county jobs and get something out of it." Harsh talk about these "traitors" returned to "Camden's street conversation" during the election season of 1928. RCKD, February 2–3, 1942.

6. RCKD, January 13, 19, February 19, May 2, July 22, 1928, February 3, 1942; MR, November 8, 1947.

7. RCKD, July 22, October 24, November 2, 5, 10, 1928; MR, November 18, 1947; Feldman, *Irony of the Solid South*, 71, 74. I am the great-great-grandson of Miles McWilliams, whose life and descendants are summarized in *HWC*, 232–34.

8. RCKD, October 6, 24, November 2, 1928, February 3, 1942; RCK/WFMR/1928; J. Wayne Flynt, *Alabama Baptists: Southern Baptists in the Heart of Dixie* (Tuscaloosa: University of Alabama Press, 1988), 359. Kennedy encountered similar sentiments among Marion Junction people. Craig Chisolm, a leading member of Prosperity ARP Church, with whom Kennedy often overnighted when preaching there, told him: "'I'll vote Republican or Socialist. . . . If Al Smith is not nominated [by Democrats] you can say 'Tom Heflin has done it.' Craig is a Kluxer, an anti-Catholic, and a Heflin man." RCKD, February 19, 1928.

9. RCKD, October 19, 1928; WJJ and JCCJ interview, November 22, 1979. On Sam Lee Jones—his complicated connections with the ARPC, sawmilling, alcohol, the KKK, leadership of the Wilcox Democratic Party Executive Committee, and his December 1934 death from heart attack at age fifty—see, for example, RCKD, January 30, February 4, 1942. After Kennedy buried him, he noted that "[he] was an ARP, a member of my church . . . a man of some good qualities and some not good." RCK/WFMR/1934.

On the Red Cross "free seeds" program, RCK initially encountered "Hoover-style bureaucracy." In 1930, the American Red Cross initiated the program to be implemented through "county extension agents of the State agricultural schools." However, as an indication of how far removed from reality the Red Cross was at this stage of the Depression, its program required a farmer to submit a "proposal stating the number of acres to go to feed crops . . . and cash crops." Such guidelines were so far removed from what Benders could do that Kennedy and W. J. Jones negotiated with the Wilcox extension agent out of Auburn, C. E. Carmack, for the Wilcox chapter to get a certain amount of vegetable seeds in bulk—seeds for carrots, peas, lettuce, pumpkins—that it then could distribute in the Bend. WJJ and JCC interview, November 22, 1979; American Red Cross, *Relief Work in the Drought of 1930–1931* (Washington, DC: American Red Cross, 1931), 56–57.

10. *AOSR, 1931*, 113; RCKD, November 6–7, 1928.

11. RCKD, November 7, 23–24, 1928.

12. RCKD, March 9, 1928, May 5, 1929.

13. RCKD, March 4, 1928; WJJ and JCCJ interview, November 22, 1979; RCK interview, May 21,1983; VJGL interview, October 1, 1987; MR interview, April 18, 1983.

14. RCKD, January 7, February 16, 18–19, 1928; WJJ interview, January 5, 1983.

15. The 1941 Camden Book Club reading list included Ernest Hemingway's *For Whom the Bell Tolls* (1940), Walter Van Tilburg Clark's *The Oxbow Incident* (1940), Helen Norris's *Something More Than Earth* (1940), Margery Sharp's *The Stone of Chastity* (1940), Gwen Bristow's *This Side of Glory* (1940) and Frances Parkinson Keyes's *Fielding's Folly* (1940). Elgin W. Mellown to RCK, January 10, 1940; *WPE*, October 13, 1927, February 2, 18, 1928; RCKD, August 2, 1928, January 13, 1941; VJGL interview, October 11, 1987, especially regarding RCK's early, futile efforts to get local support for a public library. The Starr family narrative, including the bizarre fortune connected to the famous English watercolorist, is found in *HWC*, 301. It was written by John Paul Starr's journalist-historian daughter, the late Ouida Starr Woodson. Even more on the Tepper family, including Samuel Tepper's youngest son, the blind John Jackson Tepper—"a [Charles] Dickens character" who talked regularly on the streets of Camden about the wrongness of local planters' sexually abusing slave girls, naming names, and whom RCK buried in 1939—is found in RCKD, August 2, 1928, November 3, 1939; and in RCK/WFMA/1939.

16. RCKD, June 4, July 27, 1928, July 19, 1962; Furman interview, September 24, 2015; Marian Purdue Furman to author, January 31, 2016; Peter Jenkins, "Ode to Uncle Esten," chap. 31 in *Along the Edge of America* (New York: Houghton Mifflin, 1995). On July 18, 1962, when told he no longer could drive, Esten Purifoy went to his bathroom, lay down in the tub, and killed himself with a German Luger handgun.

17. RCK/RR/1928; Constance Skinner, *Pioneers of the Old Southwest* (New Haven: Yale University Press, 1919), 1–13; William Allen White, *Woodrow Wilson: The Man, His*

Times, His Task (Boston: Houghton Mifflin, 1924), 1–5, 72–73, 86–87, 100–101; Woodrow Wilson, "The Puritan," in *Selected Literary and Political Papers and Addresses of Woodrow Wilson* (New York: Grosset and Dunlap, 1927), 102–11; and Arthur S. Link, "Woodrow Wilson: The American As Southerner," *Journal of Southern History* 36 (February 1970): 3–17, though it should be noted that Link does not address "Scotch-Irish" in this article. See also Charles Knowles Bolton, *Scotch-Irish Pioneers in Ulster and America* (Boston: Bacon and Brown, 1910); and Henry Jones Ford, *The Scotch-Irish in America* (Princeton: Princeton University Press, 1915). For full explication of Skinner's "whole freedom" within the context of British Borderlander influences persisting into the southern backcountry, see Fischer, *Albion's Seed*, 777.

18. *HWC*, 119; McCarty, *Reins of Power*, 44–84; RCKD, May 15, 1939. Violent retributive justice, as a characteristic of southern frontier life traceable to the British Borderlands, is discussed in David Hackett Fischer, *Albion's Seed: Four British Folkways in America* (New York: Oxford University Press, 1989), 766–67. Kennedy's usage of the term in this context would appear to be one of the earliest by a critic of New South life.

19. RCKD, December 7, 1928; *AOSR, 1907*, 40; WJJ and JCCJ interview, November 21, 1979, where I first encountered the killing on Clifton Road through WJJ's and JCCJ's recollections of the dinner at the Bonners' house. There is no record of this case being covered by the recently created (in 1900) *Wilcox Progressive Era*; its owner and sometime editor at the time was a prominent Jewish businessman, Sol Bloch, recently elected state senator and known for strong segregationist views as well as for initiating state legislation to found what became Alabama College, in Montevallo. *HWC*, 6.

20. WJJ and JCCJ interview, November 21, 1979; RCKD, December 7, 1928. For modern scholarship on Scotch-Irish violence and feuding see, for example, Bertram Wyatt-Brown, *Honor and Violence in the Old South* (New York: Oxford University Press, 1986), 143–44; and in the context of persisting British Borderlander influences, Fischer, *Albion's Seed*, 767–68.

21. RCKD, June 25, 1928; *HWC*, 22, 201–2, 205; *Wilcox Progress*, August 22, October 3, 1894, January 28, 1897.

22. RCKD, February 3, 1942; RCK interview, September 9, 1984; Will Liddell interview, May 20, 2019; *Wilcox Progress*, March 3, 1897; *MA*, January 26, 1897; copy of undated clipping, *Montgomery Journal*, provided by Will Liddell and in KRF/B/Horn.

23. RCKD, February 3, 1942; RCK interview, September 9, 1984, source of "abject violent feuding." I am the great-grandson of Richebourg Gaillard, whose life is summarized in *Memorial Record of Alabama*, 2 vols. (Madison, WI: Brant and Fuller, 1893), 1:1068–70.

24. Alice Foster Cook, "History of Camden and Wilcox County," [part 2], *WPE*, March 22, 1934; RCKD, May 5, 1939, February 2–3, 1942; RCK interview, September 9, 1984, the source of "abject violent feuding" and opposition to "change." See also James Wallace, *Wallace-Bruce and Closely Related Families* (Northfield, MN: Mohn Print Co., 1930), 279–363; McCarty, *Reins of Power*, 56, 60, 70.

25. RCKD, June 21, 25–27, November 23, 1928, December 30, 1929. Before hearing of the feud that affected the Negro patient, RCK regularly had encountered related sentiments about Negro health care. B. M. Miller: Negroes are "devoted to operations. If one family has one, every family on the [sharecropped] place will want one." RCKD,

September 27, 1927. And a year later he heard this from John Miller: "Virtually no white people [of Wilcox] died of influenza" in 1912 and 1918, but "many Negroes did, no doubt largely due to lack of medical attention, plus in the county there were four Negroes to every one white person." RCKD, February 1, 1929.

26. RCKD, December 30, 1929, January 24, 1930; Wyatt-Brown, *Honor and Violence*, 142–45. For a more positive opinion of Lottie Beck and her sisters, see the extensive obituary of "Mrs. Charlotte Vass Beck," *WPE*, June 16, 1938.

27. RCKD, February 17, March 12, 1931; RCK to MMK, February 17, 1944, MMK to RCK, February 17, 1971 ("clung"). The interior description of the ARP manse is based on my visits there as well Morton Rubin's, who was in the home many times in the mid-1940s and then again in the early to mid-1960s. In 1947, Rubin estimated that Kennedy had more than 7,000 books filling the study and spreading out all over the house. MR, September 30, 1947.

28. RCKD, June 28, 1928, November 15, 1929, July 28, 1930, February 2, 1933; Joseph Lindsay to RCK, January 13, 1930; RCK to Mary Conway Kennedy, June 28, 1934; Judith Paterson to author, December 1, 2012; *WPE*, March 27, 1924, July 17, 1930, September 1, 1932, April 13, 1933, May 3, 1945; MKA interview, June 27, 1989.

29. RCK, "Our Revival Meeting" (draft, 1933), RCK/UP (hereafter, unless otherwise noted, all of RCK's unpublished writings and drafts are in RCK/UP). RCK interview, July 20, 1985; RCK/S/1940; RCKD, July 10, 1940, and December 26, 1930, where he confides to himself late at night: "The periodic debacles of the capitalistic system become worse and worse . . . leading to ultimate disaster." Shortly after, he gave a sermon that included readings from Charles and Mary Beard's *Rise of American Civilization* (1927), notably, sections devoted to the rise and impact of corporate power, which he had read February 13–September 5, 1930. RCK/S/1930. For balanced discussion of causes of the Depression, see, for example, William E. Leuchtenburg, *The Perils of Prosperity, 1914–1932* (Chicago: University of Chicago Press, 1958), 96–97, 138, 184, 245, 251, 259, 272. Michael Kazin treats Bryan's "Cross of God Speech" in *A Godly Hero: The Life of William Jennings Bryan* (New York: Alfred A. Knopf, 2006). Will Rogers's comments first appeared in the *St. Petersburg Times*, November 27, 1932. The syndicated column ran in the major daily newspapers of the United States, including the *New York Times*, under the heading "Will Rogers Says."

30. *AOSR, 1931*, 560; McCarty, *Reins of Power*, 101–3; Feldman, *Politics, Society, and the Klan in Alabama, 1915–1949* (Tuscaloosa: University of Alabama Press, 1999), 199–207; Mary Stanton, *Red Black White: The Alabama Communist Party, 1930–1950* (Athens: University of Georgia, Press, 2019), 64–76; Dan T. Carter, *Scottsboro: A Tragedy of the American South* (New York: Oxford University Press, 1969), 9, 50, 106, 145–46. RCKD, March 14, October 2, 1928, February 20, March 9, August 18, September 8, December 26, 1930; *Montgomery Advertiser*, August 13–15, 22, September 7, 9, 1930; B. L. Shi to RCK, April 6, 1931; *WPE*, February 27, August 21, November 15, 1930; RCK interview, July 20, 1985. White Wilcoxons' criticism of Benjamin Meek Miller is illustrated in RCK's diary entry of May 5, 1935: "Frank Dexter reports no one in Camden likes him. He is 'selfish' and 'not sociable.' 'Nobody likes him. . . . Jim Lawler once kept books for him. He quit because of the way he treated his [sharecropping] Negroes.'" On ARPs and political/societal engagement, see the excellent analysis in Ware and Gettys, *Second Century*, 108–34, and passim.

31. Marian Purdue Furman to author, August 27, 2014; Furman interview, July 28, 2014; Feldman, *Politics, Society and the Klan*, 214–15, 223, 227, 269, 271–73; Melanie S. Morrison, *Murder on Shades Mountain* (Durham, NC: Duke University Press, 2018); Samuel L. Webb and Margaret E. Armbrester, eds., *Alabama Governors: A Political History of the State* (Tuscaloosa: University of Alabama Press, 2018), 180–84; Rogers et al., *Alabama*, 497–500. The Dexter quote is from RCKD, May 27, 1935; the Dobbins quote from Charles Dobbins, "Alabama Governors and Editors, 1930–1955," *AR* 29 (April 1976): 136–38. The feud between B. M. Miller and J. Miller Bonner extended to family members. After a 1942 visit in the home of ex-governor Miller, RCK entered into the diary: "Gov. Miller and son Ben absorbed in hoping to defeat J. Miller Bonner in race for Supreme Court. Ben's . . . only interest is in seeing Miller Bonner defeated." RCKD, January 28, 1942; MR, June 26, 1947. Bonner indeed lost the race. *MA*, May 12, 1942.

32. RCK interview, February 25, 1984; *ARP*, April 21, 1931; Ware and Gettys, *Second Century*, 350–52.

33. RCK to W. E. Barton, November 3, 1930 (copy); Dale A. Johnson, *The Vanderbilt Divinity School: Education, Content, Change* (Nashville: Vanderbilt University Press, 2001), 63–86. Henry Edmonds to G. B. Winston, February 26, 1934; J. E. McCullough to Lee Hart, March 28, 1932 (copy); "Comprehensive Examination"; "Registration, Attendance and Course Cards," all in Divinity School, RG 530, Archives and Special Collections, Heard Library, Vanderbilt University, Nashville. RCK, "Minister's Institute," RCK/UP. For more on Henry Edmonds, see Marvin Yeomans Whiting, *An Enduring Ministry: A Biography of Henry Morris Edmonds, 1878–1960* (Birmingham: William F. Edmonds and Joan McCoy Edmonds, 2007); and Henry M. Edmonds, *A Parson's Notebook* (Birmingham: Elizabeth Agee's Bookshop, 1961).

34. *MA*, March 22, 28, 1931; *WPE*, March 26, April 9, 1931; *ARP*, April 16, 21, 29, 30, 1931; RCK/S/1931. RCK interview, September 9, 1984, in which he recalled: "After the vote Miller Bonner really laid it on me. He would do that often . . . disagree with me . . . but a couple of days later he would warm back up . . . not change his mind, just be nice to me."

35. *WPE*, May 26, 1932; RCK/S/1931; WJJ interview, January 5, 1983. On the Depression and Alabama public education, see, for example, Don Eddins, *AEA: Head of the Class in Alabama Politics* (Montgomery: Alabama Education, 1997), 270–72; Ira Harvey, *History of Education Finance in Alabama History* (Auburn, AL: Truman Pierce Institute for the Advancement of Teacher Education, 1989), 136–79; and, specifically on Wilcox, *WPE*, May 26, 1932. On February 11–14, 1928, RCK read Madison Grant's *The Passing of the Great Race* (New York: Charles Scribner's Sons, 1921); other than this sermon reference, his only other comment of record on this book was in the form of extensive diary quotes from it regarding physical characteristics of Nordic and Alpine types—nothing on people of color (RCKD, April 23, 1928). In mid-July 1930, he read Ulrich B. Phillips, *Life and Labor in the Old South* (New York: Little, Brown, and Co., 1929). *Cotton snob* origins—which Kennedy did not discuss—are found in chapter 4 of D. R. Hundley, *Social Relations in Our Southern States* (New York: Henry B. Price, 1860), as cited in Phillips, *Life and Labor in the Old South*. On Phillips's many contradictions, and notably on "Cavaliers," see, for example, Singal, *The War Within*, 40, 54–55. In early August 1930, Kennedy read Thomas J. Wertenbaker, *Patrician and Plebian in Virginia* (Charlottesville:

Michie Co., 1910); and between late February 1929 and early September 1930, he read Charles and Mary Beard, *Rise of the American Civilization* (New York: MacMillan, 1927). RCK/RR/1928/1930. On Hill's "captive theology" idea, see his *Southern Churches in Crisis* (Tuscaloosa: University of Alabama Press, 2020), including an introduction by Hill reflecting on southern religious history since his classic first appeared in 1966. See also Paul Harvey, "God and Negroes and Jesus and Sin and Salvation: Racism, Racial Interchange, and Interracialism in Southern Religious History," in Beth Barton Schweiger and Don Mathews, eds., *Religion in the American South: Protestants and Others in History and Culture* (Chapel Hill: University of North Carolina Press, 2004), 284–327. Foremost among challenges to Hill's idea is Beth Barton Schweiger, *The Gospel Working Up: Progress and Pulpit in Nineteenth-Century Virginia* (New York: Oxford University Press, 2000).

Chapter 6

1. Lillian Smith, *Strange Fruit* (New York: Reynal and Hitchcock, 1944). Lillian Smith's "therapy" quote is from Fred C. Hobson, *But Now I See: The White Southern Racial Conversion Narrative* (Baton Rouge: Louisiana State University Press, 1999), 24. On the Fellowship of Southern Churchmen, see especially Robert F. Martin, "Critique of Southern Society and Vision for a New Order: The Fellowship of Southern Churchmen, 1934–1957," *Church History* 52 (March 1983): 66–80; as well as Robert F. Martin, *Howard Kester and the Struggle for Social Justice* (Charlottesville: University of Virginia Press, 1991), 160 (the "fraternity" quote) and passim; Anthony P. Dunbar, *Against the Grain: Southern Radicals and Prophets, 1929–1959* (Charlottesville: University of Virginia Press, 1981), 59–61, 74–75, 195–96, and passim; John Egerton, *Speak Now against the Day: The Generation before the Civil Rights Movement in the South* (Chapel Hill: University of North Carolina Press, 1995), 126, 153–54, 181, 172, 237–38, 289, 380, 426, 447; and David S. Burgess, *Fighting for Social Justice: The Life Story of David Burgess* (Detroit: Wayne State University Press, 2000), 90–95. For more on the FSC experience, see David L. Chappell's *A Stone of Hope: Prophetic Religion and the Death of Jim Crow* (Chapel Hill: University of North Carolina Press, 2004); and Walter Brueggmann and David Hankins, *The Prophetic Tradition: The 40th Anniversary Edition* (Minneapolis: Fortress Press, 2018).

2. "Notes from Alabama on Homo Africanus" (Draft, 1930); Harrison Leigh Flint, *Landscape Plants for the Eastern United States* (Hoboken, NJ: John Wiley and Sons, 1997), 282–83; Patricia L. Crown et al., "Ritual Black Drink Consumption at Cohokia," *Proceedings of the National Academy of Sciences of the United States of America* 35 (August 2012): 13944–49; "Frank Tait House County Road 19, Camden [near Canton Bend], AL," Alex Bush, August 31, 1936, Historic American Building Survey (Prints and Photographs Division, Library of Congress, Washington, DC); Robert S. Gamble, *The Alabama Catalog: Historic American Buildings Survey: A Guide to the Early Architecture of the State* (Tuscaloosa: University of Alabama Press, 1987), 336–37; *WPE*, September 28, 1977; RCK interview, May 21, 1983. On Kennedy and Frank Tait, see also chap. 4, note 47, above. In Wilcox lore, Myron Anderson Boynton (1843–1911) often is confused with his brother, physician Madison Eugene Boynton (1841–1912), both having been born and raised in New York. Myron served briefly as a Union soldier before coming to north Wilcox in late 1865, seeking his fortune in cotton and sharecropping. A self-avowed

"conservative Democrat," he wound up founding Catherine, Alabama, as well as its Presbyterian church. In 1888 his physician brother, also a Union Army veteran, joined Myron in Wilcox. While practicing medicine in both Camden and Selma, the doctor was part owner of the north Wilcox cotton, ginning, and mercantile businesses known as "Boynton Brothers." They likely bought and sold "Mimosa" with its large acreage as another step in their extensive brotherly entrepreneurship, offering one more fascinating chapter in Yankee business development in the Reconstruction-era South. *WPE*, November 13, 1889, July 22, 1909, May 16, 1912, December 29, 1926; *STJ*, February 25, 1927.

3. Don H. Doyle, *Faulkner County: The Historical Roots of Yoknapatawpha County* (Chapel Hill: University of North Carolina Press, 2001). An unsigned (by Harold Strauss?) review of *Sartoris* appeared in the *New York Times Book Review* of March 3, 1929. On the iconic Sartoris and Snopes families, see, for example, Richard H. King, *A Southern Renaissance: The Cultural Awakening of the American South, 1930–1955* (New York: Oxford University Press, 1980), 79–92, 125, 143–44, 153, 222.

4. Geoffrey Chaucer, *The Canterbury Tales: Rendered into English by J. U. Nicholson* (New York: Garden City Publishing Co., 1934).

5. "Notes from Alabama on Homo Africanus" (Draft, 1930).

6. "Alabama Feels Mr. Hoover's Prosperity" (Draft, 1931). Though the idea behind it traces to the Alabama Constitution of 1901, the term "Big Mule"—referencing urban industrialists and other professionals aligned with Black Belt elites—was only beginning to find currency at this time. After first surfacing, apparently, in the Alabama gubernatorial race of 1926, however, the term would be a regular part of the Alabama political discourse into the era of George Wallace. See Anne Permaloff and Carl Grafton, "Political Geography and Power Elites: Big Mules and the Alabama Constitution," in George E. Connor and Christopher W. Hannon, eds., *The Constitutionalisms of the American States* (Columbia: University of Missouri Press, 2008), 235–50.

7. RCK, "1932 Camden's Centennial Year," *MA*, December 15, 1932; RCK interview, September 9, 1984. In September 1929, RCK read Mencken's *Prejudices, Sixth Series* (New York: Alfred A. Knopf, 1927), and in September 1930, he read Mencken's *Prejudices, First Series* (New York: Alfred A. Knopf, 1919) as well as Mencken's *In Defense of Women* (New York: Alfred A. Knopf, 1918). RCK/RR/1929–30. See also Edgerton, *Speak Now against the Day*, 60; RCK/RR/1929–30.

8. RCK, "Six Cent Cotton, A Southern Tragedy," *NR* 69 (December 16, 1931): 129–30. Alongside Kennedy's piece appeared Walter Wilson's "Southern Peonage," showing how the cropper system ultimately made so many people hostages, if not slaves. With it, also, was Henry Fuller's "Sunday at Camp Hill." This analyzed the brutality experienced by "peonage" protesters—and the Christian hypocrisy behind such brutality—as demonstrated by a recent murder at Camp Hill, just north of Auburn. Fuller and Wilson, like Kennedy, were trying to become published writers. Fuller was a publisher's sales representative assigned to the southeastern market. Recently, he had been jailed in Memphis on suspicion of being a communist. Wilson was a freelance journalist working on a book about "forced labor in the United States and its colonies." It was a compatible threesome. On Tannenbaum, Ransom, and Agee, see, for example, George Brown Tindall, *The Emergence of the New South, 1913–1945* (Baton Rouge: Louisiana State University Press, 1967), 211–12, 296–98, 415, 589, 686; and Daniel Joseph Singal, *The War*

Within: From Victorian to Modernist Thought in the South, 1919–1945 (Chapel Hill: University of North Carolina Press, 1982), 210–19, 261–62.

9. RCK, "Tightening Up the Cotton Belt," *NR* 71 (August 10, 1932): 337–38. For larger context of RCK's analysis of cotton plantation dynamics, see Gavin Wright, *The Political Economy of the Cotton South* (New York: W. W. Norton, 1978), 176–80; and Charles S. Aiken, *The Cotton Plantation South since the Civil War* (Baltimore: Johns Hopkins University Press, 1998), 29–96. On Hoover and agriculture at the onset of the Depression, see Tindall, *The Emergence of the New South*, 354–56; and Kendrick A. Clements, *The Life of Herbert Hoover: Imperfect Visionary, 1918–1928* (New York: Palgrave-Macmillan, 2010), 384. President Hoover often urged that the best strategy for abolishing the poverty resulting from the 1929 Crash was a strong dose of "rugged individualism," as he asserted most notably in his final campaign speech in the 1926 election.

10. RCK interview, July 20, 1985; Howell Raines interview, May 12, 2018.

11. Kathryn Tucker Windham, "They Call It Gee's Bend," undated typescript, copies in Wilcox County Public Library, Camden, AL, and in Division of Archives and Manuscripts, Birmingham Public Library, Birmingham; Harvey H. Jackson III, *Rivers of History: Life on the Coosa, Tallapoosa, Cahaba, and Alabama* (Tuscaloosa: University of Alabama Press, 1995), 195–97.

12. Historical confusion over "the man" spans long-time contemporaneous residents to modern scholars. In 1980, for example, W. J. (Bill) Jones, who worked with RCK in the Bend in the 1930s, remembered "the man" as "E. O. Rentz." (Transcribed Interview with Mr. and Mrs. W. J. Jones, June 24, 1980, by Kathryn Tucker Windham, Gee's Bend Project Papers and Photographs, Department of Archives and Manuscripts, Birmingham Public Library, hereafter cited as "BPL Archives"). Likewise, "E. O. Rentz" appears in Windham's "They Call It Gee's Bend," 19. He turns up as "C. L. Rentz" in Mary Stanton's "Coming of Age in Gee's Bend," *AH* 114 (Fall 2014): 39. Snapshots of the life of E. O. Rentz can be seen in *WPE*, October 31, 1900, July 31, 1902, November 24, 1904, December 20, 1906; and via "Ephriam O. Rentz" on Ancestry.com. On Robert Lee Rentz, similar snapshots can be seen in *WPE*, November 28, 1907, December 16, 1915; and "Robert Lee Rentz," Ancestry.com. The two apparently worked as partners, with the elder, Ephraim, as chief owner and operator, until his death in 1924, when Robert took over. The "store" had dry goods, hardware, seed and feed, dairy products, plus a livery stable and cobbler shop.

13. Long active with the Alabama Hardware Association, Matthews also was a leader in the Methodist Church, both in Camden and in the Alabama–Northwest Florida Conference; and, from being a young man unable to afford college, provided significant scholarship assistance to the Methodists' Birmingham-Southern College and Huntingdon College. He preceded W. J. Jones as head of the Wilcox County Red Cross. He was elected to Alabama's State House in 1918, 1926, 1930, and 1934. *HWC*, 238–39; *MA*, October 3, 1963; *AOSR, 1919*, 145; *1927*, 158–59; *1931*, 225–26; and *1934*, 213.

14. *HWC*, 228–29.

15. *HWC*, 170, 226. In the early 1980s, when I interviewed Kennedy, the records of the Wilcox County Red Cross (1929–48?), undoubtedly including the Gee's Bend data, remained in moldy boxes in his garage—without my knowing it. Between the time Kennedy died, in December 1985, and the time I returned to his home to load up his papers,

in March 1986, Mrs. Kennedy—according to their daughter, Mary Conway—asked "the yard man" to take "all those moldy boxes to the dump." Here was a stunning historical loss, especially for the people of Gee's Bend, yet perhaps an understandable one, considering Kennedy family adjustments following his death. MCKD interview, March 8, 1986. The US National Archives holds the collection, "Records of the American National Red Cross, 1917–1934," which includes one item on Wilcox County, Alabama: a communication on Red Cross efforts to aid World War I veterans in Selma (Dallas County) in the early 1930s, no doubt reflecting the merger of the Dallas and Wilcox chapters.

16. RCK/WFMR/1932.

17. Transcribed Interview with Renwick C. Kennedy, June 23, 1980, by Kathryn Tucker Windham (Gee's Bend Project and Photographs, BPL Archives); RCK interview, July 20, 1985.

18. RCK, "November Morn, 1932" (Draft, 1932), in RCK/UP (all unpublished RCK writings are in this collection unless otherwise noted); *HWC*, 228.

19. RCK, "Cremation" (Draft, 1933).

20. RCK, "Bill Dickens" (Draft, 1933).

21. RCK, "Willie Watson" (Draft, 1933).

22. RCK, "One Point of View" (Draft, 1933); RCK to Bruce Blevin, June 28, 1933 (copy).

23. RCK interview, July 20, 1985.

24. RCK, "The Face of the Poor," *CC* 50 (June 21, 1933): 811–12.

25. RCK, "Military Interlude," *CC* 50 (September 13, 1933): 1144–45; RCKD, October 27, 1933.

26. RCK, "Psychic" (Draft, 1933); WJJ interview, January 5, 1983. The Klan in Tuscaloosa is discussed in Glen Feldman, *Politics, Society and the Klan in Alabama, 1915–1949* (Tuscaloosa: University of Alabama Press, 1999), 251–54.

27. RCK, "Note on Cotton," *CC* 51 (January 17, 1934): 87–88.

28. RCK, "Bookkeeping," *CC* 51 (March 28, 1934): 3–24; ; John Rex and David Mason, *Theories of Race and Ethnic Relations* (Cambridge: Cambridge University Press, 1983), 170–86, 264–321; John P. Pittman, "Double Consciousness," *Stanford Encyclopedia of Philosophy*. The "furnishing system" is detailed in Paul E. Mertz, *New Deal Policy and Southern Rural Poverty* (Baton Rouge: Louisiana State University Press, 1978), 7–9.

29. RCK, "What's Happening in the Cotton Belt," *NR* 78 (April 18, 1934): 266–67; "Recovery in the Cotton Belt," *Opportunity: Journal of Negro Life* 12 (May 1934): 134; Eddie Wayne Shell, *Evolution of the Alabama Agroecosystem* (Montgomery: New South Books, 2013), 576; Andrew M. Hood to RCK, January 13, 1934; RCK, "Commencement Address, May 10, 1934," RCK/UP.

30. *STJ*, April 16, 23, 1934; RCK to Editor, *STJ*, April 18, 1934 (copy).

31. RCK, "Before the Doctor Comes," *CC* 51 (August 8, 1934): 1020–22; RCKD, October 27, 1933, June 19, 1935; RCKD, February 8, 1938, November 28, 1967, January 2, 1968.

32. Maurice I. Bloch to RCK, April 20, 1940; W. J. Jones, "Baseball Remembrances," typescript (1979) in PWJJ; David Greenberg, *Republic of Spin: An Inside History of the American Presidency* (New York: W. W. Norton, 2016), 176–86. On January 21, 1934,

the *Montgomery Advertiser* published an extensive and positive review of Couch's *Culture in the South*, which RCK clipped and filed (KRF/C/1934). The name "Cloverleaf" also had connections to a Selma dairy products business, not coincidentally established in 1932, which was of considerable significance with the racial discord in Selma of the post–World War II era. See J. Mills Thornton III, *Dividing Lines: Municipal Politics and the Struggle for Civil Rights in Montgomery Birmingham, and Selma* (Tuscaloosa: University of Alabama Press, 2002), 395.

33. RCK, "Black Belt Aristocrats," *Social Forces* 13 (October 1934): 1–6; RCK interview, May 21, 1983; Janis Quinn interview with RCK about "Black Belt Aristocrats" in *STJ*, June 24, 1973; "Copies of 'Black Belt Aristocrats' Sent to the Following, Oct. 1934," RCK/AD; R. L. Robinson to RCK, November 2, 1934. The pattern of postbellum Black Belt planters' exercising significant influence in cities instrumental in the cotton economy—from milling to export—is explored in Don H. Doyle, *New Men, New Cities, New South: Atlanta, Charleston, Mobile, 1860–1910* (Chapel Hill: University of North Carolina Press, 1990). Well into the twenty-first century, certain Mobilians revered elements of the lifestyle of antebellum Wilcox's rich white people, notably their Greek Revival architectural accomplishments. See Cart Blackwell, "Country Living," *Mobile Bay* 37 (October 2021): 50–57.

34. Tennant McWilliams, "Viola Jefferson Goode Liddell and the Wilcox Roundtable," *AH* 122 (Fall 2006): 40–49.

35. RCK/WFMA, February 24, 1935, March 16, 1941; *HWC*, 66, 104,161, 170, 211; VJGL interview, March 6, 1984; RCKD, August 24–26, 1979; RCK, "[Comments on the Life of] Stanley Godbold, August 25, 1979," RCK/UP; *WPE*, September 23, 1987; Marian Purdue Furman to author, June 1, 2016.

36. RCK's diary is moot on the date of the dinner gathering. The author places the dinner on September 7 based on VJGL's saying it occurred "in the late summer before the article came out" and "we always met on Friday nights," as well as because of other commitments in RCK's tight schedule in August and September of that year (VJGL interview, October 11, 1987); Gould Beech to RCK, July 19, 1947; "Gould Beech," Rosenwald Fellowship Awards, Julius Rosenwald Fund Records, 1920–1948, Armistad Research Center; Nat Welch to RCK, July 24, 1947; Gould Beech to RCK, July 17, 1947. Historian Glenn Nolan Sisk explicitly credits RCK as being the first to urge the Black Belt as an "idea." Glenn Nolan Sisk, "Alabama Black Belt: A Social History, 1875–1915" (PhD diss., Duke University, 1951), 6.

37. RCK interview, May 21, 1983; VJGL interview, October 11, 1987; *STJ*, November 6, 1934. Seven years later, RCK received a presciently reflective response out of Selma. Robert James Krebs, a court reporter with the Fourth Judicial Circuit, wrote that he just had read "Black Belt Aristocrats" as well as William Faulkner's *The Hamlet* (1940). And he found the combination helped him understand more clearly the different origins and characteristics of people lumped together as "'poor whites.'" R. J. Krebs to RCK, May 14, 1940.

38. RCK, "Ox Farmers" (Draft, 1934); RCK, "Rehabilitation: Alabama Version," *CC* 51 (November 14, 1934): 1455–57. RCK interview, July 20, 1985, where he references VJGL's theory that some descendants of Wilcox plantation families openly attacked cooperating with federal programs to assist agriculture—while quietly benefiting

from them—to offset public memories of their ancestors having cooperated with the US government's Reconstruction political representatives in Wilcox.

39. *Tuscaloosa News*, November 11, 1934; RCK's "Slick Scam" quote from John Henry Bogie, who pastored the Camden Presbyterian Church in the 1940s and was a close friend of RCK: "I loved to hear Ren say that . . . he said it with such strength and he seemed to feel satisfied after he said it." Bogie interview, December 11, 2012.

40. RCK, "Fairy Story," *CC* 51 (December 19, 1934): 1620–22; *Tuscaloosa News*, January 1, 1935.

41. RCK, "Quality in the Reserve Corps," *CC* 52 (February 27, 1935): 272–74.

42. RCKD, April 8, 1935.

43. RCK, "Scottsboro Shadow," *CC* 52 (April 10, 1935): 476–78. In 1934, on the way to a synod meeting in Tennessee, Kennedy spent the night in Decatur, Alabama, where he talked with local whites about their reactions to the Scottsboro case. Back in Camden, on the night of May 10, he drafted "A Night in Decatur," a short story based on those conversations showing how they generally reflected less racism than predominant white Wilcox opinions on the case. Here was a significant subject, though the writing stands as no more than a rough start. It went to the file drawer. RCK, "A Night in Decatur" (Draft, 1934). RCK's friend from Camden, Charles Dobbins Jr.—by this time owner and editor of the *Anniston Times*—argued for the same diversity of north Alabama opinion in a letter to the *Nation*, bashing Carlton Beale's articles on north Alabama, which the magazine recently had published. The *Nation* opted not to publish Dobbins's letter; Dobbins copied RCK on all the correspondence. Charles Dobbins to RCK, 1936 (with enclosures).

44. RCK, "Roosevelt's Tenants," *CC* 52 (May 8, 1935): 608–10; VJGL interview, March 16, 1984. Rothstein's photographs appeared in John Temple Graves II, "Big World at Last Reaches Gee's Bend," *NYT*, August 22, 1937. See also Frye Gaillard, *A Hard Rain: America in the 1960s, Our Decade of Hope, Possibility, and Innocence Lost* (Montgomery: New South Books, 2018), 391–92.

45. RCK, "Note on Erskine Caldwell" (Draft, 1935); George Lang to RCK, February 6, 1939.

46. *MA*, May 9, 1935; John Bloomer, "'The Loafers in Birmingham in the Twenties," *AR* 30 (April 1977): 101–7.

47. RCK, "A Southern Suicide" (Draft, 1935). RCK read Caldwell's *Tobacco Road* in late March 1934 and T. S. Stribling's *The Store* (1932) in mid-February 1935 (RCK/RR, March 27–30, 1934, February 11–19, 1935); VJGL interview, March 16, 1984. On Tuscaloosa Klan activity leading up to the time Cason killed himself, see Feldman, *Politics, Society and the Klan*, 251–53. Among recent analyses of Clarence Cason are John M. Matthews, "Clarence Cason among the Southern Liberals," *AR* 38 (January 1985): 3–18; Wayne Flynt, "Introduction," in Clarence Cason, *90 Degrees in the Shade* (Tuscaloosa: University of Alabama Press, 1983); Bailey Thompson, "Clarence Cason's Shade: A Look at Alabama Then and Now," *AH* 60 (Spring 2001): 20–27; and Philip Biedler, "Yankee Interloper and Native Son: Carl Carmer and Clarence Cason," *Southern Cultures* 9 (March 2003): 18–35. The Cason quotes—"less interested" in southern change and "more in talking about the region," are from Cason, *90 Degrees in the Shade*, x. See also RCK/RR/1934–35. For more on Cason's family background, see, for example, *Southern Aegis* (Ashville, AL), August 16, 1916, May 22, 1924, and September 17, 1925.

48. RCK, "Alabama Dilemma," *CC* 52 (July 10 , 1935): 917–18.

49. RCK, "Sedition Bill," *CC* 52 (October 23, 1935): 1344–46; RCKD, August 23, 1935; VJGL interview, March 16, 1984; *MA*, August 3, 6, 1935; Shawn R. Tucker, *Virtues and Vices in the Arts* (Eugene, OR: Cascade, Books, 2015). While the Roundtable critiqued iterations of "Sedition Bill," RCK also hand-wrote a Yaupon vignette depicting how Negro education severely threatened two "furnishing merchants": Negroes with numerical literacy were harder to cheat. RCK, "Advancing Agent" (Draft, 1935).

50. RCK/WWMR/1935, including notes on Wilson's life; RCK, "Isolation," *CC* 52 (November 13, 1935): 1455–56; *HWC*, 48; Jeannette Steele McCall, *The First and Last Bell: A Story of Six Missions for Blacks in Wilcox County, Alabama* (Baltimore: American Literary Press, 2005), 27–29; Cynthia Griggs Fleming, *In the Shadow of Selma: The Continuing Struggle for Civil Rights in the Rural South* (Lanham, MD: Rowan and Littlefield, 2004), xiii–xiv, 21, 54, 61, 87–88; VJGL interview, October 11, 1987; Cornel West, "The Dilemma of the Black Intellectual," *Cultural Critique* 1 (Autumn 1985): 109–24.

51. RCK, "The Great Peace Celebration," *CC* 52 (December 4, 1935): 1553–54; William Penack, *For God and Country: The American Legion, 1919–1941* (Boston: Northeastern University Press, 1989); Charles Reagan Wilson, *Baptized in Blood: The Religion of the Lost Cause, 1865–1920* (Athens: University of Georgia Press, 1980), 161.

CHAPTER 7

1. RCK, "Mr. McClintock and His Tenants," *CC* 53 (April 8, 1936): 533–35. Besides giving "Eph" Evans "50 cents for food" on January 22, 1933, and again on March 1, 1934, a snapshot of RCK's financial records in this period also shows these other gifts: "to a Negro who works at Doc[k] Hayes's place . . . for meat . . . 10 cents" (September 25, 1933); "to Clarence [Robinson] at Doc[k] Hayes's place . . . for meat . . . 50 cents" (October 6, 1933); "to Clarence 70 cents" (December 26, 1933); "to a young boy from Doc[k] Hayes's place for school tuition . . . 25 cents" (December 21, 1933); "to a Negro [with last name of] Pettway . . . for a sweater . . . 59 cents" (December 21, 1933); "to a young boy at Doc[k] Hayes place for a shoe sole . . . 20 cents" (January 1, 1934); "to Morrisette for food . . . 50 cents" (March 8, 1939); "to Morrisette for doctor . . . $1.16" (April 2, 1939). On Christmas Eve, 1934, RCK married "Clarence Robinson and Rosa Wilson, ages about 22 and 20, at a Negro home near my house, no fee." William Lee ("Dock") Hayes served as Wilcox school superintendent in the early 1900s, and his family continued to live in the Canton Bend and Catherine areas in the 1930s, where one member of the family, L. H. Hayes, was a plantation overseer and truck farmer. "Doc[k] Hayes's place" apparently refers to small acreage still in the Hayes family where one or two sharecroppers lived and worked. *WPE*, April 18, May 9, 1901, January 21, 1904, July 8, 1926. See also Harold Hoffsommer, "The AAA and the Cropper," *SF* 13 (May 13, 1935): 494–502; and Jim F. Couch and Gina Couch, "New Deal Expenditures in Alabama: Was Economic Need Addressed?" *AR* 50 (July 1997): 181–84.

2. RCK, "Waste," *CC* (November 4, 1936): 1457–58. See Gerald W. Johnson, *The Wasted Land* (Chapel Hill: University of North Carolina Press, 1937), which RCK read December 17–21, 1937 (RCK/RR/1937). On "the bridge" between Progressive Era "conservationism" and more contemporary "environmentalism," see Henry L. Henderson

and David Woolner, eds., *FDR and the Environment* (New York: Palgrave Macmillan, 2005), 155–76.

3. RCK, "Legion Audit," *CC* 53 (December 16, 1936): 1688–90. On the "Bonus Bill," see David M. Kennedy, *Freedom from Fear: The American People in Depression and War* (New York: Oxford University Press, 1999), 92, 138, 279.

4. For example, between 1931 and 1939 Kennedy read Lyle Saxon, *Old Louisiana* (New York: Century Co., 1929), and Margaret Mitchell, *Gone with the Wind* (New York: Macmillan, 1936), as well as several works of the Southern Renaissance "canon": Thomas Wolfe, *Look Homeward, Angel* (New York: Charles Scribner's Sons, 1929); Virginius Dabney, *Liberalism in the South* (Chapel Hill: University of North Carolina Press, 1932); T. S. Stribling, *The Store* (New York: Doubleday, Doran, 1932); Stribling, *The Forge* (Garden City: Sun Dial Press, 1938); Stribling, *The Second Wagon* (New York: Doubleday, Doran and Co., 1935); Erskine Caldwell, *God's Little Acre* (New York: Grosset and Dunlap, 1933); William Faulkner, *Sanctuary* (New York: Jonathan Cape and Harrison Smith, 1931); Faulkner, *Absalom, Absalom!* (New York: Random House, 1936); Thomas Wolfe, "I Have a Thing to Tell You," *New Republic* 90 (March 10, 1937): 132–36; and Erskine Caldwell and Margaret Bourke-White, *You Have Seen Their Faces* (New York: Modern Age Books, 1937.) Three other books, all set in Alabama, also got his close attention: Howell Vines, *This Green Thicket World* (Boston: Little, Brown, 1936); Carl Carmer, *Stars Fell on Alabama* (New York: New York Literary Guild, 1934); and James Saxon Childers, *A Black Man and a White Man in the Deep South* (New York: Farrar and Strauss, 1936) (RCK/RR/1931–39). On major publishing houses—notably Knopf—pursuing books telling of the nonmythologized South, see Fred C. Hobson, *Serpent in Eden: H. L. Mencken in the South* (Chapel Hill: University of North Carolina Press, 1974); and James C. Cobb, *Away Down South: A History of the Southern Identity* (New York: Oxford University Press, 2005), 180–84, 197–99.

5. Drafts of all five in RCK/UP.

6. RCK later changed the real "Pigeon Creek" to the fictional "Fish Creek." But Pigeon Creek—if not the location, at least the name—seemed destined for convoluted currency. In a noted 2002 Hollywood film, "Sweet Home, Alabama," directed by Andy Tennant and starring Reese Witherspoon, Pigeon Creek became the basis for the fictional "Pigeon Creek, Alabama," as a stand-in for Greenville, Alabama. Roger Ebert, *Movie Yearbook 2004* (Kansas City, MO: Andrews McMeel, 2003), 626–27.

7. RCK, "Red Menace," *CC* 54 (December 9, 1937): 1526–27; "Forty-two Dollars" (Draft, 1937).

8. Bruce Clayton and John A. Salmond, eds., *The South Is Another Land: Essays on the Twentieth Century South* (New York: Greenwood Press, 1987), 191–94; VJGL interview, March 6, 1984.

9. Carl Fleischhauer and Beverly W. Brannan, eds., *Documenting America, 1935–1943* (Berkeley: University of California Press, 1988), 1–10, 28–29, 35–39, 58, 146–59; VJGL interview, March 16, 1984; RCKD, February 26, 1942; Robert Sonkin to RCK, February 26, 1942.

10. See also John Edgerton, *Speak Now Against the Day: The Generation Before the Civil Rights Movement in the South* (Chapel Hill: University of North Carolina Press, 1994), 60, 184, 195–97, 251–61, and passim.

11. RCK, "Life at Gee's Bend," *CC* 54 (September 1, 1937): 1072–75. On "waged constant war," see Wayne Flynt, *Alabama in the Twentieth Century* (Tuscaloosa: University of Alabama Press, 2004), 119. See also Roger Biles, *The South and the New Deal* (Lexington: University of Kentucky Press, 1994), 50–51; and Kari Frederickson, *Deep South Dynasty: The Bankheads of Alabama* (Tuscaloosa: University of Alabama Press, 2021), 277.

12. RCK, "Episode in Alabama" (Draft, 1938). See also RCK, "An Old Gospel Horse" (Draft, 1935); chapter 4, notes 10–11 above; RCK/WFMR/1936.

13. See chapter 4, note 10 above; McWilliams, "Wilcox County Slave Data."

14. "The People of Fish Creek" (Draft, 1937). RCK's notes for the "Fish Creek" manuscript are in his diary for the following dates: September 22, 26, October 1, 3, 7, 17, 20, 29, December 17, 23, 1936; October 8, February 4, March 3, 19, 24, 26, 30, April 2, 7, 15, May 21, 25, June 2, August 4, 1937; July 28, 1939; and October 2, 1940.

15. WJJ interview, January 5, 1983; RGM interview, July 9, 1983.

16. Rejection card from Macmillan, November 18, 1937; Charles B. Blanchard to RCK, October 26, 1938.

17. RCK, "History of Associate Reformed Presbyterian Church, Camden, Alabama," *WPE*, September 1, 1938.

18. RCK, "The Whipping of Lester Carlos" (Draft, 1938); RCK, "Bird Hunt," *CC* 55 (December 28, 1938): 1606–7. *The Report on the Economic Conditions of the South* (Washington, DC: Government Printing Office, 1938) went public around August 9, 1938; RCK read it August 22–23, 1938, and his copy then circulated among others of the Roundtable, according to Viola Liddell, with discussion by the Roundtable in "early fall of the year after it came out [1938]." VJGL interview, March 16, 1984; RCK/RR/1938.

19. RCK, "Is It the End of Cotton?" *CC* 55 (May 1, 1938): 591–92; Pete Daniel, "The Transformation of the Rural South," *Agricultural History* 55 (July 1981): 231–43; Charles S. Aiken, *The Cotton Plantation South since the Civil War* (Baltimore: Johns Hopkins University Press, 1998), 63–133, with especially useful comments on Morton Rubin's investigations in Wilcox County.

20. RCK, "W.P.A., Here We Come!" *CC* 55 (June 8, 1938): 728–29; Ligon A. Wilson to RCK, May 8, 1939, May 5, 1940; *HWC*, 285–86; *People and Places of Conecuh County, Alabama, 1816–1860* (Conecuh County Historical Society, n.d. [1970?]), 72; Riley, *History of Conecuh County*, 133–34; *Boston Herald*, January 13, 1899; William J. Edwards, *Twenty-five Years in the Black Belt* (Tuscaloosa: University of Alabama Press, 1993); Louis R. Harlan, ed., *The Papers of Booker T. Washington* (Champaign: University of Illinois Press, 1972), 3:530–31, 7:302–4, 408–10, 10:174–76.

21. RCK, "Life Goes on at Gee's Bend," *CC* 55 (December 1938): 1546–47; Paul E. Mertz, *New Deal Policy and Southern Rural Poverty* (Baton Rouge: Louisiana State University Press, 1978), 174–209; R. P. Yount to Ernest N. Orr, June 22, 1938 (copy); Stonewall McConnico to RCK, January 9, 1939.

22. RCK, "Government in Private Business" (Draft 1939), "One Sunday Morning" (Draft 1939), "Neither Fish Nor Fowl" (Draft 1939), "Drunk" (Draft 1939), "O, Southern Baptists" (Draft 1939), "Peter DeSoto" (Draft 1939), "Flood in Harvest" (Draft 1939), "Half-Back" (Draft 1939); RCK, "How It Happens," *CC* 56 (May 17, 1939): 641–42.

23. MR interview, April 18, 1983; MR, September 13, 1947; Charles G. Dobbins interview, October 14, 1985; RCKD, April 7, 15, 1960. *WPE*, April 21, 1960; *HWC*, 35;

W. P. Wilks, comp., *Biographical Directory of Alabama Baptists, 1920–1947* (Opelika, AL: Post Publishing Co., 1949), 87; *Alabama Baptist* 124 (November 19, 1959): 7, and 125 (April 28, 1960): 2.

24. *WPE*, September 15, 1938; *Tuscaloosa News*, September 12, 1938.

25. Ouida Starr Woodson, "A [Partial] List of Sheriffs of Wilcox County"(copy of an undated typescript in author's possession); *HWC*, 102–3,198–99, 298–300; *WPE*, January 15, February 14, 1915, August 8,1918, December 24, 1925, September 15, 1938, April 23, 1942; Delynn Jenkins Halloran, *Lummie Jenkins* (self-published, 2008); Alexandra Marvar, "The Two Faces of Lummie Jenkins," *Topic* 17 (November 2018).

26. *Anniston Star*, September 12, 1938; *Tuscaloosa News*, September 2, 1938; *BN*, September 12, 1938.

27. Among sermons with implications for Martin's death are "The Mind of Christ," "The Weeping Prophet," and "Being a Christian," RCK/S/1938–39; RCKD, January 13, 1939; WJJ interview, January 5, 1983; Eva Lips, *Savage Symphony: A Personal History of the Third Reich*, trans. Caroline Newton (New York: Random House, 1938). George F. McNeill was shot on the streets of Selma trying to arrest a wanted man (*WPE*, February 24, 1915); Thomas Jenkins Jones was shot in Camden as he attempted to place a man in the Wilcox County jail (*WPE*, February 3, 6, 1936).

28. RGM to RCK, January 10, 21, May 4, 1939; Grover Hall to RGM, January 18, 1939; WJJ to RGM, December 6, 1938; RCK to RGM, January 12, 17, 1939; all in PRGM.

29. RCK, "How It Happens," *CC* 56 (May 7, 1939): 591–92. See also RCK, "The Liquidation of Mr. Smith" (Draft, 1941).

30. *HWC*, 118–19; Miller Bonner to RCK, June 19, 1940; RCK to RGM, June 8, 1939, PRGM; RGM to RCK, May 4, 1939. In 1983, the Wilcox County superintendent of education at the time of the Tait-Martin killings, W. J. Jones, recalled that "the tongue-tied [withdrawn and timid] Monette Curtis, a member of the Klan, told me and everybody he met on the street that he was the one who shot Jonas Martin" and that "the story of the dog-boys doing the shooting was just cooked up." Though gone from Camden by the time of the Martin killing, Charles Dobbins remembered that "any number of Camden friends told [him] the same." WJJ interview, January 5, 1983; Dobbins interview, October 15, 1985. Independent from those statements, one can neither confirm nor deny that Monette Curtis shot Jonas Martin. Not long after the killing, Curtis moved to Evergreen, Alabama, where he worked as a night watchman at a mill. Reverend Roark died in 1960, Sheriff Jenkins in 1978, and Monette Curtis in 1989. I attempted to interview Curtis (in the process discovering that I was Curtis's far distant cousin) but failed.

31. MR, September 9, 1949; RCKD, May 9, 1942; RCK to Charles Dobbins, June 3, 1939 (copy); Dobbins to RCK, June 9, July 5, 1939.

32. *MA*, February 1, 1938; RCK/WFMR/1936–37; Charles R. Bell Jr. to Charles G. Dobbins, November 5, 1938 (copy). D. W. Hollingsworth to George Lang, January 17, 1946; J. McDowell Richards to Lang, January 20, 1947; both in George Lang Papers, University Libraries Special Collections, University of Alabama, Tuscaloosa (hereafter cited as Lang Papers). Lang's fascinating—and unexplored—life as a "southern white liberal" began in Scotland. He was born in the coal-mining town of Wilborne, near

Glasgow. In 1884, at age four, he moved to the Walker County, Alabama, coal-mining town of Townley, when his father accepted a mine management position with the Kansas City, Memphis & Birmingham Railway. Lang went on to become a revered philosophy professor, minister, and author. See *Anniston Star*, November 29, 1957, May 26, 1971; *Tuscaloosa News*, September 10, 1918, June 3, 1924, February 16, 1928. On Charles R. Bell Jr., see Wayne Flynt, "Growing Up Baptist in Anniston, Alabama: The Legacy of the Reverend Charles R. Bell, Jr.," in *Southern Religion and Christian Diversity in the Twentieth Century* (Tuscaloosa: University of Alabama Press, 2016), 13–36; and Charles R. Bell Jr., "A Southern Approach to the Color Issue," *CC* 61 (August 9, 1944): 923–24. When RCK received this 1944 issue of *CC*, he was a US Army chaplain on the war front near Saint-Pair-sur-Mer, France. He clipped Bell's piece and mailed it home to Mary for filing. On J. McDowell Richards, Ralph McGill, and the "Atlanta [Ministers'] Manifesto" of 1957, see James David Phillips, *Faithful Servant: The Life and Times of J. McDowell Richards* (Franklin, TN: Providence House Publishers, 2004). And for more regarding Henry Edmonds, consult Whiting, *An Enduring Ministry*, passim.

33. George Lang to RCK, February 2, July 3, 1939; J. Frederick Mills to RCK, May 8, 20, June 18, 1940; Stan Tinkler to RCK, July 17, 1939; P. D. Chisolm to RCK, August 16, 23, September 29, 1939; N. J. Warren to RCK, October 4, 1939; Clyde V. Hickerson to RCK, July 15, 28, 1940; J. McDowell Richards to RCK, September 18, 1941; N. J. Warren to RCK, October 4. Jonathan Bass, *Blessed Are the Peace Makers: Eight White Religious Leaders, Martin Luther King, Jr., and the "Letter from Birmingham Jail"* (Baton Rouge: Louisiana State University Press, 2001), 69–86, 209–12.

34. Ernest N. Orr to RCK, January 23, February 21, May 1, 1941; Andrew Hood to RCK, September 6, 1941.

35. Guy Logsdon, "Lottinville, Savoie (1906–1997)," okhistory.org; Savoie Lottinville, *The Rhetoric of History* (Norman: University of Oklahoma Press, 1976); VJGL interview, October 11, 1987; Savoie Lottinville to RCK, January 11, 14, 1941.

36. Marie Bankhead Owen to RCK, April 24, 1939; EK to RCK, February 15, September 9, 1939. Owen's "Old Order" addictions are explored in Flynt, *Alabama in the Twentieth Century*, 277, 490–93; Harvey H. Jackson III, "How Marie Bankhead Owen Almost Killed the W. P. A. *Guide* for Alabama," *AH* 56 (Spring 2000): 26–34; Frederickson, *Deep South Dynasty*, 258–66; and Whitmire, "How a Confederate Daughter Rewrote Alabama History for White Supremacy," *Mobile Register*, February 27, 2022.

37. RCK, "Poets of Fish Creek," *AHQ* 2 (May 15, 1940): 44–51; EK to RCK, February 1, June 13, 1940; *BN*, April 23, 1939; RCKD, May 20, 1941; RCK to MMK, March 30, 1944.

38. EK to RCK, February 22, December 18, 1940; VJGL to RCK, August 5, 1941; RCK interview, February 25, 1985.

39. RCK, "Alabama Black Belt," *AHQ*, 2 (Fall 1940): 282–89; RCK/RR/1937. Seven years later, when Chapel Hill anthropologist Morton Rubin conducted field studies in Wilcox County, his interviews with whites turned up regular references to "that man is just the feud'n type." MR, January 19, 1948. Owen's "Old Order" proclivities are profiled in Flynt, *Alabama in the Twentieth Century*, 277, 490–93; and in Jackson, "How Marie Bankhead Owen," 26–34. RCK's thoughts on Civil War battle damage and mass media exposure appear to anticipate some major threads of modern southern scholarship. For

example, consider Lisa M. Brady, *War upon the Land: Military Strategy and the Transformation of Southern Landscapes during the American Civil War* (Athens: University of Georgia Press, 2012); and Karen L. Cox, *Dreaming of Dixie: How the South Was Created in American Popular Culture* (Chapel Hill: University of North Carolina Press, 2011). On the "Selling of the South," see James C. Cobb, *The Selling of the South: The Southern Crusade for Industrial Development, 1936–1990* (Champaign: University of Illinois Press, 1997); and on the ending of the old plantation system, see Charles S. Aiken, *The Cotton Plantation South since the Civil War* (Baltimore: Johns Hopkins University Press, 1998), 63 and passim.

40. RCK, "Alas, Poor Yorick," *AHQ* 3 (February 1941): 405–15. See also the imaginative use of Kennedy's "Yorick" funeral analysis in Elizabeth Findley Shores, *Earline's Pink Party: The Social Rituals and Domestic Relics of a Southern Woman* (Tuscaloosa: University of Alabama Press, 2017), 128. RCK to Folks [Brothers and Sisters], April 13, 1981 (copy). The impact of World War II on Wilcox is distilled in Clinton McCarty, *Reins of Power: Racial Change and Challenge in a Southern Community* (Tallahassee: Sentry Press, 1999), 123. See also Tindall, *Emergence of the New South*, 694, 701–3; W. Jayson Hill, "Craig Field Airport and Industrial Complex (Craig Air Force Base)," Encyclopediaofalabama.org; and Flynt, *Alabama in the Twentieth Century*, 396.

Chapter 8

1. On the US move from isolationism to intervention in World War II, see George C. Herring, *The American Century and Beyond: US Foreign Relations, 1893–2014* (New York: Oxford University Press, 2017), 185–238. On southerners specifically, consult Joseph A. Fry, *Dixie Looks Abroad: The South and US Foreign Relations, 1879–1973* (Baton Rouge: Louisiana State University Press, 2002), 195–221. And on Alabamians, see Allen Cronenburg, *Forth to the Mighty Conflict: Alabama and World War II* (Tuscaloosa: University of Alabama Press, 2004). Mark G. Toulouse assays the changing foreign affairs viewpoint of the *Christian Century* in "The 'unnecessary necessity': The CENTURY in World War II," *CC* 117 (July 5–12, 2000): 725–29. Ware and Gettys, *Second Century*, 132–34, explains the fine line the ARP Synod tried to follow on the Spanish-American War and World War I as it focused on "the individual rather than society," though in this context they do not treat ARPs and World War II.

2. RCK read Charles Clayton Morrison's *Outlawry of War* (Chicago: Willet, Clark, and Colby, 1927), in early September 1928; Erich Remarque's *All Quiet on the Western Front* (Boston: Little Brown, 1929), in late September 1929; and William March's *Company K* (New York: Smith and Haas, 1933), in early August 1934 (RCK/RR/1928/1934). Paul Hutchinson's "The Portent of Hitler," *CC* 50 (October 18, 1933): 1299–1301, he read repeatedly and used in sermons through the mid-to-late 1930s. Although RCK continued to reference Charles Beard as a respected opinion on social and economic injustices in the United States, he parted with Beard over interventionism in the late 1930s and appears not to have bought any of Beard's books dissenting from FDR's foreign policy.

3. RCK, "Pulpit Diary," *CC* 58 (January 29, 1941): 151; RCK/S/1934.

4. RCK, "Black Belt Aristocrats," *Social Forces* 13 (October 1934): 81–85; RCK, "Quality in the Reserve Corps," *CC* 52 (February 27, 1935): 272–74; RCK, "Great Peace

Celebration," *CC* 52 (December 15, 1935): 1553–54; RCK, "Legion Audit," *CC* 53 (December 16, 1936): 1688–90; WJJ interview, January 5, 1983.

5. WJJ and JCCJ interview, November 21, 1979 ("Alabama first"); Robert Brinkmeyer, *The Fourth Ghost: White Southern Writers and European Fascism, 1930–1950* (Baton Rouge: Louisiana State University Press, 2009), 202; Clarence Cason, *90 Degrees in the Shade* (Chapel Hill: University of North Carolina Press, 1935), 90–107.

6. RCK/S/1939; RCK, "Pulpit Diary."

7. RCK/S/1939–40; E. N. Orr to RCK, September 5, 1939, May 30, 1940; J. Frank Robinson to RCK, December 27, 1939; and EK to RCK, June 13, 1940. On the war, including coverage of the Holocaust, see Martin Gilbert, *The Second World War: A Complete History* (New York: Henry Holt, 1989), 117–25 and passim; Deborah E. Lipstadt, *Beyond Belief: The American Press and the Coming of the Holocaust, 1933–1945* (New York: Free Press, 1993); Laurel Leff, *Buried by the Times: The Holocaust and America's Most Important Newspaper* (Cambridge: Cambridge University Press, 2005); and Robert Sorbel, *The Origins of Interventionism: The United States and the Russo-Finnish War* (New York: Literary Licensing, 1960), 109–37, 181.

8. RCK, "Pulpit Diary," 152; RCK/S/1940. After this address/sermon, one member of the Roundtable, Helen Burford Lambert—who attended both Methodist and Baptist churches in Camden—wrote RCK: "I wish I could hear you every Sunday. I do so approve of preaching in terms of 1942 rather than staying in the First Century. . . . You broaden my knowledge, enlarge my vision and increase my desire to live better." Helen Lambert to RCK, May 20, 1942.

9. RCK, "Pulpit Diary," 152; Adam Alles, "Forces That Produced Hitler," *CC* 57 (November 6, 1940): 1370–73; Lowry and Gettys, *Second Century*, 329–46; RCK interview, February 25, 1984; *NYT*, January 7, 1941 (including distillation of "Four Freedoms"). Another *NYT* clipping RCK used in sermons at this time was a letter to the editor from James W. Osborne (*NYT*, May 25, 1940), which included these words: "Should not priests, clergymen, and ministers rise up . . . and preach that the Allies are engaged in a crusade to destroy the German pagans . . . infidels . . . more venomous and powerful than the Saracens?" On social anthropology, religion, and cultural cohesiveness, see, for example, Robert A. Siegal, ed., *The Blackwell Companion to the Study of Religion* (Malden, MA: Blackwell, 2006). For recent intellectuals employing societal insecurity to help explain the embrace of certain aggressive behaviors, see Richard Hofstadter, *The Paranoid Style in American Politics* (New York: Random House, 1964); Robert Wiebe, *The Search for Order, 1877–1920* (New York: Hill and Wang, 1967); and Madeleine Albright, *Fascism: A Warning* (New York: Harper Collins, 2018).

10. RCK, "Pulpit Diary," 151–52. Despite RCK's firm interventionism by late 1940, his creative urges apparently led him to draft a Yaupon story—autobiographical up to a point—about a racially liberal and pacifist preacher who gave a strongly antiwar sermon on February 15, 1941, with the community subsequently turning on him. See "The Liquidation of Mr. Smith" (Draft, 1941).

11. RCK, "Volunteer," *CC* 58 (July 1941): 931–32; Pete Daniel, "Going among Strangers: Southern Reactions to World War II," *JAH* 77 (December 1990): 891. See also George Q. Flynn, "The Selective Service and American Blacks during World War II," *Journal of Negro History* 69 (Winter 1984): 14–25.

12. RCK, "December 7, 1941" (Draft, 1941); RCK/S/1941; RCK interview, May 2, 1983.

13. "Christmas 1941" (Draft, 1941); RCK/S/1941; George Lang to RCK, April 7, 1941; Lang to J. McDowell Richards, April 18, 1941 (copy); Richards to RCK, April 25, May 21, December 18, 1941; Dorothy Duncan to RCK, April 28, 1941; RCK to MMK, June 6, 1941; Charles Granville Hamilton to RCK, January 24, 1941; RCK/S/1941.

14. Lisa O'Neill Dobson interview, November 10, 2008; Betty Gaines Kennedy interview, November 10, 2008; RCKD, May 19, June 1, 8–9, July 9, December 19, 21–22, 1942; Daniel, "Going among Strangers," 892–93, 900, 903, 906; Michael V. R. Thomason, ed., *Mobile: The New History of Alabama's First City* (Tuscaloosa: University of Alabama Press, 2001), 148–49, 215–18, 234, 244; Clinton McCarty, *Reins of Power: Racial Change and Challenge in a Southern Community* (Tallahassee: Sentry Press, 1999), 122; Accessgenealogy.com.

15. RCK/S/1941.

16. Lottinville to RCK, March 7, 1942.

17. RCK registered with the Selective Service on February 6, 1942 (RCKD, February 16, 1942). On the Finnish relief fund, see Sorbel, *Origins of Interventionism*, 101–37; Thomas W. Martin to RCK, February 19, 22, 26, March 4, 1940. On the Defense Bond Committee, see Kennedy, *Freedom from Fear*, 626; and RCKD, February 4, 1942, January 11–12, 17, February 2–3, 1943. Pledges ranged from ten cents a month to a thousand dollars or more per year. For July 1942 through June 1943 the total raised was $3,511, placing Wilcox among the top ten Alabama counties for the War Bonds initiative—a strong accomplishment in view of the county's pervasive poverty. RCK credited this success not just to the use of Joe Lewis posters but to the extraordinary canvassing work of Joe Allen, head of Camden Academy, and Legon Wilson, head of Snow Hill Institute. In the Wilcox campaign, the majority of the money derived from white-owned businesses; Wilcox American Legion chapters stood out as "laggards." As far as "household participation" went, the Black citizens' participation was three times that of white citizens. RCKD, May 26–27, June 11, 17, July 12–14, 1942. "Vic," the bicycle, assumed a life all its own. Though the community found it "charming," to RCK it was one more indication of the ARPs' lack of vitality—lack of salary money for its preachers to be able to afford a car to help others. Camden's city code required him to have a "bicycle license." RCKD, June 12, 1942, July 14–18, 31, and August 3, 1942; RCK, "War: Causes and Possible Consequences [of World War II]" (Draft, 1942). On Thomas W. Martin, see Leah Rawls Atkins, "Thomas W. Martin," Encyclopediaofalabama.org.

18. On anthropologist Stone, see Stanton, "Coming of Age in Gee's Bend," *AH* 114 (Fall 2014): 36–43; and Olive Stone to RCK, December 12, May 31, June 4, 1942. On Presbyterian social worker Heinrich, see "Biographical Files—John C. Heinrich," Commission on Ecumenical Missions and Relations, 1883–1966, RG209, Reel 37, Archives of the United Presbyterian Church, Pittsburgh; RCKD, February 22–24, August 10, September 18, 1942; J. C. Heinrich to RCK, April 29, 1942; and John C. Heinrich, *The Psychology of the Oppressed* (London: Allen and Unwin, 1937). On "Misses Hornsby and Barnhoeff," see RCKD, September 6, 1942, and MR, February 2, 1947; and specifically on Klan threats, RCKD, February 22, June 10, August 5, 13, 1942. The growing fundamentalism of the area also is noted in MR, January 27, 1947: "Most people in WC

believe in Fundamentalism and less concern with pure theology and denominational [differences]." On Cooksville, Tennessee, native Glenn Nolan Fisk and his dissertation, see RCKD, August 10, 1942. The possibilities of ARP–Southern Presbyterian merger are reflected in RCKD, May 14, October 22, November 5, 1942, and W. L. Hill to RCK, October 22, 1942; and its larger context is given in Ware and Gettys, *Second Century*, 227–65. On Viola Liddell and this tension, see RCKD, April 20, 1942. His level of fatigue, frustration, and increased alcohol consumption shows in RCKD, March 4, 8, 24, April 7, May 31, June 9, July 8, 14–15, and August 12, 1942. They "don't give a damn" quote is from RCKD, September 5, 1942.

19. For fascinating comparisons of Percy and Cash, see Cobb, *Away Down South*, 164–69 and passim; and Fred Hobson, *Tell about the South: The Southern Rage to Explain* (Baton Rouge: Louisiana State University Press, 1983), 244–94. RCK, "By-Product of War," *CC* 60 (July 28, 1943): 865–66; and "Coat," *CC* 61 (February 9, 1944): 1175–77. On extended sharecropper poverty due to mechanization, war demand, new types of crops, and indeed New Deal policies, consult Daniel, "Going among Strangers," 910; and Morton Sosna, "More Important Than the Civil War? The Impact of World War II on the South," in James C. Cobb and Charles R. Wilson, eds., *Perspectives on the American South: An Annual Review of Society, Politics, and Culture* (New York: Routledge, 1987), especially 150–53. When Chapel Hill anthropologist Morton Rubin researched Wilcox in 1947, he noted the ongoing results of these forces, notably the growth of cattle and timber, leaving little in the economy for uneducated laborers. MR, September 6, 1947.

20. Lottinville to RCK, January 14, 1943; "War . . ." (Draft, 1942). The finished typescript of "The Yaupon Tales" is not in Kennedy's abundant papers, nor is it in the business files or the archives of the University of Oklahoma Press. This remains unsurprising. Few indeed are the presses that keep old manuscripts, published or rejected, written by relatively unknown authors. So, as with "The People of Fish Creek," the handwritten "Yaupon Tales" in the RCK papers—combined with those vignettes published—is what survives.

21. The term "Greatest Generation" gained currency through Tom Brokaw, *The Greatest Generation* (New York: Random House, 1998). However, this book also ignited a debate over how "great" the World War II generation actually was in that many of its members either tolerated or advocated any number of "not great" social institutions, such as racial segregation, gender discrimination, and extreme disparities in health care and education. Even before Brokaw's book appeared, that thought was advocated in Neil A. Wynn, "The 'Good War': The Second World War and Postwar American Society," *Journal of Contemporary History* 31 (July 1996): 463–82; and, after Brokaw's book appeared, in Kenneth Rose, *Myth and the Greatest Generation* (New York: Routledge, 2012).

22. RCKD, January 23, 1942; *AJ*, February 8, 1942, March 29, 1950; RCK/S/1942; RCK, "Pulpit Diary."

23. *Minutes of the General Synod of the Associate Reformed Presbyterian Church: One Hundred and Thirty-Eighth Session, First Church Statesville, N. C. April 22–26, 1942* (Greenville, SC: The Synod, 1942); J. Miller Bonner to RCK, August 5, 1942; A. B. Love to RCK, July 23, 1942; R. C. Grier to RCK, August 5, 1942; RCKD, October 22, 1942,

January 15–16, 25–26, 28, 31, 1943; William M. Boyce to RCK, January 5, 1942; RCK to MMK, March 7, 1944; *Sesquicentennial History*, 305–6; RCK "201" Personnel File.

24. EK to RCK, February 6, 1943; RCKD, January 1, February 8, 15, 26, 1943; RCK to MMK, February 26, 1943.

25. Memorandum from William R. Arnold, March 3, 1943 (mimeographed copy); RCKD, February 3, 27, March 3–4, 1943; Arthur Carl Piepkorn, "A Chronicle of the United States Army Chaplains School during the Second World War"(typescript, 1959, US Military Chaplains Library, Fort Jackson, SC); "Renwick C. Kennedy: Record of Attendance and Grades," Army Chaplain School—Harvard Program (US Army Museum, Fort Jackson, SC); "Application for Appointment as Chaplain: Renwick Kennedy," RCK US Army Personnel 201 File; John Brinsfield to author, March 17, 2008, RCK/RF/Brinsield. Aside from the "satisfactory" grade on his "sex sermon" (RCKD, April 2, 1943), the only blemish on RCK's Harvard Chaplaincy School record was what he called a "fully innocent bookshop violation." On the evening of March 15, Kennedy visited several Cambridge bookshops; returning to quarters ten minutes late. "Caught," he was confined to quarters the following weekend. Ralph C. Deibert to RCK, March 16, 1943. See also RCKD, March 3–April 3, 1943; Monthly Reports of Renwick C. Kennedy, Records of the Office of the Chief of Chaplains and "201" Files, 1920–1945, RG 247, NA (Military Archives Division).

26. RCKD, April 4–10, 1943; RCK interview, February 25, 1984.

27. On the background of SLO and the evolution of the 102nd Evacuation Hospital, see RCK, *History of the 102nd Evacuation Hospital* (n.p., 1946), 1–2 (hereafter cited as RCK, *History 102nd*); RCKD, November 20, 1943. On the Vasco Hale case, see Robert Jefferson, *Fighting for Hope: African American Troops of the 93rd Infantry Division in World War Two and Post-War America* (Baltimore: Johns Hopkins University Press, 2008); Tennant McWilliams, *The Chaplain's Conflict: Good and Evil in a War Hospital, 1943–1945* (College Station: Texas A&M University Press, 2012), 2–3, 25–26; and RCK interview, May 21, 1983.

28. RCK, *History 102nd*, 6–7; McWilliams, *Chaplain's Conflict*, 1–28; MMK to Dorothy Moore McNeill, March 24, 1944, PLMD; Hugh A. Kelsey to RCK, April 28, 1944; RCK to MMK, December 10, 1943, January 2, 19, 20, February 11, 1944; RCKD, April 21, November 4, December 9, 12, 1943; Ann Margaret Peterson interview, February 9, 2008.

29. Anna Marie Laws Walton interview, April 16, 2008; RCKD, April 28, May 8, June 18, October 23, 1943, July 22, 1944; McWilliams, *Chaplain's Conflict*, 76–77.

30. RCKD, June 22, November 14, 1944.

31. RCK, *History 102nd*, 8–9; RCK to MMK, July 1, 1944; RCKD, July 5, 18, 1944. In 1953, Amy Erickson and her parents—driving from Florida to their home in Illinois—stopped in Camden for a three-hour visit with RCK and MMK. Whether the nurse revealed the truth about the preacher's dancing remains unknown. RCKD, May 3, 1953.

32. McWilliams, *Chaplain's Conflict*, 41–56; VJGL to Oxford Liddell, October 30, 1943, PVJGL; Sam McNeill to Dorothy Moore McNeill, June 1, 28, July 25–26, August 10, 1944, PLMD; RCK to MMK, July 25–26, 1944; RCKD, July 20, 25–27, 1944. On context for the Battle of Saint-Lô, see Stephen E. Ambrose, *D-Day, June 6, 1944: The Climactic Battle of World War II* (New York: Simon & Schuster, 1994), 248, 515.

33. RCKD, August 8, 18–19, 24–25, 28, 1944; Sylvie Louboutin-Croc interview, June 6, 2008; Anne Vincot Bellec interview, June 6, 2008; Georges Talec interview, June 6, 2008; the diary of Mme. Christine Croc still resides at Château de Trébodennic, Ploudaniel, France. For context on the Battle of Brest, see Gilbert, *The Second World War*, 348, 596.

34. RCKD, July 25–26, 1944; RCK to MMK, July 27, 1944.

35. RCKD, August 7, 11, 1944; Louis Forget interview, January 3, 15, 2008; Marie-Thérèse Provost Dasrochas interview, February 6, March 26, 2008; Roland Dulins Duprey interview, February 6, 2008; Marie Louise Lévi-Ménard interview, February 8, 2008; RCK to "Folks," August 5, 1944 (copy); *Saint-Aubin des Préaux: Son histoire*, ([n.p.]: La Fédération de la Manche des Retraites, 1990), 37–40.

36. RCK to MMK, October 3, 5, 1944; RCKD, October 1–3, 1944.

37. McWilliams, *Chaplain's Conflict*, 74–79; RCK to MMK, October 12, 16, 1944; Sam McNeill to RCK, October 5, 1944.

38. RCKD, September 2, 7, 1943, September 10, 17, 20, October 7–10, 17, 25, 28, 1944; RCK to MMK, October 7–12, 14, 16, November 5, 10, 19, 22, 1944; *Contrat de location* (rental agreement) and *Accord de règlement* (settlement agreement) for the US Army's use of Château de Roument, Business Files, Archives of Château de Roument (Ochamps, Belgium); Jean-Christophe Coppée to author, July 17, 2008; Jean-Christophe Coppée interview, April 5, 2008; Edith and Jacques Bertin, *Evence Coppée, III: 1882–1945* (Brussels: Imprimeurs Alleur, 1991), 338–62.

39. Tom Poecker and Fred Fey, eds., *85 Joer an Der Kinnekswiss* (Ettelbruck: Print Solutions, 2017), 298–326; McWilliams, *Chaplain's Conflict*, 80–84; RCKD, November 20, 23, 27, December 11–12, 1944 ("sick at heart"); RCK to MMK, November 20–21, 1944, January 3, 25, 1945; RCK to Hayden Jones, November 28, 1944; Sam McNeill to Dorothy Moore McNeill, October 6, 15, 23, 1944, PLMD; RCK interview, September 9, 1984. See also chapter 6, note 12, and chapter 8, notes 18 and 32, above.

40. RCKD, December 14, 17–19, 1944; RCK to MMK, January 21, 1945. On the larger context for the Battle of the Bulge, see Martin, *Second World War*, 621–29.

41. McWilliams, *Chaplain's Conflict*, 86–89; "102nd Evacuation Hospital Annual Report, Submitted by Col. John F. Blatt," US Army Surgeon General, World War II, 1944–45 (RG 112, Box 406, National Archives, Military Records Division); Goodiel to Maj. Gen. Troy H. Middleton, January 3, 1945, Troy H. Middleton Papers, Personal Correspondence, 1944–45 (Archives and Special Colletions, Louisiana State University, Baton Rouge); RCKD, December 21–30, 1944; Edward J. Russell to Hugh C. Dale, March 8, 2006 (copy). On the day Goodiel was relieved of command, RCK took temporary leave from his long and severe criticism of the CO: "Goodiel left today . . . my friend" (RCKD, December 29, 1944).

42. RCKD, August 25, 27, September 4, 9, 1944, January 1–5, 11, 1945 ("bucket"); RCK to MMK, January 10, 1945 ("insane business"); RCK/S/1945 ("horrible war"); Millard E. Lumpkin to Family, January 7, 1945, in possession of Russell E. Summerlin, Delta, Alabama; Russell E. Summerlin interview, February 3, 2009; Maudine Lumpkin interview, February 4, 2009; Elizabeth Lumpkin interview, February 4, 2009.

43. RCK to MMK, January 14, 18, 21, 25–26, 1945; RCK to Dot McNeill, January 25 (copy), February 11, 1945 (copy); Dot McNeill to RCK, January 21, February 11, 1945; RCKD, January 16, 24–25, 1945.

44. RCK/S/1945; *NYT,* January 7, 1941; RCK to MMK, January 28–30, 1945. In RCK's papers, the author found the *NYT* clipping still inside this sermon. On George Kennan's many USSR assessments, notably his "Long Telegram" and "Sources of Soviet Conduct," *Foreign Affairs* 25 (July 1947): 566–82, consult for example John Lewis Gaddis, *The Cold War: A New History* (New York: Penguin, 2005), 29–32, 46–47, 61, 101.

45. RCK, *History 102nd,* 11; RCKD, March 14–15, 1945. On the larger context for the Remagen Bridge battle, see Gilbert, *The Second World War,* 646 and passim.

46. RCKD, April 6, 10, 13, 16, 25 (Buchenwald quote), 29, 1945; RCK to MMK, April 16, 18, 29, May 20, 1945 (stealing quote).

47. RCKD, May 3, 8–9, 17, 19–20, 28–29, June 12, 14, November 5, 1945; RCK to All Personnel This Command, May 19, 1945 (copy); RCK to Dorothy Mae Brown, May 28, 1945 (copy); RCK to MMK, May 19–20, 31, 1945.

48. RCKD, June 4–7, 1945; RCK to MMK, June 8, 10, 1945; William E. Kennedy to RCK, September 20, 1971; Leon Kennedy to RCK, June 1, 1970; Margaret Kennedy to RCK, April 26, 1976; William McLane Kennedy, US Army Personnel "201" File (copy in KRF/B/Kennedy); Michael W. Perry, ed., *Dachau Liberated: The Official Report* [of the US Seventh Army] (Seattle: Inkling Books, 2000). Though he practiced medicine for a long time after the war, William Kennedy's debilitating posttraumatic stress never left him. He died in 1977, living as a mentally ill invalid in Charlotte, North Carolina, with his brother, Leon. RCK's reflections on William's war torments are addressed in RCKD, September 15, 1977.

49. On VJ Day, RCK held a 3:00 p.m. service with seventy on hand, but he clearly was preoccupied with the surrounding chaos (RCKD, August 17–18, 1945). During these draw-down procedures, the 102nd first set up at Marburg, Germany, then on to sprawling "tent towns" erected by the US Army for moving the military out of Europe: Camp San Antonio, eighty-five miles west of Paris; then Camp Baltimore, near Reims, with easy access to rail lines down to Marseilles (and where RCK had to part with *Alabama II*); and finally to Calas, adjacent to Marseilles. In each of these camps, the Red Cross provided well-stocked libraries—classical literature, history, philosophy, and modern fiction. RCK appears to have been one of the relatively few GIs who went to the libraries to read and to check out books to his tent. At the camp libraries he completed a first draft of "A History of the 102nd Evacuation Hospital"; and he read Heiden's *Der Fuehrer: Hitler's Rise to Power* (Boston: Houghton Mifflin, 1944); Crane's *The Red Badge of Courage* (New York: D. Appleton and Co., 1895); Smith's *Strange Fruit*; Maugham's *Razor's Edge* (New York: Doubleday, Doran, 1944); and Wolfe's *You Can't Go Home Again* (New York: Harper and Bros., 1940). He also reunited with at least five of William Shakespeare's plays, as well as Herman Melville's *Moby-Dick* (New York: Harper and Bros., 1851). RCKD, June 21, 26, 29, July 10–11, 22, 25, 28, August 4, 15, 30, September 7, November 1–2, 1945; RCK/RR/1945; MKA to Daddy, July 2, 1945.

50. RCK/S/1945; RCKD, November 3–12, 1945, giving details of the voyage home. On the wristwatch, see RCKD, March 31, April 1–3, 1943; RCK to MMK, December 28, 1944, where he writes: "A wristwatch is a very convenient thing to have ... [if it is] doing well." See also Alexis McCrossen, *Making Modern Times: A History of Clocks, Watches, and Other Timekeepers in American Life* (Chicago: University of Chicago Press, 2013), 60–61 and passim.

51. RCKD, November 13–18, 1945.
52. RCKD, November 19, 1945.

Chapter 9
1. RCKD, November 20–25, 1945; RCK/S/1945; *WPE*, November 22, 1945.
2. RCKD, November 26, December 9, 1945.
3. Upon hearing of "good deals" on military surplus, Camdenites Burford Hollinger and James Bonner headed for the Atlanta outlet and took RCK with them. Subsequently, RCK drafted a short article on how to buy war surplus vehicles from the US government. See RCK, "How to Buy a WAA Truck" (Draft, 1947). The piece seems to have gone nowhere. RCKD, November 17, December 6, 16, 29, and 31, 1946, January 15, 1947; MCKD interview, December 22, 2008.
4. RCK, *History 102nd*, is available in NA, RG 40, Records of the US Army Adjutant General, World War II Records, 102nd Evacuation Hospital, Box 2151. On his communication with Dan Laws and many others of the 102nd see, e.g., RCKD, January 17, February 4, April 12, 26, May 21, September 16, October 10, December 15, 21, 31, 1946. For snapshots of RCK's immediate postwar consumption of alcohol—an ounce or two of hard liquor per night on average of three nights a week, but occasionally more—see RCKD, July 2, 12, August 12, 16, 1946.
5. RCK, "The Conqueror," *CC* 63 (April 17, 1946): 485–97; *Time* 47 (May 6, 1946): 24; *Newsweek* 27 (May 6, 1946): 33; *AJ*, May 13, 1946; *MA*, May 18, 1946; RCKD, December 29, 1945, January 11, April 16, 27, May 3, 1946. In mid-March 1946, as RCK worked on "The Conqueror," he went to Emmett Kilpatrick's house for dinner. That evening's diary entry: "I eat dinner with Emmett. . . . He is disgusted with present American scene. . . . We agree Europeans are more civilized. [In the war] U. S. soldiers [acted as] adolescent barbarians." RCKD, March 19, 1946. On broad reaction to "The Conqueror," see, for example, Clyde C. Harris to RCK, April 17, 1946; Kenneth R. Corliss to RCK, May 10, 1946. W. N. Smith to the Editor and H. P. Nelson to the Editor, *Time* 47 (June 3, 1946): 7–8. William H. Danforth to RCK, April 19, 1946; Frank Trinder to RCK, February 5, 1946; Lee J. Hand to RCK, May 4, 1946; Charles Lee to RCK, May 4, 1946. Bart J. Engram, May 6, 1946, and Ernest H. Tilford to the Editor, May 22, 1946, in *CC* 63 (May 22, 1946): 659. Jack Cromwell to RCK, June 4, 1946. See also Eric F. Goldman, *The Crucial Decade—and After: America, 1945–1960* (New York: Alfred A. Knopf, 1966), 33–34. Goldman's reference got sustained traction. Journalist William Manchester, himself a veteran, credited Kennedy in *The Glory and the Dream: A Narrative History of America, 1932–1972* (New York: Little, Brown, 1973), 435. So did Joseph Goulden in yet another noted synthesis of postwar America, *The Best Years, 1945–1950* (New York: Atheneum, 1976), 31. The most recent reference to RCK's World War II critique is in Michael Snape, *God and Uncle Sam: Religion and American Armed Forces in World War II* (Rochester, NY: Boydell Press, 2015), 65, 84, 31–36, 583–84.
6. RCK, "How Good Were the Army Chaplains?" *CC* 63 (June 5, 1946): 716–17; RCK, "To the Victor Goes the Spoils," *CC* 63 (July 31, 1946): 936–67; RCKD, March 18, June 26, 1946; Paul Hutchinson to RCK, May 23, 1946. In response to "How Good Were the Army Chaplains?" for example, Lyman Ward, president of the Southern Industrial Boys School, at Camp Hill, Alabama (later Lyman Ward Military Academy),

wrote RCK: "The darkest cloud on the American horizon at this time is the Roman Catholic Church. . . . They would destroy our public-school system." Lyman Ward to RCK, June 13, 1946. On the "mad duke's sword," Emmett Kilpatrick—the likely source of Kennedy's information—seems to have conflated the "provenance" of several swords. Staff Sgt. Richard B. Edwards, of Andalusia, made the gift to the Archives, but "it is a German sword from Naufdeuren, Germany. [While] initial reports attributed the sword to Leopold the Great of Breslau . . . not to the Duke of Bavaria and not from Munich . . . later research [established it as a] German sword from Naufdeuren, Germany." Scotty Kirkland to author, September 3, 2019. On Archbishop Spellman, see Snape, *God and Uncle Sam*, 138–243. On the Ervin-McKelvey wedding, see *HWC*, 230; *WPE*, August 11, 1949; MCKD interview, October 10, 2011; Bogie interview, December 11, 2012. On Marian Perdue Furman's Catholicism, see RCK to Marian Perdue, May 5, 1955 (copy); and Furman interview, January 20, 2016.

7. RCK, "Brass Hats," *CC* 63 (October 2, 1946): 1179–80; RCK, "The G. I. Gravy Train," *CC* 64 (August 6, 1947): 944–45.

8. RCK, "Military Training for Your Son," *Better Homes and Gardens* 25 (October 1946): 33, 168; RCKD, July 19, 1946. At the publisher's request, RCK did a follow-up piece, "Letter to Your Boy about Army Life," *Better Homes and Gardens* 27 (December 1948): 202–3, which emphasized the same points. Peter Crossly to RCK, January 11, August 2, 31, 1948. See also John Patrick Diggins, *Why Niebuhr Now?* (Chicago: University of Chicago Press, 2011), 62–95.

9. Gunnar Myrdal, *An American Dilemma: The Negro and Modern Democracy*, 2 vols. (New York: Harper and Bros., 1944); Walter Van Clark, *A Christian Global Strategy* (Chicago: Willet, Clark and Co., 1945). John H. Burzhardt to RCK, December 19, 1945, June 26, 1946; RCKD, February 15, 1946; Ernest N. Orr to RCK, February 27, 1946 (White's quote), and August 23, 1946; D. F. White to WJJ, March 29, 1954, in PWJJ; RCK interview, February 25, 1984, where RCK said: "[Myrdal] was wrong then and wrong now . . . unless the U. S. government really gets behind the plan . . . doubtful . . . depressing . . . really depressing." Despite no response from his congregations as well as Synod rejection, all through the mid-to-late 1940s RCK found opportunities to give sermons on the need for Americans to support various international Christian aid programs targeted at alleviating hunger and providing housing in war-torn Europe, and he contributed to these himself. For example, see RCK/S/1947; RCKD, April 15, October 7, 22, 1947. He also pled his case—where it needed less pleading—with "The World's Most Generous People," *CC* 64 (April 4, 1947): 525–26.

10. RCKD, July 21, 1946; Aubrey Williams to RCK, June 8, 1948. John Salmond, *A Southern Rebel: The Life and Times of Aubrey Willis Williams, 1890–1965* (Chapel Hill: University of North Carolina Press, 1983), 199–203, 249, and passim; Anthony Dunbar, *Against the Grain: Southern Radicals and Prophets, 1929–1959* (Charlottesville: University of Virginia Press, 1981), 117, 144, 164, 171–79, 237–40; Patricia Sullivan, *Days of Hope: Race and Democracy in the New Deal Era* (Chapel Hill: University of North Carolina Press, 1996), 111–14, 205, 220; Judith E. Sheppard, "Gould Beech," Encyclopediaofalabama. org. On 1948 politics, both Williams and Beech despised the Dixiecrats, cheered the US Supreme Court's rejection of the Boswell Amendment, and strongly criticized Alabama's subsequent use of "literacy qualification" tests to block voting by Black people. But on

the 1948 presidential nomination, Williams wanted *Southern Farmer* to endorse Truman, while Beech urged the more liberal Henry Wallace of the Progressive Party. Philosophically, RCK was more aligned with Henry Wallace, yet he pragmatically supported Truman because he thought Truman had the better chance of beating Dewey. The same pragmatism led RCK to stay clear of the split between Williams and Beech. The job overture Beech made to Troy Teachers College president, Charles Bunyan Smith, appears to have been blocked in great part by Emmett Kilpatrick, who explained to Smith that his institution was too dependent on state politics to risk hiring Beech—an open critic of the Black Belt–Big Mule axis who was not from the Black Belt. RCKD, October 29, 1948.

11. Gould Beech to RCK, July 17, November 19, 1947; RCKD, July 22, 28, 1946, August 22, 1947 (RCK's first meeting with Beech and Williams), August 30, September 11–12, December 11, 1946. RCK, "Can the Christian Faith Work on a Seven Day a Week Basis?" *SF* 107 (August 1946): 12; "Are They Our Neighbors? [Part 1]," *SF* 107 (October 1946): 13; "Are They Our Neighbors? [Part 2]," *SF* 107 (November 1946): 5; "We Need to Think of This Life, Too," *SF* 107 (December 1946): 1, 12; "Make Peace with Your Neighbor," *SF* 108 (January 1947): 11, reprinted in *MA*, February 8, 1947; "Strength for Our Time: Need for Racial Tolerance," *SF* 108 (March 1947): 13; "Veterans Make Good Citizens," *SF* 108 (April 1947): 6; "Are We Too Conservative?" *SF* 107 (May 1947): 12; "Waste in a Hungry World," *SF* 108 (June 1947): 16; "Do Our Churches Need to Fight Each Other," *SF* 108 (August 1947): 10; "Strength for Our Time: Be Liberal, Be Moral, Be Self-Sufficient," *SF* 108 (October 1947): 16; "What Do You Read?" *SF* 108 (November 1947): 17; "The Best Years of Our Life," *SF* 108 (January 1948): 17.

12. RCK, "Southwind" (Draft, 1947). On *SF* support for Folsom, Gould Beech wrote RCK: "Like the followers of Andrew Jackson, Grover Cleveland and Woodrow Wilson, we have to suffer some personal embarrassment [regarding Folsom's drinking and personal life]. But the fact is that Jim Folsom is the only American who is saying something that makes sense." Beech to RCK, January 29, 1948. During this period RCK also drafted a plea for poll tax reform, an analysis of why Black Belters voted more on personality and family connections than on policy issues, and a portrait of continuing damage done by the Black Belt's "broken aristocracy." The larger context for Kennedy's "Southwind" assessment is in Kari Frederickson, *The Dixiecrat Revolt and the End of the Solid South, 1932–1968* (Chapel Hill: University of North Carolina Press, 2001), 40–41, 48; and in Robert J. Norrell, "Labor at the Ballot Box: Alabama Politics from the New Deal to the Dixiecrat Movement," *JSH* 57 (May 1991): 201–34.

13. Dobbins interview, October 15, 1985; MR, January 27, 1948; RCK interview, February 25, 1984; RCKD, March 19, May 6, 1947. RCK's personal library included Richard Wright's *Uncle Tom's Children* (New York: Harper and Bros., 1938), including much on Wright's early years in Jim Crow Mississippi.

14. On his meeting "goal" for the Red Cross fund drive, see, for example, RCKD, February 14, 20, March 4, November 3, 1947. On Mary Conway's tearful departure for college, see RCKD, September 7, 1947. Rejected by the well-paying and tony *Country Gentleman*, the antihunting article became a national *cause célèbre*—against RCK—when it finally appeared as "Why I Gave Up Hunting," *Outdoor Life* 101 (February 1948): 266–68, and "Give Up Hunting," *Outdoor Life* 101 (April 18, 1948): 17–22. Kennedy

later suspected that *Outdoor Life* ran his article to generate angry letters to the editor in a sinister scheme to create controversy that increased subscriptions: "with more subscriptions, more people saw advertisements for guns and bought them for more killing." See also Tennant McWilliams, "Dixie's Heretic? The Great Hunting Debate of 1948," *AH* 117 (Summer 2015): 58–60.

15. The development of the Troy jobs is reflected, for example, in RCK to MMK, July 7, 1947; EK to RCK, August 4, 1947; Robert Hugh Ervin to RCK, September 27, 1947; RCKD, June 14, July 6, August 15, 1947. In 2013, ninety-three-year-old Vera Tisdale, one of Kennedy's English literature students that first summer, recalled: "It was nearly all male veterans and a few young adults like me [in the class]. All the men had been to England and Europe and knew about the different places he referenced in the class. When he lectured his eyes just lit up . . . getting to the life messages of the literature—things that could help us live our lives better. He never mentioned he was a preacher nor that he was a veteran." Vera Tisdale interview, May 7, 2012.

16. An overview of Rubin's life is found in his extensive obituary, *Boston Globe*, August 24, 2011; and in the biographical sketch in Papers of Morton Rubin, Archives and Special Collections, Northeastern University, Boston. On Howard Odum, John Gillin, the Rosenwald Foundation, and the UNC Institute for Research in the Social Sciences, see Daniel Joseph Singal, *The War Within: Victorian to Modernist Thought in the South, 1919–1945* (Chapel Hill: University of North Carolina Press, 1982), 115; and Guy Benton Johnson and Guion Griffis Johnson, *Research in Service to Society: The First Fifty Years of the Institute for Research in Social Science at the University of North Carolina* (Chapel Hill: University of North Carolina Press, 1980), 131–60.

17. MR, February 17, June 29, September 13, 1947; RCKD, June 28, 1947; and *STJ*, December 25, 1985.

18. JCCJ to author, August 6, 1976; MR, June 26–29, July 6, 25, 29, September 13, 1947; RCKD, June 9, 1947. Lillian Jones, "Prominent Research Assistant of University of N. C. Locates in Camden," *WPE*, July 3, 1947; and her follow-up, *WPE*, November 20, 1947.

19. WJJ and JCCJ interview, November 22, 1979; MR interview, April 18, 1983; MR, October 6–9, 1947; RCKD, October 6, 1947; RCK, "Miss Eleanor Elizabeth McWilliams" (Draft, 1972).

20. Betty Kennedy interviews, November 10, 2008, March 27, 2015; MR, June 26–30, July 3, 1947 ("inheritance"), July 5, 1947 ("siren"), July 12, 1947 ("new business"), July 30, 1947 (Watson, Gee's Bend quotes), August 26, 1947 ("local politics"), and September 2, 1947 ("individual violence"). Rubin's additional notes on Gee's Bend include reports on corruption of white FSA administrators—somehow "acquiring" private hunting rights to most of the land as the federal government sold it back to the Benders, which meant that most Benders seemingly could not hunt on their "own" property (MR, August 14, 1947). On hostility to new business, out of fear of increased pay rates and fear of advent of "different type" of whites imposing on traditional social order, see MR, March 2 and 20, 1948.

21. MR, July 22, August 27, September 8, 28, 1947, April 5, 1948 ("individualism . . . remembering"). On The Spot, see *STJ*, May 19–20, 1935, April 23, 1975, April 4, 1994; Wanda Stroud Anderson interview, February 27, 2013; MR interview,

April 18, 1983; MCKD interview, July 22, 2006; Horace Wilkinson interview, March 4, 2006. See also MR, January 19, 1948, where—after an afternoon of interviews with white businessmen—Rubin wrote: "Most want to live for themselves . . . alone." And also MR interview, April 18, 1983; Bogie interview, December 11, 2012; MCKD interview, June 6, 2006; VJGL interview, March 16, 1984; and George S. Bobinski, "Carnegie Libraries: Their History and Impact on American Public Library Development," *ALA Bulletin* 62 (December 1968): 1361–67.

22. MR, July 13, 21 ("conscientious . . . crusading"), and July 31, 1947. On Boswell Amendment followup, see MR, August 23, 26, 1947; as well as RCKD, November 7, 1947. On McKay, especially where Rubin writes, "McKay disliked whites' dependence on the Negro," see MR, July 20, 23, September 20, 1947. It should be noted that Rubin's assessment of McKay had to have been based on his interviews with others, for in November 1946—some six months before Rubin started work in Camden—McKay departed Camden to become pastor of students at the University of Florida, and later was a longtime Tampa minister (*Atlanta Constitution*, March 27, 1943, and *Orlando Sentinel*, January 17, 1952). On Boswell Amendment background consult Glen Feldman, *The Great Melding: War, the Dixiecrat Rebellion, and the Southern Model for America's New Conservatism* (Tuscaloosa: University of Alabama Press, 2015), 139, 165, 179–88; William D. Barnard, *Dixiecrats and Democrats: Alabama Politics 1942–1950:* (Tuscaloosa: University of Alabama Press,1974), 59–71; and Scotty Kirkland, "Mobile and the Boswell Amendment," *AR* 65 (July 2012): 205–49. In January 1948, to block some of Governor Folsom's tax plans and at the urging of Alabama Power and other large corporations, senators Bruce Henderson of Wilcox and James B. Allen of Gadsden sponsored the "Self-Starter Amendment" to the state constitution, giving the legislature the power to call more frequent sessions, effectively eliminating Governor Folsom's constitutional primacy in this matter. A statewide referendum defeated the proposed amendment. In Wilcox, while Camden voters supported the amendment 194–98—one of the negative votes being RCK's—Oak Hillians voted 19–13 against it. Similar to the Boswell Amendment, the "Self-Starter" proposal, in RCK's view, was a barometer of liberal versus conservative sentiment in the county. RCKD, January 6, 1948; Barnard, *Dixiecrats and Democrats*, 92–94, 105–7, 126; Carl Grafton and Anne Permaloff, *Big Mules and Branchheads: James E. Folsom and Political Power in Alabama* (Athens: University of Georgia Press, 1985), 103–8.

23. MR, July 3, 18 ("Herman Johnson"), September 18 ("conservative liberal"), 30 ("Hill upholds women"), November 25, 1947.

24. MR, July 3, ("liquor," "sexual habits"), October 11, 1947 ("rape"), March 9, 1948 (Bogie quote). For more on RCK's visit with Patricia Pitt Yarborough, see RCKD, August 23, 1935; and regarding Eleanor McWilliams on aristocrats and miscegenation, MR, January 9, 1948.

25. MR, November 25, 1947; MR interview, April 18, 1983.

26. MR interview, April 18, 1983; Betty Kennedy interview, March 14–15, 2021; *Boston Globe*, August 24, 2011.

27. Liddell's earlier publications were "Self-Expression: The Modern Mother's Sesame to Happiness," *HOLLAND'S: The Magazine of the South* 50 (February 1931): 30–35; "A Little Town Rolls Its Own," *Southern Literary Messenger* 3 (December 1941): 543–48;

and *Reflections in Rhyme* (Birmingham: Birmingham Publishing Co., 1944). See also RCKD, January 29, July 20, 1947; VJGL interview, March 16, 1984 (emphasis added).

28. MR, July 4, 21, 1947, March 27, 1948.

29. Thomas D. Jarrett, "The Post Reconstruction South in Miniature," *Phylon* 9 (1948): 384–85. Jarrett's distinguished career, including the presidency of Atlanta University and a postadministration life as a professor at Georgia State University, is covered in his extensive obituary, *Atlanta Journal-Constitution*, July 8, 2000.

30. Beyond Jarrett's, for a critical review see *Newark* (NJ) *News*, April 11, 1948. For mildly critical yet also positive, see *Christian Science Monitor*, May 19, 1948, and *San Diego Chronicle*, April 11, 1948. For positive appraisals see foremost the review by influential southern critic Hershel Brickell: "Dixie: Day-by-Day," *Saturday Review* 31 (May 1, 1948); but also *NYT*, March 27, 1948; *Asheville* (NC) *Citizen*, May 9, 1948; *Miami Herald*, May 28, 1948; *LAT*, April 14, 1948; and *Richmond Times-Dispatch*, April 4, 1948. A review from closer to home, "The Goodes of Gastonburg," came from a fellow Wilcoxon whom Liddell had dated once or twice in her senior year at Judson—the Birmingham-Southern College writing teacher, Richebourg McWilliams. "Free of false southern pride," McWilliams wrote, "[Liddell] blends . . . deductions from the foils of everyday life—talent of the essayist—with human zest in telling a story . . . talent of the fiction writer" (*BN*, May 8, 1948). On modern views of successes and failures of the civil rights movement, see Doug McAdams and Karena Kloos, *Deeply Divided: Racial Politics and Social Movements in Post-War America* (New York: Oxford University Press, 2014); Kahlilah L. Brown-Dean, *Identity Politics in America* (Medford, CT: Polity Press, 2019). In the mid-1970s, with copyright options opening up, *With A Southern Accent* became a possibility for re-publication by the University of Alabama Press. Ultimately that happened, but not before "some jerk" (RCK's word) sought to edit out "darky" and other "offensive language." Liddell protested vehemently, and prevailed, saying "that was the way I wrote it. . . . Why rewrite history? Use that to teach somebody!!" RCKD, August 10, 1976; VJGL interview, March 16, 1984.

31. RCKD, January 21–24, March 20, April 3, 1948; EK to RCK, July 12, 1948; Bogie interview, December 11, 2012; VJGL interview, October 1, 1987; VJGL to RCK, February 22, 1950; RCK interview, September 9, 1984.

32. RCK, "Ecumenity at the Grass Roots," *CC* 65 (February 15, 1948): 238–39; MR, July 3, September 12 ("monopoly"), 15, 1947; Bogie interview, December 11, 2012. MCKD interview, October 10, 2011, revealing, "Daddy felt Baptists did not practice what they preached, that they only were for Baptists." RCK interview, July 20, 1985, where RCK says some of the Auburn administrators were "crooked"; Paul Hutchinson to RCK, February 12, March 2, 1948; William F. Clarke to RCK, March 6, 1948. For more on illegal hunting permits in the Bend, and the "transfer"—not termination—of FSA administrators, see MR, May 19, 1948. One of the first characteristics of Camden that Morton Rubin turned up was the territoriality of Baptists. As he wrote in his Field Notes (and shared with Kennedy) "Catholics convert Negroes in Selma, and Presbyterians and Lutherans try to help Negroes in Wilcox but do not try to convert them. Regardless, all this bothers Roark who sees Negroes as 'naturally Baptist.' Camden Baptists stay angry over encroachment on 'their territory.'" So, Kennedy's was not just a relevant article; it was the culmination of long concerns told with his old satiric verve.

33. RCK, "Nowhere to Go," *CC* 65 (May 26, 1948): 510–12. RCK's attendance at Army Reserve meetings in Pine Hill gave him a new source on "local white opinion," and much of it apparently wound up in this article. RCKD, February 4, 23, 1948. On Troy teaching in summer 1948, see RCKD, May 31, June 1, 4, 1948.

34. RCK, "The Cracker Boy's Vote," *CC* 65 (October 27, 1948): 1143–44; RCKD, October 4, 1948; William E. Leuchtenburg, *The White House Looks South: Franklin D. Roosevelt, Harry Truman, and Lyndon B. Johnson* (Baton Rouge: Louisiana State University Press, 2005), 200–205.

35. MR, February 19, 1948; RCKD, April 3, July 31 ("Heroic"), December 27, 1948 (Stapp quote). "Candidates to Democratic Convention Bolt Party," *SF* 109 (April 1948): 1. On Stapp, see also Feldman, *The Great Melding*, 194.

36. Frederickson, *The Dixiecrat Revolt*, 237–38. On bifurcation of fascist racism between "intellectual" and "popular," I follow vocabulary employed in analyses of late nineteenth-century American and British racial views. But see also Angelina Saini, *Superior: The Return of Intellectual Racism* (Boston: Beacon Press, 2019). A few white southern veterans did indeed let their war experiences with Black soldiers guide them to a deeper appreciation of Black people in the polity of America; see Jennifer Brooks, *Defining the Peace: World War II Veterans, Race, and the Remaking of Southern Political Tradition* (Chapel Hill: University of North Carolina Press, 2004), 36–57. See also Steven White, *World War II and American Racial Politics* (New York: Cambridge University Press, 2019). Southerners and creation of the United Nations is analyzed in Joseph A. Fry, *Dixie Looks Abroad: The South and US Foreign Relations, 1879–1973* (Baton Rouge: Louisiana State University Press, 2002), 216–21.

37. RCK interview, September 9, 1984; Steve Crabtree, "Gallup Brain: Strom Thurmond and the 1948 Election" (December 17, 2002), Gallup.com.

CHAPTER 10

1. C. B. Smith to RCK, February 4, 9, 1948; EK to RCK, March 20, 1948. In December 1950, EK offered more "positive" perspective on himself and "work": "Emmett says he always has avoided work, [for] it brutalizes values and sensitivity . . . says you can't appreciate a flower if you have to work and slave to produce it." RCKD, December 31, 1950.

2. RCKD, November 14, 1947, January 9, April 21, 29–30, May 2, August 1, 31, 1948; EK to RCK, July 28, 1948. His renewed courtship by Montevallo Presbyterians extended from late 1948 until early June 1951, with RCK—apparently—never encouraging them but never saying no; at last, in May 1951, they gave him a final written offer, which he declined. RCKD, May 9, 27, 1951; RCK to Eva Gholson and Eugene Reynolds, June 13, 1951 (copy).

3. RCKD, May 31, June 1, Sep 13, 21, Oct 7, Dec 8, 1948; C. B. Smith to RCK, February 4, 9, 1949, July 1, 1949; EK to RCK, February 3, Mar 20, September 14, 1948, May 8, June 25, August 9, 1949, January 31, February 22, 1950; MR, March 26, 1948; Jane Shelton Dale interview, September 20, 2012. EK's problem in making it to class on time—or at all—remained a persisting problem: RCK's diary for November 10, 1949—"Emmett oversleeps. . . . I take his Amer Lit class."

4. Charles Bunyan Smith, *Autobiography, Early Years: 1891–1938* (Troy, AL: The

Author, 1973); Smith, *Troy State University* (Troy, AL: Troy State University Press, 1973); RCK, "Freshmen Are Alright," *CC* (September 7, 1949): 1033–34; Paul Hutchinson to RCK, August 25, 1949; EK to RCK, August 9, 1948. For an excellent distillation of Smith's Troy presidency, as well as all other Troy presidencies up through the early 1970s, see Margaret Pace Farmer, *One Hundred Fifty Years in Pike County, Alabama, 1821–1971* (Montgomery: Brown Printing Co., 1973), 222–28.

5. EK to RCK, May 8, June 25, 1949; Smith to RCK, July 1, 1949; Hubert Searcy to RCK, April 19, 1949; Brooks Forehand to RCK, April 20, 1949; RCK to MCKD, October 11, 1949 ("devilment").

6. RCKD, June 6, July 4, 1948; Lucy J. Spiva to RCK, December 30, 1948, January 5, August 29, September 8, 15, 1949; RCKD, January 1–2, 16 ("Best Day"), April 8, 1949, and July 30, 1950; *WPE*, January 20, 1949. Besides making major cash gifts, Lucy Spiva sponsored a unique "charm string" fundraising project for the church. And not long after the church enhancements, she sent RCK a check for $100 in "new 5 dollar bills" for him to buy himself a new portable Royal typewriter. He spent "$77.91" on it, he wrote Mary Conway, "which leaves . . . $22.09 for me to raise hell in the swamps." At age ninety-one, Lucy Spiva died on June 16, 1955. RCK buried her in Camden. RCK to MCKD, n.d. [1949], MCKD Collection; EK to Lucy Spiva, March 30, 1952 (copy); Spiva to RCK, July 18, 1952; RCKD, April 10, 1952, June 16–18, 1955.

7. RCKD, January 15, April 5–6, 1949.

8. RCKD, March 12, 22–23, 1949; *MA*, September 11, 1987.

9. Phillip Cabell, "Camden, Alabama: A Case History," *NYT*, August 28, 1949. RCK apparently wrote Cabell complimenting him on the accuracy of his article and mentioned some negative reactions locally. Cabell wrote back: "Thank you for your candid letter. I am delighted that you . . . perceived the merits of my story." Cabell Phillips to RCK, September 8, 1949. In Clinton McCarty, *Reins of Power: Racial Change and Challenge in a Southern Community* (Tallahassee: Sentry Press, 1999), 126, Kennedy's interview is misidentified with a "young minster"—possibly Jack Bogie, at Camden Presbyterian. But the interviewee cannot be anyone but Kennedy: the quotes about "minority" white sensitivities include words Kennedy had used many times before. Plus, while Bogie was moderately liberal in a private sense, by his own account to me, he pastored a Camden church dominated by highly conservative male lay leaders—often at odds with VJGL—and tried to avoid "saying things in public that would make them nervous." Regrettably, in our interview, I failed to ask Bogie about this *NYT* article. Bogie interview, December 1, 2012.

10. On Kennedy's different concepts of "minority," see chapter 7, note 21 above. For modern scholarly context on these thoughts see, for example, Leo Rangell, "Aggression, Oedipus, and Historical Perspective," *International Journal of Psychoanalysis* 53 (January 1, 1972): 3–10. Fred C. Hobson elaborates on racial views and strains of puritan guilt in *But Now I See: The White Southern Racial Conversion Narrative* (Baton Rouge: Louisiana State University Press, 1999), 1–4, 8, 33, 53, 58, and 93. The Lillian Smith quote is from *Killers of the Dream* (New York: W. W. Norton, 1949), 20.

11. E. Marcellus Nesbitt to RCK, December 6, 1949; VJGL to RCK, February 22, 1950; *MA*, February 2, 1945, September 7, 10, 1949.

12. EK to RCK, July 28, December 6, 1950; RCKD, October 2, 4, 1950; *MA*, November 26, 1950.

13. RCK/S/1950; William Faulkner, "Banquet Speech . . . December 10, 1950," in Frenz Hortz, ed., *Nobel Lectures: Literature, 1901–1967* (Amsterdam: Elsevier, 1969).

14. RCKD, March 5, May 21, June 4, 10, 1951, April 11, 1952; RCK to MMK, August 8, 1951.

15. RCK, "They Never Had It so Good," *CC* 68 (June 27, 1951): 765–66; Herbert Pierce, pastor at First Baptist Church in Wilburn, Oklahoma, complained to *CC* editors: "[Kennedy's criticism of MacArthur] reminds me of stories I have read in *The Worker* . . . and can be used without doubt for Communist propaganda." *CC* clipping, KRF/C/, June 25, 1951. When RCK received similar criticism from his own siblings, he wrote back: "Opening up a war with China . . . could have caused World War III. . . . [MacArthur] deserved to be fired, and I admire the 'little jerk in the White House' for his courage in tying a tin can to the tail of the high and mighty MacArthur. It took courage, not politics." RCK to Chums, April 4, 1951 (copy). See also RCKD, April 4, July 17, 21, 27, August 3, 8, 1951, March 11, 1952 ("Sgt. . . . Barker").

16. MR, February 23, 1948; RCKD, June 10, 1951; RCK to MMK, August 8, 1951. Kennedy's worry about Margaret's social contacts at the University of Alabama is reflected in Rubin's Field Notes for February 23, 1948; but the quote, "self-styled plantation aristocrats," uses Rubin's words elaborating on RCK's attitude as given in Rubin interview, April 18, 1983.

17. RCKD, August 14, 1951; Charles Bunyan Smith to RCK, August 15, 1951; RCK to MMK, August 15, 1951 ("Emmett needs me").

18. RCK, "Fog in August" (draft, 1951); RCKD, August 15, 1951; Margaret L. Hartley to RCK, February 20, 1952; Wilbur Hatfield to RCK, March 11, 1952; Paul Pickiel to RCK, March 10, 1952.

19. RCK interview, February 25, 1984; RCKD, April 15, 1950; RCK to Folks, October 13, 1951 (copy), Rubin to RCK, November 25, 1951; Hugh Ervin to RCK, October 1, 1951; RCK to Bogie, August 12, 1952 (copy); and Bogie to RCK, August 13, 1960. Two years later RCK gave family members another take on his being down on the ministry: "The ministry, I am sorry to say, seems to attract a lot of people of mediocre ability. I have never been very sympathetic with the idea that the average preacher would have made a better living if he had done something else. Many of them would have made a poorer living," RCK to Folks, June 18, 1962 (copy). On Troy travails, see also Violet Gross Ervin to RCK, October 2, 1951; and Hugh Ervin to RCK, February 20, 1952. Although *Plantation County* does not identify specific names with specific interviews, Rubin's Field Notes correlate interviews with names through a code, which Rubin shared with me. By the same token, any number of Wilcoxons—certainly Hugh Ervin—had little difficulty deducing who gave certain interviews referenced in the book.

20. *MA*, August 17, 1952; RCKD, March 22, May 27–28, 1952; RCK to MMK, August 14, 17, 31, 1951; W. J. Jones to RCK, October 25, 1954.

21. RCK, "Why Churches Do Not Unite," *CC* 69 (July 15, 1952): 825–27. A typical negative response was this from an ARP minister of Huntersville, North Carolina: "[Your article is] gloomy, self-righteous and proud. . . . Should I reject the will of God and change? . . . I conclude that you have very little respect for the ARP church" (Grady R. Oates to RCK, July 17, 1952.) In contrast, Rev. Samuel L. McKay, formerly of Oak Hill's Bethel ARPC and currently at a Salisbury, North Carolina, ARPC, wrote

him: "A tailor-made shoe . . . fitting the ARPs perfectly. . . . I especially like your word 'feckless.' Though there is much unrest [among ARPs], the last Synod did little . . . to settle it" (MacKay to RCK, July 15, 1952). Likewise, Aubrey N. Brown, editor of *Presbyterian Outlook*, wrote: "This is an incisive article. . . . I hope you will have good protection from the brickbats which will be hurled" (Brown to RCK, July 15, 1952). On continued stresses among ARPs and some congregations leaving for other denominations, see F. J. Blythe et al. to RCK, March 12, 1952; William Bryce Moore to RCK, April 28, May 22, June 4, 1952; *Raleigh News and Observer*, March 12, 1952.

22. RCK, "The Well Digger" (draft, 1952); the Editors [of *Reader's Digest*] to RCK, March 26, 1952, RCKD, February 11, March 26, 1952.

23. RCKD, June 8, 1948, May 8, June 14–15, October 10, 16–18, 20, 1951, January 28, September 25, October 1, 1952; *AJ*, October 17, 1951.

24. RCKD, September 25, October 14, 1952, March 7, April 19–20, 29, June 1, 4, August 14, 1953, January 5, 13, 1954; *Troy Messenger*, April 5, 1953.

25. There is no complete ancestry-profile of Alabama whites. With major assistance from Ann Potter and Yvonne Crumpler, I developed a data-level analysis of members of the Alabama legislature, 1820 to 1975—derived from ancestral studies of specific individuals, not just from census data. It suggests that early in the state's history, Black Belt whites were disproportionately a blend of English, Irish, and Scotch-Irish, with Wilcox atypically heavy with Scotch-Irish of direct Ulster-Scot dissent. And this pattern persisted in 2022. Even so, looking at Alabama overall, my data support generalizations offered by Thomas Perkins Abernethy and other scholars of early Alabama history, who used chiefly US Census data to portray Alabama whites as rarely of "pure" (my term) ancestry but rather as a "blended" (my term) people of English, Scotch-Irish (Ulster influence), Scotch, and Irish ancestry, with subsidiary strains of French, German, Scandinavian, Italian, and Greek.

26. MCKD interview, April 20, 2012; MKA interview, June 27, 1987, and April 20, 2012.

27. *MA*, November 19,1953; RCKD, November 19 ("agog"), 22–23, December 2–3, 7, 10, 14–15, 29, 1953 ("bitter"). "William J. Terry," Ancestry.com; *Heritage of Marengo County* (Clanton, AL: Heritage Publishing Consultants, 2000), 200; *BN*, November 3, 1950, August 8, 1955. As RCK returned to Troy in 1953 under these taxing circumstances, he recalled in 1983, he was unaware of the April 1953 killing of a wheelchair-bound Black woman, Della McDuffie, in a raid on her Alberta café, led by Sheriff "Lummie" Jenkins and Deputy Sheriff Edwin Tait. The event captured the attention of NAACP representatives Thurgood Marshall and John LeFlore, resulting in an investigation by the Civil Rights Division of the US Justice Department, but ultimately no charges. Only the historic Black-owned *New York Age* covered the story—slightly (*New York Age*, July 25, 1953). In a 1983 interview with the author, however, RCK raised this case as an example of the filter on news used by the local press, saying he only recently had learned of the killing. Wilcox native Sarah Woods—the Black woman who provided home health care for him in his final years—told him about it. Then he said, "There were so many others [cases of racial violence], too, that people like me never heard about at the time. It is so difficult . . . the truth is . . . Lummie kept the 1930s going right into the 1950s and later, too. That law change [of 1939] letting sheriffs succeed

themselves did not help matters—bad all around" (RCK interview, May 21, 1983). "The Della McDuffie Case," Northeastern University School of Law, Civil Rights and Restorative Justice Project, Northeastern University, Boston.

28. *AOSR, 1932-1950*; McCarty, *Reins of Power,* 127-31; RCKD, May 5, October 3, November 4, 19, 21-22, 1953.

29. "Samuel Martin Englehardt, Jr.," Ancestry.com with related Ancestry.com data on "John Englehardt," "Samuel Martin Englehardt," "Annie Floyd Pinkston," and "John H. Pinkston"; 1860 US Census Slave Schedules: Macon County, Alabama. *MA,* November 17, 1887, March 7, 1927; *WPE,* March 5, 1935, March 17, 1938; *Alabama Journal,* December 4, 1958. Donnie Williams with Wayne Greenhaw, *The Thunder of Angels: The Montgomery Bus Boycott and the People Who Broke the Back of Jim Crow* (Chicago: Lawrence Hill Books, 2006), 125-26; Neil R. McMillen, *The Citizens Council: Organized Resistance to the Second Reconstruction, 1954-1964* (Urbana: University of Illinois Press, 1994), 41-72, 220-22, 314-16, 332; *ASOR, 1955,* 278; RCK/WFMA/September 5, 1935; Numan V. Bartley, *The Rise of Massive Resistance: Race and Politics in the South during the 1950s* (Baton Rouge: Louisiana State University Press, 1969, 1999), 56, 87, 88-90, 127, 281; and Robert J. Norrell, *Reaping the Whirlwind: The Civil Rights Movement in Tuskegee* (New York: Knopf, 1985), 79-86. The probable misidentification of Englehardt as a stereoptypical and pivotal "neo-Bourbon" of massive resistance leadership also should be integrated into evolving historiographical approaches to massive resistance leadership, emphasizing neo-Bourbon influence as but a first stage succeeded by more grassroots neo-populist and then state government leadership. See, for example, Francis M. Wilhoit, *The Politics of Massive Resistance* (New York: George Braziller, 1973); and George Lewis, *Massive Resistance: The White Response to the Civil Rights Movement* (New York: Oxford University Press, 2006).

30. *MA,* November 19-20, 1953; RCKD, September 26, 1948, October 3, November 21, 1953, May 5-7, 1954, January 3, October 3, November 1, 19-20, 22-23, 30, December 7, 10, 18, 29, 1953, January 3, 6, February 4, 1955.

31. RCKD, January 5, February 1, 3, March 23, April 18, May 19, 1954; *WPE,* February 25, 1954; *BN,* May 26, 1946, August 30 1951, November 19, 1953; *Troy Messenger,* August 21, 1944, March 23, 1954, November 1, 1960, August 5, 1963; *Opp News,* February 9, 1950, July 19, 1956.

32. *WPE* (February 25, 1954) printed the W. J. Jones letter for the public, along with the condemning editorial from *Alabama* magazine and the letter from Laura Lee Moore. See also RCKD, February 21, 27, 1954 ("mighty stew"); and William J. Terry to WJJ, April 2, 1954, in PWJJ. A native of Mobile, Laura Lee (Tunsdell) Moore married Camden native Frank Lowry Moore Jr., grandson of a Wilcox Confederate soldier who rode with Confederate Gen. Joe Wheeler, and a passionate leader of the Franklin King Beck Camp of Confederate Veterans. Moore owned a livery stable and mercantile store in Camden and often served on the Wilcox Board of Equalization (tax assessment). Judge McLeod married Frank Moore's sister, Lucia. See *HWC,* 231, 245; *WPE,* April 15, 1954; and J. Mills Thornton III, *Dividing Lines: Municipal Politics and the Struggle for Civil Rights in Montgomery Birmingham, and Selma* (Tuscaloosa: University of Alabama Press, 2002), 425. Unmatched in devotion to the antebellum racial order, Klan leader and White Citizens Council activist Jesse McIntosh McLeod died on March 22, 1958,

age eighty-two. Two of the most socially liberal white Protestant ministers in Alabama at that time—both of Camden, Ren Kennedy and Camden Presbyterian's Clayton Bell—tended to him in his final painful days and on March 23 presided over his "big political funeral" starting with services at the McLeods' Coy plantation and then interment at Camden Cemetery. RCKD, March 22–23, 26, 1958; *WPE*, March 27, April 24, 1958.

33. RCKD, December 14–15, 1953, March 23–24, April 15, 30, May 3, 13–14, 17, 19, 25, June 1, July 9, 1954; RCK to Folks, June 14, 1954, where he wrote, "Dr. Smith and I won our political race . . . Dr. Austin Meadows." Of course, there was "another race" in 1954: despite a modest challenge by Laurie Battle, John Sparkman won the Democratic primary as well as the general election to be returned to the US Senate. RCK contributed to the Sparkman campaign, and RCK's papers include detailed notes on how different Wilcoxons voted in this election and others where Sparkman was a candidate. See, for example, James Bonner to Ralph H. Ford, May 7, 1954 (copy), explaining who in the county were "loyal Democrats," "McCorvey Democrats," "Ike Democrats," and "Dixiecrats"—men and women, with families well divided.

34. William Warren Rogers et al., *Alabama: History of a Deep South State* (Tuscaloosa: University of Alabama Press, 2018), 545; Numan V. Bartley, *The New South, 1945–1980* (Baton Rouge: Louisiana State University Press, 1995), 165; Bartley, *Massive Resistance*.

35. George E. Sims, *The Little Man's Big Man: James E. Folsom and Alabama Politics, 1946–1958* (Tuscaloosa: University of Alabama Press, 1985), 120–214; Grafton and Permaloff, *Big Mules and Branchheads*, 168–85; RCKD, January 17, 25, 1955.

36. *AOSR, 1956*, 277; *HWC*, 146; RCKD, April 9, 1948; April 3, May 7–8, 1954, February 4, March 15, 1955.

37. Grafton and Permaloff, *Big Mules and Branchheads*, 185–87; Cordellia Humphrey, "Senator O. J. ("Joe") Goodwyn and the Politics of Public Education in Alabama, 1955–1970," MA thesis, Auburn University at Montgomery, 1997; RCKD, April 6, October 21, 1955.

38. Grafton and Permaloff, *Big Mules and Branchheads*, 188–89; RCKD, March 15, 26, April 7, June 7, October 4–6, 11, 17, 20, 27, 31, November 3, 11, 14, 30 ("dubious"), December 10, 30 ("discouraged"), 1955; *WPE*, April 7, 1955.

39. RCKD, December 12, 1955, January 12, 19, October 22, 1956, March 19, 1965; Dan T. Carter, *The Politics of Rage: George Wallace, the Origins of the New Conservatism, and the Transformation of American Politics*, 2nd ed. (Baton Rouge: Louisiana State University Press, 1996), 112. A World War II Navy (skin diver) veteran and graduate of University of North Carolina and the Yale Law School, Hobbs, then thirty-three years old, met with RCK soon after leaving Birmingham's Bradley, Arant law firm to go into practice with John Godbold in Montgomery. By 1980, Hobbs would be judge for the US Middle District of Alabama. *MA*, September 3, 1952, December 21, 2015; Samuel L. Webb to author, May 28, 2020.

40. Grafton and Permaloff, *Big Mules and Branchheads*, 194, 197, 200–211.

41. RCK, "While the Supreme Court Ponders," *CC* 70 (March 4, 1953): 253–55; Aubrey Burns, "Segregation and the Church," *Southwest Review* 34 (Spring 1949): 121–30. In response to his article, RCK received numerous positive communications from across the nation. One of the most interesting was from the minister of Bethany Congregational Church in Los Angeles, indicating he used RCK's piece with his congregation

to stimulate greater sensitivity among the "100% Nordics" regarding greater sensitivity to people from Latin America (William I. Newman to RCK, March 2, 1953). Yet one of the most negative, if polite, came from his own siblings, jointly signed. RCK's reply showed him employing the "gaming" strategy he had used in writing about Black Belt aristocrats. While he admitted he had taken a "controversial topic"—for people like to read about "controversy"—he said, "I personally favor segregation in the South," a Menckenian slice his siblings knew well. Their return letters popped him back: their older brother, their "Presiding Elder," and their own "family liberal . . . every family needs one." RCKD, March 25, 1953; RCK interview, May 21, 1983; MCKD interview, April 20, 2011.

42. RCK to Folks, June 2, 1953 (copy); RCK to Friends, June 29, 1953 (copy).

43. Margaret Craft, "The Students Speak: Should Segregation Be Entirely Abolished in Higher Education," *Tropolitan*, October 12, 1953. Immediately after this article appeared, RCK had to deal with the complicated situation of state politicians and other local conservatives seeing the article as "terrible," while President Smith's liked it but felt concern about resultant fallout affecting his job and the institution's budget. Though there seems to have been effective damage control from Smith's perspective, the diary gives no details on how they managed the situation. RCKD, October 12–13, 1953.

44. RCK, "Alabama Book Toasters," *CC* 71 (April 7, 1954): 428–29; "Alabama School Book Act Proves Ludicrous," *Harvard Crimson*, June 17, 1954; RCKD, March 1, 1954. For context on Judge Jones, see Gene Roberts and Hank Klibanoff, *The Race Beat: The Press, the Civil Rights Struggle and the Awakening of a Nation* (New York: Random House, 2006), 238–40; Thornton, *Dividing Lines*, 96, 120, 197.

45. RCK to Folks, May 23, 1953 (copy); RCK/S/1954; RCKD, April 2, 1961.

46. RCKD, December 3, 9, 14, 29, 1954, January 3, 6, July 4, 1955, February 2 ("entertaining"), 3 ("reapportionment"), 7 (depressing"), 10 ("White Citizen Council"), April 25 ("sorriest speech"), 1956; RCK to Friends, June 11, 1956 (copy) ("Robert Ruark"), and December 10, 1956 ("never shoot at me").

47. RCKD, April 17, 1955. Though declining the proposal to join the SRC, over the next year RCK worked regularly with Clara Rutledge in various lobbying endeavors associated with the Goodwyn amendment to enhance education funding. (See, for example, RCKD, January 4, 1955.) For more on Clara Rutledge, see Mary Stanton, *Journey toward Justice: Juliette Hampton Morgan and the Montgomery Bus Boycott* (Athens: University of Georgia Press, 2006), 98–99, 151–52, 110, 124; and Hollinger F. Barnard, ed., *Outside the Magic Circle: The Autobiography of Virginia Foster Durr* (Tuscaloosa: University of Alabama Press, 1986), 243–45, 269, 315, 337.

48. RCKD, July 4, 1955 ("blowing over"). As of August 1957, when Miller Bonner had Mississippi governor Jim Coleman at the Wilcox County High School auditorium urging the WCC to stay clear of violence, in the audience of 800—many listed in *WPE*—sat Johnson as one of four vice-chairmen. *WPE*, August 29, 1957; RCKD, August 8, 1957; *MA*, August 8, 1957.

49. RCKD, May 3, 1955 ("feasible").

50. RCKD, June 4, 29, August 16, September 15, 1948, December 20, 1949, February 26, 1951, August 30, 1952, March 29, 1953. On the "morphine, opium" quote, see RCK to Family, April 19, 1960 (copy). Stages of alcoholism used in this assessment

of Kennedy are discussed in Robert M. Morse and Kevin L. Florin, "The Definition of Alcoholism," *Journal of the American Medical Association* 268 (August 26, 1992): 1012–14.

51. J. D. Salinger, *The Catcher in the Rye* (Boston: Little, Brown, and Co., 1951); William Faulkner, *Intruder in the Dust* (New York: Random House, 1951); Ralph Ellison, *The Invisible Man* (New York: Random House, 1952); Sloan Wilson, *The Man in the Gray Flannel Suit* (New York: Simon and Schuster, 1955); RCK, "While Thousands Cheered," *CC* 67 (December 6, 1950): 1154–55; "Jeremiah Buys a Field," *Pulpit* 22 (July 15 1951): 15, 18; "Drought in the South," *CC* 71 (December 1954): 1459–61; *Troy Messenger*, December 20, 1949. In this period RCK also produced two publications on higher education topics: "College English Awakening," *Clearing House* 28 (November 1953): 1157–58; and "How Good Is Progressive Education," *CC* 71 (November 10, 1954): 1366–68.

52. RCK to Folks (copies), May 27, 1955 ("peasant mentality"), January 26 ("Eisenhower radicalism"), October 17 ("unguided missile"), December 10, 1956 ("hack"). Of the many assessments of Eisenhower's lack of support for civil rights, one of the best remains John Patrick Diggins, *The Proud Decades: America in War and Peace, 1941–1960* (New York: W. W. Norton, 1988), 293–95.

53. RCK to Friends (copy), January 9, 1954 ("private club"); INK to RCK, November 23, 1949, February 7, 1950; WJJ to RCK, February 15, 1950; *ARP*, December 7, 1949, February 15, 1950, March 28, May 19, 1954; RCKD, November 23, 1949, January 18, February 11, December 31, 1950, February 2, December 21, 25, 1952, May 9–11, 1954, January 29, April 2, November 4, 1955.

Chapter 11

1. April 14, 1957; RCKD, July 10, 18, August 13, 16, October 10, 28, 1957; *The Palladium for 1957* (Troy, AL: Troy State Teachers College, 1957), 6–7.

2. Dan T. Carter, *Politics of Rage: George Wallace, the Origins of the New Conservatism, and the Transformation of American Politics* (Baton Rouge: Louisiana State University Press, 1996), 94–96; Carl Grafton and Anne Permaloff, *Big Mules and Branchheads: James E. Folsom and Political Power in Alabama* (Athens: University of Georgia Press, 1985), 70–71; J. Wayne Flynt, *Alabama in the Twentieth Century* (Tuscaloosa: University of Alabama Press, 2004), 89–90; RCKD, April 19, May 5, 1958; RCK to Folks, June 3, 1958 (copy).

3. Notes for "The Changing South," and Ralph Bridges to Bell I. Wiley, May 1, 1957, in Bell I. Wiley Papers (Manuscript, Archives, and Rare Book Library, Emory University,); *Tropolitan*, October 22, 1957; RCKD, October 23, 1957; John Inscoe, Fred A. Bailey et al., "Forum: Memphis, the Peabody, and the SHA," *JSH* 71 (November 2005): 831–64. Wiley's general opposition to racial affirmative action in higher education admissions brought many an attack his way, but he never budged from the stance. See Jordon Hill, James I. Robertson Jr., and J. H. Segar, eds., *The Bell Irvin Wiley Reader* (Baton Rouge: Louisiana State University Press, 2001), 1–16, 167–82; Krista Reese, "The Uncommon Common Man," *Emory Magazine* (Winter 2001); and James I. Robertson to author, January 4, 2015.

4. Carter, *Politics of Rage*, 68–95; J. Mills Thornton, III, *Dividing Lines: Municipal Politics and the Struggle for Civil Rights in Montgomery, Birmingham, and Selma* (Tuscaloosa:

University of Alabama Press, 2002), 36; RCKD, Jul 30, 1958 (coffee with Wallace). See also chapter 10, note 47 above.

5. Carter, *Politics of Rage*, 92–93; Grafton and Permaloff, *Big Mules and Branchheads*, 72–75; Clinton McCarty, *Reins of Power: Racial Change and Challenge in a Southern Community* (Tallahassee: Sentry Press, 1999), 145–48 and passim.

6. RCKD, May 16 (college presidents' strategy), 17 (Tennille and WSFA interviews), April 19, May 5, 6, 13, 16, June 3, 1958; RCK to Folks, June 3, 1958 (copy) ("bitter blow"), January 20, 1959 (copy) ("No Negroes").

7. On Englehardt's use of highway construction as leverage for Patterson's education initiative, a tool also used by Governor Folsom, see Grafton and Permaloff, *Big Mules and Branchheads*, 96–99 and passim. RCKD, June 11, 30, July 7, 1958, May 22, 27, June 24, 29, July 14, 15, 20, 22, 28, August 18, 20, September 30, October 21, 1959.

8. Grafton and Permaloff, *Big Mules and Branchheads*, 104–14; Howell Raines, *My Soul Is Rested: Movement Days in the Deep South Remembered* (New York: G. P. Putnam's Sons, 1977), 290–98; Numan V. Bartley, *The Rise of Massive Resistance: Race and Politics in the South during the 1950s* (Baton Rouge: Louisiana State University Press, 1969), 232; RCKD, March 2, 1960.

9. Carter, *Politics of Rage*, 90–98; Grafton and Permaloff, *Big Mules and Branchheads*, 70–72; RCKD, July 30 (Laird conversation), November 11, 1958 ("Democrats sweeping country"); RCK to Folks, November 27, 1958 ("attacking Republicans"). Laird family lines in the United States, much like those of Great Britain, are multiple and complex. Contrary to what Kennedy thought, I suspect that Kennedy and Wallace actually came from separate strains of the transatlantic Lairds. Kennedy's connections were to Samuel and Mary Gibson Laird. In 1767, when they migrated from Ulster to Cedar Springs, Abbeville County, South Carolina, they had three children—two sons and a daughter, Mary, all born in Ulster. George Wallace's great-great-great-great grandmother indeed was named Mary Laird, but she seems to have been born in Mecklenburg County, North Carolina in 1762 (Ancestry.com). A good starting point for understanding the Laird family is "Samuel Laird" (Ancestry.com); and Warren F. Spencer, *The Confederate Navy in Europe* (Tuscaloosa: University of Alabama Press, 1983).

10. Chestnutt's story is revealed in "John Calvin Chestnutt" Biographical Sketch, Presbyterian Historical Society (Philadelphia); "Sermons of John Calvin Chestnutt," submitted to ADAH; VJGL to Oxford Stroud, April 14, 1969, in PVJGL; Joel L. Alvis Jr., *Religion and Race: Southern Presbyterians, 1946–1983* (Tuscaloosa: University of Alabama Press, 1994), 98; RCKD, January 27, 1957, May 9, 1958, June 4, 1966; Calvin Chestnutt interview, February 10, 2013; Will Liddell interview, August 10, 2020; and RCK/S/1958. On Clayton Bell, see "Benjamin Clayton Bell" Biographical Sketch, Presbyterian Historical Society (Philadelphia); *Asheville Citizen-Times*, July 6, 2000; Dwayne Cox to author, December 29, 2012; *Christianity Today*, July 11, 2000; *HWC*, 185–86; RCKD, January 28, 1957, April 13, May 2, 5, 24, June 13, 1959, January 17, 31, 1960, January 16, 1963, January 29, 1964.

11. RCKD, July 9, 1960; Alfred M. Hero Jr., *The Southerner and World Affairs* (Baton Rouge: Louisiana State University Press, 1965), 11–14, 21–23, 61, 174, 273–76, 281–89, 310, 324–33; *Boston Globe*, January 22, 2006; Alfred O. Hero III interview, March 9, 2013.

12. RCKD, September 15, 1960 (including final typed copy of EK's remarks). See also RCKD, September 16, 19, 1960; and Thomas W. Martin to RCK, September 30, 1960. On Walter B. Jones, see *NYT*, August 2, 1963; and Thornton, *Dividing Lines*, 28, 96, 108, 120, 409, 447. On John S. Tilley, see *MA*, March 1, 1968; on Robert F. Hudson, see Coke Ellington, "*Montgomery Advertiser*," EncyclopediaofAlabama.org. On Thomas Bowen Hill, see Thornton, *Dividing Lines*, 124; *MA*, April 22, August 25, 1984; and on Thomas W. Martin, see Atkins, "Thomas W. Martin," Encyclopediaofalabama.org, as well as William Warren Rogers et al., *Alabama: History of a Deep South State* (Tuscaloosa: University of Alabama Press, 2018), 447, 471–72, including salient comments on Martin's hostility to the New Deal. In part because of his own persisting criticism of FDR and the New Deal, Massey Wilson never found a close friend in RCK. Still, out of long-term admiration for Wilson's wife, John T. Dale's daughter, Julia, and her sister, Laura—dignified bulwarks of Bethel ARPC—RCK regularly paid pastoral calls on Wilson even after Mrs. Wilson's death in 1948. Following these visits, he noted in the diary Wilson's perennial health problems, from heart attacks to dementia, and occasionally mentioned Tom Martin's attentions to his aging mentor. For example, see RCKD, February 4, 1948, January 27, 1956, December 28, 1959, February 25, March 3, 10, 1961, July 5, August 23, 1963, February 24, October 18, 1964. See also *HWC*, 315; and *MA*, March 30, 1966.

13. McCarty, *Reins of Power*, 138–40, 147–48; Grafton and Permaloff, *Big Mules and Branchheads*, 136–39.

14. Margaret Pace Farmer, *One Hundred Fifty Years in Pike County, Alabama, 1821–1897* (Montgomery: Brown Printing Co., 1973), 224–25; RCKD, January 1, April 4, 23, August 8, 1959.

15. On Bennett's career see *Fairhope Courier*, January 4, 1940, January 8, 1942, May 15, 1947, July 29, September 9, 1948, January 12, 1950, October 13, 1955, May 18, 1961; *Tuscaloosa News*, October 16, 2001; *Anniston Star*, July 12, 1968, June 8, 1971; E. Culpepper Clark, *The Schoolhouse Door: Segregation's Last Stand at the University of Alabama* (New York: Oxford University Press, 1993), 35, 41, 80, 111–24, 136, 165, 213, 222–25, 236, 249, 292n. The documents in the Papers of J. Jefferson Bennett (University of Alabama Special Collections, University of Alabama, Tuscaloosa) contain little on the development of his career. On RCK's early discussions with Bennett about the Troy position, see RCKD, March 12, July 20, August 20, 1959, July 26, 1960.

16. *BN*, December 3, 1954; *MA*, November 8, 1957, March 22, 1961; Miller Bonner to Sara [Bonner] Englehardt, January 23, 1960 (copy); RCKD, April 19, May 11, 19, June 15, October 29, 1959, January 26, February 2, March 25, 1960, April 18, July 26–27, September 14, 1960; J. Jefferson Bennett interview, May 8, 1998.

17. RCK to Folks (copies), November 28, 1960, February 14, 1961; RCKD, January 9, 18, 22, 31, February 6, 10, 15, 18, 20, March 3, 20, 1961; *BN*, January 8, 1961. Roland Cooper to John Patterson, January 16, 1961 (copy); Roland Cooper to Robert Locklin, February 4, 1961 (copy); RCK to Robert Locklin, February 22, 1961 (copy); RCK to John Patterson, February 22, 1961 (copy); Patterson to RCK, March 20, 1961; Harry M. Ayers to RCK, February 28, 1961; James B. Perdue to RCK, February 16, 1961; Ira D. Pruitt to RCK, February 16, 1961; John Patterson to Ira Pruitt, December 12, 1961 (copy). Roland Cooper's help had strings attached: RCK had to reimburse him—with a personal check made out to "Roland Cooper"—in the amount of $30.00

for lobbying lunches Cooper paid for out of a state account. In the same type of "transaction," Cooper often sold free UA football tickets—given him by the University—to Kennedy for $5.00 apiece. RCKD, March 25, 1961, September 9, November 12, 1966.

18. RCKD, July 26, 1960, March 21, May 17, June 15, 1961. On Skidmore's career as a prolabor state senator and 1958 candidate for lieutenant governor, see Grafton and Permaloff, *Big Mules and Branchheads*, 77; *Tuscaloosa News*, December 19, 1933, May 25, 1956, September 15, 1957; *AOSR, 1967*, 297. Shortly, RCK was in Opp, Alabama, on a student recruitment trip and ate lunch with Superintendent Vernon E. St. John, who told him that Jeff Bennett's suspicion about Skidmore likely had merit: "He thinks Skidmore engineered [Board adoption] of Randall texts English-Communication Arts for 9 through 12 grades—$1 million deal—for election of Frank Stewart." RCKD, March 3, April 6, 1961. See also RCK to Folks, March 30, 1961 (copy); *AJ*, July 2, 1961.

19. RCKD, April 19, May 2, 3, 1961. The tab for the meal—five couples—ran $30.36 with tip. When RCK presented his receipt to the Troy business office for reimbursement, President Smith—by this time, in RCK's view, "a bitter old man unreconciled to giving up his job and Frank Stewart's getting it"—already had sent word that he was not to be reimbursed. RCK had to get his reimbursement piecemeal from the different Troy employees at the dinner and covered the Stewarts' meals on his own, "all around, nothing new . . . like dealing with ARPs."

20. RCKD, January 1, 1958, July 5, 1963, April 20, 24–25, 1965, March 29, 31, 1966, January 1–3, 1968; Thomas W. Martin to RCK, September 30, 1960. Wilson's life is covered in the excellent sketch by Scott Mitchell, "Harrison Massey Wilson," *HWC*, 315. See also *WPE*, November 5, 1959; *MA*, July 11, 1954, July 19, 1962, March 30, 1966; and *AJ*, March 30, 1966, January 2, 3, 1968.

21. Grafton and Permaloff, *Big Mules and Branchheads*, 114–17; Numan V. Bartley, *The New South, 1945–1980* (Baton Rouge: Louisiana State University Press, 1995), 237–38; Bartley, *Massive Resistance*, 158–59, 180; Sheldon N. Stern, "Review: John F. Kennedy and Politics of Race and Civil Rights," *Reviews in American History* 35 (March 2007): 118–25; David Niven, *The Politics of Injustice: The Kennedys, the Freedom Rides, and the Electoral Consequences of Moral Compromise* (Knoxville: University of Tennessee Press, 2003), 1–23; RCK to Family, April 19, 1960 (copy); RCK interview, September 9, 1984.

22. RCKD, July 11, 13, 15, 28, 1960; RCK interview, September 9, 1984; John Patrick Diggins, *Proud Decades: America in War and Peace, 1941–1960* (New York: W. W. Norton, 1988), 339–42.

23. Diggins, *Proud Decades*, 342–44; RCK interview, September 9, 1984; RCK to Family, November 28, 1960 (copy); RCKD, October 13, November 3, 8, 9, December 8, 12, 1960; *MA*, October 26, 1960; *Tropolitan*, November 8, 1960.

24. RCKD, December 31, 1960.

25. RCK to Folks (copies), April 2, June 18, 1962; RCKD, March 12, May 22, 1962, August 31, 1965 (buying manse); RCKD, August 10, 1962 (Stone's visit); EK to RCK, March 8, June 23, 1962; and *MA*, July 24, 1962 (EK takes Presbyterian College position); RCKD, March 3, 1961 (church members received); RCKD, June 8, 1961; RCK to Folks, January 22, 1962 (copy) (Lee's book a "good book" and Lee's Camden visit); VJGL interview, March 16, 1984.

26. EK to RCK, October 13, 21, November 11, 13, 18, 1962, February 24, 1967;

Jane Shelton Dale to author, December 13, 2013; *WPE,* March 3, 1967 (EK's departing Presbyterian College and life shortly after); EK to RCK, January 21, 1961; RCKD, January 14, 1961 (Stone to UCLA and final decision on filming of Lee's book); RCKD, August 8, 1967 (Wilbur Ausley's Vietnam experience). On Stone's life at UCLA and afterward, see the excellent biographical sketch of her with the Olive M. Stone Papers, SHC, and Mary Stanton's "Coming of Age in Gee's Bend."

27. Bartley, *New South,* 298–99; William L. O'Neill, *Coming Apart: An Informal History of America in the 1960s* (Chicago: Ivan R. Dee, Publishers, 2005), 23–93; Niven, *Politics of Injustice,* 39–127; George C. Herring, *The American Century and Beyond: US Foreign Relations, 1893–2014* (New York: Oxford University Press, 2017), 401–30.

28. Morton Rubin, *Plantation County* (Chapel Hill: University of North Carolina Press, 1951), viii, 219–32; Rubin, "Memoir" (typescript, Rubin Papers, Archives, Northeastern University); Niven, *Politics of Injustice,*72, 80, 93–95; Thornton, *Dividing Lines,* 495–96; Howell Raines, *My Soul Is Rested: Movement Days in the Deep South Remembered* (New York: G. P. Putnam's Sons, 1977), 299–302; RCKD, August 21, 26, 1961, October 2, 1962, January 2, 1969; RCK to Family, August 22, 1961 (copy) ("no solutions"); RCK/S/1961; MR interview, April 18, 1983; WJJ interview, January 5, 1983; and RCK interview, September 9, 1984. In *Reins of Power* (130–31), Clinton McCarty briefly mentions Morton Rubin's frightening return to Camden, implying that Cooper was the key to Rubin's rescue—no doubt extrapolated from Rubin's revised edition of *Plantation County,* but quite different from Kennedy, Jones, and Rubin accounts given me. MR sent RCK a first draft of his 1963 epilogue for *Plantation County,* currently in my possession. While it is substantially the same as the published version, in a few instances one can notice differing nuances. I am not aware of what—if any—feedback RCK gave MR on this draft. On Mann as a professional and responsible person, see for example Thornton, *Dividing Lines,* 12, 121; Glen T. Eskew, *But for Birmingham: The Local and National Movements in the Civil Rights Struggle* (Chapel Hill: University of North Carolina Press, 1997), 163–64, 282; and Jack Bass, *Taming the Storm: The Life and Times of Judge Frank M. Johnson, Jr., and the South's Fight over Civil Rights* (New York: Doubleday, 1993), 176–80.

29. Herring, *The American Century and Beyond,* 420–26; Bartley, *New South,* 253; Robert J. Norrell, *Reaping the Whirlwind: The Civil Rights Movement in Tuskegee* (New York: Knopf, 1985), 128; RCK to Family, May 10, 1962 (copy) ("bitter battle"); RCK interview, September 9, 1984; RCKD, June 25, 1957, July 1, 1962.

30. RCKD, November 18, December 17, 1962.

31. Carter, *Politics of Rage,* 108; Clark, *Schoolhouse Door,* 155; Eskew, *But for Birmingham,* 24; S. Jonathan Bass, *Blessed Are the Peace Makers: Eight White Religious Leaders, Martin Luther King, Jr., and the "Letter from Birmingham Jail"* (Baton Rouge: Louisiana State University Press, 2001); Cynthia Griggs Fleming, *In the Shadow of Selma: The Continuing Struggle for Civil Rights in the Rural South* (Lanham, MD: Rowan and Littlefield, 2004), 135–58; RCKD, May 12, 1963 ("Race riots in Bhm last nights"); RCKD, May 21, 1963 ("Wallace says he will stand"); RCKD, March 13, 1963 ("Wallace . . . dull speech").

32. As late as March 1962, when Wallace made a campaign appearance at Troy State, RCK was prominent in the planning and even made it—with a big smile—into photo coverage of the event. *Troy Messenger,* March 16, 1962. But that changed quickly. RCKD, May 16, June 14, December 24, 28 (ridiculing Miller Bonner's lengthy *Alabama*

Journal endorsement of Wallace's racial views), 1962, January 14, 1963; RCK to Family (copies), January 14, April 3, June 11, 1963.

33. Thurston Clarke, *JFK's Last Hundred Days: The Transformation of a Man and the Emergence of a Great President* (New York: Penguin, 2013), 108–16; RCKD, August 28, September 2, 1963; RCK to Folks, October 21, 1963 (copy).

34. Clarke, *JFK's Last Hundred Days*, 126–362; RCKD, November 22–25, December 1, 1963; *Troy Messenger*, November 25, 1963; RCK, "Prayer upon the Assassination of John F. Kennedy," November 25, 1963, RCKD, and now filed in RCK/S/1963.

35. RCKD, November 26, 1963; RCK/S/1963; RCK to Folks, December 11, 1963 (copy).

36. Dee Albritton to Folks, November 25, 1963, included in Lena Albritton, "Letter to the Editor," *Atlanta Journal*, December 5, 1963.

Chapter 12

1. RCKD, September 19, 1964, January 12, November 13, 1966; RCK to Folks (Especially Richard) (copy), December 23, 1966. Numan V. Bartley, *The New South, 1945–1980* (Baton Rouge: Louisiana State University Press, 1995), 381–90; William Warren Rogers et al., *Alabama: History of a Deep South State* (Tuscaloosa: University of Alabama Press, 2018), 578–80; Dan T. Carter, *From George Wallace to Newt Gingrich: Race in the Conservative Counterrevolution* (Baton Rouge: Louisiana State University Press, 1999); Tennant McWilliams, "Remembering Ol' Bullet," *Troy Magazine* (Summer 2009): 14–15; *AJ*, April 11, 1959; RCKD, December 21, 1964.

2. The Wallace quote is from Carter, *Politics of Rage*, 112.

3. According to Kennedy, Stewart's first heart attack occurred while he still was state superintendent of education; RCK visited him in the hospital on November 11, 1959, and he was in bed at home for two weeks in September 1961, telling people it was lingering effects of "frost bite" from his Army days—which RCK doubted. RCKD, November 12, 1959, September 13, 20, 1961, November 2, 1962, August 23, September 6, 1963; *AJ*, March 23–24, 1964; RCK, "Remarks Made at the Funeral of Dr. Frank Ross Stewart . . . March 25, 1964" (RCK/UP).

4. James B. Perdue to Cecil Jackson, March 27, 1964 (copy) and Cecil Jackson to George C. Wallace, May 22, 1964 Governor George C. Wallace Papers, State Institution Files, 1963–64 (SG 21951); RCKD, March 26–27, 1964; David E. Shi and George Brown Tindall, *America: A Narrative History*, 10th ed. (New York: W. W. Norton, 2016), 1339–83; Carter, *Politics of Rage*, 307–64.

5. RCKD, April 7, 9, 1964; *MA*, May 21, 1955, May 30, July 29, 1956; *AJ*, November 3, 1950, July 25, 29, August 28, 1956; *BN*, August 19, 1958. Jeff Bennett yet again put his name in the "silent candidate" hat, but withdrew quickly on getting confirmation that Wallace had not forgotten his prodesegregation politics. Subsequently, UA President Rose elevated Bennett to provost and academic vice president. By 1969, however, Rose had left UA to become CEO of General Computing Corporation in Washington, DC; Rose's diplomatic executive assistant, David Mathews, was UA president; and Bennett was director of legislative affairs for the US Health Services and Mental Health Administration, in Bethesda, Maryland. In 1971, Bennett became president of the University of the South, Sewanee, Tennessee, where his continued assertiveness clashed with board

priorities, leading to his return to Alabama to finish out his visionary career as a senior member of the new University of Alabama System staff. Retired in Orange Beach, Alabama, where he had fished as a teenager in 1930s, he died in 2001. Long after their joint conniving over "Wallace College," he and Ren Kennedy remained close friends.

6. RCKD, May 11, 16, 29, June 23, 29, July 2, 11, 13, 1964; RCK to George Wallace, July 2, 1964 (copy); Carter, *Politics of Rage*, 221.

7. *Greensboro Watchman*, April 4, August 24, 1946; *AJ*, August 4, 1964; RCKD, January 1, 1966; Stephan Lesher, *George Wallace: American Populist* (Boston: Da Capo Press, 1995), 39–41, 45. Some of the early comradeship and political plotting between Adams and Wallace are reflected in letters between the two, with Adams addressing Wallace as "Geo. C." and Wallace sometimes signing off, "G. C.," in Papers of Ralph W. Adams, Vol. III, Correspondence, 1937–1984 (Lurleen B. Wallace Library, Troy University, Troy, AL). Hereafter cited as Adams Papers, this collection does not include what apparently were extensive files of business correspondence between the two while Wallace was governor, and archivists wonder if those files even exist today.

8. Carter, *Politics of Rage*, 202–3; Lesher, *George Wallace*, 274; RCKD, August 11, 18, September 16, 1964.

9. *BPH*, June 14, 1964, September 22, 1965; *MA*, May 1, June 11, 1964, June 27, 1965; *AJ*, August 21, September 12, 1964; *Mobile Register*, January 23, 1966; John E. DaLoney to Ralph Adams, Sep 10, 1965, in Adams Papers, Vol. I, 1964–65. RCK to Wallace, August 21, 1964, and Wallace to RCK, August 25, 1964, George Wallace Governor's Papers (State Institutions File, 1963–65, SG 21957). RCKD, January 8, 14, June 10, 1964. RCK was so supportive of Sparkman that, when "the silk-stocking Birmingham attorney," Republican John Grenier, came to Troy in the summer of 1966 in his campaign against Sparkman, Kennedy could not stick with his normal public diplomacy. As RCK showed Grenier around the campus, he encountered Grenier saying repeatedly that he felt good campaigning at Troy because of its conservatism. The third time Grenier said this, RCK "shocked him by saying I am a Democrat and I will vote for Sparkman" (RCKD, July 8, 1966).

10. RCKD, January 8, August 20, 28, September 5, October 1–2, 7, 29, December 16–17, 1964; WJJ interview, January 1, 1983 ("bode"); Carter, *Politics of Rage*, 221–22. In 1969, Adams was made a brigadier general in the Alabama Air National Guard (*BN*, January 31, 1969).

11. Jon Meacham, *His Truth Is Marching On: John Lewis and the Power of Hope* (New York: Random House, 2020), 16–18, 50–52; Thomas Winton Davis to author, August 23, 2021; RCKD, April 9, 1959, June 3, 1960; Jerome A. Ennels and Wesley Philip Newton, *The Wisdom of Eagles: A History of Maxwell Air Force Base* (Montgomery: River City Press, 2002); J. Mills Thornton III, *Dividing Lines: Municipal Politics and the Struggle for Civil Rights in Montgomery, Birmingham, and Selma* (Tuscaloosa: University of Alabama Press, 2002), 98.

12. Lesher, *George Wallace*, 217–18; Clark, *Schoolhouse Door*, 169, 187; Wallace to Adams, February 2 (copy) and August 12, 1965 (copy), Wallace Governor Papers (State Institutions Files, 1963–1967, SG 21951); RCKD, December 2, 1965.

13. RCKD, April 6–21, 1967, January 9, February 2, 1968 ("fried real good . . . a fool"), August 8, 25, September 6, 8, 13, 1967; Jack Bass, *Taming the Storm: The Life*

and Times of Judge Frank M. Johnson, Jr., and the South's Fight over Civil Rights (New York: Doubleday, 1993), 386–87; Cole Lawson, "A Lament for Gary Dickey," *Tropolitan*, April 17, 2014; "Academic Freedom and Tenure: Troy State University (Alabama)," *AAUP Bulletin* 54 (September 1968): 298–305; Robert F. Kennedy Jr., *Judge Frank M. Johnson, Jr: A Biography* (New York: G. P. Putnam's Sons, 1978), 104–5; "State of the States," *New South* 23 (Fall 1967): 81–110; *MA*, May 17, 19, and 23, 1967, October 19, 1996; *Troy State University and Board of Trustees of Troy State University v. Gary Dickey, 402 F.2d 515 (5th Cir 1968)*; Ralph W. Adams, *Retrospect: An Autobiographical Reveille and Taps* (Montgomery: Black Belt Communications Group, 1995), 73–74.

14. RCKD, February 2, 10, November 20, 1964, March 3, April 27, June 3–4, 14, July 1, 16, 22, 1965, June 8, 1966, June 26–27, 1969; RCK to Folks, January 1, 1966 (copy); Adams to Wallace, June 3, 1965, in Wallace Governor's Papers; Thomas Winton Davis to author, August 2, 2021. As of August 2021, Troy University had no archived institutional records on the desegregation of its main campus and no Adams-Wallace communications on this subject in files of its central administration. The Wallace papers also offer little on Troy's main-campus desegregation.

15. As an appropriate frame of reference, desegregation of higher education in the upper South had a few, far earlier developments. For example, from its Presbyterian founding in 1819, private Maryville College, in east Tennessee, had both slave and free Black people in classes with white students. In 1901 the state of Tennessee made the college segregate, which it did inconsistently. When RCK's close friend and Troy colleague, Emmett Kilpatrick, attended Maryville in 1913–16, he took classes with ("a few") Black students. As soon as the *Brown* opinion came down in 1954, Maryville returned to more robust racially mixed education. Still, even in the upper South, the first public institution to desegregate was the University of Louisville, in 1951. On these and other higher education desegregation developments, see Caroll Van West, "Maryville College," Tennesseeencyclopedia.net (2018); Clarence L. Mohr, ed., *The New Encyclopedia of Southern Culture: Education* (Chapel Hill: University of North Carolina Press, 2011), 54–60, 65–68, 128–38; William E. Nichols, "The Dilemma of the Genteel Tradition: Birmingham-Southern College in the Civil Rights Era, 1957–1965," *AR* 67 (October 2014): 340–73; Clark, *Schoolhouse Door*; Dwayne Cox, *The Village on the Plains: Auburn University, 1856–2006* (Tuscaloosa: University of Alabama Press, 2016), chaps. 7–8; Tennant S. McWillaims, *New Lights in the Valley: The Emergence of UAB* (Tuscaloosa: University of Alabama Press, 2007), 145–93; and S. Jonathan Bass, "Maintaining a Christian Environment without Federal Control: The Struggle to Integrate Samford University, 1954–1974" (typescript, 2021, in possession of S. Jonathan Bass), 12.

16. RCK/S/1964; "Presbyterians Speed Integration," *CC* 81 (May 13, 1964): 630–31; Lowry Ware and James W. Gettys, *Second Century: A History of the Associate Reformed Presbyterians, 1882–1982* (Greenville, SC: Associate Reformed Presbyterian Center, 1982), 359–64; RCK, "The Church Looks at Itself," *ARP*, June 7, 1953; RCKD, April 4, 20, May 11, 17–18, 24, June 1–3, 1964; RCK, "Minister Atones for Mental Lapse" (draft, 1964). Among other sources, the RCK quote on Jesus and alcohol is from RCK to Folks, May 11, 1977 (copy).

17. RCKD, July 30–31, August 4–8, 1964, January 29, April 29, June 8–10, July 4, 18, 29–30, September 3, 1965, May 31 ("gutsy letter"), June 11, 1966; Erskine College

and Seminary Board Minutes, April 30, July 30, October 29, 1965 (Archives of McCain Library, Erskine College and Seminary, Due West, SC); *WPE*, August 12, 1965; Ware and Gettys, *Second Century*, 359, 471–76.

18. RCKD, May 15, October 20, 1965, August 30, 1966; RCK to Folks (copies), April 8, 1965, August 23–30, 1966; *MA*, September 1, 6, 1966; Gene Roberts and Hank Klibanoff, *The Race Beat: The Press, the Civil Rights Struggle and the Awakening of a Nation* (New York: Random House, 2006), 376; Clinton McCarty, *Reins of Power: Racial Change and Challenge in a Southern Community* (Tallahassee: Sentry Press, 1999), 135–43, 146, 150, 157, 222–25, 230; Frye Gaillard, *Cradle of Freedom: Alabama and the Movement That Changed America* (Tuscaloosa: University of Alabama Press, 2004); *AJ*, April 16, 1965. The case of Byron Hale and the failure of the Bank of Pine Apple are summarized in *MA*, May 15, 1968.

19. RCKD, March 5, 7, 10–11, 15, 20–22, April 2, 5, 16, July 25, 1965; WJJ interview, January 5, 1983; John Golden interview, January 10, 1991; Maria Gitin, *This Bright Light of Ours: Stories from the Voting Rights Fight* (Tuscaloosa: University of Alabama Press, 2014), 46, 62, 82, 115, 128, 131, 231–36, 241, 253; McCarty, *Reins of Power*, 155, chap. 17; Cynthia Griggs Fleming, *In the Shadow of Selma: The Continuing Struggle for Civil Rights in the Rural South* (Lanham, MD: Rowan and Littlefield, 2004), chap. 5; *BN*, March 21, 1965; *AJ*, March 16, 1965. My account of the Jones slapping incident generally comports with that of Camden Academy faculty and students on hand that day as well as with published assessments as cited above. However, it also fleshes out the incident by giving far more on W. J. Jones's background and thoughts about the incident. Still, just as there was no single Black citizen response to the incident, there certainly was no single white citizen response, which makes one appreciate even further the late Morton Sosna's classic, *In Search of the Silent South: Southern Liberals and the Race Issue* (New York: Columbia University Press, 1977).

20. McCarty, *Reins of Power*, 155–56, 223; Donnie Williams with Wayne Greenhaw, *The Thunder of Angels: The Montgomery Bus Boycott and the People Who Broke the Back of Jim Crow* (Chicago: Lawrence Hill Books, 2006), 78, 182; *BN*, December 15, 2001; Fleming, *In the Shadow of Selma*, 163; *NYT*, January 24–25, February 20, 1966; *AJ*, January 24, 1966. The entire case file for *US v. Wilcox County Board of Education*, 494 F.2d 575 Fifth Circuit (1974) is in the National Archives of Atlanta (Morrow, GA).

21. RCKD, January 12, 1966 ("LBJ . . . very good"), March 14, 1966 ("gruesome"), February 9, 12, 1968 (Wallace's 1968 campaign); RCK to Folks, March 20, 1968 (copy), where RCK reports Adams as saying, "Wallace campaign is receiving about $20,000 a day in contributions . . . but spending $50,000 a day . . . campaign needs $10 million"; RCK to Folks, November 18, 1975 (copy) (personally "makes money" despite campaign falling behind). McCarty, *Reins of Power*, 223; Fleming, *In the Shadow of Selma*, 135–39, 154–59, 246–48, 263–69; RCK/S/1968; *ARP*, May 26, 1968; Joe Wightman to RCK, October 10, November 6, 1967. Kennedy only knew Wallace was an Air Force veteran who saw action in the Pacific Theater. Still, 1942 correspondence between Wallace and Gessner McCorvey, executive director of the Alabama Democratic Party, reveals Wallace—three months after the Pearl Harbor attack—apparently trying to get McCorvey to facilitate his running for the legislature out of the strategy that its members were exempt from military service; Wallace apparently saw military service as intruding on

his building a political career. Gessner T. McCorvey to George C. Wallace (telegram), March 2 and 4, 1942, Papers of the Executive Committee of the Alabama Democratic Party, LPR99, Box 81, folder 1, ADAH. This generally tracks with some of Wallace's wartime behavior, which undoubtedly involved high-risk service as a flight engineer and health issues, but also no strong record as a committed airman and an early, adamantly requested, exit from the Air Force right after Japan's surrender. See Carter, *Politics of Rage*, 65–66; Dan Carter to author, November 2, 2020.

22. *HWC*, 284–86; WJJ interview, January 5, 1983. See also chapter 7, note 20 above.

23. WJJ interview, January 5, 1983; Martha Simpson to WJJ, March 30, 1954, in PWJJ; *MA*, May 30, 1989; McCarty, *Reins of Power*, 149–50; RCKD, August 26, 1964, September 8, 16, 1968; *Gulley Simpson v. William J. Jones, et al., 460 So 2d 282 (1984)*, case file in ADAH.

24. *MA*, December 18, 1989, May 1, 1990; *STJ*, May 29–31, 1982; Robert J. Bullock, "Trust Funds Wilcox Scholarships," *STJ*, November 10, 2003; and *Mobile Register*, February 4, 2022. In the late 1990s one of these Wilcox high school graduates—Tyronne Quarles (1972–2020), a Black man educated as an aeronautical engineer as well as an attorney—successfully defended me in a complicated federal higher education lawsuit.

25. RCKD, March 16, 31, April 3 ("fine") ,4, 9, June 5–8 ("compassionate"), November 22 ("Fifth anniversary"), 1968; R. W. Apple Jr., "Kennedy Appeals for Nonviolence," *NYT*, April 5, 1968; Frye Gaillard, *A Hard Rain: America in the 1960s, Our Decade of Hope, Possibility, and Innocence Lost* (Montgomery: New South Books, 2018), 489; Thurston Clarke, *The Last Campaign: Robert F. Kennedy and 82 Days That Inspired America* (New York: Henry Holt, 2008), 94–97; Arthur M. Schlesinger Jr., *Robert F. Kennedy and His Times* (New York: Houghton Mifflin, 1978), 618–19. As one of several gifts by Mary Conway Kennedy and Margaret Kennedy Ausley, the author has in his possession RCK's copy of Edith Hamilton, *The Greek Way* (New York: W. W. Norton and Co., 1942), with underlining on pages 256–57 and assorted clippings on Hamilton enclosed.

26. McCarty, *Reins of Power*, 223–24; Darrell Prescott, "Benign Neglect in Wilcox County, Alabama," *Harvard Crimson*, December 4, 1970; Dobbins interview, October 15, 1985.

27. RCKD, February 24, April 20, 22, May 3–5, 9, 13, 20, July 27, August 24, November 8, 17–23 (Flynn case), December 16, 1966; Carter, *Politics of Rage*, 232, 275–76, 285–87; Lesher, *George Wallace*, 172, 353, 358, 362, 365; John Hayman, *Bitter Harvest: Richmond Flowers and the Civil Rights Revolution* (Montgomery: New South Books, 2006).

28. RCKD, April 21 ("clever"), March 9 ("Mother of Year"), December 14 ("FRAUD"), 1967, May 5, 7, 9, 1968, January 14, 1969 ("crook"). RCK to Folks (copies), March 28, 1967 ("battle"), November 8, 1969 ("Redneck"); EK to RCK, June 17, 1967 ("cold heart"). In RCK's papers, attached to EK's June 17 letter is a clipping (*MA*, June 27, 1967) of a letter to the editor from Penelope Jones, of Frisco City, Alabama (in Cooper's district), excoriating Cooper for defeating a state bill to allow eighteen-year-olds to vote and blasting him for being another crooked Alabama conservative. "The Wily Fox from Wilcox works . . . for the benefit of the Fox." See also *MA*, December 16, 1967, on Troy's new "university" status; and the unidentified clipping, dated October 24, 1967, in Adams Papers, vol. 2, 1967, listing members of Troy State University's first board of trustees.

29. RCK to Folks (copies), February 23 ("finished off"), March 16 ("turn it off"), April 7 ("scared"), 8, 16 ("good job"), May 1, 5, 6 ("new idea"), 17, 21, 26, June 6, 1970; Carter, *Politics of Rage*, 370–77, 383–89, 391–99; Gordon Harvey, "Albert Preston Brewer," encyclopediaofalabama.org; Dan T. Carter, *From George Wallace to Newt Gingrich: Race in the Conservative Counterrevolution, 1963–1994* (Baton Rouge: Louisana State University Press, 1999); RCK interview, February 25, 1984. On these Gallup polls see *NYT*, March 22 and December 31, 1970, both of which RCK clipped at the time and had not forgotten some fourteen years later.

30. In some ways American education in the 1960s grew out of World War II and Cold War science and engineering initiatives. Still, other pressing social forces also were at work on 1960s education, as summarized in Irving Bernstein, *Guns or Butter: The Presidency of Lyndon Johnson* (New York: Oxford University Press, 1994), 202–22. See also RCKD, April 4, 1967, January 2, 1969, April 8, 1970; RCK to Folks, May 24, 1971 (copy; "cold-blooded, impersonal"); VJGL, "Renwick Carlisle Kennedy, D.D.," *WPE*, May 25, 1988, repeating President Adams's remarks about Kennedy's job description at RCK's retirement reception, as excerpted from Ralph Adams to J. A. Dale, June 30, 1974 (copy).

31. On private "segregation academies" see *NYT*, March 30, 1972, and especially McCarty, *Reins of Power*, 174, 177, emphasizing that some Camden white families strongly opposed building a separate private school for white students. See, too, RCK to Folks, August 5, 1972 (copy; "100% black"); and Carla Crowder, "Private White Academies Struggle On in a Changing World," *BN*, October 27, 2002. For larger context consult Southern Education Association, *A History of Private Schools and Race in the New South*, southerneducation.org; and Sara Carr, "In Southern Towns, 'Segregation Academies' Are Still Going Strong," *Atlantic* (December 14, 2012).

32. RCKD, December 12, 1967, January 3, April 9, 11, May 28, October 13–15, 1969, February 4 ("Louisville"), April 5, 26, May 5, 24, March 7, 1971; RCK to Folks, March 15, 1971 (copy); Robert Foster to author, May 30, 2013; RCK interview, September 9, 1984; Donald M. McLeod interview, May 23, 2012; RCK interview, September 9, 1984; Dan T. Carter to author, November 2, 2020.

33. RCKD, March 10, 1969 ("sad and good"), January 19 ("puzzling"), February 2 ("desultory"), March 17 ("not as good as others"), April 8 ("race film"), September 14 ("very good"), 1970, February 2 ("dirty language"), 6, June 4–5 (weddings), 10 ("YPCU speech"), July 19, 1971; *WPE*, July 8, 1969.

34. RCK to Folks (copies), October 25, 1966, May 26, October 6 ("I smoke"), 1970; RCK to MMK, November 19, 1968 ("regamorole"); RCK to RGM, July 7, 1970, PRGM; RCKD, August 3, 4, 10–11 ("brave face"), 1970. On Duane Tway, see *AJ*, November 13, 1956, May 22, 1958, December 2, 1968; *Troy Messenger*, September 27, 1970; and *Abbeville* [Alabama] *Journal*, March 20, 1980. On Max Rafferty, consult *NYT*, November 8, 1962; *LAT*, June 14, 1982; Ralph Adams to Max Rafferty, September 2, 1970, and Rafferty to Adams, September 8, 1970, Max Rafferty Papers (Special Collections, University of Iowa Libraries, Iowa City); *MA*, August 15, 1970, January 30, June 16, 1971. Franklin Parker, "School Critic Max Rafferty (1917–1982) and the New Right," in Michael V. Belok and Joe L. Kinchelope, eds., *The New Right in Education* (Meerut, India: ANU Books, 1986), 129–40; Margaret Shannon, "Comeback of a

Left-Out Rightist," *Atlanta Journal-Constitution*, March 14, 1971; and Bennett interview, May 8, 1998 ("intolerant developer").

35. "Troy University—A Capsule History," *Tropolitan*, April 23, 1971; RCKD, June 29–30, 1971 ("Troy over"); *Troy Messenger*, June 30, 1971.

Chapter 13

1. RCKD, July 1 ("Redneck president"), September 9, 1971 ("suitcase"); *WPE*, October 29, 1970. On Sunday, September 25, 1970, RCK was not scheduled to preach because of a Protestant Union service. At the last minute, however, Camden Baptist hosted a prohibition rally that drew so many—RCK and Mary did not attend—that the Union service was canceled. On October 20, RCK cast an absentee ballot voting "yes" for legalization of alcohol in Wilcox County. RCKD, October 20, 25, 1970.

2. Kennedy's papers for 1972–75 include significant correspondence, meeting notes, and reports labeled "Indigent Health Committee." On Rosa Pettway's circumstances, see especially RCKD, June 30, July 19, October 10, 1975. RCK to Folks, November 18, 1971 (copy; "You get tired"); RCK to Pulpit Committees [of Camden, Bethel, and Prosperity Churches], January 1, 1973 (copy); RCKD, August 8, 1972 ("Henry Lewis Smith," whom RCK observed in August 1972 when he guest-preached at the Marion Junction Prosperity Church anniversary celebration; *MA*, August 5, 1972); RCKD, August 8 ("dull sermon"), December 1, 1974 ("rank Calvinist"), February 16 ("gore"), March 3, 1975 ("hell-fire"); RCKD, June 6, 1978 ("pitchfork"); *ARP*, May 22, 1974; *WPE*, July 11, 1974. RCK developed strong feeling about graduates of the Reformed Theological Seminary in Jackson, Mississippi: they represented "a Fifth Column in the ARP Synod . . . already they control two of our four presbyteries and would like to take over all of them . . . they want to take us [ARPs] into the Presbyterian Church of America. I don't like this" (RCK to Folks, June 17, 1978; copy). He was much happier when a young graduate of Erskine College and Seminary, Robert P. Brawley ("an ARP and a scholar") shortly came to Wilcox County. Even with Brawley's presence, however, RCK attended church less frequently, though he still served for a while longer as clerk of the presbytery and the session. RCKD, June 25, 1978, January 4, 1983; RCK to Folks, May 5, 1980 (copy). On Richardson and Brawley, see Lowry Ware and James W. Gettys *Second Century: A History of the Associate Reformed Presbyterians, 1882–1982* (Greenville, SC: Associate Reformed Presbyterian Center, 1982), 307.

3. RCKD, May 15, 1972 ("shabby"), September 15, 1978 (Baxley); RCKD, April 24, 1974 ("Beasley"); RCK interview, September 9, 1984 (Fob James); Samuel L. Webb and Margaret E. Armbrester, eds., *Alabama Governors: A Political History of the State* (Tuscaloosa: University of Alabama Press, 2018), 243–48.

4. RCK to Folks, August 5, 1972 (copy; "Tricky Dick"), May 5, 1975 (copy; "McGovern"), September 8, 1973 ("smell"), April 4 (copy; "crook"), November 11, 1974 (copy; "hack"), December 23, 1976 (copy; "snake"), May 21, 1981 (copy; "Peanut Farmer"). RCKD, June 1, 1971 ("evasive"), April 5, July 12, November 7, 1972 ("McGovern"), January 31 ("brilliant"), May 7 ("my boy"), August 16 ("old people"), 19 ("clod"), 1976, January 20, 1977 ("magnificent"), Aug 12, 1980 ("Ted Kennedy"). RCK interview, September 9, 1984 ("gross hypocrisy"). Craig Shirley gives an accurate treatment of the origins and uses of "rendezvous with destiny" in *Rendezvous with Destiny: Ronald Reagan and*

the Campaign That Changed America (Wilmington, DE: Intercollegiate Studies Institute, 2009), 7–8, 11, 73, though with a pro-Reagan attitude quite the opposite of RCK's. The only concession to the Republican Party RCK ever made, apparently, was to President Ford's initial vice president, "[Nelson] Rockefeller [who] might make a good president" (RCKD, December 12, 1974, January 13, 1975).

    5. RCK's getting "real news" out to Camden's Black citizens—his *"New York Times* ministry"—waned only in his last years as old age and ill health finally intruded. See, for example, RCKD, April 4, November 2, 1971, October 21, 1972, May 7, 1975, March 28, 1978, January 17, 1979, April 4, October 22, 1981. RCKD, October 15, 21, December 11, 1971 ("tires spinning"), January 21, 1975 ("altercation"); RCK to Folks, January 29, 1975 (copy; "sorry I feel this way"); RCK interview, July 20, 1985 ("frightfully lacking"); RCKD, April 3, 14, 1971 (Atmore schools). On his absentee voting see also RCKD, April 24, May 24, October 2, 1972, May 24, 1974, March 5, 1980. For larger context on racial tensions and conflict in Camden at this time, especially strong on Black perspectives, see Cynthia Griggs Fleming, *In the Shadow of Selma: The Continuing Struggle for Civil Rights in the Rural South* (Lanham, MD: Rowman and Littlefield, 2004), 187–256; *NYT*, November 20–21, 1971.

    6. *STJ*, October 5, 1969; RCKD, May 4, 1976 ("Albritton"), December 30, 1972, January 1, February 9, 1973. After its shutdown in 1965, the ferry reopened in 2006 with US government support. See ruralswalabama.org; Frye Gaillard, *A Hard Rain: America in the 1960s, Our Decade of Hope, Possibilities and Innocence Lost* (Montgomery: NewSouth Books, 2018), 392.

    7. RCKD, May 1, 2, 5, 1977; *WPE*, November 12, 2018; Amanda Walker, "Tears and Laughter: Who Was Roland Cooper?" *West Alabama Watchman*, April 30, 2016.

    8. RCKD, September 27 ("uneventful day"), December 8, 1978 ("old order"); *STJ*, February 22, 1979, September 9, 1982, March 8, 1988, February 8, 2000; "Retired Sheriff of 32 Years, Sheriff Arnold," WilcoxCountySheriff.com.

    9. RCKD, November 24, 1975 (*Dr. Zhivago*), June 22 (*Anna Karenina*), July 25 (*Doll's House*), 1978, April 19, 1979 (*King Lear*). RCK/RR/1975–79. On alcohol, for example, see RCKD, February 23, 1972, including a typical note: "Drop off M in Montgomery... go to Prattville Hi-way and buy stock of gin and vodka." See also RCKD, September 4, 1971, April 22, June 6, 27, 1972, May 5, 1973, May 21, July 13, 1974, May 11, 23, 1975, December 10, 1980, December 18, 1981. RCK's reflections on Jones's death: "Bill came by, often on Mondays, bringing vegetables and a bottle." RCK to Sisters, September 10, 1984 (copy).

    10. Though he arrived home on June 18, 1979, RCK's first diary entry after the hospital stay was on August 2, when he went to Selma to check on travel insurance for the upcoming trip. His diary reports no alcohol purchases on that Selma visit, atypical for his Selma runs, and no alcohol consumption before they departed for Europe on July 16. RCKD, July 2–16, 1979. Their trip, including occasional alcohol consumption, he recorded separately from the regular diary in "Overseas Diary Book," PRCK. See also RCKD, August 9 ("grits"), 19 (*Class Reunion*), September 4 ("commodities"), 1979, March 31, 1983 ("Sarah... good to me"). See also diary entries for October 18–30, November 5, 13, December 13, 1979, August 6, 1980, March 9, 1983.

    11. MCKD interview, July 8, 1989 ("clear head"); RCKD, May 1, 1982.

12. RCK to Folks, December 28, 1982 (copy); MCKD and MKA to author, June 16, 2013; Veronica Wood interview, September 6, 2015.

13. RCKD, January 1, 3, 10, 24 ("bath"), 7, 18 ("driving," "ride"), March 8, 1983, November 5, 1984 ("Sarah gets commodities"), March 3 ("Sarah good to me"), April 16 ("and I have chicken sandwich"), 1983, November 5–6, September 24, 1984 (Sarah Woods as transporter to polls).

14. One of the female witnesses used against Butts maintained that Butts's liberal message corrupted her to the extent that she became promiscuous—but not with Butts. Birmingham attorney, Edward L. Hardin Jr., himself the son of a noted Alabama Methodist minister, convinced the tribunal that accusations of Butts's sexual misconduct were contrived, though initially he failed to convince them that Butts had not violated certain Methodist protocols in the due process charge. With an appeal, he won Butts's acquittal on that charge, too. Still, the two-year suspension effectively lasted longer than that; conservative leaders of the Alabama and Northwest Florida Methodist Conference continued to "poison the waters" on Butts's efforts to return to active pastorate life. Ultimately, "the authorities" eased up. Butts turned around a failing church in Chickasaw, near Mobile, and succeeded mightily with another in Fort Walton Beach, Florida, whereupon the Lee sisters orchestrated his giving a celebrated series of sermons at Christ Church in Manhattan before bringing him back to Monroeville. Edward L. Hardin Jr, interview, September 26, 2008; *MA*, August 31, 1969, April 3, 1976, September 4, 1977, April 15, 20, 22, 1983. On RCK watching "Tom's t.v. church," see for example RCKD, January 2, April 3, May 2, 10, 1983; and on Butts's suspension, RCKD, August 24, September 9, 1983. See also Butts's obituary, *Mobile Press-Register*, February 19, 2021.

15. Hardin interview, September 26, 2008 (Butts); RCKD, June 29, 1975 (Adams), January 24 (Waugh), February 2–3 (Troyat), May 13 (Thoreau), June 29 (Brodie). RCKD, April 16, 1983 (last wedding); RCK/RR/1983; Betty Anderson interview, September 1, 2021.

16. RCKD, April 24–25 ("small ache"), May 10 ("do not go in"), 12 ("stomach pain"), 8 ("Starr's turn-off"), 20–21 (McWilliams), 26 ("pain . . . must cut down"), June 18, 1983 (Lee's wedding). RCK to Folks, August 8, 1983 (copy; "champagne flowed"). Years later, it felt eerie for me to find in RCK's papers my own (embarrassingly stilted) follow-up note on this interview: "Dear Reverend Kennedy, Please know that I am indebted to you for the excellent conversation we had last Saturday. . . . You have had a remarkable career—and are still having one" (Tennant McWilliams to RCK, May 24, 1983).

17. RCK to Folks, November 1, 1983 (copy; "don't get better"); RCKD, November 23–24, 1983 (Thanksgiving).

18. RCKD, December 3, 1983 (football game), July 14–28, 1984 (eating, gagging, feeding dog); MCKD, interview, July 8, 1989 (maiden names, television remote, Edith Hamilton).

19. On Sarah Woods, see RCK to Folks, March 3, 1984 ("Sarah . . . comfort"); and similar references in RCKD, May 14, August 22, September 19, October 20, 27, 29, November 14, 1985. RCKD, August 23 ("tedious"), September 9, 1984 (Bogie and McIntosh). The diary reflects RCK's regular trips to the barbershop once a month on

into the fall of 1985. He was scheduled for a haircut on November 18, 1985, but to his considerable frustration an unscheduled visitor caused him to miss it. Sarah Woods got him to the barbershop on November 20, 1985—his last such visit. RCKD, November 18, 20, 1985.

20. *Charlotte Observer*, September 17, 1977, March 30, 1981; RCK to Margaret [Kennedy Blakely], May 4, 1976 (copy; "no wish to die"); RCK to Folks, December 28, 1982 (copy; "no brothers"), February 2, 1984 (copy; "lonely"). On February 16, 1982, RCK told the diary, "Elise does not look good." On March 1, he noted "biopsy [in Selma] this morning . . . Elise has cancer of the lung . . . may live three to five weeks," though with great pain she lasted seven months. There are no diary notes regarding RCK's reaction to her death; much of the diary for July through October of 1982 does not survive. A graduate of Alabama College (now the University of Montevallo) and considered an "Alabama institution" as a phonetics/reading specialist, Elise Bonner Hickey taught elementary school in Camden (1922–52), where some knew her as "the lady who wanted poor kids to learn to read as well as rich kids." She also taught in Mobile (1952–57) and in Selma (1957–71). After a funeral service at Camden ARPC, with RCK not present, the family buried her in Camden Cemetery next to her husband, Walter C. Hickey, who predeceased her by some twenty-five years. *STJ*, April 14, 1971, September 22, 1982; Haas Strother interview, April 21, 1991 (Bonner's teaching); Mac Partin interview, April 21, 1991 ("poor kids"); MCKD, July 8, 1989 ("did not talk").

21. RCKD, August 11, 19, 1981 (Bill's stroke), May 12 ("Bill . . . pain"), June 18 ("hardly walk"), September 3 ("stroke"), 1984; RGM to WJJ, January 24, 1965, and June 23, 1974, in PWJJ; MR interview, April 18, 1983 ("did not know"); MCKD interview, July 8, 1989 ("not up to it"); RCK to Sisters, September 10, 1984 (copy; "desolate").

22. RCKD, October 1, 1984 (birthday, driving denied).

23. RCKD, December 21–26, 1984 (Viola and hedge;); MCKD interview, April 20, 2012 ("Yes, Daddy").

24. RCK to Sisters, January 2 (copy; "typing errors"), February 2 (copy; pay tax). RCKD, January 11 ("Laws"; the letter to Laws does not survive), 21 (weather report), 27–29 (RFK), February 20 ("bottle"), May 14 ("election official"), July 2 ("x-ray"), 20 ("McWilliams"), 1985. See also RCKD, July 31–November 15, 1985, for his own articulate, if wrenching, day-by-day notes of the esophagus steadily becoming nonfunctional, to the point at which he could not even drink a milkshake. MCKD interview, July 7, 1989 ("never discussed"); RCK to Folks, November 18, 1971 (copy; "deep-seated"); RCKD, November 24, 1985 (last entry). *WPE*, January 1, 1986; MCKD to author, June 6, 2013. In February 1969, RCK bought a "five-space" lot in Camden Cemetery "with coping around it" (RCK to Folks, February 18, 1969 [copy]). As early as June 1, 1971—a month before his retirement from Troy—he carefully selected "Option 3" in the State of Alabama Retirement System, which would provide "$158 a month and $79 per month for M[ary] if I die first." Then, in February 1972, RCK placed in his safe deposit box all documents related to his US Army discharge, with the note: "I am entitled to some burial expenses from the Veterans Administration, with this discharge proof." RCKD, June 1, 1971, February 10, 1972. Will L. Liddell and Ruth H. Liddell, comps., "Camden Cemetery Survey" (typescript, 2014, in possession of the author, Fairhope, AL); chapter 7, note 15 above.

Coda

1. Robert Penn Warren, *All the King's Men* (New York: Harcourt, Brace and Co., 1946), 136.

2. To my knowledge, no scientific study documents patterns in the "Scotch-Irish vote"; identifying the target in a scientific way would appear to be problematical, at the least, without DNA sampling. Still, numerous inferential and anecdotal treatments—some otherwise sophisticated and compelling—profile exceptionally strong Scotch-Irish support for Donald Trump. See, for example, Cameron Joseph, "The Scots-Irish Vote," *Atlantic*, October 6, 2009; Ian McTear, "Scotch-Irish Influence in American Democracy," *BBC News*, September 16, 2018; Adrian McKinty, "Donald Trump's Ulster Supporters," blog post, *The Psychopathology of Everyday Life*, February 12, 2016; and Yoni Applebaum, "Trump and the Borderers," *Atlantic*, April 6, 2016. For the 2020 presidential election, see the online fundraising effort urging support for Trump: Jolene Bunting, "Ulster Scots for Trump," [2020], donorbox.org. On the term, "second rise of massive resistance," I suggest its consideration to connote the evolution of a southern-based to a national-based resistance to race change from the 1950s into 1960s America as a key feature in recent "Trumpism." More than a half-century of historiographical work related to "massive resistance"—from Numan Bartley's early writings to George Lewis's and others, combined with Dan Carter's *From George Wallace to Newt Gingrich* and most recently the more broadly conceived, *The Southernization of America*, by Frye Gaillard and Cynthia Tucker—appears to support this idea. See also chapter 10, note 29 above.

3. One of the best illustrations of Cash's social-scientific thought is his pivotal use of "folkmind." See Robert Brinkmeyer, *The Fourth Ghost: White Southern Writers and European Fascism, 1930–1950* (Baton Rouge: Louisiana State University Press, 2009), 84. Connections between Gingrich and the warring Trumpism are assayed in, among other places, in McKay Coppins, "The Man Who Broke Politics," *Atlantic* (November 2018). On hostile responses to US government mask and vaccination strategies targeted at the COVID-19 pandemic, and their partial origins in hostility to US government support of desegregation in the mid-twentieth century, see the provocative essay by education policy analyst, Dustin Hornbeck, "Banning School Mask Mandates Mirrors Resistance to Integration," September 1, 2021, TheConversation.com.

4. RCK interviews, May 21, 1983, March 24, 1984.

5. Dobbins interview, October 15, 1985; MR interview, April 18, 1983.

6. Despite recurring historiographical innovations, one of the best overviews of changing waves in the "New South" movement during the years of RCK's life remains in four iconic volumes: Paul M. Gaston, *The New South Creed: A Study in Southern Mythmaking* (New York: Alfred A. Knopf, 1970); C. Vann Woodward, *Origins of the New South, 1877–1913* (Baton Rouge: Louisiana State University Press, 1951); George B. Tindall, *The Emergence of the New South, 1914–1945* (Baton Rouge: Louisiana State University Press, 1967); and Numan V. Bartley, *The New South, 1945–1980* (Baton Rouge: Louisiana State University Press, 1995).

7. RCK to Bogie, August 12, 1952 (copy); Sidney Ahlstrom, *A Religious History of the American People* (New Haven: Yale University Press, 1972), 118, 941, 1089; Kennon M. Sheldon, "Comparing Catholics' and Protestants' Religious Motivations," *International Journal for the Psychology of Religion* 16, no. 3 (November 26, 2009): 209–23.

8. John Edgerton, *Speak Now Against the Day: The Generation Before the Civil Rights Movement in the South* (Chapel Hill: University of North Carolina Press, 1994), 210, 257–58; David T. Ballantyne, *New Politics in the Old South: Ernest F. Hollings in the Civil Rights Era* (Columbia: University of South Carolina Press, 2016), 113; Scotty E. Kirkland, "Joseph N. Langan," encyclopediaofalabama.org; Jack Bass, *Taming the Storm: The Life and Times of Judge Frank M. Johnson, Jr., and the South's Fight over Civil Rights* (New York: Doubleday, 1993), 56–61; *NYT*, January 12, 2013. Among the highest profile southern white liberals who went to the war—but not to combat—were historian C. Vann Woodward, who spent the time with a US Navy desk job in Washington, DC; and Mississippi editor, Hodding Carter, whose loss of an eye in basic training resulted in his becoming a noncombat US Army journalist.

9. Brinkmeyer, *The Fourth Ghost*, 35–26; George Packer, *The Blood of the Liberals* (New York: Farrar, Straus and Giroux, 2000).

10. A. B. Love to RCK, February 22, 1950.

11. MCKD interview, March 18,1986.

BIBLIOGRAPHY

MANUSCRIPTS AND ARCHIVAL MATERIALS
Adams, Ralph. Papers. Archives of Lurleen B. Wallace Library, Troy University, Troy, AL.
Alabama Democratic Party, Executive Committee. Papers. Alabama Department of Archives and History. Montgomery.
Bennett, J. Jefferson. Papers. Hoole Special Collections, University of Alabama Libraries, Tuscaloosa.
Biographical Files. Archives of the Presbyterian Historical Society, Philadelphia.
Brickell, Hershell. Collection. Department of Archives and Special Collections, University of Mississippi Libraries, Oxford.
Château Business Files. Archives, Château de Roumont, O'Champs, Belgium.
Church of the Resurrection. Records, 1909–13. South Carolina Historical Society Archives, Charleston.
Commission on Ecumenical Missions and Relations, 1883–1966. RG209, Reel 37. Archives of the United Presbyterian Church, Pittsburgh.
Croc, Christine Chateauneuf. Diary. Château de Trébodennic, Ploudaniel, France.
Divinity School. Papers. RG 530. Archives and Special Collections, Heard Library, Vanderbilt University Archives, Nashville.
Dobbins, Charles G. Papers. Special Collections and Archives, Auburn University, Auburn, AL.
DuBose Memorial Church Training School and Theology Department: Student Records, 1925–26. Archives, Sewanee: University of the South, Sewanee, TN.
Englehardt, Samuel E., Jr. Personal Papers. Alabama Department of Archives and History, Montgomery.
Equal Justice Initiative. Archives. Montgomery.
Erskine College. Board Records. Archives, McCain Library, Erskine College and Seminary, Due West, SC.
Field Studies in the Modern Culture of the South. Records, 1945–57. Southern Historical Collection, Wilson Library, University of North Carolina, Chapel Hill.
Gulley Simpson v. William J. Jones et al. 460 So 2d 282 (1984). Case File. Alabama Department of Archives and History, Montgomery.
Jarrett, Thomas D. Papers. Archives and Research Center, Atlanta University Center Consortium, Atlanta.
Jones, William ("Bill") Junius. Papers. In possession of the author, Fairhope, AL.
Kennedy, Renwick C. Papers. Special Collections, Princeton Theological Seminary Library, Princeton.

———. Research Files. In possession of the author, Fairhope, AL.
Lang, George. Papers. Hoole Special Collections, University of Alabama Libraries, Tuscaloosa.
Latané, John Holliday. Papers. Archives of the Milton S. Eisenhower Library. Johns Hopkins University, Baltimore.
Liddell, Viola Jefferson Goode. Papers. Alabama Department of Archives and History, Montgomery.
———. Personal Papers. In possession of Ruth and Will Liddell, Camden, AL.
Liddell, Viola Jefferson Goode, and Emmett Kilpatrick. Letters, 1943. Photocopied collection in possession of the author, Fairhope, AL.
Lynching Information. Tuskegee University Archives Repository, Tuskegee University, Tuskegee, AL.
McNeill, Sam. Papers. In possession of Fleetwood Hollinger, Camden, AL.
McWilliams, Richebourg Gaillard. Papers. In possession of the author, Fairhope, AL.
Melton, William D. Papers. Office of the President, Box 4, 1923–26. University of South Carolina Archives, University of South Carolina, Columbia.
Middleton, Troy H. Papers: Personal Correspondence, 1944–45. Archives and Special Collections, Louisiana State University, Baton Rouge.
Military Personnel ["201"] Files. National Personnel Records Center, National Archives, St. Louis.
Perry, Raymond H. Papers. Special Collections and Manuscripts, University of Vermont Libraries, Burlington.
Rafferty, Max. Papers. Special Collections, University of Iowa Libraries, Iowa City.
Renwick, James. Collection. Local History Manuscripts, Edinburgh and Scottish History Collections, Central Library, George IV Bridge, Edinburgh.
Rhynus, Roland. Papers. In possession of Rolinda Rhynus Lueveno, Colton, CA.
Richards, J. McDowell. Papers. Kline Special Collections and Archives, Columbia Theological Seminary, Atlanta.
Rubin, Morton. Papers. Special Collections and Archives, Snell Library, Northeastern University, Boston.
Rutledge, Archibald. Papers. South Carolinian Library, University of South Carolina, Columbia.
State of Alabama. Certificate of Death Files. Center for Health Statistics, Alabama Department of Public Health, Montgomery.
Student Records. Archives, Princeton Theological Seminary, Princeton.
Student Records. Mudd Manuscript Library, Princeton University, Princeton.
Student Records. Special Collections, Bowling Library, Judson College, Marion, AL.
Tait Family. Papers. Alabama Department of Archives and History, Montgomery.
Troy State University and Board of Trustees of Troy State University v. Gary Dickey. 402 F.2d 515, Fifth Circuit (1968). Case File. National Archives of Atlanta, Morrow, GA.
US Army. Chief of Chaplains. Records. Military Archives Division, National Archives, College Park, MD.
———. Harvard Chaplain School. Records. US Army Museum, Fort Jackson, SC.
———. *Official Records of the War of the Rebellion*. Series 1, 53 vols. Washington, DC: Government Printing Office, 1880–1901.

———. Surgeon General. Records. Military Records Division, National Archives, College Park, MD.
US Census. Butler and Conecuh counties, AL. Slave Schedules, 1850. USGenWeb Archives. Files.usgwarchives.net.
———. Monroe County, AL. 1830. USGenWeb Archives. Files.usgwarchives.net.
———. Monroe County, AL. 1850. USGenWeb Archives. Files.usgwarchives.net.
———. Monroe County, AL. Largest Slaveholders from 1860 Slave Census Schedules and Surname Matches for African Americans on 1870 Census. Transcribed by Tom Blake, May 2001.
———. Newberry County, SC. Largest Slaveholders from 1860 Slave Schedules and Surname Matches for African Americans on 1870 Census. Transcribed by Tom Blake, May 2001.Sites.rootsweb.com.
———. Newberry County, SC. 1860 Slave Census.
———. Wilcox County, AL. 1820. Ancestry.com.
———. Wilcox County, AL. 1830. Ancestry.com.
———. Wilcox County, AL.1840. Ancestry.com.
———. Wilcox County, AL 1850. Abstracted by Scott McCoy, February 1998. Files.usgwarchives.net.
———. Wilcox County, AL. Largest Slaveholders from 1860 Slave Schedules and Surname Matches for African Americans on 1870 Census. Transcribed by Tom Blake, February 2002. Sites.rootsweb.com.
———. Wilcox County, AL. Slave Censuses, 1820–60.
United States v. Wilcox County Board of Education. 494 F. 2d 575 Fifth Circuit (1974). Case File. National Archives of Atlanta, Morrow, GA.
University of Oklahoma Press. Papers. Western History Collection, Manuscripts Division, Libraries of University of Oklahoma, Norman.
Wiley, Bell I. Papers. Manuscript, Archives, and Rare Book Library, Emory University. Atlanta.

Interviews and Oral Histories
Unless otherwise indicated, notes and tapes for these interviews are located in Renwick C. Kennedy Research Files in possession of the author, Fairhope, AL.

Anderson, Betty. Interview with author. Camden, AL, June 23 and September 1, 2021.
Anderson, Wanda Stroud. Interview with author. Birmingham, February 27, 2013.
Ausley, Margaret Kennedy. Interview with author. Nokesville, VA, June 27, 1989.
Bennett, J. Jefferson. Interview with author. Orange Beach, AL, May 8, 1998.
Blakely, Margaret Kennedy. Interview with author. Due West, SC, July 8, 2007.
Bogie, John ("Jack") Henry. Interview with author. Worcester, MA, September 11, 2012.
Bullock, Robert, and Juliette Harper. Interviews with author. Oak Hill, AL, June 2, 2009; February 22, 2010; October 10, 2014; May 7, 2016.
Butts, Thomas E. Interview with author. Monroeville, AL, July 12, 2011.
Carlisle, Charles. Interview with author. Due West, SC, July 7, 2007.
Chestnutt, Calvin. Interview with author. Montreat, NC, February 10, April 11, 2013.
Clarke, Erskine. Interview with author. Decatur, GA, September 1, 2006.

Croc, Sylvie Louboutain. Interview with author. Ploudaniel, France, March 27, 2008.
Dale, Jane Shelton. Interview with author. Camden, AL, September 20, 2012.
Dale, John Laurie, Jr. Interview with author. Oak Hill, AL, November 3, 2004.
Deroaches, Marie-Thérèse Provost. Interview with author. St. Pair-sur-Mer, France, February 8, 2008.
Dickinson, Mary Conway Kennedy. Interviews with author. Atmore, AL, March 18, 1986; July 8, 1989; June 6, 2006; October 10, 2011; April 20, 2012.
Dobbins, Charles G. Interview with author. Washington, DC, October 15, 1985.
Dobson, Lisa McNeill. Interviews with author. Camden, AL, November 10, 2008; December 16, 2008.
Duprey, Roland Dulins. Interview with author. St. Pair-sur-Mer, France, February 6, 2008.
Forget, Louis. Interviews with author. Jullouville, France, January 3 and 15, 2008.
Furman, Marian P. Interview with author. Camden, AL, September 24, 2015; January 28, 2016; April 19, 2022.
Gitin, Maria. Telephone interview with author. Capitola, CA, April 1, 2013.
Hardin, Edward L., Jr. Interview with author. Birmingham, September 26, 2008.
Hero, Alfred M., III. Telephone interview with author. Ann Arbor, MI, March 9, 2013.
Hollinger, Fleetwood. Interview with author. Camden, AL, November 10, 2008.
Hood, Renwick Carlisle. Interview with author. Pennedepie and Honfleur, France, April 9–10, 2014.
Jones, Joyce Clopton Carothers. Taped interview with author. Oak Hill, AL, November 21 and 22, 1979.
Jones, William ("Bill") Junius. Taped interviews with author. Oak Hill, AL, November 21 and 22, 1979; January 5, 1983.
———. Taped interview with Katheryn Tucker Windham. Oak Hill, AL, June 24, 1980. Gee's Bend Project: Papers and Photographs, Division of Archives and Manuscripts, Birmingham Public Library, Birmingham.
Kennedy, Betty Gaines. Interviews with author. Camden, AL, November 10, 2008; May 7, 2021.
Kennedy, Renwick C. Taped interview with author. Camden, AL, January 1, 1979.
———. Interview with author, May 21, 1983 (with Mary Moore Kennedy).
———. Taped interview with Kathryn Tucker Windham, Camden, AL, June 23, 1980. Gee's Bend Project: Papers and Photographs, Division of Archives and Manuscripts, Birmingham Public Library, Birmingham.
———. Telephone interviews with author, February 25, 1984; March 24, 1984; September 9, 1984 (with Mary Moore Kennedy); July 20, 1985.
Kidd, James. Interview with author. Fayetteville, TN, May 29, 2007.
Lévi-Ménard, Marie Louise. Interviews with author, Bréville-sur-Mer, France, February 6 and March 26, 2008.
Liddell, Viola Jefferson Goode. Interviews with author. Camden, AL, March 16, 1984; October 11, 1987.
Liddell, Will, and Ruth Liddell. Interviews with author. Camden, AL, January 12, 2012; September 23, 2015.
———. Telephone interviews with author. Montgomery, AL, June 3, 2019; August 10, 2020.

Lucas, Dominique Bindel. Interview with author. St. Martins des Champs, France, March 26, 2008.
Lumpkin, Elizabeth. Interview with author. Delta, AL, February 4, 2009.
Lumpkin, Maudine. Interview with author. Delta, AL, February 4, 2009.
Matthews-Threadgill, Sheryl. Interview with author. Camden, AL, April 14, 2022.
McLeod, Donald. Interview with author. Camden, AL, May 23, 2012.
McPhillips, Julian. Interview with author. Montgomery, February 15, 2018.
McWilliams, Richebourg Gaillard. Taped interview with author, Mobile, January 1, 1979.
———. Interviews with author. February 24, 1979; March 23, 1979; March 13, 1982; July 9, 1983.
Mitchell, Bonnie Dean. Interview with author. Oak Hill, AL, July 9, 2013.
Partin, Mac. Interview with author. Fatama, AL, April 21, 1991.
Paterson, Judith. Interview with author. Montgomery, December 3, 2012.
Peterson, Ann Margaret. Interview with author. Birmingham, February 9, 2008.
Raines, Howell. Interview with author. Fairhope, AL, May 12, 2018.
Rubin, Morton. Interview with author. Newton Heights, MA, April 18, 1983.
Strother, Haas. Interview with author. Camden, AL, April 21, 1991.
Summerlin, Russell E. Interview with author. Delta, AL, February 13, 2009.
Tisdale, Vera. Telephone interview with author. Troy, AL, May 13, 2012.
Touzé, Jean. Interview with author. Angomesnil, France, January 15, 2008.
Walton, Anna Marie Laws. Telephone interview with author. Elizabethton, TN, April 16, 2008.
Ware, Lowry. Interview with author. Due West, SC, July 8, 2007.
Wilkinson, Horace. Interview with author. Gastonburg, AL, March 4, 2006.
Wood, Veronica. Interview with author. Camden, AL, September 6, 2015.

NEWSPAPERS

Alabama Herald (1840)
Alabama Journal (1942–66)
AlabamaNews.net (2014, 2016)
Anniston Star (1927, 1937, 1958, 1968)
Asheville Citizen (1948, 2000)
Atlanta Constitution (1943)
Atlanta Journal (1963)
Atlanta Journal-Constitution (1971, 2000)
Birmingham News (1938–73, 2002)
Boston Globe (2011)
Charlotte Observer (1946, 1950, 1977)
Christian Science Monitor (1948)
Fairhope Courier (1940)
Greensboro Watchman (1946)
Los Angeles Times (1948)
Miami Herald (1948)
Mobile Register (1966, 1998, 2019, 2021–22)
Montgomery Advertiser (1930–85)

Newark News (1948)
New York Age (1953)
New York Herald Tribune (1944)
New York Post (1944)
New York Times (1921, 1925, 1932–72, 1986, 2013, 2021)
Orlando Sentinel (1952)
Raleigh News and Observer (1952)
Richmond Times-Dispatch (1948)
Russellville Courier-Democrat (1925)
San Diego Chronicle (1948)
Selma Times Journal (1927, 1934–2003)
Southern Aegis (1916, 1924–25)
Tropolitan (Troy University) (1953–74, 2014)
Troy Messenger (1944, 1949, 1953, 1962–71)
Tuscaloosa News (1918, 1933–38, 2001)
Wall Street Journal (2004)
Washington Post (1921)
Washington Times (1922, 2008)
West Alabama Watchman (2014, 2016, 2018)
Wilcox American (1977)
Wilcox Progress (1894, 1897)
Wilcox Progressive Era (1900–1985, 2018)

GENERAL SOURCES ON SOUTH CAROLINA, ALABAMA, AND BEYOND

"Academic Freedom and Tenure: Troy State University (Alabama)." AAUP Bulletin 54 (September 1968): 298–305.

Adams, Ralph W. Retrospect: An Autobiographical Reveille and Taps. Montgomery: Black Belt Communications Group, 1995.

Aiken, Charles S. *The Cotton Plantation South since the Civil War*. Baltimore: Johns Hopkins University Press, 1998.

Alabama Official and Statistical Register, 1926–80. Montgomery: Alabama Department of Archives and History.

"Alabama School Book Act Proves Ludicrous." *Harvard Crimson*, June 17, 1954.

Albright, Madeleine. *Fascism: A Warning*. New York: Harper Collins, 2018.

Alles, Adam. "Forces That Produced Hitler." *Christian Century* 57 (November 6, 1940): 1370–73.

Ambrose, Stephen. *D-Day, June 6, 1944: The Climactic Battle of World War II*. New York: Simon and Schuster, 1994.

Atkins, Leah Rawls. "Thomas W. Martin." Encyclopediaofalabama.org.

Bailey, Richard. *Neither Carpetbaggers nor Scalawags: Black Officeholders during the Reconstruction of Alabama, 1867–1878*. Montgomery: New South Books, 2010.

Ballantyne, David T. *New Politics in the Old South: Ernest F. Hollings in the Civil Rights Era*. Columbia: University of South Carolina Press, 2016.

Barnard, Hollinger F., ed. *Outside the Magic Circle: The Autobiography of Virginia Foster Durr*. Tuscaloosa: University of Alabama Press, 1986.

Barnard, William D. *Dixiecrats and Democrats: Alabama Politics 1942–1950.* Tuscaloosa: University of Alabama Press, 1974.
Bartley, Numan V. *The New South, 1945–1980.* Baton Rouge: Louisiana State University Press, 1995.
———. *The Rise of Massive Resistance: Race and Politics in the South during the 1950s.* Baton Rouge: Louisiana State University Press, 1969.
Bass, Jack. *Taming the Storm: The Life and Times of Judge Frank M. Johnson, Jr., and the South's Fight over Civil Rights.* New York: Doubleday, 1993.
Bass, S. Jonathan. *Blessed Are the Peace Makers: Eight White Religious Leaders, Martin Luther King, Jr., and the "Letter from Birmingham Jail."* Baton Rouge: Louisiana State University Press, 2001.
———. "Maintaining a Christian Environment without Federal Control: The Struggle to Integrate Samford University, 1954–1974." Typescript (2021). In possession of S. Jonathan Bass, Birmingham.
Beard, Charles, and Mary Beard. *Rise of the American Civilization.* New York: Macmillan, 1927.
Bernstein, Irvin. *Guns or Butter: The Presidency of Lyndon Johnson.* New York: Oxford University Press, 1994.
Biedler, Philip. "Yankee Interloper and Native Son: Carl Carmer and Clarence Cason." *Southern Cultures* 9 (March 2003): 18–35.
Biles, Roger. *The South and the New Deal.* Lexington: University Press of Kentucky, 1994.
Black, George F. *The Surnames of Scotland.* New York: New York Public Library, 1946.
Blakely, Margaret Kennedy. "Mary Emma Carlisle Kennedy." Undated typescript. In possession of Tennant McWilliams.
Blakley, Ralph Erskine. *Memories.* Davidson, NC: Privately printed, 1992.
Bobinski, George S. "Carnegie Libraries: Their History and Impact on American Public Library Development." *ALA Bulletin* 62 (December 1968): 1361–67.
Boykin, Edward M. *History of the Boykin Family, from Their First Settlement in Virginia, 1685, and in South Carolina, Georgia, and Alabama.* Camden, SC: Colin Macrae, 1876.
Brady, Lisa M. *War upon the Land: Military Strategy and the Transformation of Southern Landscapes during the American Civil War.* Athens: University of Georgia Press, 2012.
Bridenbaugh, Carl. *Myths and Realities: Societies of the Colonial South,* Baton Rouge: Louisiana State University Press, 1952.
Bridges, Edwin C. *Alabama: The Making of an American State.* Tuscaloosa: University of Alabama Press, 2016.
Brinkmeyer, Robert. *The Fourth Ghost: White Southern Writers and European Fascism, 1930–1950.* Baton Rouge: Louisiana State University Press, 2009.
Brokaw, Tom. *The Greatest Generation.* New York: Random House, 1998.
Brooks, Jennifer. *Defining the Peace: World War II Veterans, Race, and the Remaking of Southern Political Tradition.* Chapel Hill: University of North Carolina Press, 2004.
Brown-Dean, Kahlilah L. *Identity Politics in America.* Medford, CT: Polity Press, 2019.
Burns, Aubrey. "Segregation and the Church." *Southwest Review* 34 (Spring 1949): 121–30.
Caldwell, Erskine. *God's Little Acre.* New York: Grosset and Dunlap, 1933.

Caldwell, Erskine, and Margaret Bourke-White. *You Have Seen Their Faces*. New York: Modern Age Books, 1937.
Carlton, David L., and Peter A. Coclanis, eds. *Confronting Southern Poverty in the Great Depression: The Report on Economic Conditions in the South with Related Documents*. Boston: Bedford Books of St. Martin's Press, 1996.
Carmer, Carl. *Stars Fell on Alabama*. New York: New York Literary Guild, 1934.
Carpenter, Jesse T. *The South as a Conscious Minority, 1789–1861*. New York: New York University Press, 1930.
Carr, Sara. "In Southern Towns, 'Segregation Academies' Are Still Going Strong." *The Atlantic* (December 14, 2012).
Carrole, J. Creg, ed. *Abbeville County Family History*. Clinton, SC: Intercollegiate Press, 1979.
Carter, Dan T. *From George Wallace to Newt Gingrich: Race in the Conservative Counterrevolution, 1963–1994*. Baton Rouge: Louisiana State University Press, 1999.
———. *Politics of Rage: George Wallace, the Origins of the New Conservatism, and the Transformation of American Politics*. Baton Rouge: Louisiana State University Press, 1996.
———. *Scottsboro: A Tragedy of the American South*. New York: Oxford University Press, 1969.
Cash, W. J. *The Mind of the South*. New York: Knopf, 1941.
Cason, Clarence. *90 Degrees in the Shade*. Chapel Hill: University of North Carolina Press, 1935.
Chaucer, Geoffrey. *The Canterbury Tales: Rendered into English by J. U. Nicholson*. New York: Garden City Publishing Co., 1934.
Childers, James Saxon. *A Black Man and a White Man in the Deep South*. New York: Farrar and Strauss, 1936.
Clark, E. Culpepper. *The Schoolhouse Door: Segregation's Last Stand at the University of Alabama*. New York: Oxford University Press, 1993.
Clarke, Thurston. *JFK's Last Hundred Days: The Transformation of a Man and the Emergence of a Great President*. New York: Penguin Random House, 2013.
———. *The Last Campaign: Robert F. Kennedy and 82 Days That Inspired America*. New York: Henry Holt, 2008.
Clayton, Bruce, and John Salmond, eds. *Lives Full of Struggle and Promise*. Gainesville: University of Florida Press, 2003.
———, eds. *The South Is Another Land: Essays on the Twentieth Century South*. New York: Greenwood Press, 1987.
Clements, Kendrick A. *The Life of Herbert Hoover: Imperfect Visionary, 1918–1928*. New York: Palgrave-Macmillan, 2010.
Cobb, James C. *Away Down South: A History of the Southern Identity*. New York: Oxford University Press, 2005.
———. *The Selling of the South: The Southern Crusade for Industrial Development, 1936–1990*. Champaign: University of Illinois Press, 1997.
———. *The South and America since World War II*. New York: Oxford University Press, 2012.
Cobb, James C., and Charles R. Wilson, eds. *Perspectives on the American South: An Annual Review of Society, Politics, and Culture*. New York: Routledge, 1987.

"Coleman Carlisle" (1770–1824). Ancestry.com.
Coppins, McKay. "The Man Who Broke Politics." *The Atlantic* (November 2018).
Couch, Jim F., and Gina Couch. "New Deal Expenditures in Alabama: Was Economic Need Addressed?" *Alabama Review* 50 (July 1997): 181–84.
Cox, Dwayne. *The Village on the Plains: Auburn University, 1856–2006*. Tuscaloosa: University of Alabama Press, 2016.
Cox, Karen L. *Dreaming of Dixie: How the South Was Created in American Popular Culture*. Chapel Hill: University of North Carolina Press, 2011.
Crabtree, Steve. "Gallup Brain: Strom Thurmond and the 1948 Election." December 17, 2002. Gallup.com.
Crane, Stephen. *The Red Badge of Courage*. New York: D. Appleton and Co., 1895.
Cronenburg, Allen. *Forth to the Mighty Conflict: Alabama and World War II*. Tuscaloosa: University of Alabama Press, 2004.
Crown, Patricia L., et al. "Ritual Black Drink Consumption at Cohokia." *Proceedings of the National Academy of Sciences of the United States of America* 35 (August 2012): 13944–49.
Dabney, Virginius. *Liberalism in the South*. Chapel Hill: University of North Carolina Press, 1932.
Daniel, Pete. "Going among Strangers: Southern Reactions to World War II." *Journal of American History* 77 (December 1990): 886–911.
———. "The Transformation of the Rural South." *Agricultural History* 5 (July 1981): 231–43.
Diggins, John Patrick. *Proud Decades: America in War and Peace, 1941–1960*. New York: W. W. Norton, 1988.
———. *Rise and Fall of the American Left*. New York: Harcourt, Brace, Jovanovich, 1973.
———. *Why Niebuhr Now?* Chicago: University of Chicago Press, 2011.
Doyle, Don H. *Faulkner County: The Historical Roots of Yoknapatawpha County*. Chapel Hill: University of North Carolina Press, 2001.
———. *New Men, New Cities, New South: Atlanta, Charleston, Mobile, 1860–1910*. Chapel Hill: University of North Carolina Press, 1990.
Dyer, Frederick P., ed. *Compendium of the War of the Rebellion*. 3 vols. New York: Thomas Yoseloff, 1959.
Dykeman, Wilma, and James Stokley. *Seeds of Southern Change: The Life of Will Alexander*. Chicago: University of Chicago Press, 1962.
Eddins, Don. *AEA: Head of the Class in Alabama Politics*. Montgomery: Alabama Education, 1997.
Edgar, Walter. *South Carolina: A History*. Columbia: University of South Carolina Press, 1998.
Edgerton, John. *Speak Now Against the Day: The Generation Before the Civil Rights Movement in the South*. Chapel Hill: University of North Carolina Press, 1994.
Edmonds, Henry M. *A Parson's Notebook*. Birmingham: Elizabeth Agee's Bookshop, 1961.
Ellington, Coke. "*Montgomery Advertiser*." Encyclopediaofalabama.org.
Ellis, R. H. "The Calhoun School: Miss Charlotte Thorn's 'Lighthouse on a Hill' in Lowndes County, Alabama." *Alabama Review* 37 (July 1984): 183–201.
Ellison, Ralph. *The Invisible Man*. New York: Random House, 1952.

English, Van. *Beyond the Normal: The Centennial History of Troy State College, 1880–1986.* Troy, AL: Troy University, 1988.
Ennels, Jerome A., and Wesley Philip Newton. *The Wisdom of Eagles: A History of Maxwell Air Force Base.* Montgomery: River City Press, 2002.
Escott, Paul D., ed. *W. J. Cash and the Minds of the South.* Baton Rouge: Louisiana State University Press, 1992.
Eskew, Glen T. *But for Birmingham: The Local and National Movements in the Civil Rights Struggle.* Chapel Hill: University of North Carolina Press, 1997.
Fairclough, Adam. *A Class of Their Own: Black Teachers in the Segregated South.* Cambridge, MA: Harvard University Press, 2007.
Farmer, Margaret Pace. *One Hundred Fifty Years in Pike County, Alabama, 1821–1897.* Montgomery: Brown Printing Co., 1973.
Faukner, Neil, et al. *Creeping Socialism.* London: Public Reading Room—Bookmark, 2019.
Faulkner, William. *Absalom, Absalom!* New York: Random House, 1936.
———. *Intruder in the Dust.* New York: Random House, 1951.
———. *Sanctuary.* New York: Jonathan Cape and Harrison Smith, 1931.
———. *The Sound and the Fury.* New York: Jonathan Cape and Harrison Smith, 1929.
Feldman, Glen. *The Great Melding: War, the Dixiecrat Rebellion, and the Southern Model for America's New Conservatism.* Tuscaloosa: University of Alabama Press, 2015.
———. *The Irony of the Solid South: Democrats, Republicans and Race, 1865–1944.* Tuscaloosa: University of Alabama Press, 2013.
———. *Politics, Society, and the Klan in Alabama, 1915–1949.* Tuscaloosa: University of Alabama Press, 1999.
Fitzgerald, Michael. *Reconstruction in Alabama: From Civil War Redemption to the Cotton Belt.* Baton Rouge: Louisiana State University Press, 2017.
Fleischhauer, Carl, and Beverly W. Brannan, eds., *Documenting America, 1935–1943.* Berkeley: University of California Press, 1988.
Fleming, Walter Linwood. *Civil War and Reconstruction in Alabama.* New York: Macmillan, 1905.
Flint, Harrison Leigh. *Landscape Plants for the Eastern United States.* Hoboken, NJ: John Wiley and Sons, 1997.
Flynn, George Q. "The Selective Service and American Blacks during World War II." *Journal of Negro History* 69 (Winter 1984): 14–25.
Flynt, J. Wayne. *Alabama in the Twentieth Century.* Tuscaloosa: University of Alabama Press, 2004.
Frederickson, Kari. *Deep South Dynasty: The Bankheads of Alabama.* Tuscaloosa: University of Alabama Press, 2021.
———. *The Dixiecrat Revolt and the End of the Solid South, 1932–1968.* Chapel Hill: University of North Carolina Press, 2001.
Fry, Joseph A. *Dixie Looks Abroad: The South and U. S. Foreign Relations, 1789–1973.* Baton Rouge: Louisiana State University Press, 2002.
Gaddis, John Lewis. *The Cold War: A New History.* New York: Penguin, 2005.
Gaillard, Frye. *Cradle of Freedom: Alabama and the Movement That Changed America.* Tuscaloosa: University of Alabama Press, 2004.

———. *A Hard Rain: America in the 1960s, Our Decade of Hope, Possibilities and Innocence Lost*. Montgomery: NewSouth Books, 2018.

Gaillard, Frye, and Cynthia Tucker. *The Southernization of America: A Story of Democracy in the Balance*. Montgomery: NewSouth Books, 2022.

Garnet and Black. Columbia: University of South Carolina, 1928–36.

Gaston, Paul M. *The New South Creed: A Study in Southern Mythmaking*. New York: Knopf, 1970.

Gilbert, Martin. *The Second World War: A Complete History*. New York: Henry Holt, 1989.

Gilmore, Glenda Elizabeth. *Defying Dixie: The Radical Roots of Civil Rights, 1919–1950*. New York: W. W. Norton, 2009.

Goldman, Eric F. *The Crucial Decade—and After: America, 1945–1960*. New York: Knopf, 1966.

Grafton, Carl, and Anne Permaloff. *Big Mules and Branchheads: James E. Folsom and Political Power in Alabama*. Athens: University of Georgia Press, 1985.

Grant, Madison. *The Passing of the Great Race*. New York: Charles Scribner's Sons, 1921.

Greenberg, David. *Republic of Spin: An Inside History of the American Presidency*. New York: W. W. Norton, 2016.

Gruen, Lori. *Ethics and Animals*. Cambridge: Cambridge University Press, 2011.

———. "The Moral Status of Animals." *Stanford Encyclopedia of Philosophy*. https://plato.Stanford.edu.

Hackney, Sheldon. *Populism to Progressivism in Alabama*. Princeton: Princeton University Press, 1969.

Hahn, Maria, and Seunsook Moon. *Over There: Living with the U. S. Military Empire from World War Two to the Present*. Durham, NC: Duke University Press, 2010.

Hanks, Patrick. *Dictionary of American Family Names*. 5 vols. New York: Oxford University Press, 2006.

Harris, Stuart. *Alabama Place Names*. Huntsville: Strode Publishing, 1982.

Harvey, Gordon E. *A Question of Justice: New South Governors and Education, 1968 to 1976*. Tuscaloosa: University of Alabama Press, 2006.

Harvey, Ira. *A History of Education Finance in Alabama History*. Auburn, AL: Truman Pierce Institute for the Advancement of Teacher Education, 1989.

Hayman, John. *Bitter Harvest: Richmond Flowers and the Civil Rights Revolution*. Montgomery: New South Books, 2006.

Heiden, Konrad. *Der Fuehrer: Hitler's Rise to Power*. Boston: Houghton Mifflin, 1944.

Heinrich, John C. *The Psychology of the Oppressed*. London: Allen and Unwin, 1937.

Henderson, Henry L., and David Woolner, eds., *FDR and the Environment*. New York: Palgrave Macmillan, 2005.

Heritage of Marengo County. Clanton, AL: Heritage Publishing Consultants, 2000.

Herring, George C. *The American Century and Beyond: US Foreign Relations, 1893–2014*. New York: Oxford University Press, 2017.

Hill, Jordon, James I. Robertson Jr., and J. H. Segar, eds. *The Bell Irvin Wiley Reader*. Baton Rouge: Louisiana State University Press, 2001.

Hill, W. Jayson. "Craig Field Airport and Industrial Complex (Craig Air Force Base)." Encyclopediaofalabama.org.

Hobson, Fred C. *But Now I See: The White Southern Racial Conversion Narrative.* Baton Rouge: Louisiana State University Press, 1999.
———. *Serpent in Eden: H. L. Mencken in the South.* Chapel Hill: University of North Carolina Press, 1974.
———. *Tell about the South: The Southern Rage to Explain.* Baton Rouge: Louisiana State University Press, 1983.
Hoffsomer, Harold. "The AAA and the Cropper." *Social Forces* 13 (May 13, 1935): 494–502.
Hofstadter, Richard. *The Paranoid Style in American Politics.* New York: Random House, 1964.
Hollis, Daniel W., III. *An Alabama Newspaper Tradition: Grover C. Hall and the Hall Family.* Tuscaloosa: University of Alabama Press, 1983.
Hornbeck, Dustin. "State Efforts to Ban Mask Mandates in Schools Mirror Resistance to Integration." September 1, 2021. TheConversation.com.
Hortz, Frenz, ed. *Nobel Lectures: Literature, 1901–1967.* Amsterdam: Elsevier, 1969.
Howe, Daniel Walker. *Victorian America.* Philadelphia: University of Pennsylvania Press, 1976.
Hubbs, G. Ward. *Searching for Freedom after the Civil War: Klansman, Carpetbagger, Scalawag, and Freedman.* Tuscaloosa: University of Alabama Press, 2015.
Humphrey, Cordellia. "Senator O. J. ("Joe") Goodwyn and the Politics of Public Education in Alabama, 1955–1970." MA thesis, Auburn University at Montgomery, 1997.
Hundley, D. R. *Social Relations in Our Southern States.* New York: Henry B. Price, 1860.
Hunter-Gault, Charlayne. *In My Place.* New York: Vintage, 1993.
Inscoe, John, Fred A. Bailey, et al. "Forum: Memphis, the Peabody, and the SHA." *Journal of Southern History* 71 (November 2005): 831–64.
Jackson, Harvey H., III, ed. *Sports and Recreation.* Vol. 16 of *The New Encyclopedia of Southern Culture,* ed. Charles Reagan Wilson. Chapel Hill: University of North Carolina Press, 2011.
Jefferson, Robert. *Fighting for Hope: African American Troops of the 93rd Infantry Division in World War Two and Post-War America.* Baltimore: Johns Hopkins University Press, 2008.
Jenkins, Peter. *Along the Edge of America.* New York: Houghton Mifflin, 1995.
Johnson, Dale A. *The Vanderbilt Divinity School: Education, Content, Change.* Nashville: Vanderbilt University Press, 2001.
Johnson, Gerald W. *The Wasted Land.* Chapel Hill: University of North Carolina Press, 1937.
Johnson, Guy Benton, and Guion Griffis Johnson. *Research in Service of Society: The First Fifty Years of the Institute for Research in Social Science at the University of North Carolina.* Chapel Hill: University of North Carolina Press, 1980.
Kazin, Michael. *A Godly Hero: The Life of William Jennings Bryan.* New York: Knopf, 2006.
Kennedy, David M. *Freedom from Fear: The American People in Depression and War.* New York: Oxford University Press, 1999.
Kennedy, Robert F., Jr. *Judge Frank M. Johnson, Jr.: A Biography.* New York: G. P. Putnam's Sons, 1978.

"Kennedy Family Genealogy." Undated typescript. In possession of Richard N. Kennedy Jr., Atlanta.
King, Richard H. *A Southern Renaissance: The Cultural Awakening of the American South, 1930–1955*. New York: Oxford University Press, 1980.
Kirkland, Scotty. "Joseph N. Langan." Encyclopediaofalabama.org.
———. "Mobile and the Boswell Amendment." *Alabama Review* 65 (July 2012): 205–49.
Klein, Rachel N. *Unification of a Slave State: The Rise of the Planter Class in the South Carolina Backcountry, 1760–1808*. Chapel Hill: University of North Carolina Press, 1990.
Kolchin, Peter. *First Freedom: Responses of Alabama Blacks to Emancipation and Reconstruction* Tuscaloosa: University of Alabama Press, 2007.
Kuehl, Warren F., and Lynne K. Dunn. *Keeping the Covenant: American Interventionists and the League of Nations, 1920–1939*. Kent, OH: Kent State University Press, 1997.
Lawson, Cole. "A Lament for Gary Dickey." *Tropolitan* (April 17, 2014).
Leff, Laurel. *Buried by the Times: The Holocaust and America's Most Important Newspaper*. Cambridge: Cambridge University Press, 2005.
Lesher, Stephan. *George Wallace: American Populist*. Boston: Da Capo Press, 1995.
Leuchtenburg, William E. *The Perils of Prosperity, 1914–1932*. Chicago: University of Chicago Press, 1958.
———. *The White House Looks South: Franklin D. Roosevelt, Harry Truman, and Lyndon B. Johnson*. Baton Rouge: Louisiana State University Press, 2005.
Lewis, George. *Massive Resistance: The White Response to the Civil Rights Movement*. New York: Oxford University Press, 2006.
Lewis, Sinclair. *Elmer Gantry*. New York: Harcourt Trade Publishers, 1927.
———. *Main Street*. New York: Harcourt, Brace, and Howe, 1920.
Link, Arthur S. "Woodrow Wilson: The American As Southerner." *Journal of Southern History* 36 (February 1970): 3–17.
Lipstadt, Deborah E. *Beyond Belief: The American Press and the Coming of the Holocaust, 1933–1945*. New York: Free Press, 1993.
Logsdon, Guy. "Lottinville, Savoie (1906–1997)." okhistory.org.
Mahoney, Harry Thayer. *American Prisoners of the Bolsheviks, 1917–1922*. N.p., 2000.
Manchester, William. *The Glory and the Dream: A Narrative History of America, 1932–1972*. New York: Little, Brown, 1973.
March, William. *Company K*. New York: Smith and Haas, 1933.
"Margaret Elizabeth McLane Kennedy" (1837–1933). Ancestry.com.
Mathews, John M. "Clarence Cason among the Southern Liberals." *Alabama Review* 38 (January 1985): 3–18.
McAdams, Doug, and Karena Kloos. *Deeply Divided: Racial Politics and Social Movements in Post-War America*. New York: Oxford University Press, 2014.
McCrossen, Alexis. *Making Modern Times: A History of Clocks, Watches, and Other Timekeepers in American Life*. Chicago: University of Chicago Press, 2013.
McIlwain, Christopher Lyle. *Civil War Alabama*. Tuscaloosa: University of Alabama Press, 2016.
McMillan, James B. *Indian Place Names in Alabama*. Tuscaloosa: University of Alabama Press, 1984.

McMillen, Neil R. *The Citizens Council: Organized Resistance to the Second Reconstruction, 1954–1964*. Urbana: University of Illinois Press, 1994.

———, ed. *Remaking Dixie: The Impact of World War II on the American South*. Oxford: University Press of Mississippi, 1997.

McRae, Elizabeth Gillespie. *Mothers of Massive Resistance: White Women and the Politics of White Supremacy Massive Resistance*. New York: Oxford University Press, 2018.

McWilliams, Tennant. *The Chaplain's Conflict: Good and Evil in a War Hospital*. College Station: Texas A&M University Press, 2012.

———. "Dixie's Heretic? The Great Hunting Debate of 1948." *Alabama Heritage* 117 (Summer 2015): 58–60.

———. *New Lights in the Valley: The Emergence of UAB*. Tuscaloosa: University of Alabama Press, 2007.

———. "Remembering Ol' Bullet." *Troy Magazine* (Summer 2009): 14–15.

Meachem, Jon. *His Truth Is Marching On: John Lewis and the Power of Hope*. New York: Random House, 2020.

Melville, Herman. *Moby-Dick*. New York: Harper and Bros., 1851.

Memorial Record of Alabama. 2 vols. Madison, WI: Brant and Fuller, 1893.

Mencken, Henry L. *In Defense of Women*. New York: Knopf, 1918.

———. *Prejudices, First Series*. New York: Knopf, 1919.

———. *Prejudices, Sixth Series*. New York: Knopf, 1927.

Meriweather, Robert Lee. *The Expansion of South Carolina, 1729–1765*. Kingsport, TN: Southern Publishers, 1940.

Mertz, Paul E. *New Deal Policy and Southern Rural Poverty*. Baton Rouge: Louisiana State University Press, 1978.

Mitchell, Margaret. *Gone with the Wind*. New York: Macmillan, 1936.

Mohr, Clarence, ed. *Education*. Vol. 17 of *The New Encyclopedia of Southern Culture*, ed. Charles Reagan Wilson. Chapel Hill: University of North Carolina Press, 2011.

Morrison, Charles Clayton. *Outlawry of War*. Chicago: Willet, Clark, and Colby, 1927.

Morrison, Melanie S. *Murder on Shades Mountain*. Durham, NC: Duke University Press, 2018.

Morse, Robert M., and Kevin L. Florin. "The Definition of Alcoholism." *Journal of the American Medical Association* 268 (August 26, 1992): 1012–14.

Myrdal, Gunnar. *American Dilemma*. 2 vols. New York: Harper and Bros., 1944.

Nearing, Scott. *Where Is Civilization Going?* New York: Vanguard Press, 1927.

Nichols, William E. "The Dilemma of the Genteel Tradition: Birmingham-Southern College in the Civil Rights Era, 1957–1965." *Alabama Review* 67 (October 2014): 340–73.

Norrell, Robert J. "Labor at the Ballot Box: Alabama Politics from the New Deal to the Dixiecrat Movement." *Journal of Southern History* 57 (May 1991): 201–34.

———. *Reaping the Whirlwind: The Civil Rights Movement in Tuskegee*. New York: Knopf, 1985.

O'Neill, William L. *Coming Apart: An Informal History of America in the 1960s*. Chicago: Ivan R. Dee, Publishers, 2005.

Osterweis, Rollin G. *Romance and Nationalism in the Old South*. New Haven: Yale University Press, 1949.

Oxford Dictionary of National Biography. 20 vols. Oxford: Oxford University Press, 1937–38.
Packer, George. *Blood of the Liberals*. New York: Farrar, Straus and Giroux, 2000.
Palladium for 1957. Troy, AL: Troy State Teachers College, 1957.
Parker, Franklin. "School Critic Max Rafferty (1917–1982) and the New Right." In Michael V. Belok and Joe L. Kinchelope, eds., *The New Right in Education*. Meerut, India: ANU Books, 1986.
Parker, Omie Wall. "Hershel Brickwell: An Estimate of His Works as Critic, Author, and Lecturer." MA thesis, University of Mississippi, 1961.
Paxton, Robert O. *The Anatomy of Fascism*. New York: Knopf, 2004.
Penack, William. *For God and Country: The American Legion, 1919–1941*. Boston: Northeastern University Press, 1989.
Permaloff, Anne, and Carl Grafton. "Political Geography and Power Elites: Big Mules and the Alabama Constitution." In George E. Connor and Christopher W. Hannon, eds., *The Constitutionalisms of the American States*. Columbia: University of Missouri Press, 2008.
Perry, Michael W., ed. *Dachau Liberated: The Official Report* [of the US Seventh Army]. Seattle: Inkling Books, 2000.
Phillips, Ulrich. *Life and Labor in the Old South*. New York: Little, Brown, 1929.
Piepkorn, Arthur Carl. "A Chronicle of the United States Army Chaplains School during the Second World War." Typescript (1959). US Military Chaplains Library, Fort Jackson, SC.
Pinker, Steven. *Rationality: What It Is, Why It Seems Scarce, Why It Matters*. New York: Viking, 2021.
———. "Why We Are Not Living in a Post-Truth Era." Skeptic.com.
Pinson, Adam. "Federal Census Data on the Renwick Family of Newberry County, South Carolina." Typescript (2009). In possession of Tennant McWilliams.
Pittman, John P. "Double Consciousness." *Stanford Encyclopedia of Philosophy*. https://plato.stanford.edu/.
Poecker, Tom, and Fred Fey, eds. *85 Joer an Der Kinnekswiss*. Ettlebruck: Print Solutions, 2017.
Pope, Thomas H. *The History of Newberry County, South Carolina*. 2 vols. Columbia: University of South Carolina Press, 1973.
Pressly, Nancy. *Settling the South Carolina Backcountry: The Pressly Family and Life along Hard Labor Creek*. Alpharetta, GA: Booklogix Publishers, 2016.
Raines, Howell. "A Mentor's Presence." *New York Times*, July 20, 1986.
———. *My Soul Is Rested: Movement Days in the Deep South Remembered*. New York: G. P. Putnam's Sons, 1977.
Rangell, Leo. "Aggression, Oedipus, and Historical Perspective." *International Journal of Psychoanalysis* 53 (January 1, 1972): 3–10.
———. *The Mind of Watergate: An Exploration into the Mind of Integrity*. New York: W. W. Norton, 1980.
"Recovery in the Cotton Belt." *Opportunity: The Journal of Negro Life* 12 (May 1934): 134.
Reed, John Shelton. *Dixie Bohemia: A French Quarter Circle in the 1920s*. Baton Rouge: Louisiana State University Press, 2012.

Reed, Linda. *Simple Decency and Common Sense: The Southern Conference Movement, 1938–1963.* Bloomington: Indiana University Press, 1991.
Reese, Krista. "The Uncommon Common Man." *Emory Magazine* 76, no. 4 (Winter 2001).
Remarque, Erich. *All Quiet on the Western Front.* Boston: Little, Brown, 1929.
"Renwick/Carlisle Home." *Newberry County Historical and Museum Society Bulletin* (Fall/Winter 2005): 9–19.
Report on the Economic Conditions of the South, The. Washington, DC: Government Printing Office, 1938.
Rex, John, and David Mason. *Theories of Race and Ethnic Relations.* Cambridge: Cambridge University Press, 1983.
Riley, Benjamin F. *History of Conecuh County, Alabama.* Columbus, GA: T. Gilbert Printer, 1881.
Roberts, Gene, and Hank Klibanoff. *The Race Beat: The Press, the Civil Rights Struggle and the Awakening of a Nation.* New York: Random House, 2006.
Rogers, William Warren, Robert David Ward, Leah Rawls Atkins, and Wayne Flynt. *Alabama: History of a Deep South State.* Tuscaloosa: University of Alabama Press, 2018.
Rose, Kenneth. *Myth and the Greatest Generation: A Social History of Americans and World War II.* New York: Routledge, 2012.
Rubin, Jennifer. "Nazi Analogies Are Dangerous. But They Are Increasingly Relevant Today." *Washington Post*, September 19, 2022.
Saint-Aubin-des-Préaux: Son Histoire. N.p.: La Fédération de la Manche des Retraites, 1990.
Salinger, J. D. *The Catcher in the Rye.* Boston: Little, Brown, 1951.
Salmond, John. *A Southern Rebel: The Life and Times of Aubrey Willis Williams, 1890–1965.* Chapel Hill: University of North Carolina Press, 1983.
Sami, Angelina. *Superior: The Return of Intellectual Racism.* Boston: Beacon Press, 2019.
"Samuel Laird" (1725–1821). Ancestry.com.
"Samuel Martin Englehardt, Jr." (1912–1991). Ancestry.com.
Saxon, Lyle. *Old Louisiana.* New York: Century Co., 1929.
Schlereth, Thomas J. *Victorian America: Transformations in Everyday Life, 1876–1915.* New York: HarperCollins, 1991.
Schlesinger, Arthur M., Jr. *Robert F. Kennedy and His Times.* New York: Houghton Mifflin, 1978.
Shackelford, Edward M. *First Fifty Years of the State Teachers College at Troy, Alabama, 1887–1937.* Montgomery: Paragon Press, 1937.
Shannon, Margaret. "Comeback of a Left-Out Rightist." *Atlanta Journal Constitution*, March 14, 1971.
Shell, Eddie Wayne. *Evolution of the Alabama Agroecosystem.* Montgomery: NewSouth Books, 2013.
Sheppard, Judith E. "Gould Beech." Encyclopediaofalabama.org.
Shi, David E., and George Brown Tindall. *America: A Narrative History.* 10th ed. New York: W. W. Norton, 2016.
Shirley, Craig. *Rendezvous with Destiny: Ronald Reagan and the Campaign That Changed America.* Wilmington, DE: Intercollegiate Studies Institute, 2009.

Shores, Elizabeth Findley. *Earline's Pink Party: The Social Rituals and Domestic Relics of a Southern Woman.* Tuscaloosa: University of Alabama Press, 2017.

Shouse, Sarah Newman. *Hillbilly Realist: Herman Clarence Nixon of Possum Trot.* Tuscaloosa: University of Alabama Press, 1986.

Siegal, Robert A., ed. *The Blackwell Companion to the Study of Religion.* Malden, MA: Blackwell, 2006.

Sims, George. *The Little Man's Big Man: James E. Folsom and Alabama Politics, 1946–1958.* Tuscaloosa: University of Alabama Press, 1985.

Singal, Daniel Joseph. *The War Within: From Victorian to Modernist Thought in the South, 1919–1945.* Chapel Hill: University of North Carolina Press, 1982.

Smith, Charles Bunyan. *Autobiography, Early Years: 1891–1938.* Troy, AL: By the Author, 1973.

———. *Troy State University.* Troy, AL: Troy State University Press, 1973.

Smith, Elson C. *New Dictionary of American Family Names.* New York: Harper and Brothers, 1973.

Smith, Lillian. *Killers of the Dream.* New York: W. W. Norton, 1949.

Snape, Michael. *God and Uncle Sam: Religion and American Armed Forces in World War I.* Rochester, NY: Boydell Press, 2015.

Snyder, Timothy. "The American Abyss." *New York Times,* January 9, 2021.

Sorbel, Robert. *The Origins of Interventionism: The United States and the Russo-Finnish War.* New York: Literary Licensing, 1960.

Sosna, Morton. *In Search of the Silent South: Southern Liberals and the Race Issue.* New York: Columbia University Press, 1977.

Southern Education Association. *A History of Private Schools and Race in the New South.* Southerneducation.org.

Spencer, Warren F. *The Confederate Navy in Europe.* Tuscaloosa: University of Alabama Press, 1983.

Stabler, Carey V. "The History of the Alabama Public Health System." PhD diss., Duke University, 1944.

Stanton, Mary. *Journey toward Justice: Juliette Hampton Morgan and the Montgomery Bus Boycott.* Athens: University of Georgia Press, 2006.

———. *Red Black White: The Alabama Communist Party, 1930–1950.* Athens: University of Georgia, Press, 2019.

"State of the States." *New South* 23 (Fall 1967): 81–110.

Stern, Sheldon N. "Review: John F. Kennedy and the Politics of Race and Civil Rights." *Reviews in American History* 35 (March 2007): 118–25.

Stevenson, Bryan. *Just Mercy: A Story of Mercy and Redemption.* New York: Random House, 2014.

Stribling, T. S. *The Forge.* Garden City, NY: Sun Dial Press, 1938.

———. *The Second Wagon.* New York: Doubleday, Doran, 1935.

———. *The Store.* New York: Doubleday, Doran, 1932.

Sullivan, Patricia. *Days of Hope: Race and Democracy in the New Deal Era.* Chapel Hill: University of North Carolina Press, 1996.

Tannenbaum, Frank. *Darker Phases of the South.* New York: G. P. Putnam's, 1924.

Taylor, William R. *Cavalier and Yankee: The Old South and American Character.* New York: G. Braziller, 1961.

Thomason, Michael V. R., ed. *Mobile: The New History of Alabama's First City*. Tuscaloosa: University of Alabama Press, 2001.
Thompson, Bailey. "Clarence Cason's Shade: A Look at Alabama Then and Now." *Alabama Heritage* 60 (Spring 2001): 20–27.
Thornton, J. Mills, III. *Dividing Lines: Municipal Politics and the Struggle for Civil Rights in Montgomery, Birmingham, and Selma*. Tuscaloosa: University of Alabama Press, 2002.
———. *Politics and Power in a Slave Society: Alabama, 1800–1860*. Baton Rouge: Louisiana State University Press, 1978.
Tindall, George B. *The Emergence of the New South, 1914–1945*. Baton Rouge: Louisiana State University Press, 1967.
Toulouse, Mark G. "Origins of the *Christian Century*, 1884–1914." *Christian Century* 117 (January 26, 2000): 83–88.
———. "Progress and Relapse." The *Century* and World War I." *Christian Century* 117 (March 8, 2000): 260–64.
———. "Socializing Capitalism: The *Century* during the Great Depression." *Christian Century* 117 (April 12, 2000): 415–18.
———. "'Unnecessary Necessity': The *Century* and World War II." *Christian Century* 17 (July 5–12, 2000): 725–29.
Tucker, Shawn R. *Virtues and Vices in the Arts*. Eugene, OR: Cascade Books, 2015.
Twelve Southerners. *I'll Take My Stand: The South and the Agrarian Tradition*. New York: Harper and Brothers, 1930.
US Congress. *Congressional Record*. 102nd Cong., 2nd Sess. January 23, 1992. Washington, DC: Government Printing Office,1992.
Vines, Howell. *This Green Thicket World*. Boston: Little, Brown, 1936.
Walter, Francis Xavier. *From Preaching to Meddling: A White Minister in the Civil Rights Movement*. Montgomery, AL: NewSouth Books, 2021.
Warren, Robert Penn. *All the King's Men*. New York: Harcourt, Brace, 1946.
Webb, Samuel L. *Two-Party Politics in the One-Party South: Alabama's Hill Country, 1874–1920*. Tuscaloosa: University of Alabama Press, 1997.
Webb, Samuel L., and Margaret E. Armbrester, eds. *Alabama Governors: A Political History of the State*. Tuscaloosa: University of Alabama Press, 2018.
Weiner, Jonathan. *Social Origins of the New South: Alabama, 1860–1885*. Baton Rouge: Louisiana State University Press, 1977.
Wertenbaker, Thomas J. *Patrician and Plebian in Virginia*. Charlottesville, VA: Michie Co., 1910.
West, Caroll Van. "Maryville College." Tennesseeencyclopedia.net.
West, Cornel. "The Dilemma of the Black Intellectual." *Cultural Critique* 1 (Autumn 1985): 109–24.
White, Steven. *World War II and American Racial Politics*. New York: Cambridge University Press, 2019.
Whitmire, Kyle. "How a Confederate Daughter Rewrote Alabama History for White Supremacy." *Mobile Register*, February 27, 2002.
Wiebe, Robert. *The Search for Order, 1877–1920*. New York: Hill and Wang, 1967.
Wiggins, Sarah Woolfolk. *The Scalawags in Alabama Politics, 1865–1881*. Tuscaloosa: University of Alabama Press, 1977.

Wilhoit Francis M. *The Politics of Massive Resistance.* New York: G. Braziller, 1973.
Wilkerson, Isabele. *Caste: The Origins of Our Discontents.* New York: Random House, 2020.
"William Patton Kennedy" (1837–1892). Ancestry.com.
Williams, Donnie, and Wayne Greenhaw. *The Thunder of Angels: The Montgomery Bus Boycott and the People Who Broke the Back of Jim Crow.* Chicago: Lawrence Hill Books, 2006.
Wilson, Charles Reagan. *Baptized in Blood: The Religion of the Lost Cause, 1865–1920.* Athens: University of Georgia Press, 1980.
Wilson, Sloan. *The Man in the Gray Flannel Suit.* New York: Simon and Schuster, 1955.
Wolfe, Thomas. "I Have a Thing to Tell You." *New Republic* 90 (March 10, 1937): 132–36.
———. *Look Homeward, Angel.* New York: Scribner's, 1929.
———. *You Can't Go Home Again.* New York: Harper and Bros., 1940.
Woodward, C. Vann. *Origins of the New South, 1877–1913.* Baton Rouge: Louisiana State University Press, 1951.
Wright, Gavin. *Old South, New South: Revolutions in the Southern Economy since the Civil War.* Baton Rouge: Louisiana State University Press, 1986.
———. *The Political Economy of the Cotton South.* New York: W. W. Norton, 1978.
Wright, Richard. *Black Boy.* New York: Harper and Brothers, 1945.
———. *Uncle Tom's Children.* New York: Harper and Brothers, 1938.
Wyatt-Brown, Bertram. *Honor and Violence in the Old South.* New York: Oxford University Press, 1986.
Wyley, David Ward. *Early History of Covington County, Alabama, 1821–1871.* Huntsville, AL: By the Author, 1976.
Wynn, Neil A. "The 'Good War': The Second World War and Postwar American Society." *Journal of Contemporary History* 31 (July 1996): 463–82.

Sources on the Scotch Irish
Applebaum, Yoni. "Trump and the Borderers." *The Atlantic* (April 6, 2016).
Blethen, H. Tyler, and Curtis W. Wood, Jr., eds. *Ulster and North America: Trans-Atlantic Perspectives on the Scotch Irish.* Tuscaloosa: University of Alabama Press, 1997.
Bolton, Charles Knowles. *Scotch-Irish Pioneers in Ulster and America.* Boston: Bacon and Brown, 1910.
Bunting, Jolene. "Ulster Scots for Trump." Undated [2020]. Donorbox.org.
Cassell, Grant. *Cassell's Old and New Edinburgh.* 2 vols. London: Cassell and Co., 1822.
Crozier, Alan. "The Scotch-Irish Influence on American English." *American Speech* 59 (Winter 1984): 310–31.
Dabbs, James McBride. *Who Speaks for the South.* New York: Funk and Wagnalls, 1964.
Directory of Scots Banished to American Plantations, 1650–1775. Baltimore: Clearfield Publishers, 1983.
Fischer, David Hackett. *Albion's Seed: Four British Folkways in America.* New York: Oxford University Press, 1989.
Ford, Henry Jones. *The Scotch-Irish in America.* Princeton: Princeton University Press, 1915.
Gilbert, Bill. *Westering Man: The Life of Joseph Walker.* Norman: University of Oklahoma Press, 1985.

Griffin, Patrick. *The People with No Name: Ireland's Ulster Scots, America's Scots Irish and the Creation of a British Atlantic World, 1689–1754*. Princeton: Princeton University Press, 2001.

Harkins, Anthony, and Jeredith McCarroll, eds. *Appalachian Reckoning: A Regional Response to Hillbilly Elegy*. Morgantown: West Virginia University Press, 2019.

Herman, Arthur. *How the Scots Invented the Modern World*. New York: Three Rivers Press, 2002.

Hofstra, Warren. *Ulster to America: The Scotch-Irish Immigration Experience*. Knoxville: University of Tennessee Press, 2012.

Joseph, Cameron. "The Scots-Irish Vote." *The Atlantic* (October 6, 2009).

Leyburn, James G. *The Scotch-Irish: A Social History*. Chapel Hill: University of North Carolina Press, 1962.

Love, Dane. *Scottish Covenanter Stories: Tales from the Killing Times*. Edinburgh: Neil Wilson Publishing, 2000.

McCarthy, Karen F. *The Other Irish*. New York: Fall River Press, 2014.

McKinty, Adrian. "The Psychopathology of Everyday Life: Donald Trump's Ulster Supporters." Blog post, February 12, 2016. Adrianmckinty.blogspot.com.

McTear, Ian. "Scotch-Irish Influence in American Democracy." September 16, 2018. Bbc.com.

Moffat, Alistair. *Scotland: A History from Earliest Times*. Edinburgh: Birlinn, 2017.

Nelson, Lynn A. "Historiographical Conversations about the Backcountry: Politics." *Journal of Backcountry Studies* 2 (Autumn 2007): 1–10.

Skinner, Constance L. *Pioneers of the Old Southwest*. New Haven: Yale University Press, 1919.

Stephenson, Jean. *Scotch-Irish Migration to South Carolina, 1772*. New York: ISHI Press International, 2013.

Vance, J. D. *Hillbilly Elegy: A Memoir of Family and Culture in Crisis*. New York: Harper, 2016.

Vann, Barry A. *In Search of the Ulster Scots: The Birth and Geotheological Imaginings of a Transatlantic People, 1603–1703*. Columbia: University of South Carolina Press, 2008.

Wallace, James. *Wallace-Bruce and Closely Related Families*. Northfield, MN: Mohn Print Co., 1930.

Webb, James. *Born Fighting: How the Scots-Irish Shaped America*. New York: Broadway Books, 2004.

White, William Allen. *Woodrow Wilson: The Man, His Times, His Task*. Boston: Houghton Mifflin, 1924.

Wilson, Woodrow. *Selected Literary and Political Papers and Addresses of Woodrow Wilson*. New York: Grosset and Dunlap, 1927.

Woodward, Collin. *American Nations: A History of the Eleven Rival Regional Cultures of North America*. New York: Penguin, 2012.

Yeager, Kevin L. "The Power of Culture: The Preservation of Scots-Irish Culture in the Eighteenth-Century American Backcountry." PhD diss., Louisiana State University, 2000.

Sources on Religion and the Associate Reformed Presbyterian Church (ARPC)

Ahlstrom, Sidney. *A Religious History of the American People*. New Haven: Yale University Press, 1972.

Allison, Leon McDill. *A Short History of the Associate Reformed Presbyterian Church*. [Greenville, SC]: The [ARP] Board of Christian Education, 1984.

———. "Sketch of Erskine Theological Seminary, 1951–1968." Typescript (1968). Erskine College Archives, McCain Library, Erskine College and Seminary, Due West, SC.

Alvis, Joel T., Jr. *Religion and Race: Southern Presbyterians, 1946–1983*. Tuscaloosa: University of Alabama Press, 1994.

Bailey, Kenneth K. *Southern White Protestantism in the Twentieth Century*. New York: Harper and Row, 1964.

Brueggmann, Walter, and David Hankins. *The Prophetic Tradition: The 40th Anniversary Edition*. Minneapolis: Fortress Press, 2018.

Bullock, Robert H, Jr. "Case Studies in Twentieth Century American Unitive Protestantism: The Problem of Church Union in the Presbyterian-Reformed Family, 1937–1958." PhD diss., Princeton University, 1974.

Burgess, David S. *Fighting for Social Justice: The Life Story of David Burgess*. Detroit: Wayne State University Press, 2000.

Chappell, David L. *A Stone of Hope: Prophetic Religion and the Death of Jim Crow*. Chapel Hill: University of North Carolina Press, 2004.

Clark, Walter Van. *A Christian Global Strategy*. Chicago: Willet, Clark, and Co., 1945.

Collins, Donald E. *When the Church Bells Rang Racist: The Methodist Church and the Civil Rights Movement in Alabama*. Macon, GA: Mercer University Press, 1998.

Dunbar, Anthony. *Against the Grain: Southern Radicals and Prophets, 1929–1959*. Charlottesville: University of Virginia Press, 1981.

Ferguson, Robert Hunt. *Remaking the Rural South: Inter-racialism, Christian Socialism, and Cooperative Farming in Jim Crow Mississippi South*. Athens: University of Georgia Press, 2018.

Flynt, J. Wayne. *Alabama Baptists: Southern Baptists in the Heart of Dixie*. Tuscaloosa: University of Alabama Press, 1988.

———. *Southern Religion and Christian Diversity in the Twentieth Century*. Tuscaloosa: University of Alabama Press, 2016.

Fox, Michael Wightman. *Reinhold Niebuhr: A Biography*. New York: Pantheon, 1985.

Harvey, Paul. *Christianity and Race in the American South*. Chicago: University of Chicago Press, 2018.

Hedges, Chris. *American Fascists: The Christian Right and the War on America*. New York: Free Press, 2007.

Hill, Samuel S., Jr. *Southern Churches in Crisis*. New York: Holt, Rinehart, and Winston, 1966.

———, ed. *Southern Religion*. Vol. 1 of *New Encyclopedia of Southern Culture*, ed. Charles Reagan Wilson. Chapel Hill: University of North Carolina Press, 2006.

Howie, John. "The Life of Mr. James Renwick." *Biographia Scoticana*. Edinburgh: S. Bryce, 1781.

Jones, Peter d'A. *Christian Socialist Revival*. Princeton: Princeton University Press, 1968.
Jones, Robert P. *White Too Long: The Legacy of White Supremacy in American Christianity*. New York: Simon and Schuster, 2020.
Kennedy, Renwick C. *History of the Associate Reformed Presbyterian Church of Camden, Alabama*. N.p., n.d. [1938].
King, Ray A. *A History of the Associate Reformed Presbyterian Church*. Charlotte, NC: Board of Christian Education of the Associate Reformed Presbyterian Church, 1966.
Lathan, Robert. *History of the Associate Reformed Synod of the South*. Harrisburg, PA: By the Author, 1882.
LeFevre, Perry Deyo. "The Chicago Theological Seminary: History and Christology in the Theology of Tillich, Morrison, and Reinhold Niebuhr." PhD diss., Chicago Theological Seminary, 1946.
Lippy, Charles E., and Peter W. Williams, eds. *Encyclopedia of the American Religious Experience*. 3 vols. New York: Charles Scribner's Sons, 1988.
Loetscher, Lefferts A. *The Broadening Church: A Study of Theological Issues in the Presbyterian Church since 1869*. Philadelphia: University of Pennsylvania Press, 1954.
Martin, Robert F. "Critique of Southern Society and Vision of a New Order: The Fellowship of Southern Churchmen, 1934–1957." *Church History* 52 (March 1983): 66–80.
———. *Howard Kester and the Struggle for Social Justice*. Charlottesville: University of Virginia Press, 1991.
McCune, Rolland D. "The Formation of the New Evangelism (Part One): Historical and Theological Antecedents." *Detroit Baptist Seminary Journal* 3 (Fall 1998): 3–34.
Minutes of the General Synod of the Associate Reformed Presbyterian Church: One Hundred and Thirty-Eighth Session, First Church Statesville, N.C., April 22–26, 1942. Greenville, SC: The Synod, 1942.
Moorhead, James H. *Princeton Seminary in American Religion and Culture*. Grand Rapids, MI: William B. Eerdmans, 2012.
Nicholas, William. *Go and Be Reconciled: Alabama Methodists Confront Racial Injustice, 1954–1974*. Montgomery: NewSouth Books, 2018.
Orr, Brian J. *Testimony of the Covenant*. 2010. Available online at Lulu.com.
Phillips, James David. *Faithful Servant: The Life and Times of J. McDowell Richards*. Franklin, TN: Providence House Publishers, 2004.
Pittendreich, Maynard. *History of Erskine Theological Seminary, 1837–1976*. N.p., 1981.
Posey, Walter Brownlow. *Development of Methodism in the Old Southwest*. Nashville, TN: Vanderbilt University Press, 1933.
———. *Frontier Mission: History of Religion West of the Southern Appalachians to 1861*. Lexington: University of Kentucky Press, 1966.
———. *Influence of Slavery upon the Methodist Church in the Early South and Southwest*. N.p., 1931.
———. *Presbyterian Church in the Old Southwest*. Louisville, KY: John Knox Press, 1952.
———. *Religious Strife on the Southern Frontier*. Baton Rouge: Louisiana State University Press, 1965.
Poteat, William H. "The Banality of Evil: Darkness at the Center." Unpublished lecture,

University of North Carolina, Charlotte, 1988. Copy in possession of Tennant McWilliams.
"Presbyterians Speed Integration." *Christian Century* 81 (May 13, 1964): 630–31.
Rian, Edwin H. *The Presbyterian Conflict*. New York: Garland, 1988.
Ruble, Randall T., ed. *Bicentennial History of the Associate Reformed Presbyterian Church, 1950–2003*. N.p.: General Synod, 2003.
Schweiger, Beth Barton. *The Gospel Working Up: Progress and Pulpit in Nineteenth Century Virginia*. New York: Oxford University Press, 2000.
Schweiger, Beth Barton, and Donald G. Mathews, eds. *Religion in the American South: Protestants and Others in History and Culture*. Chapel Hill: University of North Carolina Press, 2004.
Sesquicentennial History of the Associate Reformed Presbyterian Church. Clinton, SC: Jacobs Brothers, 1951.
Sheldon, Kennon M. "Comparing Catholics' and Protestants' Religious Motivations." *International Journal for the Psychology of Religion* 16 (November 26, 2009): 209–23.
Vaughn, J. Barry. *Bishops, Bourbons, and Big Mules: A History of the Episcopal Church in Alabama*. Tuscaloosa: University of Alabama Press, 2013.
Wacker, Grant. *America's Preacher: Billy Graham and the Shaping of a Nation*. Cambridge, MA: Belknap Press, 2014.
Ware, Lowry. *A Place Called Due West*. Columbia, SC: R. L. Bryan Co. for the Author, 1997.
Ware, Lowry, and James W. Gettys. *Second Century: A History of the Associate Reformed Presbyterians, 1882–1982*. Greenville, SC: Associate Reformed Presbyterian Center, 1982.
Wells, David F. *The Princeton Theology*. Grand Rapids, MI.: Baker Book House, 1989.
———. *Southern Reformed Theology*. Grand Rapids, MI: Baker Book House, 1989.
Whiting, Marvin Yeomans. *An Enduring Ministry: A Biography of Henry Morris Edmonds, 1878–1960*. Birmingham: William F. Edmonds and Joan McCoy Edmonds, 2007.

Sources on Wilcox County, Alabama, and the Black Belt

Abernethy, Thomas P. *The Formative Period in Alabama, 1815–1828*. Tuscaloosa: University of Alabama Press, 1990.
Adelman, Bob. *Down Home: Camden, Alabama*. New York: McGraw-Hill, 1972.
Alabama State Department of Education. *Annual Reports*. 1921–32.
Arnett, William, et al., eds. *Gee's Bend: The Women and Their Quilts*. Atlanta: Tinwood Books, 2002.
Blackwell, Cart. "Country Living." *Mobile Bay* 37 (October 2021): 50–57.
Bond, Horace Mann. *Negro Education in Alabama*. Washington, DC: Associated Publishers, 1939.
Bonner, Becky, comp. and ed. "Family Facts [Known to Joyce Carothers Jones]." Typescript (1967). Copy in possession of Tennant McWilliams.
Bonner, Jo[siah] Robins. "Lieutenant Joseph Morgan Wil[l]cox." *Wilcox Progressive Era*, May 17, 1934.
Boyd, Gregory A., comp and ed. *Family Maps of Wilcox County, Alabama, With Homesteads,*

Roads, Waterways, Towns, Cemeteries, Railroads and More. Norman, OK.: Arphax Publishing, 2010.

Brooks, Daniel Fate. "The Mind of Wilcox County: An Antebellum History, 1819–1861." MA thesis, Samford University, 1984.

Bullock, Robert J. "Trust Funds Wilcox Scholarships." *Selma Times Journal*, November 10, 2003.

Callahan, Nancy. *Freedom Quilting Bee.* Tuscaloosa: University of Alabama Press, 1987.

"Charles Tait" (1768–1835). Ancestry.com.

Cochran, John Perry. "James Asbury Tait and His Plantation." MA thesis, University of Alabama, 1951.

Cook, Alice Foster. "History of Camden and Wilcox County." *Wilcox Progressive Era*, March 15, 22, 1934.

Davis, Charles S. *The Cotton Kingdom in Alabama.* Montgomery: Alabama State Department of Archives and History, 1939.

"Della McDuffie Case." Civil Rights and Restorative Justice Project, School of Law, Northeastern University, Boston.

Edwards, William J. *Twenty-Five Years in the Black Belt.* Tuscaloosa: University of Alabama Press, 1993.

"Elizabeth Martha Harriss Jones" (1825–1895). Ancestry.com.

"Ephraim Ockles Rentz" (1847–1924). Ancestry.com.

Fisk, Glenn Nolan. "Alabama Black Belt: A Social History, 1875–1917." PhD diss., Duke University, 1951.

Fleming, Cynthia Griggs. *In the Shadow of Selma: The Continuing Struggle for Civil Rights in the Rural South.* Lanham, MD: Rowman and Littlefield, 2004.

Hale, Jennifer. *Historic Plantations of Alabama's Black Belt.* Charleston, SC: History Press, 2009.

Halloran, Delynn Jenkins. *Lummie Jenkins: The Unarmed Sheriff of Wilcox County.* N.p.: By the Author, 2008.

Harper, Roland. *Resources of Southern Alabama.* Tuscaloosa: Geological Survey of Alabama, 1920.

———. "Some Relations between Soil, Climate and Civilization in the Southern Red Hills of Alabama." *South Atlantic Quarterly* 19 (July 1920): 201–15.

Henderson, Aileen Kilgore. *Eugene Allen Smith's Alabama: How a Geologist Shaped a State.* Tuscaloosa: University of Alabama Press, 2011.

Heritage of Wilcox County, Alabama. Clanton, AL: Heritage Publishing Co., 2002.

"History of St. Joseph's Catholic Church [of Camden]." Undated typescript. Copy in possession of Tennant McWilliams.

Hollingsworth, J. Selwyn. *Changes in the Population of Alabama Black Belt, 1890 to 1990.* Montgomery: Center for Demographic and Cultural Research, Auburn University at Montgomery, 1993.

Jackson, Harvey H., III. "How Marie Bankhead Owen Almost Killed the W.P.A. *Guide for Alabama.*" *Alabama Heritage* 56 (Spring 2000): 26–34.

———. *Rivers of History: Life on the Coosa, Tallapoosa, Cahaba, and Alabama.* Tuscaloosa: University of Alabama Press, 1995.

"Jessie Taylor Bonner Jones" (1869–1926). Ancestry.com.

"John Miller Bonner" (1878–1968). Ancestry.com.
Jones, Joyce Carothers. *Bethel ARP Church—Oak Hill, Alabama: Its Houses and People, 1856–1978*. Oak Hill, AL: Bethel Associate Reformed Presbyterian Church, 1978.
———. *Bethel's Shadow*. Oak Hill, AL: Bethel Associate Reformed Presbyterian Church, 1979.
Jordon, Weymouth T. *Ante-Bellum Alabama: Town and Country*. Tallahassee: Florida State University. 1957.
"Joseph Morgan Wil[l]cox" (1790–1814). Ancestry.com.
"Joshua B. Grace" (1802–1875). Ancestry.com.
"Joyce Clopton Carothers Jones" (1900–1980). Ancestry.com.
"Joyce Harriss Carothers" (1848–1907). Ancestry.com.
"Justice Smith Jones" (1884–1962). Ancestry.com.
Kennedy, Renwick C. "Alabama Black Belt." *Alabama Historical Quarterly* 2 (Fall 1940): 282–89.
———. "Black Belt Aristocrats." *Social Forces* 13 (October 1934): 81–85.
———. *Camden's Centennial Year*. Camden, AL: Wilcox Progressive Era, 1933.
———. "Life at Gee's Bend." *Christian Century* 54 (September 1, 1937): 1072–75.
———. "Rehabilitation: Alabama Version." *Christian Century* 51 (November 14, 1934): 1455–57.
———. "Roosevelt's Tenants." *Christian Century* 52 (May 8, 1935): 608–10.
———. "Scottsboro's Shadow." *Christian Century* 52 (May 1935): 476–78.
Lacefield, Jim. *The Lost Worlds in Alabama Rocks: A Guide to the State's Ancient Life and Landscapes*. Tuscaloosa: Alabama Museum of Natural History, 2013.
Liddell, Viola [Jefferson Goode]. *Grass Widow: Making My Way in Depression Alabama*. Tuscaloosa: University of Alabama Press, 2004.
———. *A Place of Springs*. Tuscaloosa: University of Alabama Press, 1982.
———. *With a Southern Accent*. Norman: University of Oklahoma Press, 1948.
Liddell, Will L., and Ruth H. Liddell, eds. *Collected [Short] Works of Viola Jefferson Goode Liddell, 1901–1998*. N.p., 2003.
———. Camden Cemetery Survey. Typescript (2014). In possession of Tennant McWilliams.
"[Martin] Van Buren Jones" (1878–1934). Ancestry.com.
Marvar, Alexandra. "The Two Faces of Lummie Jenkins." *Topic* 17 (November 2018). Topic.com.
McCall, Jeannette Steele. *The First and Last Bell: A Story of Six Missions for Blacks in Wilcox County, Alabama*. Baltimore: American Literary Press, 2005.
McCarty, Clinton. *Reins of Power: Racial Change and Challenge in a Southern Community*. Tallahassee: Sentry Press, 1999.
McDonald, Robin, and Valerie Pope Burns. *Visions of the Black Belt: A Cultural Survey of the Heart of Alabama*. Tuscaloosa: University of Alabama Press, 2015.
McWilliams, Tennant. "Viola Jefferson Goode Liddell and the Wilcox Roundtable." *Alabama Heritage* 122 (Fall 2006): 40–49.
"Memorial Bell Tower Dedicated in Wilcox County." *Birmingham Presbyterian* 14 (September 1987): 1.

Moffat, Charles Hill. "The Life of Charles Tait." PhD diss., Vanderbilt University, 1946.
Moore, Andrew, and Madison Smartt Bell. *Blue Alabama*. Bologna: Damiana, 2019.
Palmer, William Bradley. *A History of Furman, Snow Hill and Ackerville*. Birmingham: Birmingham Public Library, 1977.
Peacock, Evan, and Timothy Shauwecker, eds. *Blackland Prairies of the Gulf Coastal Plain*. Tuscaloosa: University of Alabama Press, 2003.
Pettway, Tinnie. *Gee's Bend Experiment: Poems and Tidbits about Life*. N.p. [Cropwell, AL], 2008.
Phillips, Cabell. "Camden, Alabama: A Case History." *New York Times*, August 28, 1949.
"Portrait of an Alabamian—'Rugged Oak of Wilcox.'" *Alabama* (March 8, 1937), 8–10.
Prescott, Darrell. "Benign Neglect in Wilcox County, Alabama." *Harvard Crimson* (December 4, 1970).
"Retired Sheriff of 32 Years, Sheriff Arnold." WilcoxCountySheriff.com.
"Richebourg Gaillard McWilliams" (1901–1985). Ancestry.com.
"Robert Lee Rentz" (1864–1932). Ancestry.com.
Rubin, Morton. *Plantation County*. Chapel Hill: University of North Carolina Press, 1951.
"Samuel Swift Boykin" (1868–1939). Ancestry.com.
Sisk, Glenn Nolan. "Alabama Black Belt: A Social History, 1875–1915." PhD diss., Duke University, 1951.
———. "Negro Migration in the Alabama Black Belt, 1895–1917." *Journal of Negro History* 17 (November 1953): 32–39.
Smith, Robert A., and Frances Donald Dudley. "A History of Pine Apple, Wilcox County." Typescript (1990). In possession of Tennant McWilliams.
"Solomon Boykin" (1742–1821). Ancestry.com.
Stanton, Mary. "Coming of Age in Gee's Bend." *Alabama Heritage* 114 (Fall 2014): 36–43.
Stone, Donald P. *The Fallen Prince: William J. Edwards, Black Education, and the Quest for Afro American Identity*. Snow Hill, AL: Snow Hill Press, 1989.
Stone, Olive Matthews. "Agrarian Conflict in Alabama: Sections, Races, and Classes in a Rural State, 1800–1938." PhD diss., University of North Carolina, 1939.
"Swene [Sevne] McIntosh" (1745–1827). Ancestry.com.
Tellos, Allen. "The Black Belt." *Southern Spaces* (April 19, 2004). Southernspaces.org.
Tompkins, Alma Cole. "Charles Tait." Typescript (1910). Auburn University Library, Auburn, AL.
Tower, J. Allen. "Changing Black Belt—A Geographical View." *Journal of the Alabama Academy of Sciences* 32 (January 1961): 479–84.
University of Virginia Extension Division. *Up from the Bottom: A Rehabilitation Program Pays Off at Gee's Bend*. Charlottesville: University of Virginia, 1949.
Walker, Amanda. "Tears and Laughter: Who Was Roland Cooper?" *West Alabama Watchman*, April 30, 2016.
Wilcox, Reynold Webb. *The Descendants of William Wilcoxson, Vincent Meigs, and Richard Webb*. Boston: New England Genealogical Society, 1998.
"Wilcoxon." Ancestry.com.
"William Junius Jones" (1895–1984). Ancestry.com.
Williamson, Betty Dale. "Hamburg Cemetery." Typescript (1970). Copy in possession of Tennant McWilliams.

———. "History of Bethel Church." Typescript (1982). Copy in possession of Tennant McWilliams.
Wimberly, Ronald C., and Libby V. Morris. *The Southern Black Belt: A National Perspective*. Lexington, KY: TVA Rural Studies, 1997.
Windham, Kathryn Tucker. "They Call It Gee's Bend." Undated typescript. Copies in Wilcox County Public Library, Camden, AL, and in Division of Archives and Manuscripts, Birmingham Public Library, Birmingham.
Woodson, Ouida Starr. *Men of Wilcox: They Wore Gray*. Camden, AL: O. S. Woodson, 1989.
———. "A [Partial] List of the Sheriffs of Wilcox County." Undated typescript in possession of Tennant McWilliams.
———. *Within the Bend: Stories of Wilcox*. Camden, AL: O. S. Woodson, 1989.
Young, Rosa. *Light in the Dark Belt: The Story of Rosa Young as Told by Herself*. Rev. ed. St. Louis: Concordia Publishing House, 2014.

INDEX

Abbeville County, South Carolina, 53–58, 302
Abernathy, Ralph, 302
Absalom, Absalom! (Faulkner), 123
Adams, Ralph, 330–37, 354–55
Adjusted Compensation Act, 168
A Doll's House (Ibsen), 362
Aeschylus, 26, 36, 346, 362, 380
Agricultural Adjustment Act, 167
Agricultural Marketing Act, 129
Ahoghill (Dervock, County Antrim, Ulster Ireland), 14
Alabama, 221, 284
Alabama, The (war ship), 303
"Alabama Book Toasters" (Kennedy), 292
Alabama College, 288, 301, 308, 337, 410n19. *See also* University of Montevallo
Alabama Democratic Party, 281–82, 310, 326
"Alabama Dilemma" (Kennedy), 161
Alabama Education Association, 278–79, 282, 286–87, 298, 310–11, 316, 326, 352
"Alabama Feels Mr. Hoover's Prosperity" (Kennedy), 125
Alabama Historical Quarterly, The, 188
Alabama Polytechnic Institute (Auburn University), 285; Extension Service, 127; Social Work department, 252
Alabama Power Company, 143, 201. *See also* Martin, Thomas W.; Wilson, Massey
Alabama State College, 302, 333
Alabama State Teachers Association, 352
Alabama State University, 329, 361
"Alas, Poor Yorick" (Kennedy), 191
Alberta, Alabama, 131
Albritton, Daniel ("Dee"), 323–24
Albritton, Jesse ("Tuck") McDaniel, 148
Albritton, Lee, 180

Albritton, Lena Tucker Miller, 148, 305, 323, 365, 374
Albritton, Reginald, 171, 180, 347, 360
Alexander, Will, 121
Alexander City Schools, 283
Alford, George, family, 91
Allen, James B., 334
Allen, Joe, 95, 374
Allenton, Alabama, 50, 54, 345
All Quiet on the Western Front (Remarque), 92
All the King's Men (Warren), 238
American Association of University Professors, 334
American Dilemma, The (Myrdal), 243–44, 289
American Epoch (Odom), 147
American Independent Party, 332
American Legion. *See* Kennedy, Renwick Carlisle (RCK): social concerns
Andalusia, Alabama, 67, 174, 287, 291
Anderson, Betty, xii
Andrews, Bill Glenn, 326
Andrews, George, 326
animal rights. *See* Kennedy, Renwick Carlisle (RCK): social concerns
Anna Karenina (Tolstoy), 361
Anniston Star, 182, 245, 279, 292
anti-Christ, 204, 372
Antioch Baptist Church (Camden, Alabama), 13, 95
Apple, R. W., 346–47
"Aristocracy of the Kingdom of God," 119, 374
Armistice Day, 152, 164
Armstrong, Sarah Brice, 255
Arnold, Prince, 361
ARP (Associate Reformed Presbyterian). *See individual Associate Reformed churches/ synods*
Asbury, Francis, 180

Associate Reformed Presbyterian, The, 41, 58, 187
Associate Reformed Presbyterian Synod [of the South], 19, 56, 115–17, 187, 193, 338–40, 372
Associate Reformed Presbyterian Synod of North America, 13
Athens City Schools, 283
Athens College, 329, 337
Atlanta Journal, 204
Atlanta Journal-Constitution, 354
Atlantic Charter, 263
Atlantic Monthly, 305
Atmore, Alabama, 274, 360
Ausley, Margaret Kennedy, 278, 363, 368
Ausley, Wilbur, 296, 315
Austin, Peggy, 291
Away Down South (Cobb), 81

Baker v. Carr (1962), 307, 348
Ballard, Martha Jane, 272
Bankhead, John H., II, 171, 191
Bankhead-Jones Act, 142–43, 150
Bank of Camden, 94–95, 319–20
Bank of Pine Apple, 272–73, 316, 340–41, 367, 452n18
Barbour, James, 48
Barbour County, Alabama, 285, 298, 330
Barbourville, Alabama, 44, 48
Barker, William A., 272
Barrett, Gilmer, 287
Barth, Karl, 35
Bartow (Florida) ARP Church, 27
Baruch, Bernard, 43
Bass, S. Jonathan, xii, 186, 423n33, 451n15
Battle of Bastogne, 212–13
Battle of Blakeley, 51
Battle of Brest, 211
Battle of Britain, 195
Battle of Saint-Lô, 210
Battle of the Bulge, 215–16, 308
Baxley, Bill, 357
Beard, Charles, 118, 278, 348
Beard, Mary, 118
Beasley, Jere, 357
Béchy, France, 219
Beck, Charlotte ("Lottie") Vass Tait, 89–92, 94–95, 102, 104, 109–10, 122

Beck, Franklin King, 48, 70, 90
Beck, James Tait, 109
Beck, Martha Jefferson Tait, 90
Beck, Mary Tait, 109
Beck, William Rufus King, 109
Beech, Gould, 149, 245–47, 308
"Before the Doctor Comes" (Kennedy), 144
Behavioralism (Watson), 148–49
behavioralism, 372
Bell, B. Clayton, 304
Bell, Charles R., Jr., 185–86
Bell, John, 275
Bendorff, Patrick, 172
Bennett, J. Jefferson, 288, 300–301, 308–10, 331, 336, 354–55, 377
Bergen-Belsen Concentration Camp, 211
Bermuda, Alabama, 363
Berry, Edward Walker, 154
Beth Eden (South Carolina), 15–22
Bethel ARP Church (Oak Hill, Alabama), 7–8, 51–67, 79, 98, 116–17, 205–6, 266, 274, 296, 311, 338, 344, 357, 361, 374, 439n21
Bethel ARP Church (Ora, South Carolina), 21, 33, 338
Better Homes and Gardens, 242
"Big World Reaches Gee's Bend, The" (Graves), 170–71
Bilbo, Theodore, 246
"Bill Dickens" (Kennedy), 135
Billingsley, Orzell, 342
Bindel, Bleuette, 212
"Bird Hunt" (Kennedy), 177
Birmingham City Schools, 321
Birmingham News, The, 170, 188, 279
Birmingham-Southern College, 278, 330, 337
Black Belt: geologic, 4; as an idea, 149. *See also* Kennedy, Renwick Carlisle (RCK): social concerns
"Black Belt Aristocrats" (Kennedy), 145, 245
Black Belt–Big Mule Axis, 152, 254, 279, 281, 284, 287, 300, 302, 306–7, 311, 330
"Black Belt Mainstreetism," 82
"Black Belt Today, The" (Kennedy), 187–88
Black's Bluff, Alabama, 52, 65, 104
Blakley, Ralph, 26, 28
Blanchard, Charles, 176
Blevin, Bruce, 136

Index

Blood of the Liberals, The (Packer), 379
Bogie, John ("Jack") Henry, 253–54, 274, 365–66, 376
Bolton, Charles Knowles, 12, 102
Bonclarken Conference Center, 244, 296, 339
Bonner, Annie Brice, 305
Bonner, Becky, 363, 367
Bonner, Ernest, 66, 84, 91, 108, 110, 154
Bonner, James, 315–16, 360
Bonner, James (early Alabama settler), 53–54
Bonner, Jane Elizabeth ("Elise"), 66–71, 85–93. *See also* Hickey, Elise Bonner
Bonner, Jo, 360
Bonner, John Miller, 54, 76, 98–110, 154, 162, 185, 206, 250–61, 279–82, 294–311
Bonner, Jo Robins, 304–5, 360
Bonner, Judy, 360
Bonner, Marlowe, 65–66
Bonner, Martha, 53
Bonner, Mary Larid, 53
Bonner, Mrs. William Joel, 95
Bonner, Patricia, 353
Bonner, Peggy, 53
Bonner, Roy, 314
Bonner, Samuel, 54
Bonner, William, 54
Bonner, William Joel, 55, 80, 94–95, 104
"Bookkeeping" (Kennedy), 140–42
Boston, Massachusetts, 65, 249–50
Boswell Amendment, 22, 253, 435
Bourbon Democrats, 306–7, 314
Boyce, William, 206
Boyd, Andrew ("Pat") Love, 286–87
Boyd, George Robert, 329, 332
Boykin, Matt ("Nannie") McWilliams, 2–3, 182
Boykin, Samuel Swift, 2–3, 80, 83, 85, 138, 182, 390, 402n13
Boynton, Myron, 122
"Brass Hats" (Kennedy), 242
Brewer, Albert, 349
Brewton, Alabama, 115
Brideshead Revisited (Waugh), 364
Bridgeport Landing, 52
Bridges, Edwin C., xi
Brinkley, David, 321
Brinkmeyer, Robert, 194, 378, 389n1

British Borderlands, 12, 46, 359, 372, 376–77
Broad River Group, 46, 54
Bromley, Flora James, 214
Brooks, Daniel Fate, 44
Browder v. Gayle (1956), 300
Brown, John, 317
Brown, Lonnie, 342
Brown, Marion, 222
Browning, Robert, 85
Brown v. Board of Education (1954, 1955), 280, 282, 285–86, 288–89, 295, 342
Bruce, William L., 107
Brundage, Alabama, 278
Brussels, Belgium, 213
Bryan, John, 283
Bryant, Paul ("Bear"), 364
Bryson College, 248
Buchanan, John, 326
Buchenwald Concentration Camp, 221
Bufford, Charles Lee, 360–61
"Bug Juice," 209, 213–14, 221, 223, 240, 372, 380
Bullet Park (Heller), 353
Bullock, Robert, xii
Bullock County, Alabama, 28–82, 285
Bunche, Ralph, 329
Burden, Jack, 238
Burford, Peyton, 251
Burford family, 148
Burl, Alabama, 84
Burnt Corn, Alabama, 53
Bush, George Herbert Walker, 366
Butler County, Alabama, 170
But Now I See (Hobson), 76
Butts, Thomas Lane, 363–64
Buzhardt, John H., 116
"By-Product of War" (Kennedy), 202–3

Cabell, Phillip, 268–70
Caldwell, Erskine, 26, 157, 169
Caldwell, John Daniel, 49
Caldwell, Sylvester, 26
Calhoun, John C., 16, 276–77, 371
Calhoun, Walter, 342
Calhoun Colored School, 78
Calvin, John, 83–84
"Camden, Alabama: A Case Study" (Cabell), 268–71

Camden, Alabama: general history. *See* Kennedy, Renwick Carlisle (RCK): social concerns; Wilcox County
Camden Academy, 163, 341
Camden ARP Church, 55–65, 77, 95, 176, 187, 201, 238, 249–68, 280, 323, 408n3, 458n20
Camden Bank, 106
Camden Baptist Church, 69–71, 73, 97, 106, 185, 259
Camden Book Club, 361
Camden Cemetery, 268, 369–70
Camden Centennial Celebration (Kennedy), 176
Camden Culture Club, 77, 101
Camden Exchange Cub, 203–4
Camden Methodist Church, 254
Camden National Bank, 154, 201, 248, 273, 294
Camden Presbyterian Church, 10, 132–33, 185, 201, 241, 252, 274, 303
Campbell, C. A., 133
Campbell, Will, 270
Camp Hill, Alabama, 136
Cannon's Creek (South Carolina) ARP Church, 14
Canterbury Tales, The (Chaucer), 123
"Can the Christian Faith Work on a Seven Day a Week Basis?" (Kennedy), 246
Canton Bend, Alabama, 47–48, 122
"Capsule History of Troy State University, A" (Kennedy), 355
"captive theology," 117, 413n35
Carlisle, Catherine ("Kittie") Peacock Teal, 16
Carlisle, Coleman Thomas, 15–17
Carlisle, Emma Elizabeth Renwick, 21–22, 72, 91
Carlisle, England, 15–16
Carlisle, Hubert, 22, 72, 91
Carlisle, Mary Emma, 17. *See also* Kennedy, Mary Emma Carlisle
Carlisle, Thomas Coleman, 17, 20
Carlowville, Alabama, 78, 186
Carmack, W. A., 178
Carmichael, Oliver, 288, 308
Carnegie, Andrew, 252
Carothers, Edward ("Edgar") Sadler, 85, 138, 152, 158, 276–77

Carothers, Robert ("Fitz") Russell, Jr., 85
Carothers family, 25
Carter, Dan T., xii, 156, 288, 352–53, 459n2
Carter, Jimmy, 358
Carter, P. E., 283
Cash, Wilbur J., 169, 192, 194, 202, 373, 376
Cason, Clarence, 152, 157–61, 185, 194, 276, 418n47
Catch-22 (Heller), 353
Catcher in the Rye (Salinger), 296
Catherine, Alabama, 122, 131, 259
Catherine the Great (Troyat), 364
Catholicism. *See* Boykin, Samuel Swift; Kennedy, Renwick Carlisle (RCK): social concerns; McKelvey, Connie; Purdue, Marian; Wilcox County: presidential elections of 1928 and 1960; Winters, John Albert
Cavalier Myth, The, 81, 119, 126, 146, 149
Cease Firing (Johnston), 22
Cecil, Sir Robert, 43
Charlotte, North Carolina, 42, 56, 59, 65, 72, 88
Chase City, Virginia, 162
Château de Roumont, 213–14, 221
Château de Trébodennic, 211
Chaucer, Geoffrey, 123
Chautauqua, 33–34, 78, 85
Chester County, South Carolina, 55
Chestnutt, John Calvin, 303
Chilahatchee Creek, 44
Childers, James Saxon, 160, 169
Chilton County, Alabama, 101
Choctaws, 122
Christian Century, The, 5, 36, 58, 112, 125, 134–39, 142–44, 149–56, 161–62, 168–69, 170–71, 176–79, 184–88, 196, 198, 203, 214, 241–42, 259, 272, 289, 292, 296, 312, 388
"Christian Fascism," 1
Christianity and Liberalism (Machen), 31
Christian Science Monitor, The, 257–58
Christian Socialism. *See* Kennedy, Renwick Carlisle (RCK): personal and career
Christian Strategy for the Global World, A (Clark), 243
"Christmas Sermon, 1943" (Kennedy), 323

Index

"Church and the War, The" (Kennedy), 204–5, 212, 223
"Church Looks at Itself, The" (Kennedy), 338
Citadel, The, 16
Civilian Conservation Corps, 138, 143, 153
Civil Work Administration, 142, 150–51
Civitan Clubs, 287
Clark, Jim, 340
Clarke, Erskine, xii
Class Reunion (Jaffe), 362
"Clean Feet" (Kennedy), 169
Clemson College, 25
Clifton Ferry, 110
Clio High School, 352
"Clover Belt," 145–46
"Coat" (Kennedy), 203
Cobb, James, 81, 190, 391n8, 402n13, 427n19
Cochran, Bess, 70–71, 107
Cochran, Samuel G., 70
Cochran, Sara Louisa ("Lou"), 70
Cochran, Thomas L., 107
Cold War, 219
Cole, Houston, 301
Coleman, James P., 312
Coleman, Tom, 342
Colonial Williamsburg, 345
Columbia Theological Seminary, 186, 199, 253, 304, 337, 357
Columbia University, 95, 170, 343
Columbia University Teachers College, 3, 36, 284
"Comeback of a Left-Out Rightest" (Shannon), 354
Committee of 100 Fundamentalists, 204
communists, 245, 315–16
Company K (March), 192
Conecuh County, Alabama, 135, 170
Connor, Eugene ("Bull"), 320, 340
"Conqueror, The" (Kennedy), 240–41, 245
"Conscious Minority," 1
Cook, Daniel G., 162
Cook, Mrs. Arnold, 77
Cooper, Roland, 266, 269, 279, 281, 286, 287, 300, 310, 314–18, 330, 349, 360–61
Coppée, Baron Evence von, 213
"Cotton Kingdom, The: 1931," 127

Cotton Snobs, 118, 146, 152. *See also* Kennedy, Renwick Carlisle (RCK): social concerns (white upper class)
Couch, William Terry, 147, 16
Counts, George, 278
Courthouse, Alabama, 48–49
COVID-19, 373
Covington County, Alabama, 67–68, 78, 93, 95, 99, 173–75, 285
Coy, Alabama, 81
"Cracker Boy's Vote, The" (Kennedy), 260
Craft, Margaret, 291
Craig Air Force Field, 200
Creeks, 122
Creek Wars, 47, 50
"Creeping Fascism," 1
"Cremation" (Kennedy), 134–35
crippled children (of Camden), 254
Croc, Christine, 211
Croc, Louis, 211
Crooks, Roy, 221
Cross Keys, Alabama, 280
Crucial Decade, The (Goldman), 241
Crumpler, Yvonne, xii
Cuban Missile Crisis, 319
Cullman City Schools, 283
Culp, Delos P., 301
Culture in the South (Couch), 147
Cumberland Presbyterian Church (Camden, Alabama), 55
Curtis, Monette, 76, 184, 422n30

Dabbs, Charles McBride, 84–85, 270
Dachau Concentration Camp, 222–23, 231
Dale, Frank, 8
Dale, Hugh, 56, 61, 266, 365
Dale, Hugh, Jr., 365
Dale, Jane Shelton, 314, 365
Dale, John Taylor, 66
Dale, Margaret, 363
Dale family, 25, 43, 54
Dallas County, Alabama, 78, 182, 252, 280, 328
Danforth, William H., 266
Daniel, Pete, 199, 421n19
Daniels, Jonathan, 342
Dannelly, William J., 360
Darlington, Alabama, 54

Darwin, Charles, 30, 36
Davis, John D., 31–32
Davis, Thomas Winton, xii
D-Day, 210
Dean, Bonnie, 353. *See also* Mitchell, Bonne Dean
Debs, Eugene V., 35, 135, 282
"December 7, 1941" (Kennedy), 199
Deen's Memorial ARP Church (Red Level, Alabama), 67
Dees, Morris, 334
De Graffenreid, Ryan, 326
DeKalb County, Alabama, 154
Delta, Alabama, 218
Democratic National Convention (1948), 298
Democratic Party, 258, 260–61. *See also* Kennedy, Renwick Carlisle (RCK): social concerns (Democratic Party leaders)
Demopolis, Alabama, 278
Denny, George, 152
Dent, Alice, 334
Depression. *See* Wilcox County
Der Fuehrer (Heiden), 223
Dew, Duncan, 131
Dewey, Thomas E., 260–61
Dexter, Frank, 86, 115
Dexter family, 148
Dickens, Charles, 90, 409n15
Dickey, Gary, 334, 354
Dickinson, Lawrence Edward ("Dickie"), 221, 274
Dickinson, Lee, 365
Dickinson, Mary Conway Kennedy, 274, 360, 362–70, 380. *See also* Kennedy, Mary Conway
Dietrich, Marlene, 219
Dixiecrat movement, 261
Dixon, Frank, 279
Dobbins, Charles, 115, 186, 247, 279, 287, 306, 365, 403n14, 418n43
Dobbins, John G., 69, 97–98
Dodge, Cleveland, 43
"Dog Boy," 181
Dole, Robert, 358
Dothan, Alabama, 287
Doubleday, Doran, 183–84
Draughon, Ralph, 288, 292, 301

"Dry Forks" (home), 46
Dr. Zhivago (Pasternack), 361–62
DuBois, W. E. B., 257
Duck, Tommy, 291
Dudley, Harold J., 186
Due West, South Carolina, 16, 18, 187
Due West Female Institute, 15, 17
Duke University, 164
Dulles, John Foster, 243, 296
Dunn, Ervin, 154
Dunn, Joe, 85
Dunn, Thomas, 48, 55
Dunn family, 25
Durant, Will, 299
Durr, Clifford, 294
Durr, Virginia, 294

Eastland, James, 312
Easy Rider (film), 353
ecumenicalism. *See* Kennedy, Renwick Carlisle (RCK): social concerns
"Ecumenity at the Grass Roots" (Kennedy), 258–59
Edgar, Walter B., xii
Edgecombe County, North Carolina, 16
Edict of Nantes, 35
Edmonds, Henry, 116, 147, 149, 185
Edmund Pettus Bridge, 340, 362
Edwards, Jack, 326
Edwards, William J., 178, 343
Eggleston, Ralph, 341
Eisenhower, Dwight D., 276, 294, 296, 311
Elba, Alabama, 287
Elite, The (restaurant), 206, 308
Elizabethton, Tennessee, 209, 224
Elk Valley ARP Church (Fayetteville, Tennessee), 21
Ellison, Tom, 291
Elmer Gantry (Lewis), 87
Elmore County, Alabama, 280
Elsberry (Missouri) ARP Church, 28–29
Emory University, 133, 299
Englehardt, John, 279
Englehardt, Samuel Martin, 280
Englehardt, Samuel Martin, Jr., 280–81, 286–87, 294, 298, 301–7, 309–12
Englehardt, Sara Bonner, 309
English Teacher, The, 274

"Episode in Alabama" (Kennedy), 172–73
Erdman, Charles R., 30, 32–33, 38, 207
Erickson, Amy, 210, 364
Erskiana, The, 26
Erskine College, 15, 19, 55, 95, 157, 187, 296, 314, 336–69
Erskine Theological Seminary, 17, 55, 336–39
Ervin, Hugh, 148, 184, 261, 272, 274, 298–99, 306, 313
Ervin, Samuel J., Jr., 274
Ervin, Sarah Tait, 97
Ervin, Susan Cherry, 241
Escambia County, Alabama, 285
Ettelbruck Agricultural College, 214
Eubanks, Bucknell, 258
Eufaula, Alabama, 287
Eufaula City Schools, 283
Euripides, 26
Evers, Medgar, 320
Exchange Club of Camden, 251
Extension Service, of Alabama Polytechnic Institute. *See* Alabama Polytechnic Institute

"Face of the Poor" (Kennedy), 136–38
Faerie Queene, The (Spenser), 7
Fail, Jeremiah, 52
Fails, John, 104
Fair Employment Practice's Commission, 260
"Fairy Story" (Kennedy), 153, 157
Falkenberry, Bettie Lou Albritton, 364
Farish, Hunter, 65, 345
Farish family, 345
Farm Bureau, 150, 171, 279
Farm Credit Administration, 139
Farmers and Merchants Bank (Troy, Alabama), 287
Farm Security Administration, 178, 259
"Fascism-Southern Style" (Cason), 194
"Father Was a Family Man" (Liddell), 257
Faulkner, William, 90, 123, 169, 207, 271–72, 296, 353
Fayetteville, Tennessee, 59, 328
Federal Emergency Relief Act, 142
Federal Land Bank, 139
Feldman, Glenn, 77

Fellowship of Christian Churchmen, 121
Fellowship of Christian Socialists, 35
Fellowship of Southern Churchmen, 270, 377
feuding, 102, 105, 109, 111, 113, 180, 190, 181, 191, 410n20, 410nn23–24
Fey, Fred, xii
Field, Blake, 65
Field, Blake, Jr., 314
Field, Marlow Bonner, 245
Field, Marshall, 65, 245
Fifth Column and the First Nine Stories, The (Hemingway), 195
Finland, 194, 312
First ARP Church (Gastonia, North Carolina), 7
First Presbyterian Church (Auburn, Alabama), 304
First Presbyterian Church (Norman, Oklahoma), 186
First Presbyterian Church at Selma, 186
First Presbyterian Church of Birmingham, 186
First Presbyterian Church of Montevallo, 186
First Presbyterian Church of Princeton, 32
First Presbyterian Church of Tuscaloosa, 186
First United Church of Monroeville, 364
Fite, Gilbert, 143
Flat Creek, 53–54
Flat Rock, North Carolina, 78
Fleming, Cynthia Griggs, 164
Fleming, Harold C., 377
Florala, Alabama, 287
Florence Sate College, 337
Florida Ice and Light Company, 27
Florida State University, 320
Flowers, Richmond, 287, 347–48
Flynn, Gregory, 348, 354
Flynt, Wayne, 171
"Fog in August" (Kennedy), 274
"Folk culture," 375
Folsom, James E., 244–45, 285–89, 329
"Forces That Produced Hitler" (Alles), 196
Ford, Gerald, 358
Forehand, Brooks, 267
Forest Home, Alabama, 63
Forrest, Nathan Bedford, 51–52

"Forty-Two Dollars" (Kennedy), 170
Fosdick, Raymond, 43
"Four Freedoms, The," 198, 219, 263
Fourth Ghost, The (Brinkmeyer), 194, 378, 389n1, 459n3
Frederickson, Kari, 262, 433n12
"Freedom of Choice," 329
"Freedom Riders," 302, 315–18
Freeport, Maine, 209–10, 213
"Freshmen Are Alright" (Kennedy), 267
Frownfelter, Joseph, 220
fugitives, 146–47
"Full Christianity." *See* Kennedy, Renwick Carlisle (RCK): personal and career
Furman, Alabama, 343
Furman, Marian Purdue, xii, 241–42, 432n6. *See also* Perdue, Marian Furman
Furman College, 237
Future Teachers Association, 287

Gaillard, Frye, 346, 459n2
Gaillard, Richebourg, 107
Gaines, Betty, 255. *See also* Kennedy, Betty Gaines
Gaines, Hayden Jones, 314
Gaines, Snooks Jones, 365
Gaines Ridge Dinner Club, ii
Gallic Wars, The (Caesar), 24
Gallup poll, 24
Gandhi, Mahatma, 317
Gaston, Cecil, 329
Gaston family, 147
Gee, Joseph, 13, 44–45, 130, 156
Gee's Bend, Alabama. *See* Kennedy, Renwick Carlisle (RCK): social concerns; Stone, Olive
Geneva, Alabama, 286–87, 296
Geneva County, Alabama, 285
Georgetown University, 26
Georgiana, Alabama, 73
Georgia Tech, 322–23
Gera, Germany, 221
German Youth Movement, 212
Gettys, Ebenezer, 116
Giessen, Germany, 221–22
"G. I. Gravy Train" (Kennedy), 242
Gilder's Creek (South Carolnia) ARP Church, 14

Gillian, John, 249–50
Gingrich, Newt, 373
Givhan, Walter, 280
Godbold, Mary Emma Harris, 259. *See also* Harris, Mary Emma
Godbold, Stanley David, 91, 148, 162, 305
"God Mandate." *See* Kennedy, Renwick Carlisle (RCK): personal and career
Goffs, California, 208
Golden, John, 341
Goldman, Eric, 241
Goldwater, Barry, 326, 332
Gomillion v. Lightfoot (1960), 348
Gone With the Wind (Mitchell), 189
Goode, Robert Larkin, 52
Goode family, 147
Goodiel, Carlton D., 208–9, 212–14, 216, 221
Goodwin, Tully, 287
Goodwyn, Otis James ("Joe"), 287
Goodwyn Amendment, 287–88
Grace, Joshua B., 54
Graham, Billy, 304
Grampian Hills, 44, 67
Grant, Madison, 118
Graves, Bibb, 76–77, 98, 114, 161–62
Graves, John Temple, II, 170–72
"Greatest Generation, The," 204, 258, 330, 366, 377
Great Pan-Africa Road Race, The, 265, 271
"Great Peace Celebration, The" (Kennedy), 164–65
"Great Society, The," 325
Greene, William Benton, 36
Greene County, Alabama, 131
Greensboro, North Carolina, 16
Gregg, Robert Henry, 48
Grier, Paul, 206
Grier, Robert Calvin, II, 62
Grier, William Boyce, 43, 49, 55
Grier family, 24–25, 43
Griffin, Carl, 271
Guadalcanal, 308
Guerard, Louise Elliott, 35–36. *See also* Kennedy, Louise Guerard
Gulley, Elizabeth Ann, 343
Gulley, Riley, 69

Index

Haiti, 45, 122
Hale, Byron, 316, 341
Hale, Vasco, 208
"Half-Christianity." *See* Kennedy, Renwick Carlisle (RCK): personal and career
Halifax County, Virginia, 92
Hall, Grover, 71, 73, 126
Hall, N. H., 73
Hall, Warner, 186
Hamburg, Alabama, 43, 50, 54
Hamilton, Edith, 346–47, 366, 380
Hamlet (Shakespeare), 361
Hand, Lee, 241
"Hangman's Hill" (Camden, Alabama), 163
Hanover County, Virginia, 46
Harmony, Arthur Fort, 186
Harms, Tennessee, 20–22
Harper, Jacob ("Jaki"), 266, 286, 338
Harper, Juliette, 353
Harper, Taylor Jones, 366
Harris, Mary Emma, 133, 148. *See also* Godbold, Mary Emma Harris
Harris family, 133
Harrison, Harry P., 34
Harriss, Anne Duguid, 54
Harriss, Francis, 54
Hart, Gary, 366
Hart, Sallie, 104–5
Harvard University, 3, 65, 148; Divinity School, 206–7
Harvey, Ira, 404n21
Hayneville, Alabama, 342
Heart is a Lonely Hunter, The (McCullers), 353
"Heart of Dixie," 295
Heflin, Tom, 194
Heiden, Konrad, 223
Heinrich, John C., 201
Heller, Joseph, 353
Hemingway, Ernest, 195, 204
Henderson, Bruce, 293, 302–4
Henderson, Fred, 97, 304, 316
Henderson, William, 97, 107
Henderson family, 351
Henry, Hugh McMaster, 52–58, 66, 98
Hero, Alfred O., Jr., 304–6
Hickey, Elise Bonner, 366–67. *See also* Bonner, Jane Elizabeth ("Elise")

Hickey, Walter, 88
Hickey, Walter, family, 91
Hicks, Carol, 300
Highlander Scots. *See* Scots
Hill, Herbert, 254
Hill, Lister, 246, 326, 334
Hill, Luther Leonidas, 107
Hill, Samuel S., Jr., 120
Hill, T. B., Jr., 306
Hillyer, Robert, 4
History of the 102nd Evacuation Hospital (Kennedy), 223, 240
History of the ARP Church of Camden, Alabama (Kennedy), 176
Hitler, Adolph, 3–4, 192–93, 204, 372. *See also* Kennedy, Renwick Carlisle (RCK): social concerns (racial fascism)
"Hitler Report" (McWilliams), 3–4, 50, 158, 192–94, 239
Hobbs, Samuel Earl, 288
Hobbs, Truman, 288
Hobson, Fred C., 75, 268–69, 405n35, 427n19, 438n10
Hodge, Casper, 36
Hodo, David Walker, 279, 281
Hogg, James, xii
"Hold the Line Resolution," 282–83
Holleman, Mary Ruth, 283
Hollings, Ernest F., 377–78
"Hollywood Types," 314, 317
"Holy Hamlet" (Due West, South Carolina), 19, 43, 55
"Holy Joeism," 198, 375
Homer, 380
homosexuality. *See* Kennedy, Renwick Carlisle (RCK): social concerns (World War II soldiers' behaviors)
Hood, Andrew, 143
Hood, Cy, 66, 72
Hood, Gladyce Kennedy, 26
Hood, James Boyce, 26
Hood, William, 26
Hood family, 24, 43
Hoover, Herbert. *See* Kennedy, Renwick Carlisle (RCK): social concerns (Republican Party leaders)
Hope Hull, Alabama, 161
Hopkins, Harry, 143, 151

Horn, Peter 106–7
Houston, Texas, 245, 285
Howard College. *See also* Samford University
Howells, William Dean, 35
"How Good Were the Army Chaplains?" (Kennedy), 241
"How It Happens" (Kennedy), 179–81, 183–85, 253
Hudson, R. F., 306
Hull, Marion McHenry, 204
"Humility, Not Hubris, in the Post-War World" (Kennedy), 224
Hunt, Bill, 334
Huntersville, North Carolina, 42
Huntingdon College, 237
Huntley, Chet, 321
Huntsville, Alabama, 58
Hurtsboro High School, 352
Hutchinson, Paul, 241
Hutton, Carol, 300
Huy, Belgium, 216–17
Huy Normal School, 216

Ibsen, Henry, 362
"I Have a Dream" (King), 321
I'll Take My Stand (Twelve Southerners), 82, 147
Independent Presbyterian Church (Birmingham, Alabama), 116
Institutes for the Christian Religion (Calvin), 83
International Harvester Corporation, 36, 94, 278
Intruder in the Dust (Faulkner), 296
Invisible Man, The (Ellison), 296
"Is It the End of Cotton?" (Kennedy), 177
"Isolation" (Kennedy), 162–64
Ivy League, 29–30, 33, 207, 258

Jackson, Andrew, 12, 54, 67
Jackson, Bo, 365
Jackson, Harvey H., III, xii, 131, 399n12, 423n36
Jackson, Walter, 282
Jacksonville City Schools, 283
Jacksonville State University, 337
Jaffe, Rona, 362
James, Forrest ("Fob"), 357

Jarrett, Thomas D., 257
Jeep, 239–40, 243, 248
Jefferson, Thomas, 46, 106
Jenkins, Percy Columbus ("Lummie"), 180, 316–17, 340, 342, 347, 361
Jenkins family, 180
"Jesus Was a Liberal" (Kennedy), 186
Jews: Alabama Black Belt, 73, 138, 145, 249–50, 318; Europe, 182, 194–95, 221–23, 321; US Army, 213–14; US East coast, 192
"JFK Memorial Remarks" (Kennedy), 323
Joe (film), 353
Johns Hopkins University, 81
Johnson, Frank, Jr., 333–34, 337
Johnson, Gerald, 168–69
Johnson, Herman, 252
Johnson, Lyndon B., 328, 342, 346
Johnson's Motor Court, 296, 339
Johnston, Joseph F., 16
Johnston, Mary, 22
Johnstone, Chancellor, 15
"Jolt, The," 179, 185, 187, 253, 270
Jones, Bob, 326
Jones, Clark, 89, 98, 100, 109, 145, 154
Jones, Dick, 107
Jones, Edward Nathaniel, 106
Jones, Elizabeth Martha Harriss, 50–51
Jones, Henry Ford, 102
Jones, J. Heustis, 89, 97, 100, 108
Jones, James Harvey, 50, 54
Jones, John Cargill, 106
Jones, John Paul (1837–1903), 106
Jones, John Paul (1894–1975), 259, 263
Jones, John Paul, Jr. (1878–1937), 108
Jones, Joseph, 53
Jones, Joyce, 50
Jones, Joyce Carothers Clopton, xii, 7, 2, 76, 104, 182, 206, 315, 361
Jones, Justice Smith, 78–79, 100, 116, 146, 186, 249
Jones, Lillian, 250
Jones, Martin Van Buren, 4–5, 50
Jones, Mrs. Clark, 92
Jones, Mrs. Clem, 92
Jones, Mrs. Heustis, 104
Jones, Mrs. Paul E., 104
Jones, Ralph, 287

Index

Jones, Richard Channing, 106
Jones, Robert, 53
Jones, Robert Reynolds, 98
Jones, Sam Lee, 98
Jones, Thomas Goode, 306
Jones, Thomas Jenkins, 180, 184
Jones, Thomas Warburton, 104, 108
Jones, Walter B., 293, 306
Jones, William ("Bill") Junius, xi–xii; death, 367; early years, 3, 56, 194; health issues, 202, 361–63; "Hitler Report," 2–3; J. Miller Bonner, 7, 103, 282–84, 306, 367; and Jones Resolution, 282–84; KKK, 76, 82–83, 283–84, 317–18; personality, 367; racial views, general, 7, 75–76, 163, 177, 182–84, 201, 254–55, 261, 281–84, 315, 329, 338, 341–42; and RCK, 3, 7, 153, 194, 201, 205–7, 225, 281, 311–21, 341–42, 355, 374; reading, 184, 361–62; Red Cross Gee's Bend endeavors, 100, 132–33; Simpson family connections and Mary Patton Simpson Educational Foundation, 343–45; and "slapping incident," 341–42, 452n19
Jones, William Clarence, 201
Jones family, of South Carolina, 10, 25, 43; of Virginia, 106
Jones Resolution, The, 282–84
Jordon, Jake, 279
"Journey's End, The," 255
J. Paul Jones Hospital, 362–64
Judson College, 147, 237, 252, 256, 258

Kappa Delta, 343
Katzenbach, Nicholas, 320
Kelley, Guy, 344
Kennedy, Betty Gaines, vii, xii. *See also* Gaines, Betty
Kennedy, Ebenezer, 19, 25, 27
Kennedy, Elizabeth, 20
Kennedy, Emma, 20
Kennedy, Gladyce Mildred, 20. *See also* Hood, Gladyce Kennedy
Kennedy, Isaac ("Ike") Newton, 17, 19–29, 35, 39, 59, 95, 248
Kennedy, Jesse, 79–80
Kennedy, John F. *See* Kennedy, Renwick Carlisle (RCK): social concerns (Democratic Party leaders)
Kennedy, Leon Toland, 20, 366
Kennedy, Louise Guerard, 187. *See also* Guerard, Louise Elliott
Kennedy, Margaret ("Muddie") Elizabeth McFarlan McLane, 18–20
Kennedy, Margaret, 111, 207–12, 223, 225, 239–40, 272–73. *See also* Ausley, Margaret Kennedy
Kennedy, Margaret McLane, 366
Kennedy, Mary Conway, 92–96, 102–9, 212, 225, 239, 245, 274. *See also* Dickinson, Mary Conway Kennedy
Kennedy, Mary Elizabeth Moore, 7–9, 37, 89, 93, 95, 120, 161–73, 182, 187, 202, 206–7, 211, 222–25, 248, 266–67, 278, 311, 355. *See also* Moore, Mary Elizabeth
Kennedy, Mary Emma Carlisle, 20, 21. *See also* Carlisle, Mary Emma
Kennedy, Renwick Carlisle (RCK)
—personal and career: alcohol, 202, 220, 240, 295–97, 356, 361–68, 374, 379, 431n4; birth, 20; childhood, 22–23; courtship, marriage and family, 36–42, 56–68, 72–79, 85–93, 110–11, 120, 161–73, 182, 187, 199, 202–11, 222–25, 239, 248, 266–67, 276, 311, 353, 362–68, 376; Christian Socialism/Social Gospelism, 2, 37–41, 60, 62, 82, 111, 125, 142, 193, 200, 303–4, 318, 364, 372–74, 380; personality, 121, 367, 369, 376–77, 379; family background, 11–23; "Half" and "Full" Christianity, 37, 84, 112, 119, 162, 263, 269, 318, 322, 352–53, 355, 356, 369, 372–77, 379; "God Mandate," 1, 83–84, 93, 121, 160, 187, 192, 225, 238, 244, 262, 264, 272–73, 277, 294–95, 340, 375–77; modernism, 39, 321; neo-orthodoxy, 37, 58, 111, 238, 372–73, 377; Arkansas pastorate, 39–49, 56–59, 65–68; Wilcox pastorates pre-WWII, 43–57, 61–207; Wilcox pastorates post-WWII, 237–357; personal papers, 8; physical appearance, 7, 25, 207, 366; sickness and death, 8, 362–69; Troy State College life, 244–379, 434n15, 437n33, 439n19, 446n15, 447n19, 448n31, 451n9,

451n14, 453n28, 455n35, 459n24; US Army Reserve service, 267–68, 272, 290; Victorianism, 39, 77, 321, 353; youth and education, 24–39, 40–43, 209; World War II service, 206–25; writing motivations and schedule, 64, 121–23, 138–39, 225, 293
—social concerns: Ralph Adams, 330–55; Aristocracy of the Kingdom of God, 119, 374; Black Belt defined, 4, 45, 145; Black Belt-Big Mule Axis, 114–15, 125, 153, 165, 177, 245, 279, 284, 287, 300–302, 306, 310; Black middle class, 163–64, 241, 374, 426n17; Black poor: sharecroppers, generally, 21, 114–15, 122, 127, 131, 140–42, 150, 159, 194, 199, 203, 280, 343, 419n1; of Gee's Bend, 123–24, 129–38, 143–52, 156, 168–79, 201, 259, 314, 345–47, 356, 360, 366, 409n9, 415n12, 415–16n15, 434n20, 437n32; Catholicism, 80, 98, 109, 241–42, 436; cotton prices, 94, 117–31, 142, 177–78, 127–28, 134, 142–43, 177, 203; Democratic Party leaders, 3, 26–27, 36–38, 43, 57–73, 86–87, 102–3, 128–30, 193–204, 245, 255–61, 272, 293, 298, 305, 311–13, 320–26, 346–47, 358–59, 366–68, 373–74, 378; desegregation, general, 259–60, 282–85, 290, 294–96, 299–302, 308–11, 319–21, 329, 337–38, 363, 377, at Erskine College, 337–40, at Troy State College, 289–92, 332, 335–37, 340, 349, in Wilcox, general, 256–57, 269, 305, 315, 360, 339–45, 355–60, 367, in Wilcox schools, 282–85, 342–44, 351; ecumenicalism, 34, 117, 185, 206, 241, 258–59, 275, 314; Greek philosophers, 17, 117–18, 346–47, 362, 380; KKK/lynching, 19, 68–78, 80–115, 138, 155, 159, 164, 179–85, 193, 201, 245, 273–76, 284, 300, 322, 347, 402n13, 403n14, 418n47, 441n32; liberalism, 34, 160, 186, 278, 313, 320, 325–26, 343–44, 348, 358, 374; Massive Resistance I, 281, 285–88, 302–7, 371; Massive Resistance II, 372–73, 452n2; natural environment, 81–83, 167, 177, 248, 317, 325–26, 405n32; racial fascism, in America, 1, 6,

9, 194, 197, 247, 260–64, 314–22, 342, 350–58, 371–72, 377–79, overseas, 1, 6, 9, 194, 204–13, 219, 225, 247, 260–69, 372, 377–79; Republican Party leaders, 27, 96–104, 112–16, 125–30, 136, 145, 203, 245–46, 259–62, 276, 293, 296, 303, 311–13, 325–32, 343–52, 357–59, 366, 378, 408n5, 445n9, 450n9, 456n4; Scotch-Irish, 2, 15, 21, 49, 102–3, 202, 277, 300, 325–27, 346, 351–52, 356, 367–69, 371–73, 380, 392n3, 394n14, 397n21, 410n17, 410n20, 440n25, 459n2; veterans (and American Legion), 68, 155, 164–69, 193, 202, 242, 244–47, 251, 258–60, 273, 308, 342, 355, 401n4, 410n20, 416n5, 426n17, 433n11, 437n36; violence/lynching, 6, 68–71, 78, 82–85, 103–5, 113–16, 136, 154–59, 180–85, 193–97, 213, 221, 250–53, 260–71, 278, 285–89, 293–94, 315–32, 369, 371, 375, 402n13, 403n14, 434n20, 440n27, 443n48; voting rights, general, 312–19, in Wilcox, 163, 300, 305, 341–42, 363; George Wallace, 239, 289, 293, 298–307, 312–61, 366, 371, 379, 410n24, 445n9, 448n32, 449n5, 450n7, 451n14, 452–53n21; white upper class, 49, 71–84, 90–91, 100–102, 109–26, 159, 201–2, 303, 374, 403n17, 406n47, 434n21 (*see also* Wilcox Roundtable); white middle class, 100–101; white lower class, 67–68, 72–79, 88–99, 135, 170–75, 183, 187, 201, 401n10; women, abuse of, 77, 99–100, 254–55; World War I, 25, 30, 62, 67–68, 74, 77, 86, 113, 253–55, 164, 190, 193, 270–72, 276, 308; World War II: futility of, 220; passive stage, 192–98; soldiers' positive behaviors, 213–14, 216, and negative behaviors, 209–14, 221–24, 241–42, 262–63; Yaupon idea, 5, 123–25, 134–44, 153–70, 183–91, 198–204, 214, 220–23, 256, 260, 275, 289, 290, 338, 372, 406n47, 419n49, 425n10, 427n20
Kennedy, Richard Newton, 20, 325, 366
Kennedy, Robert F., ix, 312, 317, 320–22, 329, 346–48
Kennedy, Selden, 187, 397n21
Kennedy, Ted, 358

Kennedy, William McLane, 20, 26, 209, 222–23, 274, 355, 366
Kennedy, William Patton, 17–19
Kester, Howard, 121, 270, 377
Key, Margaret, 201
Kilby Prison, 181
Killers of the Dream (Smith), 27
"Killing Time, The," 11–12, 249
Kilpatrick, Emmett: alcohol, 148, 161–62, 168, 223; Army Reserve, 247; "Cremation" model, 135; early years, 86–87, 188, 406n38, 451n15; friendship with RCK and Troy life, 86–87, 126, 146–49, 252–53, 261, 265–67, 271–73, 276–77, 289, 310–14; Marie Bankhead Owen, 188–89; marriage proposal, 272; Pan-Africa Automobile Race, 265; personality, 148, 313–14, 437n1, 437n3; political preferences, 261, 305–7, 374, 431n5; religion, 374; retirement and death, 313–14; "the trees," 314; Wilcox Roundtable, 146–48
King, Coretta Scott, 312, 363
King, Martin Luther, Jr., 186, 300, 312, 317, 320–21, 332, 346
King, William Rufus, 46, 91, 109–10
"King Cotton," 256–57
King Lear (Shakespeare), 361
King's Creek (South Carolina) ARP Church, 14, 16
Kipling, Rudyard, 27
Kirkland, Scotty, xii
Kiwanis Clubs, 287
KKK. *See* Kennedy, Renwick Carlisle (RCK): social concerns
Knight, Thomas E., 79
Kurahuas Hotel, 220

Laird, John, 303
Laird, Mary 302
Lambert, Helen Burford, 148, 253
Lamison, Alabama, 69
Lanaux, Martin, xii
"Land! Answer to Unemployment" (Ransom), 127
Lane, R. F., 338
Lang, George, 185–87, 199
Langan, Joseph N., 377–78

Lanterns on the Levy (Percy), 202
Laurens, South Carolina, 24
Lawler, Marie, 290, 300
Lawrence, Robert J., 282
Laws, Daniel, 314, 364, 368
League of Nations, 96
Lee, Alice, 364
Lee, Harper, 314–15, 363–64
"Legion Audit" (Kennedy), 168–69
Lenin, Vladimir, 332, 335
"Letter from Birmingham Jail, The" (King), 186, 320
Leuchtenburg, William E., 260
Lewis, Joe, 201
Lewis, John, 332–33
Lewis, Sinclair, 62, 87
Lewis, William, 68
"Liberty Hall" (home), 45
Liddell, John Russell, 107
Liddell, Ruth, xii
Liddell, Viola Jefferson Goode, xii, 147–49, 157, 160–61, 170, 176, 184–89, 201–2, 251–61, 268, 271, 274–76, 303–5, 314, 368, 374, 421n18, 427n18, 458n22
Liddell, Will Lithgow, 147–48, 253, 314
Liddell, Will Lithgow, Jr., xii
Liddell family, 100, 202
Life and Labor in the Old South (Phillips), 118–19
"Life at Gee's Bend" (Kennedy), 171–72
"Life Goes on at Gee's Bend" (Kennedy), 178
Lindbergh, Charles, 73
"Liquidation of Mr. Smith, The," (Kennedy), 184
Little, Brown, and Co., 176
Little, George, 287
Little Rock, Arkansas, 39, 143, 59, 77, 294
Liuzzo, Viola, 340
Livingston State College, 337
L. L. Bean Boots, 210, 213, 215
Locke, Hugh, 114
Loetscher, Frederick W., 36, 207
Long Cane Creek, South Carolina, 17
Long Cane Creek School, 36, 38
Long Roll, The (Johnston), 22
Look Magazine, 312
Losing Battles (Welty), 353
"Lost Cause," 160, 165, 169, 188, 190–91

Lottinville, Savoie, 187–88, 190, 200, 203–4, 256–58
Louboutin, Pierre, 211
Louisville High School, 352
Love, Andrew Boyce ("Coot"), 42–43, 58–59, 380
Lower Peach Tree, Alabama, 100, 252
Lowlander Scots. *See* Scots
Lowndes County, Alabama, 340, 342
Lucas, Thomas J., 51
Lucy, Autherine, 289, 293, 300, 308
Lumpkin, Ethel, 218, 268
Lumpkin, Maudine, 268
Lumpkin, Millard, 217–18, 268
Lumpkin, Willard, 217–18, 268
Luverne, Alabama, 98
lynching. *See* Kennedy, Renwick Carlisle (RCK): social concerns; McWilliams, Richebourg Gaillard

MacArthur, Douglas, 272
Machen, J. Gresham, 30, 32, 207
Macmillan Company, 176
Macon County, Alabama, 280–81, 285
Maddox, Gordon, 291
Maddox, Lester, 325
Madison Avenue, New York, 14
Main Street (Lewis), 81, 192
Malone, Wallace, 265, 271
Manchester Guardian, The, 304
Manhattan, New York, 70, 343
Man in the Gray Flannel Suit, The (Wilson), 296
Mann, Floyd, 316–18
March, William, 192, 205, 424n2
Marengo County, Alabama, 51–52
Marion Junction, Alabama, 49, 57, 78
Martha Patton Simpson Educational Foundation, 343–45
Martin, Jim, 347–48, 326
Martin, Jonas, 179–81, 182–85, 253, 270
Martin, Thomas W., 201, 306–7, 311
Mason, Littlefield, 48
Masons (white), 254
"Massive Resistance," 310, 318–24, 326. *See also* Kennedy, Renwick Carlisle (RCK): social concerns; "Second Massive Resistance Movement"

Mathews, Curtis, 70
Mathews, William J., 122
Matthews, Barnet Houser, 132–33, 415n13; hardware store, 201
Maxwell Air Force Base, 328
Mays, Benjamin, 121
McBride, Mrs. Betty, 267
McCall family, 43
McCallie School, 280
McCarthy, Eugene, 345
McCarthy, Joseph, 292–93, 331
McConnico, Stonewall, 179, 184
McConnico family, 274
McCormick County, South Carolina, 17
McCormick Theological Seminary, 27
McCrory, Cynthia, xii
McDaniel, John, 267
McDaniel, Rosa Tait, 109–10, 267
McDill, Tom (Mrs.), 25
McDonald's, 57
McDowell, William G., 116, 186
McDowell family, 133
McGovern, George, 357–58
McIntosh, Edward L., 132–33, 259
McIntosh, Harriet Louisa ("Lulu"), 133
McIntosh, Roy, 366
McIntosh, Swene, 43
McKay, E. Osborn, 253
McKellar, Dennis, 241, 246
McKelvey, Connie, 241
McKinley, Marvin, 268
McLeod, Donald M., 352
McLeod, Jesse, 84, 283–84
McNeill, Dorothy ("Dot"), 215–25. *See also* Moore, Dorothy; Paterson, Dorothy
McNeill, George F., 183, 215
McNeill, Sam, 21, 92–95, 113, 145, 201, 210–21, 268, 323
McReynolds family, 54
McWilliams, Dave, 250–51
McWilliams, Eleanor, 250
McWilliams, Enoch, 250
McWilliams, Miles Levi, 97, 250
McWilliams, Richebourg Gaillard, xii; *Alabama*, 367; Clarence Cason, 158; death, 7; "Hitler Report," 3–4, 50, 158, 192–94, 239; Miller Bonner, 367; 1930s fiction life, 3–5; racial-violence

experiences, 402n13; and RCK, 3–5, 50, 158, 183, 258; teaching career, 353–54; and Viola Jefferson Goode Liddell, 258, 436n30; and W. J. ("Bill") Jones, 367
McWilliams, Rubye, 249–52, 315, 318
McWilliams, Susan Lee Johnson, xii
McWilliams, Tennant, 365, 369
McWilliams, Will, 97, 249
Meadows, Austin, 282, 284–85, 298, 300–301, 308–9, 311, 326–29
Mellon, Andrew, 112
Mencken, Henry L., 71, 126, 190, 325
Meredith, James, 319
Metz, France, 218
Middleton family, 78
Midway, Alabama, 69
Miller, Abijah, 48
Miller, Benjamin ("Ben") Meek, Jr., 114
Miller, Benjamin Meek, 55, 76, 77, 81–83, 89, 107, 113–16, 125, 152
Miller, Clyde Purifoy, 43, 45, 56–58, 86, 95, 102, 148
Miller, John, 43–50, 52–58, 76, 86, 93, 99, 100, 107, 256
Miller, Joseph Neely, 55
Miller, Sarah Pressly, 106
Miller, Stanley, 29
Miller family, 25, 54, 102, 375
Miller's Ferry, Alabama, 110, 181
Miller's Ferry School, 243
Mills, Victor, 216–17
"Mimosa" (home), 122
Mind of the South, The (Cash), 194, 202, 373, 403n17
Mitchell, Bonnie Dean, 53, 365. *See also* Dean, Bonnie
Mitchell, Broadus, 81–82
Mitchell, Scott, 447n20
Mize, P. G., 283
Mobile College, 237
modernism, 39, 321
Mohave Desert, 208
Mohr, Clarence, xii
Monet, Claude, 101
Moniaive (Dumfriesshire County, Scotland), 12
Monroe, James, 46
Monroe County, Alabama, 285

Monroeville, Alabama, 287, 314, 363
Monteleone Hotel, 20
Montevallo Presbyterian Church, 265
Montgomery, Alabama, 245
Montgomery Advertiser, 71, 73, 98, 107, 126, 195, 245, 271, 278–79, 292, 306, 348
Montgomery Bus Boycott, 288
Montgomery County, Alabama, 287
Montgomery Examiner, 279
Montgomery Journal, 107, 325
Mont Saint-Michel, France, 212
Moore, Dorothy ("Dot"). *See also* McNeill, Dorothy; Paterson, Dorothy
Moore, Joe McReynolds ("Mac"), 70–71
Moore, John T., 95
Moore, Laura Lee, 284
Moore, Mary Elizabeth, 36–42, 56–67, 72–89. *See also* Kennedy, Mary Elizabeth Moore
Moore, R. E., 282
Mooresville, North Carolina, 38, 248
"More the Merrier, The" (Kennedy), 268
Morgan, Albion, 107
Morgan, James Bryant, 292
Mormon (unidentified), 67
Morrison, Charles Clayton, 34, 38, 137, 155, 192
Moseley, Alf, 172
Mountain Brook, Alabama, 115
Mount Zion ARP Church (Elsberry, Missouri), 28–29
Mozart, Wolfgang Amadeus, 101
"Mr. McClintock and His Tenants" (Kennedy), 166–67
Mt. Horeb (Alabama) ARP Church, 67, 78
Mt. Sanai (Alabama) ARP Church, 67
Mt. Sinai, Alabama, 95
Murphy, Harvey, 291
Myrdal, Gunnar, 243–44, 289

National Association for the Advancement of Colored People, The (NAACP), 284, 300, 302, 326
National Council of Churches, 243
National Urban League, 143
Nazism: "Creeping," 1; and fascism in Germany and US, 1. *See also* Kennedy, Renwick Carlisle (RCK): social concerns

Nearing, Scott, 62, 74
Neenah, Alabama, 44
Nelson, Byron B., 279, 308
Nelson, C. P., 283
neo-orthodoxy, 34–35, 37, 58
Nesbit, Marcellus, 270
Nettie Quill, The, 107
Nettles, Cora Belle, 144
Nettles, Sam, 287
Newberry, Emma, 49, 61, 64, 83
Newberry, John, 98
Newberry County, South Carolina, 14, 15, 56
Newberry family, 54
New Deal. *See* Kennedy, Renwick Carlisle (RCK): social concerns
"New Frontier, The," 315, 325
Newman, Julia, 283
New Orleans, Louisiana, 378
New Republic, The, 5, 95, 125–28, 134, 137, 142, 214, 240, 312
New South movement, 375–76
Newsweek, 240–41, 245
New York Times Ministry, 359, 362–63
New York University, 16
Niebuhr, Reinhold, 38, 192, 243
"1932: Camden's Centennial Year" (Kennedy), 126
Ninety Degrees in the Shade (Cason), 157–61, 185, 194
Nixon, E. D., 302
Nixon, Herman Clarence, 82, 377
Nixon, Richard M., 313, 357–58
Nobel Prize, 271–72
Norman (Oklahoma) Rotary Club, 186–87
Norris, Clarence, 154
Northeastern University, 251, 256
Norton, Ethelbert P., 301
"Note on Cotton" (Kennedy), 139–40
"Note on Erskine Caldwell" (Kennedy), 157
"Note on Trapping" (Kennedy), 169
"Notes from Alabama on Homo Africanus," 123–25, 140
"November Morn, 1932" (Kennedy), 134
Noviant-aux-Pres, France, 218, 221
"No Where to Go" (Kennedy), 259–60

Oak Hill, Alabama, 4–5, 50–51, 54, 78, 80, 84–85, 182, 205, 306, 315, 321, 363, 367

Oakley, George, 287
Oates family, 58
Oberlin College, 51
Ochamps, Belgium, 213
Odom, Howard W., 147, 149, 249
Oliver Twist (Dickens), 90
Olliff, Martin, xii
"On Aristocracy" (Kennedy), 117–20
O'Neal, Edward A., III, 171
"One Point of View" (Kennedy), 161
On the Origin of Species (Darwin), 30
Opp City Schools, 283, 287
Opportunity: The Journal of Negro Life, 143
Ora, South Carolina, 20, 24, 43
Orange Beach, Alabama, 310
Orr, Ernest N., 24, 76, 116
Orr, William W., 58
Orthodox Presbyterian Church, 31
Oswald, Lee Harvey, 321–22, 328
Outdoor Life, 248, 433–34n14
Outlawry of War, The (Morrison), 192
Owen, Marie Bankhead, 188–89, 190–91, 253
"Ox Farmers" (Kennedy), 150
Oxford, Alabama, 217
Oxford University, 187
Ozark, Alabama, 287

pacificism. *See* Kennedy, Renwick Carlisle (RCK): social concerns
Palladium, The, 298
Parker Memorial Baptist Church, 185
Parkinson, Gilbert Gordon, 27, 29–30, 116
Parks, Rosa, 288, 333
Partial Nuclear Test Ban Treaty, 321
Pascagoula, Mississippi, 202
Passing of the Great Race, The (Grant), 118
Pasternack, Boris, 362
Paterson, Dorothy ("Dot"), 268. *See also* McNeill, Dorothy ("Dot")
Paterson, Duke, 268
Patrician and Plebian in Virginia (Wertenbaker), 413n35
Patterson, Eugene, 377
Patterson, Haywood, 154
Patterson, John, 281, 289, 300–302, 309–12, 332
Patton, George, 210, 214, 218–19, 268, 371
Paxton, Robert, 1

Peabody, George F., 343
Peace Corps, 315
Pearl Harbor, 189, 199, 204
"People of Fish Creek, The" (Kennedy), 170–76, 183, 187, 189, 200
Pepper, Claude, 246
Percy, William Alexander, 202
Perdue, Marian Furman, 242
Perry, Raymond H., 51
Peterson, Willie, 115
Pettway, Ed-O, 172
Pettway, Mark, 131, 156
Pettway, Rosa Lee, 356
Petway, Cherokee Parker, 154
Phenix City High School, 352
Philadelphia, 18
Phillips, Howard, 301
Phillips, Ulrich B., 118
Phillips High School, 283
"Phony, The" (Kennedy), 293
Phylon, 257
Picauville, France, 210
Pike County Schools, 283
Pike County Teacher's Credit Union, 333
Pinckney family, 78
Pine Apple, Alabama, 67, 69, 74, 209, 272–73, 316, 340–41, 363, 367, 402n13, 452n18
Pine Barren Creek, 43, 53, 97
Pinkston, Annie Floyd, 280
Pinkston, Hattie, 280
Pinkston, James, 280
Pioneers of the Old Southwest (Skinner), 102
Plantation County (Rubin), 253, 256, 274, 316
Ploudaniel, France, 211
Plowley, Edward, 69
Plowley, William, 6
Poland, 192, 194
"Poll Tax" (Kennedy), 188
poll tax, 328
Pope, Ephreium, 69
Populist Party, 143
Porter, Frank ("Buck"), 181
Possum Bend, Alabama, 100
Powell, Adam Clayton, 288
Prairie Bluff, Alabama, 47
Prairieville, Alabama. *See* Prairie Bluff, Alabama

Pratt, Charles, First Earl of Camden, 49
Prejudices, Sixth Series (Mencken), 126
Presbyterian Church of Scotland, 11
Presbyterian Church USA, 30, 243
"Presbyterian Conflict," 30–33
presidential elections. *See* Wilcox County
Presly, James, 206
Pressly, Francis Young, 27
Pressly, Joseph Lowry, 67, 173
Pressly, Maude, 92–93
Pressly, Mrs. Maude, 25
Pressly family, 25, 54
Prince Edward County, Virginia, 106
Princeton Theological Seminary, 3, 27, 29, 30–39, 85, 112, 208, 372, 380
Princeton University, 38, 103
Prohibition. *See* Wilcox County
Prosperity ARP Church (Marion Junction, Alabama), 49, 57, 187, 202–6, 248, 265, 323, 338, 357
Prosperity ARP Church (Taft, Tennessee), 19–20
Protestant Puritanism, 268–69
Provost, Marie-Thérèse, 212
"Psychic" (Kennedy), 138
psychic crisis, 30
Psychology of the Oppressed, The (Heinrich), 201
Public Works Administration, 150
"Pulpit Diary" (Kennedy), 197–98
Purdue, Cecil, 328
Purdue, Marian, 242. *See also* Furman, Marian Perdue
Purifoy, Francis Esten, 101–2
Purifoy family, 54, 95
Pursley Creek, 52

"Quality in the Reserve Corps" (Kennedy), 153, 193

Rachel's Place, 98
racial fascism, 1, 342, 371, 373. *See also* Kennedy, Renwick Carlisle (RCK): social concerns
Rafferty, Max, 354, 357
Raines, Howell, xii, 130
Ralston Purina Company, 241
Ramage, Edward V., 186
Ransom, John Crowe, 127

rape. *See* Kennedy, Renwick Carlisle (RCK): social concerns
Ray, James Earl, 346
Razor's Edge, The (Maugham), 223
Reagan, Ronald, 358, 366
Reconstruction Finance Corporation, 150–51
Red Badge of Courage, The (Crane), 223
Red Cross. *See* Jones, William ("Bill") Junius; Kennedy, Renwick Carlisle (RCK): social concerns (Black poor); Matthews, Barnet Houser; Wilcox County
"Redeeming the Time" (Kennedy), 343
Red Hills, 13, 43
Red Level, Alabama, 67, 78–79, 95, 169, 172–74
"Rednecks," 11–12, 18, 392n2
Reeves, Ben, 287
Reformed Theological Seminary, 357, 455n2
"Rehabilitation: Alabama Version" (Kennedy), 150–51
Reichlen, Leonard, 217–18
Reivers, The (Faulkner), 353
Remagen Bridge, 220
Remington, Craig, xii
"Rendezvous with Destiny," 358–59
Rentz, Ephraim, 132–33, 150, 172
Rentz, Harriet Louisa ("Lulu") McIntosh, 133–34, 172
Rentz, Robert Lee, 132–33, 172, 374
Renwick, Emma Elizabeth, 15–17. *See also* Carlisle, Emma Elizabeth Renwick
Renwick, James ("The Martyr"), 12, 14, 16, 369, 371–72
Renwick, James William, 14
Renwick, John, 14
Renwick, John, Jr., 14
Renwick, John Simpson, 14–17
Renwick, Mary Toland, 14–15
Report on the Economic Conditions of the South, The, 176
Republican Party. *See* Kennedy, Renwick Carlisle (RCK): social concerns
Resistance (French), 211
"Responsible Living" (Kennedy), 200
Retrospect: An Autobiographical Reveille and Taps (Adams), 335
Reynolds v. Sims (1964), 348
Rhineland, 193

Rhynus, Roland, 209–10, 212, 216, 364–65
Richards, J. McDowell, 186, 204
Richardson, Harold, 357
"River View" (home), 36
Roark, Eldridge Waldo, 179–81, 185, 201
Robert F. Kennedy and His Times (Schlesinger), 368
Rockefeller Foundation, 116, 278, 284
Rockford County, Virginia, 50, 54
Rock West, Alabama, 148
Rogers, Lena Tucker Miller, 148. *See also* Albritton, Lena Tucker Miller
Rooney, Mickey, 219
Roosevelt, Eleanor, 312
Roosevelt, Franklin D. *See* Kennedy, Renwick Carlisle (RCK): social concerns (Democratic Party leaders)
"Roosevelt Hall" (Kennedy), 169
"Roosevelt's Tenants" (Kennedy), 156
Rose, Frank, 301, 333–34, 336
Rosenburg, Janette Stout, 334, 348, 354. *See also* Stout, Janette
Rosenwald Fellowship, 3, 149, 183, 249, 344
Rotary Clubs, 287
Rothstein, Arthur, 157, 170
Rousseau, Jean-Jacques, 71
Ruark, Robert, 293
Rubin, Morton, 184, 249–57, 304, 315–21, 341, 367, 375
Ruby, Jack, 322, 328
Rural Preachers Institute. *See* Vanderbilt University
Rural Rehabilitation Program (RRP), 150–51
Russellville, Arkansas, 40–43, 56–59
Rutenberg, Joe, 213–14
Rutherford family, 122
Rutledge, Clara Hard, 294, 300

Safford, Alabama, 252
Saint-Hubert, Belgium, 213
Saint-James, France, 212
Saint-Lô, France, 211
Saint-Malo, France, 211
Saint-Pair-sur-Mer, France, 212
Salem, Alabama, 95
Salem ARP Church (Loango, Alabama), 67
Samford University (Howard College), 237
Samson, Alabama, 330

Index

Sand Island, 363
Sanger, J. D., 296
San Luis Obispo, California, 207–8
San Marcos University, 138
Sartain, Auxford, 272
Sartilly, France, 212
Sartoris (Faulkner), 123
Satyricon of Petronius (Petronius), 102
Savage Symphony (Lips), 182, 195
Saxon, Lyle, 169
Scotch-Irish, 371–72
Scotch-Irish: behavior, 12–14, 20, 53, 72, 107, 371–72; historiography of, 102–3, 392n3; origins, 12–13, 102–3. *See also* Kennedy, Renwick Carlisle (RCK): social concerns; Wilcox County
Scotch Irish in America, The (Jones), 102
Scotch Irish Pioneers in Ulster and America (Bolton), 12, 102
Scots: Highlander, 45, 102; Lowland, 11, 102; Ulster, 11, 53, 102
Scottish Covenanters, 11
Scottsboro Case, 135–36, 153–56, 161, 184
"Scottsboro Shadow" (Kennedy), 153–56
Scottsburg, Virginia, 36
Searcy, Hubert, 267
Seceders, 18
"Second Massive Resistance Movement, The," 372–73, 378. *See also* "Massive Resistance"
"Sedition Bill" (Kennedy), 161
Seeds of Southern Change (Alexander), 22
"Segregation and the Church" (Burns), 289
Selden, Armistead, 326
Self, Mrs. R. L., 283
Selling of the South, The (Cobb), 190
Selma, Alabama, 247, 252
Selma Clover Leafs (baseball team), 143
Selma Stationary Shop, 85, 149, 243, 258
Selma Times-Journal, 143, 145, 149
Sepulga River, 170
Sessions, Willie, 154
Shakespeare, William, 13, 42, 175, 361
sharecroppers. *See* Kennedy, Renwick Carlisle (RCK): social concerns
Sharpe, Tammi, xii
Shavertown, Alabama, 48–49
Shawnee, Alabama, 99

Shepard, Alan, 315
Shorter, Alabama, 280
Sick, Glenn Nolan, 201
Sigma Alpha Epsilon, 280
Silver, James, 299
Simpson, James E., 246
Simpson, Martha Patton, 177, 185, 343, 344
Simpson, Ransom Overton, 177–18, 343
"Sin at the Door" (Kennedy), 74–76
Singal, Daniel Joseph, 39, 397n29, 412n35, 414n8, 434n16
"Six Cent Cotton: A Southern Tragedy" (Kennedy), 127–28
Skidmore, Edwin Weber, 310–11
Skinner, Powell, 275
Slade, Bennett, 83
slavery: ARPs, 18–19; Macon County, Alabama, 280; Newberry County, South Carolina, 15, 17; Wilcox County, Alabama, 45–46
"Slick Scam of the Real and Un-Christian Alabama Tax Code," 152
Smith, Alfred E., 96–98, 321
Smith, Bob, 154
Smith, Calvin, 205
Smith, Charles Bunyan, 247, 266, 270–333, 348
Smith, Ellison, 246
Smith, Eugene Allen, 4
Smith, Henry Lewis, 357
Smith, J. Ritchie, 30
Smith, Lillian, 69, 122, 269
Smith, Riley, 152
Snopes family, 123
Snow, Kirby, 291
Snow Hill Institute, 76, 95, 143, 169, 177–78, 343
Social Darwinism, 372
"Social Degeneration," 90
Social Forces, 147, 149, 150, 152, 249, 376
Social Gospel. *See* Kennedy, Renwick Carlisle (RCK): personal and career
"Social Regeneration," 84, 197
Social Science Research Institute. *See* University of North Carolina at Chapel Hill
"Solace of the Poor" (Kennedy), 169
Something of Value (Ruark), 293

Sonkin, Robert, 170
Sophocles, 26, 362
Sosna, Morton, 203, 452n19
South Carolina College, 25
"Southern Approach to the Color Issue, A" (Bell), 185–86
Southern Association of Colleges and Schools, 333
Southern Conference for Human Relations, 377
Southerner and World Affairs, The (Hero), 304
Southern Farmer, 245, 258
Southern Historical Association, 299
Southern Poverty Law Center, 334
Southern Presbyterian Church, 32, 201
Southern Regional Council, 294, 300, 377
Southern Renaissance, 90, 169
"Southern Strategy," 347
"Southern Suicide" (Kennedy,), 157–61
"South Shuns GOP Compromise on Racial Issue Draft Bill," 258
Southwest Review, 274, 289
"Southwind" (Kennedy), 246–47
Spa, Belgium, 215–16
Sparkman, John, 276, 326, 331
Sparks, Chauncey, 330
Speak Now Against the Day (Edgerton), 126
Spellman, Francis Joseph, 241
Spiva, Lucy McDaniel, 267
Spoon River Anthology (Masters), 102
"Spot, The," 252
Spring Hill College, 292, 337
Sprott, Laura Gaines, 283
Stabler, Clay, 313, 328–29
Stafford Hotel, 309
Stalin, Joe, 260
Stapp, Albert, 261
Stark, Willie, 238
Starr, John Paul, 101
Starr, Lucius Ernest, 101
Starr, Molly Tepper, 101
Starr, Paul Ernest, 176, 365
Stars Fell on Alabama (Carmer), 44
Staten Island, 224
State of Alabama: Board of Education, 307, 328–29; Department of Archives and History, 188, 242; Department of Education, 282–83, 285–86, 300–302, 309, 333–34, 341; Department of Highways, 281, 301, 310, 360; Department of Insurance, 330; Department of Public Safety, 316; House and Senate, 292; House Education Committee, 281; House Ways and Means Committee, 287; 1901 Constitutional Convention, 306; Public Service Commission, 330; Senate, 188; Tax Code, 152
St. Clair County, Alabama, 159
Sterkx, Eugene ("Gene"), 272, 298–99, 309–10, 313, 328, 330, 348, 353, 365
Sterling College, 208, 326
Stevenson, J. Ross, 31
Stevenson, Robert Milton, 27, 116
Stewart, Arthur, 69
Stewart, Frank, 308–11, 316, 326–28
Stewart, Margaret, 311
St. Francs of Assisi, and *stigmata*, 29
St. James Episcopal Church (Fairhope, Alabama), 308
St. John, Vernon E., 282
St. John's College, 196
St. Louis, Missouri, 29, 53
St. Mary's Episcopal Church (Camden, Alabama), 71, 90, 106, 116
Stockholm, Sweden, 271
Stone, Olive, 14, 201, 315
Store, The (Stribling), 183
Stout, Ira W., 69
Stout, Janette, 272. *See also* Rosenburg, Janette Stout
Stowe, Harriet Beecher, 22
St. Paul's Episcopal Church (Carlowville, Alabama), 78
St. Petersburg Times, 377
Strange Fruit (Smith), 122
Stribling, T. S., 169, 183
Stroud, Laurine, 252
Stroud, Oxford, 147
Stuart, Edward C., 27–29
Stuttgart, Germany, 132
Sulzberger family, 194–95

Tait, Carlotta, 96
Tait, Charles, 45–49, 89, 96
Tait, Felix, 70, 79, 90, 96, 101

Tait, Felix, III, 180
Tait, Fleet, 70, 79, 90, 97–98, 104–5, 109
Tait, Frank Shropshire, 122
Tait, Goode, 179–71, 183–85
Tait, James Asbury, 46, 52, 70, 90
Tait, Julian Marsh, 122
Tait, Mabel Jones, 109
Tait, Maggie, 122
Tait, Martha Jefferson, 48
Tait, Mary Carter, 201
Tait, Mrs. Felix, 77
Tait family, 90, 97, 274, 406n47
Talec, Aimé, 211
Talladega County, Alabama, 159
Tallassee, Alabama, 308
Talmadge, Eugene, 246
Tannenbaum, Frank, 71, 127
Teachers College Columbia University, 36
Tennessee-Alabama Presbytery (ARP), 66, 79, 91, 296, 354, 357
Tennessee Valley Authority, 143
Tennille, Frank, 300
Tennyson, Alfred, 85
Tepper, Samuel, 101
Tepper, Sol, 318, 347
Terry, William R., 278–79, 281–84, 292, 329
"Terry-Morgan Law," 293
Thaggard, Roy, 313
"They Never Had It So Good" (Kennedy), 272
"They Were Seven" (McWilliams), 4
Thomas, Norman, 259
Thomas Jefferson: An Intimate Biography (Brodie), 364
Thoreau, Henry David, 364
Thorn, Charlotte R., 78
Threadgill-Matthews, Sheryl, xii
Thunderburk, Louie, 38
Thurmond, Strom, 260–61
Tick, Tick, Tick (film), 353
Tidewater area, Virginia, 72
"Tightening Up in the Cotton Belt" (Kennedy), 128–29, 134
Tilley, John S., 306
"Time," 24, 33, 36–37. *See also* Kennedy, Renwick Carlisle (RCK): personal and career
Time Magazine, 240–41, 245

Tinker, Matthew, xii
Tobacco Road (Caldwell), 26, 157
To Kill a Mockingbird (Lee), 314–15
Toland, Mary. *See* Renwick, Mary Toland
Toledo Blade, The, 257
"Tom Fund, The," 364
"Town World," 138
Trapp, Leonard, 301, 313, 328, 348, 354
"Tribe of Isaac," 20, 366
"Trickle Down Hoax, The," 113, 125, 352
Trinder, Frank, 241
Tropolitan, The, 291, 334, 348, 355
Troyat, Henri, 364
Troy High School, 283
Troy State College, Dothan, 332
Troy State College, Montgomery, 332
Troy State Teachers College (and Troy State College, Troy State University, and Troy University), 238, 245, 247, 299, 308; desegregation of, 332–37; separated from State of Alabama Department of Education, 334. *See also* Adams, Ralph; Kennedy, Renwick Carlisle (RCK): personal and career; Smith, Charles Bunyan; Stewart, Frank
Truman, Harry. *See* Kennedy, Renwick Carlisle (RCK): social concerns (Democratic Party leaders)
Trump, Donald, 372–73
Tucker, Cynthia, 459n2
Tuesday Literary Club, 283
Tulane University, 82
Turner, Joseph Mallord William, 101
Turner, Mrs. Howard, 92
Tuscaloosa, Alabama, 131, 138, 152, 159–60. *See also* "Town World"; "University World"
Tuscaloosa County Inferior Court, 330
Tuscaloosa News, 182, 292
Tuskegee, Alabama, 280, 319
Tuskegee Institute, 304, 343
Tway, Duane, 354
Twenty-fourth Amendment, 238
Tyrone County (Ulster Ireland), 14, 16

Ulster Plantation, 11. *See also* Scots
Uncle Tom's Cabin (Stowe), 22

Uncle Tom's Children (Wright), 247
"Union [Church] Services," 95
Union County, South Carolina, 16
Union Springs, Alabama, 252
Uniontown, Alabama, 254
United Daughters of the Confederacy, 90
United Nations, 256
United Presbyterian Church, 19, 163
Unity ARP Church (Lancaster County, South Carolina), 28
Universal Studios, 314–15
University of Alabama, 273, 285, 343; Department of Philosophy, 185; desegregation of, 289–300, 320; football, 63, 95, 118 152–53; School of Law, 104, 292, 308, 330–31; School of Medicine, 292. *See also* Bennett, J. Jefferson; Carmichael, Oliver; Cason, Clarence; Denny, George; Rose, Frank
University of Alabama, Birmingham Extension Center, 333, 337
University of Alabama, Huntsville Extension Center, 337
University of Alabama, Mobile Extension Center, 337
University of Berlin, 187
University of California, Los Angeles, 315
University of Chicago, 257
University of Michigan, 325
University of Mississippi, 319
University of Mobile, 237
University of Montevallo, 337. *See also* Alabama College
University of Munich, 187
University of North Carolina at Chapel Hill: Extension Service, 38; Institute for Social Science Research, 149, 249; "Liberals," 147; Southern Historical Collection, 247, 251
University of North Carolina Press, 256
University of Oklahoma, Presbyterian Club, 186
University of Oklahoma Press, 187–88
University of South Alabama, 337
University of the South, 78, 354
University of Virginia, 104, 224
University of Wisconsin, Madison, 256

University Presbyterian Church (Tuscaloosa, Alabama), 16
"University World," 138
Upper East Side (Manhattan), 362
US Air University, 330, 333–34
US Army: Camp Kilmer, 209; Chaplaincy Corps, 206–7; Fort Riley, 247; Fort Rucker, 290–332; Q Regiment, Company G, 217; Reserve, 153; 10th Field Hospital, 222; 16th Evacuation Hospital, 217; 83rd Infantry, 33; 93rd Infantry, 208; 101st Airborne, 213; 102nd Evacuation Hospital, 207, 222 and passim. *See also* Kennedy, Renwick Carlisle (RCK): social concerns
US Civil Rights Act: of 1957, 294, 312; of 1964, 237, 336, 340
US Civil Rights Commission, 300, 307
US Department of Defense, 333
US Department of Health, Education, ad Welfare, 335
US Department of Housing and Urban Development, 336
US Department of Housing and Urban Finance Agency, 336
US Department of Justice, 285
US Economic Opportunity Act, 325
US Fifth Circuit Court Appeals, 307, 333, 342
US National Defense Education Act, 336
US Selective Service, 5, 195, 198, 201, 330, 332, 336, 426n17
US Veterans Administration, 240, 243, 459
US Voting Rights of 1965, 340, 342
US v. Wilcox County Board of Education (1974), 342
Utah Beach, 210, 317

Van de Graaff, Adrian, 131
Van de Graaff, Hargrave, 150
Van de Graaff family, 171
Vance, Rupert, 249
Vanderbilt University, 237; agrarians, 146–47; Rural Preachers Institute, 116
Vann, Barry, 11
Vaughn Memorial Hospital, 279, 362, 367, 369
VE Day, 221

Index

Victorianism, 16, 24, 39, 91, 154, 290, 321, 353; post-Victoriansm, 321
Vidette, Georgia, 28
Vietnam War, 325, 328, 345–46
Virginia Quarterly Review, 305
Volker, Joseph F., 333
Volunteers in Service to America, 347
"Volunteer Story" (Kennedy), 198
Voss, Geerhardus, 30
Vredenburg, Alabama, 44
Vredenburgh family, 45, 95, 407–8n1

Waites, Wallace L., 334, 348
Walden (Thoreau), 364
Walker, Amanda, 360–61
Walker County, Alabama, 287
Wallace, Allerae, 345
Wallace, Brent, 334
Wallace, George, 238, 289, 298–303, 307, 312, 314, 320, 325–30, 340, 347–49, 357–58, 371
Wallace, Henry, 259
Wallace, Joe, 83, 98, 133–34
Wallace, Lurleen, 346–49
Wallace Foundation, 345
"Walnut Bluff" (home), 109
Wardlaw family, 43
Ware, Lowry, xii, 77–78, 394n14
"War on Poverty," 321
Warren, Robert Penn, xii, 238, 371, 380
Warrior Creek (South Carolina) ARP Church, 14
Washington, Booker T., 177–78, 343
Washington and Lee University, 280
Washington County, Alabama, 281
"Waste" (Kennedy), 167–68
Wasted Land, The (Johnson), 168
Watergate Scandal, 357–58
Watership Down (Adams), 364
Watson, Dorothy ("Dot"), 252
Watson, John B., 148
Watson's Crossing, Alabama, 84
Way Greek, The (Hamilton), 366
Webb, Samuel L., xii
Weber, Shirley Howard, 36
Welch, Nat, 247
"Well Digger, The" (Kennedy), 275–76
Wertenbaker, Thomas J., 118

West, Cornell, 164
Westminster College, 27
Westminster Standards, 13
Westminster Theological Seminary, 31
"What's Happening in the Cotton Belt" (Kennedy), 142–43
Wheaton College, 304
Wheeler, Joseph H., 66
"When the Books Are Opened" (Kennedy), 303
Where Is Civilization Going? (Nearing), 74, 192
"While the Supreme Court Ponders" (Kennedy), 289–90
"Whipping of Lester Carloss, The," (Kennedy), 176
White, D. F., 243–44
White, S. Reese, 283
White, William Allen, 102
White "aristocracy." *See* Kennedy, Renwick Carlisle (RCK): social concerns
White Citizens' Councils (WCC) of Alabama, 280, 284, 289, 293–94, 301, 329
"White Columns" (home), 45, 101
"White Displacement Fear," 1
White House Looks South, The (Leuchtenburg), 260
White middle class. *See* Kennedy, Renwick Carlisle (RCK): social concerns
White poor. *See* Kennedy, Renwick Carlisle (RCK): social concerns
"White Supremacy," 184
Whitley Hotel, 207, 287
Whitmire, Kyle, 188
"Whole Gospel," 84, 197
"Why Churches Do Not Unite" (Kennedy), 275
"Why I Gave Up Hunting" (Kennedy), 248
Wideman's, South Carolina, 17
Wightman, Joseph, 339
Wilcox, John, 47
Wilcox Academy, 351, 357
Wilcox County, general history: Catholicism, 98, 241; Civil War, 50–52; contemporary, xi–xii; founding of, 47–48; Great Depression, 94–95, 112–16, 125, 150; KKK, 70, 74, 90, 98, 100, 183, 194, 283–84, 321; physical description, 4, 45;

presidential election of 1928, 96–99, of 1948, 259–64, of 1960, 311–14, 323–24; prohibition, 108; race relations: pre-WWII, 79–80, 192, post-WWII, 261–63, 315–17, 338–47, 358–61, 374–75; Reconstruction, 104, 107; Red Cross, 7–8, 13, 132–33, 248, 252; Scotch-Irish, 43, 49, 54, 58, 103–7, 367; slavery, 45–46; World War II life, 198–99, 200–203. *See also* Kennedy, Renwick Carlisle (RCK): social concerns

Wilcox County Board of Registrars, 300

Wilcox County High School, 143, 180, 195, 258, 273

Wilcox County Public Library, 101, 202, 252–53

Wilcox Female Institute, 55, 314

Wilcox Hotel, 8, 49, 52, 63–64, 82, 250, 329

Wilcoxon, 47

Wilcox Progress, 107

Wilcox Progressive Era, 63, 69, 70, 98, 100, 126, 162, 176, 182, 250, 283–84

Wilcox Roundtable, The, 144, 148, 157, 161–62, 170, 173, 176–77, 201, 274, 361

Wiley, Bell, 299–300, 319, 342

Wilkerson, Isabel, 1

Wilkins, Robert Bernard, 292

Wilks, William ("Bill") T., 329, 354

Williams, Aubrey, 245, 247

Williams, Bob, 291

Williams, Calvin Brice, 187

Williams, Charles B., 206

Williams, D. F., 374

Williams, Joseph, 182

Williams, Nell, 115

"Willie Watson" (Kennedy), 135

Wilson, Charles Reagan, 164

Wilson, James H., 51

Wilson, Ligon, 99

Wilson, Massey, 306, 446n12, 447n20

Wilson, Sloan, 296

Wilson, William Green, 163–64, 374

Wilson, Woodrow. *See* Kennedy, Renwick Carlisle (RCK): social concerns (Democratic Party leaders)

Wind Creek Casino, 364

Winters, John Albert, 80

Winters, Phillip, 340

With a Southern Accent (Liddell), 256–58, 268

Wolfe, Thomas, 90, 169, 223, 406n47

Woodford, John, 217–18, 221–22

Woodrow Wilson (White), 102–3

Woodrow Wilson Foundation, 72–73

Woods, Sarah McDaniel, 362–69, 374

Woods, Veronica, xii

Woodward, C. Vann, 299

Works Progress Administration, 142

World Peace Foundation, 304

World War I, 24, 67–68. *See also* Kennedy, Renwick Carlisle (RCK): personal and career; Kennedy, Renwick Carlisle (RCK): social concerns

World War II. *See* Kennedy, Renwick Carlisle (RCK): personal and career; Kennedy, Renwick Carlisle (RCK): social concerns; Wilcox County

"W.P.A., Here We Come!" (Kennedy), 177

Wright, Catherine, 300

Wright, Gavin, 16

Wright, Richard, 247, 376

Wyatt-Brown, Bertram, 109

Yale Review, 274

Yale University, 196

Yankovic, Frankie, 255

Yarborough, Patricia Pitt, 254

"Yaupon" (idea). *See* Kennedy, Renwick Carlisle (RCK): social concerns

"Yaupon Tales, The" (Kennedy), 185, 187, 200, 203–4, 256, 372

YMCA, 25

"Yoknapatawpha," 123

You Can't Go Home Again (Wolfe), 223

Young, Mary Evelyn, 55

Young family, 3, 44

Young People's Christian Union (of the ARP Synod), 353

Yount, R. P., 178

"Youpon" (home), 45, 122

"Youth March," 320

Zeus, 27, 380